What's That?

THE OXFORD VISUAL DICTIONARY
OF NEARLY EVERYTHING

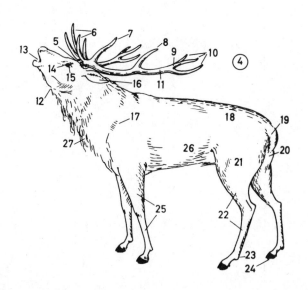

What's That?

THE OXFORD VISUAL DICTIONARY OF NEARLY EVERYTHING

Edited by John A. Pheby

Tess Press

Published by Tess Press, an imprint of
Black Dog & Leventhal Publishers, Inc.
151 West 19th Street
New York, NY 10011

Jacket design by Liz Driesbach and Lindsay Wolff

ISBN: 978-1-60376-001-0

h g f e d c b a

Printed in the United States of America

Contents

The arabic numerals are the numbers of the pictures

Preface

The *Oxford-Duden Pictorial English Dictionary* has a firmly established reputation as a uniquely useful learning aid and reference tool. It is based on the German *Bildwörterbuch*, published as Volume 3 of the twelve-volume *Duden* series of authoritative monolingual German dictionaries, and has been produced with the assistance of numerous British companies, institutions, and technical experts.

There are certain kinds of information which can be conveyed more readily and clearly by pictures than by definitions and explanations alone: an illustration will help the reader to visualize the object denoted by the word and to form an impression of the way in which objects function in their own technical field or in the everyday life of English-speaking countries. The layout of the illustrations and the text will be particularly useful to the learner. Each double page of the dictionary contains a list of the vocabulary of a subject together with a picture illustrating this vocabulary. This arrangement, and the presence of an alphabetical index, allows the book to be used in two ways: either as a key to the vocabulary of a subject or as an alphabetical dictionary in which the reader is referred to the section or sections in which the word is illustrated.

For this new edition the *Oxford-Duden Pictorial* has been revised to reflect recent developments in technical and everyday vocabulary and contains over 1,500 new items in fast-changing fields such as computing, audio and video, photography, typesetting, communications, and transport. Its wide range of vocabulary, accuracy of translation, and ease of use make it an indispensable supplement to any standard English dictionary.

Oxford, 1995   M.C.

Abbreviations

Am.	*American usage*
c.	*castrated (animal)*
coll.	*colloquial*
f.	*female (animal)*
form.	*formerly*
joc.	*jocular*
m.	*male (animal)*
poet.	*poetic*
sg.	*singular*
sim.	*similar*
y.	*young (animal)*

1 Atom I

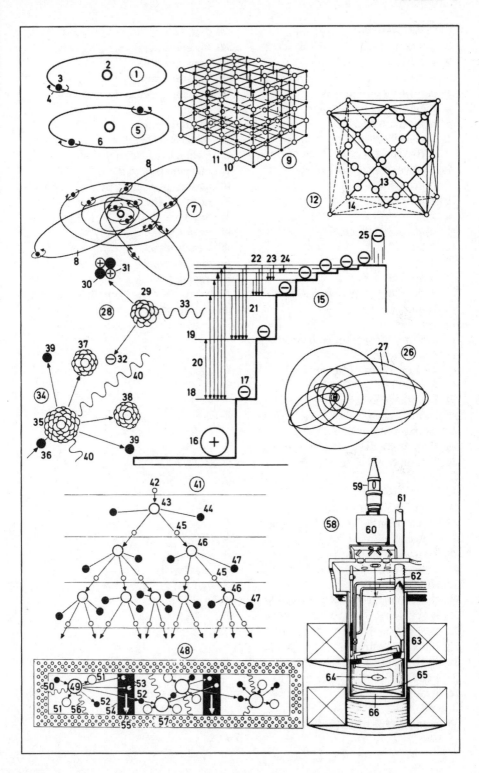

2 Atom II

1-23 **radiation detectors** (radiation meters)
1 radiation monitor
2 ionization chamber (ion chamber)
3 central electrode
4 measurement range selector
5 instrument housing
6 meter
7 zero adjustment
8-23 dosimeter (dosemeter)
8 film dosimeter
9 filter
10 film
11 film-ring dosimeter
12 filter
13 film
14 cover with filter
15 pocket meter (pen meter, pocket chamber)
16 window
17 ionization chamber (ion chamber)
18 clip (pen clip)
19 Geiger counter (Geiger-Müller counter)
20 counter tube casing
21 counter tube
22 instrument housing
23 measurement range selector
24 Wilson cloud chamber (Wilson chamber)
25 compression plate
26 cloud chamber photograph
27 cloud chamber track of an alpha particle
28 **telecobalt unit** (*coll.* cobalt bomb)
29 pillar stand
30 support cables
31 radiation shield (radiation shielding)
32 sliding shield
33 bladed diaphragm
34 light-beam positioning device
35 pendulum device (pendulum)
36 irradiation table
37 rail (track)
38 **manipulator with sphere unit**
39 handle
40 safety catch (locking lever)
41 wrist joint
42 master arm
43 clamping device (clamp)
44 tongs
45 slotted board
46 radiation shield (protective shield, protective shielding), a lead shielding wall [section]
47 grasping arm of a pair of manipulators (of a master/slave manipulator)
48 dust shield
49 **synchrotron**
50 danger zone
51 magnet
52 pumps for emptying the vacuum chamber

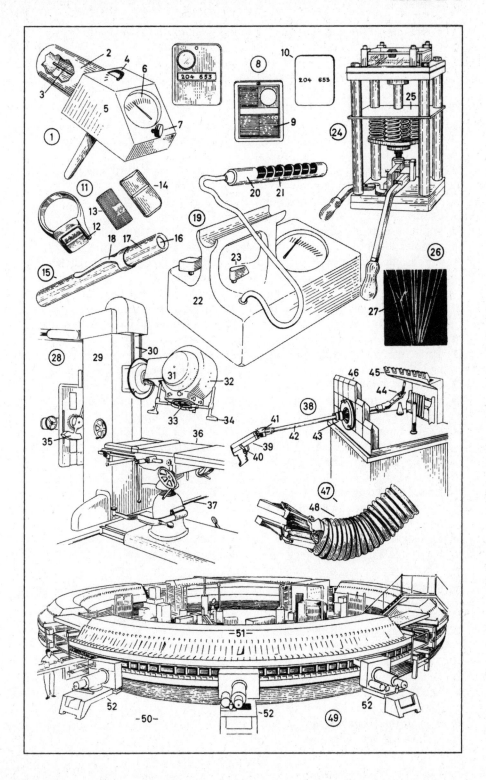

3 Astronomy I

1-35 star map of the northern sky
(northern hemisphere)

1-8 divisions of the sky

1 celestial pole with the Pole Star
(Polaris, the North Star)

2 ecliptic (apparent annual path of
the sun)

3 celestial equator (equinoctial line)

4 tropic of Cancer

5 circle enclosing circumpolar stars

6, 7 equinoctial points (equinoxes)

6 vernal equinoctial point (first point
of Aries)

7 autumnal equinoctial point

8 summer solstice

9-48 constellations (grouping of fixed
stars into figures) **and names of
stars**

9 Aquila (the Eagle) with Altair the
principal star (the brightest star)

10 Pegasus (the Winged Horse)

11 Cetus (the Whale) with Mira, a
variable star

12 Eridamus (the Celestial River)

13 Orion (the Hunter) with Rigel,
Betelgeuse and Bellatrix

14 Canis Major (the Great Dog, the
Greater Dog) with Sirius (the Dog
Star), a star of the first magnitude

15 Canis Minor (the Little Dog, the
Lesser Dog) with Procyon

16 Hydra (the Water Snake, the Sea
Serpent)

17 Leo (the Lion) with Regulus

18 Virgo (the Virgin) with Spica

19 Libra (the Balance, the Scales)

20 Serpens (the Serpent)

21 Hercules

22 Lyra (the Lyre) with Vega

23 Cygnus (the Swan, the Northern
Cross) with Deneb

24 Andromeda

25 Taurus (the Bull) with Aldebaran

26 The Pleiades (Pleiads, the Seven
Sisters), an open cluster of stars

27 Auriga (the Wagoner, the
Charioteer) with Capella

28 Gemini (the Twins) with Castor
and Pollux

29 Ursa Major (the Great Bear, the
Greater Bear, the Plough,
Charles's Wain, *Am.* the Big
Dipper) with the double star (bina-
ry star) Mizar and Alcor

30 Bootes (the Herdsman) with
Arcturus

31 Corona Borealis (the Northern
Crown)

32 Draco (the Dragon)

33 Cassiopeia

34 Ursa Minor (the Little Bear,
Lesser Bear, *Am.* Little Dipper)
with the Pole Star (Polaris, the
North Star)

35 the Milky Way (the Galaxy)

36-48 the southern sky

36 Capricorn (the Goat, the Sea
Goat)

37 Sagittarius (the Archer)

38 Scorpio (the Scorpion)

39 Centaurus (the Centaur)

40 Triangulum Australe (the
Southern Triangle)

41 Pavo (the Peacock)

42 Grus (the Crane)

43 Octans (the Octant)

44 Crux (the Southern Cross, the
Cross)

45 Argo (the Celestial Ship)

46 Carina (the Keel)

47 Pictor (the Painter)

48 Reticulum (the Net)

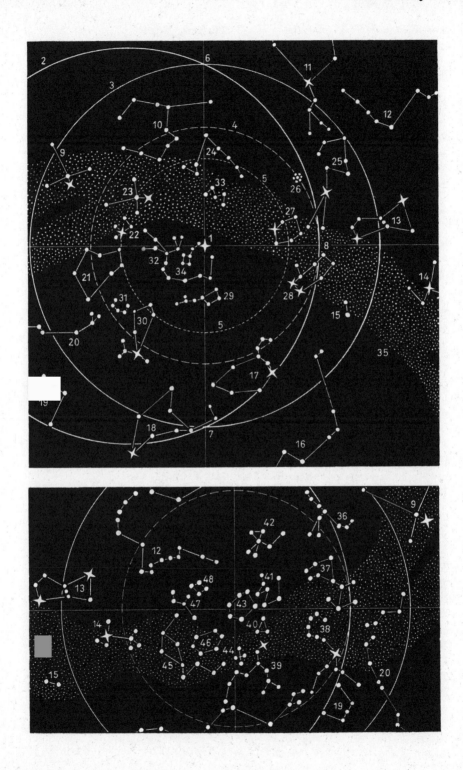

1-9 the moon
1 moon's path (moon's orbit round the earth)
2-7 lunar phases (moon's phases) (lunation)
2 new moon
3 crescent (crescent moon, waxing moon)
4 half-moon (first quarter)
5 full moon
6 half-moon (last quarter, third quarter)
7 crescent (crescent moon, waning moon)
8 the earth (terrestrial globe)
9 direction of the sun's rays
10-21 apparent path of the sun at the beginning of the seasons
10 celestial axis
11 zenith
12 horizontal plane
13 nadir
14 east point
15 west point
16 north point
17 south point
18 apparent path of the sun on 21 December
19 apparent path of the sun on 21 March and 23 September
20 apparent path of the sun on 21 June
21 border of the twilight area
22-28 rotary motions of the earth's axis
22 axis of the ecliptic
23 celestial sphere
24 path of the celestial pole [precession and nutation]
25 instantaneous axis of rotation
26 celestial pole
27 mean axis of rotation
28 polhode
29-35 solar and lunar eclipse [not to scale]
29 the sun
30 the earth
31 the moon

32 solar eclipse
33 area of the earth in which the eclipse appears total
34, 35 lunar eclipse
34 penumbra (partial shadow)
35 umbra (total shadow)
36-41 the sun
36 solar disc (disk) (solar globe, solar sphere)
37 sunspots
38 cyclones in the area of sunspots
39 corona (solar corona), observable during total solar eclipse or by means of special instruments
40 prominences (solar prominences)
41 moon's limb during a total solar eclipse
42-52 planets (planetary system, solar system) [not to scale] and planet symbols
42 the sun
43 Mercury
44 Venus
45 Earth, with the moon, a satellite
46 Mars, with two moons
47 asteroids (minor planets)
48 Jupiter
49 Saturn
50 Uranus
51 Neptune
52 Pluto, with the moon Charon
53-64 signs of the zodiac (zodiacal signs)
53 Aries (the Ram)
54 Taurus (the Bull)
55 Gemini (the Twins)
56 Cancer (the Crab)
57 Leo (the Lion)
58 Virgo (the Virgin)
59 Libra (the Balance, the Scales)
60 Scorpio (the Scorpion)
61 Sagittarius (the Archer)
62 Capricorn (the Goat, the Sea Goat)
63 Aquarius (the Water Carrier, the Water Bearer)
64 Pisces (the Fish)

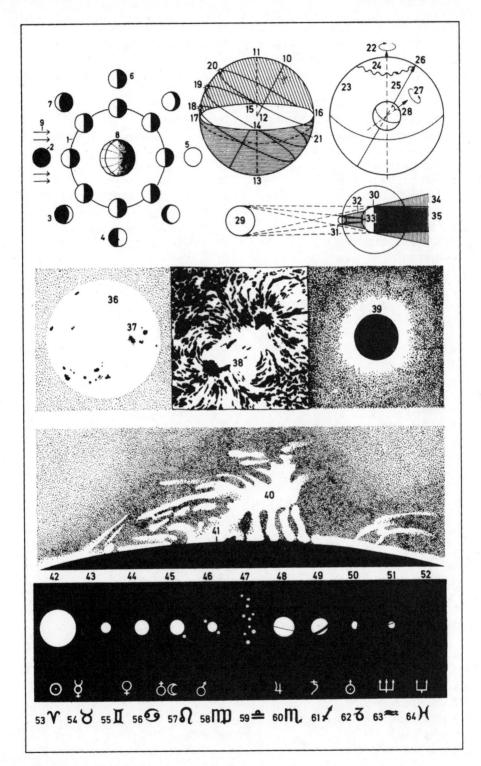

5 Astronomy III

1-16 the European Southern Observatory (ESO) on *Cerro la Silla, Chile,* an observatory [section]
1 primary mirror (main mirror) with a diameter of 3.6 m (144 inches)
2 prime focus cage with mounting for secondary mirrors
3 flat mirror for the coudé ray path
4 Cassegrain cage
5 grating spectrograph
6 spectrographic camera
7 hour axis drive
8 hour axis
9 horseshoe mounting
10 hydrostatic bearing
11 primary and secondary focusing devices
12 observatory dome, a revolving dome
13 observation opening
14 vertically movable dome shutter
15 wind screen
16 siderostat
17-28 the *Stuttgart* Planetarium [section]
17 administration, workshop, and store area
18 steel scaffold
19 glass pyramid
20 revolving arched ladder
21 projection dome
22 light stop
23 planetarium projector
24 well
25 foyer
26 theatre (*Am.* theater)
27 projection booth
28 foundation pile
29-33 the *Kitt Peak* solar observatory near *Tucson, Ariz.* [section]
29 heliostat
30 sunken observation shaft
31 water-cooled windshield
32 concave mirror
33 observation room housing the spectrograph

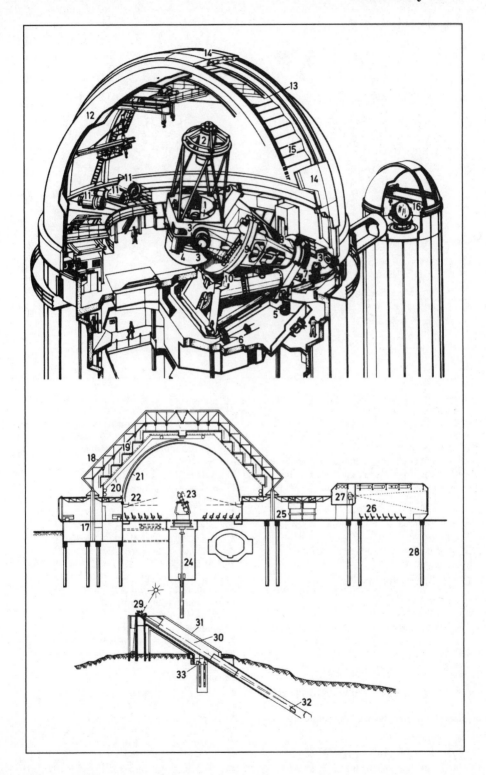

6 Moon Landing

1 Apollo spacecraft
2 service module (SM)
3 nozzle of the main rocket engine
4 directional antenna
5 manoeuvring (*Am.* maneuvering) rockets
6 oxygen and hydrogen tanks for the spacecraft's energy system
7 fuel tank
8 radiators of the spacecraft's energy system
9 command module (Apollo space capsule)
10 entry hatch of the space capsule
11 astronaut
12 lunar module (LM)
13 moon's surface (lunar surface), a dust-covered surface
14 lunar dust
15 piece of rock
16 meteorite crater
17 the earth
18-27 space suit (extra-vehicular suit)
18 emergency oxygen apparatus
19 sunglass pocket [with sunglasses for use on board]
20 life support system (life support pack), a backpack unit
21 access flap
22 space suit helmet with sun filters
23 control box of the life support pack

24 penlight pocket
25 access flap for the purge valve
26 tube and cable connections for the radio, ventilation, and water-cooling systems
27 pocket for pens, tools, etc.
28-36 descent stage
28 connector
29 fuel tank
30 engine
31 mechanism for unfolding the legs
32 main shock absorber
33 landing pad
34 ingress/egress platform (hatch platform)
35 ladder to platform and hatch
36 cardan mount for engine
37-47 ascent stage
37 fuel tank
38 ingress/egress hatch (entry/exit hatch)
39 LM manoeuvring (*Am.* maneuvering) rockets
40 window
41 crew compartment
42 rendezvous radar antenna
43 inertial measurement unit
44 directional antenna for ground control
45 upper hatch (docking hatch)
46 inflight antenna
47 docking target recess

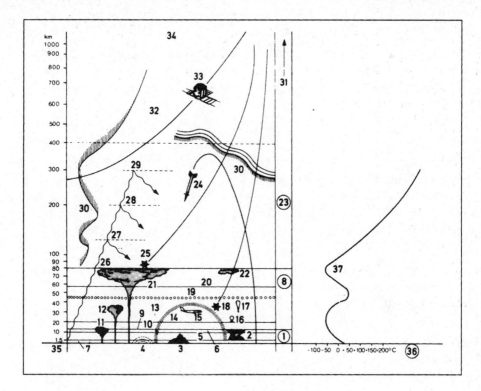

1 **the troposphere**
2 thunderclouds
3 the highest mountain, *Mount Everest* [8,882 m]
4 rainbow
5 jet stream level
6 zero level [inversion of vertical air movement]
7 ground layer (surface boundary layer)
8 **the stratosphere**
9 tropopause
10 separating layer (layer of weaker air movement)
11 atomic explosion
12 hydrogen bomb explosion
13 ozone layer
14 range of sound wave propagation
15 stratosphere aircraft
16 manned balloon
17 sounding balloon
18 meteor
19 upper limit of ozone layer

20 zero level
21 eruption of Krakatoa
22 luminous clouds (noctilucent clouds)
23 **the ionosphere**
24 range of research rockets
25 shooting star
26 short wave (high frequency)
27 E-layer (Heaviside-Kennelly Layer)
28 F_1-layer
29 F_2-layer
30 aurora (polar light)
31 **the exosphere**
32 atom layer
33 range of satellite sounding
34 fringe region
35 altitude scale
36 temperature scale (thermometric scale)
37 temperature graph

1-19 clouds and weather
1-4 clouds found in homogeneous air masses

1 cumulus (woolpack cloud), a heap cloud; *here:* cumulus humilis (fair-weather cumulus), a flat-based heap cloud

2 cumulus congestus, a heap cloud with more marked vertical development

3 stratocumulus, a layer cloud (sheet cloud) arranged in heavy masses

4 stratus (high fog), a thick, uniform layer cloud (sheet cloud)

5-12 clouds found at warm fronts

5 warm front

6 cirrus, a high to very high ice-crystal cloud, thin and assuming a wide variety of forms

7 cirrostratus, an ice-crystal cloud veil

8 altostratus, a layer cloud (sheet cloud) of medium height

9 altostratus praecipitans, a layer cloud (sheet cloud) with precipitation in its upper parts

10 nimbostratus, a rain cloud, a layer cloud (sheet cloud) of very large vertical extent which produces precipitation (rain or snow)

11 fractostratus, a ragged cloud occurring beneath nimbostratus

12 fractocumulus, a ragged cloud like 11 but with billowing shapes

13-17 clouds at cold fronts

13 cold front

14 cirrocumulus, thin fleecy cloud in the form of globular masses; *covering the sky:* mackerel sky

15 altocumulus, a cloud in the form of large globular masses

16 altocumulus castellanus and altocumulus floccus, species of 15

17 cumulonimbus, a heap cloud of very large vertical extent, to be classified under 1-4 in the case of tropical storms

18-19 types of precipitation

18 steady rain or snow covering a large area, precipitation of uniform intensity

19 shower, scattered precipitation

black arrow = cold air   white arrow = warm air

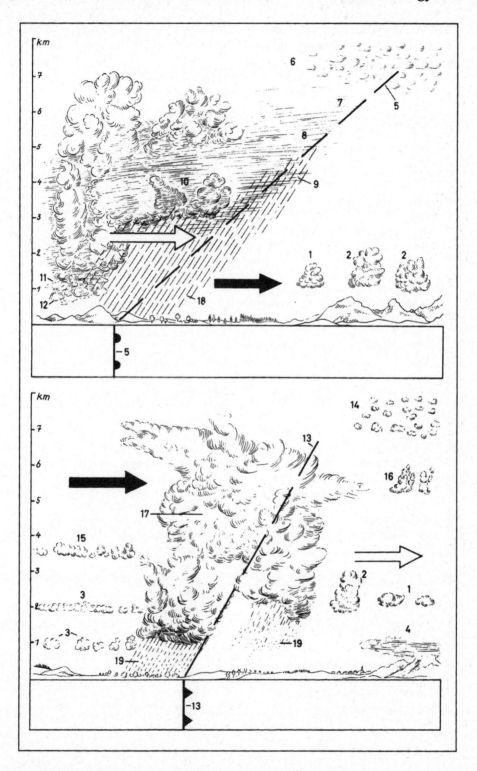

1-39 weather chart (weather map, surface chart, surface synoptic chart)

1 isobar (line of equal or constant atmospheric or barometric pressure at sea level)
2 pleiobar (isobar of over 1,000 mb)
3 meiobar (isobar of under 1,000 mb)
4 atmospheric (barometric) pressure given in millibars
5 low-pressure area (low, cyclone, depression)
6 high-pressure area (high, anticyclone)
7 observatory (meteorological watch office, weather station) or ocean station vessel (weather ship)
8 temperature

9-19 means of representing wind direction (wind-direction symbols)

9 wind-direction shaft (wind arrow)
10 wind-speed barb (wind-speed feather) indicating wind speed
11 calm
12 1-2 knots (1 knot = 1.852 kph)
13 3-7 knots
14 8-12 knots
15 13-17 knots
16 18-22 knots
17 23-27 knots
18 28-32 knots
19 58-62 knots

20-24 state of the sky (distribution of the cloud cover)

20 clear (cloudless)
21 fair
22 partly cloudy
23 cloudy
24 overcast (sky mostly or completely covered)

25-29 fronts and air currents

25 occlusion (occluded front)
26 warm front
27 cold front
28 warm airstream (warm current)
29 cold airstream (cold current)

30-39 meteorological phenomena

30 precipitation area
31 fog
32 rain
33 drizzle
34 snow
35 ice pellets (graupel, soft hail)
36 hail
37 shower
38 thunderstorm
39 lightning

40-58 climatic map

40 isotherm (line connecting points having equal mean temperature)
41 0 ° C (zero) isotherm (line connecting points having a mean annual temperature of 0 ° C)
42 isocheim (line connecting points having equal mean winter temperature)
43 isothere (line connecting points having equal mean summer temperature)
44 isohel (line connecting points having equal duration of sunshine)
45 isohyet (line connecting points having equal amounts of precipitation)

46-52 atmospheric circulation (wind systems)

46-47 calm belts

46 equatorial trough (equatorial calms, doldrums)
47 subtropical high-pressure belts (horse latitudes)
48 north-east trade winds (north-east trades, tropical easterlies)
49 south-east trade winds (south-east trades, tropical easterlies)
50 zones of the variable westerlies
51 polar wind zones
52 summer monsoon

53-58 earth's climates

53 equatorial climate: tropical zone (tropical rain zone)
54 the two arid zones (equatorial dry zones): desert and steppe zones
55 the two temperate rain zones
56 boreal climate (snow forest climate)
57, 58 polar climates
57 tundra climate
58 perpetual frost climate

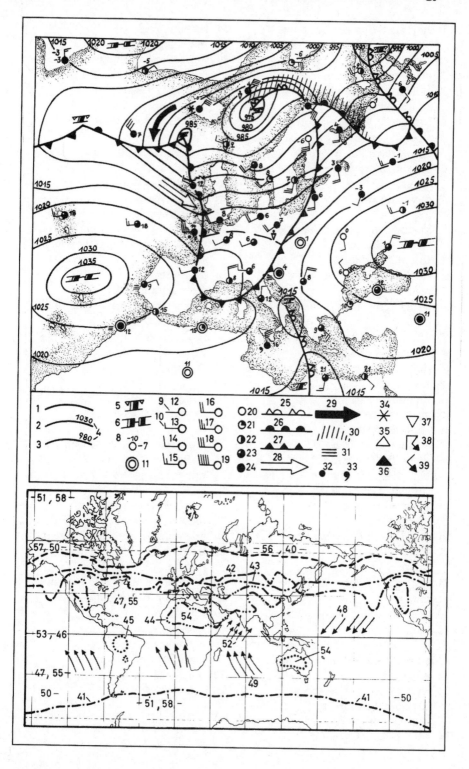

10 Meteorological Instruments

1 mercury barometer, a siphon barometer, a liquid-column barometer
2 mercury column
3 millibar scale, a millimetre (*Am.* millimeter) scale
4 barograph, a self-registering aneroid barometer
5 drum (recording drum)
6 bank of aneroid capsules (aneroid boxes)
7 recording arm
8 hygrograph
9 hygrometer element (hair element)
10 reading adjustment
11 amplitude adjustment
12 recording arm
13 recording pen
14 change gears for the clockwork drive
15 off switch for the recording arm
16 drum (recording drum)
17 time scale
18 case (housing)
19 thermograph
20 drum (recording drum)
21 recording arm
22 sensing element
23 silver-disc (silver-disk) pyrheliometer, an instrument for measuring the sun's radiant energy
24 silver disc (disk)
25 thermometer
26 wooden insulating casing
27 tube with diaphragm (diaphragmed tube)
28 wind gauge (*Am.* gage) (anemometer)
29 wind-speed indicator (wind-speed meter)
30 cross arms with hemispherical cups
31 wind-direction indicator
32 wind vane
33 aspiration psychrometer
34 dry bulb thermometer
35 wet bulb thermometer
36 solar radiation shielding
37 suction tube
38 recording rain gauge (*Am.* gage)
39 protective housing (protective casing)
40 collecting vessel
41 rain cover
42 recording mechanism
43 siphon tube
44 precipitation gauge (*Am.* gage) (rain gauge)
45 collecting vessel
46 storage vessel
47 measuring glass
48 insert for measuring snowfall
49 thermometer screen (thermometer shelter)
50 hygrograph
51 thermograph
52 psychrometer (wet and dry bulb thermometer)
53, 54 thermometers for measuring extremes of temperature
53 maximum thermometer
54 minimum thermometer
55 radiosonde assembly
56 hydrogen balloon
57 parachute
58 radar reflector with spacing lines
59 instrument housing with radiosonde [a short-wave transmitter] and antenna
60 transmissometer, an instrument for measuring visibility
61 recording instrument (recorder)
62 transmitter
63 receiver
64 weather satellite (ITOS satellite)
65 temperature regulation flaps
66 solar panel
67 television camera
68 antenna
69 solar sensor (sun sensor)
70 telemetry antenna
71 radiometer

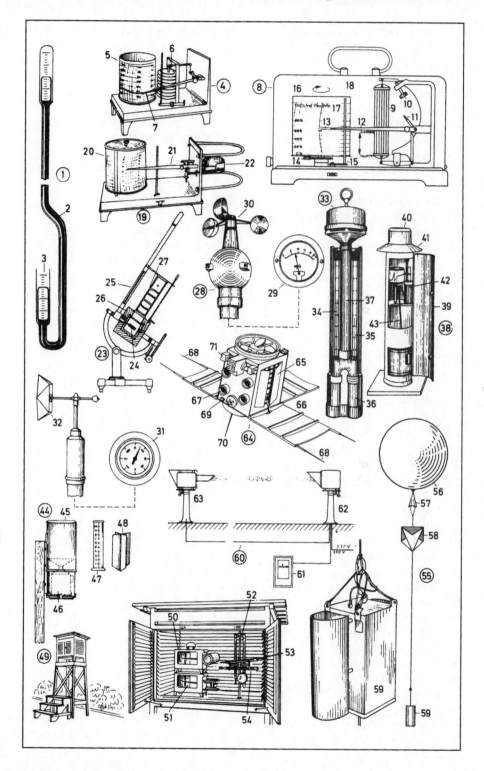

11 Physical Geography I

1-5 layered structure of the earth
1 earth's crust (outer crust of the earth, lithosphere, oxysphere)
2 hydrosphere
3 mantle
4 sima (intermediate layer)
5 core (earth core, centrosphere, barysphere)
6-12 hypsographic curve of the earth's surface
6 peak
7 continental mass
8 continental shelf (continental platform, shelf)
9 continental slope
10 deep-sea floor (abyssal plane)
11 sea level
12 deep-sea trench
13-28 volcanism (vulcanicity)
13 shield volcano
14 lava plateau
15 active volcano, a stratovolcano (composite volcano)
16 volcanic crater (crater)
17 volcanic vent
18 lava stream
19 tuff (fragmented volcanic material)
20 subterranean volcano
21 geyser
22 jet of hot water and steam
23 sinter terraces (siliceous sinter terraces, fiorite terraces, pearl sinter terraces)
24 cone
25 maar (extinct volcano)
26 tuff deposit
27 breccia
28 vent of extinct volcano
29-31 plutonic magmatism
29 batholite (massive protrusion)
30 lacolith, an intrusion
31 sill, an ore deposit
32-38 earthquake (*kinds:* tectonic quake, volcanic quake) **and seismology**
32 earthquake focus (seismic focus, hypocentre, *Am.* hypocenter)
33 epicentre (*Am.* epicenter), point on the earth's surface directly above the focus
34 depth of focus
35 shock wave
36 surface waves (seismic waves)
37 isoseismal (line connecting points of equal intensity of earthquake shock)
38 epicentral area, an area of macroseismic vibration
39 horizontal seismograph (seismometer)
40 electromagnetic damper
41 adjustment knob for the period of free oscillation of the pendulum
42 spring attachment for the suspension of the pendulum
43 mass
44 induction coils for recording the voltage of the galvanometer
45-54 effects of earthquakes
45 waterfall (cataract, falls)
46 landslide (rockslide, landslip, *Am.* rock slip)
47 talus (rubble, scree)
48 scar (scaur, scaw)
49 sink (sinkhole, swallowhole)
50 dislocation (displacement)
51 solifluction lobe (solifluction tongue)
52 fissure
53 tsunami (seismic sea wave) produced by seaquake (submarine earthquake)
54 raised beach

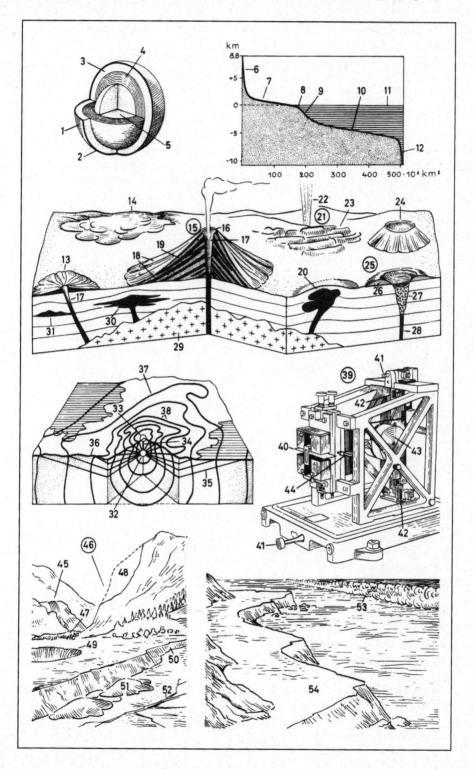

1-33 geology
1 stratification of sedimentary rock
2 strike
3 dip (angle of dip, true dip)
4-20 orogeny (orogenis, tectogenis, deformation of rocks by folding and faulting)
4-11 fault-block mountain (block mountain)
4 fault
5 fault line (fault trace)
6 fault throw
7 normal fault (gravity fault, normal slip fault, slump fault)
8-11 complex faults
8 step fault (distributive fault, multiple fault)
9 tilt block
10 horst
11 graben
12-20 range of fold mountains (folded mountains)
12 symmetrical fold (normal fold)
13 asymmetrical fold
14 overfold
15 recumbent fold (reclined fold)
16 saddle (anticline)
17 anticlinal axis
18 trough (syncline)
19 trough surface (trough plane, synclinal axis)
20 anticlinorium
21 **groundwater under pressure** (artesian water)
22 water-bearing stratum (aquifer, aquafer)
23 impervious rock (impermeable rock)
24 drainage basin (catchment area)
25 artesian well
26 rising water, an artesian spring
27 **petroleum reservoir** in an anticline
28 impervious stratum (impermeable stratum)
29 porous stratum acting as reservoir rock
30 natural gas, a gas cap

31 petroleum (crude oil)
32 underlying water
33 derrick
34 **mountainous area**
35 rounded mountain top
36 mountain ridge (ridge)
37 mountain slope
38 hillside spring
39-47 high-mountain region
39 mountain range, a massif
40 summit (peak, top of the mountain)
41 shoulder
42 saddle
43 rock face (steep face)
44 gully
45 talus (scree, detritus)
46 bridle path
47 pass (col)
48-56 glacial ice
48 firn field (firn basin, nevé)
49 valley glacier
50 crevasse
51 glacier snout
52 subglacial stream
53 lateral moraine
54 medial moraine
55 end moraine
56 glacier table

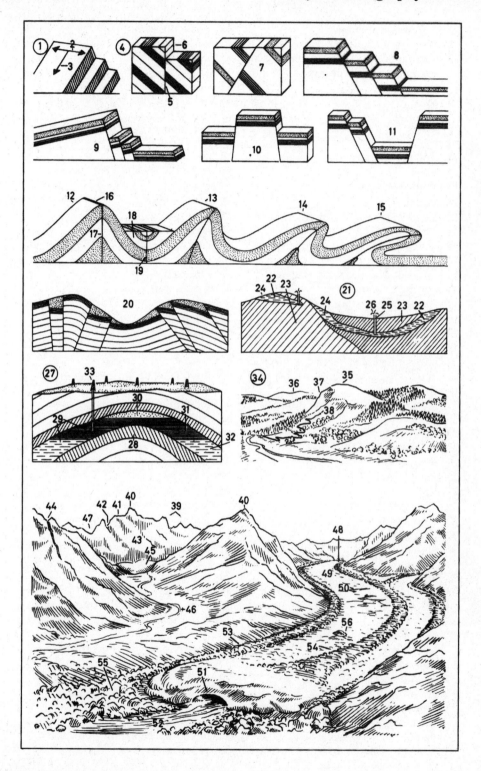

13 Physical Geography III

1-13 fluvial topography
1 river mouth, a delta
2 distributary (distributary channel), a river branch (river arm)
3 lake
4 bank
5 peninsula (spit)
6 island
7 bay (cove)
8 stream (brook, rivulet, creek)
9 levee
10 alluvial plain
11 meander (river bend)
12 meander core (rock island)
13 meadow
14-24 bog (marsh)
14 low-moor bog
15 layers of decayed vegetable matter
16 entrapped water
17 fen peat [consisting of rush and sedge]
18 alder-swamp peat
19 high-moor bog
20 layer of recent sphagnum mosses
21 boundary between layers (horizons)
22 layer of older sphagnum mosses
23 bog pool
24 swamp
25-31 cliffline (cliffs)
25 rock
26 sea (ocean)
27 surf
28 cliff (cliff face, steep rock face)
29 scree
30 [wave-cut] notch
31 abrasion platform (wave-cut platform)
32 atoll, a ring-shaped coral reef
33 lagoon
34 breach (hole)
35-44 beach
35 high-water line (high-water mark, tidemark)
36 waves breaking on the shore
37 groyne (Am. groin)
38 groyne (Am. groin) head
39 wandering dune (migratory dune, travelling, Am. traveling, dune), a dune
40 barchan (barchane, barkhan, crescentic dune)
41 ripple marks
42 hummock
43 wind cripple
44 coastal lake
45 canyon (cañon, coulee)
46 plateau (tableland)
47 rock terrace
48 sedimentary rock (stratified rock)
49 river terrace (bed)
50 joint
51 canyon river
52-56 types of valley [cross section]
52 gorge (ravine)
53 V-shaped valley (V-valley)
54 widened V-shaped valley
55 U-shaped valley (U-valley, trough valley)
56 synclinal valley
57-70 river valley
57 scarp (escarpment)
58 slip-off slope
59 mesa
60 ridge
61 river
62 flood plain
63 river terrace
64 terracette
65 pediment
66 hill
67 valley floor (valley bottom)
68 riverbed
69 sediment
70 bedrock
71-83 karst formation in limestone
71 dolina, a sink (sinkhole, swallowhole)
72 polje
73 percolation of a river
74 karst spring
75 dry valley
76 system of caverns (system of caves)
77 water level (water table) in a karst formation
78 impervious rock (impermeable rock)
79 limestone cave (dripstone cave)
80, 81 speleothems (cave formations)
80 stalactite (dripstone)
81 stalagmite
82 linked-up stalagmite and stalactite
83 subterranean river

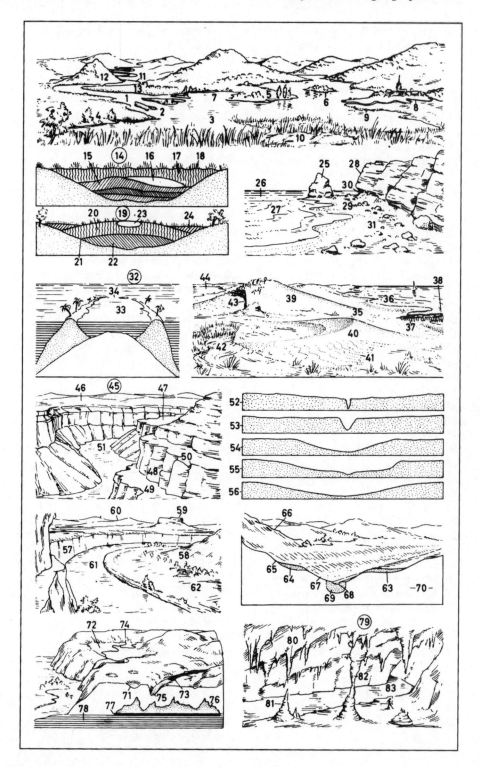

1-7 graticule of the earth (network of meridians and parallels on the earth's surface)

1 equator

2 line of latitude (parallel of latitude, parallel)

3 pole (North Pole or South Pole), a terrestrial pole (geographical pole)

4 line of longitude (meridian of longitude, meridian, terrestrial meridian)

5 Standard meridian (Prime meridian, Greenwich meridian, meridian of Greenwich)

6 latitude

7 longitude

8, 9 map projections

8 conical (conic) projection

9 cylindrical projection (Mercator projection, Mercator's projection)

10-45 map of the world

10 tropics

11 polar circles

12-18 continents

12, 13 America

12 North America

13 South America

14 Africa

15, 16 Europe and Asia

15 Europe

16 Asia

17 Australia

18 Antarctica (Antarctic Continent)

19-26 ocean (sea)

19 Pacific Ocean

20 Atlantic Ocean

21 Arctic Ocean

22 Antarctic Ocean (Southern Ocean)

23 Indian Ocean

24 Strait of Gibraltar, a sea strait

25 Mediterranean (Mediterranean Sea, European Mediterranean)

26 North Sea, a marginal sea (epeiric sea, epicontinental sea)

27-29 key (explanation of map symbols)

27 cold ocean current

28 warm ocean current

29 scale

30-45 ocean (oceanic) currents (ocean drifts)

30 Gulf Stream (North Atlantic Drift)

31 Kuroshio (Kuro Siwo, Japan Current)

32 North Equatorial Current

33 Equatorial Countercurrent

34 South Equatorial Current

35 Brazil Current

36 Somali Current

37 Agulhas Current

38 East Australian Current

39 California Current

40 Labrador Current

41 Canary Current

42 Peru Current

43 Benguela (Benguella) Current

44 West Wind Drift (Antarctic Circumpolar Drift)

45 West Australian Current

46-62 surveying (land surveying, geodetic surveying, geodesy)

46 levelling (*Am.* leveling) (geometrical measurement of height)

47 graduated measuring rod (levelling, *Am.* leveling, staff)

48 level (surveying level, surveyor's level), a surveyor's telescope

49 triangulation station (triangulation point)

50 supporting scaffold

51 signal tower (signal mast)

52-62 theodolite, an instrument for measuring angles

52 micrometer head

53 micrometer eyepiece

54 vertical tangent screw

55 vertical clamp

56 tangent screw

57 horizontal clamp

58 adjustment for the illuminating mirror

59 illuminating mirror

60 telescope

61 spirit level

62 circular adjustment

63-66 photogrammetry (phototopography)

63 air survey camera for producing overlapping series of pictures

64 stereoscope

65 pantograph

66 stereoplanigraph

Map I 14

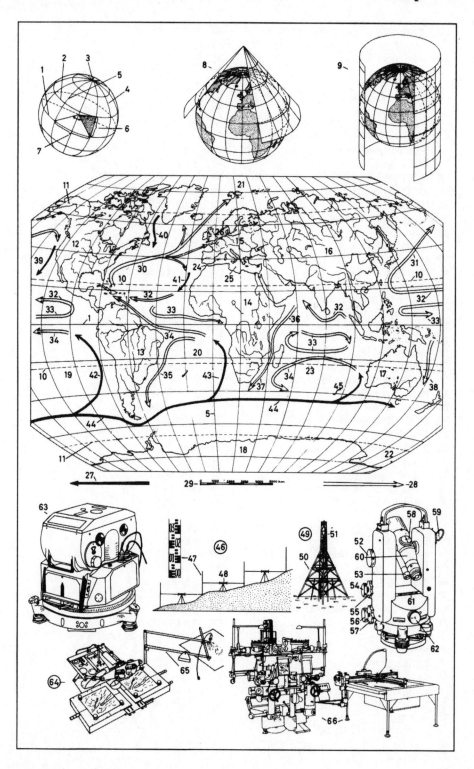

1-114 map signs (map symbols, conventional signs) on a 1: 25 000 map
1 coniferous wood (coniferous trees)
2 clearing
3 forestry office
4 deciduous wood (non-coniferous trees)
5 heath (rough grassland, rough pasture, heath and moor, bracken)
6 sand or sand hills
7 beach grass
8 lighthouse
9 mean low water
10 beacon
11 submarine contours
12 train ferry
13 lightship
14 mixed wood (mixed trees)
15 brushwood
16 motorway with slip road (*Am.* freeway with on-ramp, freeway with acceleration lane)
17 trunk road
18 grassland
19 marshy grassland
20 marsh
21 main line railway (*Am.* trunk line)
22 road over railway
23 branch line
24 signal box (*Am.* switch tower)
25 local line
26 level crossing
27 halt
28 residential area
29 water gauge (*Am.* gage)
30 good, metalled road
31 windmill
32 thorn house (graduation house, salina, salt-works)
33 broadcasting station (wireless or television mast)
34 mine
35 disused mine
36 secondary road (B road)
37 works
38 chimney
39 wire fence
40 bridge over railway
41 railway station (*Am.* railroad station)
42 bridge under railway
43 footpath
44 bridge for footpath under railway
45 navigable river
46 pontoon bridge
47 vehicle ferry
48 mole
49 beacon
50 stone bridge
51 town or city
52 market place (market square)
53 large church with two towers
54 public building
55 road bridge
56 iron bridge
57 canal
58 lock
59 jetty
60 foot ferry (foot passenger ferry)
61 chapel (church) without tower or spire
62 contours
63 monastery or convent
64 church landmark
65 vineyard
66 weir
67 aerial ropeway
68 view point
69 dam
70 tunnel
71 triangulation station (triangulation point)
72 remains of a building
73 wind pump
74 fortress
75 ox-bow lake
76 river
77 watermill
78 footbridge
79 pond
80 stream (brook, rivulet, creek)
81 water tower
82 spring
83 main road (A road)
84 cutting
85 cave
86 lime kiln
87 quarry
88 clay pit
89 brickworks
90 narrow-gauge (*Am.* narrow gage) railway
91 goods depot (freight depot)
92 monument
93 site of battle
94 country estate, a demesne
95 wall
96 stately home
97 park
98 hedge

Map II 15

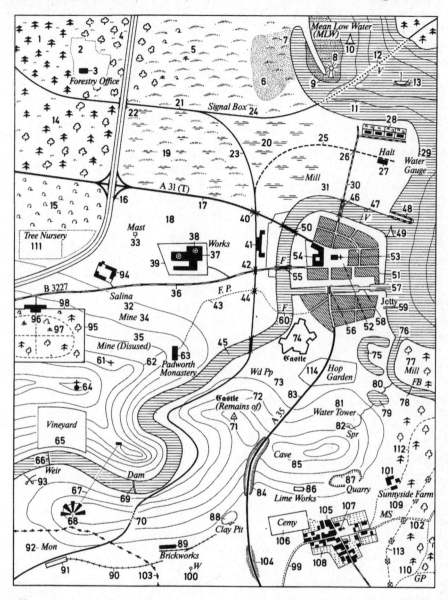

99 poor or unmetalled road
100 well
101 farm
102 unfenced path (unfenced track)
103 district boundary
104 embankment
105 village
106 cemetery
107 church or chapel with spire
108 orchard
109 milestone
110 guide post
111 tree nursery
112 ride (aisle, lane, section line)
113 electricity transmission line
114 hop garden

1-54 the human body
1-18 head
1 vertex (crown of the head, top of the head)
2 occiput (back of the head)
3 hair
4-17 face
4-5 forehead
4 frontal eminence (frontal protuberance)
5 superciliary arch
6 temple
7 eye
8 zygomatic bone (malar bone, jugal bone, cheekbone)
9 cheek
10 nose
11 nasolabial fold
12 philtrum
13 mouth
14 angle of the mouth (labial commissure)
15 chin
16 dimple (fossette) in the chin
17 jaw
18 ear
19-21 neck
19 throat
20 hollow of the throat
21 nape of the neck
22-41 trunk
22-25 back
22 shoulder
23 shoulderblade (scapula)
24 loins
25 small of the back
26 armpit
27 armpit hair
28-30 thorax (chest)
28-29 breasts (breast, mamma)
28 nipple
29 areola
30 bosom
31 waist
32 flank (side)
33 hip
34 navel

35-37 abdomen (stomach)
35 upper abdomen
36 abdomen
37 lower abdomen
38 groin
39 pudenda (vulva)
40 seat (backside, *coll.* bottom)
41 anal groove (anal cleft)
42 gluteal fold (gluteal furrow)
43-54 limbs
43-48 arm
43 upper arm
44 crook of the arm
45 elbow
46 forearm
47 hand
48 fist (clenched fist, clenched hand)
49-54 leg
49 thigh
50 knee
51 popliteal space
52 shank
53 calf
54 foot

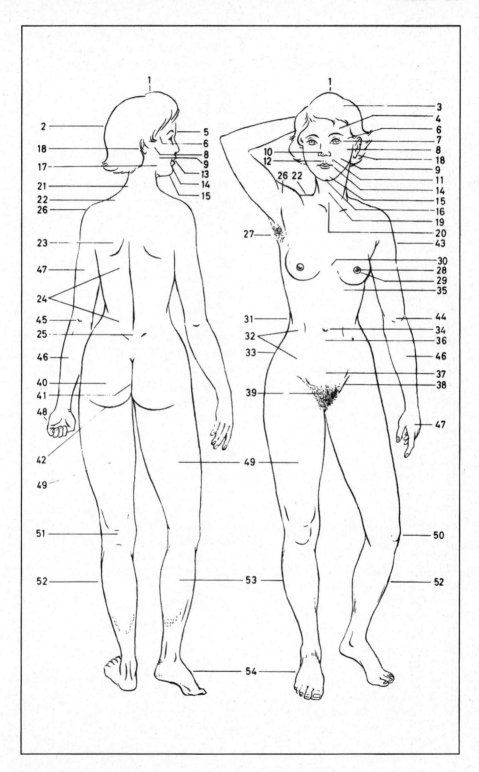

17 Man II

1-29 **skeleton** (bones)
1 skull
2-5 **vertebral column** (spinal column, spine, backbone)
2 cervical vertebra
3 dorsal vertebra (thoracic vertebra)
4 lumbar vertebra
5 coccyx (coccygeal vertebra)
6, 7 **shoulder girdle**
6 collarbone (clavicle)
7 shoulderblade (scapula)
8-11 **thorax** (chest)
8 breastbone (sternum)
9 true ribs
10 false ribs
11 costal cartilage
12-14 **arm**
12 humerus
13 radius
14 ulna
15-17 **hand**
15 carpus
16 metacarpal bone (metacarpal)
17 phalanx (phalange)
18-21 **pelvis**
18 ilium (hip bone)
19 ischium
20 pubis
21 sacrum
22-25 **leg**
22 femur (thigh bone, thigh)
23 patella (kneecap)
24 fibula (splint bone)
25 tibia (shinbone)
26-29 **foot**
26 tarsal bones (tarsus)
27 calcaneum (heelbone)
28 metatarsus
29 phalanges
30-41 **skull**
30 frontal bone
31 left parietal bone
32 occipital bone
33 temporal bone
34 external auditory canal
35 lower jawbone (lower jaw, mandible)

36 upper jawbone (upper jaw, maxilla)
37 zygomatic bone (cheekbone)
38 sphenoid bone (sphenoid)
39 ethmoid bone (ethmoid)
40 lachrimal (lacrimal) bone
41 nasal bone
42-55 **head** [section]
42 cerebrum (great brain)
43 pituitary gland (pituitary body, hypophysis cerebri)
44 corpus callosum
45 cerebellum (little brain)
46 pons (pons cerebri, pons cerebelli)
47 medulla oblongata (brain stem)
48 spinal cord
49 oesophagus (esophagus, gullet)
50 trachea (windpipe)
51 epiglottis
52 tongue
53 nasal cavity
54 sphenoidal sinus
55 frontal sinus
56-65 **organ of equilibrium and hearing**
56-58 **external ear**
56 auricle
57 ear lobe
58 external auditory canal
59-61 **middle ear**
59 tympanic membrane
60 tympanic cavity
61 auditory ossicles: hammer, anvil, and stirrup (malleus, incus, and stapes)
62-64 **inner ear** (internal ear)
62 labyrinth
63 cochlea
64 auditory nerve
65 eustachian tube

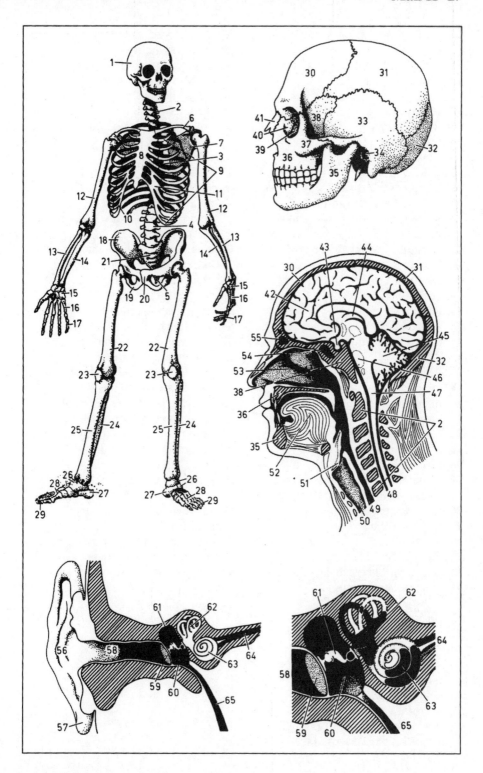

1-21 blood circulation (circulatory system)

1 common carotid artery, an artery
2 jugular vein, a vein
3 temporal artery
4 temporal vein
5 frontal artery
6 frontal vein
7 subclavian artery
8 subclavian vein
9 superior vena cava
10 arch of the aorta (aorta)
11 pulmonary artery [with venous blood]
12 pulmonary vein [with arterial blood]
13 lungs
14 heart
15 inferior vena cava
16 abdominal aorta (descending portion of the aorta)
17 iliac artery
18 iliac vein
19 femoral artery
20 tibial artery
21 radial artery

22-33 nervous system

22 cerebrum (great brain)
23 cerebellum (little brain)
24 medulla oblongata (brain stem)
25 spinal cord
26 thoracic nerves
27 brachial plexus
28 radial nerve
29 ulnar nerve
30 great sciatic nerve [lying posteriorly]
31 femoral nerve (anterior crural nerve)
32 tibial nerve
33 peroneal nerve

34-64 musculature (muscular system)

34 sternocleidomastoid muscle (sternomastoid muscle)
35 deltoid muscle
36 pectoralis major (greater pectoralis muscle, greater pectoralis)
37 biceps brachii (biceps of the arm)
38 triceps brachii (triceps of the arm)
39 brachioradialis
40 flexor carpi radialis (radial flexor of the wrist)
41 thenar muscle
42 serratus anterior
43 obliquus externus abdominis (external oblique)
44 rectus abdominis
45 sartorius
46 vastus lateralis and vastus medialis
47 tibialis anterior
48 tendo calcaneus (Achilles' tendon)
49 abductor hallucis (abductor of the hallux), a foot muscle
50 occipitalis
51 splenius of the neck
52 trapezius
53 infraspinatus
54 teres minor (lesser teres)
55 teres major (greater teres)
56 extensor carpi radialis longus (long radial extensor of the wrist)
57 extensor communis digitorum (common extensor of the digits)
58 flexor carpi ulnaris (ulnar flexor of the wrist)
59 latissimus dorsi
60 gluteus maximus
61 biceps femoris (biceps of the thigh)
62 gastrocnemius, medial and lateral heads
63 extensor communis digitorum (common extensor of the digits)
64 peroneus longus (long peroneus)

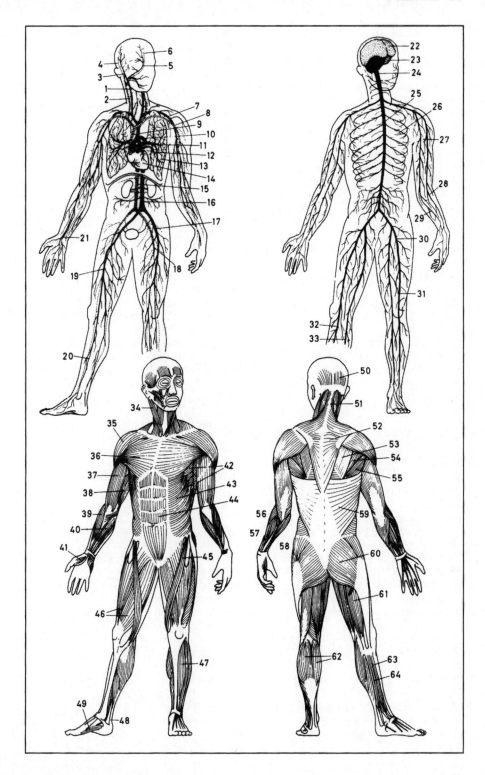

19 Man IV

1-13 head and neck
1 sternocleidomastoid muscle (sternomastoid muscle)
2 occipitalis
3 temporalis (temporal, temporal muscle)
4 occipito frontalis (frontalis)
5 orbicularis oculi
6 muscles of facial expression
7 masseter
8 orbicularis oris
9 parotid gland
10 lymph node (submandibular lymph gland)
11 submandibular gland (submaxillary gland)
12 muscles of the neck
13 Adam's apple (laryngeal prominence) [in men only]

14-37 mouth and pharynx
14 upper lip
15 gum
16-18 teeth (set of teeth)
16 incisors
17 canine tooth (canine)
18 premolar (bicuspid) and molar teeth (premolars and molars)
19 angle of the mouth (labial commissure)
20 hard palate
21 soft palate (velum palati, velum)
22 uvula
23 palatine tonsil (tonsil)
24 pharyngeal opening (pharynx)
25 tongue
26 lower lip
27 upper jaw (maxilla)

28-37 tooth
28 periodontal membrane (periodontium, pericementum)
29 cement (dental cementum, crusta petrosa)
30 enamel
31 dentine (dentin)
32 dental pulp (tooth pulp, pulp)
33 nerves and blood vessels
34 incisor
35 molar tooth (molar)
36 root (fang)
37 crown

38-51 eye
38 eyebrow (supercilium)
39 upper eyelid (upper palpebra)
40 lower eyelid (lower palpebra)
41 eyelash (cilium)
42 iris

43 pupil
44 eye muscles (ocular muscles)
45 eyeball
46 vitreous body
47 cornea
48 lens
49 retina
50 blind spot
51 optic nerve

52-63 foot
52 big toe (great toe, first toe, hallux, digitus I)
53 second toe (digitus II)
54 third toe (digitus III)
55 fourth toe (digitus IV)
56 little toe (digitus minimus, digitus V)
57 toenail
58 ball of the foot
59 lateral malleolus (external malleolus, outer malleolus, malleolus fibulae)
60 medial malleolus (internal malleolus, inner malleolus, malleolus tibulae, malleolus medialis)
61 instep (medial longitudinal arch, dorsum of the foot, dorsum pedis)
62 sole of the foot
63 heel

64-83 hand
64 thumb (pollex, digitus I)
65 index finger (forefinger, second finger, digitus II)
66 middle finger (third finger, digitus medius, digitus III)
67 ring finger (fourth finger, digitus anularis, digitus IV)
68 little finger (fifth finger, digitus minimus, digitus V)
69 radial side of the hand
70 ulnar side of the hand
71 palm of the hand (palma manus)

72-74 lines of the hand
72 life line (line of life)
73 head line (line of the head)
74 heart line (line of the heart)
75 ball of the thumb (thenar eminence)
76 wrist (carpus)
77 phalanx (phalange)
78 finger pad
79 fingertip
80 fingernail (nail)
81 lunule (lunula) of the nail
82 knuckle
83 back of the hand (dorsum of the hand, dorsum manus)

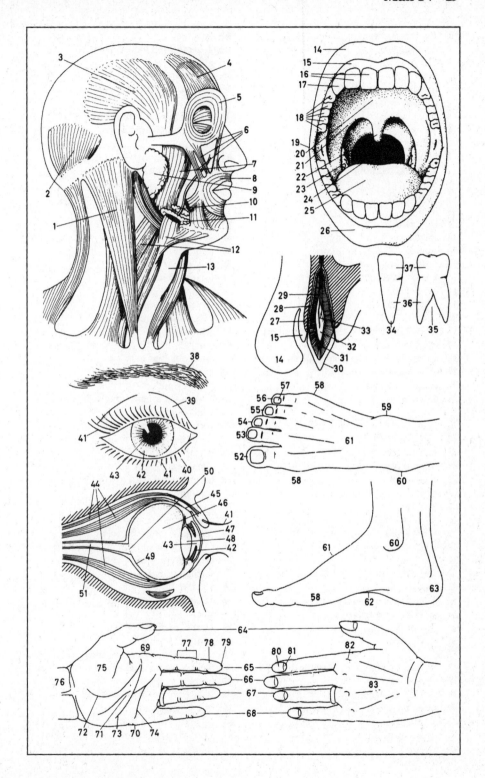

1-57 internal organs [front view]
1 thyroid gland
2, 3 larynx
2 hyoid bone (hyoid)
3 thyroid cartilage
4 trachea (windpipe)
5 bronchus
6, 7 lung
6 right lung
7 upper pulmonary lobe (upper lobe of the lung) [section]
8 heart
9 diaphragm
10 liver
11 gall bladder
12 spleen
13 stomach
14-22 intestines (bowel)
14-16 small intestine (intestinum tenue)
14 duodenum
15 jejunum
16 ileum
17-22 large intestine (intestinum crassum)
17 caecum (cecum)
18 appendix (vermiform appendix)
19 ascending colon
20 transverse colon
21 descending colon
22 rectum
23 oesophagus (esophagus, gullet)
24, 25 heart
24 auricle
25 anterior longitudinal cardiac sulcus
26 diaphragm
27 spleen
28 right kidney
29 suprarenal gland
30, 31 left kidney [longitudinal section]
30 calyx (renal calyx)
31 renal pelvis
32 ureter
33 bladder
34, 35 liver [from behind]
34 falciform ligament of the liver
35 lobe of the liver
36 gall bladder
37, 38 common bile duct
37 hepatic duct (common hepatic duct)
38 cystic duct
39 portal vein (hepatic portal vein)
40 oesophagus (esophagus, gullet)
41, 42 stomach
41 cardiac orifice
42 pylorus
43 duodenum

44 pancreas
45-57 heart [longitudinal section]
45 atrium
46, 47 valves of the heart
46 tricuspid valve (right atrioventricular valve)
47 bicuspid valve (mitral valve, left atrioventricular valve)
48 cusp
49 aortic valve
50 pulmonary valve
51 ventricle
52 ventricular septum (interventricular septum)
53 superior vena cava
54 aorta
55 pulmonary artery
56 pulmonary vein
57 inferior vena cava
58 peritoneum
59 sacrum
60 coccyx (coccygeal vertebra)
61 rectum
62 anus
63 anal sphincter
64 perineum
65 pubic symphisis (symphisis pubis)
66-77 male sex organs [longitudinal section]
66 penis
67 corpus cavernosum and spongiosum of the penis (erectile tissue of the penis)
68 urethra
69 glans penis
70 prepuce (foreskin)
71 scrotum
72 right testicle (testis)
73 epididymis
74 spermatic duct (vas deferens)
75 Cowper's gland (bulbourethral gland)
76 prostate (prostate gland)
77 seminal vesicle
78 bladder
79-88 female sex organs [longitudinal section]
79 uterus (matrix, womb)
80 cavity of the uterus
81 fallopian tube (uterine tube, oviduct)
82 fimbria (fimbriated extremity)
83 ovary
84 follicle with ovum (egg)
85 os uteri externum
86 vagina
87 lip of the pudendum (lip of the vulva)
88 clitoris

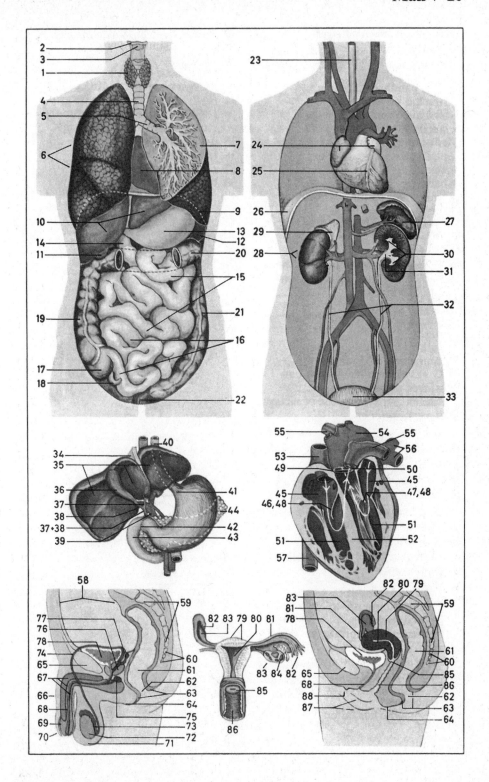

21 First Aid

1-13 emergency bandages
1 arm bandage
2 triangular cloth used as a sling (an arm sling)
3 head bandage (capeline)
4 first aid kit
5 first aid dressing
6 sterile gauze dressing
7 adhesive plaster (sticking plaster)
8 wound
9 bandage
10 emergency splint for a broken limb (fractured limb)
11 fractured leg (broken leg)
12 splint
13 headrest
14-17 measures for stanching the blood flow (tying up (ligature) of a blood vessel)
14 pressure points of the arteries
15 emergency tourniquet on the thigh
16 walking stick used as a screw
17 compression bandage
18-23 rescue and transport of an injured person
18 Rautek grip (for rescue of a car accident victim)
19 helper
20 injured person (casualty)
21 chair grip
22 carrying grip
23 emergency stretcher of sticks and a jacket
24-27 positioning of an unconscious person and artificial respiration (resuscitation)
24 coma position
25 unconscious person
26 mouth-to-mouth resuscitation (*variation:* mouth-to-nose resuscitation)
27 resuscitator (respiratory apparatus, resuscitation apparatus), a respirator (artificial breathing device)
28-33 methods of rescue in ice accidents

28 person who has fallen through the ice
29 rescuer
30 rope
31 table (or similar device)
32 ladder
33 self-rescue
34-38 rescue of a drowning person
34 method of release (release grip, release) to free rescuer from the clutch of a drowning person
35 drowning person
36 lifesaver
37, 38 towing (tows)
37 double shoulder tow
38 head tow

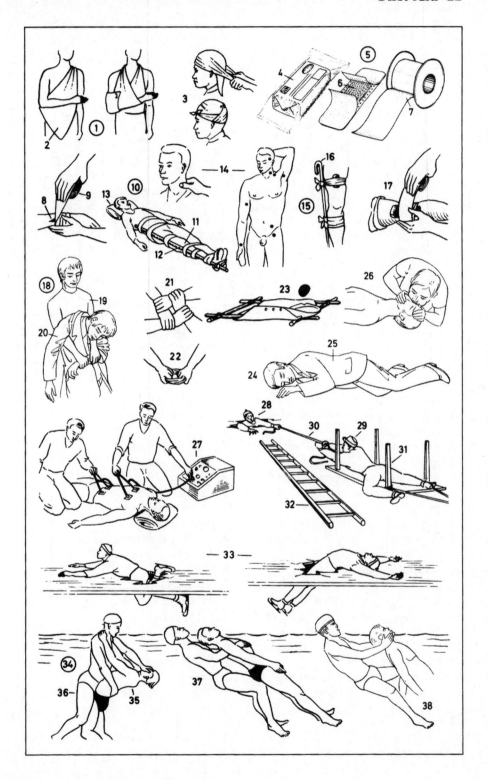

1-74 **general practice** (*Am.* physician's office)
1 **waiting room**
2 patient
3 patients with appointments (for a routine check-up or renewal of prescription)
4 magazines [for waiting patients]
5 reception
6 patients file
7 eliminated index cards
8 medical record (medical card)
9 health insurance certificate
10 advertising calendar (publicity calendar)
11 appointments book
12 correspondence file
13 automatic telephone answering and recording set (telephone answering device)
14 radiophone
15 microphone
16 illustrated chart
17 wall calendar
18 telephone
19 [doctor's] assistant
20 prescription
21 telephone index
22 medical dictionary
23 pharmacopoeia (list of registered medicines)
24 franking machine (*Am.* postage meter)
25 stapler
26 diabetics file
27 dictating machine
28 paper punch
29 doctor's stamp
30 ink pad
31 pencil holder
32-74 **surgery**
32 chart of eyegrounds
33 doctor's bag (doctor's case)
34 intercom
35 medicine cupboard
36 swab dispenser

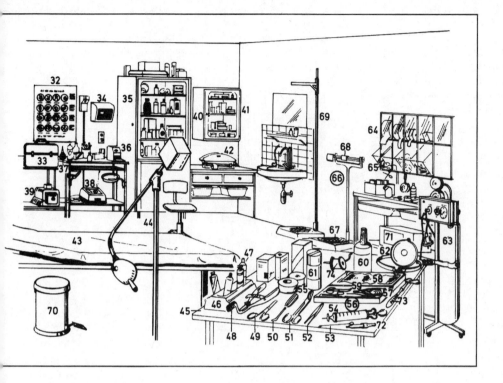

37 inflator (Politzer bag)	**57** curved surgical needle
38 electrotome	**58** sterile gauze
39 steam sterilizer	**59** needle holder
40 cabinet	**60** spray for disinfecting the skin
41 medicine samples (from the pharmaceutical industry)	**61** thread container
	62 ophthalmoscope
42 baby scales	**63** freezer for cryosurgery
43 examination couch	**64** dispenser for plasters and small pieces of equipment
44 directional lamp	
45 instrument table	**65** disposable hypodermic needles and syringes
46 tube holder	
47 tube of ointment	**66** scales, sliding-weight scales
48-50 instruments for minor surgery	**67** weighing platform
48 mouth gag	**68** sliding weight (jockey)
49 Kocher's forceps	**69** height gauge (*Am.* gage)
50 scoop (curette)	**70** waste bin (*Am.* trash bin)
51 angled scissors	**71** hot-air sterilizer
52 forceps	**72** pipette
53 olive-pointed (bulb-headed) probe	**73** percussor
54 syringe for irrigations of the ear or bladder	**74** aural speculum (auriscope, aural syringe)
55 adhesive plaster (sticking plaster)	
56 surgical suture material	

1 consulting room
2 general practitioner
3-21 instruments for gynaecological and proctological examinations
3 warming the instruments up to body temperature
4 examination couch
5 colposcope
6 binocular eyepiece
7 miniature camera
8 cold light source
9 cable release
10 bracket for the leg support
11 leg support (leg holder)
12 holding forceps (sponge holder)
13 vaginal speculum
14 lower blade of the vaginal speculum
15 platinum loop (for smears)
16 rectoscope
17 biopsy forceps used with the rectoscope (proctoscope)
18 insufflator for proctoscopy (rectoscopy)

19 proctoscope (rectal speculum)
20 urethroscope
21 guide for inserting the proctoscope
22 diathermy unit (short-wave therapy apparatus)
23 radiator
24 inhaling apparatus (inhalator)
25 basin [for sputum]
26-31 ergometry
26 bicycle ergometer
27 monitor (for visual display of the ECG and of pulse and respiratory rates when performing work)
28 ECG (electrocardiograph)
29 suction electrodes
30 strap-on electrodes for the limbs
31 spirometer (for measuring respiratory functions)
32 measuring blood pressure
33 sphygmomanometer
34 inflatable cuff
35 stethoscope
36 microwave treatment unit

37 faradization unit (for applying low-frequency currents with different pulse shapes)
38 automatic tuner
39 short-wave therapy apparatus
40 timer
41-59 laboratory
41 medical laboratory technician
42 capillary tube stand for blood sedimentation
43 measuring cylinder
44 automatic pipette
45 kidney dish
46 portable ECG machine for emergency use
47 automatic pipetting device
48 constant temperature water bath
49 tap with water jet pump
50 staining dish (for staining blood smears, sediments, and other smears)

51 binocular research microscope
52 pipette stand for photometry
53 computer and analyser for photometry
54 photometer
55 potentiometric recorder
56 transforming section
57 laboratory apparatus (laboratory equipment)
58 urine sediment chart
59 centrifuge

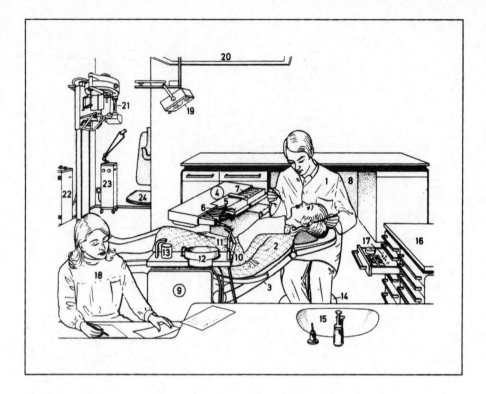

1 dentist (dental surgeon)
2 patient
3 dentist's chair
4 dental instruments
5 instrument tray
6 drills with different handpieces
7 medicine case
8 storage unit (for dental instruments)
9 assistant's unit
10 multi-purpose syringe (for cold and warm water, spray, or air)
11 suction apparatus
12 basin
13 water glass, filled automatically
14 stool
15 washbasin
16 instrument cabinet
17 drawer for drills
18 dentist's assistant
19 dentist's lamp
20 ceiling light

21 X-ray apparatus for panoramic pictures
22 X-ray generator
23 microwave treatment unit, a radiation unit
24 seat
25 denture (set of false teeth)
26 bridge (dental bridge)
27 prepared stump of the tooth
28 crown (*kinds:* gold crown, jacket crown)
29 porcelain tooth (porcelain pontic)
30 filling
31 post crown
32 facing
33 diaphragm
34 post
35 carborundum disc (disk)
36 grinding wheel
37 burs
38 flame-shaped finishing bur
39 fissure burs

40 diamond point
41 mouth mirror
42 mouth lamp
43 cautery
44 platinum-iridium electrode
45 tooth scalers
46 probe
47 extraction forceps
48 tooth-root elevator
49 bone chisel
50 spatula
51 mixer for filling material
52 synchronous timer
53 hypodermic syringe for injection of local anaesthetic
54 hypodermic needle
55 matrix holder
56 impression tray
57 spirit lamp

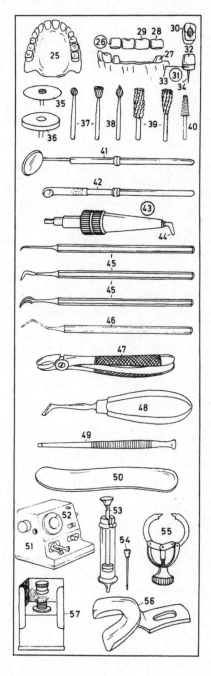

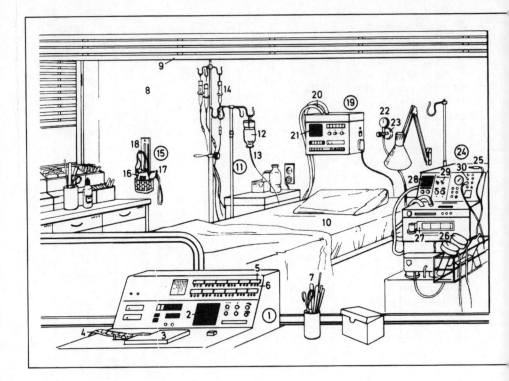

1-30 intensive care unit

1-9 control room

1 central control unit for monitoring heart rhythm (cardiac rhythm) and blood pressure
2 electrocardiogram monitor (ECG monitor)
3 recorder
4 recording paper
5 patient's card
6 indicator lights (with call buttons for each patient)
7 spatula
8 window (observation window, glass partition)
9 blind
10 bed (hospital bed)
11 stand for infusion apparatus
12 infusion bottle
13 tube for intravenous drips
14 infusion device for water-soluble medicaments
15 sphygmomanometer
16 cuff
17 inflating bulb
18 mercury manometer
19 bed monitor
20 connecting lead to the central control unit
21 electrocardiogram monitor (ECG monitor)
22 manometer for the oxygen supply
23 wall connection for oxygen treatment
24 mobile monitoring unit
25 electrode lead to the short-term pacemaker
26 electrodes for shock treatment
27 ECG recording unit
28 electrocardiogram monitor (ECG monitor)
29 control switches and knobs (controls) for adjusting the monitor
30 control buttons for the pacemaker unit
31 **pacemaker** (cardiac pacemaker)

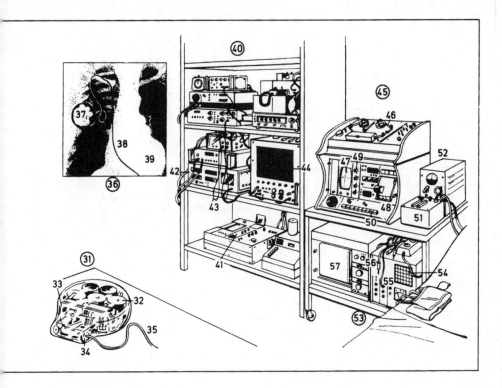

32 mercury battery
33 programmed impulse generator
34 electrode exit point
35 electrode
36 implantation of the pacemaker
37 internal cardiac pacemaker (internal pacemaker, pacemaker)
38 electrode inserted through the vein
39 cardiac silhouette on the X-ray
40 **pacemaker control unit**
41 electrocardiograph (ECG recorder)
42 automatic impulse meter
43 ECG lead to the patient
44 monitor unit for visual monitoring of the pacemaker impulses
45 long-term ECG analyser
46 magnetic tape for recording the ECG impulses during analysis
47 ECG monitor
48 automatic analysis on paper of the ECG rhythm

49 control knob for the ECG amplitude
50 program selector switches for the ECG analysis
51 charger for the pacemaker batteries
52 battery tester
53 pressure gauge (*Am.* gage) for the right cardiac catheter
54 trace monitor
55 pressure indicator
56 connecting lead to the paper recorder
57 paper recorder for pressure traces

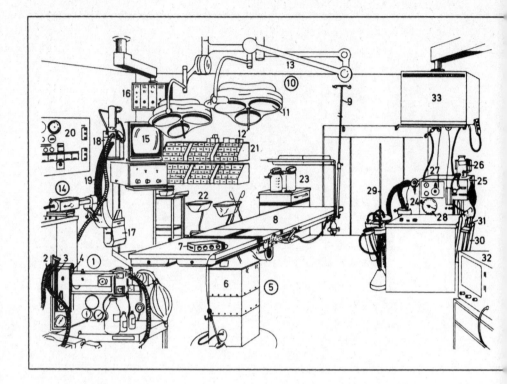

1-54 surgical unit
1-33 operating theatre (*Am.* theater)
1 anaesthesia and breathing apparatus (respiratory machine)
2 inhalers (inhaling tubes)
3 flowmeter for nitrous oxide
4 oxygen flow meter
5 pedestal operating table
6 table pedestal
7 control device (control unit)
8 adjustable top of the operating table
9 stand for intravenous drips
10 swivel-mounted shadow-free operating lamp
11 individual lamp
12 handle
13 swivel arm
14 mobile fluoroscope
15 monitor of the image converter
16 monitor [back]
17 tube
18 image converter
19 C-shaped frame
20 control panel for the air-conditioning
21 surgical suture material
22 mobile waste tray
23 containers for unsterile (unsterilized) pads
24 anaesthesia and respiratory apparatus
25 respirator
26 fluothane container (halothane container)
27 ventilation control knob
28 indicator with pointer for respiratory volume
29 stand with inhalers (inhaling tubes) and pressure gauges (*Am.* gages)
30 catheter holder
31 catheter in sterile packing
32 sphygmograph
33 monitor

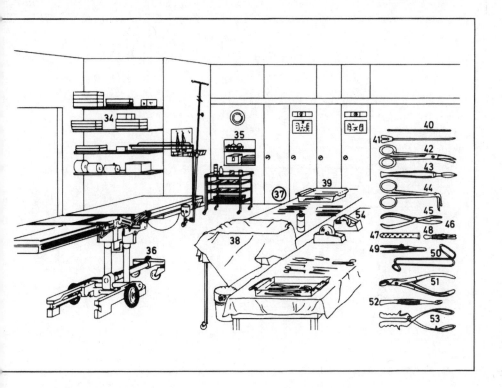

34-54 preparation and sterilization room
34 dressing material
35 small sterilizer
36 carriage of the operating table
37 mobile instrument table
38 sterile cloth
39 instrument tray
40-53 surgical instruments
40 olive-pointed (bulb-headed) probe
41 hollow probe
42 curved scissors
43 scalpel (surgical knife)
44 ligature-holding forceps
45 sequestrum forceps
46 jaw
47 drainage tube
48 surgeon's tourniquet
49 artery forceps
50 blunt hook
51 bone nippers (bone-cutting forceps)

52 scoop (curette) for erasion (curettage)
53 obstetrical forceps
54 roll of plaster

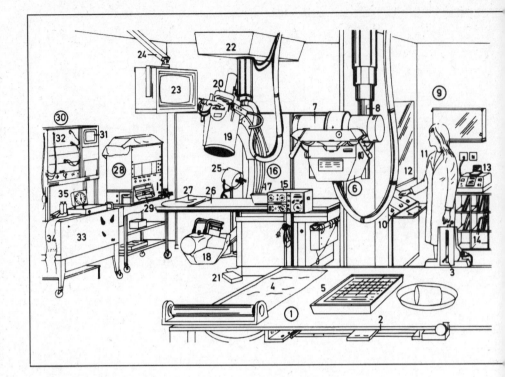

1-35 X-ray unit
1 X-ray examination table
2 support for X-ray cassettes
3 height adjustment of the central beam for lateral views
4 compress for pyelography and cholecystography
5 instrument basin
6 X-ray apparatus for pyelograms
7 X-ray tube
8 telescopic X-ray support
9 central X-ray control unit
10 control panel (control desk)
11 radiographer (X-ray technician)
12 window to the angiography room
13 oxymeter
14 pyelogram cassettes
15 contrast medium injector
16 X-ray image intensifier
17 C-shaped frame
18 X-ray head with X-ray tube
19 image converter with converter tube

20 film camera
21 foot switch
22 mobile mounting
23 monitor
24 swivel-mounted monitor support
25 operating lamp
26 angiographic examination table
27 pillow
28 eight-channel recorder
29 recording paper
30 catheter gauge (*Am.* gage) unit for catheterization of the heart
31 six-channel monitor for pressure graphs and ECG
32 slide-in units of the pressure transducer
33 paper recorder unit with developer for photographic recording
34 recording paper
35 timer

36-50 spirometry
36 spirograph for pulmonary function tests

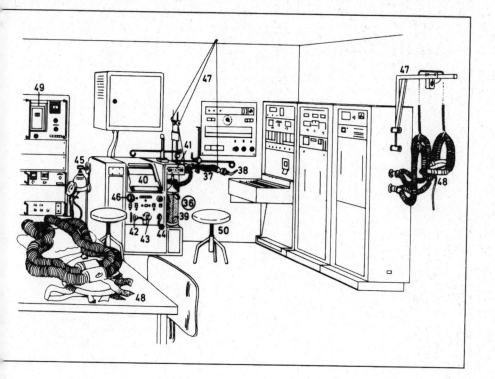

37 breathing tube
38 mouthpiece
39 soda-lime absorber
40 recording paper
41 control knobs for gas supply
42 O_2 stabilizer
43 throttle valve
44 absorber attachment
45 oxygen cylinder
46 water supply
47 tube support
48 mask
49 CO_2 consumption meter
50 stool for the patient

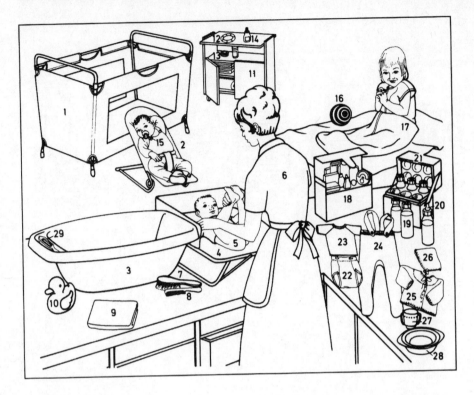

1 collapsible cot	22 rubber baby pants for disposable nappies (*Am.* diapers)
2 bouncing cradle	
3 baby bath	23 vest
4 changing top	24 leggings
5 baby (new-born baby)	25 baby's jacket
6 mother	26 hood
7 hairbrush	27 baby's cup
8 comb	28 baby's plate, a stay-warm plate
9 hand towel	29 thermometer
10 toy duck	
11 changing unit	
12 teething ring	
13 cream jar	
14 box of baby powder	
15 dummy	
16 ball	
17 sleeping bag	
18 layette box	
19 feeding bottle	
20 teat	
21 bottle warmer	

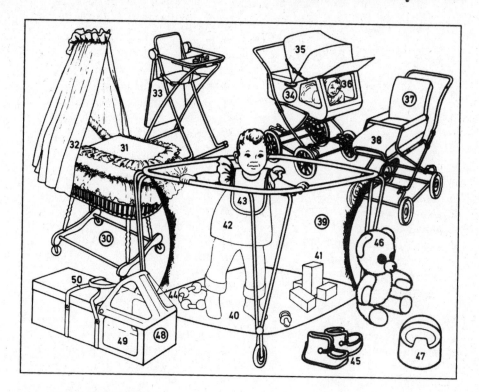

30 bassinet, a wicker pram
31 set of bassinet covers
32 canopy
33 baby's high chair, a folding chair
34 pram (baby-carriage) [with windows]
35 folding hood
36 window
37 pushchair (*Am.* stroller)
38 foot-muff (*Am.* foot-bag)
39 play pen
40 floor of the play pen
41 building blocks (building bricks)
42 small child
43 bib
44 rattle (baby's rattle)
45 bootees
46 teddy bear
47 potty (baby's pot)
48 carrycot
49 window
50 handles

29 Children's Clothes

1-12 baby clothes
1 pram suit
2 hood
3 pram jacket (matinée coat)
4 pompon (bobble)
5 bootees
6 sleeveless vest
7 envelope-neck vest
8 wrapover vest
9 baby's jacket
10 rubber baby pants
11 playsuit
12 two-piece suit
13-30 infants' wear
13 child's sundress, a pinafore dress
14 frilled shoulder strap
15 shirred top
16 sun hat
17 one-piece jersey suit
18 front zip (*Am.* zipper)
19 catsuit (playsuit)
20 motif (appliqué)
21 romper
22 playsuit (romper suit)
23 coverall (sleeper and strampler)
24 dressing gown (bath robe)
25 children's shorts
26 braces (*Am.* suspenders)
27 children's T-shirt
28 jersey dress (knitted dress)
29 embroidery
30 children's ankle socks
31-47 school children's wear
31 raincoat
32 leather shorts (lederhosen)
33 staghorn button
34 braces (*Am.* suspenders)
35 flap
36 girl's dirndl
37 cross lacing
38 snow suit (quilted suit)
39 quilt stitching (quilting)
40 dungarees (bib and brace)
41 bib skirt (bib top pinafore)
42 tights
43 sweater (jumper)

44 pile jacket
45 leggings
46 girl's skirt
47 child's jumper
48-68 teenagers' clothes
48 girl's overblouse (overtop)
49 slacks
50 girl's skirt suit
51 jacket
52 skirt
53 knee-length socks
54 girl's coat
55 tie belt
56 girl's bag
57 woollen (*Am.* woolen) hat
58 girl's blouse
59 culottes
60 boy's trousers
61 boy's shirt
62 anorak
63 inset pockets
64 hood drawstring (drawstring)
65 knitted welt
66 parka coat (parka)
67 drawstring (draw cord)
68 patch pockets

30 Ladies' Wear I (Winter Wear)

1 mink jacket
2 cowl neck jumper
3 cowl collar
4 knitted overtop
5 turndown collar
6 turn-up (turnover) sleeve
7 polo neck jumper
8 pinafore dress
9 blouse (with revers collar)
10 shirt-waister dress, a button-through dress
11 belt
12 winter dress
13 piping
14 cuff
15 long sleeve
16 quilted waistcoat
17 quilt stitching (quilting)
18 leather trimming
19 winter slacks
20 striped polo jumper
21 boiler suit (dungarees, bib and brace)
22 patch pocket
23 front pocket
24 bib
25 wrapover dress (wrap-around dress)
26 shirt
27 peasant-style dress
28 floral braid
29 tunic (tunic top)
30 ribbed cuff
31 quilted design
32 pleated skirt
33 two-piece knitted dress
34 boat neck, a neckline
35 turn-up
36 kimono sleeve
37 knitted design
38 lumber-jacket
39 cable pattern
40 shirt-blouse
41 loop fastening
42 embroidery
43 stand-up collar
44 cossack trousers

45 two-piece combination (shirt top and long skirt)
46 tie (bow)
47 decorative facing
48 cuff slit
49 side slit
50 tabard
51 inverted pleat skirt
52 godet
53 evening gown
54 pleated bell sleeve
55 party blouse
56 party skirt
57 trouser suit (slack suit)
58 suede jacket
59 fur trimming
60 fur coat (*kinds:* Persian lamb, broadtail, mink, sable)
61 winter coat (cloth coat)
62 fur cuff (fur-trimmed cuff)
63 fur collar (fur-trimmed collar)
64 loden coat
65 cape
66 toggle fastenings
67 loden skirt
68 poncho-style coat
69 hood

31 Ladies' Wear II (Summer Wear)

1 skirt suit
2 jacket
3 skirt
4 inset pocket
5 decorative stitching
6 dress and jacket combination
7 piping
8 pinafore dress
9 summer dress
10 belt
11 two-piece dress
12 belt buckle
13 wrapover (wrap-around) skirt
14 pencil silhouette
15 shoulder buttons
16 batwing sleeve
17 overdress
18 kimono yoke
19 tie belt
20 summer coat
21 detachable hood
22 summer blouse
23 lapel
24 skirt
25 front pleat
26 dirndl (dirndl dress)
27 puffed sleeve
28 dirndl necklace
29 dirndl blouse
30 bodice
31 dirndl apron
32 lace trimming (lace), cotton lace
33 frilled apron
34 frill
35 smock overall
36 house frock (house dress)
37 poplin jacket
38 T-shirt
39 ladies' shorts
40 trouser turn-up
41 waistband
42 bomber jacket
43 stretch welt
44 Bermuda shorts
45 saddle stitching
46 frill collar
47 knot

48 culotte
49 twin set
50 cardigan
51 sweater
52 summer (lightweight) slacks
53 jumpsuit
54 turn-up
55 zip (*Am.* zipper)
56 patch pocket
57 scarf (neckerchief)
58 denim suit
59 denim waistcoat
60 jeans (denims)
61 overblouse
62 turned-up sleeve
63 stretch belt
64 halter top
65 knitted overtop
66 drawstring waist
67 short-sleeved jumper
68 V-neck (vee-neck)
69 turndown collar
70 knitted welt
71 shawl

32 Underwear, Nightwear

1-15 ladies' underwear (ladies' under-
clothes, lingerie)
1 brassière (bra)
2 pantie-girdle
3 pantie-corselette
4 longline brassière (longline bra)
5 stretch girdle
6 suspender
7 vest
8 pantie briefs
9 ladies' knee-high stocking
10 long-legged (long leg) panties
11 long pants
12 tights (pantie-hose)
13 slip
14 waist slip
15 bikini briefs
16-21 ladies' nightwear
16 nightdress (nightgown, nightie)
17 pyjamas (*Am.* pajamas)
18 pyjama top
19 pyjama trousers
20 housecoat
21 vest and shorts set [for leisure wear
and as nightwear]
22-29 men's underwear (men's under-
clothes)
22 string vest
23 string briefs
24 front panel
25 sleeveless vest
26 briefs
27 trunks
28 short-sleeved vest
29 long johns
30 braces (*Am.* suspenders)
31 braces clip
32-34 men's socks
32 knee-length sock
33 elasticated top
34 long sock
35-37 men's nightwear
35 dressing gown
36 pyjamas (*Am.* pajamas)
37 nightshirt
38-47 men's shirts
38 casual shirt

39 belt
40 cravat
41 tie
42 knot
43 dress shirt
44 frill (frill front)
45 cuff
46 cuff link
47 bow-tie

1-67 men's fashion

1 single-breasted suit, a men's suit
2 jacket
3 suit trousers
4 waistcoat (vest)
5 lapel
6 trouser leg with crease
7 dinner dress, an evening suit
8 silk lapel
9 breast pocket
10 dress handkerchief
11 bow-tie
12 side pocket
13 tailcoat (tails), evening dress
14 coat-tail
15 white waistcoat (vest)
16 white bow-tie
17 casual suit
18 pocket flap
19 front yoke
20 denim suit
21 denim jacket
22 jeans (denims)
23 waistband
24 beach suit
25 shorts
26 short-sleeved jacket
27 tracksuit
28 tracksuit top with zip
29 tracksuit bottoms
30 cardigan
31 knitted collar
32 men's short-sleeved pullover (men's short-sleeved sweater)
33 short-sleeved shirt
34 shirt button
35 turn-up
36 knitted shirt
37 casual shirt
38 patch pocket
39 casual jacket
40 knee-breeches
41 knee strap
42 knee-length sock
43 leather jacket
44 bib and brace overalls
45 adjustable braces (*Am.* suspenders)
46 front pocket
47 trouser pocket
48 fly
49 rule pocket
50 check shirt
51 men's pullover
52 heavy pullover
53 knitted waistcoat (vest)
54 blazer
55 jacket button
56 overall
57 trenchcoat
58 coat collar
59 coat belt
60 poplin coat
61 coat pocket
62 fly front
63 car coat
64 coat button
65 scarf
66 cloth coat
67 glove

34 Hairstyles and Beards

1-25 men's beards and hairstyles
(haircuts)
1 long hair worn loose
2 allonge periwig (full-bottomed
wig), a wig; *shorter and smoother:*
bob wig, toupet
3 curls
4 bag wig (purse wig)
5 pigtail wig
6 queue (pigtail)
7 bow (ribbon)
8 handlebars (handlebar moustache,
Am. mustache)
9 centre (*Am.* center) parting
10 goatee (goatee beard), chintuft
11 closely-cropped head of hair (crew
cut)
12 whiskers
13 Vandyke beard (stiletto beard,
bodkin beard), with waxed moustache (*Am.* mustache)
14 side parting
15 full beard (circular beard, round
beard)
16 tile beard
17 shadow
18 head of curly hair
19 military moustache (*Am.* mustache) (English-style moustache)
20 partly bald head
21 bald patch
22 bald head
23 stubble beard (stubble, short beard
bristles)
24 side-whiskers (sideboards, side-
burns)
25 clean shave
26 Afro look (for men and women)
27-38 ladies' hairstyles (coiffures,
women's and girls' hairstyles)
27 ponytail
28 swept-back hair (swept-up hair,
pinned-up hair)
29 bun (chignon)
30 plaits (bunches)
31 chaplet hairstyle (Gretchen style)
32 chaplet (coiled plaits)
33 curled hair
34 shingle (shingled hair, bobbed
hair)
35 pageboy style
36 fringe (*Am.* bangs)
37 earphones
38 earphone (coiled plait)

1-21 ladies' hats and caps

1 milliner making a hat
2 hood
3 block
4 decorative pieces
5 sombrero
6 mohair hat with feathers
7 model hat with fancy appliqué
8 linen cap (jockey cap)
9 hat made of thick candlewick yarn
10 woollen (*Am.* woolen) hat (knitted hat)
11 mohair hat
12 cloche with feathers
13 large men's hat made of sisal with corded ribbon
14 trilby-style hat with fancy ribbon
15 soft felt hat
16 Panama hat with scarf
17 peaked mink cap
18 mink hat
19 fox hat with leather top
20 mink cap
21 slouch hat trimmed with flowers

22-40 men's hats and caps
22 trilby hat (trilby)
23 loden hat (Alpine hat)
24 felt hat with tassels (Tyrolean hat, Tyrolese hat)
25 corduroy cap
26 woollen (*Am.* woolen) hat
27 beret
28 German sailor's cap ('Prinz Heinrich' cap)
29 peaked cap (yachting cap)
30 sou'wester (southwester)
31 fox cap with earflaps
32 leather cap with fur flaps
33 musquash cap
34 astrakhan cap, a real or imitation astrakhan cap
35 boater
36 (grey, *Am.* gray, or black) top hat made of silk taffeta; *collapsible:* crush hat (opera hat, claque)
37 sun hat (lightweight hat) made of cloth with small patch pocket
38 wide-brimmed hat
39 toboggan cap (skiing cap, ski cap)
40 workman's cap

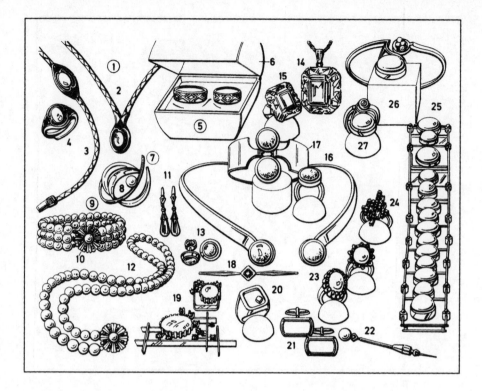

1 set of jewellery (*Am.* jewelry)
2 necklace
3 bracelet
4 ring
5 wedding rings
6 wedding ring box
7 brooch, a pearl brooch
8 pearl
9 cultured pearl bracelet
10 clasp, a white gold clasp
11 pendant earrings (drop earrings)
12 cultured pearl necklace
13 earrings
14 gemstone pendant
15 gemstone ring
16 choker (collar, neckband)
17 bangle
18 diamond pin
19 modern-style brooches
20 man's ring
21 cuff links
22 tiepin
23 diamond ring with pearl

24 modern-style diamond ring
25 gemstone bracelet
26 asymmetrical bangle
27 asymmetrical ring
28 ivory necklace
29 ivory rose
30 ivory brooch
31 jewel box (jewel case)
32 pearl necklace
33 bracelet watch
34 coral necklace
35 charms
36 coin bracelet
37 gold coin
38 coin setting
39 link
40 signet ring
41 engraving (monogram)
42-86 cuts and forms

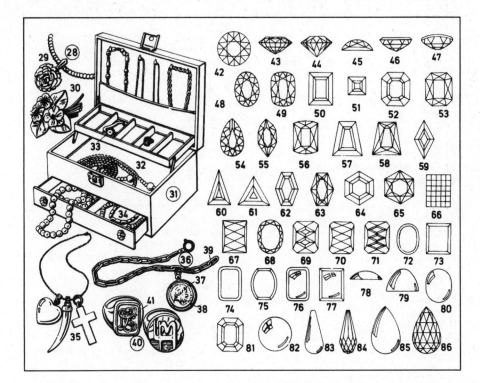

42-71 faceted stones
42, 43 standard round cut
44 brilliant cut
45 rose cut
46 flat table
47 table en cabochon
48 standard cut
49 standard antique cut
50 rectangular step-cut
51 square step-cut
52 octagonal step-cut
53 octagonal cross-cut
54 standard pear-shape (pendeloque)
55 marquise (navette)
56 standard barrel-shape
57 trapezium step-cut
58 trapezium cross-cut
59 rhombus step-cut
60, 61 triangular step-cut
62 hexagonal step-cut
63 oval hexagonal cross-cut
64 round hexagonal step-cut
65 round hexagonal cross-cut

66 chequer-board cut
67 triangle cut
68-71 fancy cuts
72-77 ring gemstones
72 oval flat table
73 rectangular flat table
74 octagonal flat table
75 barrel-shape
76 antique table en cabochon
77 rectangular table en cabochon
78-81 cabochons
78 round cabochon (simple cabochon)
79 high dome (high cabochon)
80 oval cabochon
81 octagonal cabochon
82-86 spheres and pear-shapes
82 plain sphere
83 plain pear-shape
84 faceted pear-shape
85 plain drop
86 faceted briolette

37 Types of Dwelling

1-53 detached house
1 basement
2 ground floor (*Am.* first floor)
3 upper floor (first floor, *Am.* second floor)
4 loft
5 roof, a gable roof (saddle roof, saddle-back roof)
6 gutter
7 ridge
8 verge with bargeboards
9 eaves, rafter-supported eaves
10 chimney
11 gutter
12 swan's neck (swan-neck)
13 rainwater pipe (downpipe, *Am.* downspout, leader)
14 vertical pipe, a cast-iron pipe
15 gable (gable end)
16 glass wall
17 base course (plinth)
18 balcony
19 parapet
20 flower box
21 French window (French windows) opening on to the balcony
22 double casement window
23 single casement window
24 window breast with window sill
25 lintel (window head)
26 reveal
27 cellar window
28 rolling shutter
29 rolling shutter frame
30 window shutter (folding shutter)
31 shutter catch
32 garage with tool shed
33 espalier
34 batten door (ledged door)
35 fanlight with mullion and transom
36 terrace
37 garden wall with coping stones
38 garden light
39 steps
40 rockery (rock garden)
41 outside tap (*Am.* faucet) for the hose
42 garden hose
43 lawn sprinkler
44 paddling pool
45 stepping stones
46 sunbathing area (lawn)
47 deck-chair
48 sunshade (garden parasol)
49 garden chair
50 garden table
51 frame for beating carpets
52 garage driveway
53 fence, a wooden fence

54-57 housing estate (housing development)
54 house on a housing estate (on a housing development)
55 pent roof (penthouse roof)
56 dormer (dormer window)
57 garden

58-63 terraced house [one of a row of terraced houses], **stepped**
58 front garden
59 hedge
60 pavement (*Am.* sidewalk, walkway)
61 street (road)
62 street lamp (street light)
63 litter bin (*Am.* trash bin)

64-68 house divided into two flats (*Am.* house divided into two apartments, duplex house)
64 hip (hipped) roof
65 front door
66 front steps
67 canopy
68 flower window (window for house plants)

69-71 pair of semi-detached houses divided into four flats (*Am.* apartments)
69 balcony
70 sun lounge (*Am.* sun parlor)
71 awning (sun blind, sunshade)

72-76 block of flats (*Am.* apartment building, apartment house) with access balconies
72 staircase
73 balcony
74 studio flat (*Am.* studio apartment)
75 sun roof, a sun terrace
76 open space

77-81 multi-storey block of flats (*Am.* multi-story apartment building, multistory apartment house)
77 flat roof
78 pent roof (shed roof, lean-to roof)
79 garage
80 pergola
81 staircase window
82 high-rise block of flats (*Am.* high-rise apartment building, high-rise apartment house)
83 penthouse

84-86 weekend house, a timber house
84 horizontal boarding
85 natural stone base course (natural stone plinth)
86 strip windows (ribbon windows)

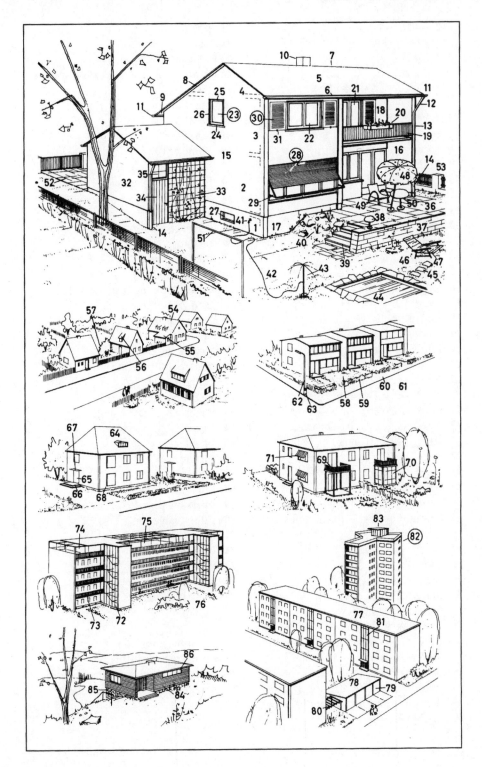

38 Roof and Boiler Room

1-29 attic
1 roof cladding (roof covering)
2 skylight
3 gangway
4 cat ladder (roof ladder)
5 chimney
6 roof hook
7 dormer window (dormer)
8 snow guard (roof guard)
9 gutter
10 rainwater pipe (downpipe, *Am.* downspout, leader)
11 eaves
12 pitched roof
13 trapdoor
14 hatch
15 ladder
16 stile
17 rung
18 loft (attic)
19 wooden partition
20 lumber room door (boxroom door)
21 padlock
22 hook [for washing line]
23 clothes line (washing line)
24 expansion tank for boiler
25 wooden steps and balustrade
26 string (*Am.* stringer)
27 step
28 handrail (guard rail)
29 baluster
30 lightning conductor (lightning rod)
31 **chimney sweep** (*Am.* chimney sweeper)
32 brush with weight
33 shoulder iron
34 sack for soot
35 flue brush
36 broom (besom)
37 broomstick (broom handle)
38-81 hot-water heating system, full central heating
38-43 boiler room
38 coke-fired central heating system
39 ash box door (*Am.* cleanout door)
40 flueblock

41 poker
42 rake
43 coal shovel
44-60 oil-fired central heating system
44 oil tank
45 manhole
46 manhole cover
47 tank inlet
48 dome cover
49 tank bottom valve
50 fuel oil (heating oil)
51 air-bleed duct
52 air vent cap
53 oil level pipe
54 oil gauge (*Am.* gage)
55 suction pipe
56 return pipe
57 central heating furnace (oil heating furnace)
58-60 oil burner
58 fan
59 electric motor
60 covered pilot light
61 charging door
62 inspection window
63 water gauge (*Am.* gage)
64 furnace thermometer
65 bleeder
66 furnace bed
67 control panel
68 hot water tank (boiler)
69 overflow pipe (overflow)
70 safety valve
71 main distribution pipe
72 lagging
73 valve
74 flow pipe
75 regulating valve
76 radiator
77 radiator rib
78 room thermostat
79 return pipe (return)
80 return pipe [in two-pipe system]
81 smoke outlet (smoke extract)

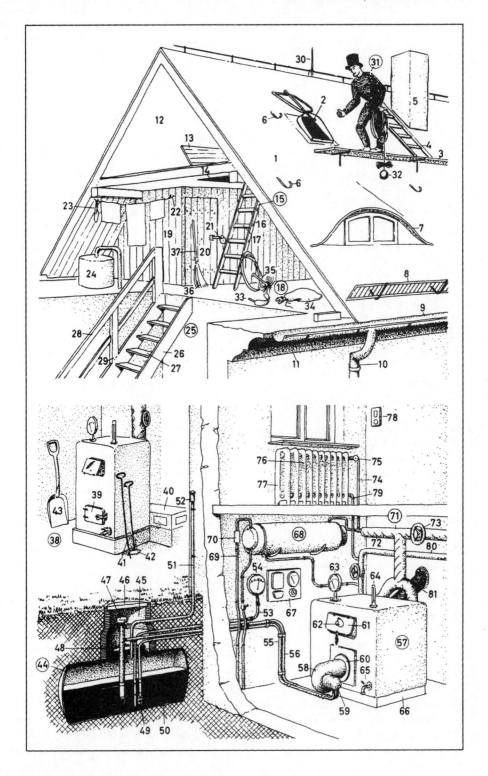

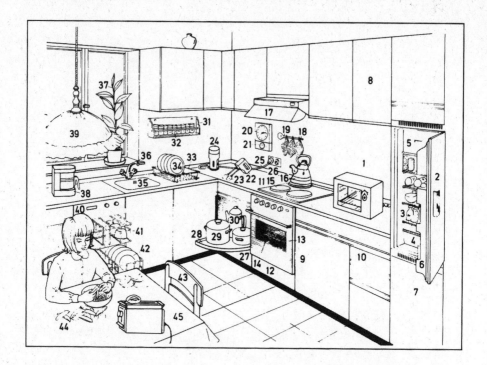

1 microwave oven (microwave)
2 refrigerator (fridge, *Am.* icebox)
3 refrigerator shelf
4 salad drawer
5 freezing compartment
6 bottle rack (in storage door)
7 upright freezer
8 wall cupboard, a kitchen cupboard
9 base unit
10 cutlery drawer
11 work surface (worktop)

12-17 cooker unit
12 electric cooker (*also:* gas cooker)
13 oven
14 oven window
15 hotplate, an automatic high-speed plate
16 kettle (whistling kettle)
17 cooker hood
18 pot holder
19 pot holder rack
20 kitchen clock
21 timer
22 hand mixer
23 whisk

24 electric coffee grinder (with rotating blades)
25 lead
26 wall socket
27 corner unit
28 revolving shelf
29 pot (cooking pot)
30 jug
31 spice rack
32 spice jar

33-36 sink unit
33 dish drainer
34 tea plate
35 sink
36 water tap (*Am.* faucet); *here:* mixer tap (*Am.* mixing faucet)
37 pot plant, a foliage plant
38 coffee maker
39 kitchen lamp
40 dishwasher (dishwashing machine)
41 dish rack
42 dinner plate
43 kitchen chair
44 kitchen table
45 toaster

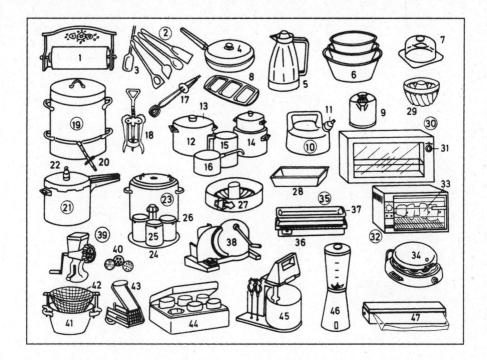

1 general-purpose roll holder with kitchen roll (paper towels)
2 set of wooden spoons
3 mixing spoon
4 frying pan
5 Thermos jug
6 set of bowls
7 cheese dish with glass cover
8 three-compartment dish
9 lemon squeezer
10 whistling kettle
11 whistle
12-16 pan set
12 pot (cooking pot)
13 lid
14 casserole dish
15 milk pot
16 saucepan
17 immersion heater
18 corkscrew [with levers]
19 juice extractor
20 tube clamp (tube clip)
21 pressure cooker
22 pressure valve
23 fruit preserver

24 removable rack
25 preserving jar
26 rubber ring
27 spring form
28 cake tin
29 cake tin
30 microwave oven (microwave)
31 timer
32 rotisserie
33 spit
34 electric waffle iron
35 sliding-weight scales
36 sliding weight
37 scale pan
38 food slicer
39 mincer (*Am.* meat chopper)
40 blades
41 chip pan
42 basket
43 potato chipper
44 yoghurt maker
45 mixer
46 blender
47 bag sealer

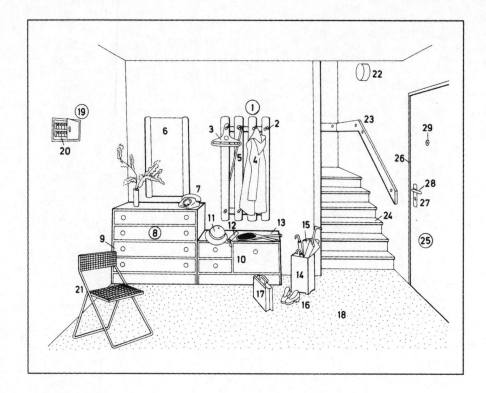

1-29 hall (entrance hall)
1 coat rack
2 coat hook
3 coat hanger
4 rain cape
5 walking stick
6 hall mirror
7 telephone
8 chest of drawers for shoes, etc.
9 drawer
10 seat
11 ladies' hat
12 telescopic umbrella
13 tennis rackets (tennis racquets)
14 umbrella stand
15 umbrella
16 shoes
17 briefcase
18 fitted carpet
19 fuse box
20 miniature circuit breaker
21 tubular steel chair
22 stair light

23 handrail
24 step
25 front door
26 door frame
27 door lock
28 door handle
29 spyhole

1-20 **wall units** (shelf units)
2 side wall
3 bookshelf
4 row of books
5 display cabinet unit
6 cupboard base unit
7 cupboard unit
8 television set (TV set)
9 stereo system (stereo equipment)
10 speaker (loudspeaker)
11 pipe rack
12 pipe
13 globe
14 brass kettle
15 telescope
16 mantle clock
17 bust
18 encyclopaedia [in several volumes]
19 room divider
20 drinks cupboard
21-26 **upholstered suite** (seating group)

21 armchair
22 arm
23 seat cushion (cushion)
24 settee
25 back cushion
26 [round] corner section
27 scatter cushion
28 coffee table
29 ashtray
30 tray
31 whisky (whiskey) bottle
32 soda water bottle (soda bottle)
33-34 **dining set**
33 dining table
34 chair
35 net curtain
36 indoor plants (houseplants)

1 wardrobe (*Am.* clothes closet)	**19** bedroom lamp
2 linen shelf	**20** picture
3 cane chair	**21** picture frame
4-13 double bed (*sim.:* double divan)	**22** bedside rug
4-6 bedstead	**23** fitted carpet
4 foot of the bed	**24** dressing stool
5 bed frame	**25** dressing table
6 headboard	**26** perfume spray
7 bedspread	**27** perfume bottle
8 duvet, a quilted duvet	**28** powder box
9 sheet, a linen sheet	**29** dressing-table mirror (mirror)
10 mattress, a foam mattress with drill tick	
11 [wedge-shaped] bolster	
12, 13 pillow	
12 pillowcase (pillowslip)	
13 tick	
14 bookshelf [attached to the headboard]	
15 reading lamp	
16 electric alarm clock	
17 bedside cabinet	
18 drawer	

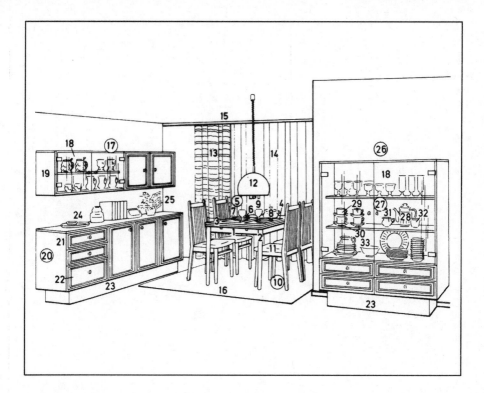

1-11 dining set
1 dining table
2 table leg
3 table top
4 place mat
5 place (place setting, cover)
6 soup plate (deep plate)
7 dinner plate
8 soup tureen
9 wineglass
10 dining chair
11 seat
12 lamp (pendant lamp)
13 curtains
14 net curtain
15 curtain rail
16 carpet
17 wall unit
18 glass door
19 shelf
20 sideboard
21 cutlery drawer
22 linen drawer

23 base
24 round tray
25 pot plant
26 china cabinet (display cabinet)
27 coffee set (coffee service)
28 coffee pot
29 coffee cup
30 saucer
31 milk jug
32 sugar bowl
33 dinner set (dinner service)

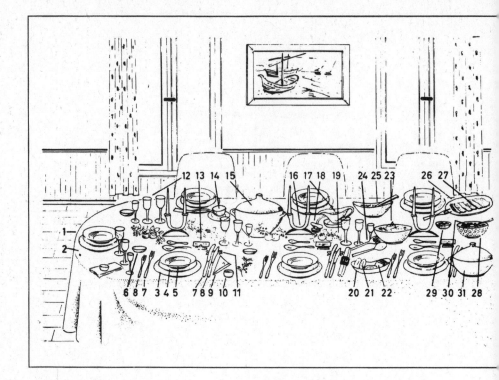

1 dining table
2 tablecloth, a damask cloth
3-12 place (place setting, cover)
3 bottom plate
4 dinner plate
5 deep plate (soup plate)
6 dessert plate (dessert bowl)
7 knife and fork
8 fish knife and fork
9 serviette (napkin, table napkin)
10 serviette ring (napkin ring)
11 knife rest
12 wineglasses
13 place card
14 soup ladle
15 soup tureen (tureen)
16 candelabra
17 sauceboat (gravy boat)
18 sauce ladle (gravy ladle)
19 table decoration
20 bread basket
21 roll
22 slice of bread
23 salad bowl
24 salad servers
25 vegetable dish
26 meat plate (*Am.* meat platter)
27 roast meat (roast)
28 fruit dish
29 fruit bowl
30 fruit (stewed fruit)
31 potato dish
32 serving trolley
33 vegetable plate (*Am.* vegetable platter)
34 toast
35 cheeseboard
36 butter dish
37 open sandwich
38 filling
39 sandwich
40 fruit bowl
41 almonds (*also:* potato crisps, peanuts)
42 oil and vinegar bottle
43 ketchup (catchup, catsup)
44 sideboard
45 electric hotplate
46 corkscrew
47 crown cork bottle opener (crown
cork opener), a bottle opener

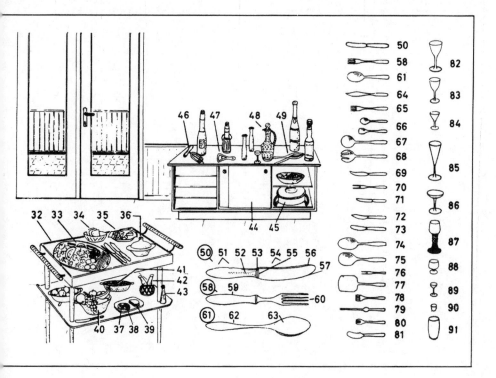

48 liqueur decanter
49 nutcrackers (nutcracker)
50 knife
51 handle
52 tang (tongue)
53 ferrule
54 blade
55 bolster
56 back
57 edge (cutting edge)
58 fork
59 handle
60 prong (tang, tine)
61 spoon; *here:* dessert spoon, soup spoon
62 handle
63 bowl
64 fish knife
65 fish fork
66 dessert spoon (fruit spoon)
67 salad spoon
68 salad fork
69, 70 carving set (serving cutlery)
69 carving knife

70 serving fork
71 fruit knife
72 cheese knife
73 butter knife
74 vegetable spoon, a serving spoon
75 potato server (serving spoon for potatoes)
76 cocktail fork
77 asparagus server (asparagus slice)
78 sardine server
79 lobster fork
80 oyster fork
81 caviare knife
82 white wine glass
83 red wine glass
84 sherry glass (madeira glass)
85, 86 champagne glasses
85 tapered glass
86 champagne glass, a crystal glass
87 rummer
88 brandy glass
89 liqueur glass
90 spirit glass
91 beer glass

1 wall units (shelf units)
2 wardrobe door (*Am.* clothes closet
  door)
3 body
4 side wall
5 trim
6 two-door cupboard unit
7 bookshelf unit (bookcase unit)
  [with glass door]
8 books
9 display cabinet
10 record player
11 drawer
12 decorative biscuit tin
13 soft toy animal
14 television set (TV set)
15 records (discs)
16 bed unit
17 scatter cushion
18 bed unit drawer
19 bed unit shelf
20 magazines
21 desk unit (writing unit)

22 desk
23 desk mat (blotter)
24 table lamp
25 wastepaper basket
26 desk drawer
27 desk chair
28 arm
29 kitchen unit
30 wall cupboard
31 cooker hood
32 electric cooker
33 refrigerator (fridge, *Am.* icebox)
34 dining table
35 table runner
36 oriental carpet
37 standard lamp

1 children's bed, a bunk bed
2 storage box
3 mattress
4 pillow
5 ladder
6 soft toy elephant, a cuddly toy animal
7 soft toy dog
8 cushion
9 fashion doll
10 doll's pram
11 sleeping doll
12 canopy
13 blackboard
14 counting beads
15 toy horse for rocking and pulling
16 rockers
17 children's book
18 compendium of games
19 ludo
20 chessboard
21 children's cupboard
22 linen drawer
23 drop-flap writing surface

24 notebook (exercise book)
25 school books
26 pencil (*also:* crayon, felt tip pen, ballpoint pen)
27 toy shop
28 counter
29 spice rack
30 display
31 assortment of sweets (*Am.* candies)
32 bag of sweets (*Am.* candies)
33 scales
34 cash register
35 toy telephone
36 shop shelves (goods shelves)
37 wooden train set
38 dump truck, a toy lorry (toy truck)
39 tower crane
40 concrete mixer
41 large soft toy dog
42 dice cup

1-20 pre-school education (nursery education)
1 nursery teacher
2 nursery child
3 handicraft
4 glue
5 watercolour (*Am.* watercolor) painting
6 paintbox
7 paintbrush
8 glass of water
9 jigsaw puzzle (puzzle)
10 jigsaw puzzle piece
11 coloured (*Am.* colored) pencils (wax crayons)
12 modelling (*Am.* modeling) clay (Plasticine)
13 clay figures (Plasticine figures)
14 modelling (*Am.* modeling) board
15 chalk (blackboard chalk)
16 blackboard
17 counting blocks
18 felt pen (felt tip pen)
19 shapes game

20 group of players
21-32 toys
21 building and filling cubes
22 construction set
23 children's books
24 doll's pram, a wicker pram
25 baby doll
26 canopy
27 building bricks (building blocks)
28 wooden model building
29 wooden train set
30 rocking teddy bear
31 doll's pushchair
32 fashion doll
33 child of nursery school age
34 cloakroom

1 bath
2 mixer tap (*Am.* mixing faucet) for hot and cold water
3 foam bath (bubble bath)
4 toy duck
5 bath salts
6 bath sponge (sponge)
7 bidet
8 towel rail
9 terry towel
10 toilet roll holder (*Am.* bathroom tissue holder)
11 toilet paper (*coll.* loo paper, *Am.* bathroom tissue)
12 toilet (lavatory, W.C., *coll.* loo)
13 toilet pan (toilet bowl)
14 toilet lid with terry cover
15 toilet seat
16 cistern
17 flushing lever
18 pedestal mat
19 tile
20 ventilator (extraction vent)
21 soap dish
22 soap
23 hand towel
24 washbasin
25 overflow
26 hot and cold water tap
27 washbasin pedestal with trap (antisyphon trap)
28 tooth glass (tooth mug)
29 electric toothbrush
30 detachable brush heads
31 mirrored bathroom cabinet
32 fluorescent lamp
33 mirror
34 drawer
35 powder box
36 mouthwash
37 electric shaver
38 aftershave lotion
39 shower cubicle
40 shower curtain
41 adjustable shower head
42 shower nozzle
43 shower adjustment rail
44 shower base
45 waste pipe
46 bathroom mule
47 bathroom scales
48 bath mat
49 medicine cabinet

50 Household Appliances and Utensils

1-20 irons
1 electric ironing machine
2 electric foot switch
3 roller covering
4 ironing head
5 sheet
6 electric iron (lightweight iron)
7 sole-plate
8 temperature selector
9 handle (iron handle)
10 pilot light
11 steam, spray, and dry iron
12 filling inlet
13 spray nozzle for damping the washing
14 steam hole (steam slit)
15 ironing table
16 ironing board (ironing surface)
17 ironing-board cover
18 iron well
19 aluminium (*Am.* aluminum) frame
20 sleeve board
21 linen bin
22 dirty linen

23-34 washing machines and driers
23 automatic washing machine
24 washing drum
25 safety latch (safety catch)
26 program selector control
27 front soap dispenser [with several compartments]
28 tumble drier
29 drum
30 front door with ventilation slits
31 worktop
32 airer
33 clothes line (washing line)
34 extending airer
35 stepladder (steps), an aluminium (*Am.* aluminum) ladder
36 stile
37 prop
38 tread (rung)

39-43 shoe care utensils
39 tin of shoe polish
40 shoe spray, an impregnating spray
41 shoe brush
42 brush for applying polish
43 tube of shoe polish
44 clothes brush
45 carpet brush

46 broom
47 bristles
48 broom head
49 broomstick (broom handle)
50 screw thread
51 washing-up brush
52 pan (dustpan)

53-86 floor and carpet cleaning
53 brush
54 bucket (pail)
55 floor cloth (cleaning rag)
56 scrubbing brush
57 carpet sweeper
58 upright vacuum cleaner
59 changeover switch
60 swivel head
61 bag-full indicator
62 dust bag container
63 handle
64 tubular handle
65 flex hook
66 wound-up flex
67 all-purpose nozzle
68 cylinder vacuum cleaner
69 swivel coupling
70 extension tube
71 floor nozzle (*sim.:* carpet beater nozzle)
72 suction control
73 bag-full indicator
74 sliding fingertip suction control
75 hose (suction hose)
76 combined carpet sweeper and shampooer
77 electric lead (flex)
78 plug socket
79 carpet beater head (*sim.:* shampooing head, brush head)
80 all-purpose vacuum cleaner (wet and dry vacuum cleaner)
81 castor
82 motor unit
83 lid clip
84 coarse dirt hose
85 special accessory (special attachment) for coarse dirt
86 dust container
87 shopper (shopping trolley)

1-35 flower garden
1 pergola
2 deck-chair
3 lawn rake (wire-tooth rake)
4 garden rake
5 Virginia creeper (American ivy, woodbine), a climbing plant (climber, creeper)
6 rockery (rock garden)
7 rock plants; *varieties:* stonecrop (wall pepper), houseleek, dryas, aubretia
8 pampas grass
9 garden hedge
10 blue spruce
11 hydrangeas
12 oak (oak tree)
13 birch (birch tree)
14 garden path
15 edging
16 garden pond
17 flagstone (stone slab)
18 water lily
19 tuberous begonias
20 dahlias
21 watering can (*Am.* sprinkling can)
22 weeding hoe
23 lupin
24 marguerites (oxeye daisies, white oxeye daisies)
25 standard rose
26 gerbera
27 iris
28 gladioli
29 chrysanthemums
30 poppy
31 blazing star
32 snapdragon (antirrhinum)
33 lawn
34 dandelion
35 sunflower

1-32 allotment (fruit and vegetable garden)

1, 2, 16, 17, 29 dwarf fruit trees (espaliers, espalier fruit trees)

1 quadruple cordon, a wall espalier
2 vertical cordon
3 tool shed (garden shed)
4 water butt (water barrel)
5 climbing plant (climber, creeper, rambler)
6 compost heap
7 sunflower
8 garden ladder (ladder)
9 perennial (flowering perennial)
10 garden fence (paling fence, paling)
11 standard berry tree
12 climbing rose (rambling rose) on the trellis arch
13 bush rose (standard rose tree)
14 summerhouse (garden house)
15 Chinese lantern (paper lantern)
16 pyramid tree (pyramidal tree, pyramid), a free-standing espalier

17 double horizontal cordon
18 flower bed, a border
19 berry bush (gooseberry bush, currant bush)
20 concrete edging
21 standard rose (standard rose tree)
22 border with perennials
23 garden path
24 allotment holder
25 asparagus patch (asparagus bed)
26 vegetable patch (vegetable plot)
27 scarecrow
28 runner bean (*Am.* scarlet runner), a bean plant on poles (bean poles)
29 horizontal cordon
30 standard fruit tree
31 tree stake
32 hedge

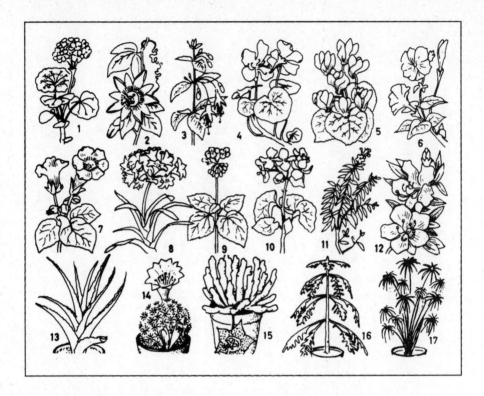

1 pelargonium (crane's bill), a geranium
2 passion flower (Passiflora), a climbing plant (climber, creeper)
3 fuchsia, an anagraceous plant
4 nasturtium (Indian cress, tropaeolum)
5 cyclamen, a primulaceous herb
6 petunia, a solanaceous herb
7 gloxinia (Sinningia), a gesneriaceous plant
8 Clivia minata, an amaryllis (narcissus)
9 African hemp (Sparmannia), a tiliaceous plant, a linden plant
10 begonia
11 myrtle (common myrtle, Myrtus)
12 azalea, an ericaceous plant
13 aloe, a liliaceous plant
14 globe thistle (Echinops)
15 stapelia (carrion flower), an asclepiadaceous plant
16 Norfolk Island Pine (an araucaria grown as an ornamental)
17 galingale, a cyperacious plant of the sedge family

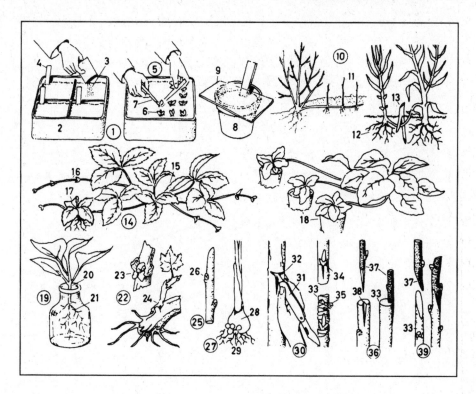

1 seed sowing (sowing)
2 seed pan
3 seed
4 label
5 pricking out (pricking off, transplanting)
6 seedling (seedling plant)
7 dibber (dibble)
8 flower pot (pot)
9 sheet of glass
10 propagation by layering
11 layer
12 layer with roots
13 forked stick used for fastening
14 propagation by runners
15 parent (parent plant)
16 runner
17 small rooted leaf cluster
18 setting in pots
19 cutting in water
20 cutting (slip, set)
21 root
22 bud cutting on vine tendril

23 scion bud, a bud
24 sprouting (shooting) cutting
25 stem cutting (hardwood cutting)
26 bud
27 propagation by bulbils (brood bud
   bulblets)
28 old bulb
29 bulbil (brood bud bulblet)
30-39 grafting (graftage)
30 budding; *here:* shield budding
31 budding knife
32 T-cut
33 support (stock, rootstock)
34 inserted scion bud
35 raffia layer (bast layer)
36 side grafting
37 scion (shoot)
38 wedge-shaped notch
39 splice grafting

1-51 market garden (*Am.* truck garden, truck farm)
1 tool shed
2 water tower (water tank)
3 market garden (*Am.* truck garden, truck farm), a tree nursery
4 hothouse (forcing house, warm house)
5 glass roof
6 [roll of] matting (straw matting, reed matting, shading)
7 boiler room (boiler house)
8 heating pipe (pressure pipe)
9 shading panel (shutter)
10, 11 ventilators (vents)
10 ventilation window (window vent, hinged ventilator)
11 ridge vent
12 potting table (potting bench)
13 riddle (sieve, garden sieve, upright sieve)
14 garden shovel (shovel)

15 heap of earth (composted earth, prepared earth, garden mould, *Am.* mold)
16 hotbed (forcing bed, heated frame)
17 hotbed vent (frame vent)
18 vent prop
19 sprinkler (sprinkling device)
20 gardener (nursery gardener, grower, commercial grower)
21 cultivator (hand cultivator, grubber)
22 plank
23 pricked-out seedlings (pricked-off seedlings)
24 forced flowers [forcing]
25 potted plants (plants in pots, pot plants)
26 watering can (*Am.* sprinkling can)
27 handle
28 rose
29 water tank
30 water pipe

31 bale of peat
32 warm house (heated greenhouse)
33 cold house (unheated greenhouse)
34 wind generator
35 wind wheel
36 wind vane
37 shrub bed, a flower bed
38 hoop edging
39 vegetable plot
40 plastic tunnel (polythene green-
    house)
41 ventilation flap
42 central path
43 vegetable crate
44 tomato plant
45, 46 nursery hand
47 tub plant
48 tub
49 orange tree
50 wire basket
51 seedling box

1 dibber (dibble)
2 spade
3 lawn rake (wire-tooth rake)
4 rake
5 ridging hoe
6 trowel
7 combined hoe and fork
8 sickle
9 gardener's knife (pruning knife, billhook)
10 asparagus cutter (asparagus knife)
11 tree pruner (long-handled pruner)
12 semi-automatic spade
13 three-pronged cultivator
14 tree scraper (bark scraper)
15 lawn aerator (aerator)
16 pruning saw (saw for cutting branches)
17 battery-operated hedge trimmer
18 motor cultivator
19 electric drill
20 gear
21 cultivator attachment
22 fruit picker
23 tree brush (bark brush)
24 sprayer for pest control
25 lance
26 hose reel (reel and carrying cart)
27 garden hose
28 motor lawn mower (motor mower)
29 grassbox
30 two-stroke motor
31 electric lawn mower (electric mower)
32 electric lead (electric cable)
33 cutting unit
34 hand mower
35 cutting cylinder
36 blade
37 riding mower
38 brake lock
39 electric starter
40 brake pedal
41 cutting unit
42 tip-up trailer
43 revolving sprinkler, a lawn sprinkler
44 revolving nozzle
45 hose connector
46 oscillating sprinkler
47 wheelbarrow
48 grass shears
49 hedge shears
50 secateurs (pruning shears)

57 Vegetables (Vegetable Plants)

1-11 leguminous plants
(Leguminosae)
1 pea, a plant with a papilionaceous corola
2 pea flower
3 pinnate leaf
4 pea tendril, a leaf tendril
5 stipule
6 legume (pod), a seed vessel (pericarp, legume)
7 pea [seed]
8 bean plant (bean), a climbing plant (climber, creeper); *varieties:* broad bean (runner bean, *Am.* scarlet runner), climbing bean (climber, pole bean), scarlet runner bean; *smaller:* dwarf French bean (bush bean)
9 bean flower
10 twining beanstalk
11 bean [pod with seeds]
12 tomato
13 cucumber
14 asparagus
15 radish
16 white radish
17 carrot
18 stump-rooted carrot
19 parsley
20 horse-radish
21 leeks
22 chives
23 pumpkin (*Am.* squash); *sim.:* melon
24 onion
25 onion skin
26 kohlrabi
27 celeriac
28-34 brassicas (leaf vegetables)
28 chard (Swiss chard, seakale beet)
29 spinach
30 Brussels sprouts (sprouts)
31 cauliflower
32 cabbage (round cabbage, head of cabbage), a brassica; *cultivated races (cultivars):* green cabbage, red cabbage
33 savoy (savoy cabbage)
34 kale (curly kale, kail), a winter green
35 scorzonera (black salsify)
36-40 salad plants
36 lettuce (cabbage lettuce, head of lettuce)
37 lettuce leaf
38 corn salad (lamb's lettuce)
39 endive (endive leaves)
40 chicory (succory, salad chicory)
41 globe artichoke
42 sweet pepper (Spanish paprika)

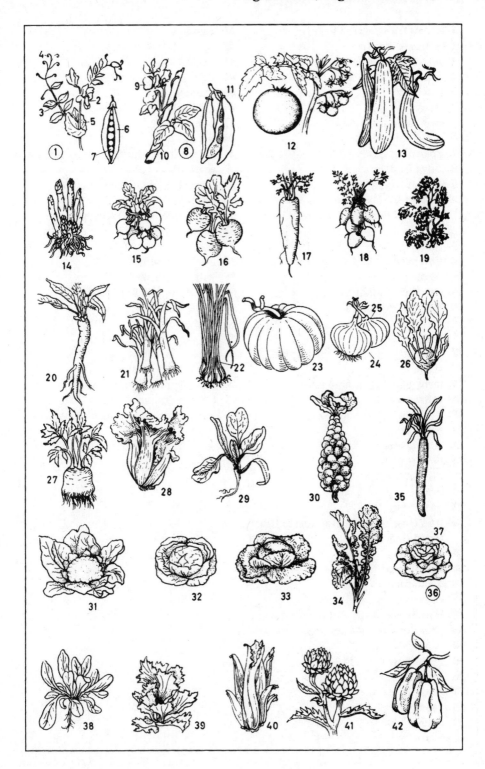

58 Soft Fruit and Pomes

1-30 soft fruit (berry bushes)

1-15 Ribes

1 gooseberry bush
2 flowering gooseberry cane
3 leaf
4 flower
5 magpie moth larva
6 gooseberry flower
7 epignyous ovary
8 calyx (sepals)
9 gooseberry, a berry
10 currant bush
11 cluster of berries
12 currant
13 stalk
14 flowering cane of the currant
15 raceme
16 strawberry plant; *varieties:* wild strawberry (woodland strawberry), garden strawberry, alpine strawberry
17 flowering and fruit-bearing plant
18 rhizome
19 ternate leaf (trifoliate leaf)
20 runner (prostrate stem)
21 strawberry, a pseudocarp
22 epicalyx
23 achene (seed)
24 flesh (pulp)
25 raspberry bush
26 raspberry flower
27 flower bud (bud)
28 fruit (raspberry), an aggregate fruit (compound fruit)
29 blackberry
30 thorny tendril

31-61 pomiferous plants

31 pear tree; *wild:* wild pear tree
32 flowering branch of the pear tree
33 pear [longitudinal section]
34 pear stalk (stalk)
35 flesh (pulp)
36 core (carpels)
37 pear pip (seed), a fruit pip
38 pear blossom
39 ovules
40 ovary
41 stigma
42 style
43 petal
44 sepal
45 stamen
46 quince tree
47 quince leaf
48 stipule
49 apple-shaped quince [longitudinal section]
50 pear-shaped quince [longitudinal section]
51 apple tree; *wild:* crab apple tree
52 flowering branch of the apple tree
53 leaf
54 apple blossom
55 withered flower
56 apple [longitudinal section]
57 apple skin
58 flesh (pulp)
59 core (apple core, carpels)
60 apple pip, a fruit pip
61 apple stalk (stalk)
62 codling moth (codlin moth)
63 burrow (tunnel)
64 larva (grub, caterpillar) of a small moth
65 wormhole

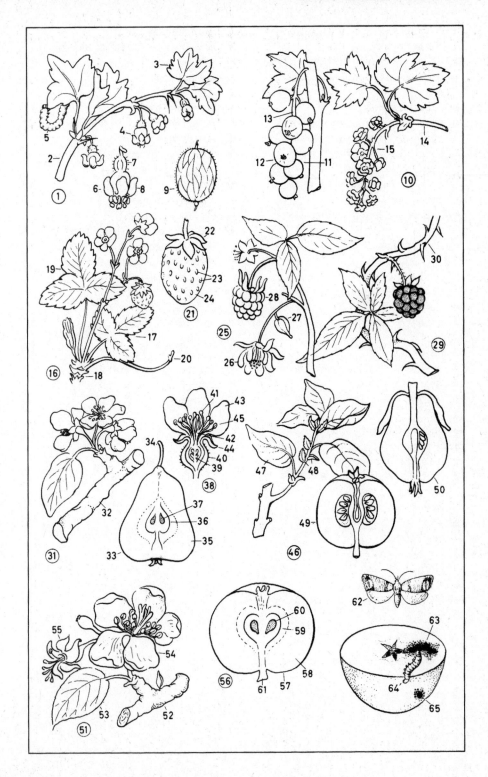

59 Drupes and Nuts

1-36 drupes (drupaceous plants)
1-18 cherry tree
1 flowering branch of the cherry tree (branch of the cherry tree in blossom)
2 cherry leaf
3 cherry flower (cherry blossom)
4 peduncle (pedicel, flower stalk)
5 cherry; *varieties:* sweet cherry (heart cherry), wild cherry (bird cherry), sour cherry, morello cherry (morello)
6-8 cherry (cherry fruit) [cross section]
6 flesh (pulp)
7 cherry stone
8 seed
9 flower (blossom) [cross section]
10 stamen
11 petal
12 sepal
13 pistil
14 ovule enclosed in perigynous ovary
15 style
16 stigma
17 leaf
18 nectary (honey gland)
19-23 plum tree
19 fruit-bearing branch
20 oval, black-skinned plum
21 plum leaf
22 bud
23 plum stone
24 greengage
25 mirabelle (transparent gage), a plum
26-32 peach tree
26 flowering branch (branch in blossom)
27 peach flower (peach blossom)
28 flower shoot
29 young leaf (sprouting leaf)
30 fruiting branch
31 peach
32 peach leaf
33-36 apricot tree
33 flowering apricot branch (apricot branch in blossom)
34 apricot flower (apricot blossom)
35 apricot
36 apricot leaf
37-51 nuts
37-43 walnut tree
37 flowering branch of the walnut tree
38 female flower
39 male inflorescence (male flowers, catkins with stamens)
40 alternate pinnate leaf
41 walnut, a drupe (stone fruit)
42 soft shell (cupule)
43 walnut, a drupe (stone fruit)
44-51 hazel tree (hazel bush), an anemophilous shrub (a wind-pollinating shrub)
44 flowering hazel branch
45 male catkin
46 female inflorescence
47 leaf bud
48 fruit-bearing branch
49 hazelnut (hazel, cobnut, cob), a drupe (stone fruit)
50 involucre (husk)
51 hazel leaf

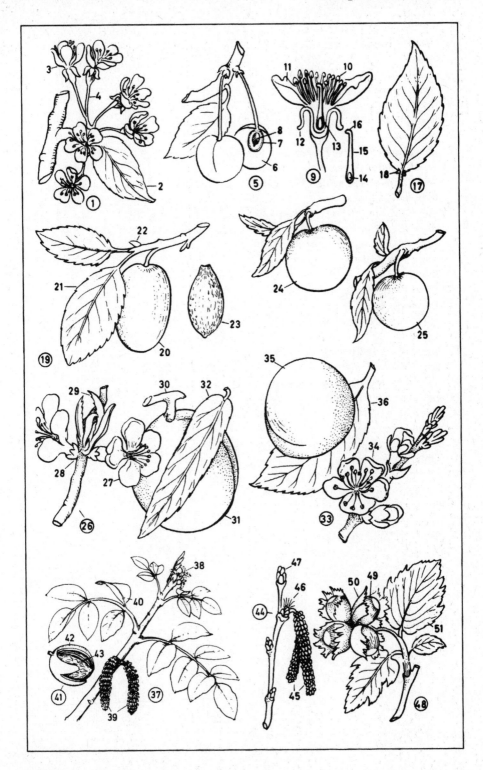

1 snowdrop (spring snowflake)
2 garden pansy (heartsease pansy), a pansy
3 trumpet narcissus (trumpet daffodil, Lent lily), a narcissus
4 poet's narcissus (pheasant's eye, poet's daffodil); *sim.:* polyanthus narcissus
5 bleeding heart (lyre flower), a fumariaceous flower
6 sweet william (bunch pink), a carnation
7 gillyflower (gilliflower, clove pink, clove carnation)
8 yellow flag (yellow water flag, yellow iris), an iris
9 tuberose
10 columbine (aquilegia)
11 gladiolus (sword lily)
12 Madonna lily (Annunciation lily, Lent lily), a lily
13 larkspur (delphinium), a ranunculaceous plant
14 moss pink (moss phlox), a phlox
15 garden rose (China rose)
16 rosebud, a bud
17 double rose
18 rose thorn, a thorn
19 gaillardia
20 African marigold (tagetes)
21 love-lies-bleeding, an amaranthine flower
22 zinnia
23 pompon dahlia, a dahlia

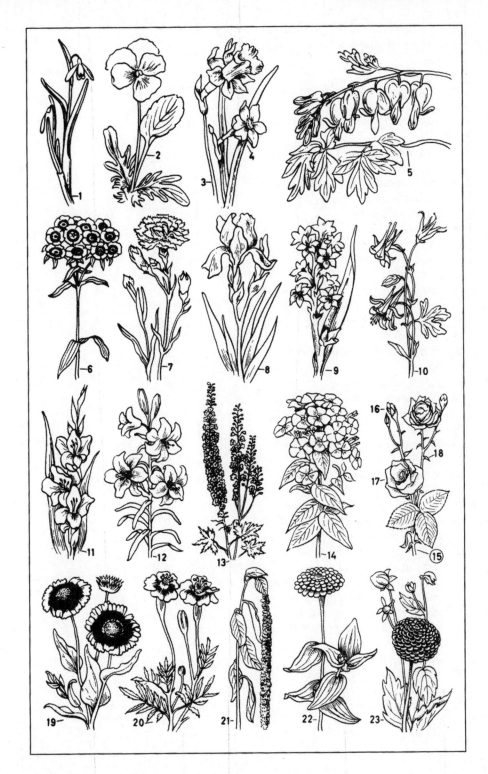

61 Weeds

1 corn flower (bluebottle), a centaury
2 corn poppy (field poppy), a poppy
3 bud
4 poppy flower
5 seed capsule containing poppy
   seeds
6 corn cockle (corn campion, crown-
   of-the-field)
7 corn marigold (field marigold), a
   chrysanthemum
8 corn camomile (field camomile,
   camomile, chamomile)
9 shepherd's purse
10 flower
11 fruit (pouch-shaped pod)
12 common groundsel
13 dandelion
14 flower head (capitulum)
15 infructescence
16 hedge mustard, a mustard
17 stonecrop
18 wild mustard (charlock, runch)
19 flower
20 fruit, a siliqua (pod)
21 wild radish (jointed charlock)
22 flower
23 fruit (siliqua, pod)
24 common orache (common orach)
25 goosefoot
26 field bindweed (wild morning
   glory), a bindweed
27 scarlet pimpernel (shepherd's
   weatherglass, poor man's weatherglass, eye-bright)
28 wild barley (wall barley)
29 wild oat
30 common couch grass (couch, quack
   grass, quick grass, quitch grass,
   scutch grass, twitch grass, witch-
   grass); *sim.:* bearded couch grass,
   sea couch grass
31 gallant soldier
32 field eryngo (Watling Street
   thistle), a thistle
33 stinging nettle, a nettle

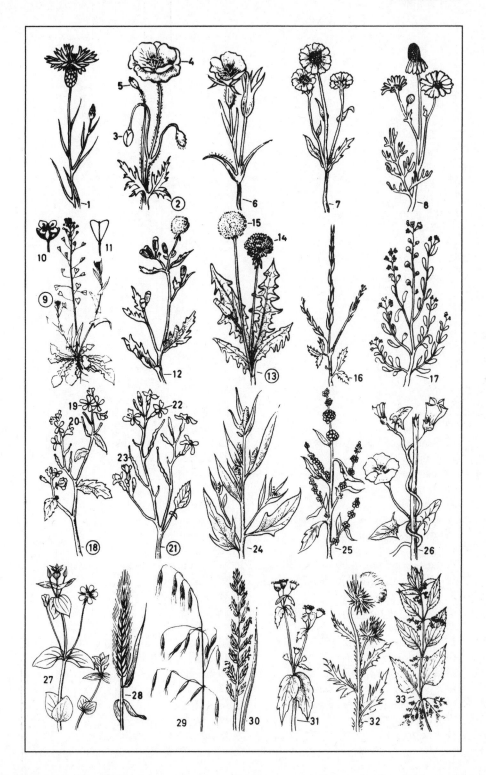

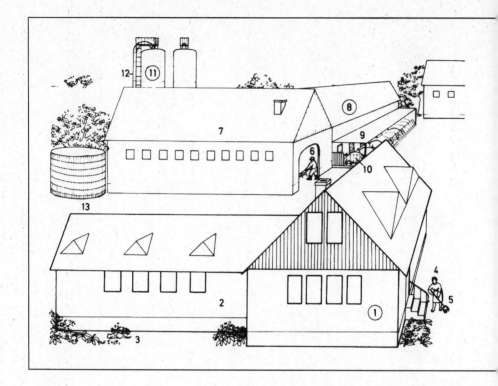

1 house
2 stable
3 house cat (cat)
4 farmer's wife
5 broom
6 farmer
7 cowshed
8 pigsty (sty, *Am.* pigpen, hogpen)
9 outdoor trough
10 pig
11 above-ground silo (fodder silo)
12 silo pipe (standpipe for filling the silo)
13 liquid manure silo
14 outhouse
15 machinery shed
16 sliding door
17 door to the workshop
18 three-way tip-cart, a transport vehicle
19 tipping cylinder
20 shafts

21 manure spreader (fertilizer spreader, manure distributor)
22 spreader unit (distributor unit)
23 spreader cylinder (distributor cylinder)
24 movable scraper floor
25 side planking (side board)
26 wire mesh front
27 sprinkler cart
28 sprinkler stand
29 sprinkler, a revolving sprinkler
30 sprinkler hoses
31 farmyard
32 watchdog
33 calf
34 dairy cow (milch-cow, milker)
35 farmyard hedge
36 chicken
37 cock (*Am.* rooster)
38 tractor
39 tractor driver
40 all-purpose trailer

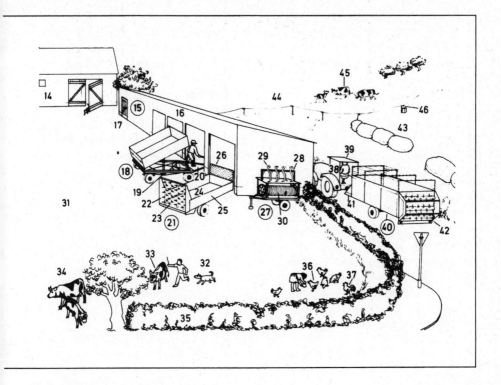

41 [folded] pick-up attachment
42 unloading unit
43 polythene silo, a fodder silo
44 meadow
45 grazing cattle
46 electrified fence

63 Agriculture (Farming)

1-41 work in the fields
1 fallow (fallow field, fallow ground)
2 boundary stone
3 boundary ridge, a balk (baulk)
4 field
5 swingletree (*Am.* whiffletree, whippletree)
6 plough (*Am.* plow)
7 clod
8 furrow
9 stone
10-12 sowing
10 sower
11 seedlip
12 seed corn (seed)
13 field guard
14 chemical fertilizer (artificial fertilizer); *kinds:* potash fertilizer, phosphoric acid fertilizer, lime fertilizer, nitrogen fertilizer
15 cartload of manure (farmyard manure, dung)
16 oxteam (team of oxen, *Am.* span of oxen)
17 fields (farmland)
18 farm track (farm road)
19-30 hay harvest (haymaking)
19 rotary mower with swather (swath reaper)
20 connecting shaft (connecting rod)
21 power take-off (power take-off shaft)
22 meadow
23 swath (swathe)
24 tedder (rotary tedder)
25 tedded hay
26 rotary swather
27 trailer with pick-up attachment
28 fence rack (rickstand), a drying rack for hay
29 rickstand, a drying rack for hay
30 hay tripod
31-41 grain harvest and seedbed preparation
31 combine harvester
32 cornfield
33 stubble field
34 bale of straw
35 straw baler (straw press), a high-pressure baler
36 swath (swathe) of straw (windrow of straw)
37 hydraulic bale loader
38 trailer
39 manure spreader
40 four-furrow plough (*Am.* plow)
41 combination seed-harrow

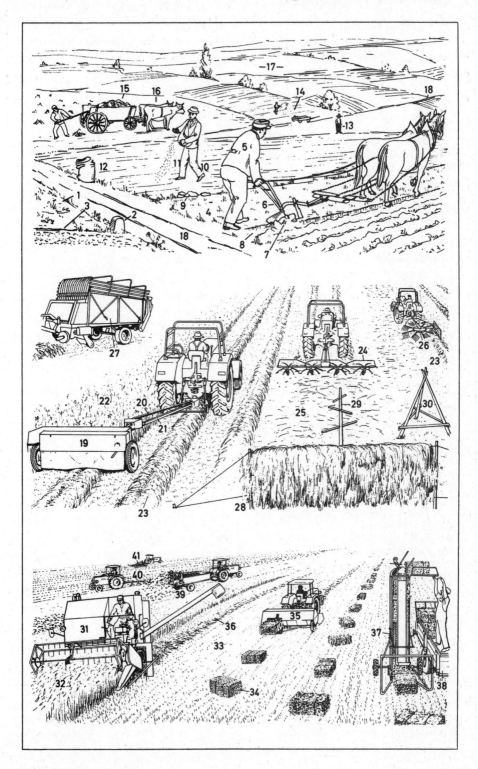

64 Agricultural Machinery I

1-33 combine harvester (combine)
1 divider
2 grain lifter
3 cutter bar
4 pick-up reel, a spring-tine reel
5 reel gearing
6 auger
7 chain and slat elevator
8 hydraulic cylinder for adjusting the cutting unit
9 stone catcher (stone trap)
10 awner
11 concave
12 threshing drum (drum)
13 revolving beater [for freeing straw from the drum and preparing it for the shakers]
14 straw shaker (strawwalker)
15 fan for compressed-air winnowing
16 preparation level
17 louvred-type sieve
18 sieve extension
19 shoe sieve (reciprocating sieve)
20 grain auger
21 tailings auger
22 tailings outlet
23 grain tank
24 grain tank auger
25 augers feeding to the grain tank unloader
26 grain unloader spout
27 observation ports for checking tank contents
28 six-cylinder diesel engine
29 hydraulic pump with oil reservoir
30 driving axle gearing
31 driving wheel tyre (*Am.* tire)
32 rubber-tyred (*Am.* rubber-tired) wheel on the steering axle
33 driver's position
34-39 self-propelled forage harvester (self-propelled field chopper)
34 cutting drum (chopper drum)
35 corn head
36 cab (driver's cab)
37 swivel-mounted spout (discharge pipe)
38 exhaust
39 rear-wheel steering system
40-45 rotary swather
40 cardan shaft
41 running wheel
42 double spring tine
43 crank
44 swath rake
45 three-point linkage
46-58 rotary tedder
46 tractor
47 draw bar

48 cardan shaft
49 power take-off (power take-off shaft)
50 gearing (gears)
51 frame bar
52 rotating head
53 tine bar
54 double spring tine
55 guard rail
56 running wheel
57 height adjustment crank
58 wheel adjustment
59-84 potato harvester
59 control levers for the lifters of the digger and the hopper and for adjusting the shaft
60 adjustable hitch
61 drawbar
62 drawbar support
63 cardan shaft connection
64 press roller
65 gearing (gears) for the hydraulic system
66 disc (disk) coulter (*Am.* colter) (rolling coulter)
67 three-bladed share
68 disc (disk) coulter (*Am.* colter) drive
69 open-web elevator
70 agitator
71 multi-step reduction gearing
72 feeder
73 haulm stripper (flail rotor)
74 rotary elevating drum
75 mechanical tumbling separator
76 haulm conveyor with flexible haulm strippers
77 haulm conveyor agitator
78 haulm conveyor drive with V-belt
79 studded rubber belt for sorting vines, clods and stones
80 trash conveyor
81 sorting table
82 rubber-disc (rubber-disk) rollers for presorting
83 discharge conveyor
84 endless-floor hopper
85-96 beet harvester
85 topper
86 feeler
87 topping knife
88 feeler support wheel with depth adjustment
89 beet cleaner
90 haulm elevator
91 hydraulic pump
92 compressed-air reservoir
93 oil tank (oil reservoir)
94 tensioning device for the beet elevator
95 beet elevator belt
96 beet hopper

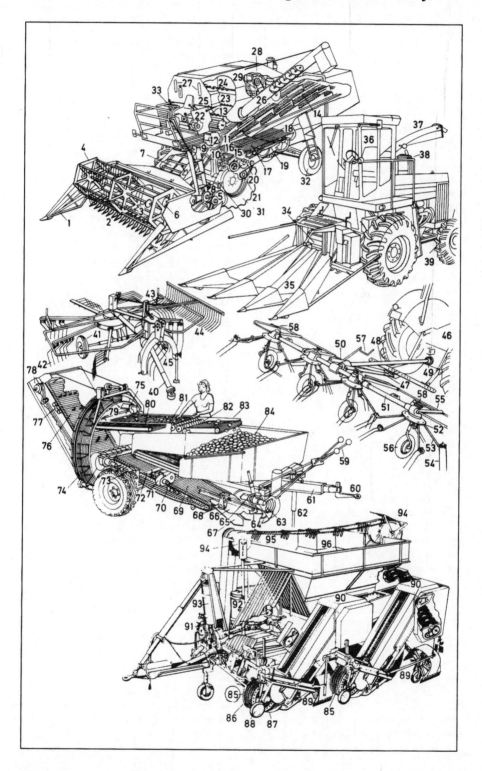

65 Agricultural Machinery II

1 **wheel plough** (*Am.* plow), a single-bottom plough *[form.]*
2 handle
3 plough (*Am.* plow) stilt (plough handle)
4-8 **plough** (*Am.* **plow**) **bottom**
4 mouldboard (*Am.* moldboard)
5 landside
6 sole (slade)
7 ploughshare (share, *Am.* plowshare)
8 frog (frame)
9 beam (plough beam, *Am.* plowbeam)
10 knife coulter (*Am.* colter), a coulter
11 skim coulter (*Am.* colter)
12 guide-chain crossbar
13 guide chain
14-19 **forecarriage**
14 adjustable yoke
15 land wheel
16 furrow wheel
17 hake chain
18 draught beam (drawbar)
19 hake
20 **tractor** (general-purpose tractor)
21 cab frame (roll bar)
22 seat
23 power take-off gear-change (gearshift)
24-29 **power lift**
24 ram piston
25 lifting rod adjustment
26 drawbar frame
27 top link
28 lower link
29 lifting rod
30 drawbar coupling
31 live power take-off (live power take-off shaft, take-off shaft)
32 differential gear (differential)
33 floating axle
34 torque converter lever
35 gear-change (gearshift)
36 multi-speed transmission
37 fluid clutch (fluid drive)
38 power take-off gear
39 main clutch
40 power take-off gear-change (gearshift) with power take-off clutch
41 hydraulic power steering and reversing gears
42 fuel tank
43 float lever
44 four-cylinder diesel engine
45 oil sump and pump for the pressure-feed lubrication system
46 fresh oil tank
47 track rod (*Am.* tie rod)
48 front axle pivot pin
49 front axle suspension
50 front coupling (front hitch)
51 radiator
52 fan
53 battery
54 oil bath air cleaner (oil bath air filter)
55 **cultivator** (grubber)
56 sectional frame
57 spring tine
58 share, a diamond-shaped share (*sim.:* chisel-shaped share)
59 depth wheel
60 depth adjustment
61 coupling (hitch)
62 **reversible plough** (*Am.* plow), a mounted plough
63 depth wheel
64-67 **plough** (*Am.* plow) **bottom,** a general-purpose plough bottom
64 mouldboard (*Am.* moldboard)
65 ploughshare (share, *Am.* plowshare), a pointed share
66 sole (slade)
67 landside
68 skim coulter (*Am.* colter)
69 disc (disk) coulter (*Am.* colter) (rolling coulter)
70 plough (*Am.* plow) frame
71 beam (plough beam, *Am.* plowbeam)
72 three-point linkage
73 swivel mechanism
74 **drill**
75 seed hopper
76 drill coulter (*Am.* colter)
77 delivery tube, a telescopic tube
78 feed mechanism
79 gearbox
80 drive wheel
81 track indicator
82 **disc (disk) harrow,** a semimounted implement
83 discs (disks) in X-configuration
84 plain disc (disk)
85 serrated-edge disc (disk)
86 quick hitch
87 **combination seed-harrow**
88 three-section spike-tooth harrow
89 three-section rotary harrow
90 frame

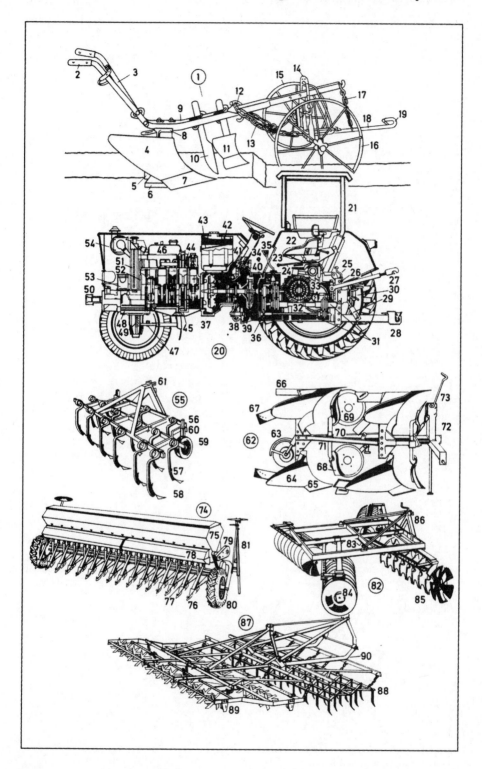

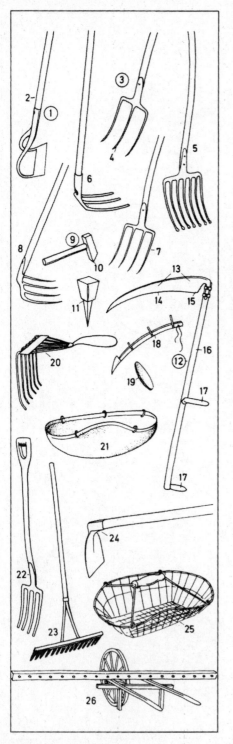

1 draw hoe (garden hoe)
2 hoe handle
3 three-pronged (three-tined) hay fork (fork)
4 prong (tine)
5 potato fork
6 potato hook
7 four-pronged (four-tined) manure fork (fork)
8 manure hoe
9 whetting hammer [for scythes]
10 peen (pane)
11 whetting anvil [for scythes]
12 scythe
13 scythe blade
14 cutting edge
15 heel
16 snath (snathe, snead, sneath)
17 handle
18 scythe sheath
19 whetstone (scythestone)
20 potato rake
21 potato planter
22 digging fork (fork)
23 wooden rake (rake, hayrake)
24 hoe (potato hoe)
25 potato basket, a wire basket
26 clover broadcaster

1 oscillating spray line
2 stand (steel chair)
3 portable irrigation system
4 revolving sprinkler
5 standpipe coupler
6 elbow with cardan joint (cardan coupling)
7 pipe support (trestle)
8 pump connection
9 delivery valve
10 pressure gauge (*Am.* gage) (manometer)
11 centrifugal evacuating pump
12 basket strainer
13 channel
14 chassis of the p.t.o.-driven pump (power take-off-driven pump)
15 p.t.o.-driven (power take-off-driven) pump
16 cardan shaft
17 tractor
18 long-range irrigation unit
19 drive connection

20 turbine
21 gearing (gears)
22 adjustable support
23 centrifugal evacuating pump
24 wheel
25 pipe support
26 polyester pipe
27 sprinkler nozzle
28 quick-fitting pipe connection with cardan joint
29 M-cardan
30 clamp
31 V-cardan
32 revolving sprinkler, a field sprinkler
33 nozzle
34 breaker
35 breaker spring
36 stopper
37 counterweight
38 thread

68 Arable Crops

1-47 arable crops (agricultural produce, farm produce)

1-37 varieties of grain (grain, cereals, farinaceous plants, bread-corn)

1 rye (*also:* corn, 'corn' often meaning the main cereal of a country or region; in Northern Germany: rye; in Southern Germany and Italy: wheat; in Sweden: barley; in Scotland: oats; in North America: maize; in China: rice)

2 ear of rye, a spike (head)

3 spikelet

4 ergot, a grain deformed by fungus [shown with mycelium]

5 corn stem after tillering

6 culm (stalk)

7 node of the culm

8 leaf (grain leaf)

9 leaf sheath (sheath)

10 spikelet

11 glume

12 awn (beard, arista)

13 seed (grain, kernel, farinaceous grain)

14 embryo plant

15 seed

16 embryo

17 root

18 root hair

19 grain leaf

20 leaf blade (blade, lamina)

21 leaf sheath

22 ligule (ligula)

23 wheat

24 spelt

25 seed; *unripe:* green spelt, a soup vegetable

26 barley

27 oat panicle, a panicle

28 millet

29 rice

30 rice grain

31 maize (Indian corn, *Am.* corn); *varieties:* popcorn, dent corn, flint corn (flint maize, *Am.* Yankee corn), pod corn (*Am.* cow corn, husk corn), soft corn (*Am.* flour corn, squaw corn), sweet corn

32 female inflorescence

33 husk (shuck)

34 style

35 male inflorescence (tassel)

36 maize cob (*Am.* corn cob)

37 maize kernel (grain of maize)

38-45 root crops

38 potato plant (potato), a tuberous plant; *varieties:* round, round-oval (pear-shaped), flat-oval, long, kidney-shaped potato; *according to colour:* white (*Am.* Irish), yellow, red, purple potato

39 seed potato (seed tuber)

40 potato tuber (potato, tuber)

41 potato top (potato haulm)

42 flower

43 poisonous potato berry (potato apple)

44 sugar beet, a beet

45 root (beet)

46 beet top

47 beet leaf

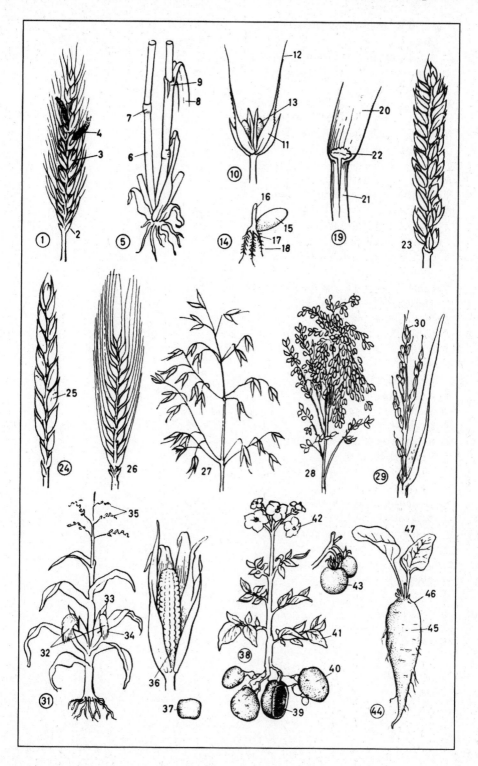

69 Fodder Plants (Forage Plants)

1-28 fodder plants (forage plants) for tillage

1 red clover (purple clover)
2 white clover (Dutch clover)
3 alsike clover (alsike)
4 crimson clover
5 four-leaf (four-leaved) clover
6 kidney vetch (lady's finger, lady-finger)
7 flower
8 pod
9 lucerne (lucern, purple medick)
10 sainfoin (cock's head, cockshead)
11 bird's foot (bird-foot, bird's foot trefoil)
12 corn spurrey (spurrey, spurry), a spurrey (spurry)
13 common comfrey, one of the borage family (Boraginaceae)
14 flower (blossom)
15 field bean (broad bean, tick bean, horse bean)
16 pod
17 yellow lupin
18 common vetch
19 chick-pea
20 sunflower
21 mangold (mangelwurzel, mangold-wurzel, field mangel)
22 false oat (oat-grass)
23 spikelet
24 meadow fescue grass, a fescue
25 cock's foot (cocksfoot)
26 Italian ryegrass; *sim.:* perennial ryegrass (English ryegrass)
27 meadow foxtail, a paniculate grass
28 greater burnet saxifrage

1-14 mastiffs
1 bulldog
2 ear, a rose-ear
3 muzzle
4 nose
5 foreleg
6 forepaw
7 hind leg
8 hind paw
9 pug (pug dog)
10 boxer
11 withers
12 tail, a docked tail
13 collar
14 Great Dane
15-18 terriers
15 wire-haired fox terrier
16 bull terrier
17 Scotch terrier (Scottish terrier)
18 Bedlington terrier
19 Pekinese (Pekingese, Pekinese dog, Pekinese dog)
20-22 spitzes

20 spitz (Pomeranian)
21 chow (chow-chow)
22 husky
23, 24 greyhounds (*Am.* grayhounds)
23 Afghan (Afghan hound)
24 greyhound (*Am.* grayhound), a courser
25 Alsatian (German sheepdog, *Am.* German shepherd), a police dog, watch dog, and guide dog
26 flews (chaps)
27 Dobermann terrier

28 dog brush
29 dog comb
30 lead (dog lead, leash); *for hunting:*
     leash
31 muzzle
32 feeding bowl (dog bowl)
33 bone
34 Newfoundland dog
35 schnauzer
36 poodle; *sim. and smaller:* pygmy
     (pigmy) poodle
37 St. Bernard (St. Bernard dog)
38-43 hunting dogs
38 cocker spaniel
39 dachshund, a terrier
40 German pointer
41 English setter
42 trackhound
43 pointer, a trackhound

71 Horse I

1-6 **equitation** (high school riding, haute école)
1 piaffe
2 walk
3 passage
4 levade (pesade)
5 capriole
6 courbette (curvet)
7-25 **harness**
7-13, 25 bridle
7-11 **headstall** (headpiece, halter)
7 noseband
8 cheek piece (cheek strap)
9 browband (front band)
10 crownpiece
11 throatlatch (throatlash)
12 curb chain
13 curb bit
14 hasp (hook) of the hame (*Am.* drag hook)
15 pointed collar, a collar
16 trappings (side trappings)
17 saddle-pad
18 girth
19 backband
20 shaft chain (pole chain)
21 pole
22 trace
23 second girth (emergency girth)
24 trace
25 reins (*Am.* lines)
26-36 **breast harness**
26 blinker (*Am.* blinder, winker)
27 breast collar ring
28 breast collar (Dutch collar)
29 fork
30 neck strap
31 saddle-pad
32 loin strap
33 reins (rein, *Am.* line)
34 crupper (crupper-strap)
35 trace
36 girth (belly-band)
37-49 **saddles**
37-44 **stock saddle** (*Am.* western saddle)
37 saddle seat

38 pommel horn (horn)
39 cantle
40 flap (*Am.* fender)
41 bar
42 stirrup leather
43 stirrup (stirrup iron)
44 blanket
45-49 **English saddle** (cavalry saddle)
45 seat
46 cantle
47 flap
48 roll (knee roll)
49 pad
50, 51 **spurs**
50 box spur (screwed jack spur)
51 strapped jack spur
52 curb bit
53 gag bit (gag)
54 currycomb
55 horse brush (body brush, dandy brush)

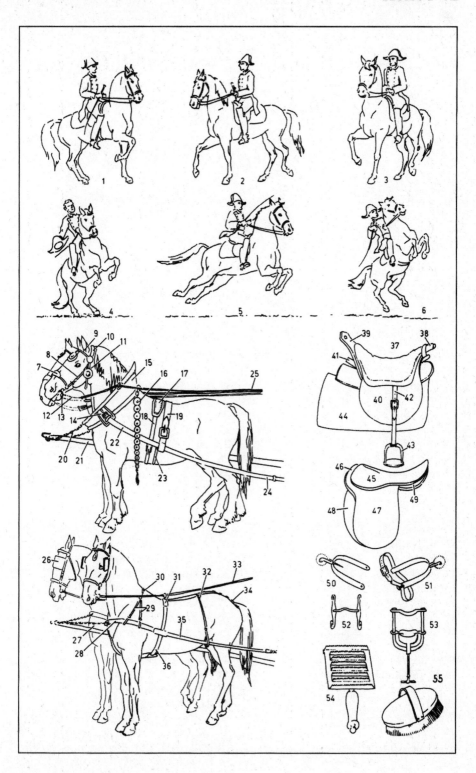

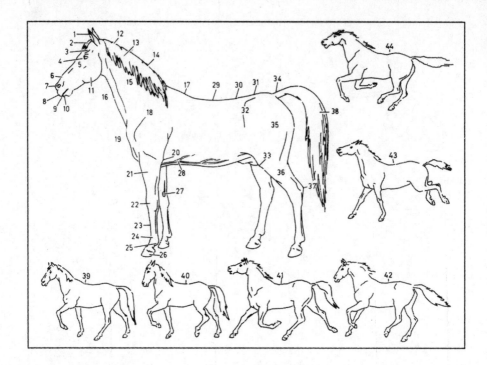

1-38 **points** of the horse
1-11 **head** (horse's head)
1 ear
2 forelock
3 forehead
4 eye
5 face
6 nose
7 nostril
8 upper lip
9 mouth
10 underlip (lower lip)
11 lower jaw
12 crest (neck)
13 mane (horse's mane)
14 crest (horse's crest)
15 neck
16 throat (*Am.* throatlatch, throat-lash)
17 withers
18-27 **forehand**
18 shoulder
19 breast
20 elbow
21 forearm
22-26 **forefoot**
22 knee (carpus, wrist)
23 cannon
24 fetlock
25 pastern
26 hoof
27 chestnut (castor), a callosity
28 spur vein
29 back
30 loins (lumbar region)
31 croup (rump, crupper)
32 hip
33-37 **hind leg**
33 stifle (stifle joint)
34 root (dock) of the tail
35 haunch
36 gaskin
37 hock
38 tail
39-44 **gaits** of the horse
39 walk
40 pace
41 trot
42 canter (hand gallop)
43, 44 full gallop
43 full gallop at the moment of descent on to the two forefeet
44 full gallop at the moment when all four feet are off the ground

Abbreviations:
m. = male; *c.* = castrated;
f. = female; *y.* = young

1-8 cattle and horses
1 cow, a ruminant; *m.* bull; *c.* ox; *f.* cow; *y.* calf
2 horse; *m.* stallion; *c.* gelding; *f.* mare; *y.* foal
3 donkey
4 pack saddle (carrying saddle)
5 pack (load)
6 tufted tail
7 tuft
8 mule, a cross between a male donkey and a mare
9 pig, a cloven-hoofed animal; *m.* boar; *f.* sow; *y.* piglet
10 pig's snout (snout)
11 pig's ear
12 curly tail
13 sheep; *m.* ram; *c.* wether; *f.* ewe; *y.* lamb
14 goat
15 goat's beard
16 dog, a Leonberger; *m.* dog; *f.* bitch; *y.* pup (puppy, whelp)

17 cat, an Angora cat (Persian cat); *m.* tom (tom cat)
18-36 small domestic animals
18 rabbit; *m.* buck; *f.* doe
19-36 poultry (domestic fowl)
19-26 chicken
19 hen
20 crop (craw)
21 cock (*Am.* rooster); *c.* capon
22 cockscomb (comb, crest)
23 lap
24 wattle (gill, dewlap)
25 falcate (falcated) tail
26 spur
27 guinea fowl
28 turkey; *m.* turkey cock (gobbler); *f.* turkey hen
29 fan tail
30 peacock
31 peacock's feather
32 eye (ocellus)
33 pigeon; *m.* cock pigeon
34 goose; *m.* gander; *y.* gosling
35 duck; *m.* drake; *y.* duckling
36 web (palmations) of webbed foot (palmate foot)

74 Poultry Farming (Poultry Keeping), Egg Production

1-27 poultry farming (intensive poultry management)
1-17 straw yard (strawed yard) **system**
1 fold unit for growing stock (chick unit)
2 chick
3 brooder (hover)
4 adjustable feeding trough
5 pullet fold unit
6 drinking trough
7 water pipe
8 litter
9 pullet
10 ventilator
11-17 broiler rearing (rearing of broiler chickens)
11 chicken run (*Am.* fowl run)
12 broiler chicken (broiler)
13 mechanical feeder (self-feeder, feed dispenser)
14 chain
15 feed supply pipe
16 mechanical drinking bowl (mechanical drinker)
17 ventilator
18 battery system (cage system)
19 battery (laying battery)
20 tiered cage (battery cage, stepped cage)
21 feeding trough
22 egg collection by conveyor
23-27 mechanical feeding and dunging (manure removal, droppings removal)
23 rapid feeding system for battery feeding (mechanical feeder)
24 feed hopper
25 endless-chain feed conveyor (chain feeder)
26 water pipe (liquid feed pipe)
27 dunging chain (dunging conveyor)
28 setting and hatching machine
29 ventilation drum [for the setting compartment]
30 hatching compartment (hatcher)
31 metal trolley for hatching trays
32 hatching tray
33 ventilation drum motor
34-53 egg productions
34 egg collection system (egg collection)
35 multi-tier transport
36 collection by pivoted fingers
37 drive motor
38 sorting machine
39 conveyor trolley
40 fluorescent screen
41 suction apparatus (suction box) for transporting eggs
42 shelf for empty and full egg boxes
43 egg weighers
44 grading
45 egg box
46 fully automatic egg-packing machine
47 radioscope box
48 radioscope table
49-51 feeder
49 suction transporter
50 vacuum line
51 supply table
52 automatic counting and grading
53 packing box dispenser
54 leg ring
55 wing tally (identification tally)
56 bantam
57 laying hen
58 hen's egg (egg)
59 eggshell, an egg integument
60 shell membrane
61 air space
62 white [of the egg] (albumen)
63 chalaza (*Am.* treadle)
64 vitelline membrane (yolk sac)
65 blastodisc (germinal disc, cock's tread, cock's treadle)
66 germinal vesicle
67 white
68 yolk

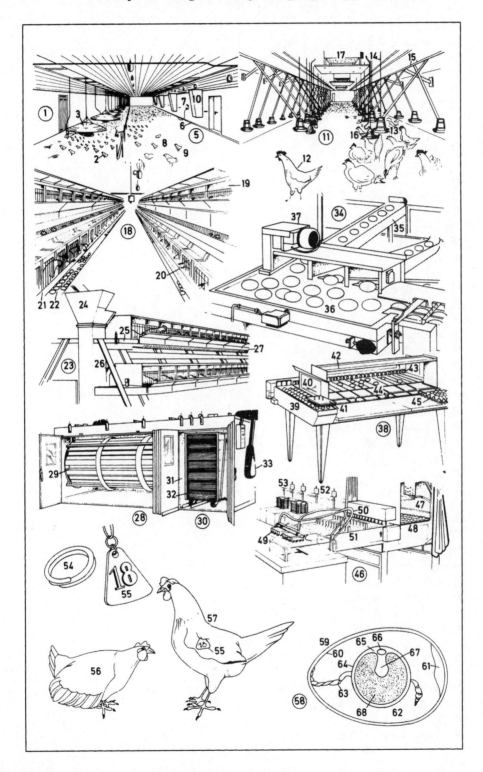

75 Rearing (*Am.* Raising) of Livestock

1 **stable**
2 horse stall (stall, horse box, box)
3 feeding passage
4 pony
5 bars
6 litter
7 bale of straw
8 ceiling light
9 **sheep pen**
10 mother sheep (ewe)
11 lamb
12 double hay rack
13 hay
14 **dairy cow shed**
15-16 tether
15 chain
16 rail
17 dairy cow (milch-cow, milker)
18 udder
19 teat
20 manure gutter
21 manure removal by sliding bars
22 short standing
23 **milking parlour** (*Am.* parlor), a
    herringbone parlour
24 working passage
25 milker (*Am.* milkman)
26 teat cup cluster
27 milk pipe
28 air line
29 vacuum line
30 teat cup
31 window
32 pulsator
33 release phase
34 squeeze phase
35 **pigsty** (*Am.* pigpen, hogpen)
36 pen for young pigs
37 feeding trough
38 partition
39 pig, a young pig
40 farrowing and store pen
41 sow
42 piglets (*Am.* shoats, shotes) (suck-
    ing pigs [for first 8 weeks])
43 farrowing rails
44 liquid manure channel

1-48 **dairy** (dairy plant)
1 **milk reception**
2 milk tanker
3 raw milk pump
4 flowmeter, an oval (elliptical) gear meter
5 raw milk storage tank
6 gauge (*Am.* gage)
7 **central control room**
8 chart of the dairy
9 flow chart (flow diagram)
10 storage tank gauges (*Am.* gages)
11 control panel
12-48 **milk processing area**
12 sterilizer (homogenizer)
13 milk heater; *sim.:* cream heater
14 cream separator
15 fresh milk tanks
16 tank for sterilized milk
17 skim milk (skimmed milk) tank
18 buttermilk tank
19 cream tank
20 fresh milk filling and packing plant
21 filling machine for milk cartons; *sim.:* milk tub filler
22 milk carton
23 conveyor belt (conveyor)
24 shrink-sealing machine
25 pack of twelve in shrink foil
26 ten-litre filling machine
27 heat-sealing machine
28 plastic sheets
29 heat-sealed bag
30 crate
31 cream maturing vat
32 butter shaping and packing machine
33 butter churn, a creamery butter machine for continuous butter making
34 butter supply pipe
35 shaping machine
36 packing machine
37 branded butter in 250 g packets
38 plant for producing curd cheese (curd cheese machine)
39 curd cheese pump
40 cream supply pump
41 curds separator
42 sour milk vat
43 stirrer
44 curd cheese packing machine
45 packeted curd cheese
46 bottle-capping machine (capper)
47 cheese machine
48 rennet vat

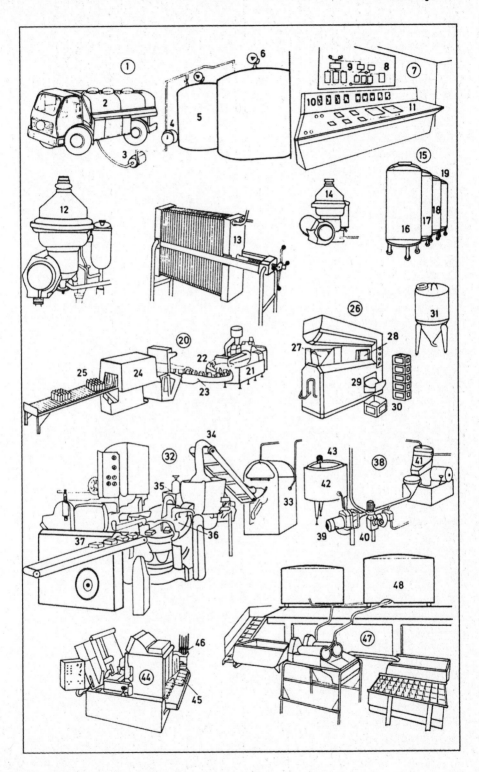

77 Bees and Beekeeping (Apiculture)

1-25 bee (honey-bee, hive-bee)
1, 4-5 castes (social classes) of bees
1 worker (worker bee)
2 three simple eyes (ocelli)
3 load of pollen on the hind leg
4 queen (queen bee)
5 drone (male bee)
6-9 left hind leg of a worker
6 pollen basket
7 pollen comb (brush)
8 double claw
9 suctorial pad
10-19 abdomen of the worker
10-14 stinging organs
10 barb
11 sting
12 sting sheath
13 poison sac
14 poison gland
15-19 stomachic-intestinal canal
15 intestine
16 stomach
17 contractile muscle
18 honey bag (honey sac)
19 oesophagus (esophagus, gullet)
20-24 compound eye
20 facet
21 crystal cone
22 light-sensitive section
23 fibre (*Am.* fiber) of the optic nerve
24 optic nerve
25 wax scale
26-30 cell
26 egg
27 cell with the egg in it
28 young larva
29 larva (grub)
30 chrysalis (pupa)
31-43 honeycomb
31 brood cell
32 sealed (capped) cell with chrysalis (pupa)
33 sealed (capped) cell with honey (honey cell)
34 worker cells
35 storage cells, with pollen
36 drone cells

37 queen cell
38 queen emerging from her cell
39 cap (capping)
40 frame
41 distance piece
42 [artificial] honeycomb
43 septum (foundation, comb foundation)
44 queen's travelling (*Am.* traveling) box
45-50 beehive, a frame hive (movable-frame hive, movable-comb hive)
45 super (honey super) with honeycombs
46 brood chamber with breeding combs
47 queen-excluder
48 entrance
49 flight board (alighting board)
50 window
51 old-fashioned bee shed
52 straw hive (skep), a hive
53 swarm (swarm cluster) of bees
54 swarming net (bag net)
55 hooked pole
56 apiary (bee house)
57 beekeeper (apiarist, *Am.* beeman)
58 bee veil
59 bee smoker
60 natural honeycomb
61 honey extractor (honey separator)
62-63 strained honey (honey)
62 honey pail
63 honey jar
64 honey in the comb
65 wax taper
66 wax candle
67 beeswax
68 bee sting ointment

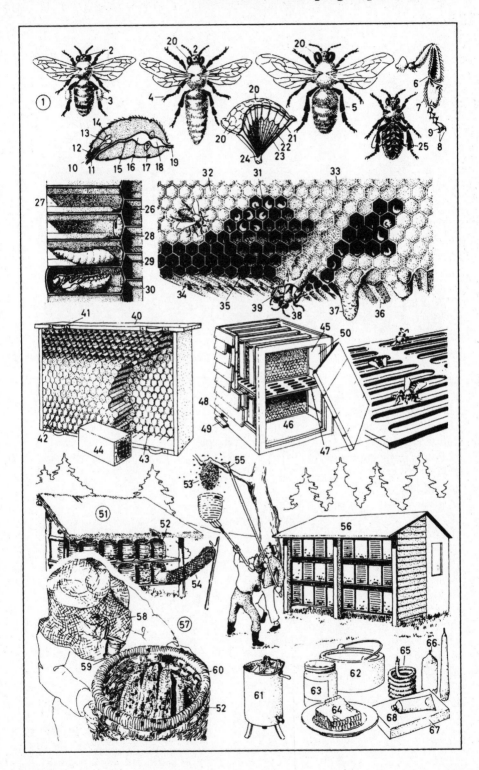

1-21 vineyard area
1 vineyard using wire trellises for training vines
2-9 vine (*Am.* grapevine)
2 vine shoot
3 long shoot
4 vine leaf
5 bunch of grapes (cluster of grapes)
6 vine stem
7 post (stake)
8 guy (guy wire)
9 wire trellis
10 tub for grape gathering
11 grape gatherer
12 secateurs for pruning vines
13 wine grower (viniculturist, viticulturist)
14 dosser carrier
15 dosser (pannier)
16 crushed grape transporter
17 grape crusher
18 hopper
19 three-sided flap extension
20 platform
21 vineyard tractor, a narrow-track tractor

1-22 wine cellar (wine vault)
1 vault
2 wine cask
3 wine vat, a concrete vat
4 stainless steel vat (*also:* vat made of synthetic material)
5 propeller-type high-speed mixer
6 propeller mixer
7 centrifugal pump
8 stainless steel sediment filter
9 semi-automatic circular bottling machine
10 semi-automatic corking machine
11 bottle rack
12 cellarer's assistant
13 bottle basket
14 wine bottle
15 wine jug
16 wine tasting
17 head cellarman
18 cellarman
19 wineglass
20 inspection apparatus [for spot-checking samples]
21 horizontal wine press
22 humidifier

1-19 fruit pests
1 gipsy (gypsy) moth
2 batch (cluster) of eggs
3 caterpillar
4 chrysalis (pupa)
5 small ermine moth, an ermine moth
6 larva (grub)
7 tent
8 caterpillar skeletonizing a leaf
9 fruit-surface-eating tortrix moth (summer fruit tortrix moth)
10 appleblossom weevil, a weevil
11 punctured, withered flower (blossom)
12 hole for laying eggs
13 lackey moth
14 caterpillar
15 eggs
16 winter moth, a geometrid
17 caterpillar
18 cherry fruit fly, a borer
19 larva (grub, maggot)

20-27 vine pests
20 downy mildew, a mildew, a disease causing leaf drop
21 grape affected with downy mildew
22 grape-berry moth
23 first-generation larva of the grape-berry moth (*Am.* grape worm)
24 second-generation larva of the grape-berry moth (*Am.* grape worm)
25 chrysalis (pupa)
26 root louse, a grape phylloxera
27 root gall (knotty swelling of the root, nodosity, tuberosity)
28 brown-tail moth
29 caterpillar
30 batch (cluster) of eggs
31 hibernation cocoon
32 woolly apple aphid (American blight), an aphid
33 gall caused by the woolly apple aphid
34 woolly apple aphid colony

35 San-José scale, a scale insect (scale louse)
36 larvae (grubs) [*male* elongated, *female* round]

37-55 field pests
37 click beetle, a snapping beetle (*Am.* snapping bug)
38 wireworm, larva of the click beetle
39 flea beetle
40 Hessian fly, a gall midge (gall gnat)
41 larva (grub)
42 turnip moth, an earth moth
43 chrysalis (pupa)
44 cutworm, a caterpillar
45 beet carrion beetle
46 larva (grub)
47 large cabbage white butterfly
48 caterpillar of the small cabbage white butterfly
49 brown leaf-eating weevil, a weevil
50 feeding site
51 sugar beet eelworm, a nematode (a threadworm, hairworm)
52 Colorado beetle (potato beetle)
53 mature larva (grub)
54 young larva (grub)
55 eggs

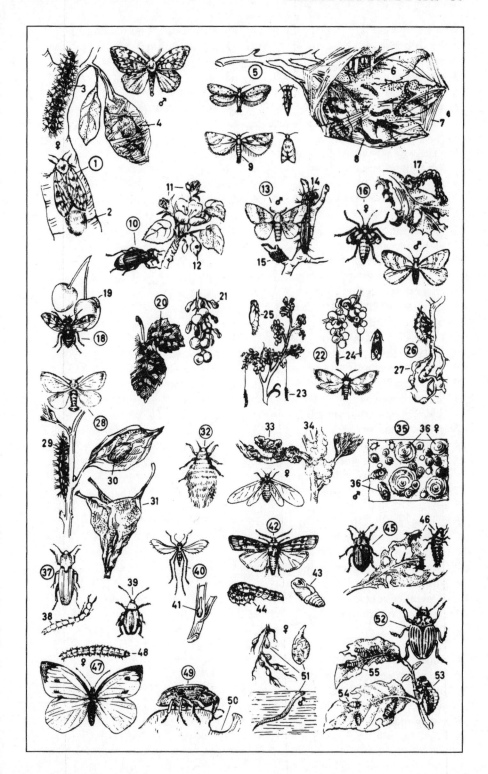

81 House Insects, Food Pests, and Parasites

1-14 house insects
1 lesser housefly
2 common housefly
3 chrysalis (pupa, coarctate pupa)
4 stable fly (biting housefly)
5 trichotomous antenna
6 wood louse (slater, *Am.* sow bug)
7 house cricket
8 wing with stridulating apparatus (stridulating mechanism)
9 house spider
10 spider's web
11 earwig
12 caudal pincers
13 clothes moth, a moth
14 silverfish (*Am.* slicker), a bristletail

15-30 food pests (pests to stores)
15 cheesefly
16 grain weevil (granary weevil)
17 cockroach (black beetle)
18 meal beetle (meal worm beetle, flour beetle)
19 spotted bruchus
20 larva (grub)
21 chrysalis (pupa)
22 leather beetle (hide beetle)
23 yellow meal beetle
24 chrysalis (pupa)
25 cigarette beetle (tobacco beetle)
26 maize billbug (corn weevil)
27 one of the Cryptolestes, a grain pest
28 Indian meal moth
29 Angoumois grain moth (Angoumois moth)
30 Angoumois grain moth caterpillar inside a grain kernel

31-42 parasites of man
31 round worm (maw worm)
32 female
33 head
34 male
35 tapeworm, a flatworm
36 head, a suctorial organ
37 sucker
38 crown of hooks
39 bug (bed bug, *Am.* chinch)
40 crab louse (a human louse)
41 clothes louse (body louse, a human louse)
42 flea (human flea, common flea)
43 tsetse fly
44 malaria mosquito

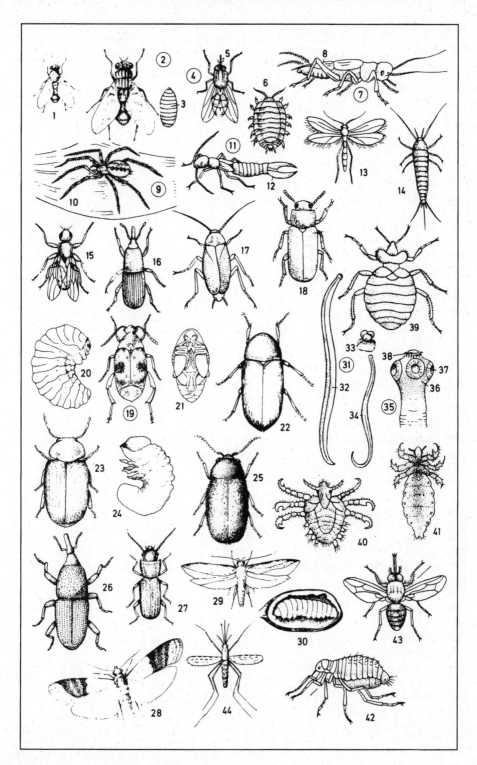

82 Forest Pests

1 cockchafer (May bug), a lamellicorn
2 head
3 antenna (feeler)
4 thoracic shield (prothorax)
5 scutellum
6-8 legs
6 front leg
7 middle leg
8 back leg
9 abdomen
10 elytron (wing case)
11 membranous wing
12 cockchafer grub, a larva
13 chrysalis (pupa)
14 processionary moth, a nocturnal moth (night-flying moth)
15 moth
16 caterpillars in procession
17 nun moth (black arches moth)
18 moth
19 eggs
20 caterpillar
21 chrysalis (pupa) in its cocoon
22 typographer beetle, a bark beetle
23-24 galleries under the bark
23 egg gallery
24 gallery made by larva
25 larva (grub)
26 beetle
27 pine hawkmoth, a hawkmoth
28 pine moth, a geometrid
29 male moth
30 female moth
31 caterpillar
32 chrysalis (pupa)
33 oak-gall wasp, a gall wasp
34 oak gall (oak apple), a gall
35 wasp
36 larva (grub) in its chamber
37 beech gall
38 spruce-gall aphid
39 winged aphid
40 pineapple gall
41 pine weevil
42 beetle (weevil)
43 green oak roller moth (green oak tortrix), a leaf roller
44 caterpillar
45 moth
46 pine beauty
47 caterpillar
48 moth

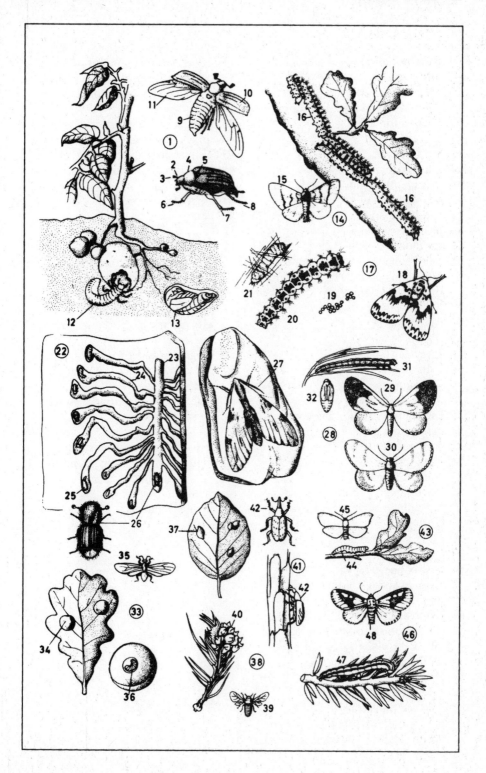

1 area spraying
2 tractor-mounted sprayer
3 spray boom
4 fan nozzle
5 spray fluid tank
6 foam canister for blob marking
7 spring suspension
8 spray
9 blob marker
10 foam feed pipe
11 vacuum fumigator (vacuum fumigation plant) of a tobacco factory
12 vacuum chamber
13 bales of raw tobacco
14 gas pipe
15 mobile fumigation chamber for fumigating nursery saplings, vine layers, seeds, and empty sacks with hydrocyanic (prussic) acid
16 gas circulation unit
17 tray
18 spray gun
19 twist grip (control grip, handle) for regulating the jet
20 finger guard
21 control lever (operating lever)
22 spray tube
23 cone nozzle
24 hand spray
25 plastic container
26 hand pump
27 pendulum spray for hop growing on slopes
28 pistol-type nozzle
29 spraying tube
30 hose connection
31 tube for laying poisoned bait
32 fly swat
33 soil injector (carbon disulphide, Am. carbon disulfide, injector) for killing the vine root louse
34 foot lever (foot pedal, foot treadle)
35 gas tube
36 mousetrap
37 vole and mole trap
38 mobile orchard sprayer, a wheelbarrow sprayer (carriage sprayer)

39 spray tank
40 screw-on cover
41 direct-connected motor-driven pump with petrol motor
42 pressure gauge (Am. gage) (manometer)
43 plunger-type knapsack sprayer
44 spray canister with pressure chamber
45 piston pump lever
46 hand lance with nozzle
47 semi-mounted sprayer
48 vineyard tractor
49 fan
50 spray fluid tank
51 row of vines
52 dressing machine (seed-dressing machine) for dry-seed dressing (seed dusting)
53 dedusting fan (dust removal fan) with electric motor
54 bag filter
55 bagging nozzle
56 dedusting screen (dust removal screen)
57 water canister [containing water for spraying]
58 spray unit
59 conveyor unit with mixing screw
60 container for disinfectant powder with dosing mechanism
61 castor
62 mixing chamber

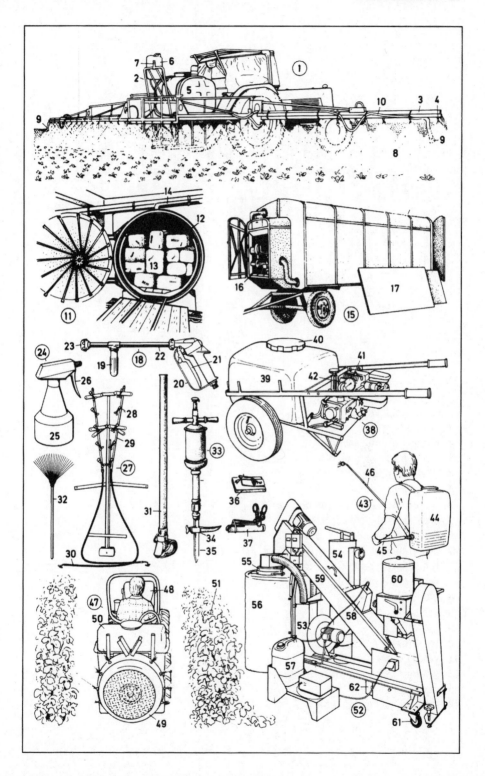

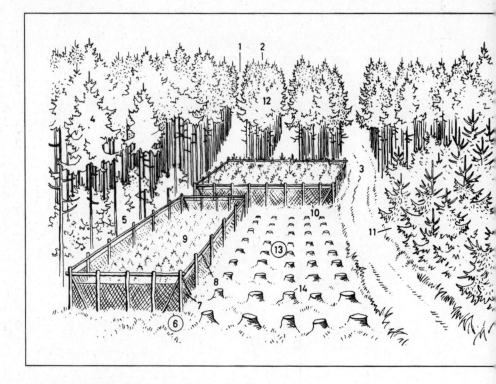

1-34 forest, a wood
1 ride (aisle, lane, section line)
2 compartment (section)
3 wood haulage way, a forest track
4-14 clear-felling system
4 standing timber
5 underwood (underbrush, under-
   growth, brushwood, *Am.* brush)
6 seedling nursery, a tree nursery
7 deer fence (fence), a wire netting
   fence (protective fence for
   seedlings); *sim.:* rabbit fence
8 guard rail
9 seedlings
10, 11 young trees
10 tree nursery after transplanting
11 young plantation
12 young plantation after brashing
13 clearing
14 tree stump (stump, stub)

15-37 wood cutting (timber cutting, tree felling, *Am.* lumbering)
15 timber skidded to the stack (stacked timber, *Am.* yarded timber)
16 stack of logs, one cubic metre (*Am.* meter) of wood
17 post (stake)
18 forest labourer (woodsman, *Am.* logger, lumberer, lumberjack, lumberman, timberjack) turning (*Am.* canting) timber
19 bole (tree trunk, trunk, stem)
20 feller numbering the logs
21 steel tree calliper (caliper)
22 power saw (motor saw) cutting a bole
23 safety helmet with visor and ear pieces
24 annual rings
25 hydraulic felling wedge
26 protective clothing [orange top, green trousers]
27 felling with a power saw (motor saw)
28 undercut (notch, throat, gullet, mouth, sink, kerf, birdsmouth)
29 back cut
30 sheath holding felling wedge
31 log
32 free-cutting saw for removing underwood and weeds
33 circular saw (or activated blade) attachment
34 power unit (motor)
35 canister of viscous oil for the saw chain
36 petrol canister (*Am.* gasoline canister)
37 felling of small timber (of small-sized thinnings) (thinning)

1 axe (*Am.* ax)
2 edge (cutting edge)
3 handle (helve)
4 felling wedge (falling wedge) with wood insert and ring
5 riving hammer (cleaving hammer, splitting hammer)
6 lifting hook
7 cant hook
8 barking iron (bark spud)
9 peavy
10 slide calliper (caliper) (calliper square)
11 billhook, a knife for lopping
12 revolving die hammer (marking hammer, marking iron, *Am.* marker)
13 power saw (motor saw)
14 saw chain
15 safety brake for the saw chain, with finger guard
16 saw guide
17 accelerator lock
18 snedding machine (trimming machine, *Am.* knotting machine, limbing machine)
19 feed rolls
20 flexible blade
21 hydraulic arm
22 trimming blade
23 debarking (barking, bark stripping) of boles
24 feed roller
25 cylinder trimmer
26 rotary cutter
27 short-haul skidder
28 loading crane
29 log grips
30 post
31 Ackermann steering system
32 log dump
33 number (identification number)
34 skidder
35 front blade (front plate)
36 crush-proof safety bonnet (*Am.* safety hood)
37 Ackermann steering system
38 cable winch
39 cable drum
40 rear blade (rear plate)
41 boles with butt ends held off the ground
42 haulage of timber by road
43 tractor (tractor unit)
44 loading crane
45 hydraulic jack
46 cable winch
47 post
48 bolster plate
49 rear bed (rear bunk)

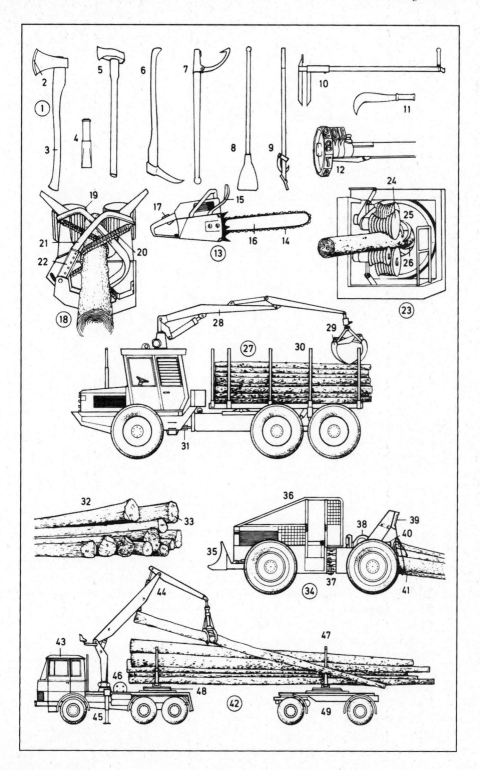

1-52 kinds of hunting
1-8 stalking (deer stalking, *Am.* still-hunting) in the game preserve
1 huntsman (hunter)
2 hunting clothes
3 knapsack
4 sporting gun (sporting rifle, hunting rifle)
5 huntsman's hat
6 field glasses, binoculars
7 gun dog
8 track (trail, hoofprints)
9-12 hunting in the rutting season and the pairing season
9 hunting screen (screen, *Am.* blind)
10 shooting stick (shooting seat, seat stick)
11 blackcock, displaying
12 rutting stag
13 hind, grazing
14-17 hunting from a raised hide
(raised stand)

14 raised hide (raised stand, high seat)
15 herd within range
16 game path (*Am.* runway)
17 roebuck, hit in the shoulder and killed by a finishing shot
18 phaeton
19-27 types of trapping
19 trapping of small predators
20 box trap (trap for small predators)
21 bait
22 marten, a small predator
23 ferreting (hunting rabbits out of their warrens)
24 ferret
25 ferreter
26 burrow (rabbit burrow, rabbit hole)
27 net (rabbit net) over the burrow opening

28 feeding place for game (winter feeding place)
29 poacher
30 carbine, a short rifle
31 boar hunt
32 wild sow (sow, wild boar)
33 boarhound (hound, hunting dog; *collectively:* pack, pack of hounds)
34-39 beating (driving, hare hunting)
34 aiming position
35 hare, furred game (ground game)
36 retrieving
37 beater
38 bag (kill)
39 cart for carrying game
40 waterfowling (wildfowling, duck shooting, *Am.* duck hunting)
41 flight of wild ducks, winged game
42-46 falconry (hawking)
42 falconer
43 reward, a piece of meat

44 falcon's hood
45 jess
46 falcon, a hawk, a male hawk (tiercel) swooping (stooping) on a heron
47-52 shooting from a butt
47 tree to which birds are lured
48 eagle owl, a decoy bird (decoy)
49 perch
50 decoyed bird, a crow
51 butt for shooting crows or eagle owls
52 gun slit

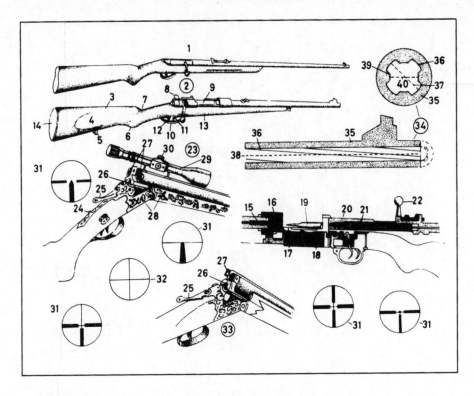

1-40 sporting guns (sporting rifles, hunting rifles)

1 single-loader (single-loading rifle)

2 repeating rifle, a small-arm (firearm), a repeater (magazine rifle, magazine repeater)

3, 4, 6, 13 stock

3 butt

4 cheek [on the left side]

5 sling ring

6 pistol grip

7 small of the butt

8 safety catch

9 lock

10 trigger guard

11 second set trigger (firing trigger)

12 hair trigger (set trigger)

13 foregrip

14 butt plate

15 cartridge chamber

16 receiver

17 magazine

18 magazine spring

19 ammunition (cartridge)

20 chamber

21 firing pin (striker)

22 bolt handle (bolt lever)

23 triple-barrelled (triple-barreled) rifle, a self-cocking gun

24 reversing catch; *in various guns:* safety catch

25 sliding safety catch

26 rifle barrel (rifled barrel)

27 smooth-bore barrel

28 chasing

29 telescopic sight (riflescope, telescope sight)

30 graticule adjuster screws

31-32 graticule (sight graticule)

31 various graticule systems

32 cross wires (*Am.* cross hairs)

33 over-and-under shotgun

34 rifled gun barrel

35 barrel casing

36 rifling

37 rifling calibre (*Am.* caliber)

38 bore axis

39 land

40 calibre (bore diameter, *Am.* caliber)

41-48 hunting equipment
41 double-edged hunting knife
42 [single-edged] hunting knife
43-47 calls for luring game (for calling game)
43 roe call
44 hare call
45 quail call
46 stag call
47 partridge call
48 bow trap (bow gin), a jaw trap
49 small-shot cartridge
50 cardboard case
51 small-shot charge
52 felt wad
53 smokeless powder (*different kind:* black powder)
54 cartridge
55 full-jacketed cartridge
56 soft-lead core
57 powder charge
58 detonator cap
59 percussion cap
60 hunting horn
61-64 rifle cleaning kit
61 cleaning rod
62 cleaning brush
63 cleaning tow
64 pull-through (*Am.* pull-thru)
65 sights
66 notch (sighting notch)
67 back sight leaf
68 sight scale division
69 back sight slide
70 notch [to hold the spring]
71 front sight (foresight)
72 bead
73 **ballistics**
74 azimuth
75 angle of departure
76 angle of elevation
77 apex (zenith)
78 angle of descent
79 ballistic curve

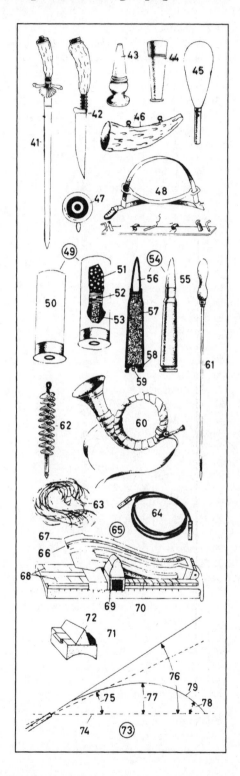

1-27 red deer

1 hind (red deer), a young hind or a dam; *collectively:* antlerless deer, *(y.)* calf

2 tongue

3 neck

4 rutting stag

5-11 antlers

5 burr (rose)

6 brow antler (brow tine, brow point, brow snag)

7 bez antler (bay antler, bay, bez tine)

8 royal antler (royal, tray)

9 surroyal antlers (surroyals)

10 point (tine)

11 beam (main trunk)

12 head

13 mouth

14 larmier (tear bag)

15 eye

16 ear

17 shoulder

18 loin

19 scut (tail)

20 rump

21 leg (haunch)

22 hind leg

23 dew claw

24 hoof

25 foreleg

26 flank

27 collar (rutting mane)

28-39 roe (roe deer)

28 roebuck (buck)

29-31 antlers (horns)

29 burr (rose)

30 beam with pearls

31 point (tine)

32 ear

33 eye

34 doe (female roe), a female fawn or a barren doe

35 loin

36 rump

37 leg (haunch)

38 shoulder

39 fawn, *(m.)* young buck, *(f.)* young doe

40-41 fallow deer

40 fallow buck, a buck with palmate (palmated) antlers, *(f.)* doe

41 palm

42 red fox, *(m.)* dog, *(f.)* vixen, *(y.)* cub

43 eyes

44 ear

45 muzzle (mouth)

46 pads (paws)

47 brush (tail)

48 badger, *(f.)* sow

49 tail

50 paws

51 wild boar, *(m.)* boar, *(f.)* wild sow (sow), *(y.)* young boar

52 bristles

53 snout

54 tusk

55 shield

56 hide

57 dew claw

58 tail

59 hare, *(m.)* buck, *(f.)* doe

60 eye

61 ear

62 scut (tail)

63 hind leg

64 foreleg

65 rabbit

66 blackcock

67 tail

68 falcate (falcated) feathers

69 hazel grouse (hazel hen)

70 partridge

71 horseshoe (horseshoe marking)

72 wood grouse (capercaillie)

73 beard

74 axillary marking

75 tail (fan)

76 wing (pinion)

77 common pheasant, a pheasant, *(m.)* cock pheasant (pheasant cock), *(f.)* hen pheasant (pheasant hen)

78 plumicorn (feathered ear, ear tuft, ear, horn)

79 wing

80 tail

81 leg

82 spur

83 snipe

84 bill (beak)

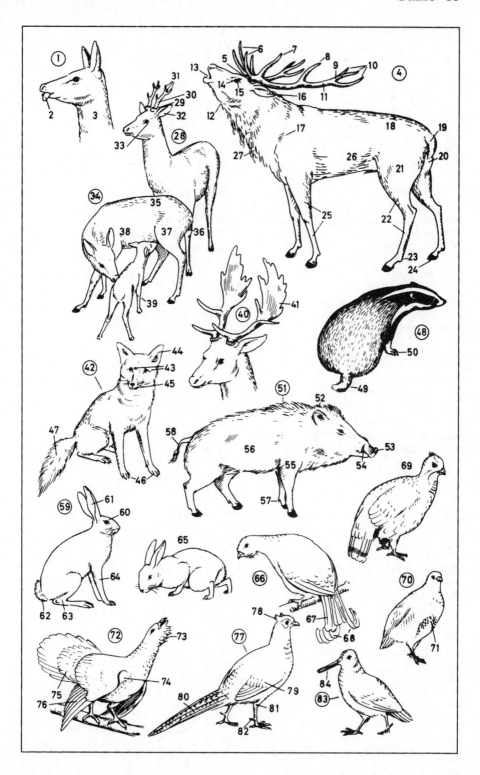

89 Fish Farming (Fish Culture, Pisciculture) and Angling

1-19 fish farming (fish culture, pisciculture)
1 cage in running water
2 hand net (landing net)
3 semi-oval barrel for transporting fish
4 vat
5 trellis in the overflow
6 trout pond; *sim.:* carp pond, a fry pond, fattening pond, or cleansing pond
7 water inlet (water supply pipe)
8 water outlet (outlet pipe)
9 monk
10 screen
11-19 hatchery
11 stripping the spawning pike (seed pike)
12 fish spawn (spawn, roe, fish eggs)
13 female fish (spawner, seed fish)
14 trout breeding (trout rearing)
15 Californian incubator
16 trout fry
17 hatching jar for pike
18 long incubation tank
19 Brandstetter egg-counting board
20-94 angling
20-31 bottom fishing (coarse fishing)
20 line shooting
21 coils
22 cloth (rag) or paper
23 rod rest
24 bait tin
25 fish basket (creel)
26 fishing for carp from a boat
27 rowing boat (fishing boat)
28 keep net
29 drop net
30 pole (punt pole, quant pole)
31 casting net
32 two-handed side cast with fixed-spool reel
33 initial position
34 point of release
35 path of the rod tip
36 trajectory of the baited weight
37-94 fishing tackle
37 fishing pliers
38 filleting knife
39 fish knife
40 disgorger (hook disgorger)
41 bait needle
42 gag
43-48 floats
43 sliding cork float
44 plastic float
45 quill float
46 polystyrene float
47 oval bubble float
48 lead-weighted sliding float

49-58 rods
49 solid glass rod
50 cork handle (cork butt)
51 spring-steel ring
52 top ring (end ring)
53 telescopic rod
54 rod section
55 bound handle (bound butt)
56 ring
57 carbon-fibre rod; *sim.:* hollow glass rod
58 all-round ring (butt ring for long cast), a steel bridge ring
59-64 reels
59 multiplying reel (multiplier reel)
60 line guide
61 fixed-spool reel (stationary-drum reel)
62 bale arm
63 fishing line
64 controlling the cast with the index finger
65-76 baits
65 fly
66 artificial nymph
67 artificial earthworm
68 artificial grasshopper
69 single-jointed plug (single-jointed wobbler)
70 double-jointed plug (double-jointed wobbler)
71 round wobbler
72 wiggler
73 spoon bait (spoon)
74 spinner
75 spinner with concealed hook
76 long spinner
77 swivel
78 cast (leader)
79-87 hooks
79 fish hook
80 point of the hook with barb
81 bend of the hook
82 spade (eye)
83 open double hook
84 limerick
85 closed treble hook (triangle)
86 carp hook
87 eel hook
88-92 leads (lead weights)
88 oval lead (oval sinker)
89 lead shot
90 pear-shaped lead
91 plummet
92 sea lead
93 fish ladder (fish pass, fish way)
94 stake net

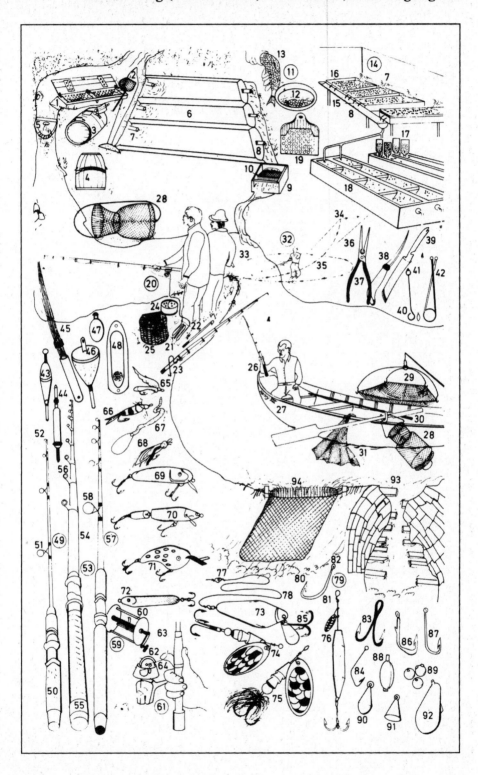

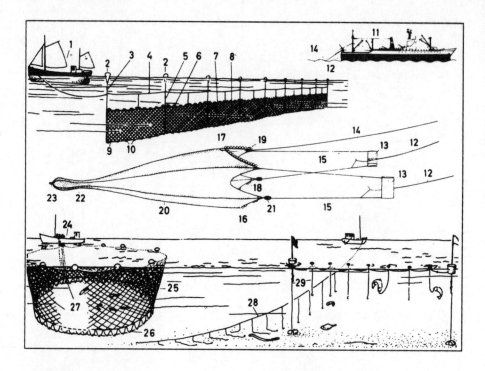

1-23 deep-sea fishing
1-10 drift net fishing
1 herring lugger (fishing lugger, lugger)
2-10 herring drift net
2 buoy
3 buoy rope
4 float line
5 seizing
6 wooden float
7 headline
8 net
9 footrope
10 sinkers (weights)
11-23 trawl fishing (trawling)
11 factory ship, a trawler
12 warp (trawl warp)
13 otter boards
14 net sonar cable
15 wire warp
16 wing
17 net sonar device
18 footrope
19 spherical floats
20 belly

21 1,800 kg iron weight
22 cod end (cod)
23 cod line for closing the cod end
24-29 inshore fishing
24 fishing boat
25 ring net cast in a circle
26 cable for closing the ring net
27 closing gear
28-29 long-line fishing (long-lining)
28 long line
29 suspended fishing tackle

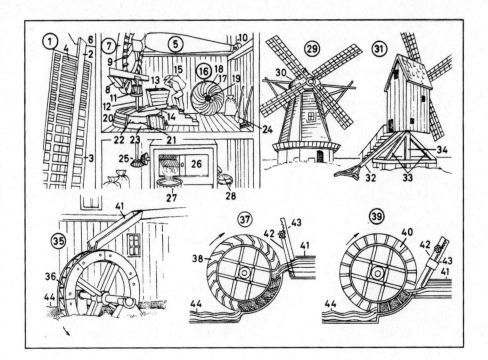

1-34 windmill
1 windmill vane (windmill sail, wind-mill arm)
2 stock (middling, back, radius)
3 frame
4 shutter
5 wind shaft (sail axle)
6 sail top
7 brake wheel
8 brake
9 wooden cog
10 pivot bearing (step bearing)
11 wallower
12 mill spindle
13 hopper
14 shoe (trough, spout)
15 miller
16 millstone
17 furrow (flute)
18 master furrow
19 eye
20 hurst (millstone casing)
21 set of stones (millstones)
22 runner (upper millstone)
23 bed stone (lower stone, bedder)
24 wooden shovel
25 bevel gear (bevel gearing)
26 bolter (sifter)
27 wooden tub (wooden tun)
28 flour
29 smock windmill (Dutch windmill)
30 rotating (revolving) windmill cap
31 post windmill (German windmill)
32 tailpole (pole)
33 base
34 post
35-44 watermill
35 overshot mill wheel (high-breast mill wheel), a mill wheel (water-wheel)
36 bucket (cavity)
37 middleshot mill wheel (breast mill wheel)
38 curved vane
39 undershot mill wheel
40 flat vane
41 headrace (discharge flume)
42 mill weir
43 overfall (water overfall)
44 millstream (millrace, *Am.* raceway)

1-41 preparation of malt (malting)
1 malting tower (maltings)
2 barley hopper
3 washing floor with compressed-air washing unit
4 outflow condenser
5 water-collecting tank
6 condenser for the steep liquor
7 coolant collecting plant
8 steeping floor (steeping tank, dressing floor)
9 cold water tank
10 hot water tank
11 pump room
12 pneumatic plant
13 hydraulic plant
14 ventilation shaft (air inlet and outlet)
15 exhaust fan
16-18 kilning floors
16 drying floor
17 burner ventilator
18 curing floor
19 outlet duct from the kiln
20 finished malt collecting hopper
21 transformer station
22 cooling compressors
23 green malt (germinated barley)
24 turner (plough)
25 central control room with flow diagram
26 screw conveyor
27 washing floor
28 steeping floor
29 drying kiln
30 curing kiln
31 barley silo
32 weighing apparatus
33 barley elevator
34 three-way chute (three-way tippler)
35 malt elevator
36 cleaning machine
37 malt silo
38 corn removal by suction
39 sacker
40 dust extractor

41 barley reception
42-53 mashing process in the mash-house
42 premasher (converter) for mixing grist and water
43 mash tub (mash tun) for mashing the malt
44 mash copper (mash tun, *Am.* mash kettle) for boiling the mash
45 dome of the tun
46 propeller (paddle)
47 sliding door
48 water (liquor) supply pipe
49 brewer (master brewer, masher)
50 lauter tun for settling the draff (grains) and filtering off the wort
51 lauter battery for testing the wort for quality
52 hop boiler (wort boiler) for boiling the wort
53 ladle-type thermometer (scoop thermometer)

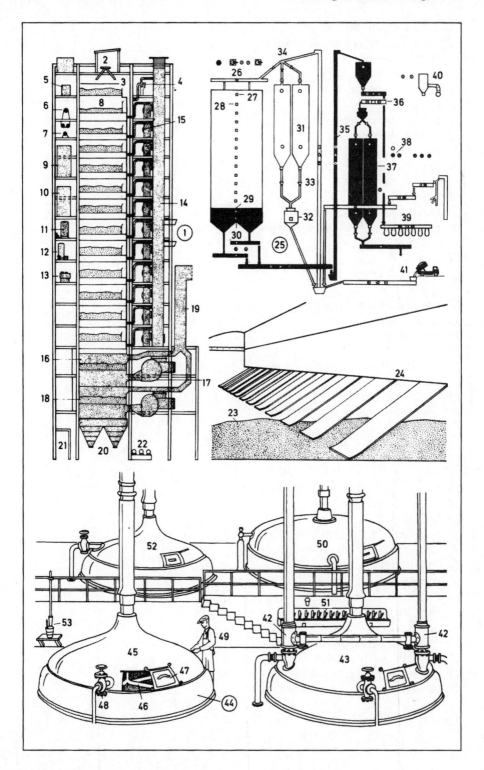

93 Brewing II

1-31 brewery (brewhouse)
1-5 wort cooling and break removal
   (trub removal)
1 control desk (control panel)
2 whirlpool separator for removing
   the hot break (hot trub)
3 measuring vessel for the kieselguhr
4 kieselguhr filter
5 wort cooler
6 pure culture plant for yeast (yeast
   propagation plant)
7 fermenting cellar
8 fermentation vessel (fermenter)
9 fermentation thermometer (mash
   thermometer)
10 mash
11 refrigeration system
12 lager cellar
13 manhole to the storage tank
14 broaching tap
15 beer filter
16 barrel store
17 beer barrel, an aluminium (*Am.*
   aluminum) barrel
18 bottle-washing plant
19 bottle-washing machine (bottle
   washer)
20 control panel
21 cleaned bottles
22 bottling
23 forklift truck (fork truck, forklift)
24 stack of beer crates
25 beer can
26 beer bottle, a Eurobottle with bottled beer; *kinds of beer:* light beer
   (lager, light ale, pale ale or bitter),
   dark beer (brown ale, mild),
   Pilsener beer, Munich beer, malt
   beer, strong beer (bock beer),
   porter, ale, stout, Salvator beer,
   wheat beer, small beer
27 crown cork (crown cork closure)
28 disposable pack (carry-home pack)
29 non-returnable bottle (single-trip
   bottle)
30 beer glass
31 head

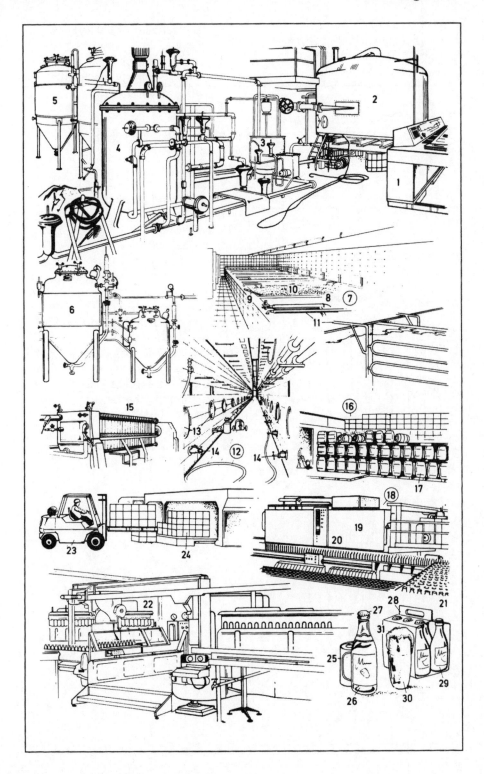

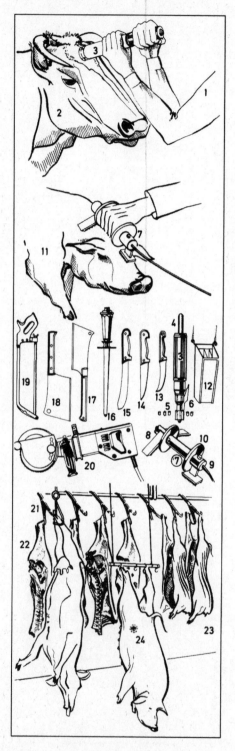

1 slaughterman (*Am.* slaughterer, killer)
2 animal for slaughter, an ox
3 captive-bolt pistol (pneumatic gun), a stunning device
4 bolt
5 cartridges
6 release lever (trigger)
7 electric stunner
8 electrode
9 lead
10 hand guard (insulation)
11 pig (*Am.* hog) for slaughter
12 knife case
13 flaying knife
14 sticking knife (sticker)
15 butcher's knife (butcher knife)
16 steel
17 splitter
18 cleaver (butcher's cleaver, meat axe (*Am.* meat ax))
19 bone saw (butcher's saw)
20 meat saw for sawing meat into cuts
21-24 **cold store** (cold room)
21 gambrel (gambrel stick)
22 quarter of beef
23 side of pork
24 meat inspector's stamp

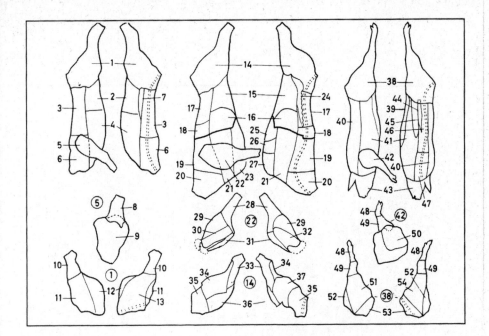

left: meat side;
right: bone side

1-13 *animal:* **calf;** *meat:* **veal**
1 leg with hind knuckle
2 flank
3 loin and rib
4 breast (breast of veal)
5 shoulder with fore knuckle
6 neck with scrag (scrag end)
7 best end of loin (of loin of veal)
8 fore knuckle
9 shoulder
10 hind knuckle
11 roasting round (oyster round)
12 cutlet for frying or braising
13 undercut (fillet)
14-37 *animal:* **ox;** *meat:* **beef**
14 round with rump and shank
15-16 flank
15 thick flank
16 thin flank
17 sirloin
18 prime rib (fore ribs, prime fore rib)
19 middle rib and chuck
20 neck
21 flat rib
22 leg of mutton piece (bladebone) with shin
23 brisket (brisket of beef)
24 fillet (fillet of beef)
25 hind brisket

26 middle brisket
27 breastbone
28 shin
29 leg of mutton piece
30 bladebone [meat side]
31 part of top rib
32 bladebone [bone side]
33 shank
34 silverside
35 rump
36 thick flank
37 top side
38-54 *animal:* **pig;** *meat:* **pork**
38 leg with knuckle and trotter
39 ventral part of the belly
40 back fat
41 belly
42 bladebone with knuckle and trotter
43 head (pig's head)
44 fillet (fillet of pork)
45 leaf fat (pork flare)
46 loin (pork loin)
47 spare rib
48 trotter
49 knuckle
50 butt
51 fore end (ham)
52 round end for boiling
53 fat end
54 gammon steak

1-30 butcher's shop

1-4 meat

1 ham on the bone
2 flitch of bacon
3 smoked meat
4 piece of loin (piece of sirloin)
5 lard

6-11 sausages

6 price label
7 mortadella
8 scalded sausage; *kinds:* Vienna sausage (Wiener), Frankfurter sausage (Frankfurter)
9 collared pork (*Am.* headcheese)
10 ring of [Lyoner] sausage
11 pork sausages; *also:* beef sausages
12 cold shelves
13 meat salad (diced meat salad)
14 cold meats (*Am.* cold cuts)
15 pâté
16 mince (mincemeat, minced meat)
17 knuckle of pork
18 basket for special offers

19 price list for special offers
20 special offer
21 freezer
22 pre-packed joints
23 deep-frozen ready-to-eat meal
24 chicken
25 canned food
26 can
27 canned vegetables
28 canned fish
29 salad cream
30 soft drinks

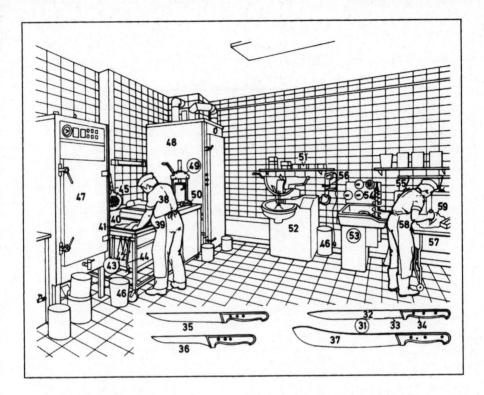

31-59 manufacture of sausages
31-37 butcher's knives
31 slicer
32 knife blade
33 saw teeth
34 knife handle
35 carver (carving knife)
36 boning knife
37 butcher's knife (butcher knife)
38 butcher (master butcher)
39 butcher's apron
40 meat-mixing trough
41 sausage meat
42 scraper
43 skimmer
44 sausage fork
45 scalding colander
46 waste bin (*Am.* trash bin)
47 cooker, for cooking with steam or
   hot air
48 smoke house
49 sausage filler (sausage stuffer)
50 feed pipe (supply pipe)

51 containers for vegetables
52 mincing machine for sausage meat
53 mincing machine (meat mincer,
   mincer, *Am.* meat grinder)
54 plates (steel plates)
55 meathook (butcher's hook)
56 bone saw
57 chopping board
58 butcher, cutting meat
59 piece of meat

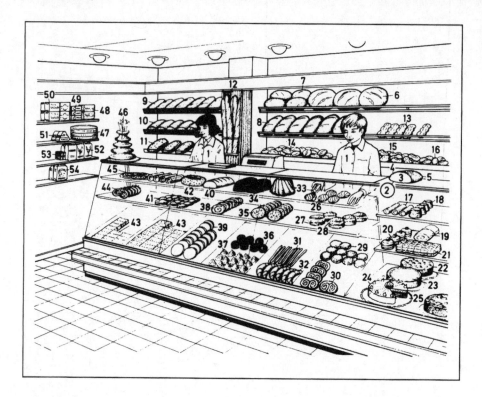

1-54 baker's shop
1 shop assistant (*Am.* salesgirl, saleslady)
2 bread (loaf of bread, loaf)
3 crumb
4 crust (bread crust)
5 crust (*Am.* heel)
6-12 kinds of bread (breads)
6 round loaf, a wheat and rye bread
7 small round loaf
8 long loaf (bloomer), a wheat and rye bread
9 white loaf
10 pan loaf, a wholemeal rye bread
11 yeast bread (*Am.* stollen)
12 French loaf (baguette, French stick)
13-16 rolls
13 brown roll
14 white roll
15 finger roll
16 rye-bread roll
17-47 cakes (confectionery)
17 cream roll

18 vol-au-vent, a puff pastry (*Am.* puff paste)
19 Swiss roll (*Am.* jelly roll)
20 tartlet
21 cream slice
22-24 flans (*Am.* pies) **and gateaux** (torten)
22 fruit flan (*kinds:* strawberry flan, cherry flan, gooseberry flan, peach flan, rhubarb flan)
23 cheesecake
24 cream cake (*Am.* cream pie) (*kinds:* butter-cream cake, Black Forest gateau)
25 cake plate
26 meringue
27 cream puff
28 whipped cream
29 doughnut (*Am.* bismarck)
30 Danish pastry
31 saltstick (Salzstange) (*also:* caraway roll, caraway stick)
32 croissant (crescent roll, *Am.* crescent)

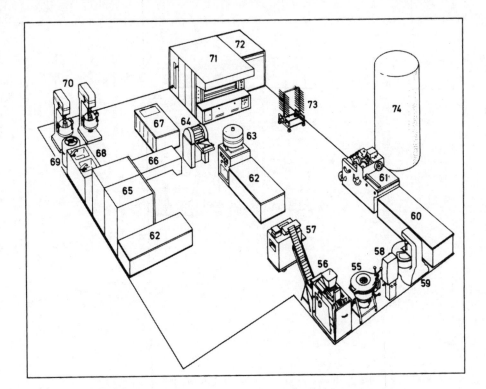

33 ring cake (gugelhupf)
34 slab cake with chocolate icing
35 streusel cakes
36 marshmallow
37 coconut macaroon
38 pastry whirl
39 iced bun
40 sweet bread
41 plaited bun (plait)
42 Frankfurter garland cake
43 slices (*kinds:* streusel slices, sugared slices, plum slices)
44 pretzel
45 wafer (*Am.* waffle)
46 tree cake (baumkuchen)
47 flan case
48-50 **wrapped bread**
48 wholemeal bread (*also:* wheatgerm bread)
49 pumpernickel (wholemeal rye bread)
50 crispbread
51 gingerbread (*Am.* lebkuchen)
52 flour (*kinds:* wheat flour, rye flour)
53 yeast (baker's yeast)

54 rusks (French toast)
55-74 **bakery** (bakehouse)
55 kneading machine (dough mixer)
56-57 **bread unit**
56 divider
57 moulder (*Am.* molder)
58 premixer
59 dough mixer
60 workbench
61 roll unit
62 workbench
63 divider and rounder (rounding machine)
64 crescent-forming machine
65 freezers
66 oven [for baking with fat]
67-70 **confectionery unit**
67 cooling table
68 sink
69 boiler
70 whipping unit [with beater]
71 reel oven (oven)
72 fermentation room
73 fermentation trolley
74 flour silo

1-87 **grocer's shop** (grocer's, delicatessen shop, *Am.* grocery store, delicatessen store), a retail shop (*Am.* retail store)
1 window display
2 poster (advertisement)
3 cold shelves
4 sausages
5 cheese
6 roasting chicken (broiler)
7 poulard, a fattened hen
8-11 **baking ingredients**
8 raisins; *sim.:* sultanas
9 currants
10 candied lemon peel
11 candied orange peel
12 computing scale, a rapid scale
13 shop assistant (*Am.* salesclerk)
14 goods shelves (shelves)
15-20 **canned food**
15 canned milk
16 canned fruit (cans of fruit)
17 canned vegetables
18 fruit juice
19 sardines in oil, a can of fish
20 canned meat (cans of meat)
21 margarine

22 butter
23 coconut oil, a vegetable oil
24 oil; *kinds:* salad oil, olive oil, sunflower oil, wheatgerm oil, groundnut oil
25 vinegar
26 stock cube
27 bouillon cube
28 mustard
29 pickled gherkin
30 soup seasoning
31 shop assistant (*Am.* salesgirl, saleslady)
32-34 **pastas**
32 spaghetti
33 macaroni
34 noodles
35-39 **cereal products**
35 pearl barley
36 semolina
37 rolled oats (porridge oats, oats)
38 rice
39 sago
40 salt
41 grocer (*Am.* groceryman), a shopkeeper (tradesman, retailer, *Am.* storekeeper)

42 capers
43 customer
44 receipt (sales check)
45 shopping bag
46-49 wrapping material
46 wrapping paper
47 adhesive tape
48 paper bag
49 cone-shaped paper bag
50 blancmange powder
51 whole-fruit jam (preserve)
52 jam
53-55 sugar
53 cube sugar
54 icing sugar (*Am.* confectioner's sugar)
55 refined sugar in crystals
56-59 spirits
56 whisky (whiskey)
57 rum
58 liqueur
59 brandy (cognac)
60-64 wine in bottles (bottled wine)
60 white wine
61 Chianti
62 vermouth
63 sparkling wine

64 red wine
65-68 tea, coffee, etc.
65 coffee (pure coffee)
66 cocoa
67 coffee
68 tea bag
69 electric coffee grinder
70 coffee roaster
71 roasting drum
72 sample scoop
73 price list
74 freezer
75-86 confectionery (*Am.* candies)
75 sweet (*Am.* candy)
76 drops
77 toffees
78 bar of chocolate
79 chocolate box
80 chocolate, a sweet
81 nougat
82 marzipan
83 chocolate liqueur
84 Turkish delight
85 croquant
86 truffle
87 soda water

1-96 supermarket, a self-service food store
1 shopping trolley
2 customer
3 shopping bag
4 entrance to the sales area
5 barrier
6 sign (notice) banning dogs
7 dogs tied by their leads
8 basket
9 **bread and cake counter** (bread counter, cake counter)
10 display counter for bread and cakes
11 kinds of bread (breads)
12 rolls
13 croissants (crescent rolls, *Am.* crescents)
14 round loaf
15 gateau
16 pretzel [made with yeast dough]
17 shop assistant (*Am.* salesgirl, saleslady)
18 customer
19 sign listing goods
20 fruit flan
21 slab cake
22 ring cake
23 **cosmetics gondola,** a gondola (sales shelves)

24 canopy
25 hosiery shelf
26 stockings (nylons)
27-35 toiletries (cosmetics)
27 jar of cream (cream; *kinds:* moisturising cream, day cream, night-care cream, hand cream)
28 packet of cotton wool
29 talcum powder
30 packet of cotton wool balls
31 toothpaste
32 nail varnish (nail polish)
33 shaving cream
34 bath salts
35 sanitary articles
36, 37 pet foods
36 complete dog food
37 packet of dog biscuits
38 bag of cat litter
39 **cheese counter**
40 whole cheese
41 Swiss cheese (Emmental cheese) with holes
42 Edam cheese, a round cheese
43 gondola for dairy products
44 long-life milk; *also:* pasteurized milk, homogenized milk
45 plastic milk bag

46 cream	**71** **drinks gondola**
47 butter	**72** soft drinks
48 margarine	**73** can of beer
49 box of cheeses	**74** bottle of fruit juice
50 box of eggs	**75** can of fruit juice
51 **fresh meat counter** (meat counter)	**76** bottle of wine
52 ham on the bone	**77** bottle of Chianti
53 meat (meat products)	**78** bottle of champagne
54 sausages	**79** emergency exit
55 ring of pork sausage	**80** **fruit and vegetable counter**
56 ring of blood sausage	**81** vegetable basket
57 freezer	**82** tomatoes
58-61 **frozen food**	**83** cucumbers
58 poulard	**84** cauliflower
59 turkey leg (drumstick)	**85** pineapple
60 boiling fowl	**86** apples
61 frozen vegetables	**87** pears
62 **gondola for baking ingredients and**	**88** scales for weighing fruit
cereal products	**89** grapes (bunches of grapes)
63 wheat flour	**90** bananas
64 sugar loaf	**91** can
65 packet of noodles	**92** **checkout**
66 salad oil	**93** cash register
67 packet of spice	**94** cashier
68-73 **tea, coffee, etc.**	**95** chain
68 coffee	**96** assistant departmental manager
69 packet of tea	
70 instant coffee	

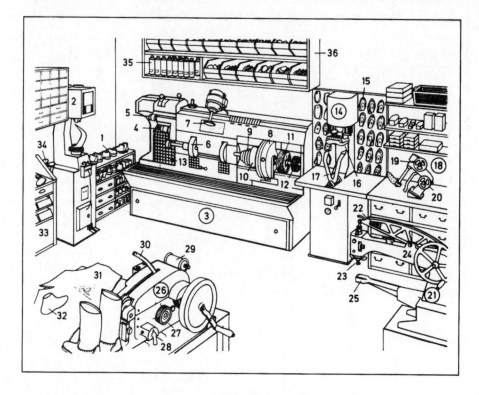

1-68 shoemaker's workshop (boot-
maker's workshop)
1 finished (repaired) shoes
2 auto-soling machine
3 finishing machine
4 heel trimmer
5 sole trimmer
6 scouring wheel
7 naum keag
8 drive unit (drive wheel)
9 iron
10 buffing wheel
11 polishing brush
12 horsehair brush
13 extractor grid
14 automatic sole press
15 press attachment
16 pad
17 press bar
18 stretching machine
19 width adjustment
20 length adjustment
21 stitching machine

22 power regulator (power control)
23 foot
24 handwheel
25 arm
26 sole stitcher (sole-stitching
machine)
27 foot bar lever
28 feed adjustment (feed setting)
29 bobbin (cotton bobbin)
30 thread guide (yarn guide)
31 sole leather
32 [wooden] last
33 workbench
34 last
35 dye spray
36 shelves for materials

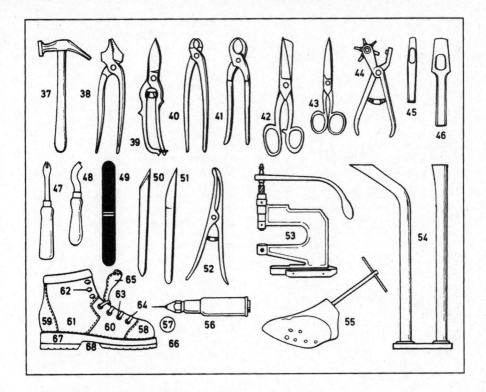

37 shoemaker's hammer
38 shoemaker's pliers (welt pincers)
39 sole-leather shears
40 small pincers (nippers)
41 large pincers (nippers)
42 upper-leather shears
43 scissors
44 revolving punch (rotary punch)
45 punch
46 punch with handle
47 nail puller
48 welt cutter
49 shoemaker's rasp
50 cobbler's knife (shoemaker's knife)
51 skiving knife (skife knife, paring knife)
52 toecap remover
53 eyelet, hook, and press-stud setter
54 stand (with iron lasts)
55 width-setting tree
56 nail grip
57 boot

58 toecap
59 counter
60 vamp
61 quarter
62 hook
63 eyelet
64 lace (shoelace, bootlace)
65 tongue
66 sole
67 heel
68 shank (waist)

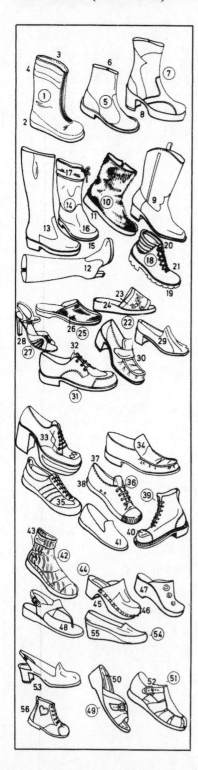

1 winter boot
2 PVC sole (plastic sole)
3 high-pile lining
4 nylon
5 men's boot
6 inside zip (*Am.* zipper)
7 men's high leg boot
8 platform sole (platform)
9 Western boot (cowboy boot)
10 pony-skin boot
11 cemented sole
12 ladies' boot
13 men's high leg boot
14 seamless PVC waterproof wellington boot
15 natural-colour (*Am.* natural-color) sole
16 toecap
17 tricot lining (knitwear lining)
18 hiking boot
19 grip sole
20 padded collar
21 tie fastening (lace fastening)
22 open-toe mule
23 terry upper
24 polo outsole
25 mule
26 corduroy upper
27 evening sandal (sandal court shoe)
28 high heel (stiletto heel)
29 court shoe (*Am.* pump)
30 moccasin
31 shoe, a tie shoe (laced shoe, Oxford shoe, *Am.* Oxford)
32 tongue
33 high-heeled shoe (shoe with raised heel)
34 casual
35 trainer (training shoe)
36 tennis shoe
37 counter (stiffening)
38 natural-colour (*Am.* natural-color) rubber sole
39 heavy-duty boot (*Am.* stogy, stogie)
40 toecap
41 slipper
42 woollen (*Am.* woolen) slip sock
43 knit stitch (knit)
44 clog
45 wooden sole
46 soft-leather upper
47 sabot
48 toe post sandal
49 ladies' sandal
50 surgical footbed (sock)
51 sandal
52 shoe buckle (buckle)
53 sling-back court shoe (*Am.* sling pump)
54 fabric court shoe
55 wedge heel
56 baby's first walking boot

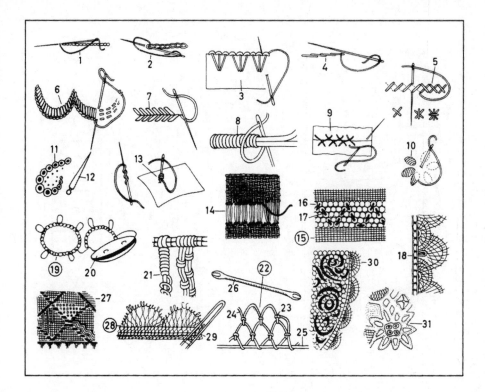

1 backstitch seam
2 chain stitch
3 ornamental stitch
4 stem stitch
5 cross stitch
6 buttonhole stitch (button stitch)
7 fishbone stitch
8 overcast stitch
9 herringbone stitch (Russian stitch, Russian cross stitch)
10 satin stitch (flat stitch)
11 eyelet embroidery (broderie anglaise)
12 stiletto
13 French knot (French dot, knotted stitch, twisted knot stitch)
14 hem stitch work
15 tulle work (tulle lace)
16 tulle background (net background)
17 darning stitch
18 pillow lace (bobbin lace, bone lace); *kinds:* Valenciennes, Brussels lace

19 tatting
20 tatting shuttle (shuttle)
21 knotted work (macramé)
22 filet (netting)
23 netting loop
24 netting thread
25 mesh pin (mesh gauge)
26 netting needle
27 open work
28 gimping (hairpin work)
29 gimping needle (hairpin)
30 needlepoint lace (point lace, needlepoint); *kinds:* reticella lace, Venetian lace, Alencon lace; *sim.:* with metal thread: filigree work
31 braid embroidery (braid work)

1-27 dressmaker's workroom
1 dressmaker
2 tape measure (measuring tape), a metre (*Am.* meter) tape measure
3 cutting shears
4 cutting table
5 model dress
6 dressmaker's model (dressmaker's dummy, dress form)
7 model coat
8 sewing machine
9 drive motor
10 drive belt
11 treadle
12 sewing machine cotton (sewing machine thread) [on bobbin]
13 cutting template
14 seam binding
15 button box
16 remnant
17 movable clothes rack
18 hand-iron press
19 presser (ironer)
20 steam iron
21 water feed pipe
22 water container
23 adjustable-tilt ironing surface
24 lift device for the iron
25 steam extractor
26 foot switch controlling steam extraction
27 pressed non-woven woollen (*Am.* woolen) fabric

1-32 tailor's workroom

1 triple mirror	22 tailor
2 lengths of material	23 shaping pad
3 suiting	24 tailor's chalk (French chalk)
4 fashion journal (fashion magazine)	25 workpiece
5 ashtray	26 steam press (steam pressing unit)
6 fashion catalogue	27 swivel arm
7 workbench	28 pressing cushion (pressing pad)
8 wall shelves (wall shelf unit)	29 iron
9 cotton reel	30 hand-ironing pad
10 small reels of sewing silk	31 clothes brush
11 hand shears	32 pressing cloth
12 combined electric and treadle sewing machine	
13 treadle	
14 dress guard	
15 band wheel	
16 bobbin thread	
17 sewing machine table	
18 sewing machine drawer	
19 seam binding	
20 pincushion	
21 marking out	

1-39 ladies' hairdressing salon and beauty salon (*Am.* beauty parlor, beauty shop)

1-16 hairdresser's tools
1 bowl containing bleach
2 detangling brush
3 bleach tube
4 curler [used in dyeing]
5 curling tongs (curling iron)
6 comb (back comb, side comb)
7 haircutting scissors
8 thinning scissors (*Am.* thinning shears)
9 thinning razor
10 hairbrush
11 hair clip
12 roller
13 curl brush
14 curl clip
15 dressing comb
16 stiff-bristle brush
17 adjustable hairdresser's chair
18 footrest

19 dressing table
20 salon mirror (mirror)
21 electric clippers
22 warm-air comb
23 hand mirror (hand glass)
24 hairspray (hair-fixing spray)
25 drier, a swivel-mounted drier
26 swivel arm of the drier
27 round base
28 shampoo unit
29 shampoo basin
30 hand spray (shampoo spray)
31 service tray
32 shampoo bottle
33 hair drier (hand hair drier, hand-held hair drier)
34 cape (gown)
35 hairdresser
36 perfume bottle
37 bottle of toilet water
38 wig
39 wig block

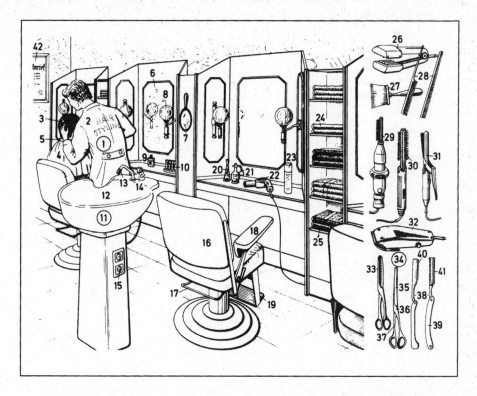

1-42 men's salon (men's hairdressing salon, barber's shop, *Am.* barbershop)

1 hairdresser (barber)
2 overalls (hairdresser's overalls)
3 hairstyle (haircut)
4 cape (gown)
5 paper towel
6 salon mirror (mirror)
7 hand mirror (hand glass)
8 light
9 toilet water
10 hair tonic
11 shampoo unit
12 shampoo basin
13 hand spray (shampoo spray)
14 mixer tap (*Am.* mixing faucet)
15 sockets, e.g. for hair drier
16 adjustable hairdresser's chair (barber's chair)
17 height-adjuster bar (height adjuster)
18 armrest
19 footrest
20 shampoo
21 perfume spray
22 hair drier (hand hair drier, hand-held hair drier)
23 setting lotion in a spray can
24 hand towels for drying hair
25 towels for face compresses
26 crimping iron
27 neck brush
28 dressing comb
29 warm-air comb
30 warm-air brush
31 curling tongs (hair curler, curling iron)
32 electric clippers
33 thinning scissors (*Am.* thinning shears)
34 haircutting scissors; *sim.:* styling scissors
35 scissor-blade
36 pivot
37 handle
38 open razor (straight razor)
39 razor handle
40 edge (cutting edge, razor's edge, razor's cutting edge)
41 thinning razor
42 diploma

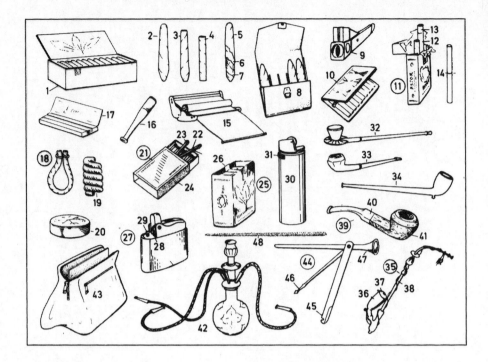

1 cigar box
2 cigar; *kinds:* Havana cigar (Havana), Brazilian cigar, Sumatra cigar
3 cigarillo
4 cheroot
5 wrapper
6 binder
7 filler
8 cigar case
9 cigar cutter
10 cigarette case
11 cigarette packet (*Am.* pack)
12 cigarette, a filter-tipped cigarette
13 cigarette tip; *kinds:* cork tip, gold tip
14 Russian cigarette
15 cigarette roller
16 cigarette holder
17 packet of cigarette papers
18 pigtail (twist of tobacco)
19 chewing tobacco; *a piece:* plug (quid, chew)
20 snuff box, containing snuff
21 matchbox
22 match
23 head (match head)
24 striking surface
25 packet of tobacco; *kinds:* fine cut, shag, navy plug

26 revenue stamp
27 petrol cigarette lighter (petrol lighter)
28 flint
29 wick
30 gas cigarette lighter (gas lighter), a disposable lighter
31 flame regulator
32 chibonk (chibonque)
33 short pipe
34 clay pipe (Dutch pipe)
35 long pipe
36 pipe bowl (bowl)
37 bowl lid
38 pipe stem (stem)
39 briar pipe
40 mouthpiece
41 sand-blast finished or polished briar grain
42 hookah (narghile, narghileh), a water pipe
43 tobacco pouch
44 smoker's companion
45 pipe scraper
46 pipe cleaner
47 tobacco presser
48 pipe cleaner

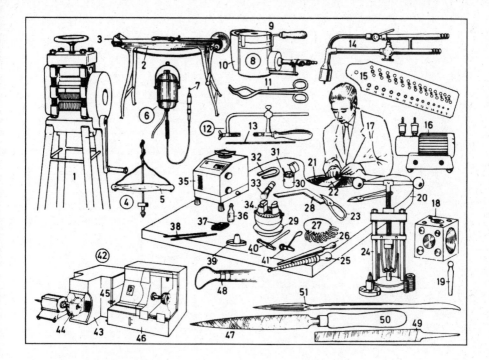

1 wire and sheet roller
2 drawbench (drawing bench)
3 wire (gold or silver wire)
4 archimedes drill (drill)
5 crossbar
6 suspended (pendant) electric drilling machine
7 spherical cutter (cherry)
8 melting pot
9 fireclay top
10 graphite crucible
11 crucible tongs
12 piercing saw (jig saw)
13 piercing saw blade
14 soldering gun
15 thread tapper
16 blast burner (blast lamp) for soldering
17 goldsmith
18 swage block
19 punch
20 workbench (bench)
21 bench apron
22 needle file
23 metal shears
24 wedding ring sizing machine
25 ring gauge (*Am.* gage)
26 ring-rounding tool

27 ring gauge (*Am.* gage)
28 steel set-square
29 (circular) leather pad
30 box of punches
31 punch
32 magnet
33 bench brush
34 engraving ball (joint vice, clamp)
35 gold and silver balance (assay balance), a precision balance
36 soldering flux (flux)
37 charcoal block
38 stick of solder
39 soldering borax
40 shaping hammer
41 chasing (enchasing) hammer
42 polishing and burnishing machine
43 dust exhauster (vacuum cleaner)
44 polishing wheel
45 dust collector (dust catcher)
46 buffing machine
47 round file
48 bloodstone (haematite, hematite)
49 flat file
50 file handle
51 polishing iron (burnisher)

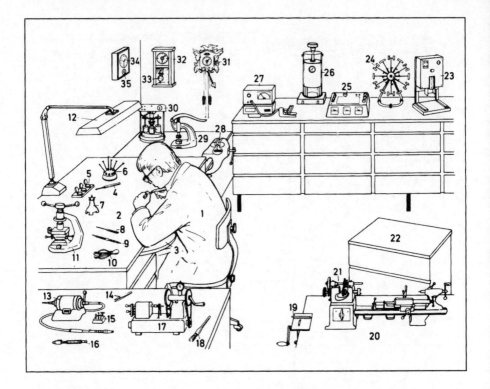

1 watchmaker; *also:* clockmaker
2 workbench
3 armrest
4 oiler
5 oil stand
6 set of screwdrivers
7 clockmaker's anvil
8 broach, a reamer
9 spring pin tool
10 hand-removing tool
11 watchglass-fitting tool
12 workbench lamp, a multi-purpose lamp
13 multi-purpose motor
14 tweezers
15 polishing machine attachments
16 pin vice (pin holder)
17 burnisher, for burnishing, polishing, and shortening of spindles
18 dust brush
19 cutter for metal watch straps
20 precision bench lathe (watchmaker's lathe)

21 drive-belt gear
22 workshop trolley for spare parts
23 ultrasonic cleaner
24 rotating watch-testing machine for automatic watches
25 watch-timing machine for electronic components
26 testing device for waterproof watches
27 electronic timing machine
28 vice (*Am.* vise)
29 watchglass-fitting tool for armoured (*Am.* armored) glasses
30 [automatic] cleaning machine for conventional cleaning
31 cuckoo clock (Black Forest clock)
32 wall clock (regulator)
33 compensation pendulum
34 kitchen clock
35 timer

1 electronic wristwatch
2 digital display (a light-emitting diode (LED) display; *also:* a liquid crystal display, LCD)
3 hour and minute button (on 6, also for setting the analogue (*Am.* analog) display)
4 date and second button
5 strap (watch strap)
6 multifunction electronic watch
7 analogue (*Am.* analog) display
8 alarm button
9 stopwatch button
10 rotating bezel (time-lapse indicator ring)
11 calendar clock (alarm clock)
12 digital display with flip-over numerals
13 alarm indicator
14 stop button
15 forward and backward wind knob
16 grandfather clock
17 face
18 clock case
19 pendulum
20 striking weight
21 time weight
22 sundial
23 hourglass (egg timer)
24-35 components of an automatic watch
(automatic wristwatch, self-winding watch)
24 weight (rotor)
25 stone (jewel, jewelled bearing) a synthetic ruby
26 click
27 click wheel
28 clockwork (clockwork mechanism)
29 bottom train plate
30 spring barrel
31 balance wheel
32 escape wheel
33 crown wheel
34 winding crown
35 drive mechanism
36 principle of the electronic quartz watch
37 quartz
38 power source (a button cell)
39 hour hand
40 minute hand
41 wheels
42 stepping motor (stepper motor)
43 frequency divider (integrated circuit)
44 decoder

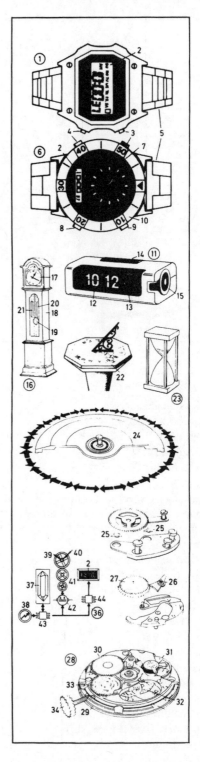

1-19 sales premises
1-4 spectacle fitting
1 optician
2 customer
3 trial frame
4 mirror
5 stand with spectacle frames (display of frames, range of spectacles)
6 sunglasses (sun spectacles)
7 metal frame
8 tortoiseshell frame (shell frame)
9 spectacles (glasses)
10-14 spectacle frame
10 fitting (mount) of the frame
11 bridge
12 pad bridge
13 side
14 side joint
15 spectacle lens, a bifocal lens
16 hand mirror (hand glass)
17 binoculars
18 monocular telescope (tube)
19 microscope

20-47 optician's workshop
20 workbench
21 universal centring (centering) apparatus
22 centring (centering) suction holder
23 sucker
24 edging machine
25 formers for the lens edging machine
26 inserted former
27 rotating printer
28 abrasive wheel combination
29 control unit
30 machine part
31 cooling water pipe
32 cleaning fluid
33 focimeter (vertex refractionometer)
34 metal-blocking device
35 abrasive wheel combination and forms of edging
36 roughing wheel for preliminary surfacing

37 fining lap for positive and negative lens surfaces
38 fining lap for special and flat lenses
39 plano-concave lens with a flat surface
40 plano-concave lens with a special surface
41 concave and convex lens with a special surface
42 convex and concave lens with a special surface
43 ophthalmic test stand
44 phoropter with ophthalmometer and optometer (refractometer)
45 trial lens case
46 collimator
47 acuity projector

1 laboratory and research microscope, *Leitz system*
2 stand
3 base
4 coarse adjustment
5 fine adjustment
6 illumination beam path (illumination path)
7 illumination optics
8 condenser
9 microscope (microscopic, object) stage
10 mechanical stage
11 objective turret (revolving nosepiece)
12 binocular head
13 beam-splitting prisms
14 transmitted-light microscope with camera and polarizer, *Zeiss system*
15 stage base
16 aperture-stop slide
17 universal stage
18 lens panel
19 polarizing filter
20 camera
21 focusing screen
22 discussion tube arrangement
23 wide-field metallurgical microscope, a reflected-light microscope (microscope for reflected light)
24 matt screen (ground glass screen, projection screen)
25 large-format camera
26 miniature camera
27 base plate
28 lamphouse
29 mechanical stage
30 objective turret (revolving nosepiece)
31 surgical microscope
32 pillar stand
33 field illumination
34 photomicroscope
35 miniature film cassette
36 photomicrographic camera attachment for large-format or television camera
37 surface-finish microscope
38 light section tube
39 rack and pinion
40 zoom stereomicroscope
41 zoom lens
42 dust counter
43 measurement chamber
44 data output
45 analogue (*Am.* analog) output
46 measurement range selector
47 digital display (digital readout)
48 dipping refractometer for examining food
49 microscopic photometer
50 photometric light source
51 measuring device (photomultiplier, multiplier phototube)
52 light source for survey illumination
53 remote electronics
54 universal wide-field microscope
55 adapter for camera or projector attachment
56 eyepiece focusing knob
57 filter pick-up
58 handrest
59 lamphouse for incident (vertical) illumination
60 lamphouse connector for transillumination
61 wide-field stereomicroscope
62 interchangeable lenses (objectives)
63 incident (vertical) illumination (incident top lighting)
64 fully automatic microscope camera, a camera with photomicro mount adapter
65 film cassette
66 universal condenser for research microscope 1
67 universal-type measuring machine for photogrammetry (phototheodolite)
68 photogrammetric camera
69 motor-driven level, a compensator level
70 electro-optical distance-measuring instrument
71 stereometric camera
72 horizontal base
73 one-second theodolite

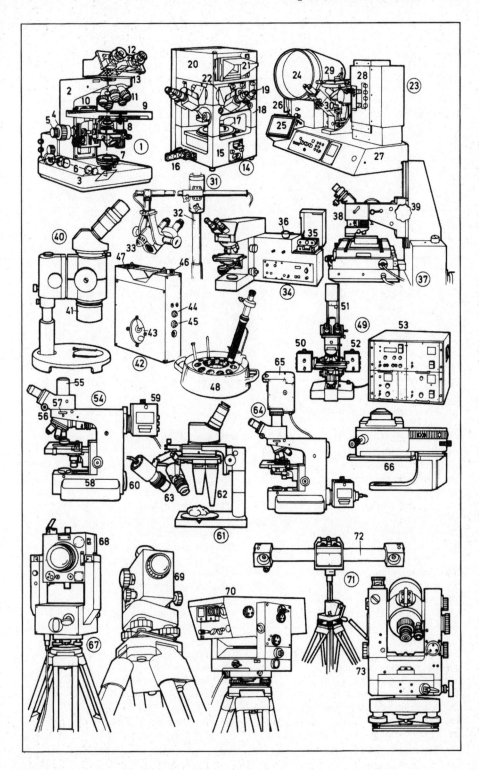

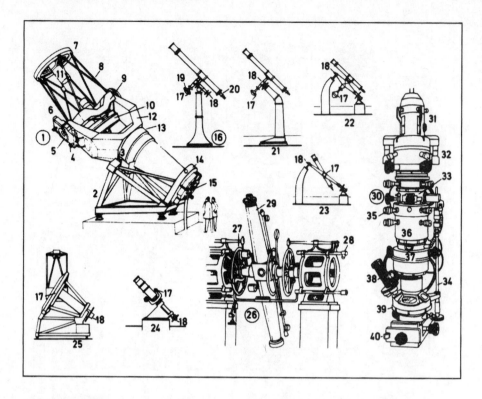

1 **2.2 m reflecting telescope** (reflector)
2 pedestal (base)
3 axial-radial bearing
4 declination gear
5 declination axis
6 declination bearing
7 front ring
8 tube (body tube)
9 tube centre (*Am.* center) section
10 primary mirror (main mirror)
11 secondary mirror (deviation mirror, corrector plate)
12 fork mounting (fork)
13 cover
14 guide bearing
15 main drive unit of the polar axis
16-25 telescope mountings (telescope mounts)
16 refractor (refracting telescope) on a German-type mounting
17 declination axis
18 polar axis
19 counterweight (counterpoise)
20 eyepiece
21 knee mounting with a bent column

22 English-type axis mounting (axis mount)
23 English-type yoke mounting (yoke mount)
24 fork mounting (fork mount)
25 horseshoe mounting (horseshoe mount)
26 meridian circle
27 divided circle (graduated circle)
28 reading microscope
29 meridian telescope
30 electron microscope
31-39 microscope tube (microscope body, body tube)
31 electron gun
32 condensers
33 specimen insertion air lock
34 control for the specimen stage adjustment
35 control for the objective apertures
36 objective lens
37 intermediate image screen
38 telescope magnifier
39 final image tube
40 photographic chamber for film and plate magazines

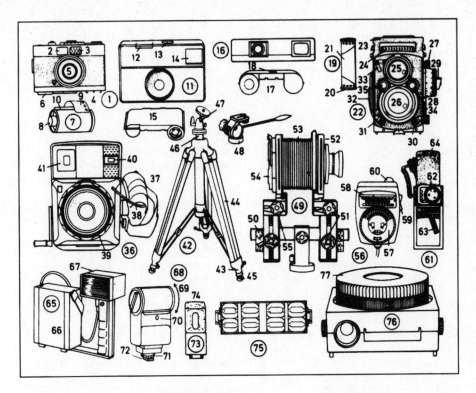

1	miniature camera (35 mm camera)	25 viewing lens
2	viewfinder eyepiece	26 object lens
3	meter cell	27 spool knob
4	accessory shoe	28 distance setting (focus setting)
5	flush lens	29 exposure meter using needle-matching system
6	rewind handle (rewind, rewind crank)	30 flash contact
7	miniature film cassette (135 film cassette, 35 mm cassette)	31 shutter release

1   miniature camera (35 mm camera)
2   viewfinder eyepiece
3   meter cell
4   accessory shoe
5   flush lens
6   rewind handle (rewind, rewind crank)
7   miniature film cassette (135 film cassette, 35 mm cassette)
8   film spool
9   film with leader and perforations
10 cassette slit (cassette exit slot)
11 cartridge-loading camera
12 shutter release (shutter release button)
13 flash cube contact
14 rectangular viewfinder
15 126 cartridge (instamatic cartridge)
16 pocket camera (subminiature camera)
17 110 cartridge (subminiature cartridge)
18 film window
19 120 rollfilm
20 rollfilm spool
21 backing paper
22 twin-lens reflex camera
23 folding viewfinder hood (focusing hood)
24 meter cell

25 viewing lens
26 object lens
27 spool knob
28 distance setting (focus setting)
29 exposure meter using needle-matching system
30 flash contact
31 shutter release
32 film transport (film advance, film wind)
33 flash switch
34 aperture-setting control
35 shutter speed control
36 large-format hand camera (press camera)
37 grip (handgrip)
38 cable release
39 distance-setting ring (focusing ring)
40 rangefinder window
41 multiple-frame viewfinder (universal viewfinder)
42 tripod
43 tripod leg
44 tubular leg
45 rubber foot
46 central column
47 ball and socket head
48 cine camera pan and tilt head
49 large-format folding camera
50 optical bench
51 standard adjustment
52 lens standard

53 bellows
54 camera back
55 back standard adjustment
56 hand-held exposure meter (exposure meter)
57 calculator dial
58 scales (indicator scales) with indicator needle (pointer)
59 range switch (high/low range selector)
60 diffuser for incident light measurement
61 probe exposure meter for large-format cameras
62 meter
63 probe
64 dark slide
65 battery-portable electronic flash (battery-portable electronic flash unit)
66 power pack unit (battery)
67 flash head
68 single-unit electronic flash (flashgun)
69 swivel-mounted reflector
70 photodiode
71 foot
72 hot-shoe contact
73 flash cube unit
74 flash cube
75 flash bar (AGFA)
76 slide projector
77 rotary magazine

1-24 system camera (fully automatic miniature single-lens reflex camera)
1 main switch
2 function adjustment button (to set exposure adjustment value, drive mode, and focus area)
3 exposure mode button
4 accessory shoe
5 program reset button
6 data panel (data monitor, data display)
7 card on/off key
8 function selector key
9 chip program card
10 card door
11 card window
12 battery chamber
13 remote control terminal
14 shutter release (shutter release button)
15 autofocus (AF) illuminator and self-timer light
16 manual shutter control [up/down control]
17 reflex mirror
18 autofocus sensor, a CCD image converter (image sensor)
19 bayonet mounting ring
20 aperture setting button
21 lens release
22 focus-mode switch (to switch to manual focusing)
23 autofocus zoom lens, a × 3 zoom lens (35–105 mm)
24 aperture and autofocus contacts
25-35 viewfinder screen (focusing screen, matt screen), a micro-honeycombed focusing screen
25 flash-on signal
26 flash-ready signal
27 focus signals
28 wide focus area
29 shutter speed display
30 manual-exposure compensation-value indicator
31 aperture or exposure adjustment indicator
32 spot metering indicator
33 spot metering area
34 centre focus area
35 focus area indicator
36-42 LCD data panel (data monitor)
36 program exposure-mode indicator

37 frame counter
38 function indicators
39 aperture or exposure adjustment indicator
40 shutter speed or film speed (film sensitivity) indicator
41 film transport indicator
42 function pointer
43 interchangeable lenses (autofocus lenses, AF lenses)
44 fisheye lens (fisheye)
45 wide-angle lens (short focal-length lens)
46 standard lens
47 medium focal-length lens
48 telephoto lens (long focal-length lens), a zoom lens (variable focus lens, varifocal lens)
49 long-focus lens
50 mirror lens
51 tele converter
52 data back
53 ten-metre (*Am.* ten-meter) film back (magazine back)
54-74 accessories for close-up and macro shots
54 extension tube
55 adapter ring
56 reversing ring
57 lens in retrofocus position
58 bellows unit (extension bellows, close-up bellows attachment)
59 focusing stage
60 slide-copying attachment
61 slide-copying adapter
62 cable release
63 copying stand (copy stand)
64 arm of the copying stand (copy stand)
65 rifle grip
66 table(-top) tripod (mini tripod)
67 ever-ready case
68 lens case
69 soft-leather lens pouch
70 camera bag, of metallic construction: aluminium (*Am.* aluminum) case
71 film container
72 filter case
73 second body
74 ring flash for macro shots

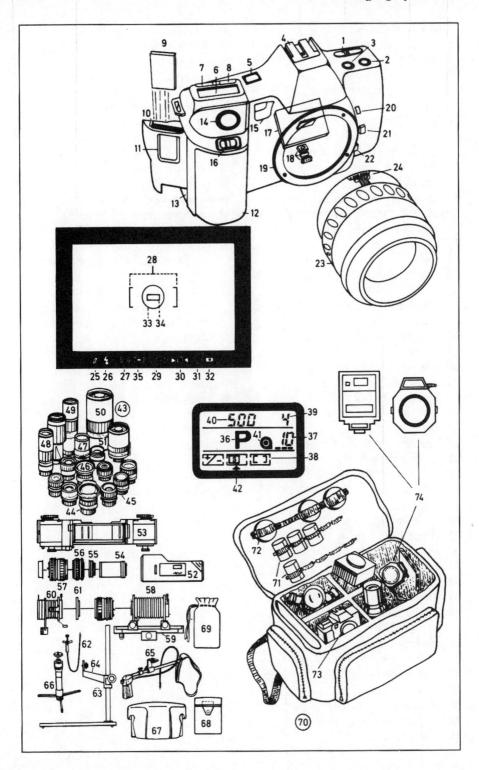

1-60 darkroom equipment
1 developing tank
2 spiral (developing spiral, tank reel)
3 multi-unit developing tank
4 multi-unit tank spiral
5 daylight-loading tank
6 loading chamber
7 film transport handle
8 developing tank thermometer
9 collapsible bottle for developing solution
10 chemical bottles for first developer, stop bath, colour developer, bleach-hardener, stabilizer
11 measuring cylinders
12 funnel
13 tray thermometer (dish thermometer)
14 film clip
15 wash tank (washer)
16 water supply pipe
17 water outlet pipe
18 laboratory timer (timer)
19 automatic film agitator
20 developing tank
21 darkroom lamp (safelight)
22 filter screen
23 film drier (drying cabinet)
24 exposure timer
25 developing dish (developing tray)
26 enlarger
27 baseboard
28 angled column
29 lamphouse (lamp housing)
30 negative carrier
31 bellows
32 lens
33 friction drive for fine adjustment
34 height adjustment (scale adjustment)
35 masking frame (easel)
36 colour (*Am.* color) analyser
37 colour (*Am.* color) analyser lamp
38 probe lead
39 exposure time balancing knob
40 colour (*Am.* color) enlarger
41 enlarger head

42 column
43-45 colour-mixing (*Am.* color-mixing) knob
43 magenta filter adjustment (minus green filter adjustment)
44 yellow filter adjustment (minus blue filter adjustment)
45 cyan filter adjustment (minus red filter adjustment)
46 red swing filter
47 print tongs
48 processing drum
49 squeegee
50 range (assortment) of papers
51 colour (*Am.* color) printing paper, a packet of photographic printing paper
52 colour (*Am.* color) chemicals (colour processing chemicals)
53 enlarging meter (enlarging photometer)
54 adjusting knob with paper speed scale
55 probe
56 semi-automatic thermostatically controlled developing dish
57 rapid print drier (heated print drier)
58 glazing sheet
59 pressure cloth
60 automatic processor (machine processor)

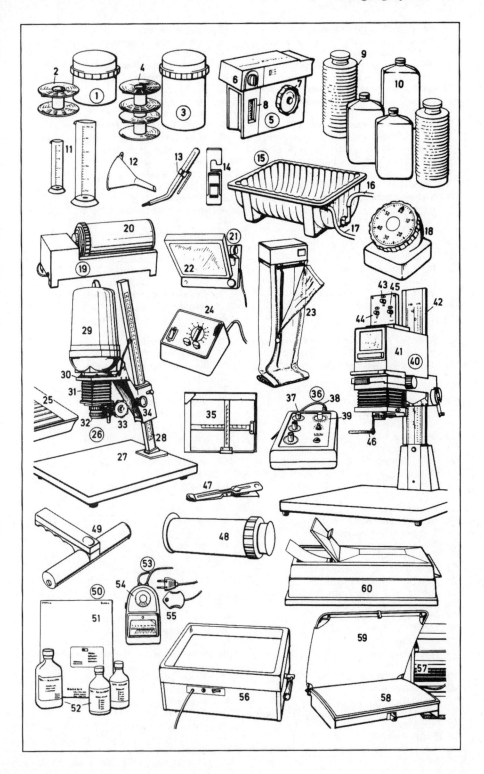

1 **cine camera,** a Super-8 sound camera
2 interchangeable zoom lens (variable focus lens, varifocal lens)
3 distance setting (focus setting) and manual focal length setting
4 aperture ring (aperture-setting ring, aperture control ring) for manual aperture setting
5 handgrip with battery chamber
6 shutter release with cable release socket
7 pilot tone or pulse generator socket for the sound recording equipment (with the dual film-tape system)
8 sound connecting cord for microphone or external sound source (in single-system recording)
9 remote control socket (remote control jack)
10 headphone socket (*sim.:* earphone socket)
11 autofocus override switch
12 filming speed selector
13 sound recording selector switch for automatic or manual operation
14 eyepiece with eyecup
15 diopter control ring (dioptric adjustment ring)
16 recording level control (audio level control, recording sensitivity selector)
17 manual/automatic exposure control switch
18 film speed setting
19 power zooming arrangement
20 automatic aperture control
21 **sound track system**
22 sound camera
23 telescopic microphone boom
24 microphone
25 microphone connecting lead (microphone connecting cord)
26 **mixing console** (mixing desk, mixer)
27 inputs from various sound sources
28 output to camera
29 **Super-8 sound film cartridge**
30 film gate of the cartridge
31 feed spool
32 take-up spool
33 recording head (sound head)
34 transport roller (capstan)
35 rubber pinch roller (capstan idler)
36 guide step (guide notch)
37 exposure meter control step
38 conversion filter step (colour, *Am.* color, conversion filter step)
39 **single-8 cassette**
40 film gate opening
41 unexposed film
42 exposed film
43 **16 mm camera**
44 reflex finder (through-the-lens reflex finder)
45 magazine
46-49 **lens head**
46 lens turret (turret head)
47 telephoto lens
48 wide-angle lens
49 normal lens (standard lens)
50 winding handle
51 **compact Super-8 camera**
52 footage counter
53 macro zoom lens
54 zooming lever
55 macro lens attachment (close-up lens)
56 macro frame (mount for small originals)
57 **underwater housing** (underwater case)
58 direct-vision frame finder
59 measuring rod
60 stabilizing wing
61 grip (handgrip)
62 locking bolt
63 control lever (operating lever)
64 porthole
65 **synchronization start** (sync start)
66 professional press-type camera
67 cameraman
68 camera assistant (sound assistant)
69 handclap marking sync start
70 **dual film-tape recording using a tape recorder**
71 pulse-generating camera
72 pulse cable
73 cassette recorder
74 microphone
75 **dual film-tape reproduction**
76 tape cassette
77 synchronization unit
78 cine projector
79 film feed spool
80 take-up reel (take-up spool), an automatic take-up reel (take-up spool)
81 **sound projector**
82 sound film with magnetic stripe (sound track, track)
83 automatic-threading button
84 trick button
85 volume control
86 reset button
87 fast and slow motion switch
88 forward, reverse, and still projection switch
89 splicer for wet splices
90 hinged clamping plate
91 **film viewer** (animated viewer editor)
92 foldaway reel arm
93 rewind handle (rewinder)
94 viewing screen
95 film perforator (film marker)
96 **six-turntable film and sound cutting table** (editing table, cutting bench, animated sound editor)
97 monitor
98 control buttons (control well)
99 film turntable
100 first sound turntable, e.g. for live sound
101 second sound turntable for post-sync sound
102 film and tape synchronizing head

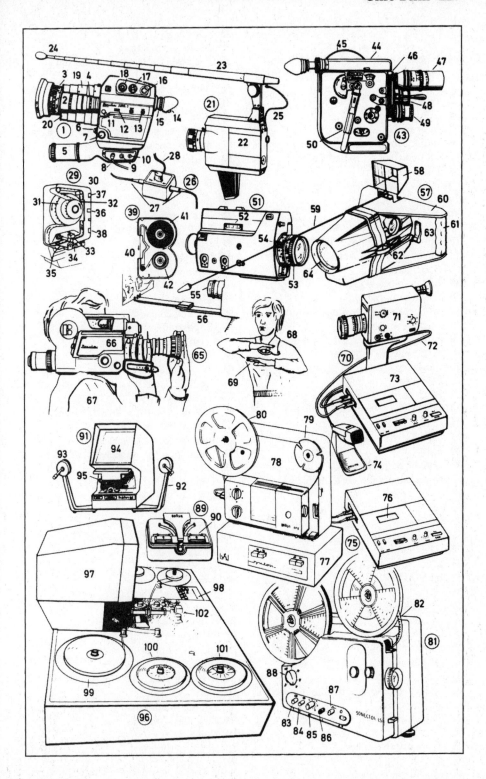

1-49 carcase (carcass, fabric) [house construction, carcassing]
1 basement of tamped (rammed) concrete
2 concrete base course
3 cellar window (basement window)
4 outside cellar steps
5 utility room window
6 utility room door
7 ground floor (*Am.* first floor)
8 brick wall
9 lintel (window head)
10 reveal
11 jamb
12 window ledge (window sill)
13 reinforced concrete lintel
14 upper floor (first floor, *Am.* second floor)
15 hollow-block wall
16 concrete floor
17 work platform (working platform)
18 bricklayer (*Am.* brickmason)
19 bricklayer's labourer (*Am.* laborer); *also:* builder's labourer
20 mortar trough
21 chimney
22 cover (boards) for the staircase
23 scaffold pole (scaffold standard)
24 platform railing
25 angle brace (angle tie) in the scaffold
26 ledger
27 putlog (putlock)
28 plank platform (board platform)
29 guard board
30 scaffolding joint with chain or lashing or whip or bond
31 builder's hoist
32 mixer operator
33 concrete mixer, a gravity mixer
34 mixing drum
35 feeder skip
36 concrete aggregate [sand and gravel]
37 wheelbarrow
38 hose (hosepipe)
39 mortar pan (mortar trough, mortar tub)
40 stack of bricks
41 stacked shutter boards (lining boards)
42 ladder
43 bag of cement
44 site fence, a timber fence
45 signboard (billboard)
46 removable gate
47 contractors' name plates

48 site hut (site office)
49 building site latrine
50-57 bricklayer's (*Am.* brickmason's) **tools**
50 plumb bob (plummet)
51 thick lead pencil
52 trowel
53 bricklayer's (*Am.* brickmason's) hammer (brick hammer)
54 mallet
55 spirit level
56 laying-on trowel
57 float
58-68 masonry bonds
58 brick (standard brick)
59 stretching bond
60 heading bond
61 racking (raking) back
62 English bond
63 stretching course
64 heading course
65 English cross bond (Saint Andrew's cross bond)
66 chimney bond
67 first course
68 second course
69-82 excavation
69 profile (*Am.* batterboard) [fixed on edge at the corner]
70 intersection of strings
71 plumb bob (plummet)
72 excavation side
73 upper edge board
74 lower edge board
75 foundation trench
76 navvy (*Am.* excavator)
77 conveyor belt (conveyor)
78 excavated earth
79 plank roadway
80 tree guard
81 mechanical shovel (excavator)
82 shovel bucket (bucket)
83-91 plastering
83 plasterer
84 mortar trough
85 screen
86-89 ladder scaffold
86 standard ladder
87 boards (planks, platform)
88 diagonal strut (diagonal brace)
89 railing
90 guard netting
91 rope-pulley hoist

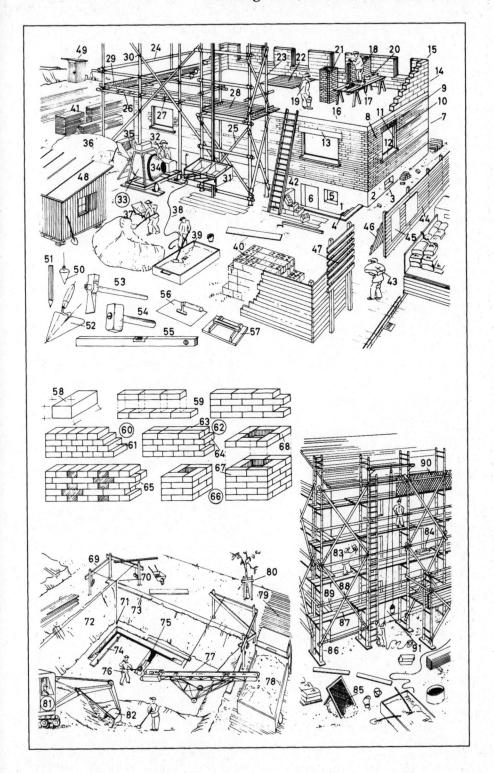

**1-89 reinforced concrete (ferrocon-
crete) construction**
1 reinforced concrete (ferroconcrete)
skeleton construction
2 reinforced concrete (ferroconcrete)
frame
3 inferior purlin
4 concrete purlin
5 ceiling joist
6 arch (flank)
7 rubble concrete wall
8 reinforced concrete (ferroconcrete)
floor
9 concreter (concretor), flattening out
10 projecting reinforcement (*Am.* connection rebars)
11 column box
12 joist shuttering
13 shuttering strut
14 diagonal bracing
15 wedge
16 board
17 sheet pile wall (sheet pile, sheet
piling)
18 shutter boards (lining boards)
19 circular saw (buzz saw)
20 bending table
21 bar bender (steel bender)
22 hand steel shears
23 reinforcing steel (reinforcement
rods)
24 pumice concrete hollow block
25 partition wall, a timber wall
26 concrete aggregate [gravel and sand
of various grades]
27 crane track
28 tipping wagon (tipping truck)
29 concrete mixer
30 cement silo
31 tower crane (tower slewing crane)
32 bogie (*Am.* truck)
33 counterweight
34 tower
35 crane driver's cabin (crane driver's
cage)
36 jib (boom)
37 bearer cable
38 concrete bucket
39 sleepers (*Am.* ties)
40 chock
41 ramp
42 wheelbarrow
43 safety rail

44 site hut
45 canteen
46 tubular steel scaffold (scaffolding)
47 standard
48 ledger tube
49 tie tube
50 shoe
51 diagonal brace
52 planking (platform)
53 coupling (coupler)
**54-76 formwork (shuttering) and rein-
forcement**
54 bottom shuttering (lining)
55 side shutter of a purlin
56 cut-in bottom
57 cross beam
58 cramp iron (cramp, dog)
59 upright member, a standard
60 strap
61 cross piece
62 stop fillet
63 strut (brace, angle brace)
64 frame timber (yoke)
65 strap
66 reinforcement binding
67 cross strut (strut)
68 reinforcement
69 distribution steel
70 stirrup
71 projecting reinforcement (*Am.* connection rebars)
72 concrete (heavy concrete)
73 column box
74 bolted frame timber (bolted yoke)
75 nut (thumb nut)
76 shutter board (shuttering board)
77-89 tools
77 bending iron
78 adjustable service girder
79 adjusting screw
80 round bar reinforcement
81 distance piece (separator, spacer)
82 Torsteel
83 concrete tamper
84 mould (*Am.* mold) for concrete test
cubes
85 concreter's tongs
86 sheeting support
87 hand shears
88 immersion vibrator (concrete vibrator)
89 vibrating cylinder (vibrating head,
vibrating poker)

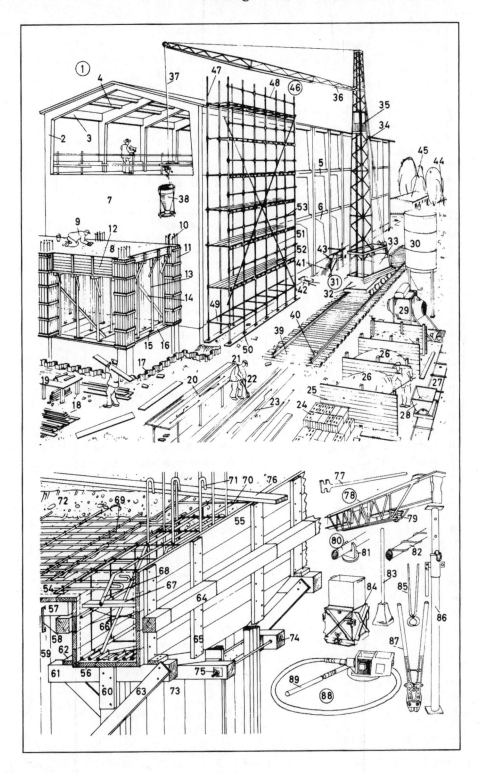

1-59 carpenter's yard
1 stack of boards (planks)
2 long timber (*Am.* lumber)
3 sawing shed
4 carpenter's workshop
5 workshop door
6 handcart
7 roof truss
8 tree [used for topping out ceremony], with wreath
9 timber wall
10 squared timber (building timber, scantlings)
11 drawing floor
12 carpenter
13 safety helmet
14 cross-cut saw, a chain saw
15 chain guide
16 saw chain
17 mortiser (chain cutter)
18 trestle (horse)
19 beam mounted on a trestle
20 set of carpenter's tools
21 electric drill
22 dowel hole
23 mark for the dowel hole
24 beams
25 post (stile, stud, quarter)
26 corner brace
27 brace (strut)
28 base course (plinth)
29 house wall (wall)
30 window opening
31 reveal
32 jamb
33 window ledge (window sill)
34 cornice
35 roundwood (round timber)
36 floorboards
37 hoisting rope
38 ceiling joist (ceiling beam, main beam)
39 wall joist
40 wall plate
41 trimmer (trimmer joist, *Am.* header, header joist)
42 dragon beam (dragon piece)
43 false floor (inserted floor)
44 floor filling of breeze, loam, etc.
45 fillet (cleat)
46 stair well (well)
47 chimney
48 framed partition (framed wall)
49 wall plate
50 girt
51 window jamb, a jamb
52 corner stile (corner strut, corner stud)
53 principal post
54 brace (strut) with skew notch
55 nogging piece
56 sill rail
57 window lintel (window head)
58 head (head rail)
59 filled-in panel (bay, pan)

60-82 carpenter's tools
60 hand saw
61 bucksaw
62 saw blade
63 compass saw (keyhole saw)
64 plane
65 auger (gimlet)
66 screw clamp (cramp, holdfast)
67 mallet
68 two-handed saw
69 try square
70 broad axe (*Am.* broadax)
71 chisel
72 mortise axe (mortice axe, *Am.* mortise ax)
73 axe (*Am.* ax)
74 carpenter's hammer
75 claw head (nail claw)
76 folding rule
77 carpenter's pencil
78 iron square
79 drawknife (drawshave, drawing knife)
80 shaving
81 bevel
82 mitre square (*Am.* miter square, miter angle)

83-96 building timber
83 undressed timber (*Am.* rough lumber)
84 heartwood (duramen)
85 sapwood (sap, alburnum)
86 bark (rind)
87 baulk (balk)
88 halved timber
89 wane (waney edge)
90 quarter baulk (balk)
91 plank (board)
92 end-grained timber
93 heartwood plank (heart plank)
94 unsquared (untrimmed) plank (board)
95 squared (trimmed) board
96 slab (offcut)

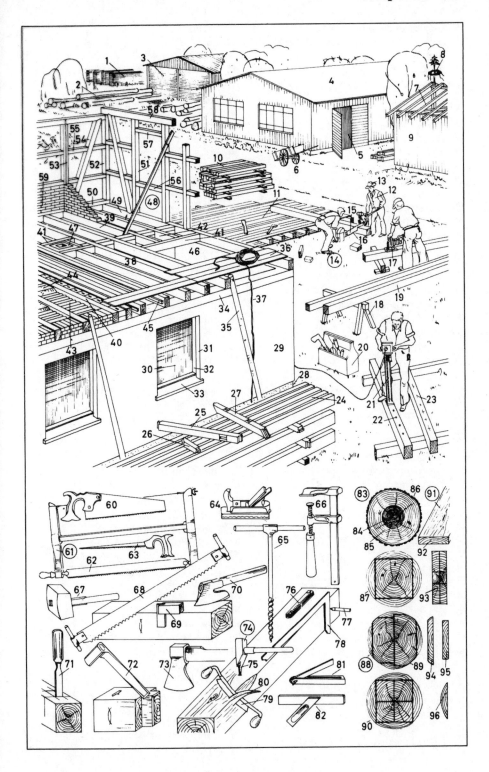

121 Roof, Timber Joints

1-26 styles and parts of roofs
1 gable roof (saddle roof, saddleback roof)
2 ridge
3 verge
4 eaves
5 gable
6 dormer window (dormer)
7 pent roof (shed roof, lean-to roof)
8 skylight
9 fire gable
10 hip (hipped) roof
11 hip end
12 hip (arris)
13 hip (hipped) dormer window
14 ridge turret
15 valley (roof valley)
16 hipped-gable roof (jerkin head roof)
17 partial-hip (partial-hipped) end
18 mansard roof (*Am.* gambrel roof)
19 mansard dormer window
20 sawtooth roof
21 north light
22 broach roof
23 eyebrow
24 conical broach roof
25 imperial dome (imperial roof)
26 weather vane

27-83 roof structures of timber
27 rafter roof
28 rafter
29 roof beam
30 diagonal tie (cross tie, sprocket piece, cocking piece)
31 arris fillet (tilting fillet)
32 outer wall
33 beam head
34 collar beam roof (trussed rafter roof)
35 collar beam (collar)
36 rafter
37 strutted collar beam roof structure
38 collar beams
39 purlin
40 post (stile, stud)
41 brace
42 unstrutted (king pin) roof structure
43 ridge purlin
44 inferior purlin
45 rafter head (rafter end)
46 purlin roof with queen post and pointing sill
47 pointing sill
48 ridge beam (ridge board)

49 simple tie
50 double tie
51 purlin
52 purlin roof structure with queen post
53 tie beam
54 joist (ceiling joist)
55 principal rafter
56 common rafter
57 angle brace (angle tie)
58 brace (strut)
59 ties
60 hip (hipped) roof with purlin roof structure
61 jack rafter
62 hip rafter
63 jack rafter
64 valley rafter
65 queen truss
66 main beam
67 summer (summer beam)
68 queen post (truss post)
69 brace (strut)
70 collar beam (collar)
71 trimmer (*Am.* header)
72 solid-web girder
73 lower chord
74 upper chord
75 boarding
76 purlin
77 supporting outer wall
78 roof truss
79 lower chord
80 upper chord
81 post
82 brace (strut)
83 support

84-98 timber joints
84 mortise (mortice) and tenon joint
85 forked mortise (mortice) and tenon joint
86 halving (halved) joint
87 simple scarf joint
88 oblique scarf joint
89 dovetail halving
90 single skew notch
91 double skew notch
92 wooden nail
93 pin
94 clout nail (clout)
95 wire nail
96 hardwood wedges
97 cramp iron (timber dog, dog)
98 bolt

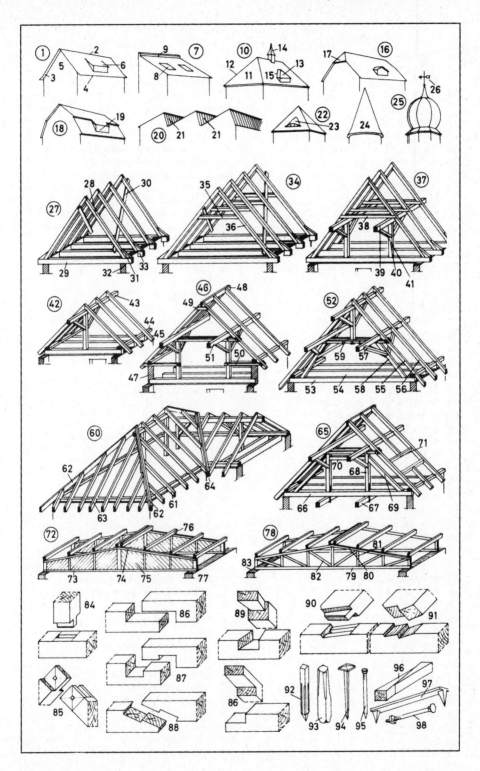

122 Roof and Roofer

1 tiled roof
2 plain-tile double-lap roofing
3 ridge tile
4 ridge course tile
5 under-ridge tile
6 plain (plane) tile
7 ventilating tile
8 ridge tile
9 hip tile
10 hipped end
11 valley (roof valley)
12 skylight
13 chimney
14 chimney flashing, made of sheet zinc
15 ladder hook
16 snow guard bracket
17 battens (slating and tiling battens)
18 batten gauge (*Am.* gage)
19 rafter
20 tile hammer
21 lath axe (*Am.* ax)
22 hod
23 hod hook
24 opening (hatch)
25 gable (gable end)
26 toothed lath
27 soffit
28 gutter
29 rainwater pipe (downpipe)
30 swan's neck (swan-neck)
31 pipe clip
32 gutter bracket
33 tile cutter
34 scaffold
35 safety wall
36 eaves
37 outer wall
38 exterior rendering
39 frost-resistant brickwork
40 inferior purlin
41 rafter head (rafter end)
42 eaves fascia
43 double lath (tilting lath)
44 insulating boards
45-60 tiles and tile roofings
45 split-tiled roof
46 plain (plane) tile
47 ridge course
48 slip
49 eaves course
50 plain-tiled roof
51 nib
52 ridge tile
53 pantiled roof
54 pantile
55 pointing
56 Spanish-tiled roof (*Am.* mission-tiled roof)
57 under tile
58 over tile
59 interlocking tile
60 flat interlocking tile
61-89 slate roof
61 roof boards (roof boarding, roof sheathing)
62 roofing paper (sheathing paper); *also:* roofing felt (*Am.* rag felt)
63 cat ladder (roof ladder)
64 coupling hook
65 ridge hook
66 roof trestle
67 trestle rope
68 knot
69 ladder hook
70 scaffold board
71 slater
72 nail bag
73 slate hammer
74 slate nail, a galvanized wire nail
75 slater's shoe, a bast or hemp shoe
76 eaves course (eaves joint)
77 corner bottom slate
78 roof course
79 ridge course (ridge joint)
80 gable slate
81 tail line
82 valley (roof valley)
83 box gutter (trough gutter, parallel gutter)
84 slater's iron
85 slate
86 back
87 head
88 front edge
89 tail
90-103 asphalt-impregnated paper roofing and corrugated asbestos cement roofing
90 asphalt-impregnated paper roof
91 width [parallel to the gutter]
92 gutter
93 ridge
94 join
95 width [at right angles to the gutter]
96 felt nail (clout nail)
97 corrugated asbestos cement roof
98 corrugated sheet
99 ridge capping piece
100 lap
101 wood screw
102 rust-proof zinc cup
103 lead washer

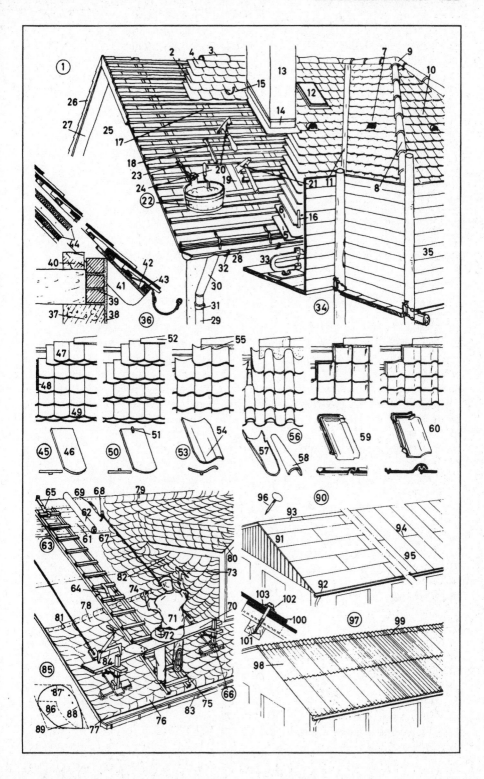

123 Floor, Ceiling, Staircase Construction

1 basement wall, a concrete wall
2 footing (foundation)
3 foundation base
4 damp course (damp-proof course)
5 waterproofing
6 rendering coat
7 brick paving
8 sand bed
9 ground
10 shuttering
11 peg
12 hardcore
13 oversite concrete
14 cement screed
15 brickwork base
16 basement stairs, solid concrete stairs
17 block step
18 curtail step (bottom step)
19 top step
20 nosing
21 skirting (skirting board, *Am.* mopboard, washboard, scrub board, base)
22 balustrade of metal bars
23 ground-floor (*Am.* first-floor) landing
24 front door
25 foot scraper
26 flagstone paving
27 mortar bed
28 concrete ceiling, a reinforced concrete slab
29 ground-floor (*Am.* first-floor) brick wall
30 ramp
31 wedge-shaped step
32 tread
33 riser
34-41 landing
34 landing beam
35 ribbed reinforced concrete floor
36 rib
37 steel-bar reinforcement
38 subfloor (blind floor)
39 level layer
40 finishing layer
41 top layer (screed)
42-44 dog-legged staircase, a staircase without a well

42 curtail step (bottom step)
43 newel post (newel)
44 outer string (*Am.* outer stringer)
45 wall string (*Am.* wall stringer)
46 staircase bolt
47 tread
48 riser
49 wreath piece (wreathed string)
50 balustrade
51 baluster
52-62 intermediate landing
52 wreath
53 handrail (guard rail)
54 head post
55 landing beam
56 lining board
57 fillet
58 lightweight building board
59 ceiling plaster
60 wall plaster
61 false ceiling
62 strip flooring (overlay flooring, parquet strip)
63 skirting board (*Am.* mopboard, washboard, scrub board, base)
64 beading
65 staircase window
66 main landing beam
67 fillet (cleat)
68, 69 false ceiling
68 false floor (inserted floor)
69 floor filling (plugging, pug)
70 laths
71 lathing
72 ceiling plaster
73 subfloor (blind floor)
74 parquet floor with tongued-and-grooved blocks
75 quarter-newelled (*Am.* quarter-neweled) staircase
76 winding staircase (spiral staircase) with open newels (open-newel staircase)
77 winding staircase (spiral staircase) with solid newels (solid-newel staircase)
78 newel (solid newel)
79 handrail

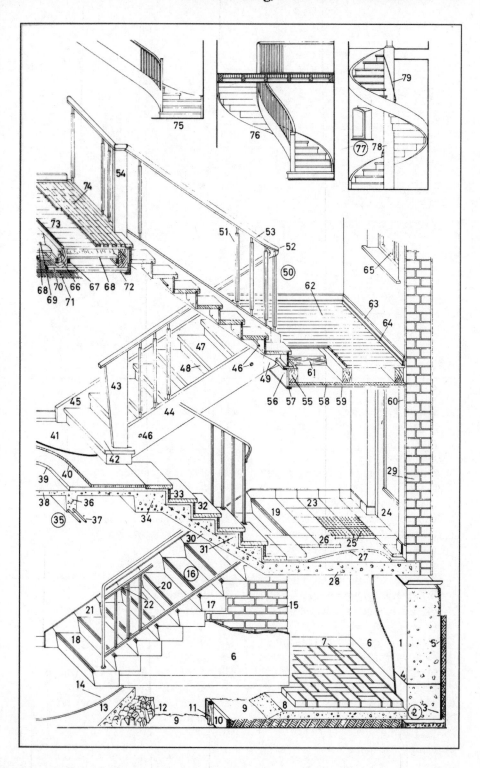

1 glazier's workshop
2 frame wood samples (frame samples)
3 frame wood
4 mitre joint (mitre, *Am.* miter joint, miter)
5 sheet glass; *kinds:* window glass, frosted glass, patterned glass, crystal plate glass, thick glass, milk glass, laminated glass (safety glass, shatterproof glass)
6 cast glass; *kinds:* stained glass, ornamental glass, raw glass, bull's-eye glass, wired glass, line glass (lined glass)
7 mitring (*Am.* mitering) machine
8 glassworker (e.g. building glazier, glazier, decorative glass worker)
9 glass holder
10 piece of broken glass
11 lead hammer
12 lead knife
13 came (lead came)
14 leaded light
15 workbench
16 pane of glass
17 putty
18 glazier's hammer
19 glass pliers
20 glazier's square
21 glazier's rule
22 glazier's beam compass
23 eyelet
24 glazing sprig
25, 26 glass cutters
25 diamond glass cutter
26 steel-wheel (steel) glass cutter
27 putty knife
28 pin wire
29 panel pin
30 mitre (*Am.* miter) block (mitre box) [with saw]
31 mitre (*Am.* miter) shoot (mitre board)

1 metal shears (tinner's snips, *Am.* tinner's shears)
2 elbow snips (angle shears)
3 gib
4 lapping plate
5-7 propane soldering apparatus
5 propane soldering iron, a hatchet iron
6 soldering stone, a sal-ammoniac block
7 soldering fluid (flux)
8 beading iron for forming reinforcement beading
9 angled reamer
10 workbench (bench)
11 beam compass (trammel, *Am.* beam trammel)
12 electric hand die
13 hollow punch
14 chamfering hammer
15 beading swage (beading hammer)
16 abrasive-wheel cutting-off machine
17 plumber
18 mallet
19 mandrel
20 socket (tinner's socket)
21 block
22 anvil
23 stake
24 circular saw (buzz saw)
25 flanging, swaging, and wiring machine
26 sheet shears (guillotine)
27 screw-cutting machine (thread-cutting machine, die stocks)
28 pipe-bending machine (bending machine, pipe bender)
29 welding transformer
30 bending machine (rounding machine) for shaping funnels

126 Plumber, Gas Fitter, Heating Engineer

1 gas fitter and plumber
2 stepladder
3 safety chain
4 stop valve
5 gas meter
6 bracket
7 service riser
8 distributing pipe
9 supply pipe
10 pipe-cutting machine
11 pipe repair stand
12-25 gas and water appliances
12, 13 geyser, an instantaneous water heater
12 gas water heater
13 electric water heater
14 toilet cistern
15 float
16 bell
17 flush pipe
18 water inlet
19 flushing lever (lever)
20 radiator
21 radiator rib
22 two-pipe system
23 flow pipe
24 return pipe
25 gas heater
26-37 plumbing fixtures
26 trap (anti-syphon trap)
27 mixer tap (*Am.* mixing faucet) for washbasins
28 hot tap
29 cold tap
30 extendible shower attachment
31 water tap (pillar tap) for washbasins
32 spindle top
33 shield
34 draw-off tap (*Am.* faucet)
35 supatap
36 swivel tap
37 flushing valve
38-52 fittings
38 joint with male thread
39 reducing socket (reducing coupler)
40 elbow screw joint (elbow coupling)
41 reducing socket (reducing coupler) with female thread
42 screw joint

43 coupler (socket)
44 T-joint (T-junction joint, tee)
45 elbow screw joint with female thread
46 bend
47 T-joint (T-junction joint, tee) with female taper thread
48 ceiling joint
49 reducing elbow
50 cross
51 elbow joint with male thread
52 elbow joint
53-57 pipe supports
53 saddle clip
54 spacing bracket
55 plug
56 pipe clips
57 two-piece spacing clip
58-86 plumber's tools, gas fitter's tools
58 gas pliers
59 footprints
60 combination cutting pliers
61 water pump pliers
62 flat-nose pliers
63 nipple key
64 round-nose pliers
65 pincers
66 adjustable S-wrench
67 screw wrench
68 shifting spanner
69 screwdriver
70 compass saw (keyhole saw)
71 hacksaw frame
72 hand saw
73 soldering iron
74 blowlamp (blowtorch) [for soldering]
75 sealing tape
76 tin-lead solder
77 club hammer
78 hammer
79 spirit level
80 steel-leg vice (*Am.* vise)
81 pipe vice (*Am.* vise)
82 pipe-bending machine
83 former (template)
84 pipe cutter
85 hand die
86 screw-cutting machine (thread-cutting machine)

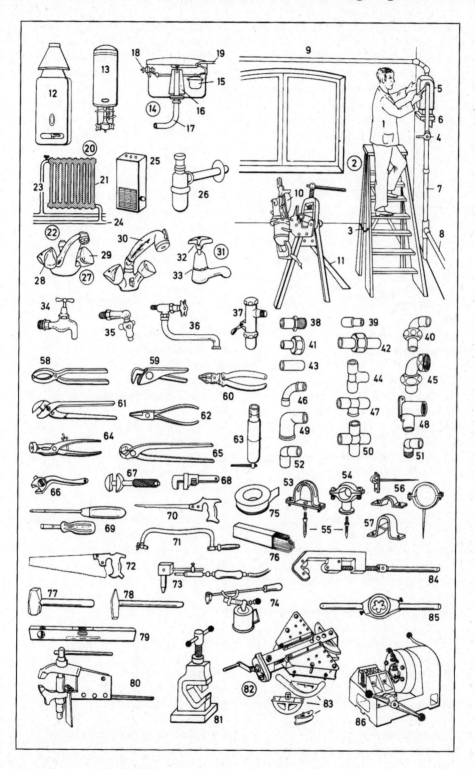

1 electrician (electrical fitter, wire-man)
2 bell push (doorbell) for low-voltage safety current
3 house telephone with call button
4 [flush-mounted] rocker switch
5 [flush-mounted] earthed socket (wall socket, plug point, *Am.* wall outlet, convenience outlet, outlet)
6 [surface-mounted] earthed double socket (double wall socket, double plug point, *Am.* double wall outlet, double convenience outlet, double outlet)
7 switched socket (switch and socket)
8 four-socket (four-way) adapter
9 earthed plug
10 extension lead (*Am.* extension cord)
11 extension plug
12 extension socket
13 surface-mounted three-pole earthed socket [for three-phase circuit] with neutral conductor
14 three-phase plug
15 electric bell (electric buzzer)
16 pull-switch (cord-operated wall switch)
17 dimmer switch [for smooth adjustment of lamp brightness]
18 drill-cast rotary switch
19 miniature circuit breaker (screw-in circuit breaker, fuse)
20 resetting button
21 set screw [for fuses and miniature circuit breakers]
22 underfloor mounting (underfloor sockets)
23 hinged floor socket for power lines and communication lines
24 sunken floor socket with hinged lid (snap lid)
25 surface-mounted socket outlet (plug point) box
26 pocket torch, a torch (*Am.* flashlight)
27 dry cell battery
28 contact spring
29 strip of thermoplastic connectors
30 steel draw-in wire (draw wire) with threading key, and ring attached
31 electricity meter cupboard
32 electricity meter
33 miniature circuit breakers (miniature circuit breaker consumer unit)
34 insulating tape (*Am.* friction tape)
35 fuse holder
36 circuit breaker (fuse), a fuse cartridge with fusible element
37 colour (*Am.* color) indicator [showing current rating]
38, 39 contact maker
40 cable clip
41 universal test meter (multiple meter for measuring current and voltage)
42 thermoplastic moisture-proof cable
43 copper conductor
44 three-core cable
45 electric soldering iron
46 screwdriver
47 water pump pliers
48 shock-resisting safety helmet
49 tool case
50 round-nose pliers
51 cutting pliers
52 junior hacksaw
53 combination cutting pliers
54 insulated handle
55 continuity tester
56 electric light bulb (general service lamp, filament lamp)
57 glass bulb (bulb)
58 coiled-coil filament
59 screw base
60 lampholder
61 fluorescent tube
62 bracket for fluorescent tubes
63 electrician's knife
64 wire strippers
65 bayonet fitting
66 three-pin socket with switch
67 three-pin plug
68 fuse carrier with fuse wire
69 light bulb with bayonet fitting

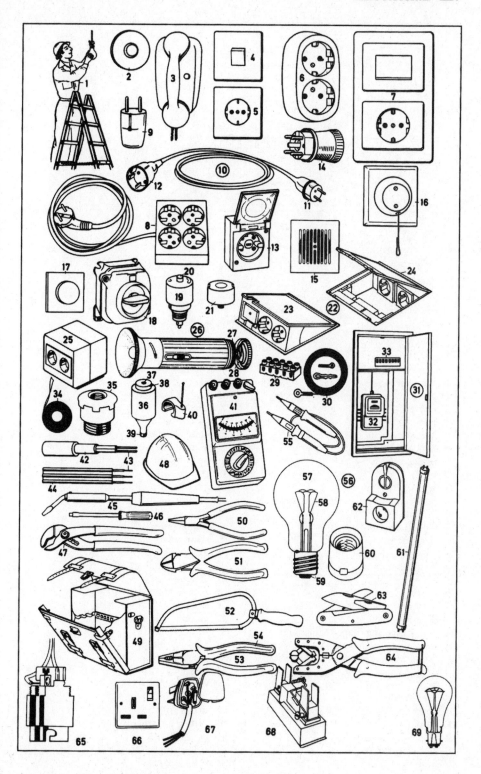

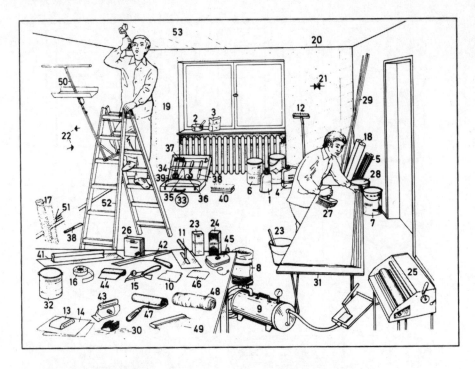

1-17 preparation of surfaces
1 wallpaper-stripping liquid (stripper)
2 plaster (plaster of Paris)
3 filler
4 glue size (size)
5 lining paper, a backing paper
6 primer
7 fluate
8 shredded lining paper
9 wallpaper-stripping machine (stripper)
10 scraper
11 smoother
12 perforator
13 sandpaper block
14 sandpaper
15 stripping knife
16 masking tape
17 strip of sheet metal [on which wallpaper is laid for cutting]
18-53 wallpapering (paper hanging)
18 wallpaper (*kinds:* wood pulp paper, wood chip paper, fabric wallhangings, synthetic wallpaper, metallic paper, natural (*e.g.* wood or cork) paper, tapestry wallpaper)
19 length of wallpaper
20 butted paper edges
21 matching edge
22 non-matching edge
23 wallpaper paste
24 heavy-duty paste
25 pasting machine
26 paste [for the pasting machine]
27 paste brush
28 emulsion paste
29 picture rail
30 beading pins
31 pasteboard (paperhanger's bench)
32 gloss finish
33 paperhanging kit
34 shears (bull-nosed scissors)
35 filling knife
36 seam roller
37 hacking knife
38 knife (trimming knife)
39 straightedge
40 paperhanging brush
41 wallpaper-cutting board
42 cutter
43 trimmer
44 plastic spatula
45 chalked string
46 spreader
47 paper roller
48 flannel cloth
49 dry brush
50 ceiling paperhanger
51 overlap angle
52 paperhanger's trestles
53 ceiling paper

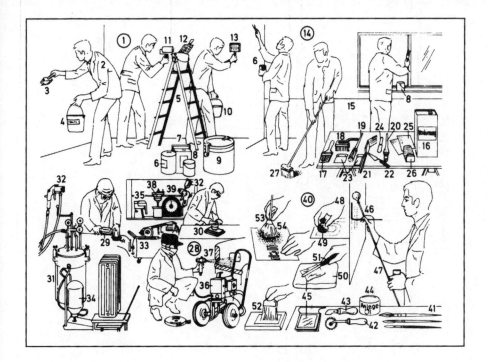

1 **painting**
2 painter
3 paintbrush
4 emulsion paint (emulsion)
5 stepladder
6 can (tin) of paint
7, 8 cans (tins) of paint
7 can (tin) with fixed handle
8 paint kettle
9 drum of paint
10 paint bucket
11 paint roller
12 grill [for removing excess paint from the roller]
13 stippling roller
14 **varnishing**
15 oil-painted dado
16 canister for thinner
17 flat brush for larger surfaces (flat wall brush)
18 stippler
19 fitch
20 cutting-in brush
21 radiator brush (flay brush)
22 paint scraper
23 scraper
24 putty knife
25 sandpaper
26 sandpaper block
27 floor brush

28 **sanding and spraying**
29 grinder
30 sander
31 pressure pot
32 spray gun
33 compressor (air compressor)
34 flow coating machine for flow coating radiators, etc.
35 hand spray
36 airless spray unit
37 airless spray gun
38 efflux viscometer
39 seconds timer
40 **lettering and gilding**
41 lettering brush (signwriting brush, pencil)
42 tracing wheel
43 stencil knife
44 oil gold size
45 gold leaf
46 outline drawing
47 mahlstick
48 pouncing
49 pounce bag
50 gilder's cushion
51 gilder's knife
52 sizing gold leaf
53 filling in the letters with stipple paint
54 gilder's mop

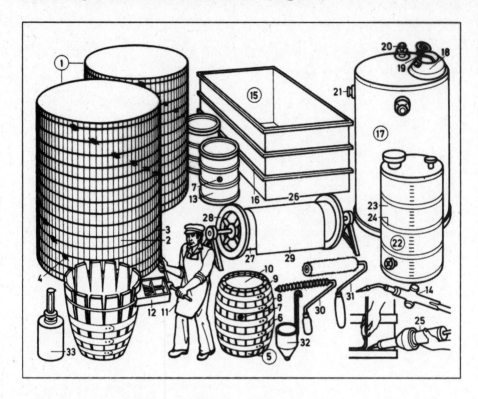

1-33 cooper's and tank construction engineer's workshops
1 tank
2 circumference made of staves (staved circumference)
3 iron rod
4 turnbuckle
5 barrel (cask)
6 body of barrel (of cask)
7 bunghole
8 band (hoop) of barrel
9 barrel stave
10 barrelhead (heading)
11 cooper
12 trusser
13 drum
14 gas welding torch
15 staining vat, made of thermoplastics
16 iron reinforcing bands
17 storage container, made of glass fibre (*Am.* glass fiber) reinforced polyester resin
18 manhole
19 manhole cover with handwheel
20 flange mount
21 flange-type stopcock
22 measuring tank
23 shell (circumference)
24 shrink ring
25 hot-air gun
26 roller made of glass fibre (*Am.* glass fiber) reinforced synthetic resin
27 cylinder
28 flange
29 glass cloth
30 grooved roller
31 lambskin roller
32 ladle for testing viscosity
33 measuring vessel for hardener

1-25 furrier's workroom
1 furrier
2 steam spray gun
3 steam iron
4 beating machine
5 cutting machine for letting out furskins
6 uncut furskin
7 let-out strips (let-out sections)
8 fur worker
9 fur-sewing machine
10 blower for letting out
11-21 furskins
11 mink skin
12 fur side
13 leather side
14 cut furskin
15 lynx skin before letting out
16 let-out lynx skin
17 fur side
18 leather side
19 let-out mink skin
20 lynx fur, sewn together (sewn)
21 broadtail
22 fur marker
23 fur worker
24 mink coat
25 ocelot coat

1-73 joiner's workshop
1-28 joiner's tools
1 wood rasp
2 wood file
3 compass saw (keyhole saw)
4 saw handle
5 [square-headed] mallet
6 try square
7-11 chisels
7 bevelled-edge chisel (chisel)
8 mortise (mortice) chisel
9 gouge
10 handle
11 framing chisel (cant chisel)
12 glue pot in water bath
13 glue pot (glue well), an insert for joiner's glue
14 handscrew
15-28 planes
15 smoothing plane
16 jack plane
17 toothing plane
18 handle (toat)
19 wedge
20 plane iron (cutter)
21 mouth
22 sole
23 side
24 stock (body)
25 rebate (rabbet) plane
26 router plane (old woman's tooth)
27 spokeshave
28 compass plane
29-37 woodworker's bench
29 foot
30 front vice (*Am.* vise)
31 vice (*Am.* vise) handle
32 vice (*Am.* vise) screw
33 jaw
34 bench top
35 well
36 bench stop (bench holdfast)
37 tail vice (*Am.* vise)
38 cabinet maker (joiner)
39 trying plane
40 shavings
41 wood screw

42 saw set
43 mitre (*Am.* miter) box
44 tenon saw
45 thicknesser (thicknessing machine)
46 thicknessing table with rollers
47 kick-back guard
48 chip-extractor opening
49 chain mortising machine (chain mortiser)
50 endless mortising chain
51 clamp (work clamp)
52 knot hole moulding (*Am.* molding) machine
53 knot hole cutter
54 quick-action chuck
55 hand lever
56 change-gear handle
57 sizing and edging machine
58 main switch
59 circular-saw (buzz saw) blade
60 height (rise and fall) adjustment wheel
61 V-way
62 framing table
63 extension arm (arm)
64 trimming table
65 fence
66 fence adjustment handle
67 clamp lever
68 board-sawing machine
69 swivel motor
70 board support
71 saw carriage
72 pedal for raising the transport rollers
73 blockboard

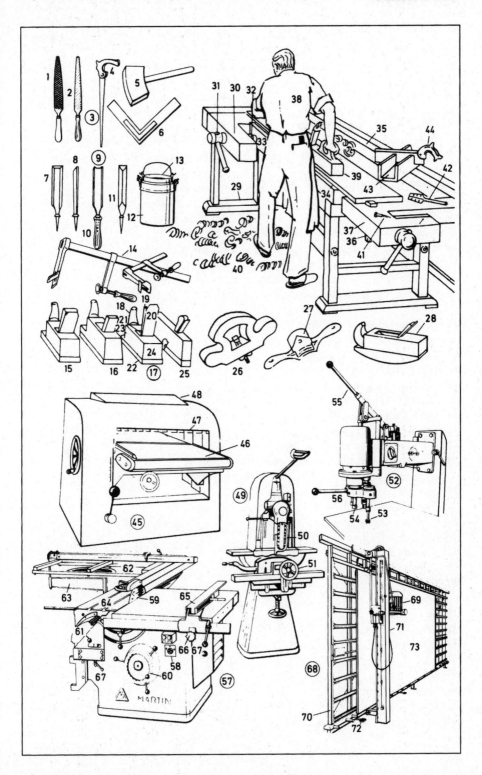

133 Joiner II

1 veneer-peeling machine (peeling machine, peeler)
2 veneer
3 veneer-splicing machine
4 nylon-thread cop
5 sewing mechanism
6 dowel hole boring machine (dowel hole borer)
7 boring motor with hollow-shaft boring bit
8 clamp handle
9 clamp
10 clamping shoe
11 stop bar
12 edge sander (edge-sanding machine)
13 tension roller with extension arm
14 sanding belt regulator (regulating handle)
15 endless sanding belt (sand belt)
16 belt-tensioning lever
17 canting table (tilting table)
18 belt roller
19 angling fence for mitres (*Am.* miters)
20 opening dust hood
21 rise adjustment of the table
22 rise adjustment wheel for the table
23 clamping screw for the table rise adjustment
24 console
25 foot of the machine
26 edge-veneering machine
27 sanding wheel
28 sanding dust extractor
29 splicing head
30 single-belt sanding machine (single-belt sander)
31 belt guard
32 band wheel cover
33 extractor fan (exhaust fan)
34 frame-sanding pad
35 sanding table
36 fine adjustment
37 fine cutter and jointer
38 saw carriage with chain drive

39 trailing cable hanger (trailing cable support)
40 air extractor pipe
41 rail
42 frame-cramping (frame-clamping) machine
43 frame stand
44 workpiece, a window frame
45 compressed-air line
46 pressure cylinder
47 pressure foot
48 frame-mounting device
49 rapid-veneer press
50 bed
51 press
52 pressure piston

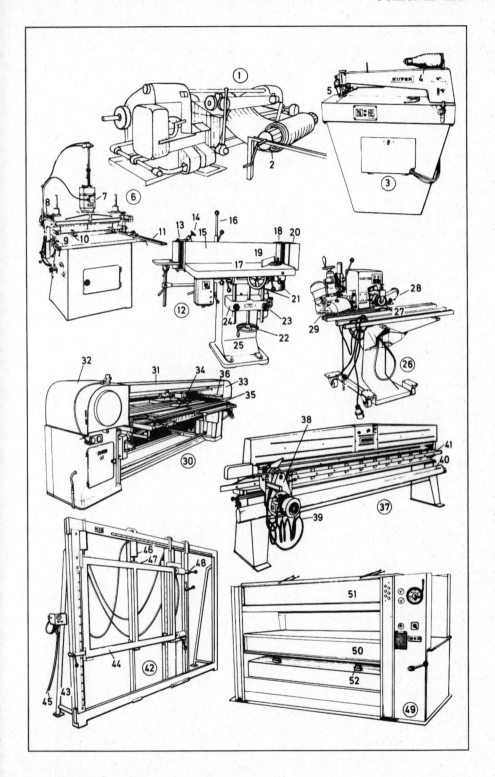

1-34 tool cupboard (tool cabinet) for do-it-yourself work
1 smoothing plane
2 set of fork spanners (fork wrenches, open-end wrenches)
3 hacksaw
4 screwdriver
5 cross-point screwdriver
6 saw rasp
7 hammer
8 wood rasp
9 roughing file
10 small vice (*Am.* vise)
11 corner pipe wrench
12 water pump pliers
13 pincers
14 all-purpose wrench
15 wire stripper and cutter
16 electric drill
17 hacksaw
18 plaster cup
19 soldering iron
20 tin-lead solder wire
21 lamb's wool polishing bonnet
22 rubber backing disc (disk)
23 grinding wheel
24 wire wheel brush
25 sanding discs (disks)
26 try square
27 hand saw
28 universal cutter
29 spirit level
30 firmer chisel
31 centre (*Am.* center) punch
32 nail punch
33 folding rule (rule)
34 storage box for small parts
35 tool box
36 woodworking adhesive
37 stripping knife
38 adhesive tape
39 storage box with compartments for nails, screws, and plugs
40 machinist's hammer
41 collapsible workbench (collapsible bench)
42 jig

43 electric percussion drill (electric hammer drill)
44 pistol grip
45 side grip
46 gearshift switch
47 handle with depth gauge (*Am.* gage)
48 chuck
49 twist bit (twist drill)
50-55 attachments for an electric drill
50 combined circular saw (buzz saw) and bandsaw
51 wood-turning lathe
52 circular saw attachment
53 orbital sanding attachment (orbital sander)
54 drill stand
55 hedge-trimming attachment (hedge trimmer)
56 soldering gun
57 soldering iron
58 high-speed soldering iron
59 upholstery, upholstering an armchair
60 fabric (material) for upholstery
61 do-it-yourself enthusiast

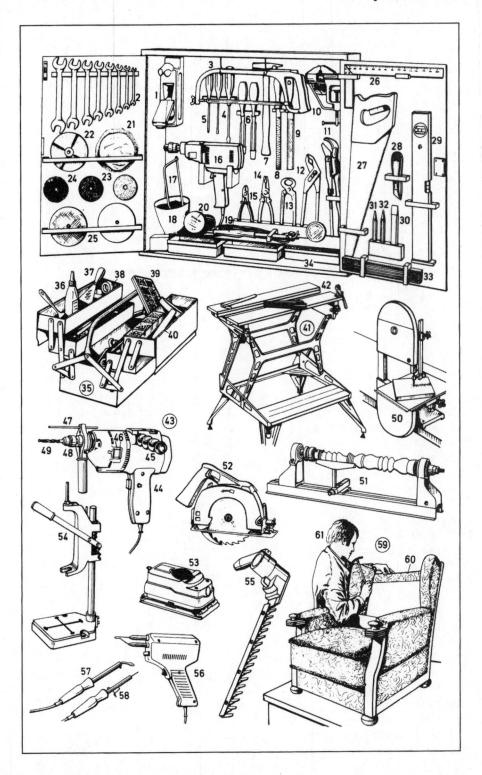

1-26 turnery (turner's workshop)
1 wood-turning lathe (lathe)
2 lathe bed
3 starting resistance (starting resistor)
4 gearbox
5 tool rest
6 chuck
7 tailstock
8 centre (*Am.* center)
9 driving plate with pin
10 two-jaw chuck
11 live centre (*Am.* center)
12 fretsaw
13 fretsaw blade
14, 15, 24 turning tools
14 thread chaser, for cutting threads in wood
15 gouge, for rough turning
16 spoon bit (shell bit)
17 hollowing tool
18 outside calliper (caliper)
19 turned work (turned wood)
20 master turner (turner)
21 [piece of] rough wood
22 drill
23 inside calliper (caliper)
24 parting tool
25 glass paper (sandpaper, emery paper)
26 shavings

1-40 basket making (basketry, basketwork)
1-4 weaves (strokes)
1 randing
2 rib randing
3 oblique randing
4 randing, a piece of wickerwork (screen work)
5 weaver
6 stake
7 workboard: *also:* lapboard
8 screw block
9 hole for holding the block
10 stand
11 chip basket (spale basket)
12 chip (spale)
13 soaking tub
14 willow stakes (osier stakes)
15 willow rods (osier rods)
16 basket, a piece of wickerwork (basketwork)
17 border
18 woven side
19 round base
20 woven base
21 slath
22-24 covering a frame
22 frame
23 end
24 rib
25 upsett
26 grass; *kinds:* esparto grass, alfalfa grass
27 rush (bulrush, reed mace)
28 reed
29 raffia (bast)
30 straw
31 bamboo cane
32 rattan (ratan) chair cane
33 basket maker
34 bending tool
35 cutting point (bodkin)
36 rapping iron
37 pincers
38 picking knife
39 shave
40 hacksaw

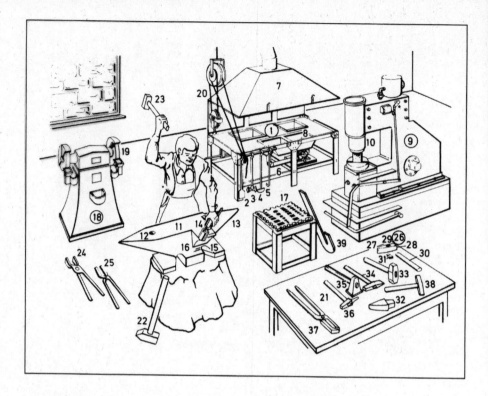

1-8 hearth (forge) with blacksmith's fire
1 hearth (forge)
2 shovel (slice)
3 swab
4 rake
5 poker
6 blast pipe (tue iron)
7 chimney (cowl, hood)
8 water trough (quenching trough, bosh)
9 power hammer
10 ram (tup)
11-16 anvil
11 anvil
12 flat beak (beck, bick)
13 round beak (beck, bick)
14 auxiliary table
15 foot
16 upsetting block
17 swage block
18 tool-grinding machine (tool grinder)
19 grinding wheel
20 block and tackle
21 workbench (bench)
22-39 blacksmith's tools
22 sledge hammer
23 blacksmith's hand hammer
24 flat tongs
25 round tongs
26 parts of the hammer
27 peen (pane, pein)
28 face
29 eye
30 haft
31 cotter punch
32 hardy (hardie)
33 set hammer
34 sett (set, sate)
35 flat-face hammer (flatter)
36 round punch
37 angle tongs
38 blacksmith's chisel (scaling hammer, chipping hammer)
39 moving iron (bending iron)

1 compressed-air system
2 electric motor
3 compressor
4 compressed-air tank
5 compressed-air line
6 percussion screwdriver
7 pedestal grinding machine (floor grinding machine)
8 grinding wheel
9 guard
10 trailer
11 brake drum
12 brake shoe
13 brake lining
14 testing kit
15 pressure gauge (*Am.* gage)
16 brake-testing equipment, a rolling road
17 pit
18 braking roller
19 meter (recording meter)
20 precision lathe for brake drums
21 lorry wheel

22 boring mill
23 power saw, a hacksaw (power hacksaw)
24 vice (*Am.* vise)
25 saw frame
26 coolant supply pipe
27 riveting machine
28 trailer frame (chassis) under construction
29 inert-gas welding equipment
30 rectifier
31 control unit
32 CO_2 cylinder
33 anvil
34 hearth (forge) with blacksmith's fire
35 trolley for gas cylinders
36 vehicle under repair, a tractor

139 Hammer Forging (Smith Forging) and Drop Forging

1 continuous furnace with grid hearth for annealing of round stock
2 discharge opening (discharge door)
3 gas burners
4 charging door
5 counterblow hammer
6 upper ram
7 lower ram
8 ram guide
9 hydraulic drive
10 column
11 short-stroke drop hammer
12 ram (tup)
13 upper die block
14 lower die block
15 hydraulic drive
16 frame
17 anvil
18 forging and sizing press
19 standard
20 table
21 disc (disk) clutch
22 compressed-air pipe
23 solenoid valve
24 air-lift gravity hammer (air-lift drop hammer)
25 drive motor
26 hammer (tup)
27 foot control (foot pedal)
28 preshaped (blocked) workpiece
29 hammer guide
30 hammer cylinder
31 anvil
32 mechanical manipulator to move the workpiece in hammer forging
33 dogs
34 counterweight
35 hydraulic forging press
36 crown
37 cross head
38 upper die block
39 lower die block
40 anvil
41 hydraulic piston
42 pillar guide
43 rollover device
44 burden chain (chain sling)
45 crane hook
46 workpiece
47 gas furnace (gas-fired furnace)
48 gas burner
49 charging opening
50 chain curtain
51 vertical-lift door
52 hot-air duct
53 air preheater
54 gas pipe
55 electric door-lifting mechanism
56 air blast

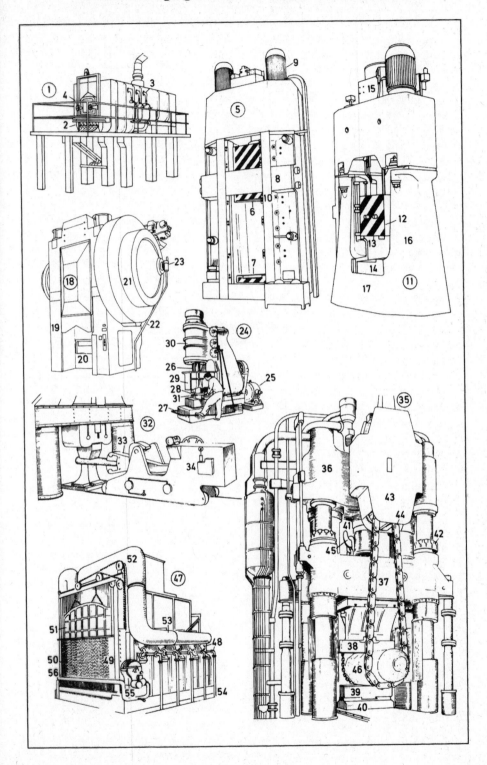

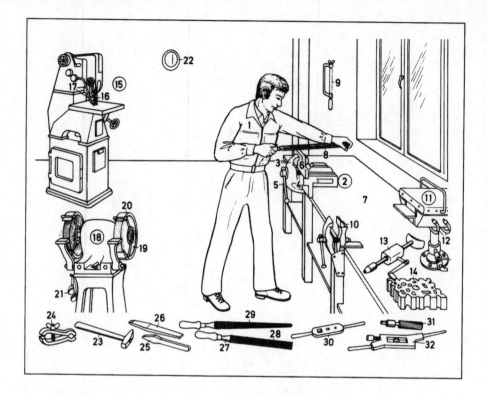

1-22 metalwork shop (mechanic's workshop, fitter's workshop, locksmith's workshop)

1 metalworker (*e.g.* mechanic, fitter, locksmith; *form. also:* wrought-iron craftsman)
2 parallel-jaw vice (*Am.* vise)
3 jaw
4 screw
5 handle
6 workpiece
7 workbench (bench)
8 files (*kinds:* rough file, smooth file, precision file)
9 hacksaw
10 leg vice (*Am.* vise), a spring vice
11 muffle furnace, a gas-fired furnace
12 gas pipe
13 hand brace (hand drill)
14 swage block
15 filing machine
16 file
17 compressed-air pipe
18 grinding machine (grinder)
19 grinding wheel
20 guard
21 goggles (safety glasses)
22 safety helmet
23 machinist's hammer
24 hand vice (*Am.* vise)
25 cape chisel (cross-cut chisel)
26 flat chisel
27 flat file
28 file cut (cut)
29 round file (*also:* half-round file)
30 tap wrench
31 reamer
32 die (die and stock)

33-35 key
33 stem (shank)
34 bow
35 bit
36-43 door lock, a mortise (mortice) lock
36 back plate
37 spring bolt (latch bolt)
38 tumbler
39 bolt
40 keyhole
41 bolt guide pin
42 tumbler spring
43 follower, with square hole
44 cylinder lock (safety lock)
45 cylinder (plug)
46 spring
47 pin
48 safety key, a flat key
49 lift-off hinge
50 hook-and-ride band
51 strap hinge
52 vernier calliper (caliper) gauge (*Am.* gage)
53 feeler gauge (*Am.* gage)
54 vernier depth gauge (*Am.* gage)
55 vernier
56 straightedge
57 square
58 breast drill
59 twist bit (twist drill)
60 screw tap (tap)
61 halves of a screw die
62 screwdriver
63 scraper (*also:* pointed triangle scraper)
64 centre (*Am.* center) punch
65 round punch
66 flat-nose pliers
67 detachable-jaw cut nippers
68 gas pliers
69 pincers

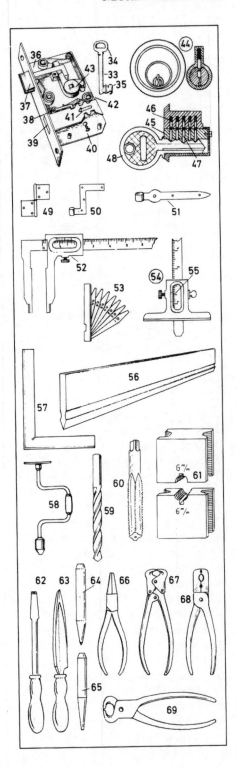

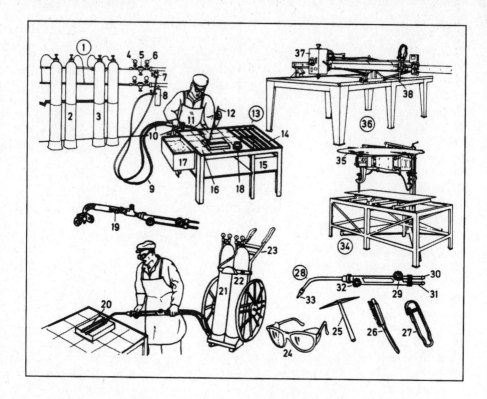

1 gas cylinder manifold
2 acetylene cylinder
3 oxygen cylinder
4 high-pressure manometer
5 pressure-reducing valve (reducing valve, pressure regulator)
6 low-pressure manometer
7 stop valve
8 hydraulic back-pressure valve for low-pressure installations
9 gas hose
10 oxygen hose
11 welding torch (blowpipe)
12 welding rod (filler rod)
13 welding bench
14 grating
15 scrap box
16 bench covering of chamotte slabs
17 water tank
18 welding paste (flux)
19 welding torch (blowpipe) with cutting attachment and guide tractor
20 workpiece

21 oxygen cylinder
22 acetylene cylinder
23 cylinder trolley
24 welding goggles
25 chipping hammer
26 wire brush
27 torch lighter (blowpipe lighter)
28 welding torch (blowpipe)
29 oxygen control
30 oxygen connection
31 gas connection (acetylene connection)
32 gas control (acetylene control)
33 welding nozzle
34 cutting machine
35 circular template
36 universal cutting machine
37 tracing head
38 cutting nozzle

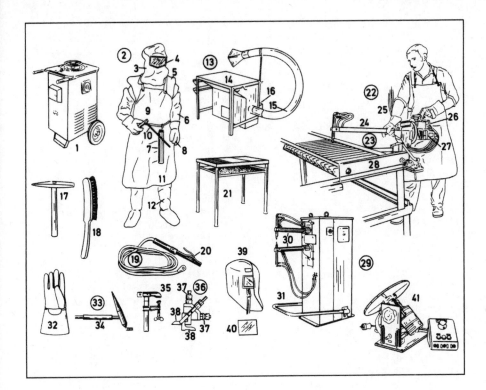

1 welding transformer	**23** spot welding electrode holder
2 arc welder	**24** electrode arm
3 arc welding helmet	**25** power supply (lead)
4 flip-up window	**26** electrode-pressure cylinder
5 shoulder guard	**27** welding transformer
6 protective sleeve	**28** workpiece
7 electrode case	**29** foot-operated spot welder
8 three-fingered welding glove	**30** welder electrode arms
9 electrode holder	**31** foot pedal for welding pressure
10 electrode	adjustment
11 leather apron	**32** five-fingered welding glove
12 shin guard	**33** inert-gas torch for inert-gas welding
13 welding table with fume extraction	(gas-shielded arc welding)
equipment	**34** inert-gas (shielding-gas) supply
14 table top	**35** work clamp (earthing clamp)
15 movable extractor duct	**36** fillet gauge (*Am.* gage) (weld
16 extractor support	gauge) [for measuring throat thick-
17 chipping hammer	ness]
18 wire brush	**37** micrometer
19 welding lead	**38** measuring arm
20 electrode holder	**39** arc welding helmet
21 welding bench	**40** filter lens
22 spot welding	**41** small turntable

143 Sections, Bolts, and Machine Parts

[material: steel, brass, aluminium (*Am.* aluminium), plastics, etc.; in the following, steel was chosen as an example]

1 angle iron (angle)
2 leg (flange)

3-7 steel girders
3 T-iron (tee-iron)
4 vertical leg
5 flange
6 H-girder (H-beam)
7 E-channel (channel iron)
8 round bar
9 square iron (*Am.* square stock)
10 flat bar
11 strip steel
12 iron wire

13-50 screws and bolts
13 hexagonal-head bolt
14 head
15 shank
16 thread
17 washer
18 hexagonal nut
19 split pin
20 rounded end
21 width of head (of flats)
22 stud
23 point (end)
24 castle nut (castellated nut)
25 hole for the split pin
26 cross-head screw, a sheet-metal screw (self-tapping screw)
27 hexagonal socket head screw
28 countersunk-head bolt
29 catch
30 locknut (locking nut)
31 bolt (pin)
32 collar-head bolt
33 set collar (integral collar)
34 spring washer (washer)
35 round nut, an adjusting nut
36 cheese-head screw, a slotted screw
37 tapered pin
38 screw slot (screw slit, screw groove)
39 square-head bolt
40 grooved pin, a cylindrical pin
41 T-head bolt
42 wing nut (fly nut, butterfly nut)
43 rag bolt
44 barb
45 wood screw
46 countersunk head
47 wood screw thread
48 grub screw
49 pin slot (pin slit, pin groove)
50 round end
51 nail (wire nail)
52 head
53 shank
54 point
55 roofing nail

56 riveting (lap riveting)

57-60 rivet
57 set head (swage head, die head), a rivet head
58 rivet shank
59 closing head
60 pitch of rivets
61 shaft
62 chamfer (bevel)
63 journal
64 neck
65 seat
66 keyway
67 conical seat (cone)
68 thread
69 ball bearing, an antifriction bearing
70 steel ball (ball)
71 outer race
72 inner race
73, 74 keys
73 sunk key (feather)
74 gib (gib-headed key)
75, 76 needle roller bearing
75 needle cage
76 needle
77 castle nut (castellated nut)
78 split pin
79 casing
80 casing cover
81 grease nipple (lubricating nipple)
82-96 gear wheels, cog wheels
82 stepped gear wheel
83 cog (tooth)
84 space between teeth
85 keyway (key seat, key slot)
86 bore
87 herringbone gear wheel
88 spoke (arm)
89 helical gearing (helical spur wheel)
90 sprocket
91 bevel gear wheel (bevel wheel)
92, 93 spiral toothing
92 pinion
93 crown wheel
94-96 epicyclic gear (planetary gear)
94 planet wheels
95 internal gear
96 sun wheel (sun gear)
97-107 absorption dynamometer
97 shoe brake (check brake, block brake)
98 brake pulley
99 brake shaft (brake axle)
100 brake block (brake shoe)
101 pull rod
102 brake magnet
103 brake weight
104 band brake
105 brake band
106 brake lining
107 adjusting screw, for even application of the brake

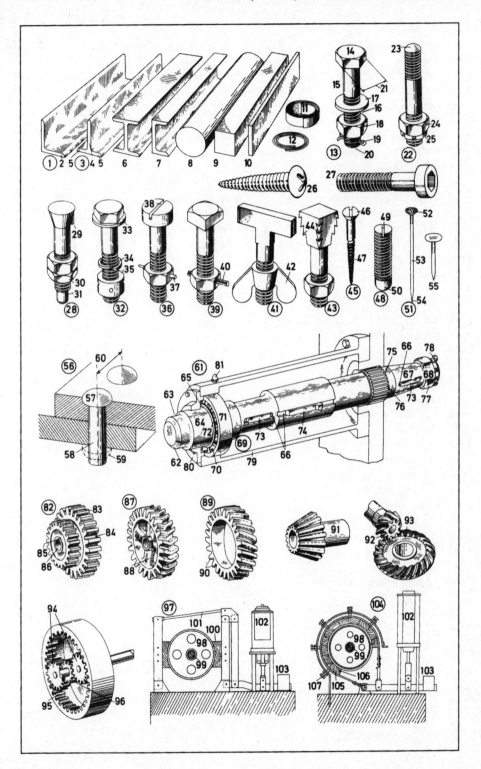

144 Coal Mine

1-51 **coal mine** (colliery, pit)
1 pithead gear (headgear)
2 winding engine house
3 pithead frame (head frame)
4 pithead building
5 processing plant
6 sawmill
7-11 **coking plant**
7 battery of coke ovens
8 larry car (larry, charging car)
9 coking coal tower
10 coke-quenching tower
11 coke-quenching car
12 gasometer
13 power plant (power station)
14 water tower
15 cooling tower
16 mine fan
17 depot
18 administration building (office building, offices)
19 tip heap (spoil heap)
20 cleaning plant
21-51 **underground workings** (underground mining)
21 ventilation shaft
22 fan drift
23 cage-winding system with cages
24 main shaft
25 skip-winding system
26 winding inset
27 staple shaft
28 spiral chute
29 gallery along seam
30 lateral
31 cross-cut
32 tunnelling (*Am.* tunneling) machine
33-37 **longwall faces**
33 horizontal ploughed longwall face
34 horizontal cut longwall face
35 vertical pneumatic pick longwall face
36 diagonal ram longwall face
37 goaf (gob, waste)
38 air lock
39 transportation of men by cars
40 belt conveying
41 raw coal bunker
42 charging conveyor
43 transportation of supplies by monorail car
44 transportation of men by monorail car
45 transportation of supplies by mine car
46 drainage
47 sump (sink)
48 capping
49 [layer of] coal-bearing rock
50 coal seam
51 fault

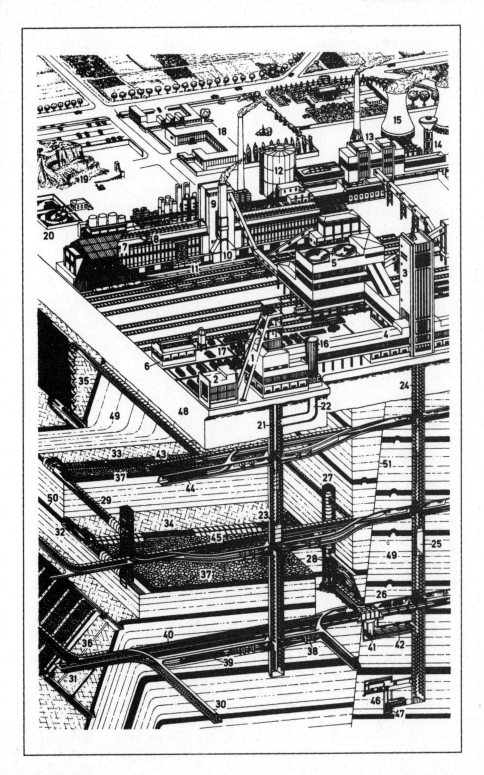

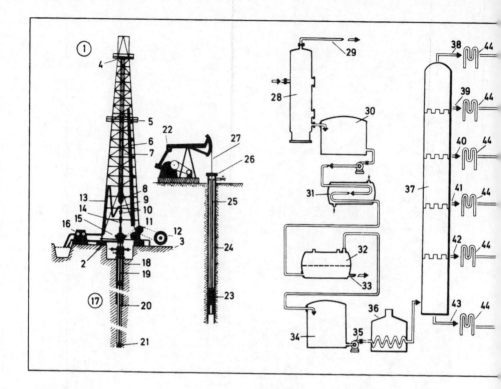

1-21 oil drilling
1 drilling rig
2 substructure
3 crown safety platform
4 crown blocks
5 working platform, an intermediate platform
6 drill pipes
7 drilling cable (drilling line)
8 travelling (*Am.* traveling) block
9 hook
10 [rotary] swivel
11 hoist
12 engine
13 standpipe and rotary hose
14 kelly
15 rotary table
16 slush pump (mud pump)
17 well
18 casing
19 drilling pipe
20 tubing
21 drilling bit; *kinds:* fishtail (blade) bit, rock (*Am.* roller) bit, core bit

22-27 oil (crude oil) production
22 pumping unit (pump)
23 plunger
24 tubing
25 sucker rods (pumping rods)
26 stuffing box
27 polish (polished) rod
28-35 treatment of crude oil [diagram]
28 gas separator
29 gas pipe (gas outlet)
30 wet oil tank (wash tank)
31 water heater
32 water and brine separator
33 salt water pipe (salt water outlet)
34 oil tank
35 trunk pipeline for oil [to the refinery or transport by tanker lorry (*Am.* tank truck), oil tanker or pipeline]
36-64 processing of crude oil [diagram]
36 oil furnace (pipe still)
37 fractionating column (distillation column) with trays
38 top gases (tops)

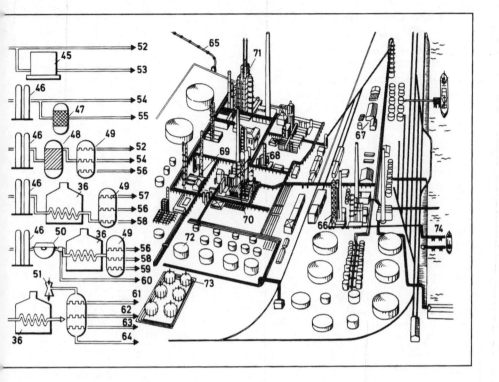

39 light distillation products
40 heavy distillation products
41 petroleum
42 gas oil component
43 residue
44 condenser (cooler)
45 compressor
46 desulphurizing (desulphurization, *Am.* desulfurizing, desulfurization) plant
47 reformer (hydroformer, platformer)
48 catalytic cracker (cat cracker)
49 distillation column
50 de-waxing (wax separation)
51 vacuum equipment
52-64 oil products
52 fuel gas
53 liquefied petroleum gas (liquid gas)
54 regular grade petrol (*Am.* gasoline)
55 super grade petrol (*Am.* gasoline)
56 diesel oil

57 aviation fuel
58 light fuel oil
59 heavy fuel oil
60 paraffin (paraffin oil, kerosene)
61 spindle oil
62 lubricating oil
63 cylinder oil
64 bitumen
65-74 oil refinery
65 pipeline (oil pipeline)
66 distillation plants
67 lubricating oil refinery
68 desulphurizing (desulphurization, *Am.* desulfurizing, desulfurization) plant
69 gas-separating plant
70 catalytic cracking plant
71 catalytic reformer
72 storage tank
73 spherical tank
74 tanker terminal

1-39 drilling rig (oil rig)
1-37 drilling platform
1 power station
2 generator exhausts
3 revolving crane (pedestal crane)
4 piperack
5 turbine exhausts
6 materials store
7 helicopter deck (heliport deck, heliport)
8 elevator
9 production oil and gas separator
10 test oil and gas separators (test separators)
11 emergency flare stack
12 derrick
13 diesel tank
14 office building
15 cement storage tanks
16 drinking water tank
17 salt water tank
18 jet fuel tanks
19 lifeboats
20 elevator shaft
21 compressed-air reservoir
22 pumping station
23 air compressor
24 air lock
25 seawater desalination plant
26 inlet filters for diesel fuel
27 gas cooler
28 control panel for the separators
29 toilets (lavatories)
30 workshop
31 pig trap [the 'pig' is used to clean the oil pipeline]
32 control room
33 accommodation modules (accommodation)
34 high-pressure cementing pumps
35 lower deck
36 middle deck
37 top deck (main deck)
38 substructure
39 mean sea level

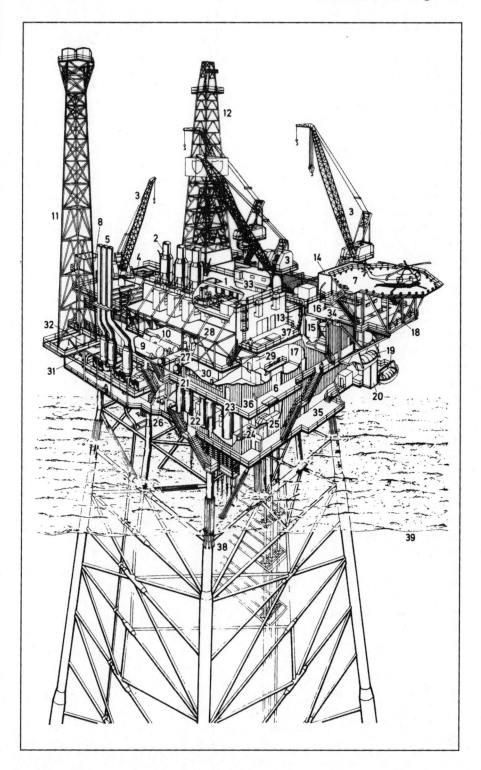

147 Iron and Steel Works

1-20 blast furnace plant
1 blast furnace, a shaft furnace
2 furnace incline (lift) for ore and flux or coke
3 skip hoist
4 charging platform
5 receiving hopper
6 bell
7 blast furnace shaft
8 smelting section
9 slag escape
10 slag ladle
11 pig iron (crude iron, iron) runout
12 pig iron (crude iron, iron) ladle
13 downtake
14 dust catcher, a dust-collecting machine
15 hot-blast stove
16 external combustion chamber
17 blast main
18 gas pipe
19 hot-blast pipe
20 tuyère
21-69 steelworks
21-30 Siemens-Martin open-hearth furnace
21 pig iron (crude iron, iron) ladle
22 feed runner
23 stationary furnace
24 hearth
25 charging machine
26 scrap iron charging box
27 gas pipe
28 gas regenerator chamber
29 air feed pipe
30 air regenerator chamber
31 [bottom-pouring] steel-casting ladle with stopper
32 ingot mould (*Am.* mold)
33 steel ingot
34-44 pig-casting machine
34 pouring end
35 metal runner
36 series (strand) of moulds (*Am.* molds)
37 mould (*Am.* mold)
38 catwalk

39 discharging chute
40 pig
41 travelling (*Am.* traveling) crane
42 top-pouring pig iron (crude iron, iron) ladle
43 pouring ladle lip
44 tilting device (tipping device, *Am.* dumping device)
45-50 oxygen-blowing converter (L-D converter, Linz-Donawitz converter)
45 conical converter top
46 mantle
47 solid converter bottom
48 fireproof lining (refractory lining)
49 oxygen lance
50 tapping hole (tap hole)
51-54 Siemens electric low-shaft furnace
51 feed
52 electrodes [arranged in a circle]
53 bustle pipe
54 runout
55-69 Thomas converter (basic Bessemer converter)
55 charging position for molten pig iron
56 charging position for lime
57 blow position
58 discharging position
59 tilting device (tipping device, *Am.* dumping device)
60 crane-operated ladle
61 auxiliary crane hoist
62 lime bunker
63 downpipe
64 tipping car (*Am.* dump truck)
65 scrap iron feed
66 control desk
67 converter chimney
68 blast main
69 wind box

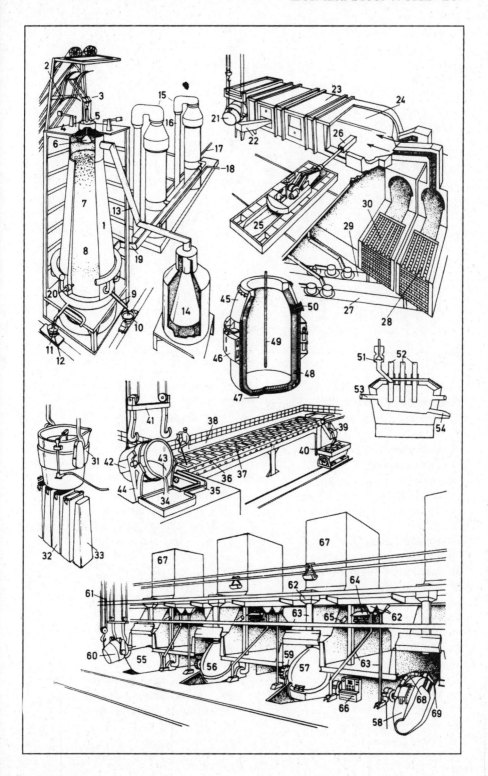

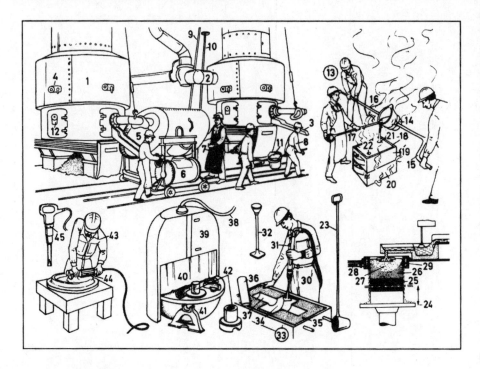

1-45 iron foundry
1-12 melting plant
1 cupola furnace (cupola), a melting furnace
2 blast main (blast inlet, blast pipe)
3 tapping spout
4 spyhole
5 tilting-type [hot-metal] receiver
6 mobile drum-type ladle
7 melter
8 founder (caster)
9 tap bar (tapping bar)
10 bott stick (*Am.* bot stick)
11 molten iron
12 slag spout
13 casting team
14 hand shank
15 double handle (crutch)
16 carrying bar
17 skimmer rod
18 closed moulding (*Am.* molding) box
19 upper frame (cope)
20 lower frame (drag)
21 runner (runner gate, down-gate)

22 riser (riser gate)
23 hand ladle
24-29 continuous casting
24 sinking pouring floor
25 solidifying pig
26 solid stage
27 liquid stage
28 water-cooling system
29 mould (*Am.* mold) wall
30-37 moulding (*Am.* molding) department (moulding shop)
30 moulder (*Am.* molder)
31 pneumatic rammer
32 hand rammer
33 open moulding (*Am.* molding) box
34 pattern
35 moulding (*Am.* molding) sand
36 core
37 core print
38-45 cleaning shop (fettling shop)
38 steel grit or sand delivery pipe
39 rotary-table shot-blasting machine
40 grit guard
41 revolving table
42 casting

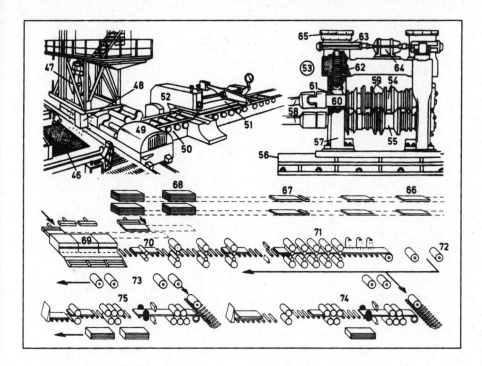

43 fettler
44 pneumatic grinder
45 pneumatic chisel
46-75 rolling mill
46 soaking pit
47 soaking pit crane
48 ingot
49 ingot tipper
50 roller table
51 workpiece
52 bloom shears
53 two-high mill
54-55 set of rolls (set of rollers)
54 upper roll (upper roller)
55 lower roll (lower roller)
56-60 roll stand
56 base plate
57 housing (frame)
58 coupling spindle
59 groove
60 roll bearing
61-65 adjusting equipment
61 chock
62 main screw
63 gear

64 motor
65 indicator for rough and fine adjustment
66-75 continuous rolling mill train for the manufacture of strip [diagram]
66-68 processing of semi-finished product
66 semi-finished product
67 gas cutting installation
68 stack of finished steel sheets
69 continuous reheating furnaces
70 blooming train
71 finishing train
72 coiler
73 stock of coils for sale
74 5 mm shearing train
75 10 mm shearing train

1 **centre** (*Am.* center) **lathe**
2 headstock with gear control (geared headstock)
3 reduction drive lever
4 lever for normal and coarse threads
5 speed change lever
6 leadscrew reverse-gear lever
7 change-gear box
8 feed gearbox (Norton tumbler gear)
9 levers for changing the feed and thread pitch
10 feed gear lever (tumbler lever)
11 switch lever for right or left hand action of main spindle
12 lathe foot (footpiece)
13 leadscrew handwheel for traversing of saddle (longitudinal movement of saddle)
14 tumbler reverse lever
15 feed screw
16 apron (saddle apron, carriage apron)
17 lever for longitudinal and transverse motion
18 drop (dropping) worm (feed trip, feed tripping device) for engaging feed mechanisms
19 lever for engaging half nut of leadscrew (lever for clasp nut engagement)
20 lathe spindle
21 tool post
22 top slide (tool slide, tool rest)
23 cross slide
24 bed slide
25 coolant supply pipe
26 tailstock centre (*Am.* center)
27 barrel (tailstock barrel)
28 tailstock barrel clamp lever
29 tailstock
30 tailstock barrel adjusting handwheel
31 lathe bed
32 leadscrew
33 feed shaft
34 reverse shaft for right and left hand motion and engaging and disengaging
35 four-jaw chuck (four-jaw independent chuck)
36 gripping jaw
37 three-jaw chuck (three-jaw self-centring, *Am.* self-centering, chuck)
38 **turret lathe**

39 cross slide
40 turret
41 combination toolholder (multiple turning head)
42 top slide
43 star wheel
44 coolant tray for collecting coolant and swarf
45-53 lathe tools
45 tool bit holder (clamp tip tool) for adjustable cutting tips
46 adjustable cutting tip (clamp tip) of cemented carbide or oxide ceramic
47 shapes of adjustable oxide ceramic tips
48 lathe tool with cemented carbide cutting edge
49 tool shank
50 brazed cemented carbide cutting tip (cutting edge)
51 internal facing tool (boring tool) for corner work
52 general-purpose lathe tool
53 parting (parting-off) tool
54 lathe carrier
55 driving (driver) plate
56-72 measuring instruments
56 plug gauge (*Am.* gage)
57 'GO' gauging (*Am.* gaging) member (end)
58 'NOT GO' gauging (*Am.* gaging) member (end)
59 calliper (caliper, snap) gauge (*Am.* gage)
60 'GO' side
61 'NOT GO' side
62 micrometer
63 measuring scale
64 graduated thimble
65 frame
66 spindle (screwed spindle)
67 vernier calliper (caliper) gauge (*Am.* gage)
68 depth gauge (*Am.* gage) attachment rule
69 vernier scale
70 outside jaws
71 inside jaws
72 vernier depth gauge (*Am.* gage)

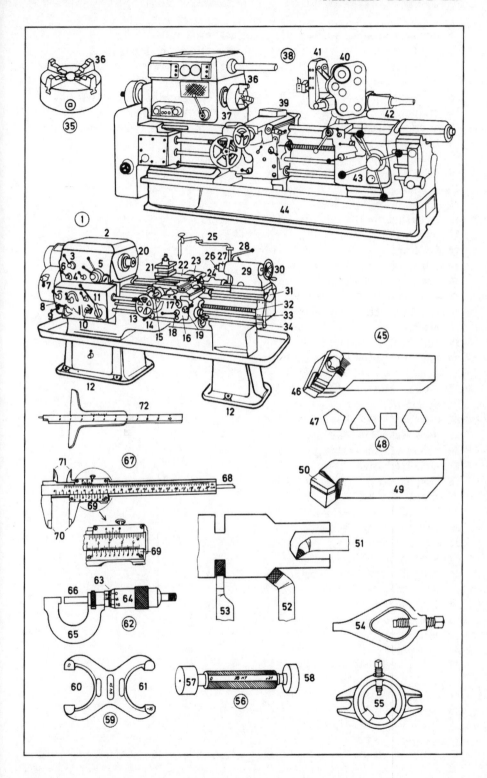

150 Machine Tools II

1 **universal grinding machine**
2 headstock
3 wheelhead slide
4 grinding wheel
5 tailstock
6 grinding machine bed
7 grinding machine table
8 **two-column planing machine** (two-column planer)
9 drive motor, a direct current motor
10 column
11 planer table
12 cross slide (rail)
13 tool box
14 **hacksaw**
15 clamping device
16 saw blade
17 saw frame
18 **radial** (radial-arm) **drilling machine**
19 bed (base plate)
20 block for workpiece
21 pillar
22 lifting motor
23 drill spindle
24 arm
25 **universal milling machine**
26 milling machine table
27 table feed drive
28 switch lever for spindle rotation speed
29 control box (control unit)
30 vertical milling spindle
31 vertical drive head
32 horizontal milling spindle
33 end support for steadying horizontal spindle
34 machine tap
35 **articulated robot,** an industrial robot
36 base plate
37 rotating column (base rotating axis)
38 shoulder joint
39 upper arm
40 elbow joint
41 tubular forearm
42 wrist joint
43 gripper mounting flange
44 gripper
45 fingers
46 upright robot (linear-axis robot, rectilinear robot)
47 portal robot (gantry robot)

258

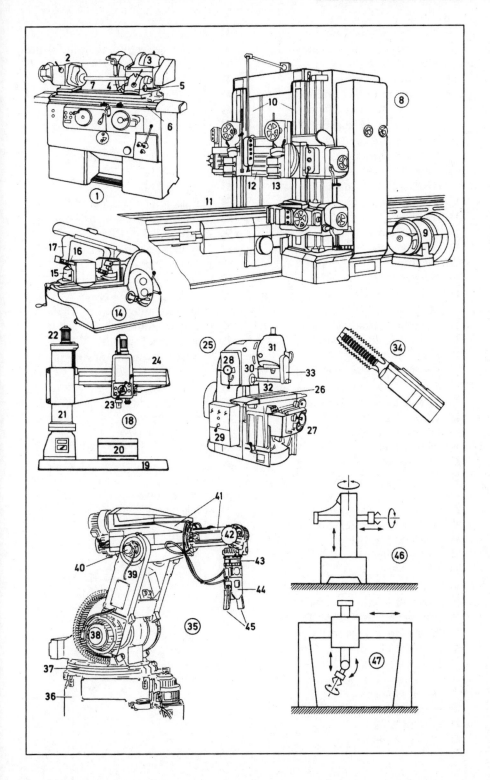

1 drawing board
2 drafting machine with parallel motion
3 adjustable knob
4 drawing head (adjustable set square)
5 drawing board adjustment
6 drawing table
7 set square (triangle)
8 triangle
9 T-square (tee-square)
10 rolled drawing
11 diagram
12 time schedule
13 paper stand
14 roll of paper
15 cutter
16 technical drawing (drawing, design)
17 front view (front elevation)
18 side view (side elevation)
19 plan
20 surface not to be machined
21 surface to be machined
22 surface to be superfinished
23 visible edge
24 hidden edge
25 dimension line
26 arrow head
27 section line
28 section A–B
29 hatched surface
30 centre (Am. center) line
31 title panel (title block)
32 technical data
33 ruler (rule)
34 triangular scale
35 erasing shield
36 drawing ink cartridge
37 holders for tubular drawing pens
38 set of tubular drawing pens
39 hygrometer
40 cap with indication of nib size
41 pencil-type eraser
42 eraser
43 erasing knife
44 erasing knife blade
45 clutch-type pencil
46 pencil lead (refill lead, refill, spare lead)
47 glass eraser
48 glass fibres (Am. fibers)
49 ruling pen
50 cross joint
51 index plate
52 compass with interchangeable attachments
53 compass head
54 needle point attachment
55 pencil point attachment
56 needle
57 lengthening arm (extension bar)
58 ruling pen attachment
59 pump compass (drop compass)
60 piston
61 ruling pen attachment
62 pencil attachment
63 drawing ink container
64 spring bow (rapid adjustment, ratchet-type) compass
65 spring ring hinge
66 spring-loaded fine adjustment for arcs
67 right-angle needle
68 tubular ink unit
69 stencil lettering guide (lettering stencil)
70 circle template
71 ellipse template

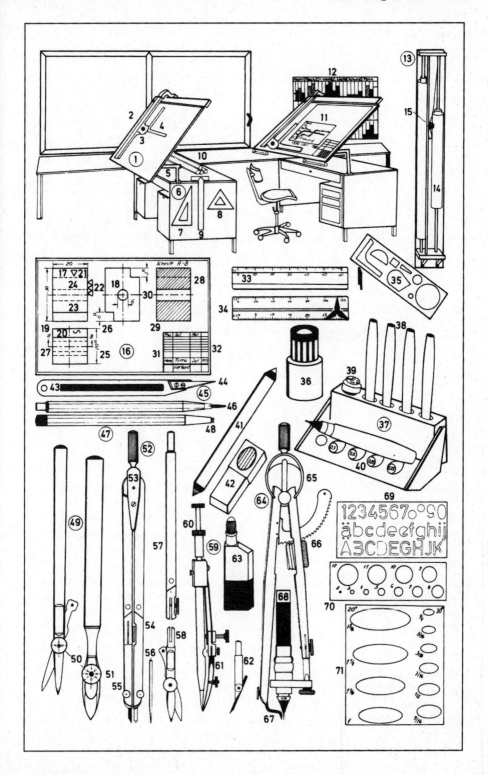

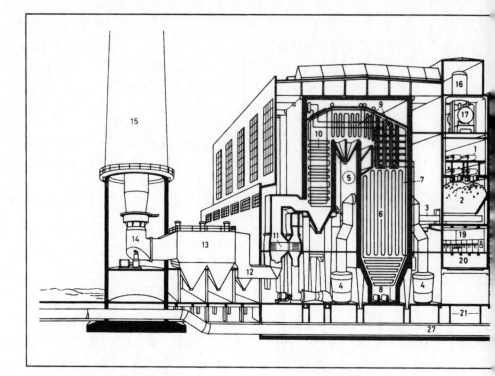

1-28 steam-generating station, an electric power plant

1-21 boiler house

1 coal conveyor
2 coal bunker
3 travelling-grate (*Am.* traveling-grate) stoker
4 coal mill
5 steam boiler, a water-tube boiler (radiant-type boiler)
6 burners
7 water pipes
8 ash pit (clinker pit)
9 superheater
10 water preheater
11 air preheater
12 gas flue
13 electrostatic precipitator
14 induced-draught (*Am.* induced-draft) fan
15 chimney (smokestack)
16 de-aerator
17 feedwater tank

18 boiler feed pump
19 control room
20 cable tunnel
21 cable vault
22 turbine house
23 steam turbine with alternator
24 surface condenser
25 low-pressure preheater
26 high-pressure preheater (economizer)
27 cooling water pipe
28 control room

29-35 outdoor substation, a substation
29 busbars
30 power transformer, a mobile (transportable) transformer
31 stay poles (guy poles)
32 high-voltage transmission line
33 high-voltage conductor
34 air-blast circuit breaker (circuit breaker)
35 surge diverter (*Am.* lightning arrester, arrester)

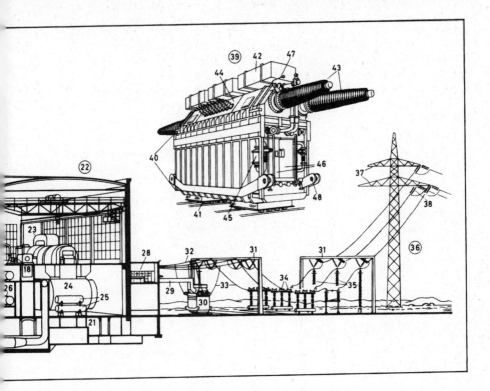

36 overhead line support, a lattice
     steel tower
37 cross arm (traverse)
38 strain insulator
39 **mobile (transportable) transformer**
     (power transformer, transformer)
40 transformer tank
41 bogie (*Am.* truck)
42 oil conservator
43 primary voltage terminal (primary
     voltage bushing)
44 low-voltage terminals (low-voltage
     bushings)
45 oil-circulating pump
46 oil cooler
47 arcing horn
48 transport lug

1-8 control room
1-6 control console (control desk)
1 control board (control panel) for the alternators
2 master switch
3 signal light
4 feeder panel
5 monitoring controls for the switching systems
6 controls
7 revertive signal panel
8 matrix mimic board
9-18 transformer
9 oil conservator
10 breather
11 oil gauge (*Am.* gage)
12 feed-through terminal (feed-through insulator)
13 on-load tap changer
14 yoke
15 primary winding (primary)
16 secondary winding (secondary, low-voltage winding)
17 core
18 tap (tapping)
19 **transformer connection**
20 star connection (star network, Y-connection)
21 delta connection (mesh connection)
22 neutral point
23-30 steam turbine, a turbogenerator unit
23 high-pressure cylinder
24 medium-pressure cylinder
25 low-pressure cylinder
26 three-phase generator (generator)
27 hydrogen cooler
28 leakage steam path
29 jet nozzle
30 turbine monitoring panel with measuring instruments
31 automatic voltage regulator
32 synchro
33 **cable box**
34 conductor

35 feed-through terminal (feed-through insulator)
36 core
37 casing
38 filling compound (filler)
39 lead sheath
40 lead-in tube
41 cable
42 **high voltage cable,** for three-phase current
43 conductor
44 metallic paper (metallized paper)
45 tracer (tracer element)
46 varnished-cambric tape
47 lead sheath
48 asphalted paper
49 jute serving
50 steel tape or steel wire armour (*Am.* armor)
51-62 air-blast circuit breaker, a circuit breaker
51 compressed-air tank
52 control valve (main operating valve)
53 compressed-air inlet
54 support insulator, a hollow porcelain supporting insulator
55 interrupter
56 resistor
57 auxiliary contacts
58 current transformer
59 voltage transformer (potential transformer)
60 operating mechanism housing
61 arcing horn
62 spark gap

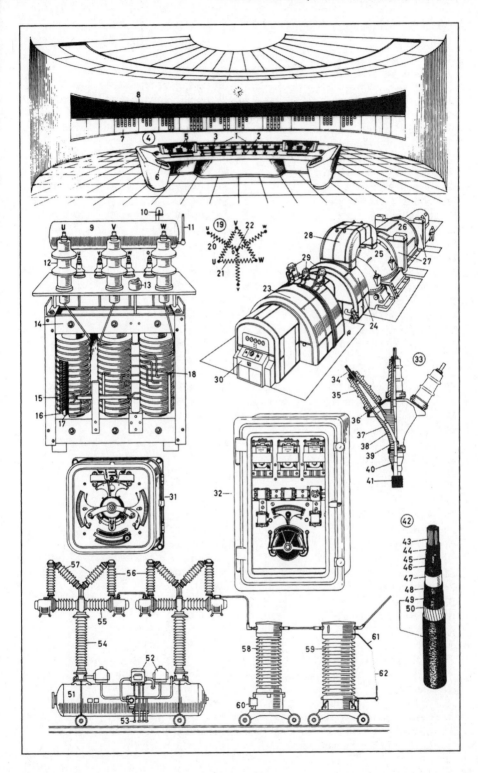

1 **fast-breeder reactor** (fast breeder) [diagram]
2 primary circuit (primary loop, primary sodium system)
3 reactor
4 fuel rods (fuel pins)
5 primary sodium pump
6 heat exchanger
7 secondary circuit (secondary loop, secondary sodium system)
8 secondary sodium pump
9 steam generator
10 cooling water flow circuit
11 steam line
12 feedwater line
13 feed pump
14 steam turbine
15 generator
16 transmission line
17 condenser
18 cooling water
19 **nuclear reactor,** a pressurized-water reactor (nuclear power plant, atomic power plant)
20 concrete shield (reactor building)
21 steel containment (steel shell) with air extraction vent
22 reactor pressure vessel
23 control rod drive
24 control rods
25 primary coolant pump
26 steam generator
27 fuel-handling hoists
28 fuel storage
29 coolant flow passage
30 feedwater line
31 prime steam line
32 manway
33 turbogenerator set
34 turbogenerator
35 condenser
36 service building
37 exhaust gas stack
38 polar crane
39 cooling tower, a dry cooling tower
40 pressurized-water system
41 reactor
42 primary circuit (primary loop)
43 circulation pump (recirculation pump)
44 heat exchanger (steam generator)
45 secondary circuit (secondary loop, feedwater steam circuit)
46 steam turbine
47 generator
48 cooling system
49 boiling water system [diagram]
50 reactor
51 steam and recirculation water flow paths
52 steam turbine
53 generator
54 circulation pump (recirculation pump)
55 coolant system (cooling with water from river)
56 **radioactive waste storage** in salt mine
57-68 geological structure of abandoned salt mine converted for disposal of radioactive waste (nuclear waste)
57 Lower Keuper
58 Upper Muschelkalk
59 Middle Muschelkalk
60 Lower Muschelkalk
61 Bunter downthrow
62 residue of leached (lixiviated) Zechstein (Upper Permian)
63 Aller rock salt
64 Leine rock salt
65 Stassfurt seam (potash salt seam, potash salt bed)
66 Stassfurt salt
67 grenzanhydrite
68 Zechstein shale
69 shaft
70 minehead buildings
71 storage chamber
72 storage of medium-active waste in salt mine
73 511 m level
74 protective screen (anti-radiation screen)
75 lead glass window
76 storage chamber
77 drum containing radioactive waste
78 television camera
79 charging chamber
80 control desk (control panel)
81 upward ventilator
82 shielded container
83 490 m level

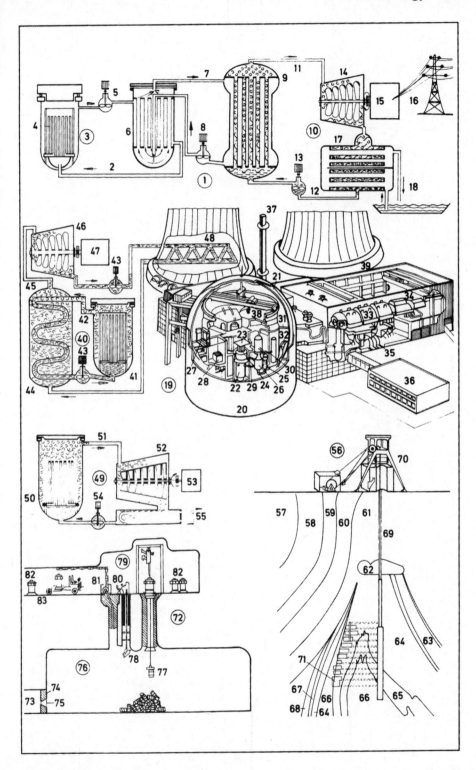

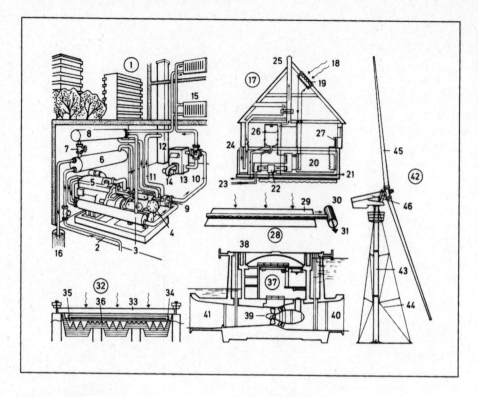

1 heat pump system
2 source water inlet
3 cooling water heat exchanger
4 compressor
5 natural-gas or diesel engine
6 evaporator
7 pressure release valve
8 condenser
9 waste-gas heat exchanger
10 flow pipe
11 vent pipe
12 chimney
13 boiler
14 fan
15 radiator
16 sink
17-36 utilization of solar energy
17 solar (solar-heated) house
18 solar radiation (sunlight, insolation)
19 collector
20 hot reservoir (heat reservoir)
21 power supply
22 heat pump
23 water outlet
24 air supply
25 flue

26 hot water supply
27 radiator heating
28 flat plate solar collector
29 blackened receiver surface with asphalted aluminium (*Am.* aluminum) foil
30 steel tube
31 heat transfer fluid
32 flat plate solar collector, containing solar cell
33 glass cover
34 solar cell
35 air ducts
36 insulation
37 tidal power plant [section]
38 dam
39 reversible turbine
40 turbine inlet for water from the sea
41 turbine inlet for water from the basin
42 wind power plant (wind generator aerogenerator)
43 truss tower
44 guy wire
45 rotor
46 generator with variable pitch for power regulation

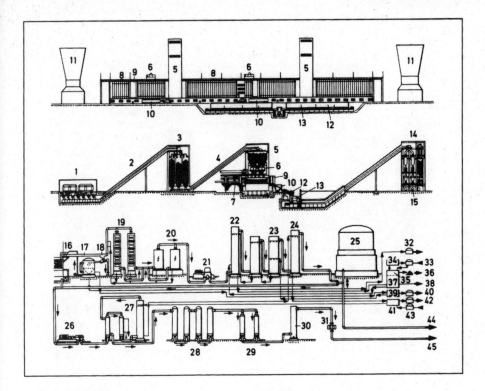

1-15 coking plant
1 dumping of coking coal
2 belt conveyor
3 blending bunker
4 service bunker conveyor
5 service bunker
6 larry car (larry, charging car)
7 pusher ram
8 battery of coke ovens
9 coke guide
10 quenching car, with engine
11 quenching tower
12 coke loading bay (coke wharf)
13 coke wharf conveyor
14 screening of coke and breeze
15 coke loading
16-45 coke-oven gas processing
16 discharge (release) of gas from the coke ovens
17 gas-collecting main
18 coal tar extraction
19 gas cooler
20 electrostatic precipitator
21 gas extractor
22 hydrogen sulphide (*Am.* hydrogen sulfide) scrubber (hydrogen sulphide wet collector)
23 ammonia scrubber (ammonia wet collector)

24 benzene (benzol) scrubber
25 gas holder
26 gas compressor
27 debenzoling by cooler and heat exchanger
28 desulphurization (*Am.* desulfurization) of pressure gas
29 gas cooling
30 gas drying
31 gas meter
32 crude tar tank
33 sulphuric acid (*Am.* sulfuric acid) supply
34 production of sulphuric acid (*Am.* sulfuric acid)
35 production of ammonium sulphate (*Am.* ammonium sulfate)
36 ammonium sulphate (*Am.* ammonium sulfate)
37 recovery plant for recovering the scrubbing agents
38 waste water discharge
39 phenol extraction from the gas water
40 crude phenol tank
41 production of crude benzol (crude benzene)
42 crude benzol (crude benzene) tank
43 scrubbing oil tank
44 low-pressure gas main
45 high-pressure gas main

1 sawmill	23 roller table
2 vertical frame saw (*Am.* gang mill)	24 undercut swing saw
3 saw blades	25 piling
4 feed roller	26 roller trestles
5 guide roller	27 gantry crane
6 fluting (grooving, grooves)	28 crane motor
7 oil pressure gauge (*Am.* gage)	29 pivoted log grips
8 saw frame	30 roundwood (round timber)
9 feed indicator	31 log dump
10 log capacity scale	32 squared timber store
11 auxiliary carriage	33 sawn logs
12 carriage	34 planks
13 log grips	35 boards (planks)
14 remote control panel	36 squared timber
15 carriage motor	37 stack bearer
16 truck for splinters (splints)	
17 endless log chain (*Am.* jack chain)	
18 stop plate	
19 log-kicker arms	
20 cross conveyor	
21 washer (washing machine)	
22 cross chain conveyor for sawn timber	

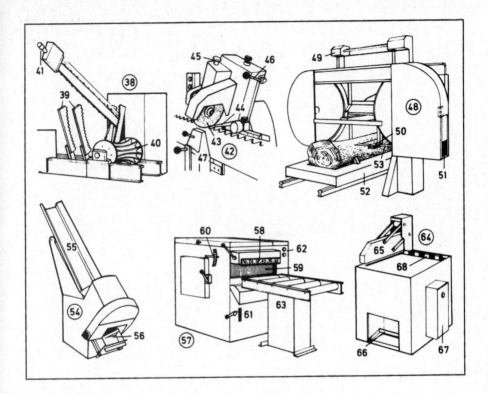

38 automatic cross-cut chain saw
39 log grips
40 feed roller
41 chain-tensioning device
42 saw-sharpening machine
43 grinding wheel (teeth grinder)
44 feed pawl
45 depth adjustment for the teeth grinder
46 lifter (lever) for the grinder chuck
47 holding device for the saw blade
48 horizontal bandsaw for sawing logs
49 height adjustment
50 chip remover
51 chip extractor
52 carriage
53 bandsaw blade
54 automatic blocking saw
55 feed channel
56 discharge opening
57 twin edger (double edger)
58 breadth scale (width scale)
59 kick-back guard (plates)

60 height scale
61 in-feed scale
62 indicator lamps
63 feed table
64 undercut swing saw
65 automatic hold-down with protective hood
66 foot switch
67 distribution board (panelboard)
68 length stop

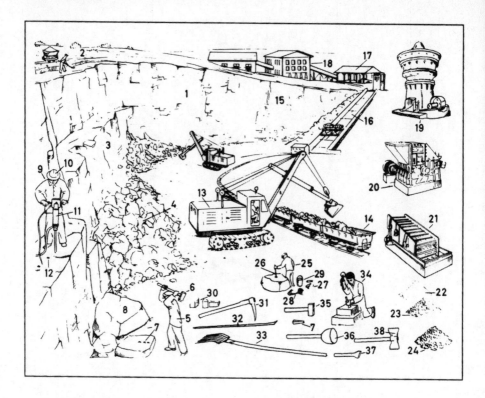

1 **quarry,** an open-cast working
2 overburden
3 working face
4 loose rock pile (blasted rock)
5 quarryman (quarrier), a quarry worker
6 sledge hammer
7 wedge
8 block of stone
9 driller
10 safety helmet
11 hammer drill (hard-rock drill)
12 borehole
13 universal excavator
14 large-capacity truck
15 rock face
16 inclined hoist
17 primary crusher
18 stone-crushing plant
19 coarse rotary (gyratory) crusher; *sim.:* fine rotary (gyratory) crusher
20 hammer crusher (impact crusher)
21 vibrating screen
22 screenings (fine dust)
23 stone chippings
24 crushed stone
25 shot firer
26 measuring rod
27 blasting cartridge
28 fuse (blasting fuse)
29 plugging sand (stemming sand) bucket
30 dressed stone
31 pick
32 crowbar (pinch bar)
33 fork
34 stonemason
35-38 stonemason's tools
35 stonemason's hammer
36 mallet
37 drove chisel (drove, boaster, broad chisel)
38 dressing axe (*Am.* ax)

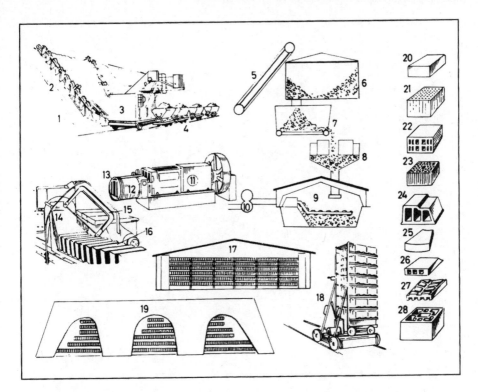

1 clay pit
2 loam, an impure clay (raw clay)
3 overburden excavator, a large-scale excavator
4 narrow-gauge (*Am.* narrow-gage) track system
5 inclined hoist
6 souring chambers
7 box feeder (feeder)
8 edge runner mill (edge mill, pan grinding mill)
9 rolling plant
10 double-shaft trough mixer (mixer)
11 extrusion press (brick-pressing machine)
12 vacuum chamber
13 die
14 clay column
15 cutter (brick cutter)
16 unfired brick (green brick)
17 drying shed
18 mechanical finger car (stacker truck)

19 circular kiln (brick kiln)
20 solid brick (building brick)
21, 22 perforated bricks and hollow blocks
21 perforated brick with vertical perforations
22 hollow clay block with horizontal perforations
23 hollow clay block with vertical perforations
24 floor brick
25 compass brick (radial brick, radiating brick)
26 hollow flooring block
27 paving brick
28 cellular brick [for fireplaces] (chimney brick)

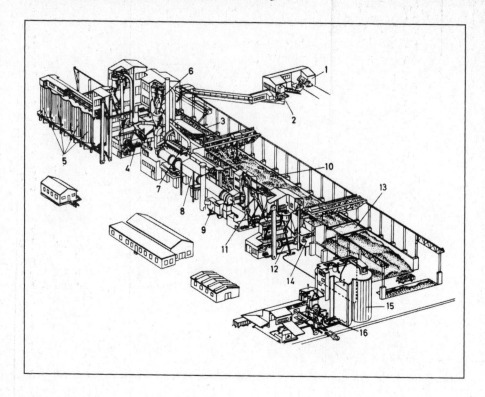

1 raw materials (limestone, clay and marl)
2 hammer crusher (hammer mill)
3 raw material store
4 raw mill for simultaneously grinding and drying the raw materials with exhaust gas from the heat exchanger
5 raw meal silos
6 heat exchanger (cyclone heat exchanger)
7 dust collector (an electrostatic precipitator) for the heat exchanger exhaust from the raw mill
8 rotary kiln
9 clinker cooler
10 clinker store
11 primary air blower
12 cement-grinding mill
13 gypsum store
14 gypsum crusher
15 cement silo
16 cement-packing plant

1 grinding cylinder (ball mill) for the preparation of the raw material in water
2 sample sagger (saggar, seggar), with aperture for observing the firing process
3 bottle kiln (beehive kiln) [diagram]
4 firing mould (*Am.* mold)
5 tunnel kiln
6 Seger cone (pyrometric cone, *Am.* Orton cone) for measuring high temperatures
7 de-airing pug mill (de-airing pug press), an extrusion press
8 clay column
9 thrower throwing a ball (bat) of clay
10 slug of clay
11 turntable; *sim.:* potter's wheel
12 filter press
13 filter cake
14 jiggering, with a profiling tool; *sim.:* jollying

15 plaster mould (*Am.* mold) for slip casting
16 turntable glazing machine
17 porcelain painter (china painter)
18 hand-painted vase
19 repairer
20 pallet (modelling, *Am.* modeling, tool)
21 shards (sherds, potsherds)

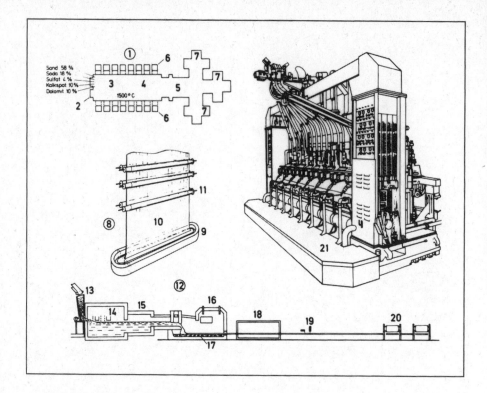

1-20 sheet glass production (flat glass production)
1 glass furnace (tank furnace) for the Fourcault process [diagram]
2 filling end, for feeding in the batch (frit)
3 melting bath
4 refining bath (fining bath)
5 working baths (working area)
6 burners
7 drawing machines
8 Fourcault glass-drawing machine
9 slot
10 glass ribbon (ribbon of glass, sheet of glass) being drawn upwards
11 rollers (drawing rolls)
12 float glass process
13 batch (frit) feeder (funnel)
14 melting bath
15 cooling tank
16 float bath in a protective inert-gas atmosphere

17 molten tin
18 annealing lehr
19 automatic cutter
20 stacking machines
21 IS (individual-section) machine, a bottle-making machine

22-37 blowing processes
22 blow-and-blow process
23 introduction of the gob of molten glass
24 first blowing
25 suction
26 transfer from the parison mould (*Am.* mold) to the blow mould (*Am.* mold)
27 reheating
28 blowing (suction, final shaping)
29 delivery of the completed vessel
30 press-and-blow process
31 introduction of the gob of molten glass
32 plunger

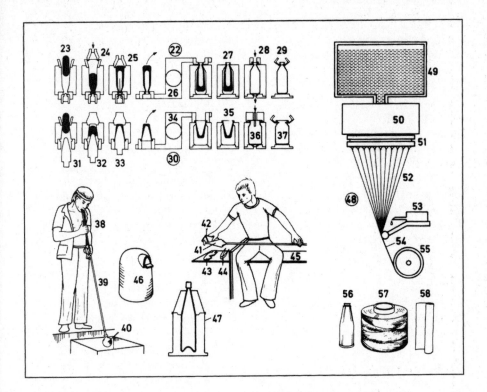

33 pressing
34 transfer from the press mould (*Am.* mold) to the blow mould (*Am.* mold)
35 reheating
36 blowing (suction, final shaping)
37 delivery of the completed vessel
38-47 glassmaking (glassblowing, glassblowing by hand, glass forming)
38 glassmaker (glassblower)
39 blowing iron
40 gob
41 hand-blown goblet
42 clappers for shaping the base (foot) of the goblet
43 trimming tool
44 tongs
45 glassmaker's chair (gaffer's chair)
46 covered glasshouse pot
47 mould (*Am.* mold), into which the parison is blown

48-55 production of glass fibre (*Am.* glass fiber)
48 continuous filament process
49 glass furnace
50 bushing containing molten glass
51 bushing tips
52 glass filaments
53 sizing
54 strand (thread)
55 spool
56-58 glass fibre (*Am.* glass fiber) **products**
56 glass yarn (glass thread)
57 sleeved glass yarn (glass thread)
58 glass wool

163　Cotton Spinning I

1-13 supply of cotton
1　ripe cotton boll
2　full cop (cop wound with weft yarn)
3　compressed cotton bale
4　jute wrapping
5　steel band
6　identification mark of the bale
7　bale opener (bale breaker)
8　cotton-feeding brattice
9　cotton feed
10　dust extraction fan
11　duct to the dust-collecting chamber
12　drive motor
13　conveyor brattice
14　**double scutcher** (machine with two scutchers)
15　lap cradle
16　rack head
17　starting handle
18　handwheel, for raising and lowering the rack head
19　movable lap-turner
20　calender rollers
21　cover for the perforated cylinders
22　dust escape flue (dust discharge flue)
23　drive motors (beater drive motors)
24　beater driving shaft
25　three-blade beater (Kirschner beater)
26　grid [for impurities to drop]
27　pedal roller (pedal cylinder)
28　control lever for the pedal roller, a pedal lever
29　variable change-speed gear
30　cone drum box
31　stop and start levers for the hopper
32　wooden hopper delivery roller
33　hopper feeder
34　**carding machine** (card, carding engine)
35　card can (carding can), for receiving the coiled sliver
36　can holder
37　calender rollers
38　carded sliver (card sliver)

39　vibrating doffer comb
40　start-stop lever
41　grinding-roller bearing
42　doffer
43　cylinder
44　flat clearer
45　flats
46　supporting pulleys for the flats
47　scutcher lap (carded lap)
48　scutcher lap holder
49　drive motor with flat belt
50　main drive pulley (fast-and-loose drive pulley)
51　principle of the card (of the carding engine)
52　fluted feed roller
53　licker-in (taker-in, licker-in roller)
54　licker-in undercasing
55　cylinder undercasing
56　**combing machine** (comber)
57　drive gearbox (driving gear)
58　laps ready for combing
59　calender rollers
60　comber draw box
61　counter
62　coiler top
63　principle of the comber
64　lap
65　bottom nipper
66　top nipper
67　top comb
68　combing cylinder
69　plain part of the cylinder
70　needled part of the cylinder
71　detaching rollers
72　carded and combed sliver

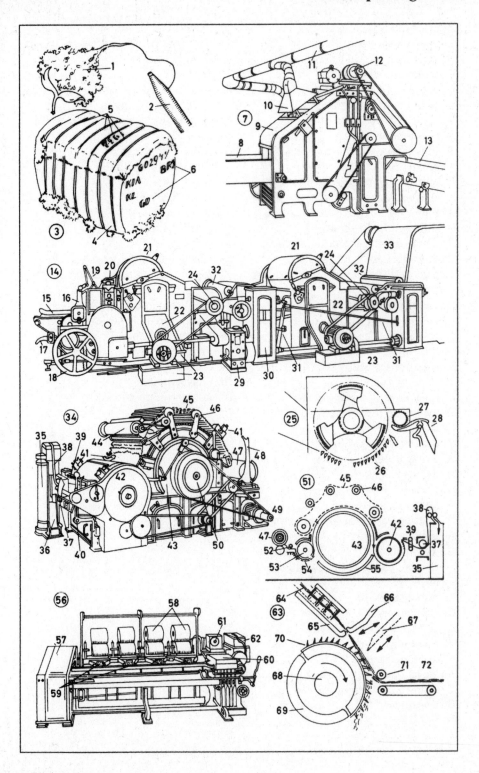

1 **draw frame**
2 gearbox with built-in motor
3 sliver cans
4 broken thread detector roller
5 doubling of the slivers
6 stopping handle
7 draw frame cover
8 indicator lamps (signal lights)
9 simple four-roller draw frame [diagram]
10 bottom rollers (lower rollers), fluted steel rollers
11 top rollers (upper rollers) covered with synthetic rubber
12 doubled slivers before drafting
13 thin sliver after drafting
14 high-draft system (high-draft draw frame) [diagram]
15 feeding-in of the sliver
16 leather apron (composition apron)
17 guide bar
18 light top roller (guide roller)
19 high-draft speed frame (fly frame, slubbing frame)
20 sliver cans
21 feeding of the slivers to the drafting rollers
22 drafting rollers with top clearers
23 roving bobbins
24 fly frame operator (operative)
25 flyer
26 frame end plate
27 intermediate yarn-forming frame
28 bobbin creel (creel)
29 roving emerging from the drafting rollers
30 lifter rail (separating rail)
31 spindle drive
32 stopping handle
33 gearbox, with built-on motor
34 **ring frame** (ring spinning frame)
35 three-phase motor
36 motor base plate (bedplate)
37 lifting bolt [for motor removal]
38 control gear for spindle speed
39 gearbox

40 change wheels for varying the spindle speed [to change the yarn count]
41 full creel
42 shafts and levers for raising and lowering the ring rail
43 spindles with separators
44 suction box connected to the front roller underclearers
45 **standard ring spindle**
46 spindle shaft
47 roller bearing
48 wharve (pulley)
49 spindle catch
50 spindle rail
51 ring and traveller (*Am.* traveler)
52 top of the ring tube (of the bobbin)
53 yarn (thread)
54 ring fitted into the ring rail
55 traveller (*Am.* traveler)
56 yarn wound onto the bobbin
57 **doubling frame**
58 creel, with cross-wound cheeses
59 delivery rollers
60 bobbins of doubled yarn

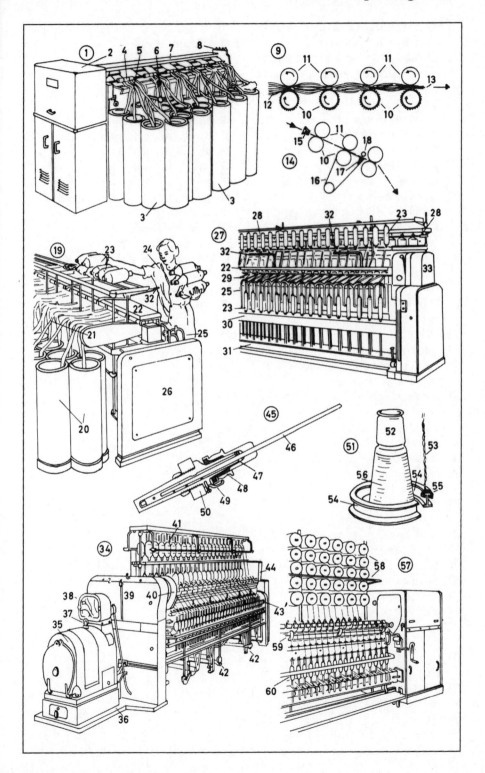

165 Weaving I

1-57 processes preparatory to weaving
1 cone-winding frame
2 travelling (*Am.* traveling) blower
3 guide rail, for the travelling (*Am.* traveling) blower
4 blowing assembly
5 blower aperture
6 superstructure for the blower rail
7 full-cone indicator
8 cross-wound cone
9 cone creel
10 grooved cylinder
11 guiding slot for cross-winding the threads
12 side frame, housing the motor
13 tension and slub-catching device
14 off-end framing with filter
15 yarn package, a ring tube or mule cop
16 yarn package container
17 starting and stopping lever
18 self-threading guide
19 broken thread stop motion
20 thread clearer
21 weighting disc (disk) for tensioning the thread
22 warping machine
23 fan
24 cross-wound cone
25 creel
26 adjustable comb
27 warping machine frame
28 yarn length recorder
29 warp beam
30 beam flange
31 guard rail
32 driving drum (driving cylinder)
33 belt drive
34 motor
35 release for starting the driving drum
36 screw for adjusting the comb setting
37 drop pins, for stopping the machine when a thread breaks
38 guide bar
39 drop pin rollers
40 indigo dying and sizing machine
41 take-off stand
42 warp beam
43 warp
44 wetting trough
45 immersion roller
46 squeeze roller (mangle)
47 dye liquor padding trough
48 air oxidation passage
49 washing trough
50 drying cylinders for pre-drying
51 tension compensator (tension equalizer)
52 sizing machine
53 drying cylinders
54 *for cotton:* stenter; *for wool:* tenter
55 beaming machine
56 sized warp beam
57 rollers

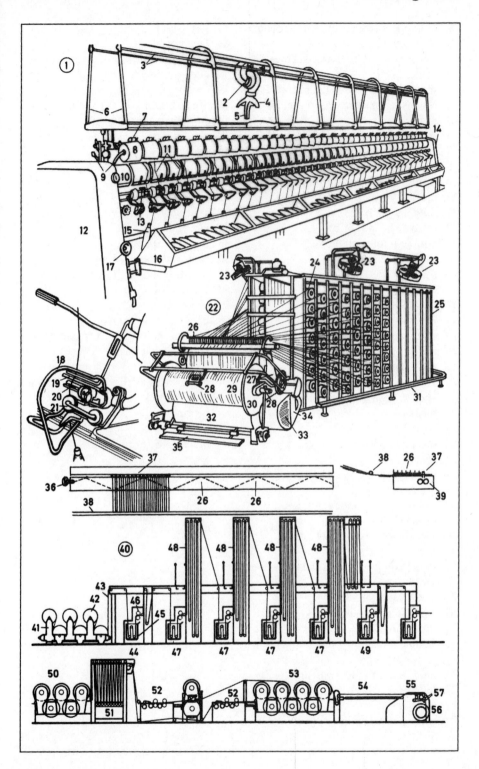

1 **weaving machine** (automatic loom)
2 pick counter (tachometer)
3 shaft (heald shaft, heald frame) guide
4 shafts (heald shafts, heald frames)
5 rotary battery for weft replenishment
6 sley (slay) cap
7 weft pirn
8 starting and stopping handle
9 shuttle box, with shuttles
10 reed
11 selvedge (selvage)
12 cloth (woven fabric)
13 temple (cloth temple)
14 electric weft feeler
15 flywheel
16 breast beam board
17 picking stick (pick stick)
18 electric motor
19 cloth take-up motion
20 cloth roller (fabric roller)
21 can for empty pirns
22 lug strap, for moving the picking stick
23 fuse box
24 loom framing
25 metal shuttle tip
26 shuttle
27 heald (heddle, wire heald, wire heddle)
28 eye (eyelet, heald eyelet, heddle eyelet)
29 eye (shuttle eye)
30 pirn
31 metal contact sleeve for the weft feeler
32 slot for the feeler
33 spring-clip pirn holder
34 drop wire
35 weaving machine (automatic loom) [side elevation]
36 heald shaft guiding wheels
37 backrest
38 lease rods
39 warp (warp thread)
40 shed
41 sley (slay)
42 race board
43 stop rod blade for the stop motion
44 bumper steel
45 bumper steel stop rod
46 breast beam
47 cloth take-up roller
48 warp beam
49 beam flange
50 crankshaft
51 crankshaft wheel
52 connector
53 sley (slay)
54 lam rods
55 camshaft wheel
56 camshaft (tappet shaft)
57 tappet (shedding tappet)
58 treadle lever
59 let-off motion
60 beam motion control
61 rope of the warp let-off motion
62 let-off weight lever
63 control weight [for the treadle]
64 picker with leather or bakelite pad
65 picking stick buffer
66 picking cam
67 picking bowl
68 picking stick return spring

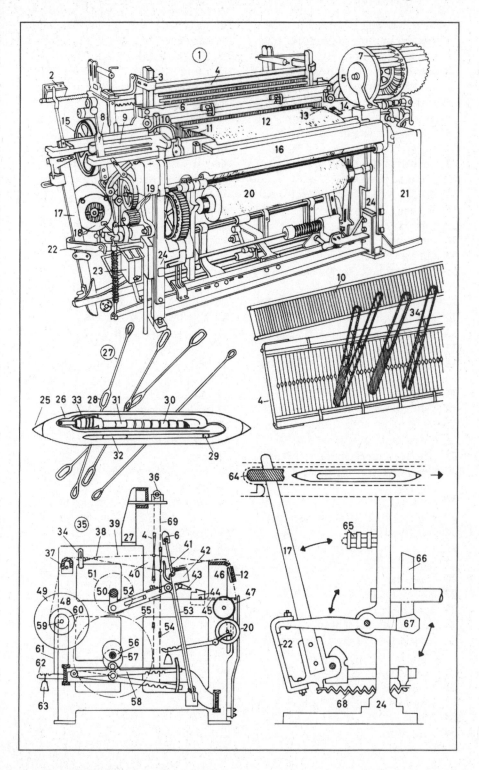

1-66 hosiery mill

1 circular knitting machine for the manufacture of tubular fabric
2 yarn guide support post (thread guide support post)
3 yarn guide (thread guide)
4 bottle bobbin
5 yarn-tensioning device
6 yarn feeder
7 handwheel for rotating the machine by hand
8 needle cylinder (cylindrical needle holder)
9 tubular fabric
10 fabric drum (fabric box, fabric container)
11 needle cylinder (cylindrical needle holder) [section]
12 latch needles arranged in a circle
13 cam housing
14 needle cams
15 needle trick
16 cylinder diameter (*also:* diameter of tubular fabric)
17 thread (yarn)
18 Cotton's patent flat knitting machine for ladies' fully-fashioned hose
19 pattern control chain
20 side frame
21 knitting head
22 starting rod
23 Raschel warp-knitting machine
24 warp (warp beam)
25 yarn-distributing (yarn-dividing) beam
26 beam flange
27 row of needles
28 needle bar
29 fabric (Raschel fabric) [curtain lace and net fabrics] on the fabric roll
30 handwheel
31 motor drive gear
32 take-down weight
33 frame
34 base plate
35 hand flat (flat-bed) knitting machine
36 thread (yarn)
37 return spring
38 support for springs
39 carriage
40 feeder-selecting device
41 carriage handles
42 scale for regulating size of stitches
43 course counter (tachometer)
44 machine control lever
45 carriage rail
46 back row of needles
47 front row of needles
48 knitted fabric
49 tension bar
50 tension weight
51 needle bed showing knitting action
52 teeth of knock-over bit
53 needles in parallel rows
54 yarn guide (thread guide)
55 needle bed
56 retaining plate for latch needles
57 guard cam
58 sinker
59 needle-raising cam
60 needle butt
61 latch needle
62 loop
63 pushing the needle through the fabric
64 yarn guide (thread guide) placing yarn in the needle hook
65 loop formation
66 casting off of loop

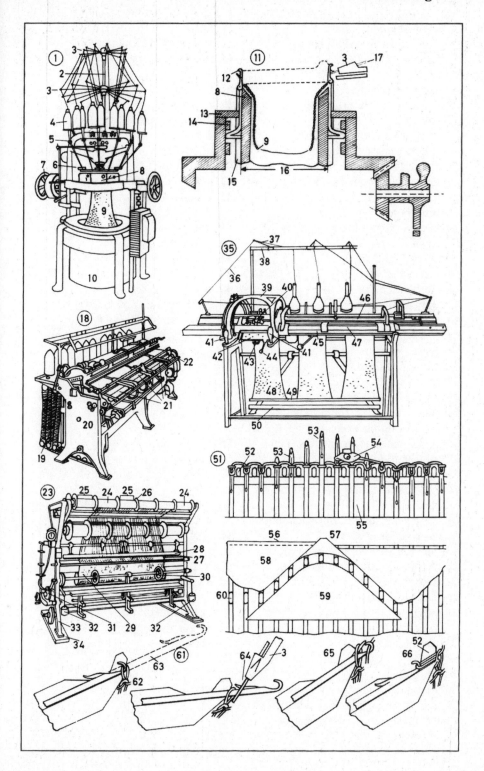

1-65 finishing

1 rotary milling (fulling) machine for felting the woollen (*Am.* woolen) fabric
2 pressure weights
3 top milling roller (top fulling roller)
4 drive wheel of bottom milling roller (bottom fulling roller)
5 fabric guide roller
6 bottom milling roller (bottom fulling roller)
7 draft board
8 open-width scouring machine for finer fabrics
9 fabric being drawn off the machine
10 drive gearbox
11 water inlet pipe
12 drawing-in roller
13 scroll-opening roller
14 pendulum-type hydro-extractor (centrifuge), for extracting liquors from the fabric
15 machine base
16 casing over suspension
17 outer casing containing rotating cage (rotating basket)
18 hydro-extractor (centrifuge) lid
19 stop-motion device (stopping device)
20 automatic starting and braking device
21 *for cotton:* stenter; *for wool:* tenter
22 air-dry fabric
23 operator's (operative's) platform
24 feeding of fabric by guides onto stenter (tenter) pins or clips
25 electric control panel
26 initial overfeed to produce shrink-resistant fabric when dried
27 thermometer
28 drying section
29 air outlet
30 plaiter (fabric-plaiting device)
31 wire-roller fabric-raising machine for producing raised or nap surface
32 drive gearbox
33 unraised cloth
34 wire-covered rollers
35 plaiter (cuttling device)
36 raised fabric
37 plaiting-down platform
38 rotary press (calendering machine), for press finishing
39 fabric
40 control buttons and control wheels
41 heated press bowl
42 rotary cloth-shearing machine
43 suction slot, for removing loose fibres (*Am.* fibers)
44 doctor blade (cutting cylinder)
45 protective guard
46 rotating brush
47 curved scray entry
48 treadle control
49 [non-shrinking] decatizing (decating) fabric-finishing machine
50 perforated decatizing (decating) cylinder
51 piece of fabric
52 cranked control handle
53 ten-colour (*Am.* ten-color) roller printing machine
54 base of the machine
55 drive motor
56 blanket [of rubber or felt]
57 fabric after printing (printed fabric)
58 electric control panel (control unit)
59 screen printing
60 mobile screen frame
61 squeegee
62 pattern stencil
63 screen table
64 fabric gummed down on table ready for printing
65 screen printing operator (operative)

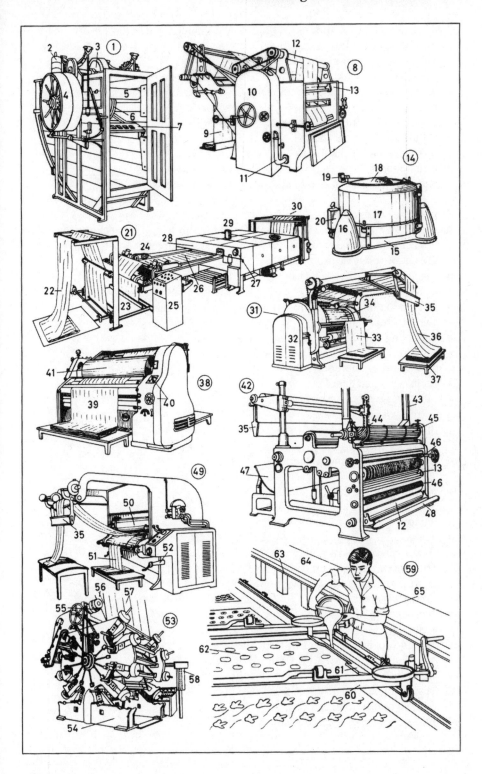

1-34 manufacture of **continuous filament and staple fibre** (*Am.* fiber) **viscose rayon yarns** by means of the viscose process

1-12 from raw material to viscose rayon

1 basic material [beech and spruce cellulose in form of sheets]

2 mixing cellulose sheets

3 caustic soda

4 steeping cellulose sheets in caustic soda

5 pressing out excess caustic soda

6 shredding the cellulose sheets

7 maturing (controlled oxidation) of the alkali-cellulose crumbs

8 carbon disulphide (*Am.* carbon disulfide)

9 conversion of alkali-cellulose into cellulose xanthate

10 dissolving the xanthate in caustic soda for the preparation of the viscose spinning solution

11 vacuum ripening tanks

12 filter presses

13-27 from viscose to viscose rayon thread

13 metering pump

14 multi-holed spinneret (spinning jet)

15 coagulating (spinning) bath for converting (coagulating) viscose (viscous solution) into solid filaments

16 Godet wheel, a glass pulley

17 Topham centrifugal pot (box) for twisting the filaments into yarn

18 viscose rayon cake

19-27 processing of the cake

19 washing

20 desulphurizing (desulphurization, *Am.* desulfurizing, desulfurization)

21 bleaching

22 treating of cake to give filaments softness and suppleness

23 hydro-extraction to remove surplus moisture

24 drying in heated room

25 winding yarn from cake into cone form

26 cone-winding machine

27 viscose rayon yarn on cone ready for use

28-34 from viscose spinning solution to viscose rayon staple fibre (*Am.* fiber)

28 filament tow

29 overhead spray washing plant

30 cutting machine for cutting filament tow to desired length

31 multiple drying machine for cut-up staple fibre (*Am.* fiber) layer (lap)

32 conveyor belt (conveyor)

33 baling press

34 bale of viscose rayon ready for dispatch (despatch)

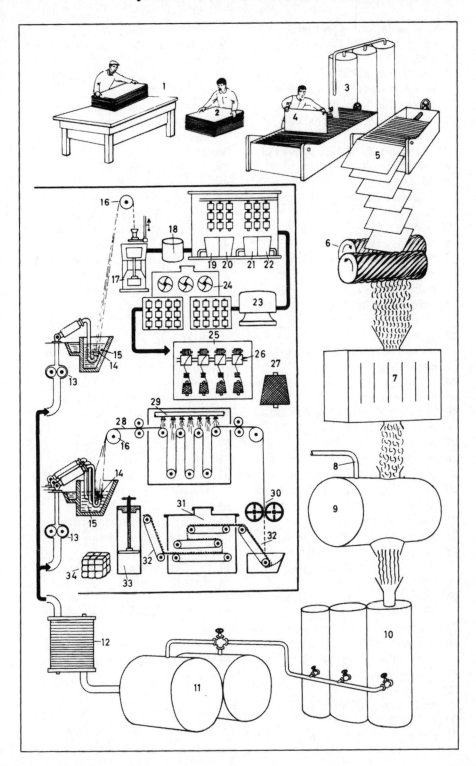

1-62 manufacture of **polyamide** (nylon 6, perlon) **fibres** (*Am.* fibers)

1 coal [raw material for manufacture of polyamide (nylon 6, perlon) fibres (*Am.* fibers)]

2 coking plant for dry coal distillation

3 extraction of coal tar and phenol

4 gradual distillation of tar

5 condenser

6 benzene extraction and dispatch (despatch)

7 chlorine

8 benzene chlorination

9 monochlorobenzene (chlorobenzene)

10 caustic soda solution

11 evaporation of chlorobenzene and caustic soda

12 autoclave

13 sodium chloride (common salt), a by-product

14 phenol (carbolic acid)

15 hydrogen inlet

16 hydrogenation of phenol to produce raw cyclohexanol

17 distillation

18 pure cyclohexanol

19 oxidation (dehydrogenation)

20 formation of cyclohexanone (pimehinketone)

21 hydroxylamine inlet

22 formation of cyclohexanoxime

23 addition of sulphuric acid (*Am.* sulfuric acid) to effect molecular rearrangement

24 ammonia to neutralize sulphuric acid (*Am.* sulfuric acid)

25 formation of caprolactam oil

26 ammonium sulphate (*Am.* ammonium sulfate) solution

27 cooling cylinder

28 caprolactam

29 weighing apparatus

30 melting pot

31 pump

32 filter

33 polymerization in the autoclave

34 cooling of the polyamide

35 solidification of the polyamide

36 vertical lift (*Am.* elevator)

37 extractor for separating the polyamide from the remaining lactam oil

38 drier

39 dry polyamide chips

40 chip container

41 top of spinneret for melting the polyamide and forcing it through spinneret holes (spinning jets)

42 spinneret holes (spinning jets)

43 solidification of polyamide filaments in the cooling tower

44 collection of extruded filaments into thread form

45 preliminary stretching (preliminary drawing)

46 stretching (cold-drawing) of the polyamide thread to achieve high tensile strength

47 final stretching (final drawing)

48 washing of yarn packages

49 drying chamber

50 rewinding

51 polyamide cone

52 polyamide cone ready for dispatch (despatch)

53 mixer

54 polymerization under vacua

55 stretching (drawing)

56 washing

57 finishing of tow for spinning

58 drying of tow

59 crimping of tow

60 cutting of tow into normal staple lengths

61 polyamide staple

62 bale of polyamide staple

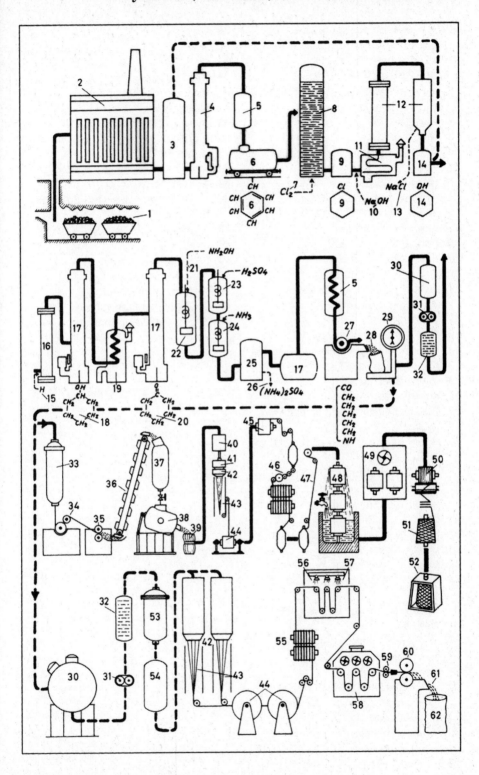

1-29 **weaves** [black squares: warp thread raised, weft thread lowered; white squares: weft thread raised, warp thread lowered]
1 plain weave (tabby weave) [weave viewed from above]
2 warp thread
3 weft thread
4 draft (point paper design) for plain weave
5 threading draft
6 denting draft (reed-threading draft)
7 raised warp thread
8 lowered warp thread
9 tie-up of shafts in pairs
10 treadling diagram
11 draft for basket weave (hopsack weave, matt weave)
12 pattern repeat
13 draft for warp rib weave
14 section of warp rib fabric, a section through the warp
15 lowered weft thread
16 raised weft thread
17 first and second warp threads [raised]
18 third and fourth warp threads [lowered]
19 draft for combined rib weave
20 selvedge (selvage) thread draft (additional shafts for the selvedge)
21 draft for the fabric shafts
22 tie-up of selvedge (selvage) shafts
23 tie-up of fabric shafts
24 selvedge (selvage) in plain weave
25 section through combination rib weave
26 thread interlacing of reversible warp-faced cord
27 draft (point paper design) for reversible warp-faced cord
28 interlacing points
29 weaving draft for honeycomb weave in the fabric
30-48 basic knits
30 loop, an open loop

31 head
32 side
33 neck
34 head interlocking point
35 neck interlocking point
36 closed loop
37 mesh [with inlaid yarn]
38 diagonal floating yarn (diagonal floating thread)
39 loop interlocking at the head
40 float
41 loose floating yarn (loose floating thread)
42 course
43 inlaid yarn
44 tuck and miss stitch
45 pulled-up tuck stitch
46 staggered tuck stitch
47 2×2 tuck and miss stitch
48 double pulled-up tuck stitch

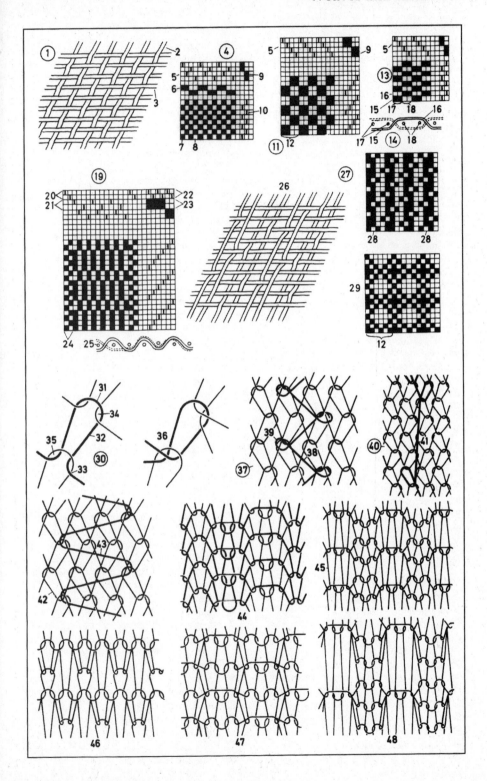

1-52 sulphate (*Am.* sulfate) pulp mill (kraft pulp mill) [in diagram form]
1 chippers with dust extractor
2 rotary screen (riffler)
3 chip packer (chip distributor)
4 blower
5 disintegrator (crusher, chip crusher)
6 dust-settling chamber
7 digester
8 liquor preheater
9 control tap
10 swing pipe
11 blow tank (diffuser)
12 blow valve
13 blow pit (diffuser)
14 turpentine separator
15 centralized separator
16 jet condenser (injection condenser)
17 storage tank for condensate
18 hot water tank
19 heat exchanger
20 filter
21 presorter
22 centrifugal screen
23 rotary sorter (rotary strainer)
24 concentrator (thickener, decker)
25 vat (chest)
26 collecting tank for backwater (low box)
27 conical refiner (cone refiner, Jordan, Jordan refiner)
28 black liquor filter
29 black liquor storage tank
30 condenser
31 separators
32 heaters (heating elements)
33 liquor pump
34 heavy liquor pump
35 mixing tank
36 salt cake storage tank (sodium sulphate storage tank)
37 dissolving tank (dissolver)
38 steam heater
39 electrostatic precipitator
40 air pump
41 storage tank for the uncleared green liquor
42 concentrator (thickener, decker)
43 green liquor preheater
44 concentrator (thickener, decker) for the weak wash liquor (wash water)
45 storage tank for the weak liquor
46 storage tank for the cooking liquor
47 agitator (stirrer)
48 concentrator (thickener, decker)
49 causticizing agitators (causticizing stirrers)
50 classifier
51 lime slaker
52 reconverted lime
53-65 groundwood mill (mechanical pulp mill) [diagram]
53 continuous grinder (continuous chain grinder)
54 strainer (knotter)
55 pulp water pump
56 centrifugal screen
57 screen (sorter)
58 secondary screen (secondary sorter)
59 rejects chest
60 conical refiner (cone refiner, Jordan, Jordan refiner)
61 pulp-drying machine (pulp machine)
62 concentrator (thickener, decker)
63 waste water pump (white water pump, pulp water pump)
64 steam pipe
65 water pipe
66 continuous grinder (continuous chain grinder)
67 feed chain
68 groundwood
69 reduction gear for the feed chain drive
70 stone-dressing device
71 grinding stone (grindstone, pulpstone)
72 spray pipe
73 conical refiner (cone refiner, Jordan, Jordan refiner)
74 handwheel for adjusting the clearance between the knives (blades)
75 rotating bladed cone (rotating bladed plug)
76 stationary bladed shell
77 inlet for unrefined cellulose (chemical wood pulp, chemical pulp) or groundwood pulp (mechanical pulp)
78 outlet for refined cellulose (chemical wood pulp, chemical pulp) or groundwood pulp (mechanical pulp)
79-86 stuff (stock) preparation plant [diagram]
79 conveyor belt (conveyor) for loading cellulose (chemical wood pulp, chemical pulp) or groundwood pulp (mechanical pulp)
80 pulper
81 dump chest
82 cone breaker
83 conical refiner (cone refiner, Jordan, Jordan refiner)
84 refiner
85 stuff chest (stock chest)
86 machine chest (stuff chest)

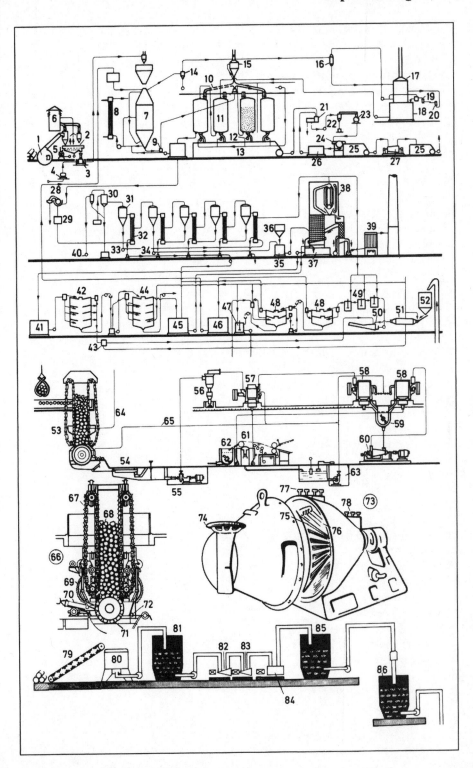

1 stuff chest (stock chest, machine chest), a mixing chest for stuff (stock)

2-10 laboratory apparatus (laboratory equipment) for analysing stuff (stock) and paper

2 Erlenmeyer flask

3 volumetric flask

4 measuring cylinder

5 Bunsen burner

6 tripod

7 petri dish

8 test tube rack

9 balance for measuring basis weight

10 micrometer

11 centrifugal cleaners ahead of the breastbox (headbox, stuff box) of a paper machine

12 standpipe

13-28 paper machine (production line) [diagram]

13 feed-in from the machine chest (stuff chest) with sand table (sand trap, riffler) and knotter

14 wire (machine wire)

15 vacuum box (suction box)

16 suction roll

17 first wet felt

18 second wet felt

19 first press

20 second press

21 offset press

22 drying cylinder (drier)

23 dry felt (drier felt)

24 size press

25 cooling roll

26 calender rolls

27 machine hood

28 delivery reel

29-35 blade coating machine (blade coater)

29 raw paper (body paper)

30 web

31 coater for the top side

32 infrared drier

33 heated drying cylinder

34 coater for the underside (wire side)

35 reel of coated paper

36 calender (super-calender)

37 hydraulic system for the press rolls

38 calender roll

39 unwind station

40 lift platform

41 rewind station (rewinder, re-reeler, reeling machine, re-reeling machine)

42 roll cutter

43 control panel

44 cutter

45 web

46-51 papermaking by hand

46 vatman

47 vat

48 mould (*Am.* mold)

49 coucher (couchman)

50 post ready for pressing

51 felt

1 **hand-setting room** (hand-composing room)
2 composing frame
3 case (typecase)
4 case cabinet (case rack)
5 hand compositor (compositor, typesetter, maker-up)
6 manuscript (typescript)
7 sorts (types, type characters, characters)
8 rack (case) for furniture (spacing material)
9 standing type rack (standing matter rack)
10 storage shelf (shelf for storing formes, *Am.* forms)
11 standing type (standing matter)
12 galley
13 composing stick (setting stick)
14 composing rule (setting rule)
15 type (type matter, matter)
16 page cord
17 bodkin
18 tweezers
19 **Linotype line-composing (line-casting, slug-composing, slug-casting) machine, a multi-magazine machine**
20 distributing mechanism (distributor)
21 type magazines with matrices (matrixes)
22 elevator carrier for distributing the matrices (matrixes)
23 assembler
24 spacebands
25 casting mechanism
26 metal feeder
27 machine-set matter (cast lines, slugs)
28 matrices (matrixes) for hand-setting (sorts)
29 Linotype matrix
30 teeth for the distributing mechanism (distributor)
31 face (type face, matrix)

32-45 **monotype single-unit composing (typesetting) and casting machine** (monotype single-unit composition caster)
32 monotype standard composing (typesetting) machine (keyboard)
33 paper tower
34 paper ribbon
35 justifying scale
36 unit indicator
37 keyboard
38 compressed-air hose
39 monotype casting machine (monotype caster)
40 automatic metal feeder
41 pump compression spring (pump pressure spring)
42 matrix case (die case)
43 paper tower
44 galley with types (letters, characters, cast single types, cast single letters)
45 electric heater (electric heating unit)
46 matrix case (die case)
47 type matrices (matrixes) (letter matrices)
48 guide block for engaging with the cross-slide guide

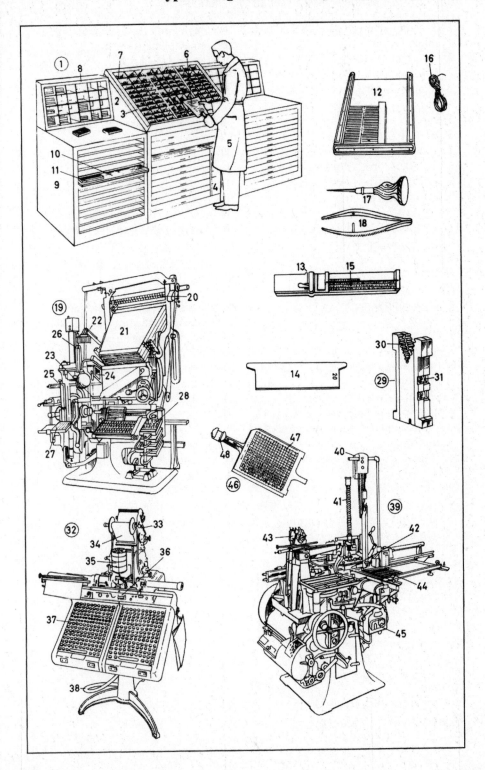

1-17 composition (type matter, type)
1 initial (initial letter)
2 bold type (bold, boldfaced type, heavy type, boldface)
3 semibold type (semibold)
4 line
5 space
6 ligature (double letter)
7 italic type (italics)
8 light face type (light face)
9 extra bold type (extra bold)
10 bold condensed type (bold condensed)
11 majuscule (capital letter, capital, upper case letter)
12 minuscule (small letter, lower case letter)
13 letter spacing (interspacing)
14 small capitals
15 break
16 indention
17 space
18 **type sizes** [one typographic point = 0.376 mm (Didot system), 0.351 mm (Pica system)]
19 six-to-pica (2 points)
20 half nonpareil (four-to-pica) (3 points)
21 brilliant (4 points); *sim.:* diamond (4^1/$_2$ points)
22 pearl (5 points); *sim.:* ruby (*Am.* agate) (5^1/$_2$ points)
23 nonpareil (6 points); *sim.:* minionette (6^1/$_2$ points)
24 minion (7 points)
25 brevier (8 points)
26 bourgeois (9 points)
27 long primer (10 points)
28 pica (12 points)
29 English (14 points)
30 great primer (two-line brevier, *Am.* Columbian) (16 points)
31 paragon (two-line primer) (20 points)
32-37 typefounding (type casting)
32 punch cutter
33 graver (burin, cutter)
34 magnifying glass (magnifier)
35 punch blank (die blank)
36 finished steel punch (finished steel die)
37 punched matrix (stamped matrix, strike, drive)
38 **type** (type character, character)
39 **head**
40 shoulder
41 counter
42 face (type face)
43 type line (bodyline)
44 height to paper (type height)
45 height of shank (height of shoulder)
46 body size (type size, point size)
47 nick
48 set (width)
49 **matrix-boring machine** (matrix-engraving machine), a special-purpose boring machine
50 stand
51 cutter (cutting head)
52 cutting table
53 pantograph carriage
54 V-way
55 pattern
56 pattern table
57 follower
58 pantograph
59 matrix clamp
60 cutter spindle
61 drive motor

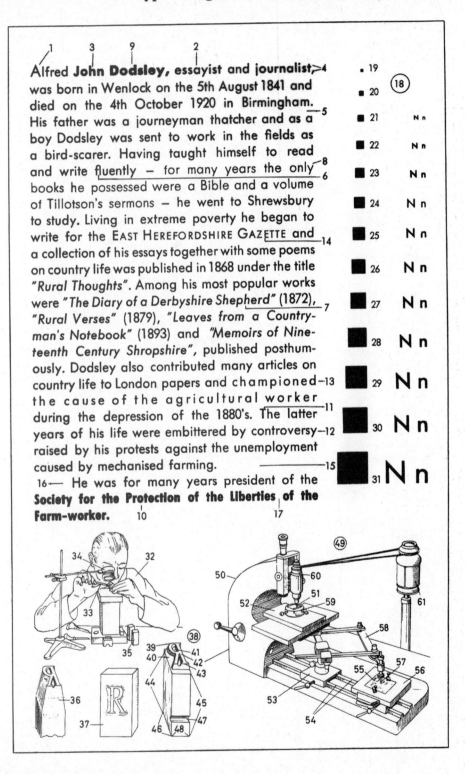

Alfred **John Dodsley,** essayist and journalist, was born in Wenlock on the 5th August 1841 and died on the 4th October 1920 in Birmingham. His father was a journeyman thatcher and as a boy Dodsley was sent to work in the fields as a bird-scarer. Having taught himself to read and write fluently — for many years the only books he possessed were a Bible and a volume of Tillotson's sermons — he went to Shrewsbury to study. Living in extreme poverty he began to write for the EAST HEREFORDSHIRE GAZETTE and a collection of his essays together with some poems on country life was published in 1868 under the title "Rural Thoughts". Among his most popular works were "The Diary of a Derbyshire Shepherd" (1872), "Rural Verses" (1879), "Leaves from a Countryman's Notebook" (1893) and "Memoirs of Nineteenth Century Shropshire", published posthumously. Dodsley also contributed many articles on country life to London papers and championed the cause of the agricultural worker during the depression of the 1880's. The latter years of his life were embittered by controversy raised by his protests against the unemployment caused by mechanised farming. He was for many years president of the **Society for the Protection of the Liberties of the Farm-worker.**

176 Typesetting Room III (Phototypesetting, Photocomposition, Photosetting)

1-21 phototypesetting **configurations**
1 off-line configuration
2, 3 data capture
2 terminal for keying unformatted text
3 text capture and correction terminal
4 layout terminal (page-layout terminal)
5 data carrier, a diskette (floppy disk)
6 (photo)typesetting unit (photo-typesetter)
7 on-line configuration
8 make-up terminal (page make-up terminal)
9 central processing unit (typesetting computer)
10 magnetic tape unit (magnetic tape drive)
11 disk store
12 printer, a laser printer
13 phototypesetting machine (photo-typesetter)
14 text capture (text-capture terminal)
15 typesetter (keyboarder or typographer)
16 screen (monitor)
17 floppy disk drive
18 computer and memory unit with central processing unit and hard disk
19 mouse, an input device
20 mouse mat
21 keyboard, an input device
22 **direct-entry phototypesetter**
23-33 **desktop publishing** (DTP)
23 diskette (floppy disk) with text, layout, and graphics programs
24 scanner (flat-bed scanner)
25 personal computer (PC) or work-station
26 printout (computer printout)
27 raster image processor (RIP)
28 laser phototypesetter
29 proof
30 high-resolution graphics screen, a large-format colour monitor
31 display window
32 typographic parameters
33 (typographic) command window
34 film copier
35-46 **cathode ray tube** (CRT) **typesetter**
35 scanning system
36 scan-generating (scanning) cath-ode ray tube (CRT)
37 lens
38 character grid (matrix case)
39 condenser lens
40 photomultiplier
41 output system
42 video amplifier
43 character-generating tube (CRT character generator)
44 exposure plane
45 matrix case
46 guide claw

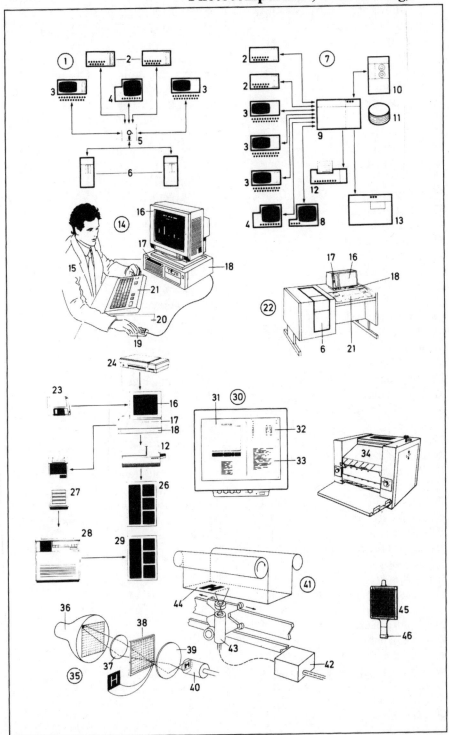

1 overhead process camera (over-head copying camera)
2 focusing screen (ground glass screen)
3 hinged screen holder
4 graticule
5 control console
6 hinged bracket-mounted control panel
7 percentage focusing charts
8 vacuum film holder
9 screen magazine
10 bellows
11 standard
12 register device
13 overhead gantry
14 copyboard
15 copyholder
16 lamp bracket
17 xenon lamp
18 copy (original)
19 retouching and stripping desk
20 illuminated screen
21 height and angle adjustment
22 copyboard
23 linen tester, a magnifying glass
24 universal process and reproduction camera
25 camera body
26 bellows
27 lens carrier
28 angled mirror
29 stand
30 copyboard
31 halogen lamp
32 vertical process camera, a compact camera
33 camera body
34 focusing screen (ground glass screen)
35 vacuum back
36 control panel
37 flash lamp
38 mirror for right-reading images
39 scanner (colour, *Am.* color, correction unit)
40 base frame
41 lamp compartment
42 xenon lamp housing
43 feed motors
44 transparency arm
45 scanning drum
46 scanning head
47 mask-scanning head
48 mask drum
49 recording space
50 daylight cassette
51 colour (*Am.* color) computer with control unit and selective colour correction
52 engraving machine
53 seamless engraving adjustment
54 drive clutch
55 clutch flange
56 drive unit
57 machine bed
58 equipment carrier
59 bed slide
60 control panel
61 bearing block
62 tailstock
63 scanning head
64 copy cylinder
65 centre (*Am.* center) bearing
66 engraving system
67 printing cylinder
68 cylinder arm
69 electronics (electronic) cabinet
70 computers
71 program input
72 automatic film processor for scanner films

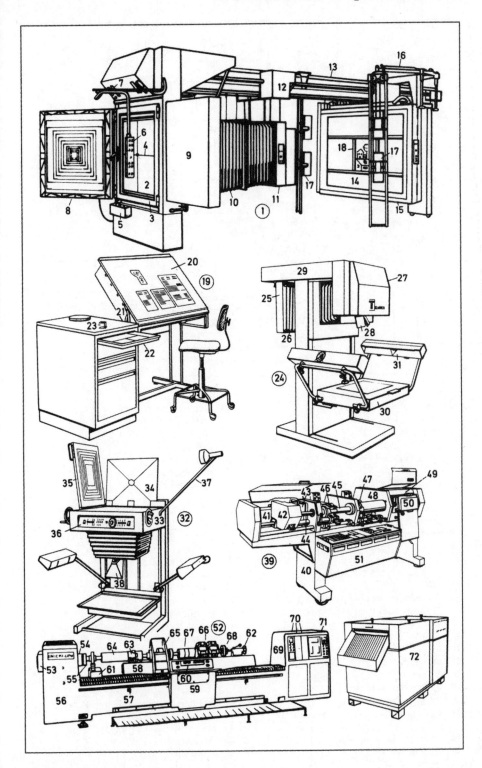

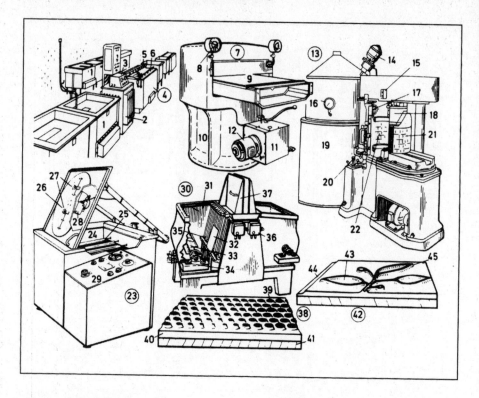

1-6 electrotyping plant
1 cleaning tank
2 rectifier
3 measuring and control unit
4 electroplating tank (electroplating bath, electroplating vat)
5 anode rod (with copper anodes)
6 plate rod (cathode)
7 **hydraulic moulding (*Am.* molding) press**
8 pressure gauge (*Am.* gage) (manometer)
9 apron
10 round base
11 hydraulic pressure pump
12 drive motor
13 **curved plate casting machine** (curved electrotype casting machine)
14 motor
15 control knobs
16 pyrometer
17 mouth piece
18 core
19 melting furnace
20 starting lever
21 cast curved plate (cast curved electrotype) for rotary printing
22 fixed mould (*Am.* mold)
23 **etching machine**

24 etching tank with etching solution (etchant, mordant) and filming agent (film former)
25 paddles
26 turntable
27 plate clamp
28 drive motor
29 control unit
30 **twin etching machine**
31 etching tank (etching bath) [in section]
32 photoprinted zinc plate
33 paddle
34 outlet cock (drain cock, *Am.* faucet)
35 plate rack
36 control switches
37 lid
38 **halftone photoengraving** (halftone block, halftone plate), a block (plate, printing plate)
39 dot (halftone dot), a printing element
40 etched zinc plate
41 block mount (block mounting, plate mount, plate mounting)
42 **line block** (line engraving, line etching, line plate, line cut)
43 non-printing, deep-etched areas
44 flange (bevel edge)
45 sidewall

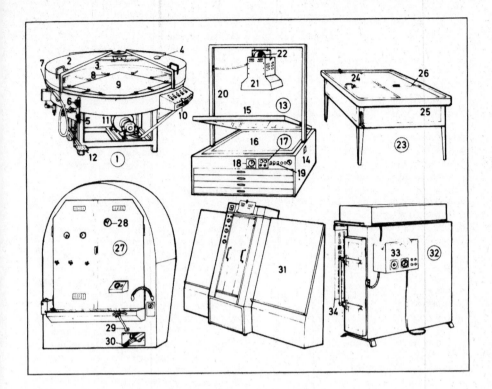

1 plate whirler (whirler, plate-coating machine) for coating offset plates
2 sliding lid
3 electric heater
4 temperature gauge (*Am.* gage)
5 water connection for the spray unit
6 spray unit
7 hand spray
8 plate clamps
9 zinc plate (*also:* magnesium plate, copper plate)
10 control panel
11 drive motor
12 brake pedal
13 vacuum printing frame (vacuum frame, printing-down frame)
14 base of the vacuum printing frame (vacuum frame, printing-down frame)
15 plate glass frame
16 coated offset plate
17 control panel

18 exposure timer
19 vacuum pump switches
20 support
21 point light exposure lamp, a quartz-halogen lamp
22 fan blower
23 stripping table (make-up table) for stripping films
24 crystal glass screen
25 light box
26 straightedge rules
27 vertical plate-drying cabinet
28 hygrometer
29 speed control
30 brake pedal
31 processing machine for presensitized plates
32 burning-in oven for glue-enamel plates (diazo plates)
33 control box (control unit)
34 diazo plate

1 four-colour (*Am.* four-color) rotary offset press (rotary offset machine, web-
 offset press)
2 roll of unprinted paper (blank paper)
3 reel stand (carrier for the roll of
 unprinted paper)
4 forwarding rolls
5 side margin control (margin control,
 side control, side lay control)
6-13 inking units (inker units)
6, 8, 10, 12 inking units (inker units) in the
 upper printing unit
6, 7 perfecting unit (double unit) for yellow
7, 9, 11, 13 inking units (inker units) in the
 lower printing unit
8, 9 perfecting unit (double unit) for cyan
10, 11 perfecting unit (double unit) for
 magenta
12, 13 perfecting unit (double unit) for
 black
14 drier
15 folder (folder unit)
16 control desk
17 sheet
18 four-colour (*Am.* four-color) rotary offset press (rotary offset machine, web-
 offset press) [diagram]
19 reel stand
20 side margin control (margin control,
 side control, side lay control)
21 inking rollers (ink rollers, inkers)
22 ink duct (ink fountain)
23 damping rollers (dampening rollers,
 dampers, dampeners)
24 blanket cylinder
25 plate cylinder
26 route of the paper (of the web)
27 drier
28 chilling rolls (cooling rollers, chill
 rollers)
29 folder (folder unit)
30 four-colour (*Am.* four-color) sheet-fed
 offset machine (offset press) [diagram]
31 sheet feeder (feeder)
32 feed table (feed board)
33 route of the sheets through swing-grip-
 pers to the feed drum
34 feed drum
35 impression cylinder
36 transfer drums (transfer cylinders)
37 blanket cylinder
38 plate cylinder
39 damping unit (dampening unit)
40 inking unit (inker unit)
41 printing unit
42 delivery cylinder

43 chain delivery
44 delivery pile
45 delivery unit (delivery mechanism)
46 single-colour (*Am.* single-color) offset
 press (offset machine)
47 pile of paper (sheets, printing paper)
48 sheet feeder (feeder), an automatic pile
 feeder
49 feed table (feed board)
50 inking rollers (ink rollers, inkers)
51 inking unit (inker unit)
52 damping rollers (dampening rollers,
 dampers, dampeners)
53 plate cylinder, a zinc plate
54 blanket cylinder, a steel cylinder with
 rubber blanket
55 pile delivery unit for the printed sheets
56 gripper bar, a chain gripper
57 pile of printed paper (printed sheets)
58 guard for the V-belt (vee-belt) drive
59 single-colour (*Am.* single-color) offset
 press (offset machine) [diagram]
60 inking unit (inker unit) with inking
 rollers (ink rollers, inkers)
61 damping unit (dampening unit) with
 damping rollers (dampening rollers,
 dampers, dampeners)
62 plate cylinder
63 blanket cylinder
64 impression cylinder
65 delivery cylinders with grippers
66 drive wheel
67 feed table (feed board)
68 sheet feeder (feeder)
69 pile of unprinted paper (blank paper,
 unprinted sheets, blank sheets)
70 small sheet-fed offset press
71 inking unit (inker unit)
72 suction feeder
73 pile feeder
74 instrument panel (control panel) with
 counter, pressure gauge (*Am.* gage), air
 regulator, and control switch for the
 sheet feeder (feeder)
75 flat-bed offset press (offset machine)
 ('Mailänder' proofing press, proof
 press)
76 inking unit (inker unit)
77 inking rollers (ink rollers, inkers)
78 bed (press bed, type bed, forme bed,
 Am. form bed)
79 cylinder with rubber blanket
80 starting and stopping lever for the printing unit
81 impression-setting wheel (impression-
 adjusting wheel)

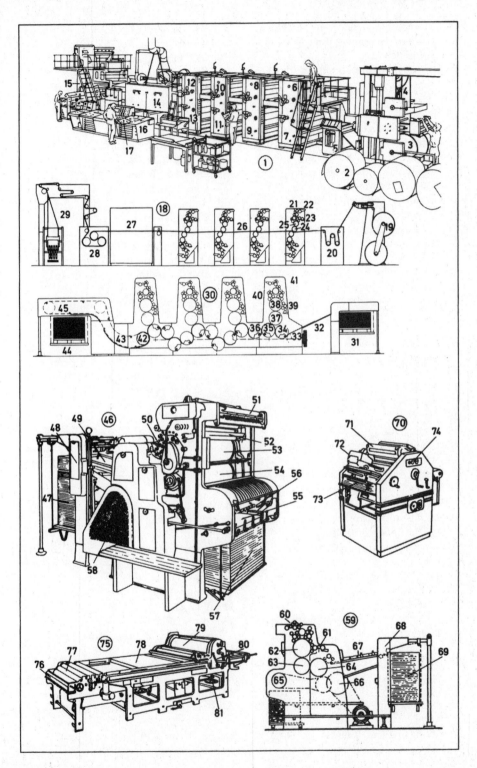

1-65 presses (machines) for letterpress printing (letterpress printing machines)
1 **two-revolution flat-bed cylinder press**
2 impression cylinder
3 lever for raising or lowering the cylinder
4 feed table (feed board)
5 automatic sheet feeder (feeder) [operated by vacuum and air blasts]
6 air pump for the feeder and delivery
7 inking unit (inker unit) with distributing rollers (distributor rollers, distributors) and forme rollers (*Am.* form rollers)
8 ink slab (ink plate) inking unit (inker unit)
9 delivery pile for printed paper
10 sprayer (anti set-off apparatus, anti set-off spray) for dusting the printed sheets
11 interleaving device
12 foot pedal for starting and stopping the press
13 **platen press** (platen machine, platen) [in section]
14 paper feed and delivery (paper feeding and delivery unit)
15 platen
16 toggle action (toggle-joint action)
17 bed (type bed, press bed, forme bed, *Am.* form bed)
18 forme rollers (*Am.* form rollers) (forme-inking, *Am.* form-inking, rollers)
19 inking unit (inker unit) for distributing the ink (printing ink)
20 **stop-cylinder press** (stop-cylinder machine)
21 feed table (feed board)
22 feeder mechanism (feeding apparatus, feeder)
23 pile of unprinted paper (blank paper, unprinted sheets, blank sheets)
24 guard for the sheet feeder (feeder)
25 pile of printed paper (printed sheets)
26 control mechanism
27 forme rollers (*Am.* form rollers) (forme-inking, *Am.* form-inking, rollers)
28 inking unit (inker unit)

29 [Heidelberg] **platen press** (platen machine, platen)
30 feed table (feed board) with pile of unprinted paper (blank paper, unprinted sheets, blank sheets)
31 delivery table
32 starting and stopping lever
33 delivery blower
34 spray gun (sprayer)
35 air pump for vacuum and air blasts
36 **locked-up forme** (*Am.* form)
37 type (type matter, matter)
38 chase
39 quoin
40 length of furniture
41 **rotary letterpress press** (rotary letterpress machine, web-fed letterpress machine) for newspapers of up to 16 pages
42 slitters for dividing the width of the web
43 web
44 impression cylinder
45 jockey roller (compensating roller, compensator, tension roller)
46 roll of paper
47 automatic brake
48 first printing unit
49 perfecting unit
50 inking unit (inker unit)
51 plate cylinder
52 second printing unit
53 former
54 tachometer with sheet counter
55 folder (folder unit)
56 folded newspaper
57 **inking unit** (inker unit) for the rotary press (web-fed press) [in section]
58 web
59 impression cylinder
60 plate cylinder
61 forme rollers (*Am.* form rollers) (forme-inking, *Am.* form-inking, rollers)
62 distributing rollers (distributor rollers, distributors)
63 lifter roller (ductor, ductor roller)
64 duct roller (fountain roller, ink fountain roller)
65 ink duct (ink fountain)

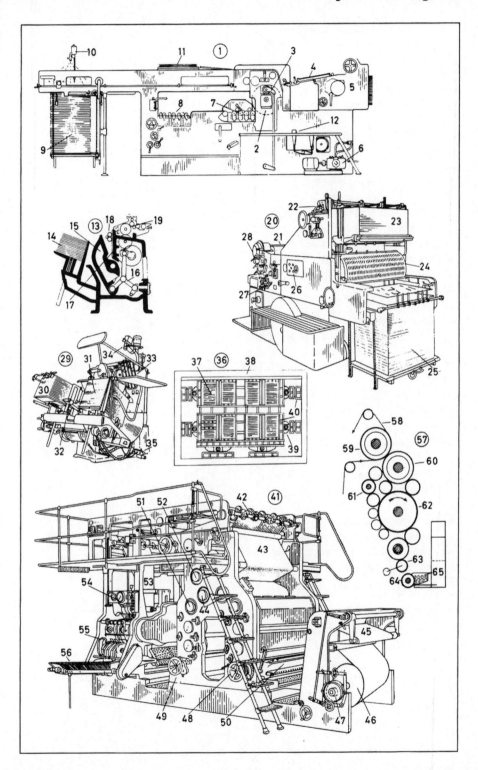

182 Photogravure (Gravure Printing, Intaglio Printing)

1 exposure of the carbon tissue (pigment paper)
2 vacuum frame
3 exposing lamp, a bank of quartz-halogen lamps
4 point source lamp
5 heat extractor
6 carbon tissue transfer machine (laydown machine, laying machine)
7 polished copper cylinder
8 rubber roller for pressing on the printed carbon tissue (pigment paper)
9 cylinder-processing machine
10 gravure cylinder coated with carbon tissue (pigment paper)
11 developing tank
12 staging
13 developed cylinder
14 retoucher painting out (stopping out)
15 etching machine
16 etching tank with etching solution (etchant, mordant)
17 printed gravure cylinder
18 gravure etcher
19 calculator dial
20 timer
21 revising (correcting) the cylinder
22 etched gravure cylinder
23 ledge
24 multicolour (*Am.* multicolor) rotogravure press
25 exhaust pipe for solvent fumes
26 reversible printing unit
27 folder (folder unit)
28 control desk
29 newspaper delivery unit
30 conveyor belt (conveyor)
31 bundled stack of newspapers

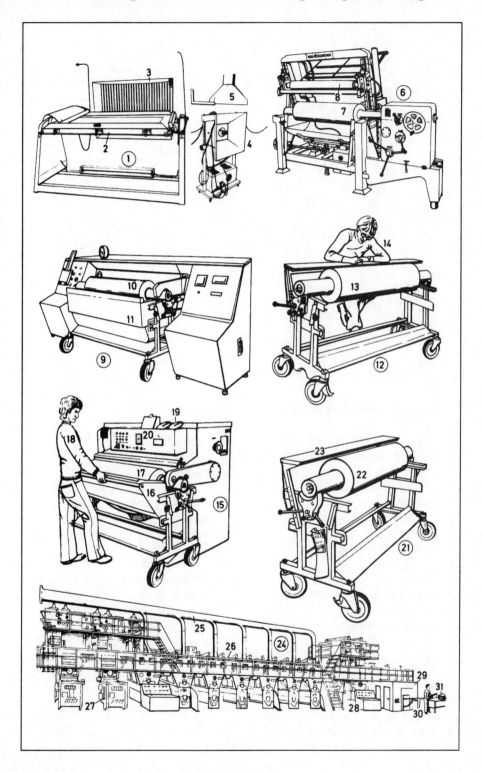

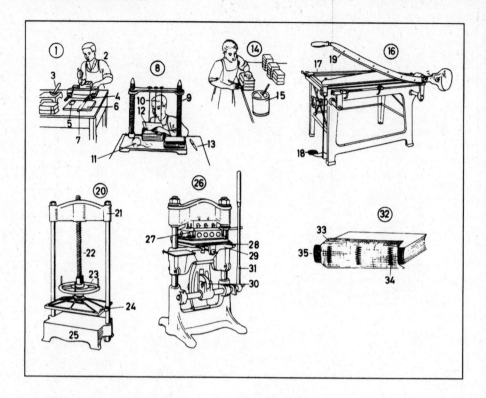

1-35 hand bookbindery (hand
bindery)
1 gilding the spine of the book
2 gold finisher (gilder), a bookbinder
3 fillet
4 holding press (finishing press)
5 gold leaf
6 gold cushion
7 gold knife
8 sewing (stitching)
9 sewing frame
10 sewing cord
11 ball of thread (sewing thread)
12 section (signature)
13 bookbinder's knife
14 gluing the spine
15 glue pot
16 board cutter (guillotine)
17 back gauge (*Am.* gage)
18 clamp with foot pedal
19 cutting blade
20 standing press, a nipping press
21 head piece (head beam)

22 spindle
23 handwheel
24 platen
25 bed (base)
26 gilding (gold blocking) and
embossing press, a hand-lever
press; *sim.:* toggle-joint press
(toggle-lever press)
27 heating box
28 sliding plate
29 embossing platen
30 toggle action (toggle-joint action)
31 hand lever
32 book sewn on gauze (mull, scrim)
(book block)
33 gauze (mull, scrim)
34 sewing (stitching)
35 headband

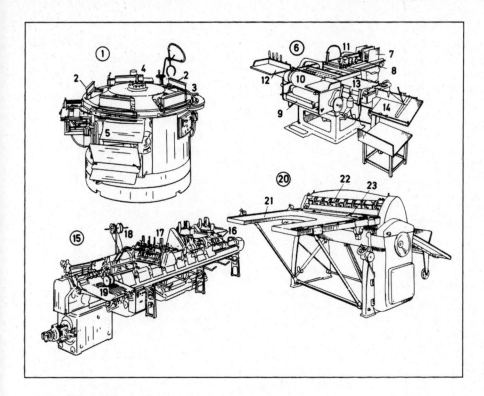

1-23 bookbinding machines
1 adhesive binder (perfect binder)
  for short runs
2 manual feed station
3 cutoff knife and roughing station
4 gluing mechanism
5 delivery (book delivery)
6 case maker (case-making machine)
7 board feed hoppers
8 pick-up suckers
9 glue tank
10 cover cylinder
11 picker head
12 feed table for covering materials
  [linen, paper, leather]
13 pressing mechanism
14 delivery table
15 gang stitcher (gathering and wire-
  stitching machine, gatherer and
  wire stitcher)
16 sheet feeder (sheet-feeding station)
17 folder-feeding station

18 stitching wire feed mechanism
19 delivery table
20 rotary board cutter (rotary board-
  cutting machine)
21 feed table with cut-out section
22 rotary cutter
23 feed guide

1-35 bookbinding machines
1 guillotine (guillotine cutter, automatic guillotine cutter)
2 control panel
3 clamp
4 back gauge (*Am.* gage)
5 calibrated pressure adjustment [to clamp]
6 illuminated cutting scale
7 single-hand control for the back gauge (*Am.* gage)
8 combined buckle and knife folding machine (combined buckle and knife folder)
9 feed table (feed board)
10 fold plates
11 stop for making the buckle fold
12 cross fold knives
13 belt delivery for parallel-folded signatures
14 third cross fold unit
15 delivery tray for cross-folded signatures
16 sewing machine (book-sewing machine)
17 spool holder
18 thread cop (thread spool)
19 gauze roll holder (mull roll holder, scrim roll holder)
20 gauze (mull, scrim)
21 needle cylinders with sewing needles
22 sewn book
23 delivery
24 reciprocating saddle
25 sheet feeder (feeder)
26 feed hopper
27 casing-in machine
28 joint and side pasting attachment
29 blade
30 preheater unit
31 gluing machine for whole-surface, stencil, edge, and strip gluing
32 glue tank
33 glue roller
34 feed table
35 delivery

36 book
37 dust jacket (dust cover, book jacket, wrapper), a publisher's wrapper
38 jacket flap
39 blurb
40-42 binding
40 cover (book cover, case)
41 spine (backbone, back)
42 tailband (footband)
43-47 preliminary matter (prelims, front matter)
43 half-title
44 half-title (bastard title, fly title)
45 title page
46 full title (main title)
47 subtitle
48 publisher's imprint (imprint)
49 fly leaf (endpaper, endleaf)
50 handwritten dedication
51 bookplate (ex libris)
52 open book
53 page
54 fold
55-58 margin
55 back margin (inside margin, gutter)
56 head margin (upper margin)
57 fore edge margin (outside margin, fore edge)
58 tail margin (foot margin, tail, foot)
59 type area
60 chapter heading
61 asterisk
62 footnote
63 page number
64 double-column page
65 column
66 running title (running head)
67 caption
68 marginal note (side note)
69 signature (signature code)
70 attached bookmark (attached bookmarker)
71 loose bookmark (loose bookmarker)

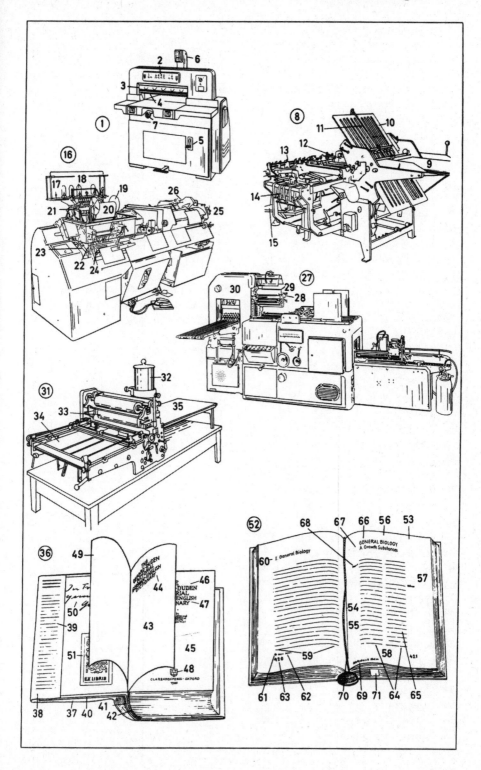

1-54 carriages (horse-drawn vehicles)
1-3, 26-39, 45, 51-54 carriages and coaches (coach wagons)
1 berlin
2 wagonette; *larger:* brake (break)
3 coupé; *sim.:* brougham
4 front wheel
5 coach body
6 dashboard (splashboard)
7 footboard
8 coach box (box, coachman's seat, driver's seat)
9 lamp (lantern)
10 window
11 door (coach door)
12 door handle (handle)
13 footboard (carriage step, coach step, step, footpiece)
14 fixed top
15 spring
16 brake (brake block)
17 back wheel (rear wheel)
18 dogcart, a one-horse carriage
19 shafts (thills, poles)
20 lackey (lacquey, footman)
21 livery
22 braided (gallooned) collar
23 braided (gallooned) coat
24 braided (gallooned) sleeve
25 top hat
26 hackney carriage (hackney coach, cab, growler, *Am.* hack)
27 stableman (groom)
28 coach horse (carriage horse, cab horse, thill horse, thiller)
29 hansom cab (hansom), a cabriolet, a one-horse chaise (one-horse carriage)
30 shafts (thills, poles)
31 reins (rein, *Am.* line)
32 coachman (driver) with inverness
33 covered char-a-banc (brake, break), a pleasure vehicle
34 gig (chaise)
35 barouche
36 landau, a two-horse carriage; *sim.:* landaulet, landaulette
37 omnibus (horse-drawn omnibus)
38 phaeton
39 Continental stagecoach (mail-coach, diligence); *also:* road coach
40 mailcoach driver
41 posthorn
42 hood
43 post horses (relay horses, relays)
44 tilbury
45 troika (Russian three-horse carriage)
46 leader
47 wheeler (wheelhorse, pole horse)
48 English buggy
49 American buggy
50 tandem
51 vis-à-vis
52 collapsible hood (collapsible top)
53 mailcoach (English stagecoach)
54 covered (closed) chaise

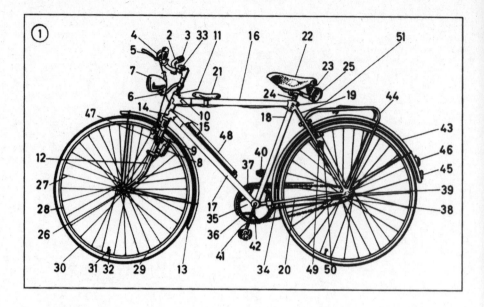

1 bicycle (cycle, *coll.* bike, *Am.*
wheel), a gent's bicycle, a touring
bicycle (touring cycle, roadster)
2 handlebar (handlebars), a touring
cycle handlebar
3 handlebar grip (handgrip, grip)
4 bicycle bell
5 hand brake (front brake), a rim
brake
6 lamp bracket
7 headlamp (bicycle lamp)
8 dynamo
9 pulley
10-12 front forks
10 handlebar stem
11 steering head
12 fork blades (fork ends)
13 front mudguard (*Am.* front fender)
14-20 bicycle frame
14 steering tube (fork column)
15 head badge
16 crossbar (top tube)
17 down tube
18 seat tube
19 seat stays
20 chain stays
21 child's seat (child carrier seat)
22 bicycle saddle

23 saddle springs
24 seat pillar
25 tool bag
26-32 wheel (front wheel)
26 hub
27 spoke
28 rim (wheel rim)
29 spoke nipple (spoke flange, spoke
end)
30 tyre (*Am.* tire) (pneumatic tyre,
high-pressure tyre); *inside:* tube
(inner tube); *outside:* tyre (outer
case, cover)
31 valve, a tube valve with valve tube
or a patent valve with ball
32 valve sealing cap
33 bicycle speedometer with milometer
34 kick stand (prop stand)
35-42 bicycle drive (chain drive)
35-39 chain transmission
35 chain wheel
36 chain, a roller chain
37 chain guard
38 sprocket wheel (sprocket)
39 wing nut (fly nut, butterfly nut)
40 pedal
41 crank
42 bottom bracket bearing

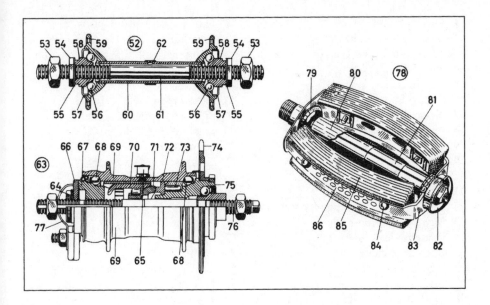

43 rear mudguard (*Am.* rear fender)	**67** brake arm cone
44 luggage carrier (carrier)	**68** bearing cup with ball bearings in
45 reflector	ball race
46 rear light (rear lamp)	**69** hub shell (hub body, hub barrel)
47 footrest	**70** brake casing
48 bicycle pump	**71** brake cone
49 bicycle lock, a wheel lock	**72** driver
50 patent key	**73** driving barrel
51 cycle serial number (factory num-	**74** sprocket
ber, frame number)	**75** thread head
52 front hub (front hub assembly)	**76** axle
53 wheel nut	**77** bracket
54 locknut (locking nut)	**78** bicycle pedal (pedal, reflector
55 washer (slotted cone adjusting	pedal)
washer)	**79** cup
56 ball bearing	**80** spindle
57 dust cap	**81** axle
58 cone (adjusting cone)	**82** dust cap
59 centre (*Am.* center) hub	**83** pedal frame
60 spindle	**84** rubber stud
61 axle	**85** rubber block (rubber tread)
62 clip covering lubrication hole	**86** glass reflector
(lubricator)	
63 free-wheel hub with back-pedal	
brake (with coaster brake)	
64 safety nut	
65 lubricator	
66 brake arm	

1 folding bicycle
2 hinge (*also:* locking lever)
3 adjustable handlebar (handlebars)
4 adjustable saddle
5 stabilizers
6 motor-assisted bicycle
7 air-cooled two-stroke engine
8 telescopic forks
9 tubular frame
10 fuel tank (petrol tank, *Am.* gasoline tank)
11 semi-rise handlebars
12 two-speed gear-change (gearshift)
13 high-back polo saddle
14 swinging-arm rear fork
15 upswept exhaust
16 heat shield
17 drive chain
18 crash bar (roll bar)
19 speedometer (*coll.* speedo)
20 battery-powered moped, an electrically-powered vehicle
21 swivel saddle
22 battery compartment
23 wire basket
24 touring moped (moped)
25 pedal crank (pedal drive, starter pedal)
26 single-cylinder two-stroke engine
27 spark-plug cap
28 fuel tank (petrol tank, *Am.* gasoline tank)
29 moped headlamp (front lamp)
30-35 handlebar fittings
30 twist grip throttle control (throttle twist grip)
31 twist grip (gear-change, gearshift)
32 clutch lever
33 hand brake lever
34 speedometer (*coll.* speedo)
35 rear-view mirror (mirror)
36 front wheel drum brake (drum brake)
37 Bowden cables (brake cables)
38 stop and tail light unit
39 light motorcycle with kickstarter

40 housing for instruments with speedometer and electronic rev counter (revolution counter)
41 telescopic shock absorber
42 twin seat
43 kickstarter
44 pillion footrest, a footrest
45 handlebar (handlebars)
46 chain guard
47 motor scooter (scooter)
48 removable side panel
49 tubular frame
50 metal fairings
51 prop stand (stand)
52 foot brake
53 horn (hooter)
54 hook for handbag or briefcase
55 foot gear-change control (foot gearshift control)
56 high-riser; *sim.:* Chopper
57 high-rise handlebar (handlebars)
58 imitation motorcycle fork
59 banana saddle
60 chrome bracket

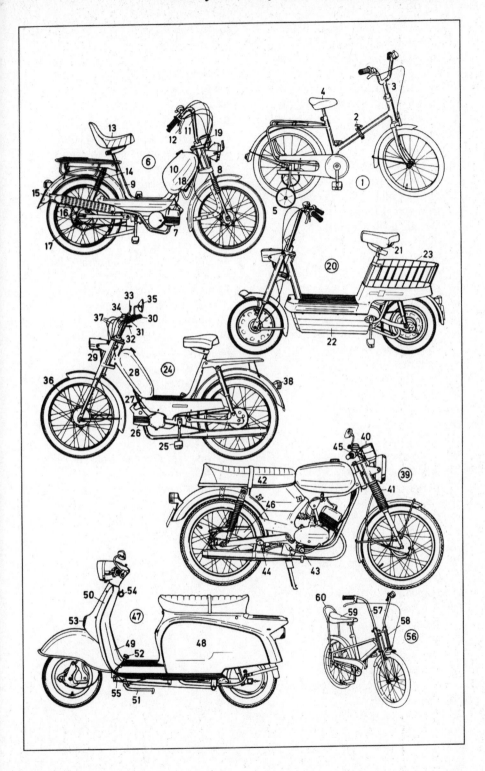

1 lightweight motorcycle (light motorcycle) [50 cc]
2 fuel tank (petrol tank, *Am.* gasoline tank)
3 air-cooled single-cylinder four-stroke engine (with overhead camshaft)
4 carburettor (*Am.* carburetor)
5 intake pipe
6 five-speed gearbox
7 swinging-arm rear fork
8 number plate (*Am.* license plate)
9 stop and tail light (rear light)
10 headlight (headlamp)
11 front drum brake
12 brake cable (brake line), a Bowden cable
13 rear drum brake
14 racing-style twin seat
15 upswept exhaust
16 scrambling motorcycle (cross-country motorcycle) [125 cc], a light motorcycle
17 lightweight cradle frame
18 number disc (disk)
19 solo seat
20 cooling ribs
21 motorcycle stand
22 motorcycle chain
23 telescopic shock absorber
24 spokes
25 rim (wheel rim)
26 motorcycle tyre (*Am.* tire)
27 tyre (*Am.* tire) tread
28 gear-change lever (gearshift lever)
29 twist grip throttle control (throttle twist grip)
30 rear-view mirror (mirror)
31-58 heavy (heavyweight, large-capacity) motorcycles
31 heavyweight motorcycle with water-cooled engine
32 front disc (disk) brake
33 disc (disk) brake calliper (caliper)
34 floating axle
35 water cooler
36 fuel tank (petrol tank, *Am.* gasoline tank)
37 indicator (indicator light, turn indicator light)
38 kickstarter
39 water-cooled engine
40 speedometer
41 rev counter (revolution counter)
42 rear indicator (indicator light)
43 heavy (heavyweight, high-performance) machine with fairing [1000 cc]
44 integrated streamlining, an integrated fairing
45 indicator (indicator light, turn indicator light)
46 anti-mist windscreen (*Am.* windshield)
47 horizontally-opposed twin engine with cardan transmission
48 light alloy wheel
49 four-cylinder machine [400 cc]
50 air-cooled four-cylinder four-stroke engine
51 four-pipe megaphone exhaust pipe
52 electric starter button
53 sidecar machine
54 sidecar body
55 sidecar crash bar
56 sidelight (*Am.* sidemarker lamp)
57 sidecar wheel
58 sidecar windscreen (*Am.* windshield)

1 eight-cylinder V (vee) fuel-injection spark-ignition engine (Otto-cycle engine)
2 cross-section of spark-ignition engine (Otto-cycle internal combustion engine)
3 sectional view of five-cylinder in-line diesel engine
4 cross-section of diesel engine
5 two-rotor Wankel engine (rotary engine)
6 single-cylinder two-stroke internal combustion engine
7 fan
8 fan clutch for viscous drive
9 ignition distributor (distributor) with vacuum timing control
10 double roller chain
11 camshaft bearing
12 air-bleed duct
13 oil pipe for camshaft lubrication
14 camshaft, an overhead camshaft
15 venturi throat
16 intake silencer (absorption silencer, *Am.* absorption muffler)
17 fuel pressure regulator
18 inlet manifold
19 cylinder crankcase
20 flywheel
21 connecting rod (piston rod)
22 cover of crankshaft bearing
23 crankshaft
24 oil bleeder screw (oil drain plug)
25 roller chain of oil pump drive
26 vibration damper
27 distributor shaft for the ignition distributor (distributor)
28 oil filler neck
29 diaphragm spring
30 control linkage
31 fuel supply pipe (*Am.* fuel line)
32 fuel injector (injection nozzle)
33 rocker arm
34 rocker arm mounting
35 spark plug (sparking plug) with suppressor
36 exhaust manifold
37 piston with piston rings and oil scraper ring
38 engine mounting
39 dog flange (dog)
40 crankcase
41 oil sump (sump)
42 oil pump
43 oil filter
44 starter motor (starting motor)
45 cylinder head
46 exhaust valve
47 dipstick
48 cylinder head cover
49 double bushing chain
50 warm-up regulator
51 tapered needle for idling adjustment
52 fuel pressure pipe (fuel pressure line)
53 fuel leak line (drip fuel line)
54 injection nozzle (spray nozzle)
55 heater plug
56 thrust washer
57 intermediate gear shaft for the injection pump drive
58 injection timer unit
59 vacuum pump (low-pressure regulator)
60 cam for vacuum pump
61 water pump (coolant pump)
62 cooling water thermostat
63 thermo time switch
64 fuel hand pump
65 injection pump
66 glow plug
67 oil pressure limiting valve
68 rotor
69 seal
70 torque converter
71 single-plate clutch
72 multi-speed gearing (multi-step gearing)
73 port liners in the exhaust manifold for emission control
74 disc (disk) brake
75 differential gear (differential)
76 generator
77 foot gear-change control (foot gearshift control)
78 dry multi-plate clutch
79 cross-draught (*Am.* cross-draft) carburettor (*Am.* carburetor)
80 cooling ribs
81 V-belt (fan belt)

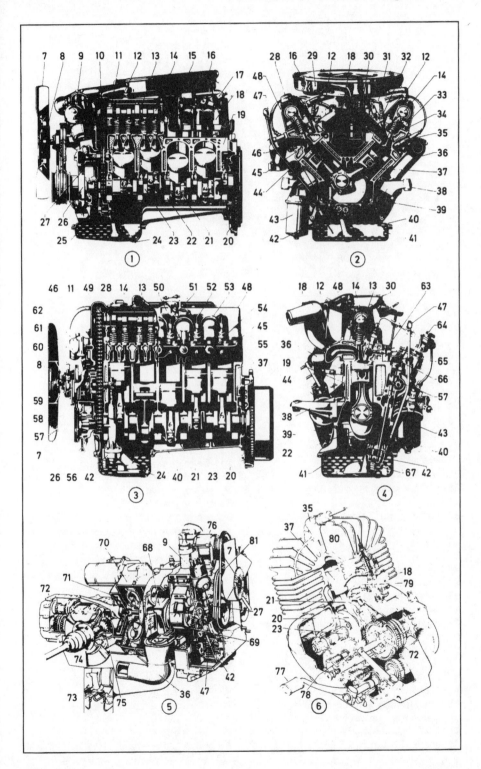

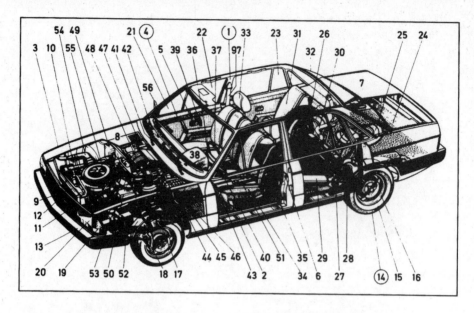

1-56 motor car (car, *Am.* automobile,
auto), a passenger vehicle
1 monocoque body (unitary body)
2 chassis, the understructure of the body
3 front wing (*Am.* front fender)
4 car door
5 door handle
6 door lock
7 boot lid (*Am.* trunk lid)
8 bonnet (*Am.* hood)
9 radiator
10 cooling water pipe
11 radiator grill
12 badging
13 rubber-covered front bumper (*Am.*
front fender)
14 car wheel, a disc (disk) wheel
15 car tyre (*Am.* automobile tire)
16 rim (wheel rim)
17-18 disc (disk) brake
17 brake disc (disk) (braking disc)
18 calliper (caliper)
19 front indicator light (front turn indicator light)
20 headlight (headlamp) with main beam
(high beam), dipped beam (low beam),
sidelight (side lamp, *Am.* sidemarker
lamp)
21 windscreen (*Am.* windshield), a
panoramic windscreen
22 crank-operated car window
23 quarter light (quarter vent)

24 boot (*Am.* trunk)
25 spare wheel
26 damper (shock absorber)
27 trailing arm
28 coil spring
29 silencer (*Am.* muffler)
30 automatic ventilation system
31 rear seats
32 rear window
33 adjustable headrest (head restraint)
34 driver's seat, a reclining seat
35 reclining backrest
36 passenger seat
37 steering wheel
38 centre (*Am.* center) console containing
speedometer (*coll.* speedo), revolution
counter (rev counter, tachometer),
clock, fuel gauge (*Am.* gage), water
temperature gauge, oil temperature
gauge
39 inside rear-view mirror
40 left-hand wing mirror
41 windscreen wiper (*Am.* windshield
wiper)
42 defroster vents
43 carpeting
44 clutch pedal (*coll.* clutch)
45 brake pedal (*coll.* brake)
46 accelerator pedal (*coll.* accelerator)
47 inlet vent
48 blower fan
49 brake fluid reservoir

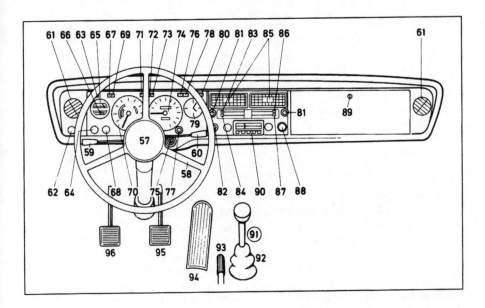

50 battery
51 exhaust pipe
52 front running gear with front wheel drive
53 engine mounting
54 intake silencer (*Am.* intake muffler)
55 air filter (air cleaner)
56 right-hand wing mirror
57-90 dashboard (fascia panel)
57 controlled-collapse steering column
58 steering wheel spoke
59 indicator and dimming switch
60 wiper/washer switch and horn
61 side window blower
62 sidelight, headlight, and parking light switch
63 fog lamp warning light
64 fog headlamp and rear lamp switch
65 fuel gauge (*Am.* gage)
66 water temperature gauge (*Am.* gage)
67 warning light for rear fog lamp
68 hazard flasher switch
69 main beam warning light
70 electric rev counter (revolution counter)
71 fuel warning light
72 warning light for the hand brake and dual-circuit brake system
73 oil pressure warning light
74 speedometer (*coll.* speedo) with trip mileage recorder
75 starter and steering lock

76 warning lights for turn indicators and hazard flashers
77 switch for the courtesy light and reset button for the trip mileage recorder
78 ammeter
79 electric clock
80 warning light for heated rear window
81 switch for the leg space ventilation
82 rear window heating switch
83 ventilation switch
84 temperature regulator
85 fresh-air inlet and control
86 fresh-air regulator
87 warm-air regulator
88 cigar lighter
89 glove compartment (glove box) lock
90 car radio
91 gear lever (gearshift lever), a floor-type gear-change
92 leather gaiter
93 hand brake lever
94 accelerator pedal
95 brake pedal
96 clutch pedal
97 seat belt (safety belt)

1-15 carburettor (*Am.* carburetor), a down-draught (*Am.* down-draft) carburettor
1 idling jet (slow-running jet)
2 idling air jet (idle air bleed)
3 air correction jet
4 compensating airstream
5 main airstream
6 choke flap
7 plunger
8 venturi
9 throttle valve (butterfly valve)
10 emulsion tube
11 idle mixture adjustment screw
12 main jet
13 fuel inlet (*Am.* gasoline inlet) (inlet manifold)
14 float chamber
15 float
16-27 pressure-feed lubricating system
16 oil pump
17 oil sump
18 sump filter
19 oil cooler
20 oil filter
21 main oil gallery (drilled gallery)
22 crankshaft drilling (crankshaft tributary, crankshaft bleed)
23 crankshaft bearing (main bearing)
24 camshaft bearing
25 connecting-rod bearing
26 gudgeon pin (piston pin)
27 bleed
28-47 four-speed synchromesh gearbox
28 clutch pedal
29 crankshaft
30 drive shaft (propeller shaft)
31 starting gear ring
32 sliding sleeve for 3rd and 4th gear
33 synchronizing cone
34 helical gear wheel for 3rd gear
35 sliding sleeve for 1st and 2nd gear
36 helical gear wheel for 1st gear
37 lay shaft
38 speedometer drive
39 helical gear wheel for speedometer drive
40 main shaft
41 gearshift rods
42 selector fork for 1st and 2nd gear
43 helical gear wheel for 2nd gear
44 selector head with reverse gear
45 selector fork for 3rd and 4th gear
46 gear lever (gearshift lever)
47 gear-change pattern (gearshift pattern, shift pattern)
48-55 disc (disk) brake [assembly]
48 brake disc (disk) (braking disc)
49 calliper (caliper), a fixed calliper with friction pads
50 servo cylinder (servo unit)
51 brake shoes
52 brake lining
53 outlet to brake line
54 wheel cylinder
55 return spring
56-59 steering gear (worm-and-nut steering gear)
56 steering column
57 worm gear sector
58 steering drop arm
59 worm
60-64 water-controlled heater
60 air intake
61 heat exchanger (heater box)
62 blower fan
63 flap valve
64 defroster vent
65-71 live axle (rigid axle)
65 propeller shaft
66 trailing arm
67 rubber bush
68 coil spring
69 damper (shock absorber)
70 Panhard rod
71 stabilizer bar
72-84 MacPherson strut unit
72 body-fixing plate
73 upper bearing
74 suspension spring
75 piston rod
76 suspension damper
77 rim (wheel rim)
78 stub axle
79 steering arm
80 track-rod ball-joint
81 trailing link arm
82 bump rubber (rubber bonding)
83 lower bearing
84 lower suspension arm

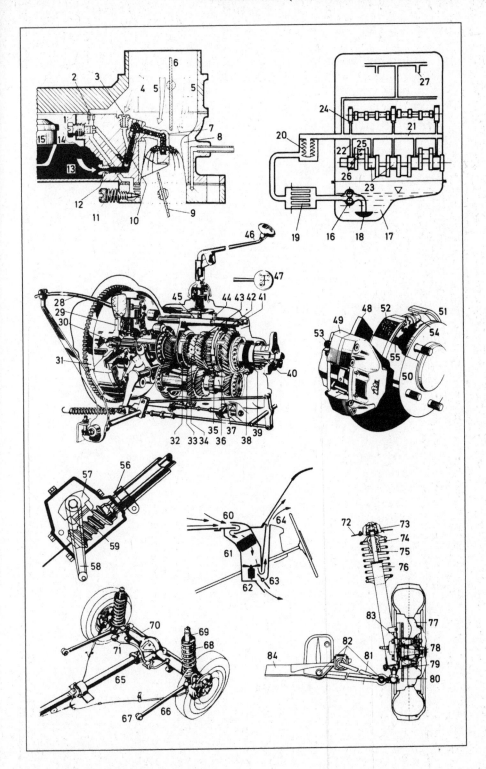

1-36 car models (*Am.* automobile models)

1 four-door touring saloon (*Am.* four-door sedan) in the upper-middle range

2 driver's door

3 rear door

4-10 four-door saloon (*Am.* four-door sedan) **and four-door hatchback in the middle range**

4 **saloon** (*Am.* sedan)

5 headrests (head restraints)

6 front seat

7 rear seat (back seat)

8 **fastback saloon** (*Am.* fastback sedan) (stubback saloon, *Am.* stubback sedan)

9 tailgate

10 fastback (stubback)

11 **cross-country vehicle** with all-wheel drive (four-wheel drive)

12 spare wheel

13 roll bar

14 **cabriolet sports coupe** (cabriolet sports car)

15 integral seat

16 automatic hood (*Am.* top) (power-operated hood, *Am.* top)

17 **estate car** (estate, shooting brake, *Am.* station wagon)

18 boot space (luggage compartment)

19 **small three-door car**

20 back (tailgate)

21 sill

22 folding back seat

23 boot (luggage compartment, *Am.* trunk)

24 (sliding) sunroof (steel sliding sunroof)

25 **three-door hatchback**

26 **roadster** (sports cabrio, sports cabriolet), a two-seater

27 hard top

28 **sports coupe,** a two-plus-two (two-seater with occasional seats)

29 fastback

30 occasional seat

31 low-profile tyre (*Am.* tire) (wide wheel)

32 **gran turismo car** (GT car)

33 integral bumper (*Am.* integral fender)

34 rear spoiler

35 back

36 front spoiler

1 light cross-country lorry (light truck, pick-up truck) with all-wheel drive (four-wheel drive)
2 cab (driver's cab)
3 loading platform (body)
4 spare tyre (*Am.* spare tire), a cross-country tyre
5 light lorry (light truck, pick-up truck)
6 platform truck
7 medium van
8 sliding side door [for loading and unloading]
9 minibus
10 folding top (sliding roof)
11 rear door
12 hinged side door
13 luggage compartment
14 passenger seat
15 cab (driver's cab)
16 air inlet
17 motor coach (coach, bus)
18 luggage locker
19 hand luggage (suitcase, case)
20 heavy lorry (heavy truck, heavy motor truck)
21 tractive unit (tractor, towing vehicle)
22 trailer (drawbar trailer)
23 swop platform (body)
24 three-way tipper (three-way dump truck)
25 tipping body (dump body)
26 hydraulic cylinder
27 supported container platform
28 articulated vehicle, a vehicle tanker
29 tractive unit (tractor, towing vehicle)
30-33 semi-trailer (skeletal)
30 tank
31 turntable
32 undercarriage
33 spare wheel
34 midi bus [for short-route town operations]
35 outward-opening doors
36 double-deck bus (double-decker bus)
37 lower deck (lower saloon)
38 upper deck (upper saloon)
39 boarding platform
40 trolley bus
41 current collector
42 trolley (trolley shoe)
43 overhead wires
44 trolley bus trailer
45 pneumatically sprung rubber connection

1-55 **agent's garage** (distributor's garage, *Am.* specialty shop)

1-23 diagnostic test bay
1 computer
2 main computer socket
3 computer harness (computer cable)
4 switch from automatic to manual
5 slot for program cards
6 printout machine (printer)
7 condition report (data printout)
8 master selector (hand control)
9 light read-out [green: OK; red: not OK]
10 rack for program cards
11 mains button
12 switch for fast readout
13 firing sequence insert
14 shelf for used cards
15 cable boom
16 oil temperature sensor
17 test equipment for wheel and steering alignment

18 right-hand optic plate
19 actuating transistors
20 projector switch
21 check light for wheel alignment, a row of photocells
22 check light for steering alignment, a row of photocells
23 power screwdriver
24 beam setter
25 hydraulic lift
26 adjustable arm of hydraulic lift
27 hydraulic lift pad
28 excavation
29 pressure gauge (*Am.* gage)
30 grease gun
31 storage box for small parts
32 wall chart [of spare parts]

33 automatic computer test
34 motor car (car, *Am.* automobile, auto), a passenger vehicle
35 engine compartment
36 bonnet (*Am.* hood)
37 bonnet support (*Am.* hood support)
38 computer harness (computer cable)
39 main computer socket
40 oil temperature sensor
41 wheel mirror for visual wheel and steering alignment
42 tool trolley
43 tools
44 impact wrench
45 torque wrench
46 body hammer (roughing-out hammer)
47 vehicle under repair, a minibus

48 car location number
49 rear engine
50 tailgate
51 exhaust system
52 exhaust repair
53 motor car mechanic (motor vehicle mechanic, *Am.* automotive mechanic)
54 air hose
55 intercom

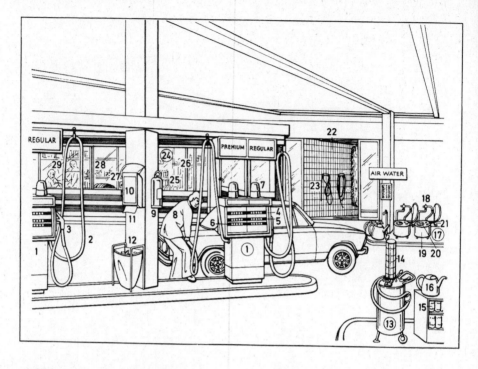

1-29 service station (petrol station, filling station, *Am.* gasoline station, gas station), a self-service station
1 petrol (*Am.* gasoline) pump (blending pump) for unleaded (lead-free) premium grade and regular petrol (*Am.* gasoline) (*sim.:* for derv)
2 hose (petrol pump, *Am.* gasoline pump, hose)
3 nozzle
4 cash readout
5 volume readout
6 price display
7 indicator light
8 driver using self-service petrol pump (*Am.* gasoline pump)
9 fire extinguisher
10 paper-towel dispenser
11 paper towel
12 litter receptacle
13 two-stroke blending pump
14 meter
15 engine oil

16 oil can
17 tyre pressure gauge (*Am.* tire pressure gage)
18 air hose
19 static air tank
20 pressure gauge (*Am.* gage) (manometer)
21 air filler neck
22 repair bay (repair shop)
23 car-wash hose, a hose (hosepipe)
24 accessory shop
25 petrol can (*Am.* gasoline can)
26 rain cape
27 car tyres (*Am.* automobile tires)
28 car accessories
29 cash desk (console)

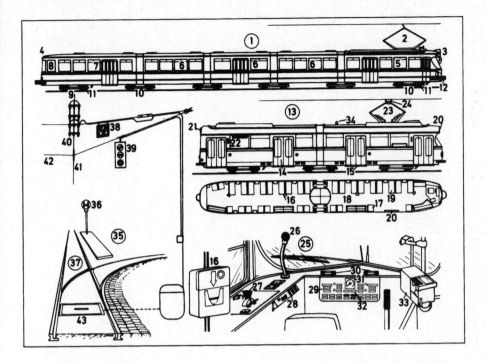

1 twelve-axle articulated railcar for interurban rail service
2 current collector
3 head of the railcar
4 rear of the railcar
5 carriage A containing the motor
6 carriage B (*also:* carriages C and D)
7 carriage E containing the motor
8 rear controller
9 driving bogie
10 carrying bogie
11 wheel guard
12 bumper (*Am.* fender)
13 six-axle articulated railcar ('Mannheim' type) for tram (*Am.* streetcar, trolley) and urban rail services
14 entrance and exit door, a double folding door
15 step
16 ticket-cancelling machine
17 single seat
18 standing room portion
19 double seat
20 route (number) and destination sign
21 route sign (number sign)
22 indicator (indicator light)
23 pantograph (current collector)

24 carbon or aluminium (*Am.* aluminum) alloy trolley shoes
25 driver's position
26 microphone
27 controller
28 radio equipment (radio communication set)
29 dashboard
30 dashboard lighting
31 speedometer
32 buttons controlling doors, windscreen wipers, internal and external lighting
33 ticket counter with change machine
34 radio antenna
35 tram stop (*Am.* streetcar stop, trolley stop)
36 tram stop sign (*Am.* streetcar stop sign, trolley stop sign)
37 electric change points
38 points signal (switch signal)
39 points change indicator
40 trolley wire contact point
41 trolley wire (overhead contact wire)
42 overhead cross wire
43 electric (*also:* electrohydraulic, electromechanical) points mechanism

1-5 road layers
1 anti-frost layer
2 bituminous sub-base course
3 base course
4 binder course
5 bituminous surface
6 kerb (curb)
7 kerbstone (curbstone)
8 paving (pavement)
9 pavement (*Am.* sidewalk, walk-way)
10 gutter
11 pedestrian crossing (zebra crossing, *Am.* crosswalk)
12 street corner
13 street
14 electricity cables
15 telephone cables
16 telephone cable pipeline
17 cable manhole with cover (with manhole cover)
18 lamp post with lamp
19 electricity cables for technical installations
20 subscribers' (*Am.* customers') telephone lines
21 gas main
22 water main
23 drain
24 drain cover
25 drain pipe
26 waste pipe
27 combined sewer
28 district heating main
29 underground tunnel

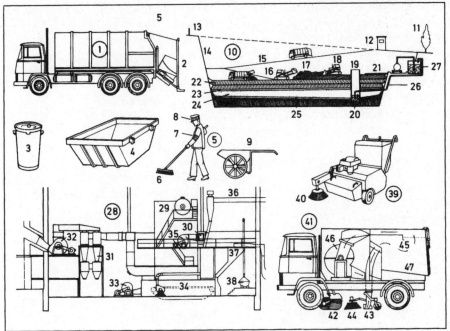

1 refuse collection vehicle (*Am.* garbage truck)	24 morainic filter layer
2 dustbin-tipping device (*Am.* garbage can dumping device), a dust-free emptying system	25 drainage layer
	26 drain pipe
	27 water tank
3 dustbin (*Am.* garbage can, trash can)	28 refuse (*Am.* garbage) incineration unit
4 refuse container (*Am.* garbage container)	29 furnace
5 road sweeper (*Am.* street sweeper)	30 oil-firing system
6 broom	31 separation plant
7 fluorescent armband	32 extraction fan
8 cap with fluorescent band	33 low-pressure fan for the grate
9 road sweeper's (*Am.* street sweeper's) barrow	34 continuous feed grate
	35 fan for the oil-firing system
10 controlled tip (*Am.* sanitary landfill, sanitary fill)	36 conveyor for separately incinerated material
11 screen	37 coal feed conveyor
12 weigh office	38 truck for carrying fuller's earth
13 fence	39 mechanical sweeper
14 embankment	40 circular broom
15 access ramp	41 road-sweeping lorry (street-cleaning lorry, street cleaner)
16 bulldozer	
17 refuse (*Am.* garbage)	42 cylinder broom
18 bulldozer for dumping and compacting	43 suction port
19 pump shaft	44 feeder broom
20 waste water pump	45 air flow
21 porous cover	46 fan
22 compacted and decomposed refuse	47 dust collector
23 gravel filter layer	

1-54 road-building machinery
1 shovel (power shovel, excavator)
2 machine housing
3 caterpillar mounting (*Am.* caterpillar tractor)
4 digging bucket arm (dipper stick)
5 digging bucket (bucket)
6 digging bucket (bucket) teeth
7 tipper (dump truck), a heavy lorry (*Am.* truck)
8 tipping body (*Am.* dump body)
9 reinforcing rib
10 extended front
11 cab (driver's cab)
12 bulk material
13 concrete scraper, an aggregate scraper
14 skip hoist
15 mixing drum (mixer drum), a mixing machine
16 caterpillar hauling scraper
17 scraper blade
18 levelling (*Am.* leveling) blade (smoothing blade)
19 grader (motor grader)
20 scarifier (ripper, road ripper, rooter)
21 grader levelling (*Am.* leveling) blade (grader ploughshare, *Am.* plowshare)
22 blade-slewing gear (slew turntable)
23 light railway (narrow-gauge, *Am.* narrow-gage, railway)
24 light railway (narrow-gauge, *Am.* narrow-gage) diesel locomotive
25 trailer wagon (wagon truck, skip)
26 tamper (rammer) *heavier:* frog
27 guide rods
28 bulldozer
29 bulldozer blade
30 pushing frame
31 road-metal spreading machine (macadam spreader, stone spreader)
32 tamping beam
33 sole-plate
34 side stop
35 side of storage bin

36 three-wheeled roller, a road roller
37 roller
38 all-weather roof
39 mobile diesel-powered air compressor
40 oxygen cylinder
41 self-propelled gritter
42 spreading flap
43 surface finisher
44 side stop
45 bin
46 tar-spraying machine (bituminous distributor) with tar and bitumen heater
47 tar storage tank
48 fully automatic asphalt drying and mixing plant
49 bucket elevator (elevating conveyor)
50 asphalt-mixing drum (asphalt mixer drum)
51 filler hoist
52 filler opening
53 binder injector
54 mixed asphalt outlet
55 typical cross-section of a bituminous road
56 grass verge
57 crossfall
58 asphalt surface (bituminous layer, bituminous coating)
59 base (base course)
60 hardcore sub-base course (Telford base) or gravel sub-base course, an anti-frost layer
61 sub-drainage
62 perforated cement pipe
63 drainage ditch
64 soil covering

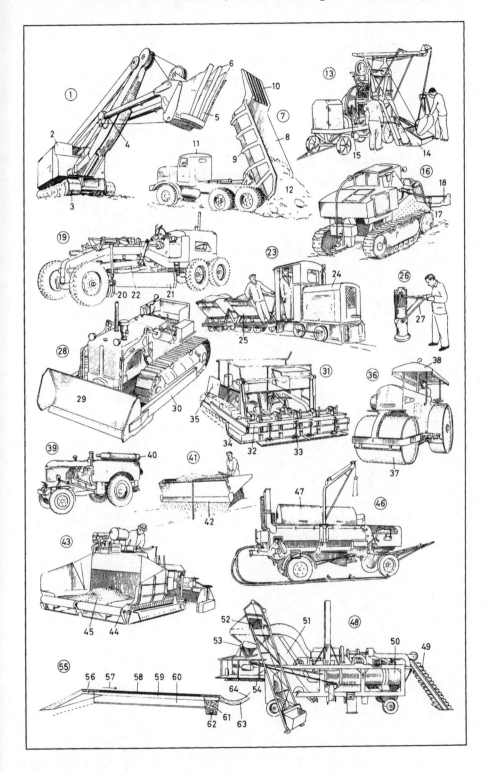

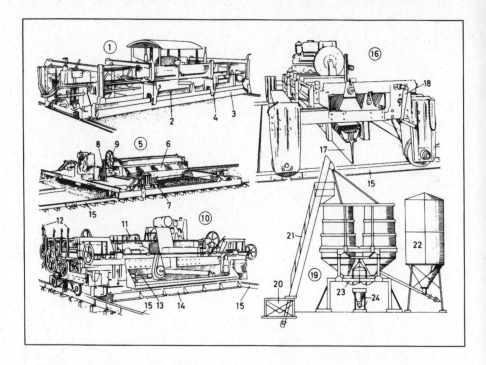

1-24 concrete road construction
(highway construction)
1 subgrade grader
2 tamping beam (consolidating beam)
3 levelling (*Am.* leveling) beam
4 roller guides for the levelling (*Am.* leveling) beam
5 concrete spreader
6 concrete spreader box
7 cable guides
8 control levers
9 handwheel for emptying the boxes
10 concrete-vibrating compactor
11 gearing (gears)
12 control levers (operating levers)
13 axle drive shaft to vibrators (tampers) of vibrating beam
14 screeding board (screeding beam)
15 road form
16 joint cutter
17 joint-cutting blade
18 crank for propelling machine
19 concrete-mixing plant, a stationary central mixing plant, an automatic batching and mixing plant
20 collecting bin
21 bucket elevator
22 cement store
23 concrete mixer
24 concrete pump hopper

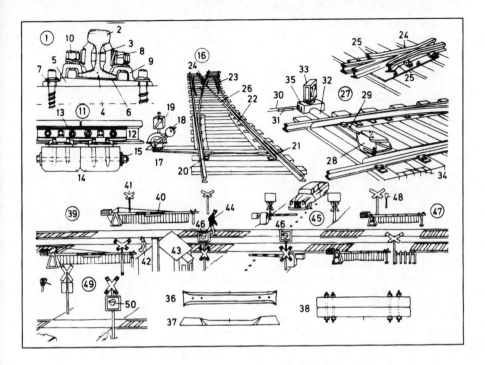

1-38 line (track)
1 rail
2 rail head
3 web (rail web)
4 rail foot (rail bottom)
5 sole-plate (base plate)
6 cushion
7 coach screw (coach bolt)
8 lock washers (spring washers)
9 rail clip (clip)
10 T-head bolt
11 rail joint (joint)
12 fishplate
13 fishbolt
14 coupled sleeper (*Am.* coupled tie, coupled crosstie)
15 coupling bolt
16 manually-operated points (manually-operated switch)
17 switch stand
18 weight
19 points signal (switch signal, points signal lamp, switch signal lamp)
20 pull rod
21 switch blade (switch tongue)
22 slide chair
23 check rail (guard rail)
24 frog
25 wing rail
26 closure rail
27 remote-controlled points (remote-controlled switch)

28 point lock (switch lock)
29 stretcher bar
30 point wire
31 turnbuckle
32 channel
33 electrically illuminated points signal (switch signal)
34 trough
35 points motor with protective casing
36 steel sleeper (*Am.* steel tie, steel crosstie)
37 concrete sleeper (*Am.* concrete tie, concrete crosstie)
38 coupled sleeper (*Am.* coupled tie, coupled crosstie)
39-50 level crossings (*Am.* grade crossings)
39 protected level crossing (*Am.* protected grade crossing)
40 barrier (gate)
41 warning cross (*Am.* crossbuck)
42 crossing keeper (*Am.* gateman)
43 crossing keeper's box (*Am.* gateman's box)
44 linesman (*Am.* trackwalker)
45 half-barrier crossing
46 warning light
47 intercom-controlled crossing; *sim.:* telephone-controlled crossing
48 intercom system
49 unprotected level crossing (*Am.* unprotected grade crossing)
50 warning light

1-6 stop signals (main signals)
1 stop signal (main signal), a semaphore signal in 'stop' position
2 signal arm (semaphore arm)
3 electric stop signal (colour light, *Am.* color light, signal) at 'stop'
4 signal position: 'proceed at low speed'
5 signal position: 'proceed'
6 substitute signal
7-24 distant signals
7 semaphore signal at 'be prepared to stop at next signal'
8 supplementary semaphore arm
9 colour light (*Am.* color light) distant signal at 'be prepared to stop at next signal'
10 signal position: 'be prepared to proceed at low speed'
11 signal position: 'proceed main signal ahead'
12 semaphore signal with indicator plate showing a reduction in braking distance of more than 5%
13 triangle (triangle sign)
14 colour light (*Am.* color light) distant signal with indicator light for showing reduced braking distance
15 supplementary white light
16 distant signal indicating 'be prepared to stop at next signal' (yellow light)
17 second distant signal (distant signal with supplementary light, without indicator plate)
18 distant signal with speed indicator
19 distant speed indicator
20 distant signal with route indicator
21 route indicator
22 distant signal without supplementary arm in position: 'be prepared to stop at next signal'
23 distant signal without supplementary arm in 'be prepared to proceed' position
24 distant signal identification plate
25-44 supplementary signals
25 stop board for indicating the stopping point at a control point
26-29 approach signs
26 approach sign 100 m from distant signal
27 approach sign 175 m from distant signal
28 approach sign 250 m from distant signal
29 approach sign at a distance of 5% less than the braking distance on the section
30 chequered sign indicating stop signals (main signals) not positioned immediately to the right of or over the line (track)
31, 32 stop boards to indicate the stopping point of the front of the train

33 stop board indicating 'be prepared to stop'
34, 35 snow plough (*Am.* snowplow) signs
34 'raise snow plough (*Am.* snowplow)' sign
35 'lower snow plough (*Am.* snowplow)' sign
36-44 speed restriction signs
36-38 speed restriction sign [maximum speed $3 \times 10 = 30$ kph]
36 sign for day running
37 speed code number
38 illuminated sign for night running
39 commencement of temporary speed restriction
40 termination of temporary speed restriction
41 speed restriction sign for a section with a permanent speed restriction [maximum speed $5 \times 10 = 50$ kph]
42 commencement of permanent speed restriction
43 speed restriction warning sign [only on main lines]
44 speed restriction sign [only on main lines]
45-52 point signals (switch signals)
45-48 single points (single switches)
45 route straight ahead (main line)
46 [right] branch
47 [left] branch
48 branch [seen from the frog]
49-52 double crossover
49 route straight ahead from left to right
50 route straight ahead from right to left
51 turnout to the left from the left
52 turnout to the right from the right
53 **manually-operated signal box** (*Am.* signal tower, switch tower)
54 lever mechanism
55 points lever (switch lever) [blue], a lock lever
56 signal lever [red]
57 catch
58 route lever
59 block instruments
60 block section panel
61 **electrically-operated signal box** (*Am.* signal tower, switch tower)
62 points (switch) and signal knobs
63 lock indicator panel
64 track and signal indicator
65 **track diagram control layout**
66 track diagram control panel (domino panel)
67 push buttons
68 routes
69 intercom system

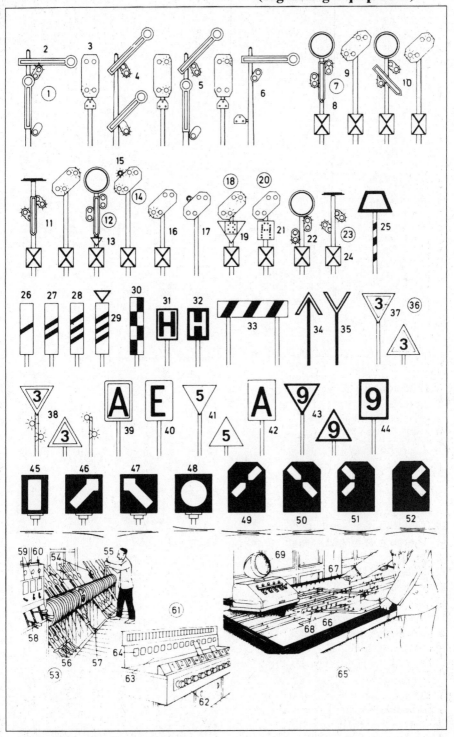

1 parcels office
2 parcels
3 basket [with lock]
4 luggage counter
5 platform scale with dial
6 suitcase (case)
7 luggage sticker
8 luggage receipt
9 luggage clerk
10 poster (advertisement)
11 station post box (*Am.* station mail-box)
12 station guide
13 station restaurant
14 waiting room
15 map of the town (street map)
16 timetable (*Am.* schedule)
17 ticket machine
18 arrivals and departures board (timetable)
19 arrival timetable (*Am.* arrival schedule)
20 departure timetable (*Am.* departure schedule)

21 left luggage lockers
22 change machine
23 tunnel to the platforms
24 passengers
25 steps to the platforms
26 station bookstall (*Am.* station bookstand)
27 left luggage office (left luggage)
28 travel centre (*Am.* center); *also:* accommodation bureau
29 information office (*Am.* information bureau)
30 station clock
31 bank branch with foreign exchange counter
32 indicator board showing exchange rates
33 railway map (*Am.* railroad map)
34 ticket office
35 ticket counter
36 ticket
37 revolving tray
38 grill

39 ticket clerk (*Am.* ticket agent)
40 pane of glass (window)
41 pocket timetable (*Am.* pocket train schedule)
42 luggage rest
43 first aid station
44 Travellers' (*Am.* Travelers') Aid
45 railway (*Am.* railroad) information clerk
46 official timetable (official railway guide, *Am.* train schedule)

1 platform	22 destination indicator
2 steps to the platform	23 departure time indicator
3 bridge	24 delay indicator
4 platform number	25 suburban train, a railcar
5 platform roofing	26 special compartment
6 passengers	27 platform loudspeaker
7-12 luggage	28 station sign
7 suitcase (case)	29 electric trolley (electric truck)
8 luggage label	30 loading foreman
9 hotel sticker	31 porter (*Am.* redcap)
10 travelling (*Am.* traveling) bag	32 barrow
11 hat box	33 drinking fountain
12 umbrella, a walking-stick umbrella	34 electric Eurocity express; *also:* IC
13 offices	express (Intercity express)
14 platform	35 electric locomotive, an express
15 crossing	locomotive
16 news trolley	36 collector bow (sliding bow)
17 news vendor (*Am.* news dealer)	37 secretarial compartment
18 reading matter for the journey	38 destination board
19 edge of the platform	39 wheel tapper
20 railway policeman (*Am.* railroad	40 wheel-tapping hammer
policeman)	41 station foreman
21 destination board	42 signal

43 red cap
44 inspector
45 pocket timetable (*Am.* pocket train schedule)
46 platform clock
47 starting signal
48 platform lighting
49 refreshment kiosk
50 beer bottle
51 newspaper
52 parting kiss
53 embrace
54 platform seat
55 litter bin (*Am.* trash bin)
56 platform post box (*Am.* platform mailbox)
57 platform telephone
58 trolley wire (overhead contact wire)
59-61 track
59 rail
60 sleeper (*Am.* tie, crosstie)
61 ballast (bed)

206 Goods Station (Freight Depot)

1 ramp (vehicle ramp); *sim.:* livestock ramp
2 electric truck
3 trailer
4 part loads (*Am.* package freight,
  less-than-carload freight); *in general traffic:* general goods in general
  consignments (in mixed consignments)
5 crate
6 goods van (*Am.* freight car)
7 goods shed (*Am.* freight house)
8 loading strip
9 loading dock
10 bale of peat
11 bale of linen (of linen cloth)
12 fastening (cord)
13 wicker bottle (wickered bottle,
  demijohn)
14 trolley
15 goods lorry (*Am.* freight truck)
16 forklift truck (fork truck, forklift)
17 loading siding
18 bulky goods
19 small railway-owned (*Am.* rail-
  road-owned) container
20 showman's caravan (*sim.* circus
  caravan)
21 flat wagon (*Am.* flat freight car)
22 loading gauge (*Am.* gage)
23 bale of straw
24 flat wagon (*Am.* flatcar) with side
  stakes
25 fleet of lorries (*Am.* trucks)
26-39 **goods shed** (*Am.* freight house)
26 goods office (forwarding office,
  Am. freight office)
27 part-load goods (*Am.* package
  freight)
28 forwarding agent (*Am.* freight
  agent, shipper)
29 loading foreman
30 consignment note (waybill)
31 weighing machine
32 pallet
33 porter

34 electric cart (electric truck)
35 trailer
36 loading supervisor
37 goods shed door (*Am.* freight
  house door)
38 rail (slide rail)
39 roller
40 weighbridge office
41 weighbridge
42 marshalling yard (*Am.* classification yard, switch yard)
43 shunting engine (shunting locomotive, shunter, *Am.* switch engine,
  switcher)
44 marshalling yard signal box (*Am.*
  classification yard switch tower)
45 yardmaster
46 hump
47 sorting siding (classification siding,
  classification track)
48 rail brake (retarder)
49 slipper brake (slipper)
50 storage siding (siding)
51 buffer (buffers, *Am.* bumper)
52 wagon load (*Am.* carload)·
53 warehouse
54 container station
55 gantry crane
56 lifting gear (hoisting gear)
57 container
58 container wagon (*Am.* container
  car)
59 semi-trailer

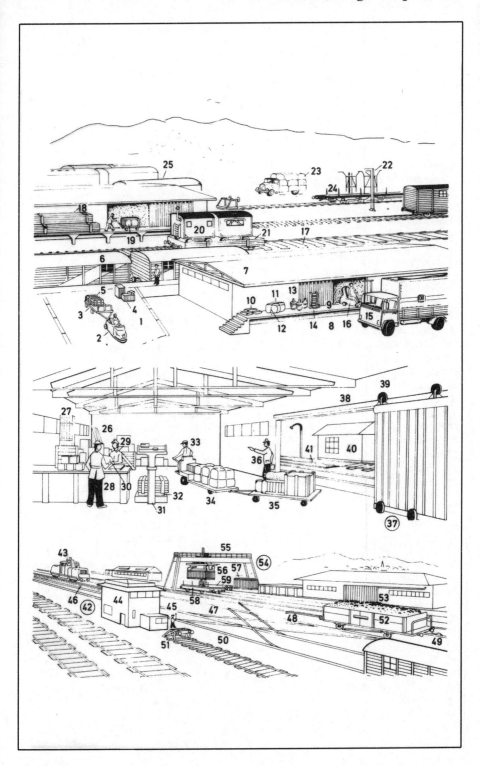

1-21 express train coach (express train carriage, express train car, corridor compartment coach), a passenger coach
1 side elevation (side view)
2 coach body
3 underframe (frame)
4 bogie (truck) with steel and rubber suspension and shock absorbers
5 battery containers (battery boxes)
6 steam and electric heat exchanger for the heating system
7 sliding window
8 rubber connecting seal
9 ventilator
10-21 plan
10 second-class section
11 corridor
12 folding seat (tip-up seat)
13 passenger compartment (compartment)
14 compartment door
15 washroom
16 toilet (lavatory, WC)
17 first-class section
18 swing door
19 sliding connecting door
20 door
21 vestibule
22-32 dining car (restaurant car, diner)
22-25 side elevation (side view)
22 door
23 loading door
24 current collector for supplying power during stops
25 battery boxes (battery containers)
26-32 plan
26 staff washroom
27 storage cupboard
28 washing-up area
29 kitchen
30 electric oven with eight hotplates
31 counter
32 dining compartment
33 dining car kitchen
34 chef (head cook)
35 kitchen cabinet
36 sleeping car (sleeper)
37 side elevation (side view)
38-42 plan
38 two-seat twin-berth compartment (two-seat two-berth compartment, *Am.* bedroom)

39 folding doors
40 washstand
41 office
42 toilet (lavatory, WC)
43 express train compartment
44 upholstered reclining seat
45 armrest
46 ashtray in the armrest
47 adjustable headrest
48 antimacassar
49 mirror
50 coat hook
51 luggage rack
52 compartment window
53 fold-away table (pull-down table)
54 heating regulator
55 litter receptacle
56 curtain
57 footrest
58 corner seat
59 open car
60 side elevation (side view)
61-72 plan
61 open carriage
62 row of single seats
63 row of double seats
64 reclining seat
65 seat upholstery
66 backrest
67 headrest
68 down-filled headrest cushion with nylon cover
69 armrest with ashtray
70 cloakroom
71 luggage compartment
72 toilet (lavatory, WC)
73 buffet car (quick-service buffet car), a self-service restaurant car
74 side elevation (side view)
75 current collector for supplying power during stops
76 plan
77 dining compartment
78-79 buffet (buffet compartment)
78 customer area
79 serving area
80 kitchen
81 staff compartment
82 staff toilet (staff lavatory, staff WC)
83 food compartments
84 plates
85 cutlery
86 till (cash register)

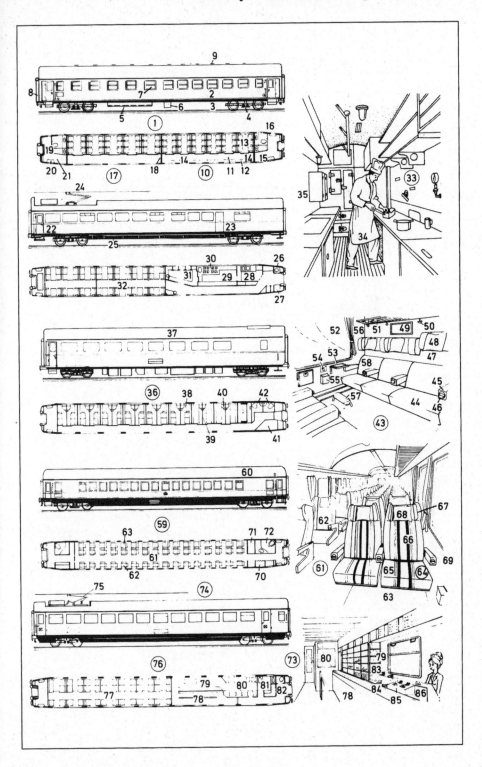

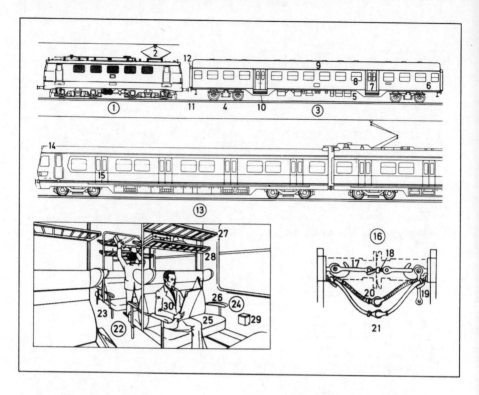

1-30 local train service
1-12 local train (short-distance train)
1 electric locomotive
2 current collector
3 four-axled coach (four-axled car) for short-distance routes, a passenger coach (passenger car)
4 bogie (truck) [with disc (disk) brakes]
5 underframe (frame)
6 coach body with metal panelling (*Am.* paneling)
7 double folding doors
8 compartment window
9 open carriage
10 entrance
11 connecting corridor
12 rubber connecting seal
13 light railcar, a short-distance railcar
14 cab (driver's cab, *Am.* engineer's cab)
15 carriage door
16 connecting hoses and coupling
17 coupling link
18 tensioning device (coupling screw with tensioning lever)
19 unlinked coupling
20 heating coupling hose (steam coupling hose)
21 coupling hose (connecting hose) for the compressed-air braking system
22 second-class section
23 central gangway
24 compartment
25 upholstered seat
26 armrest
27 luggage rack
28 hat and light luggage rack
29 ashtray
30 passenger

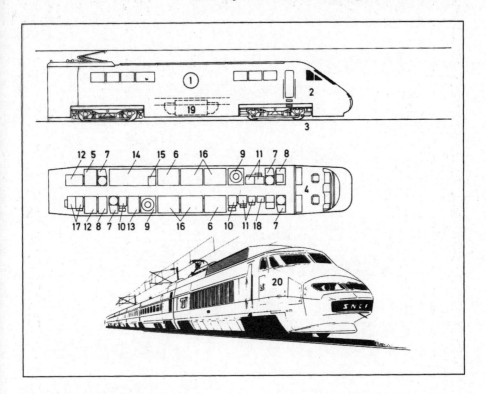

1-19 Intercity Express
1 German Federal Railway trainset
2 driving unit (power car)
3 driving bogie with traction motors
4 cab (driver's cab, *Am.* engineer's cab)
5 power supply (traction current filter)
6 contactors (converters, inductance)
7 traction motor blower
8 inductance protection (converter)
9 oil-cooling plant
10 converter for the auxiliaries
11 electronics
12 control current equipment
13 auxiliaries (switchgear)
14 pneumatic equipment
15 air-conditioning plant
16 main current converters
17 measuring equipment (diagnosis)
18 continuous automatic train-running control
19 transformer

20 **TGV** (Train à Grande Vitesse) of the Société Nationale des Chemins de Fer Français (SNCF)

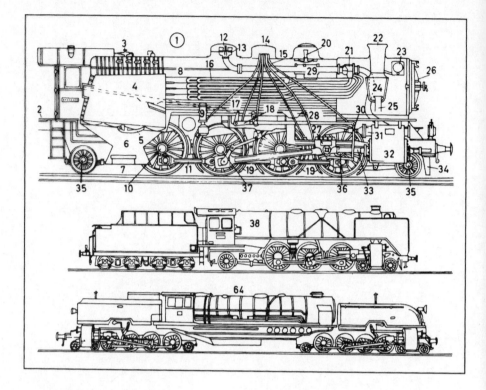

1-69 steam locomotives

2-37 locomotive boiler and driving gear

2 tender platform with coupling
3 safety valve for excess boiler pressure
4 firebox
5 drop grate
6 ashpan with damper doors
7 bottom door of the ashpan
8 smoke tubes (flue tubes)
9 feed pump
10 axle bearing
11 coupling rod
12 steam dome
13 regulator valve (regulator main valve)
14 sand dome
15 sand pipes (sand tubes)
16 boiler (boiler barrel)
17 fire tubes or steam tubes
18 reversing gear (steam reversing gear)
19 sand pipes

20 feed valve
21 steam collector
22 chimney (smokestack, smoke outlet and waste steam exhaust)
23 feedwater preheater (feedwater heater, economizer)
24 spark arrester
25 blast pipe
26 smokebox door
27 cross head
28 mud drum
29 top feedwater tray
30 combination lever
31 steam chest
32 cylinder
33 piston rod with stuffing box (packing box)
34 guard iron (rail guard, *Am.* pilot, cowcatcher)
35 carrying axle (running axle, dead axle)
36 coupled axle
37 driving axle
38 express locomotive with tender

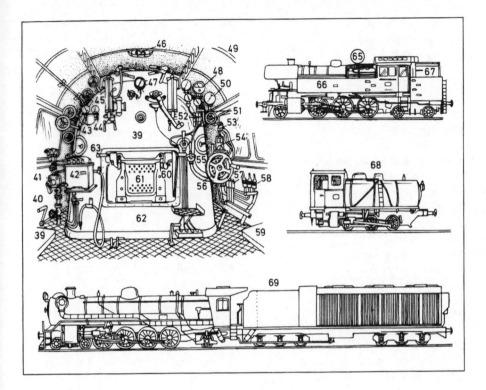

39-63 cab (driver's cab, *Am.* engineer's cab)

39 fireman's seat

40 drop grate lever

41 line steam injector

42 automatic lubricant pump (automatic lubricator)

43 preheater pressure gauge (*Am.* gage)

44 carriage heating pressure gauge (*Am.* gage)

45 water gauge (*Am.* gage)

46 light

47 boiler pressure gauge (*Am.* gage)

48 distant-reading temperature gauge (*Am.* gage)

49 cab (driver's cab, *Am.* engineer's cab)

50 brake pressure gauge (*Am.* gage)

51 whistle valve handle

52 driver's timetable (*Am.* engineer's schedule)

53 driver's brake valve (*Am.* engineer's brake valve)

54 speed recorder (tachograph)

55 sanding valve

56 reversing wheel

57 emergency brake valve

58 release valve

59 driver's seat (*Am.* engineer's seat)

60 firehole shield

61 firehole door

62 vertical boiler

63 firedoor handle handgrip

64 articulated locomotive (Garratt locomotive)

65 tank locomotive

66 water tank

67 fuel tender

68 steam storage locomotive (fireless locomotive)

69 condensing locomotive (locomotive with condensing tender)

1 **electric locomotive**
2 current collector
3 main switch
4 high-tension transformer
5 roof cable
6 traction motor
7 inductive train control system
8 main air reservoir
9 whistle
10-18 plan of locomotive
10 transformer with tap changer
11 oil cooler with blower
12 oil-circulating pump
13 tap changer driving mechanism
14 air compressor
15 traction motor blower
16 terminal box
17 capacitors for auxiliary motors
18 commutator cover
19 **cab** (driver's cab, *Am.* engineer's cab)
20 controller handwheel
21 dead man's handle
22 driver's brake valve (*Am.* engineer's brake valve)
23 ancillary brake valve (auxiliary brake valve)
24 pressure gauge (*Am.* gage)
25 bypass switch for the dead man's handle
26 tractive effort indicator
27 train heating voltage indicator
28 contact wire voltage indicator (overhead wire voltage indicator)
29 high-tension voltage indicator
30 on/off switch for the current collector
31 main switch
32 sander switch (sander control)
33 anti-skid brake switch
34 visual display for the ancillary systems
35 speedometer
36 running step indicator
37 clock
38 controls for the inductive train control system

39 cab heating switch
40 whistle lever
41 **contact wire maintenance vehicle** (overhead wire maintenance vehicle), a diesel railcar
42 work platform (working platform)
43 ladder
44-54 mechanical equipment of the contact wire maintenance vehicle
44 air compressor
45 blower oil pump
46 generator
47 diesel engine
48 injection pump
49 silencer (*Am.* muffler)
50 change-speed gear
51 cardan shaft
52 wheel flange lubricator
53 reversing gear
54 torque converter bearing
55 **accumulator railcar** (battery railcar)
56 battery box (battery container)
57 cab (driver's cab, *Am.* engineer's cab)
58 second-class seating arrangement
59 toilet (lavatory, WC)
60 **fast electric multiple-unit train**
61 front railcar
62 driving trailer car

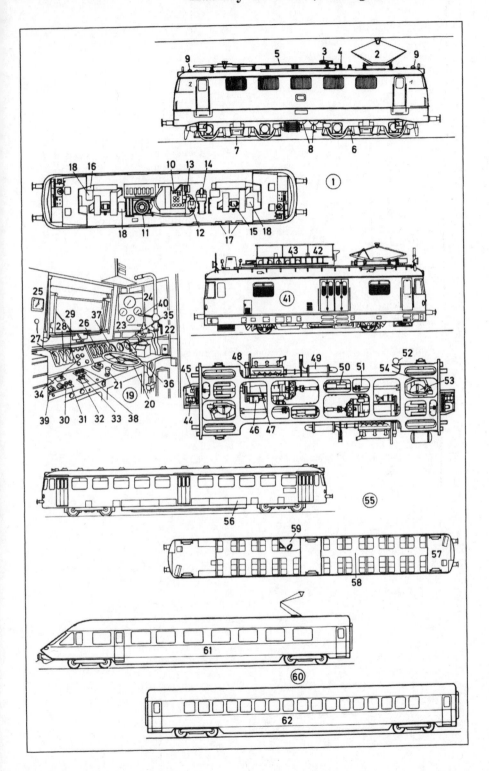

1-84 diesel locomotives
1 **diesel-hydraulic locomotive,** a mainline locomotive (diesel locomotive) for medium passenger and goods service (freight service)
2 bogie (truck)
3 wheel and axle set
4 main fuel tank
5 cab (driver's cab, *Am.* engineer's cab) of a diesel locomotive
6 main air pressure gauge (*Am.* gage)
7 brake cylinder pressure gauge (*Am.* gage)
8 main air reservoir pressure gauge (*Am.* gage)
9 speedometer
10 auxiliary brake
11 driver's brake valve (*Am.* engineer's brake valve)
12 controller handwheel
13 dead man's handle
14 inductive train control system
15 signal lights
16 clock
17 voltage meter for the train heating system
18 current meter for the train heating system
19 engine oil temperature gauge (*Am.* gage)
20 transmission oil temperature gauge (*Am.* gage)
21 cooling water temperature gauge (*Am.* gage)
22 revolution counter (rev counter, tachometer)
23 radio telephone
24 diesel-hydraulic locomotive [plan and elevation]
25 diesel engine
26 cooling unit
27 fluid transmission
28 wheel and axle drive
29 cardan shaft
30 starter motor
31 instrument panel
32 driver's control desk (*Am.* engineer's control desk)
33 hand brake
34 air compressor with electric motor
35 equipment locker
36 heat exchanger for transmission oil
37 engine room ventilator
38 magnet for the inductive train control system
39 train heating generator

40 casing of the train heating system transformer
41 preheater
42 exhaust silencer (*Am.* exhaust muffler)
43 auxiliary heat exchanger for the transmission oil
44 hydraulic brake
45 tool box
46 starter battery
47 **diesel-hydraulic locomotive** for light and medium shunting service
48 exhaust silencer (*Am.* exhaust muffler)
49 bell and whistle
50 yard radio
51-67 elevation of locomotive
51 diesel engine with supercharged turbine
52 fluid transmission
53 output gear box
54 radiator
55 heat exchanger for the engine lubricating oil
56 fuel tank
57 main air reservoir
58 air compressor
59 sand boxes
60 reserve fuel tank
61 auxiliary air reservoir
62 hydrostatic fan drive
63 seat with clothes compartment
64 hand brake wheel
65 cooling water
66 ballast
67 engine and transmission control wheel
68 **small diesel locomotive** for shunting service
69 exhaust casing
70 horn
71 main air reservoir
72 air compressor
73 eight-cylinder diesel engine
74 Voith transmission with reversing gear
75 heating oil tank (fuel oil tank)
76 sand box
77 cooling unit
78 header tank for the cooling water
79 oil bath air cleaner (oil bath air filter)
80 hand brake wheel
81 control wheel
82 coupling
83 cardan shaft
84 louvred shutter

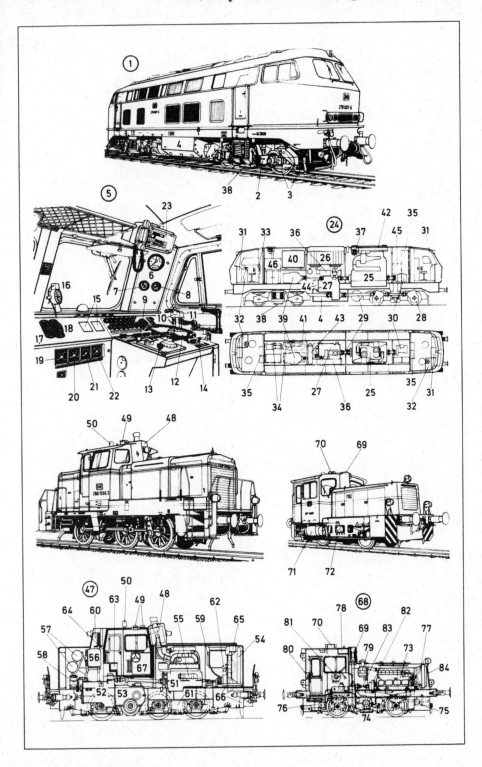

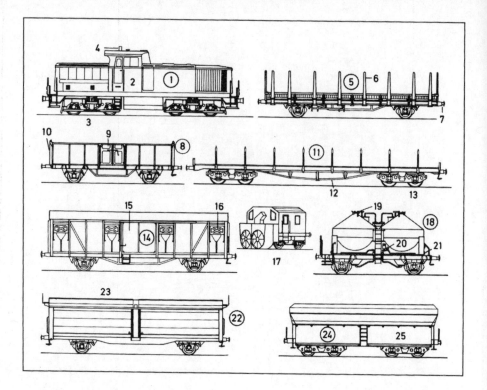

1 diesel-hydraulic locomotive
2 cab (driver's cab, *Am.* engineer's cab)
3 wheel and axle set
4 aerial for the yard radio
5 standard flat wagon (*Am.* standard flatcar)
6 hinged steel stanchion (stanchion)
7 buffers
8 standard open goods wagon (*Am.* standard open freight car)
9 revolving side doors
10 hinged front
11 standard flat wagon (*Am.* standard flatcar) with bogies
12 sole bar reinforcement
13 bogie (truck)
14 covered goods van (covered goods wagon, *Am.* boxcar)
15 sliding door
16 ventilation flap

17 snow blower (rotary snow plough, *Am.* snowplow), a track-clearing vehicle
18 wagon (*Am.* car) with pneumatic discharge
19 filler hole
20 compressed-air supply
21 discharge connection valve
22 goods van (*Am.* boxcar) with sliding roof
23 roof opening
24 bogie open self-discharge wagon (*Am.* bogie open self-discharge freight car)
25 discharge flap (discharge door)

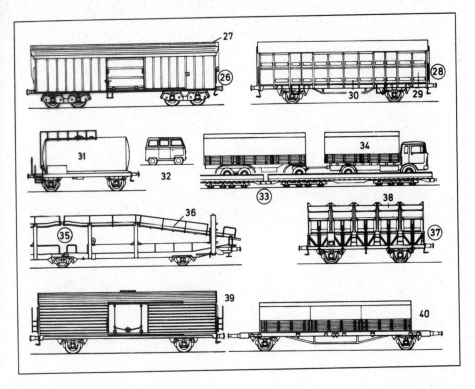

26 bogie wagon with swivelling (*Am.* swiveling) roof

27 swivelling (*Am.* swiveling) roof

28 large-capacity wagon (*Am.* large-capacity car) for small livestock

29 sidewall with ventilation flaps (slatted wall)

30 ventilation flap

31 tank wagon (*Am.* tank car)

32 track inspection railcar

33 open special wagons (*Am.* open special freight cars)

34 lorry (*Am.* truck) with trailer

35 two-tier car carrier (double-deck car carrier)

36 hinged upper deck

37 tipper wagon (*Am.* dump car) with skips

38 skip

39 general-purpose refrigerator wagon (refrigerator van, *Am.* refrigerator car)

40 interchangeable bodies for flat wagons (*Am.* flatcars)

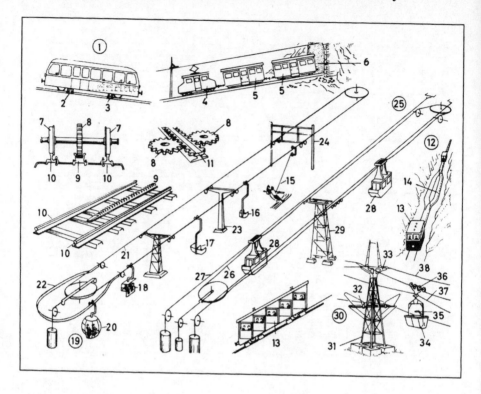

38 suspension cable (supporting cable)
39 **valley station** (lower station)
40 tension weight shaft
41 tension weight for the suspension cable (supporting cable)
42 tension weight for the haulage cable
43 tension cable pulley
44 suspension cable (supporting cable)
45 haulage cable
46 balance cable (lower cable)
47 auxiliary cable (emergency cable)
48 auxiliary-cable tensioning mechanism (emergency-cable tensioning mechanism)
49 haulage cable rollers
50 spring buffer (*Am.* spring bumper)
51 valley station platform (lower station platform)
52 cabin (cableway gondola, ropeway gondola, suspension line gondola), a large-capacity cabin
53 pulley cradle
54 suspension gear
55 stabilizer
56 guide rail
57 **top station** (upper station)
58 suspension cable guide (supporting cable guide)
59 suspension cable anchorage (supporting cable anchorage)
60 haulage cable rollers
61 haulage cable guide wheel
62 haulage cable driving pulley
63 main drive
64 standby drive
65 control room
66 **cabin pulley cradle**
67 main pulley cradle
68 double cradle
69 two-wheel cradle
70 running wheels
71 suspension cable brake (supporting cable brake), an emergency brake in case of haulage cable failure
72 suspension gear bolt
73 haulage cable sleeve
74 balance cable sleeve (lower cable sleeve)
75 derailment guard
76 **cable supports** (ropeway supports, suspension line supports, intermediate supports)
77 pylon, a framework support
78 tubular steel pylon, a tubular steel support
79 suspension cable guide rail (supporting cable guide rail, support guide rail)
80 support truss, a frame for work on the cable
81 base of the support

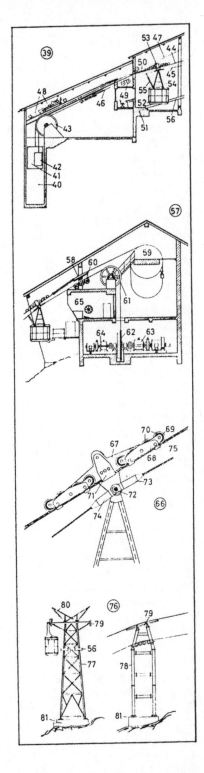

1 cross-section of a bridge
2 orthotropic roadway (orthotropic deck)
3 truss (bracing)
4 diagonal brace (diagonal strut)
5 hollow tubular section
6 deck slab
7 solid-web girder bridge (beam bridge)
8 road surface
9 top flange
10 bottom flange
11 fixed bearing
12 movable bearing
13 clear span
14 span
15 rope bridge (primitive suspension bridge)
16 carrying rope
17 suspension rope
18 woven deck (woven decking)
19 stone arch bridge, a solid bridge
20 arch
21 pier
22 statue
23 trussed arch bridge
24 truss element
25 trussed arch
26 arch span
27 abutment (end pier)
28 spandrel-braced arch bridge
29 abutment (abutment pier)
30 bridge strut
31 crown
32 covered bridge of the Middle Ages (the *Ponte Vecchio* in Florence)
33 goldsmiths' shops
34 steel lattice bridge
35 counterbrace (crossbrace, diagonal member)
36 vertical member
37 truss joint
38 portal frame
39 suspension bridge
40 suspension cable
41 suspender (hanger)
42 tower
43 suspension cable anchorage
44 tied beam [with roadway]
45 abutment
46 cable-stayed bridge
47 inclined tension cable
48 inclined cable anchorage
49 reinforced concrete bridge
50 reinforced concrete arch
51 inclined cable system (multiple cable system)
52 flat bridge, a plate girder bridge
53 stiffener
54 pier
55 bridge bearing
56 cutwater
57 straits bridge, a bridge built of precast elements
58 precast construction unit
59 viaduct
60 valley bottom
61 reinforced concrete pier
62 scaffolding
63 lattice swing bridge
64 turntable
65 pivot pier
66 pivoting half (pivoting section, pivoting span, movable half) of bridge
67 flat swing bridge
68 middle section
69 pivot
70 parapet (handrailing)

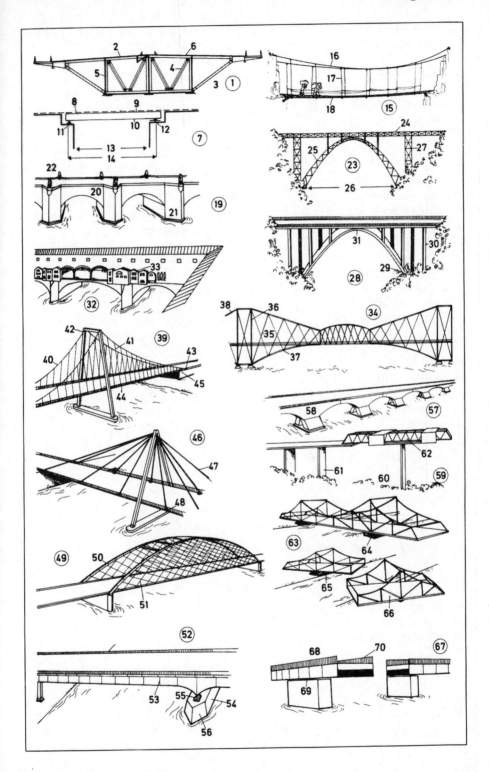

1 **cable ferry** (*also:* chain ferry), a passenger ferry
2 ferry rope (ferry cable)
3 river branch (river arm)
4 river island (river islet)
5 collapsed section of riverbank, flood damage
6 **motor ferry**
7 ferry landing stage (motorboat landing stage)
8 pile foundations
9 current (flow, course)
10 **flying ferry** (river ferry), a car ferry
11 ferry boat
12 buoy (float)
13 anchorage
14 harbour (*Am.* harbor) for laying up river craft
15 **ferry boat** (punt)
16 pole (punt pole, quant pole)
17 ferryman
18 blind river branch (blind river arm)
19 groyne (*Am.* groin)
20 groyne (*Am.* groin) head
21 fairway (navigable part of river)
22 **train of barges**
23 river tug
24 tow rope (tow line, towing hawser)
25 barge (freight barge, cargo barge, lighter)
26 bargeman (bargee, lighterman)
27 **towing** (hauling, haulage)
28 towing mast
29 towing engine
30 towing track; *form.:* tow path (towing path)
31 river after river training
32 **dike** (dyke, main dike, flood wall, winter dike)
33 drainage ditch
34 dike (dyke) drainage sluice
35 wing wall
36 outfall
37 drain (infiltration drain)
38 berm (berme)
39 top of dike (dyke)
40 dike (dyke) batter (dike slope)
41 flood bed (inundation area)
42 flood containment area
43 current meter
44 kilometre (*Am.* kilometer) sign
45 dikereeve's (dykereeve's) house (dikereeve's cottage); *also:* ferryman's house (cottage)
46 dikereeve (dykereeve)
47 dike (dyke) ramp
48 summer dike (summer dyke)
49 levee (embankment)
50 sandbags
51-55 **bank protection** (bank stabilization, revetment)
51 riprap
52 alluvial deposit (sand deposit)
53 fascine (bundle of wooden sticks)
54 wicker fences
55 stone pitching
56 **floating dredging machine** (dredger), a multi-bucket ladder dredge
57 bucket elevator chain
58 dredging bucket
59 **suction dredger** (hydraulic dredger) with trailing suction pipe or barge sucker
60 centrifugal pump
61 back scouring valve
62 suction pump, a jet pump with scouring nozzles

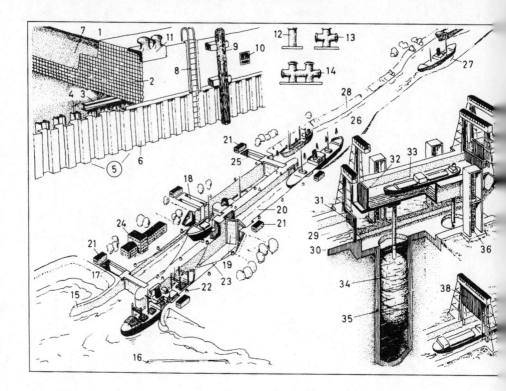

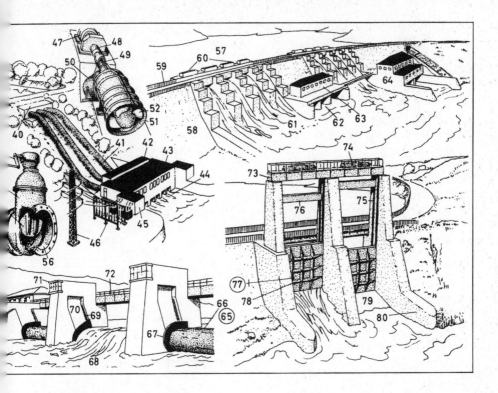

39-46 pumping plant and reservoir
39 forebay
40 surge tank
41 pressure pipeline
42 valve house (valve control house)
43 turbine house (pumping station)
44 discharge structure (outlet structure)
45 control station
46 transformer station
47-52 axial-flow pump (propeller pump)
47 drive motor
48 gear
49 drive shaft
50 pressure pipe
51 suction head
52 impeller wheel
53-56 sluice valve (sluice gate)
53 crank drive
54 valve housing
55 sliding valve (sliding gate)
56 discharge opening
57-64 dam (barrage)
57 reservoir (storage reservoir, impound-
ing reservoir, impounded reservoir)
58 masonry dam
59 crest of dam

60 spillway (overflow spillway)
61 stilling basin (stilling box, stilling pool)
62 scouring tunnel (outlet tunnel, waste
water outlet)
63 valve house (valve control house)
64 power station
65-72 rolling dam (weir), a barrage; *other
system:* shutter weir
65 roller, a barrier
66 roller top
67 flange
68 submersible roller
69 rack track
70 recess
71 hoisting gear cabin
72 service bridge (walkway)
73-80 sluice dam
73 hoisting gear bridge
74 hoisting gear (winding gear)
75 guide groove
76 counterweight (counterpoise)
77 sluice gate (floodgate)
78 reinforcing rib
79 dam sill (weir sill)
80 wing wall

1-6 Germanic rowing boat [ca. AD 400]; the Nydam boat
1 stern post
2 steersman
3 oarsman
4 stem post (stem)
5 oar, for rowing
6 rudder (steering oar), a side rudder, for steering
7 **dugout,** a hollowed-out tree trunk
8 paddle
9-12 trireme, a Roman warship
9 ram
10 forecastle (fo'c'sle)
11 grapple (grapnel, grappling iron), for fastening the enemy ship alongside
12 three banks (tiers) of oars
13-17 Viking ship (longship, dragon ship) [Norse]
13 helm (tiller)
14 awning crutch with carved horses' heads
15 awning
16 dragon figurehead
17 shield
18-26 cog (Hansa cog, Hansa ship)
18 anchor cable (anchor rope, anchor hawser)
19 forecastle (fo'c'sle)
20 bowsprit
21 furled (brailed-up) square sail
22 town banner (city banner)
23 aftercastle (sterncastle)
24 rudder, a stem rudder
25 elliptical stern (round stern)
26 wooden fender
27-43 caravel (carvel) ['Santa Maria' 1492]
27 admiral's cabin
28 spanker boom
29 mizzen (mizen, mutton spanker, lateen spanker), a lateen sail
30 lateen yard
31 mizzen (mizen) mast
32 lashing

33 mainsail (main course), a square sail
34 bonnet, a removable strip of canvas
35 bowline
36 bunt line (martinet)
37 main yard
38 main topsail
39 main topsail yard
40 mainmast
41 foresail (fore course)
42 foremast
43 spritsail
44-50 galley [15th to 18th century], a slave galley
44 lantern
45 cabin
46 central gangway
47 slave driver with whip
48 galley slaves
49 covered platform in the forepart of the ship
50 gun
51-60 ship of the line (line-of-battle ship) [18th to 19th century], a three-decker
51 jib boom
52 fore topgallant sail
53 main topgallant sail
54 mizzen (mizen) topgallant sail
55-57 gilded stern
55 upper stern
56 stern gallery
57 quarter gallery, a projecting balcony with ornamental portholes
58 lower stern
59 gunports for broadside fire
60 gunport shutter

1-72 rigging (rig, tackle) and sails of a bark (barque)
1-9 masts
1 bowsprit with jib boom
2-4 foremast
2 lower foremast
3 fore topmast
4 fore topgallant mast
5-7 mainmast
5 lower mainmast
6 main topmast
7 main topgallant mast
8, 9 mizzen (mizen) mast
8 lower mizzen (lower mizen)
9 mizzen (mizen) topmast
10-19 standing rigging
10 forestay, mizzen (mizen) stay, mainstay
11 fore topmast stay, main topmast stay, mizzen (mizen) topmast stay
12 fore topgallant stay, mizzen (mizen) topgallant stay, main topgallant stay
13 fore royal stay (main royal stay)
14 jib stay
15 bobstay
16 shrouds
17 fore topmast rigging (main topmast rigging, mizzen (mizen) topmast rigging)
18 fore topgallant rigging (main topgallant rigging)
19 backstays
20-31 fore-and-aft sails
20 fore topmast staysail
21 inner jib
22 outer jib
23 flying jib
24 main topmast staysail
25 main topgallant staysail
26 main royal staysail
27 mizzen (mizen) staysail
28 mizzen (mizen) topmast staysail
29 mizzen (mizen) topgallant staysail
30 mizzen (mizen, spanker, driver)
31 gaff topsail
32-45 spars

32 foreyard
33 lower fore topsail yard
34 upper fore topsail yard
35 lower fore topgallant yard
36 upper fore topgallant yard
37 fore royal yard
38 main yard
39 lower main topsail yard
40 upper main topsail yard
41 lower main topgallant yard
42 upper main topgallant yard
43 main royal yard
44 spanker boom
45 spanker gaff
46 footrope
47 lifts
48 spanker boom topping lift
49 spanker peak halyard
50 foretop
51 fore topmast crosstrees
52 maintop
53 main topmast crosstrees
54 mizzen (mizen) top
55-66 square sails
55 foresail (fore course)
56 lower fore topsail
57 upper fore topsail
58 lower fore topgallant sail
59 upper fore topgallant sail
60 fore royal
61 mainsail (main course)
62 lower main topsail
63 upper main topsail
64 lower main topgallant sail
65 upper main topgallant sail
66 main royal sail
67-71 running rigging
67 braces
68 sheets
69 spanker sheet
70 spanker vangs
71 bunt line
72 reef

1-5 sail shapes
1 gaffsail (*small:* trysail, spencer)
2 jib
3 lateen sail
4 lugsail
5 spritsail
6-8 single-masted sailing boats (*Am.* sailboats)
6 tjalk
7 leeboard
8 cutter
9, 10 mizzen (mizen) masted sailing boats (*Am.* sailboats)
9 ketch-rigged sailing barge
10 yawl
11-17 two-masted sailing boats (*Am.* sailboats)
11-13 topsail schooner
11 mainsail
12 boom foresail
13 square foresail
14 brigantine
15 half-rigged mast with fore-and-aft sails
16 full-rigged mast with square sails
17 brig
18-27 three-masted sailing vessels (three-masters)
18 three-masted schooner
19 three-masted topsail schooner
20 bark (barque) schooner
21-23 bark (barque) [cf. illustration of rigging and sails in plate 219]
21 foremast
22 mainmast
23 mizzen (mizen) mast
24-27 full-rigged ship
24 mizzen (mizen) mast
25 crossjack yard (crojack yard)
26 crossjack (crojack)
27 ports
28-31 four-masted sailing ships (four-masters)
28 four-masted schooner
29 four-masted bark (barque)
30 mizzen (mizen) mast
31 four-masted full-rigged ship

32-34 five-masted bark (barque)
32 skysail
33 middle mast
34 mizzen (mizen) mast
35-37 development of sailing ships over 400 years
35 five-masted full-rigged ship 'Preussen' 1902-10
36 English clipper ship 'Spindrift' 1867
37 caravel (carvel) 'Santa Maria' 1492

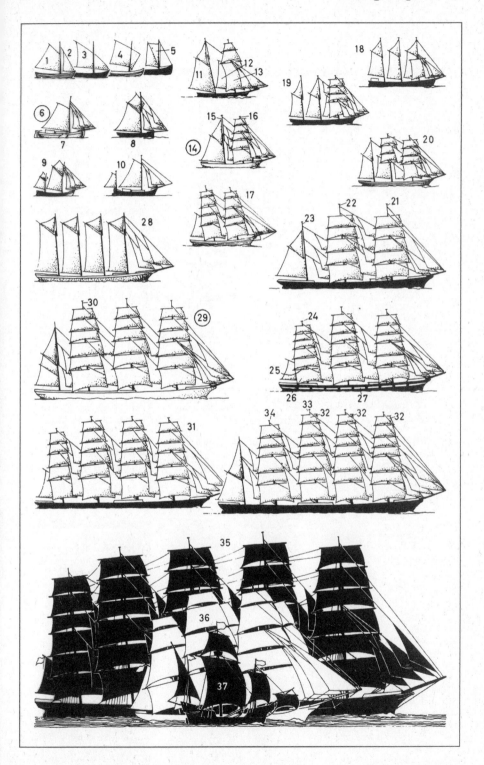

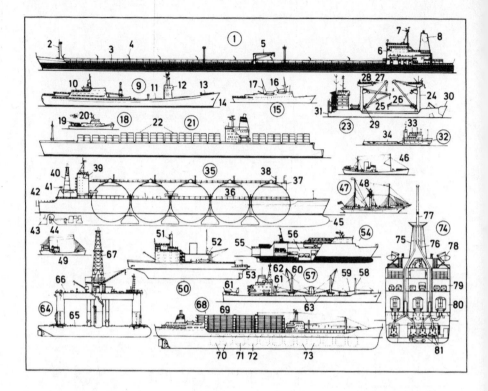

machinery
66 drilling platform
67 derrick
68 **cattleship** (cattle vessel)
69 superstructure for transporting livestock
70 fresh water tanks
71 fuel tank
72 dung tank
73 fodder tanks
74 **train ferry** [cross section]
75 funnel
76 exhaust pipes
77 mast
78 ship's lifeboat hanging at
   the davit
79 car deck
80 main deck (train deck)
81 main engines
82 **passenger liner** (liner,
   ocean liner)
83 stem
84 funnel with lattice casing
85 flag dressing (rainbow
   dressing, string of flags
   extending over mast-
   heads, e.g., on the maiden
   voyage)
86 **trawler,** a factory ship
87 gallows

88 stern ramp
89 **container ship**
90 loading bridge (loading
   platform)
91 sea ladder (jacob's ladder,
   rope ladder)
92 **barge and push tug
   assembly**
93 push tug
94 tug-pushed dumb barge
   (tug-pushed lighter)
95 pilot boat
96 **combined cargo and passenger liner**
97 passengers disembarking
   by boat
98 accommodation ladder
99 coaster (coasting vessel)
100 customs or police launch
101-128 **excursion steamer**
   (pleasure steamer)
101-106 lifeboat launching
   gear
101 davit
102 wire rope span
103 lifeline
104 tackle
105 block
106 fall
107 ship's lifeboat (ship's

boat) covered with tar-
   paulin
108 stem
109 passenger
110 steward
111 deck-chair
112 deck hand
113 deck bucket
114 boatswain (bo's'n, bo'sun,
   bosun)
115 tunic
116 awning
117 stanchion
118 ridge rope (jackstay)
119 lashing
120 bulwark
121 guard rail
122 handrail (top rail)
123 companion ladder (companionway)
124 lifebelt (lifebuoy)
125 lifebuoy light (lifebelt
   light, signal light)
126 officer of the watch
   (watchkeeper)
127 reefer (*Am.* pea jacket)
128 binoculars

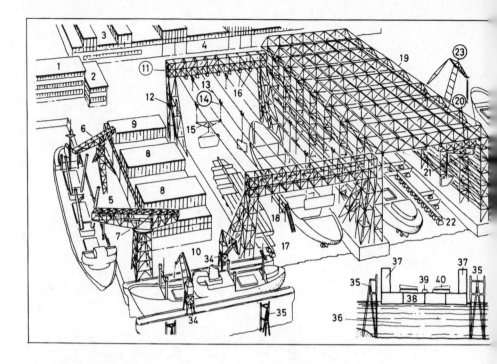

1-43 shipyard (shipbuilding yard, dock-yard, *Am.* navy yard)
1 administrative offices
2 ship-drawing office
3, 4 shipbuilding sheds
3 mould (*Am.* mold) loft
4 erection shop
5-9 fitting-out quay
5 quay
6 tripod crane
7 hammer-headed crane
8 engineering workshop
9 boiler shop
10 repair quay
11-26 slipways (slips, building berths, building slips, stocks)
11-18 cable crane berth, a slipway (building berth)
11 slipway portal
12 bridge support
13 crane cable
14 crab (jenny)
15 cross piece
16 crane driver's cabin (crane driver's cage)
17 slipway floor
18 staging, a scaffold
19-21 frame slipway

19 slipway frame
20 overhead travelling (*Am.* traveling) crane (gantry crane)
21 slewing crab
22 keel in position
23 luffing jib crane, a slipway crane
24 crane rails (crane track)
25 gantry crane
26 gantry (bridge)
27 trestles (supports)
28 crab (jenny)
29 hull frames in position
30 ship under construction
31-33 dry dock
31 dock floor (dock bottom)
32 dock gates (caisson)
33 pumping station (power house)
34-43 floating dock (pontoon dock)
34 dock crane (dockside crane), a jib crane
35 fender pile
36-43 working of docks
36 dock basin
37, 38 dock structure
37 side tank (side wall)
38 bottom tank (bottom pontoon)
39 keel block
40 bilge block (bilge shore, side support)

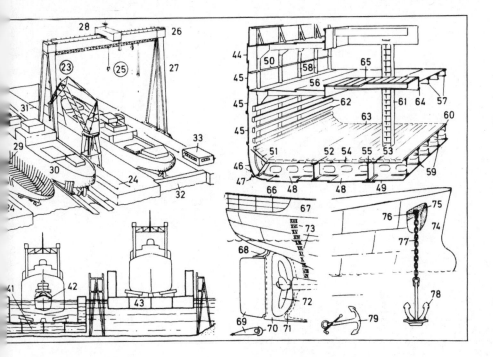

41-43 docking a ship
41 flooded floating dock
42 tug towing the ship
43 emptied (pumped-out) dock
44-61 structural parts of the ship
44-56 longitudinal structure
44-49 shell (shell plating, skin)
44 sheer strake
45 side strake
46 bilge strake
47 bilge keel
48 bottom plating
49 flat plate keel (keel plate)
50 stringer (side stringer)
51 tank margin plate
52 longitudinal side girder
53 centre (*Am.* center) plate girder (centre girder, kelson, keelson, vertical keel)
54 tank top plating (tank top, inner bottom plating)
55 centre (*Am.* center) strake
56 deck plating
57 deck beam
58 frame (rib)
59 floor plate
60 cellular double bottom
61 hold pillar (pillar)

62, 63 dunnage
62 side battens (side ceiling, spar ceiling)
63 ceiling (floor ceiling)
64, 65 hatchway
64 hatch coaming
65 hatch cover (hatchboard)
66-72 stern
66 guard rail
67 bulwark
68 rudder stock
69, 70 Oertz rudder
69 rudder blade (rudder)
70, 71 stern frame
70 rudder post
71 propeller post (screw post)
72 ship's propeller (ship's screw)
73 draught (draft) marks
74-79 bow
74 stem, a bulbous stem (bulbous bow)
75 hawse
76 hawse pipe
77 anchor cable (chain cable)
78 stockless anchor (patent anchor)
79 stocked anchor

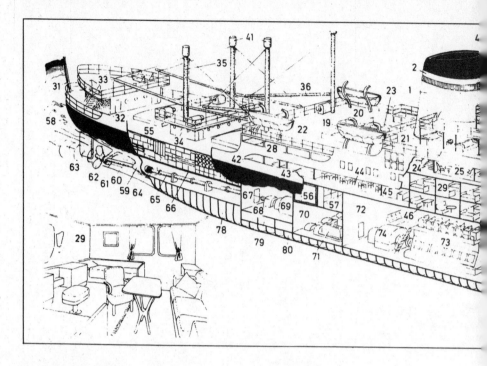

1-71 combined cargo and passenger ship [of the older type]
1 funnel
2 funnel marking
3 siren (fog horn)
4-11 compass platform (compass bridge, compass flat, monkey bridge)
4 antenna lead-in (antenna down-lead)
5 radio direction finder (RDF) antenna (direction finder antenna, rotatable loop antenna, aural null loop antenna)
6 magnetic compass (mariner's compass)
7 morse lamp (signalling, *Am.* signaling, lamp)
8 radar antenna (radar scanner)
9 code flag signal
10 code flag halyards
11 triatic stay (signal stay)
12-18 bridge deck (bridge)
12 radio room
13 captain's cabin
14 navigating bridge
15 starboard sidelight [green; port sidelight red]
16 wing of bridge
17 shelter (weather cloth, dodger)
18 wheelhouse
19-21 boat deck
19 ship's lifeboat
20 davit
21 officer's cabin
22-27 promenade deck
22 sun deck (lido deck)
23 swimming pool
24 companion ladder (companionway)
25 library (ship's library)
26 lounge
27 promenade
28-30 A-deck
28 semi-enclosed deck space
29 double-berth cabin, a cabin
30 de luxe cabin
31 ensign staff
32-47 B-deck (main deck)
32 after deck
33 poop
34 deckhouse
35 samson (sampson) post (king post)
36 derrick boom (cargo boom)
37 crosstrees (spreader)
38 crow's nest
39 topmast
40 forward steaming light

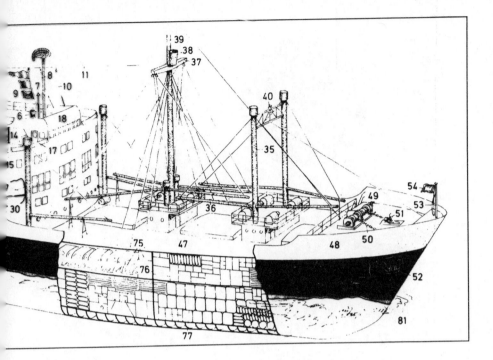

41 ventilator lead
42 galley (caboose, cookroom, ship's kitchen)
43 ship's pantry
44 dining room
45 purser's office
46 single-berth cabin
47 foredeck
48 forecastle (fo'c'sle)
49-51 **ground tackle**
49 windlass
50 anchor cable (chain cable)
51 compressor (chain compressor)
52 anchor
53 jackstaff
54 jack
55 after holds
56 cold storage room (insulated hold)
57 store room
58 wake
59 shell bossing (shaft bossing)
60 tail shaft (tail end shaft)
61 shaft strut (strut, spectacle frame, propeller strut, propeller bracket)
62 three-blade ship's propeller (ship's screw)
63 rudder blade (rudder)

64 stuffing box
65 propeller shaft
66 shaft alley (shaft tunnel)
67 thrust block
68-74 **diesel-electric drive**
68 electric engine room
69 electric motor
70 auxiliary engine room
71 auxiliary engines
72 main engine room
73 main engine, a diesel engine
74 generator
75 forward holds
76 tween deck
77 cargo
78 ballast tank (deep tank) for water ballast
79 fresh water tank
80 fuel tank
81 bow wave

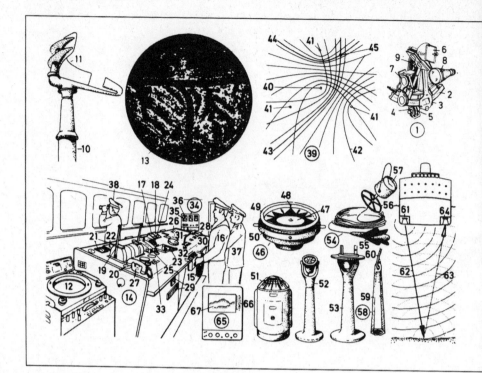

1 **sextant**
2 graduated arc
3 index bar (index arm)
4 decimal micrometer
5 vernier
6 index mirror
7 horizon glass (horizon mirror)
8 telescope
9 grip (handgrip)
10-13 **radar equipment** (radar apparatus)
10 radar pedestal
11 revolving radar reflector
12 radar display unit (radar screen)
13 radar image (radar picture)
14-38 **wheelhouse**
14 steering and control position
15 ship's wheel for controlling the rudder mechanism
16 helmsman (*Am.* wheelsman)
17 rudder angle indicator
18 automatic pilot (autopilot)
19 control lever for the variable-pitch propeller (reversible propeller, feathering propeller, feathering screw)
20 propeller pitch indicator

21 main engine revolution indicator
22 ship's speedometer (log)
23 control switch for bow thruster (bow-manoeuvring, *Am.* maneuvering, propeller)
24 echo recorder (depth recorder, echograph)
25 engine telegraph (engine order telegraph)
26 controls for the anti-rolling system (for the stabilizers)
27 local-battery telephone
28 shipping traffic radio telephone
29 navigation light indicator panel (running light indicator panel)
30 microphone for ship's address system
31 gyro compass (gyroscopic compass), a compass repeater
32 control button for the ship's siren (ship's fog horn)
33 main engine overload indicator
34 Decca position-finder (Decca Navigator)
35 rough focusing indicator
36 fine focusing indicator

37 navigating officer
38 captain
39 **Decca navigation system**
40 master station
41 slave station
42 null hyperbola
43 hyperbolic position line 1
44 hyperbolic position line 2
45 position (fix, ship fix)
46-53 **compasses**
46 liquid compass (fluid compass, spirit compass, wet compass), a magnetic compass
47 compass card
48 lubber's line (lubber's mark, lubber's point)
49 compass bowl
50 gimbal ring
51-53 gyro compass (gyroscopic compass, gyro compass unit)
51 master compass (master gyro compass)
52 compass repeater (gyro repeater)
53 compass repeater with pelorus
54 **patent log** (screw log, mechanical log, towing log, taffrail log, speedometer)
55 rotator
56 governor

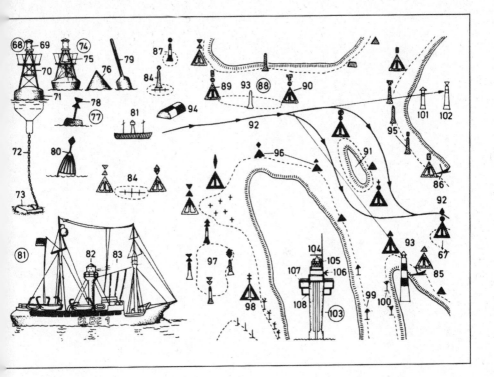

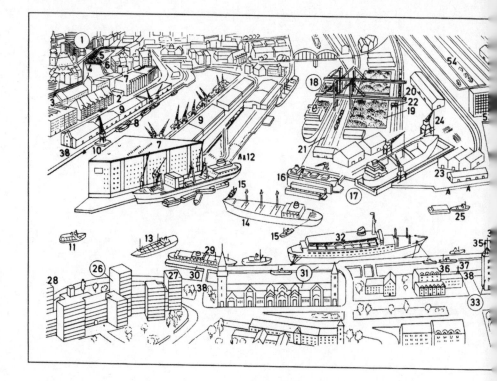

1 dock area
2 free port (foreign trade zone)
3 free zone frontier (free zone enclosure)
4 customs barrier
5 customs entrance
6 port custom house
7 entrepôt
8 barge (dumb barge, lighter)
9 break-bulk cargo transit shed (general cargo transit shed, package cargo transit shed)
10 floating crane
11 harbour (*Am.* harbor) ferry (ferryboat)
12 fender (dolphin)
13 bunkering boat
14 break-bulk carrier (general cargo ship)
15 tug
16 floating dock (pontoon dock)
17 dry dock

18 coal wharf
19 coal bunker
20 transporter loading bridge
21 quayside railway
22 weighing bunker
23 warehouse
24 quayside crane
25 launch and lighter
26 port hospital
27 quarantine wing
28 Institute of Tropical Medicine
29 excursion steamer (pleasure steamer)
30 jetty
31 passenger terminal
32 liner (passenger liner, ocean liner)
33 meteorological office, a weather station
34 signal mast (signalling mast)
35 storm signal
36 port administration offices
37 tide level indicator
38 quayside road (quayside roadway)

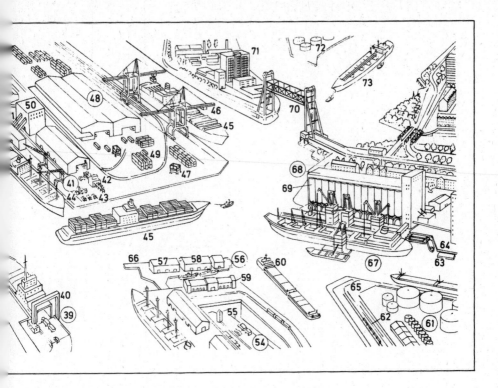

39 roll-on roll-off (ro-ro) system (roll-on roll-off operation)
40 gantry
41 truck-to-truck system (truck-to-truck operation)
42 foil-wrapped unit loads
43 pallets
44 forklift truck (fork truck, forklift)
45 container ship
46 transporter container-loading bridge
47 container carrier truck
48 container terminal (container berth)
49 unit load
50 cold store
51 conveyor belt (conveyor)
52 fruit storage shed (fruit warehouse)
53 office building
54 urban motorway (*Am.* freeway)
55 harbour (*Am.* harbor) tunnels
56 fish dock

57 fish market
58 auction room
59 fish-canning factory
60 push tow
61 tank farm
62 railway siding
63 landing pontoon (landing stage)
64 quay
65 breakwater (mole)
66 pier (jetty), a quay extension
67 bulk carrier
68 silo
69 silo cylinder
70 lift bridge
71 industrial plant
72 storage tanks
73 tanker

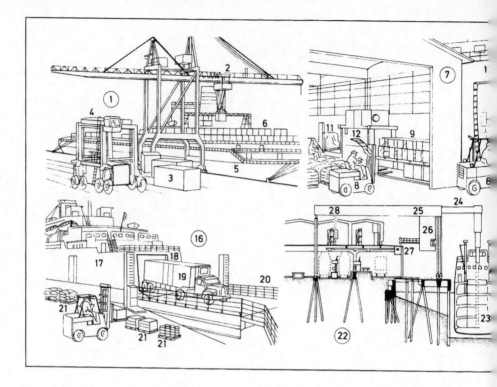

1 container terminal (container berth), a modern cargo-handling berth
2 transporter container-loading bridge (loading bridge); *sim.:* transtainer crane (transtainer)
3 container
4 truck (carrier)
5 all-container ship
6 containers stowed on deck
7 truck-to-truck handling (horizontal cargo handling with pallets)
8 forklift truck (fork truck, forklift)
9 unitized foil-wrapped load (unit load)
10 flat pallet, a standard pallet
11 unitized break-bulk cargo
12 heat sealing machine
13 break-bulk carrier (general cargo ship)
14 cargo hatchway
15 receiving truck on board ship
16 multi-purpose terminal

17 roll-on roll-off ship (ro-ro-ship)
18 stern port (stern opening)
19 driven load, a lorry (*Am.* truck)
20 ro-ro depot
21 unitized load (unitized package)
22 banana-handling terminal [section]
23 seaward tumbler
24 jib
25 elevator bridge
26 chain sling
27 lighting station
28 shore-side tumbler for loading trains and lorries (*Am.* trucks)

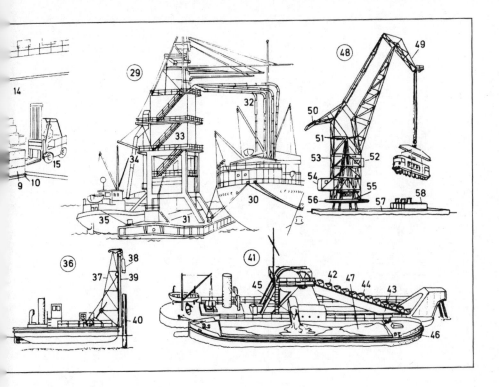

29 bulk cargo handling
30 bulk carrier
31 floating bulk-cargo elevator
32 suction pipes
33 receiver
34 delivery pipe
35 bulk transporter barge
36 floating pile driver
37 pile driver frame
38 pile hammer
39 driving guide rail
40 pile
41 bucket dredger, a dredger
42 bucket chain
43 bucket ladder
44 dredger bucket
45 chute
46 hopper barge
47 spoil
48 floating crane
49 jib (boom)
50 counterweight (counterpoise)
51 adjusting spindle
52 crane driver's cabin (crane driver's cage)
53 crane framework
54 winch house
55 control platform
56 turntable
57 pontoon, a pram
58 engine superstructure (engine mounting)

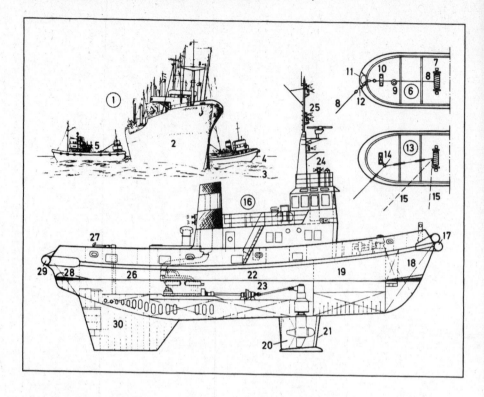

1 salvaging (salving) of a ship run aground
2 ship run aground (damaged vessel)
3 sandbank; *also:* quicksand
4 open sea
5 tug (salvage tug)
6-15 towing gear
6 towing gear for towing at sea
7 towing winch (towing machine, towing engine)
8 tow rope (tow line, towing hawser)
9 tow rope guide
10 cross-shaped bollard
11 hawse hole
12 anchor cable (chain cable)
13 towing gear for work in harbours (*Am.* harbors)
14 guest rope
15 position of the tow rope (tow line, towing hawser)
16 tug (salvage tug) [vertical elevation]
17 bow fender (pudding fender)

18 forepeak
19 living quarters
20 Schottel propeller
21 Kort vent
22 engine and propeller room
23 clutch coupling
24 compass platform (compass bridge, compass flat, monkey bridge)
25 fire-fighting equipment
26 stowage
27 tow hook
28 afterpeak
29 stern fender
30 main manoeuvring (*Am.* maneuvering) keel

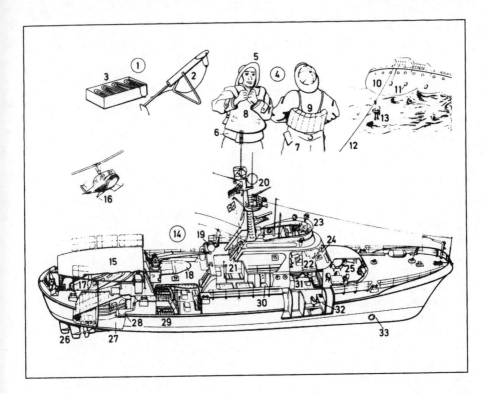

1 rocket apparatus (rocket gun, line-throwing gun)
2 life rocket (rocket)
3 rocket line (whip line)
4 oilskins
5 sou'wester (southwester)
6 oilskin jacket
7 oilskin coat
8 inflatable life jacket
9 cork life jacket (cork life preserver)
10 stranded ship (damaged vessel)
11 oil bag, for trickling oil on the water surface
12 lifeline
13 breeches buoy
14 rescue cruiser
15 helicopter landing deck
16 rescue helicopter
17 daughter boat
18 inflatable boat (inflatable dinghy)
19 life raft
20 fire-fighting equipment for fires at sea

21 hospital unit with operating cabin and exposure bath
22 navigating bridge
23 upper tier of navigating bridge
24 lower tier of navigating bridge
25 messroom
26 rudders and propeller (screw)
27 stowage
28 foam can
29 side engines
30 shower
31 coxswain's cabin
32 crew member's single-berth cabin
33 bow propeller

1-14 wing configurations
1 high-wing monoplane (high-wing plane)
2 span (wing span)
3 shoulder-wing monoplane (shoulder-wing plane)
4 midwing monoplane (midwing plane)
5 low-wing monoplane (low-wing plane)
6 triplane
7 upper wing
8 middle wing (central wing)
9 lower wing
10 biplane
11 strut
12 cross bracing wires
13 sesquiplane
14 low-wing monoplane (low-wing plane) with cranked wings (inverted gull wings)

15-22 wing shapes
15 elliptical wing
16 rectangular wing
17 tapered wing
18 crescent wing
19 delta wing
20 swept-back wing with semi-positive sweepback
21 swept-back wing with positive sweepback
22 ogival wing (ogee wing)

23-36 tail shapes (tail unit shapes, empennage shapes)
23 normal tail (normal tail unit)
24, 25 vertical tail (vertical stabilizer and rudder)
24 vertical stabilizer (vertical fin, tail fin)
25 rudder
26, 27 horizontal tail
26 tailplane (horizontal stabilizer)
27 elevator
28 cruciform tail (cruciform tail unit)
29 T-tail (T-tail unit)
30 lobe

31 V-tail (vee-tail, butterfly tail)
32 double tail unit (twin tail unit)
33 end plate
34 double tail unit (twin tail unit) of a twin-boom aircraft
35 raised horizontal tail with double booms
36 triple tail unit
37 **system of flaps**
38 extensible slat
39 spoiler
40 double-slotted Fowler flap
41 outer aileron (low-speed aileron)
42 inner spoiler (landing flap, lift dump)
43 inner aileron (all-speed aileron)
44 brake flap (air brake)
45 basic profile
46-48 plain flaps (simple flaps)
46 normal flap
47 slotted flap
48 double-slotted flap
49, 50 split flaps
49 plain split flap (simple split flap)
50 zap flap
51 extending flap
52 Fowler flap
53 slat
54 profiled leading-edge flap (droop flap)
55 Krüger flap

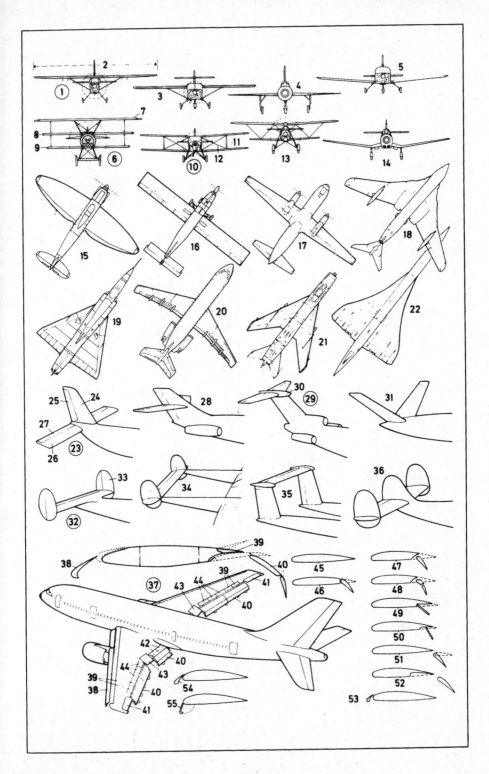

1-31 cockpit of a single-engine (single-engined) racing and passenger aircraft (racing and passenger plane)
1 instrument panel
2 air-speed (*Am.* airspeed) indicator
3 artificial horizon (gyro horizon)
4 altimeter
5 radio compass (automatic direction finder)
6 magnetic compass
7 boost gauge (*Am.* gage)
8 tachometer (rev counter, revolution counter)
9 cylinder temperature gauge (*Am.* gage)
10 accelerometer
11 chronometer
12 turn indicator with ball
13 directional gyro
14 vertical speed indicator (rate-of-climb indicator, variometer)
15 VOR radio direction finder [*VOR: very high frequency omnidirectional range*]
16 left tank fuel gauge (*Am.* gage)
17 right tank fuel gauge (*Am.* gage)
18 ammeter
19 fuel pressure gauge (*Am.* gage)
20 oil pressure gauge (*Am.* gage)
21 oil temperature gauge (*Am.* gage)
22 radio and radio navigation equipment
23 map light
24 wheel (control column, control stick) for operating the ailerons and elevators
25 co-pilot's wheel
26 switches
27 rudder pedals
28 co-pilot's rudder pedals
29 microphone for the radio
30 throttle lever (throttle control)
31 mixture control
32-66 single-engine (single-engined) racing and passenger aircraft (racing and passenger plane)
32 propeller (airscrew)
33 spinner
34 flat four engine
35 cockpit
36 pilot's seat
37 co-pilot's seat
38 passenger seats
39 hood (canopy, cockpit hood, cockpit canopy)
40 steerable nose wheel
41 main undercarriage unit (main landing gear unit)
42 step
43 wing
44 right navigation light (right position light)
45 spar
46 rib
47 stringer (longitudinal reinforcing member)
48 fuel tank
49 landing light
50 left navigation light (left position light)
51 electrostatic conductor
52 aileron
53 landing flap
54 fuselage (body)
55 frame (former)
56 chord
57 stringer (longitudinal reinforcing member)
58 vertical tail (vertical stabilizer and rudder)
59 vertical stabilizer (vertical fin, tail fin)
60 rudder
61 horizontal tail
62 tailplane (horizontal stabilizer)
63 elevator
64 warning light (anticollision light)
65 dipole antenna
66 long-wire antenna (long-conductor antenna)
67-72 principal manoeuvres (*Am.* maneuvers) of the aircraft (aeroplane, plane, *Am.* airplane)
67 pitching
68 lateral axis
69 yawing
70 vertical axis (normal axis)
71 rolling
72 longitudinal axis

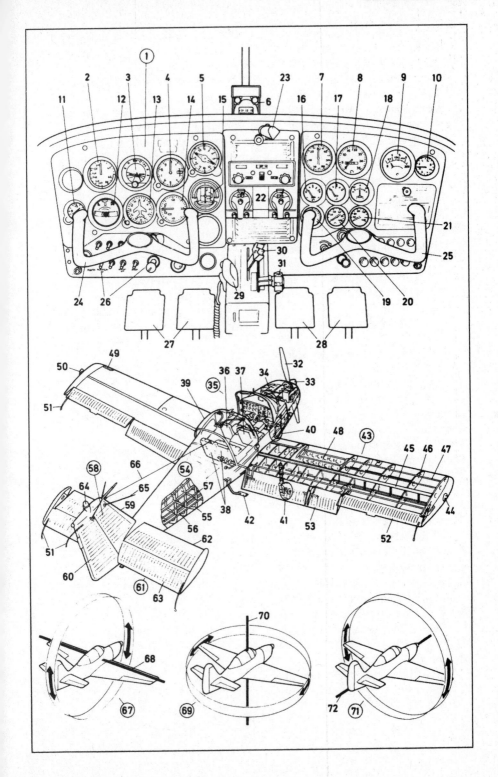

1-33 types of aircraft (aeroplanes, planes, *Am.* airplanes)

1-6 propeller-driven aircraft (aeroplanes, planes, *Am.* airplanes)

1 single-engine (single-engined) racing and passenger aircraft (racing and passenger plane), a low-wing monoplane (low-wing plane)

2 single-engine (single-engined) passenger aircraft, a high-wing monoplane (high-wing plane)

3 twin-engine (twin-engined) business and passenger aircraft (business and passenger plane)

4 short/medium haul airliner, a turboprop plane (turbopropeller plane, propeller-turbine plane)

5 turboprop engine (turbopropeller engine)

6 vertical stabilizer (vertical fin, tail fin)

7-33 jet planes (jet aeroplanes, jets, *Am.* jet airplanes)

7 twin-jet business and passenger aircraft (business and passenger plane)

8 fence

9 wing-tip tank (tip tank)

10 rear engine

11 twin-jet short/medium haul airliner

12 tri-jet medium haul airliner

13 four-jet long haul airliner

14 wide-body long haul airliner (jumbo jet)

15 supersonic airliner *[Concorde]*

16 droop nose

17 **twin-jet wide-body airliner** for short/medium haul routes (airbus)

18 radar nose (radome, radar dome) with weather radar antenna

19 cockpit

20 galley

21 cargo hold (hold, underfloor hold)

22 passenger cabin with passenger seats

23 retractable nose undercarriage unit (retractable nose landing gear unit)

24 nose undercarriage flap (nose gear flap)

25 centre (*Am.* center) passenger door

26 engine pod with engine (turbojet engine, jet turbine engine, jet engine, jet turbine)

27 electrostatic conductors

28 retractable main undercarriage unit (retractable main landing gear unit)

29 side window

30 rear passenger door

31 toilet (lavatory, WC)

32 pressure bulkhead

33 auxiliary engine (auxiliary gas turbine) for the generator unit

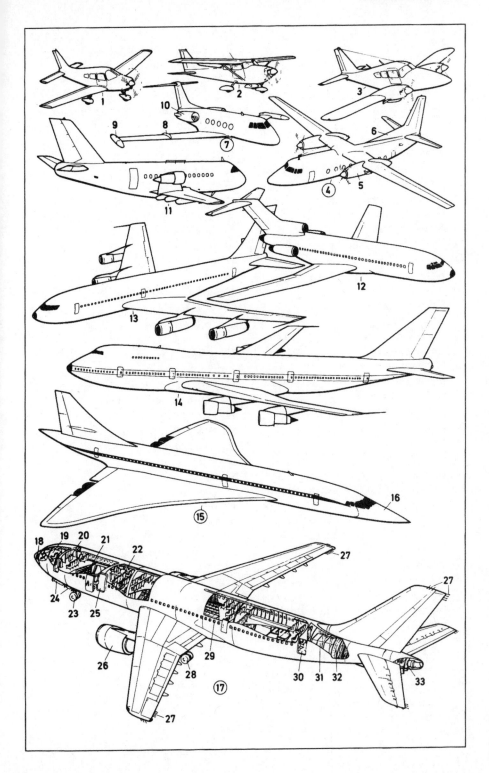

1 **flying boat,** a seaplane
2 hull
3 stub wing (sea wing)
4 tail bracing wires
5 floatplane (float seaplane), a seaplane
6 float
7 vertical stabilizer (vertical fin, tail fin)
8 **amphibian** (amphibian flying boat)
9 hull
10 retractable undercarriage (retractable landing gear)
11-25 helicopters
11 light multirole helicopter
12, 13 main rotor
12 rotary wing (rotor blade)
13 rotor head
14 tail rotor (anti-torque rotor)
15 landing skids
16 flying crane
17 turbine engines
18 lifting undercarriage
19 lifting platform
20 reserve tank
21 transport helicopter
22 rotors in tandem
23 rotor pylon
24 turbine engine
25 tail loading gate
26-32 V/STOL aircraft (vertical/short take-off and landing aircraft)
26 tilt-wing aircraft, a VTOL aircraft (vertical take-off and landing aircraft)
27 tilt wing in vertical position
28 contrarotating tail propellers
29 gyrodyne
30 turboprop engine (turbopropeller engine)
31 convertiplane
32 tilting rotor in vertical position
33-60 aircraft engines (aero engines)
33-50 jet engines (turbojet engines, jet turbine engines, jet turbines)
33 front fan-jet

34 fan
35 low-pressure compressor
36 high-pressure compressor
37 combustion chamber
38 fan-jet turbine
39 nozzle (propelling nozzle, propulsion nozzle)
40 turbines
41 bypass duct
42 aft fan-jet
43 fan
44 bypass duct
45 nozzle (propelling nozzle, propulsion nozzle)
46 bypass engine
47 turbines
48 mixer
49 nozzle (propelling nozzle, propulsion nozzle)
50 secondary air flow (bypass air flow)
51 turboprop engine (turbopropeller engine), a twin-shaft engine
52 annular air intake
53 high-pressure turbine
54 low-pressure turbine
55 nozzle (propelling nozzle, propulsion nozzle)
56 shaft
57 intermediate shaft
58 gear shaft
59 reduction gear
60 propeller shaft

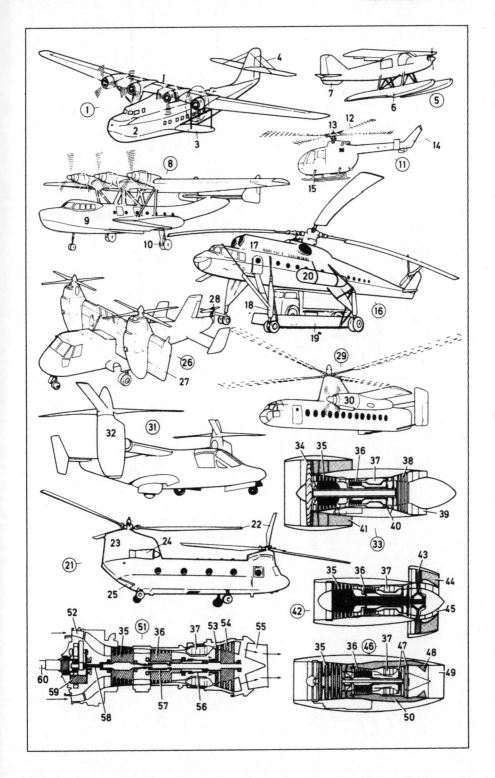

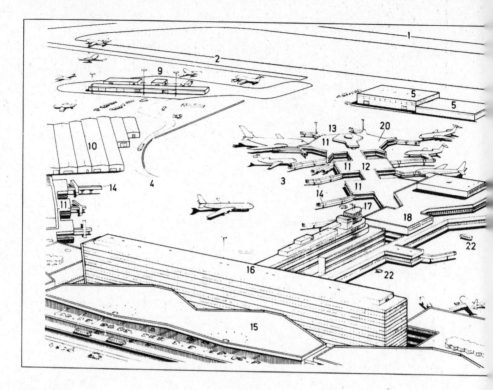

1 runway	**22** service vehicles, e.g. baggage loaders, water tankers, galley loaders, toilet-cleaning vehicles, ground power units, tankers	**35** 'buses'
2 taxiway		**36** 'entrance'
3 apron		**37** 'exit'
4 apron taxiway		**38** 'baggage reclaim'
5 baggage terminal		**39** 'luggage lockers'
6 tunnel entrance to the baggage terminal	**23** aircraft tractor (aircraft tug)	**40** 'telephone – emergency calls only'
7 airport fire service	**24-53** airport information symbols (pictographs)	**41** 'emergency exit'
8 fire appliance building		**42** 'passport check'
9 mail and cargo terminal	**24** 'airport'	**43** 'press facilities'
10 cargo warehouse	**25** 'departures'	**44** 'doctor'
11 assembly point	**26** 'arrivals'	**45** 'chemist' (*Am.* 'druggist')
12 pier	**27** 'transit passengers'	
13 pierhead	**28** 'waiting room' ('lounge')	**46** 'showers'
14 airbridge		**47** 'gentlemen's toilet' ('gentlemen')
15 departure building (terminal)	**29** 'assembly point' ('meeting point', 'rendezvous point')	
16 administration building		**48** 'ladies' toilet' ('ladies')
17 control tower (tower)	**30** 'spectators' terrace'	**49** 'chapel'
18 waiting room (lounge)	**31** 'information'	**50** 'restaurant'
19 airport restaurant	**32** 'taxis'	**51** 'change'
20 spectators' terrace	**33** 'car hire'	**52** 'duty free shop'
21 aircraft in loading position (nosed in)	**34** 'trains'	**53** 'hairdresser'

1 **Saturn V 'Apollo' booster** (booster rocket) [overall view]
2 Saturn V 'Apollo' booster (booster rocket) [overall sectional view]
3 first rocket stage (S-IC)
4 F-1 engines
5 heat shield (thermal protection shield)
6 aerodynamic engine fairings
7 aerodynamic stabilizing fins
8 stage separation retro-rockets, 8 rockets arranged in 4 pairs
9 kerosene (RP-1) tank [capacity: 811,000 litres]
10 liquid oxygen (LOX, LO_2) supply lines, total of 5
11 anti-vortex system (device for preventing the formation of vortices in the fuel)
12 liquid oxygen (LOX, LO_2) tank [capacity: 1,315,000 litres]
13 anti-slosh baffles
14 compressed-helium bottles (helium pressure bottles)
15 diffuser for gaseous oxygen
16 inter-tank connector (inter-tank section)
17 instruments and system-monitoring devices
18 second rocket stage (S-II)
19 J-2 engines
20 heat shield (thermal protection shield)
21 engine mounts and thrust structure
22 acceleration rockets for fuel acquisition
23 liquid hydrogen (LH_2) suction line
24 liquid oxygen (LOX, LO_2) tank [capacity: 1,315,000 litres]
25 standpipe
26 liquid hydrogen (LH_2) tank [capacity: 1,020,000 litres]
27 fuel level sensor
28 work platform (working platform)
29 cable duct
30 manhole
31 *S-IC/S-II* inter-stage connector (inter-stage section)

32 compressed-gas container (gas pressure vessel)
33 third rocket stage *(S-IVB)*
34 J-2 engine
35 nozzle (thrust nozzle)
36 *S-II/S-IVB* inter-stage connector (inter-stage section)
37 four second-stage *(S-II)* separation retro-rockets
38 attitude control rockets
39 liquid oxygen (LOX, LO_2) tank [capacity: 77,200 litres]
40 fuel line duct
41 liquid hydrogen (LH_2) tank [capacity: 253,000 litres]
42 measuring probes
43 compressed-helium tanks (helium pressure vessels)
44 tank vent
45 forward frame section
46 work platform (working platform)
47 cable duct
48 acceleration rockets for fuel acquisition
49 aft frame section
50 compressed-helium tanks (helium pressure vessels)
51 liquid hydrogen (LH_2) line
52 liquid oxygen (LOX, LO_2) line
53 24-panel instrument unit
54 LM hangar (lunar module hangar)
55 LM (lunar module)
56 Apollo SM (service module), containing supplies and equipment
57 SM (service module) main engine
58 fuel tank
59 nitrogen tetroxide tank
60 pressurized gas delivery system
61 oxygen tanks
62 fuel cells
63 manoeuvring (*Am.* maneuvering) rocket assembly
64 directional antenna assembly
65 space capsule (command section)
66 launch phase escape tower

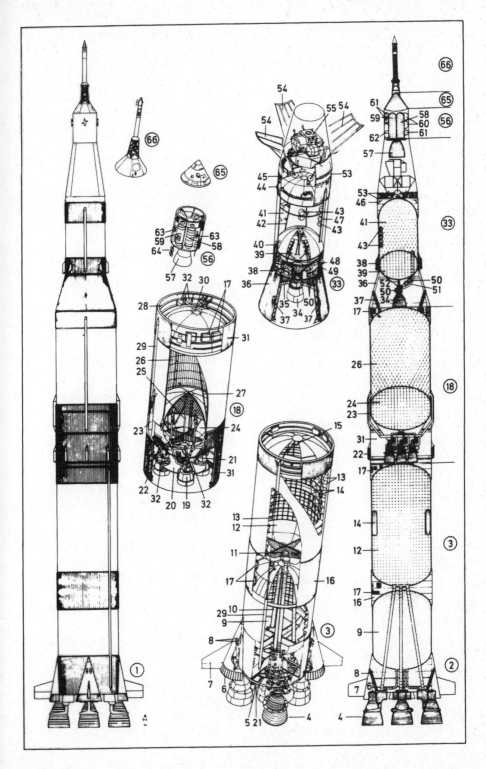

1-45 Space Shuttle-Orbiter

1 twin-spar (two-spar, double-spar) vertical fin
2 engine compartment structure
3 fin post
4 fuselage attachment [of payload bay doors]
5 upper thrust mount
6 lower thrust mount
7 keel
8 heat shield
9 waist longeron
10 integrally machined (integrally milled) main rib
11 integrally stiffened light alloy skin
12 lattice girder
13 payload bay insulation
14 payload bay door
15 low-temperature surface insulation
16 flight deck (crew compartment)
17 captain's seat (commander's seat)
18 pilot's seat (co-pilot's seat)
19 forward pressure bulkhead
20 carbon fibre reinforced nose cone
21 forward fuel tanks
22 avionics consoles
23 automatic flight control panel
24 upward observation windows
25 forward observation windows
26 entry hatch to payload bay
27 air lock
28 ladder to lower deck
29 payload manipulator arm
30 hydraulically steerable nose wheel
31 hydraulically operated main landing gear
32 removable (reusable) carbon fibre reinforced leading edge [of wing]
33 movable elevon sections
34 heat-resistant elevon structure
35 main liquid hydrogen (LH$_2$) supply
36 main liquid-fuelled rocket engine
37 nozzle (thrust nozzle)
38 coolant feed line
39 engine control system
40 heat shield

41 high-pressure liquid hydrogen (LH$_2$) pump
42 high-pressure liquid oxygen (LOX, LO$_2$) pump
43 thrust vector control system
44 electromechanically controlled orbital manoeuvring (*Am.* maneuvering) main engine
45 nozzle fuel tanks (thrust nozzle fuel tanks)
46 **jettisonable liquid hydrogen and liquid oxygen tank** (fuel tank)
47 integrally stiffened annular rib (annular frame)
48 hemispherical end rib (end frame)
49 aft attachment to Orbiter
50 liquid hydrogen (LH$_2$) line
51 liquid oxygen (LOX, LO$_2$) line
52 manhole
53 surgebaffle system (slosh baffle system)
54 pressure line to liquid hydrogen tank
55 electrical system bus
56 liquid oxygen (LOX, LO$_2$) line
57 pressure line to liquid oxygen tank
58 **recoverable solid-fuel rocket** (solid rocket booster)
59 auxiliary parachute bay
60 compartment housing the recovery parachutes and the forward separation rocket motors
61 cable duct
62 aft separation rocket motors
63 aft skirt
64 swivel nozzle (swivelling, *Am.* swiveling, nozzle)
65 **Spacelab** (space laboratory, space station)
66 multi-purpose laboratory (orbital workshop)
67 astronaut
68 gimbal-mounted telescope
69 measuring instrument platform
70 spaceflight module
71 crew entry tunnel

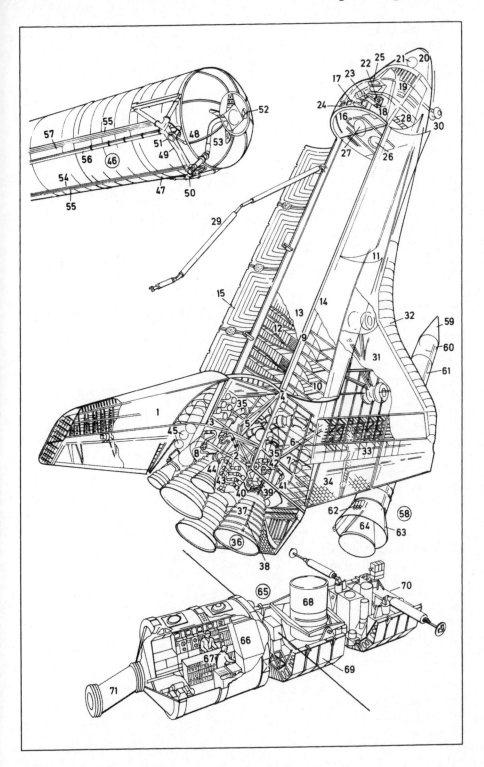

1-30 main hall
1 parcels counter
2 parcels scales
3 parcel
4 stick-on address label with parcel registration slip
5 glue pot
6 small parcel
7 franking machine (*Am.* postage meter) for parcel registration cards
8 telephone box (telephone booth, telephone kiosk, call box)
9 coin-box telephone (pay phone, public telephone)
10 telephone directory rack
11 directory holder
12 telephone directory (telephone book)
13 post office boxes
14 post office box
15 stamp counter
16 counter clerk (counter officer)
17 company messenger
18 record of posting book
19 counter stamp machine
20 stamp book
21 sheet of stamps
22 security drawer
23 change rack
24 letter scales
25 paying-in (*Am.* deposit), post office savings, and pensions counter
26 accounting machine
27 franking machine for money orders and paying-in slips (*Am.* deposit slips)
28 change machine (*Am.* changemaker)
29 receipt stamp
30 hatch
31-44 letter-sorting installation
31 letter feed
32 stacked letter containers
33 feed conveyor
34 intermediate stacker
35 coding station
36 pre-distributor channel
37 process control computer
38 distributing machine
39 video coding station
40 screen
41 address display
42 address
43 post code (postal code, *Am.* zip code)
44 keyboard
45 handstamp
46 roller stamp
47 franking machine
48 feed mechanism
49 delivery mechanism
50-55 postal collection and delivery
50 postbox (*Am.* mailbox)
51 collection bag
52 post office van (mail van)
53 postman (*Am.* mail carrier, letter carrier, mailman)
54 delivery pouch (postman's bag, mailbag)
55 letter-rate item
56-60 postmarks
56 postmark advertisement
57 date stamp postmark
58 charge postmark
59 special postmark
60 roller postmark
61 stamp (postage stamp)
62 perforations

1-41 telephone
1 dial telephone
2 handset (telephone receiver)
3 receiver cord (handset cord)
4 telephone cable (telephone cord)
5 telephone casing (telephone cover)
6 emergency numbers
7 line number
8 dial
9 compact telephone (slimline telephone), an added-feature telephone
10 earpiece (receiver)
11 keypad with number and function keys (feature keys)
12 last number redial button
13 abbreviated dialling key
14 speaker key (loudspeaker key)
15 mouthpiece
16 line reset button
17 speaker (loudspeaker)
18 call indicator
19 push-button telephone, an added-feature telephone
20 display
21 lock
22 novelty telephone, an added-feature telephone
23 (telephone) cradle
24 dummy crank
25 detachable keypad
26 cordless (tele)phone (radiophone, mobile phone)
27 aerial
28 battery strength light
29 out of signal-range indicator
30 power switch
31 cardphone
32 split display showing call charges
33 language select button for the display
34 follow-on call button
35 phonecard slot
36 phonecard (*here:* telephone credit card)
37 phonecard symbol
38 cardholder's name
39 card number
40 arrow indicating direction of insertion
41 chips
42-62 ISDN (Integrated Services Digital Network)
42 multifunction telecommunications terminal (ISDN workstation)
43 screen (monitor) for viewdata, video telephone, and Teletex
44 central processing and memory unit

45 fax unit (fax)
46 input device (keyboard)
47 telephone receiver (link to the telephone network)
48 acoustic coupler (modem)
49 telecontrol network (TEMEX network)
50 public telephone network (switched telephone network)
51 telecontrol centres
52 TEMEX main control centre
53 TEMEX transmission equipment
54 telecommunications line (telephone line)
55 TEMEX network termination
56 slave station
57 telecontrol terminal equipment
58 telecontrol terminal equipment (detector, sensor, *or* control equipment)
59 glass-break detector
60 temperature controller
61 emergency call
62 meter (electricity meter)
63 communications satellite
64 solar panel (solar paddle, solar array, solar generator)
65 antenna module
66 receiving antenna for control commands
67 parabolic antennas
68 communications module
69 propulsion module
70 broadcasting satellite (television satellite)
71 service module
72 fuel tanks
73 control jets
74 earth station
75 parabolic antenna
76 main reflector
77 feed antenna
78 radio beams
79 satellite broadcasting, satellite television, and cable television
80 broadcasting satellite
81 television studio
82 television tower
83 cablehead station
84 terrestrial broadcasting
85 satellite broadcasting
86 line-of-sight link (microwave link)
87 cable network
88 cable connections

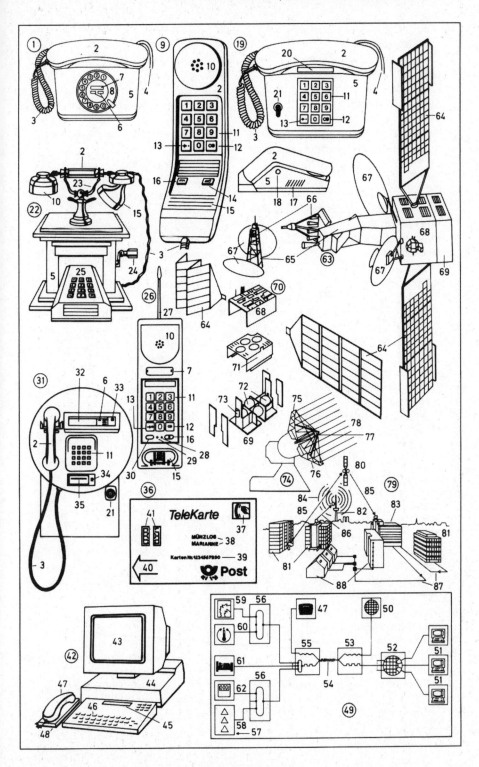

1-6 central recording channel of a radio station
1 monitoring and control panel
2 data display terminal (video data terminal, video monitor) for visual display of computer-controlled programmes (*Am.* programs)
3 amplifier and mains power unit
4 magnetic sound recording and playback deck for $^1/_4$" magnetic tape
5 magnetic tape, a $^1/_4$" tape
6 film spool holder
7-15 radio switching centre (*Am.* center) control room
7 monitoring and control panel
8 talkback speaker
9 local-battery telephone
10 talkback microphone
11 data display terminal (video data terminal)
12 teleprinter
13 input keyboard for computer data
14 telephone switchboard panel
15 monitoring speaker (control speaker)
16-26 broadcasting centre (*Am.* center)
16 recording room
17 production control room (control room)
18 studio
19 sound engineer (sound control engineer)
20 sound control desk (sound control console)
21 newsreader (newscaster)
22 duty presentation officer
23 telephone for phoned reports
24 record turntable
25 recording room mixing console (mixing desk, mixer)
26 sound technician (sound mixer, sound recordist)
27-53 television post-sync studio
27 sound production control room (sound control room)
28 dubbing studio (dubbing theatre, *Am.* theater)
29 studio table
30 visual signal
31 electronic stopclock
32 projection screen
33 monitor
34 studio microphone
35 sound effects box
36 microphone socket panel
37 recording speaker (recording loudspeaker)
38 control room window (studio window)
39 producer's talkback microphone
40 local-battery telephone
41 sound control desk (sound control console)
42 group selector switch
43 visual display
44 limiter display (clipper display)
45 control modules
46 pre-listening buttons
47 slide control
48 universal equalizer (universal corrector)
49 input selector switches
50 pre-listening speaker
51 tone generator
52 talkback speaker
53 talkback microphone
54-59 pre-mixing room for transferring and mixing 16 mm, 17.5 mm, 35 mm perforated magnetic film
54 sound control desk (sound control console)
55 compact magnetic tape recording and playback equipment
56 single playback deck
57 central drive unit
58 single recording and playback deck
59 rewind bench
60-65 final picture quality checking room
60 preview monitor
61 programme (*Am.* program) monitor
62 stopclock
63 vision mixer (vision-mixing console, vision-mixing desk)
64 talkback system (talkback equipment)
65 camera monitor (picture monitor)

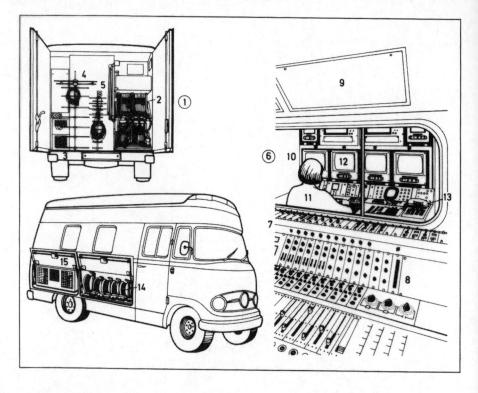

1-15 outside broadcast (OB) vehicle
  (television OB van; *also:* sound OB
  van, radio OB van)
1-4 rear equipment section of the OB
  vehicle
2 camera cable
3 cable connection panel
4 television (TV) reception aerial
  (receiving aerial) for Channel I
5 television (TV) reception aerial
  (receiving aerial) for Channel II
6 **interior equipment (on-board**
  equipment) of the OB vehicle
7 sound production control room
  (sound control room)
8 sound control desk (sound control
  console)
9 monitoring loudspeaker
10 vision control room (video control
  room)
11 video controller (vision controller)
12 camera monitor (picture monitor)

13 on-board telephone (intercommu-
  nication telephone)
14 microphone cables
15 air-conditioning plant

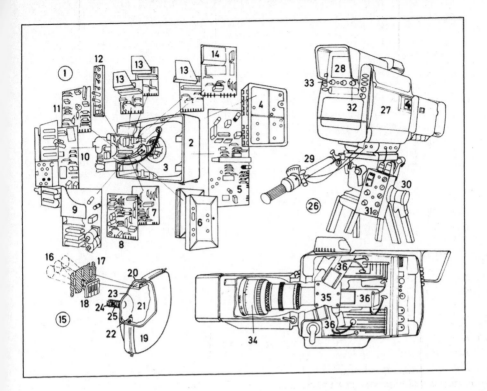

1 **colour** (*Am.* color) **television** (TV) **receiver** (colour television set) of modular design
2 television cabinet
3 television tube (picture tube)
4 IF (intermediate frequency) amplifier module
5 colour (*Am.* color) decoder module
6 VHF and UHF tuner
7 horizontal synchronizing module
8 vertical deflection module
9 horizontal linearity control module
10 horizontal deflection module
11 control module
12 convergence module
13 colour (*Am.* color) output stage module
14 sound module
15 colour (*Am.* color) picture tube
16 electron beams
17 shadow mask with elongated holes
18 strip of fluorescent (luminescent, phosphorescent) material
19 coating (film) of fluorescent material
20 inner magnetic screen (screening)
21 vacuum
22 temperature-compensated shadow mask mount
23 centring (*Am.* centering) ring for the deflection system
24 electron gun assembly
25 rapid heat-up cathode
26 **television (TV) camera**
27 camera head
28 camera monitor
29 control arm (control lever)
30 focusing adjustment
31 control panel
32 contrast control
33 brightness control
34 zoom lens
35 beam-splitting prism (beam splitter)
36 pick-up unit (colour, *Am.* color, pick-up tube)

1-17 stereo system (hi-fi system), a midi system

1 **hi-fi stack**
2 rack lid (rack dust cover, [housing] lid)
3 rack (housing) with glass door
4 record player (record deck, analogue [*Am.* analog] record player)
5 tuner (receiver, radio tuner)
6 amplifier (power amplifier)
7 double cassette deck (double cassette recorder)
8 CD player (compact disc player)
9 cassette rack
10 record and compact disc rack
11 castor
12 **speaker** (loudspeaker), a three-way bass reflex speaker
13 tweeter, a dome tweeter or piezo tweeter
14 mid-range speaker (squawker)
15 bass speaker (woofer)
16 port
17 infrared remote control [unit] (IR remote control [unit])
18 **record player** (record deck, analogue [*Am.* analog] record player)
19 turntable with direct drive or belt drive
20 strobe light (strobe speed control)
21 pitch control
22 rpm display
23 stop button
24 auto-return button
25 rpm selector (speed selector)
26 cue button (down)
27 cue button (up)
28 stylus (needle)
29 pick-up
30 size selector (record size selector)
31 tone arm (pick-up arm)
32 tone arm support (pick-up arm support)
33 stylus pressure control
34 anti-skate control
35 tone arm counterweight (pick-up arm counterweight)
36 lid (dust cover)
37 **tuner** (receiver, radio tuner)
38 power switch
39 tuning button (tuning control)

40 manual and automatic tuning selection button with muting
41 stereo/mono selection button
42 strength-of-signal display button
43 memory button
44 station selection buttons
45 frequency selection buttons ([wave] band selection buttons)
46 station select display
47 fluorescent digital display indicating wave band, frequency, and strength of signal
48 LED indicator for stereo and mono mode and automatic tuning
49 **amplifier** (power amplifier)
50 function select buttons for the turntable, tuner, cassette deck (tape deck), CD player, and monitor (tape monitor)
51 filter buttons (high and low filter buttons)
52 bass control
53 treble control
54 balance control
55 loudness button
56 volume control
57 headphone socket
58 speaker select buttons
59 LED display, a multifunction display
60 function display
61 **receiver,** a combined tuner-amp[lifier]
62 display select button
63 liquid crystal display (LCD), a multifunction display
64 [graphic] equalizer, a 2×7 band [graphic] equalizer
65 equalizer slide controls
66 LED-display spectrum analyser
67 **headphones** (stereo headphones)
68 ear pads (ear cushions)
69, 70 **microphones**
69 directional microphone (stereo directional microphone)
70 electret condenser microphone with omnidirectional pick-up characteristic

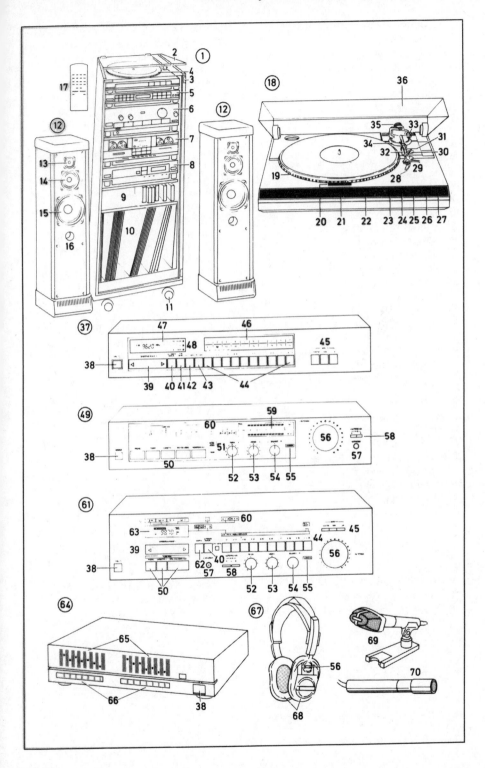

1 **cassette deck** (cassette recorder)
2 power switch
3 [stop and] eject button
4 cassette holder (cassette drive, cassette transport)
5 dust cover
6 counter (tape counter)
7-12 **transport buttons**
7 stop button
8 rewind button
9 play buttons for both directions (bi-directional play buttons)
10 fast forward button
11 record button
12 pause button
13 counter reset button
14 noise reduction buttons (Dolby select buttons)
15 auto-reverse buttons
16 recording level control
17 microphone sockets
18 headphone socket
19 level indicator display (VU meter), an LED display
20 tape type indicator (tape-bias indicator), an LED display
21 **double cassette deck** (double cassette recorder)
22 play button
23 [stop and] eject button
24 high-speed dubbing button
25 function select button
26 recording indicator light
27 on-off light (power indicator light)
28 **CD player** (compact disc player, digital compact disc player)
29 CD drawer
30 open/close button for the CD drawer
31 search button and index search button
32 skip buttons (skip-track buttons)
33 headphone volume control
34 function select buttons
35 programming, track and disc repeat, and pause indicators
36 LED display
37 remaining time and track-index indicators
38 **portable radio recorder** with integral CD player
39 handle
40 [radio] receiver (receiver and amplifier)

41 CD player
42 quartz clock with digital display and timer
43 double cassette recorder
44 loudspeaker
45-49 **audio-cassette** (cassette)
45-47 types of tape
45 ferric cassette (iron oxide cassette, normal cassette)
46 chrome dioxide cassette (chrome cassette)
47 metal cassette (metal oxide cassette)
48 tape type indication (indicating hole)
49 record-protected cassettes
50 **world receiver** for receiving ultra-short wave (USW), medium wave (MW), long wave (LW), and short wave (SW)
51 aerial (rod aerial), a telescopic aerial
52 function buttons
53 station select buttons
54 manual tuning knob
55 liquid crystal display (LCD) showing waveband, frequency, and memory number
56 (sliding) volume control
57 **cassette player** (Walkman® with radio)
58 headphones
59 equalizer, a 3-band equalizer
60 **portable CD player** (Discman®)
61 compact disc (CD)
62 lid
63 casing with transport, amplifier, display, and function buttons
64 **compact hi-fi system** (compact stereo system)
65 amplifier section
66 **DAT recorder** (digital cassette recorder) (DAT = Digital Audio Tape)
67 infrared sensor (IR sensor) for the remote control
68 input selection buttons for mono, analogue (*Am.* analog), and digital signals
69 index and program selection buttons
70 index number display
71 auto-scan button
72 end-record search button

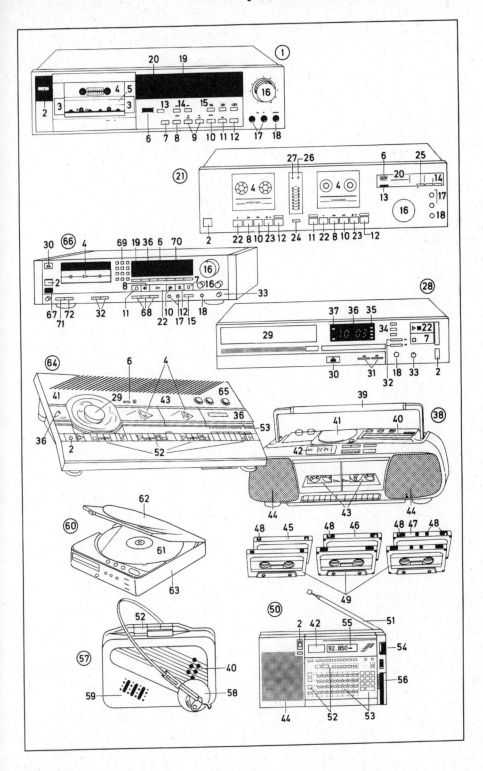

1 camcorder (camera recorder), *form:* two-component system (separate camera and recorder)
2 pocket camcorder, a video-8 camcorder
3 lens, a x6 zoom lens (11-66 mm)
4 viewfinder (ocular)
5 CCD image converter (image sensor) and high-speed shutter, a half-inch chip with shutter functions
6 video cassette
7 videotape
8 head drum
9 autofocus motor
10 built-in microphone (integral microphone)
11 VHS head drum (VHS: Video Home System)
12 erase head
13 guide pin
14 tape guide
15 capstan
16 audio sync head
17 pinch roller
18 video head
19 grooves in the wall of the head drum to promote air cushion formation
20 VHS track format
21 direction of tape movement
22 direction of recording
23 video track, a slant track (only a few tracks shown)
24 sound track (audio track)
25 sync track
26 sync head
27 sound head (audio head)
28 video head
29 video recorder
30 infrared remote control
31 program scale (program dial), a multidisplay
32 cassette compartment
33 jog shuttle knob for forward or reverse movement of the [video] picture

34 multidisc player
35 infrared remote control
36 disc drawer
37-41 disc formats
37 single compact disc (single CD)
38 audio CD
39 video CD
40 small laser disc (20 cm)
41 large laser disc (30 cm)
42 laser scanning system
43 [disc] spindle
44 laser-head tracing spindle
45 laser head (laser unit)

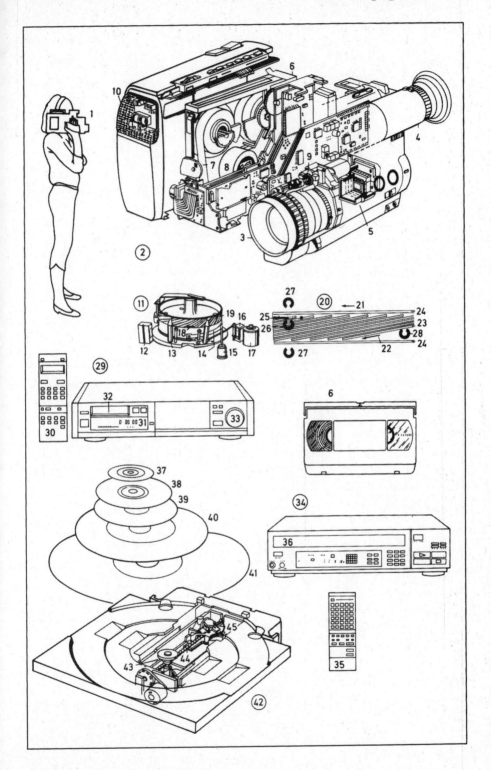

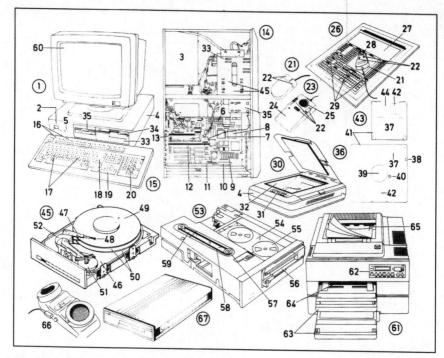

1 **personal computer** (PC; *sim.:* laptop)
2 power switch
3 power supply (power pack)
4 housing
5 fixed-disk access light
6 main memory
7 coprocessor socket
8 central processing unit (CPU), a microprocessor
9 cache memory (cache controller)
10 expansion memory slot
11 graphics card slot
12 combined fixed and floppy disk controller
13 serial and parallel communication card
14 **PC tower** *interior view*
15-67 **peripherals**
15-32 **built-in devices**
15 **keyboard**
16 function keys
17 letter keys and number keys (numeric keys)
18 enter key (return key)
19 cursor keys
20 number [key]pad (numeric [key]pad)
21 **mouse**
22 mouse buttons
23 **trackerball** (trackball)
24 handrest
25 roller ball
26 **digitizing tablet** (digitizer, *also:* graphics tablet)

27 graphics area
28 cross hairs
29 receiving grids
30 **scanner**
31 control panel with function keys
32 scanning surface
33-59 **mass storage devices** (magnetic stores, magnetic memories)
33-44 **disk drives** (drives, floppy disk drives)
33 minifloppy disk drive (5 ¼ inch [floppy] disk drive)
34 latch
35 microfloppy disk drive (3 ½ inch [floppy] disk drive)
36-44 **diskettes** (disks, floppy disks, floppies)
36 minifloppy (minifloppy disk, 5 ¼ inch disk, flexible disk)
37 label
38 write-protect notch
39 hole for engaging the drive hub
40 registration hole
41 disk cover (envelope)
42 access slot for the read-write head
43 microfloppy (3 ½ inch [floppy] disk)
44 sliding shutter
45 **fixed-disk drive** (fixed disk, hard disk)
46 base plate
47 access arm (actuator)
48 read-write head

49 drive motor for the aluminium (*Am.* aluminum) platters, a spindle drive motor
50 magnetic-coated aluminium (*Am.* aluminum) platters
51 read-write head drive motor, a linear motor or stepping motor (stepper motor)
52 data, address, and control bus
53 **magnetic tape unit** (magnetic tape drive, streamer)
54 magnetic tape
55 magnetic tape reel
56 magnetic tape cassette (magnetic tape cartridge)
57 drive post
58 drive band
59 drive motor
60-65 **output devices**
60 **screen** (monitor, display) a high-resolution colour (*Am.* color) monitor
61 **printer,** a dot-matrix printer (*here:* laser printer; *also:* inkjet printer, needle printer)
62 control panel with function keys and display
63 paper tray (paper cassette)
64 paper feed path
65 paper output tray
66, 67 **devices for long-distance data transmission**
66 acoustic coupler
67 modem

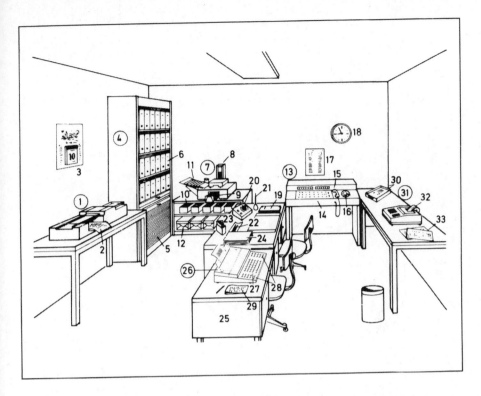

1-33 receptionists office (secretary's office)
1   fax machine
2   transmitted or received copy
3   wall calendar
4   filing cabinet
5   tambour door (roll-up door)
6   file (document file)
7   transfer-type addressing machine
8   vertical stencil magazine
9   stencil ejection
10 stencil storage drawer
11 paper feed
12 stock of notepaper
13 switchboard (internal telephone exchange)
14 push-button keyboard for internal connections
15 handset
16 dial
17 internal telephone list
18 master clock (main clock)
19 folder containing documents, correspondence, etc. for signing (to be signed)
20 intercom (office intercom)
21 pen
22 pen and pencil tray
23 card index
24 stack (set) of forms
25 typing desk
26 electronic memory typewriter
27 keyboard
28 function keys
29 shorthand pad (*Am.* steno pad)
30 letter tray
31 office calculator
32 printer
33 business letter

1-36 executive's office

1 swivel chair
2 desk
3 desk top
4 desk drawer
5 cupboard (storage area) with door
6 desk mat (blotter)
7 business letter
8 appointments diary
9 desk set
10 intercom (office intercom)
11 desk lamp
12 pocket calculator (electronic calculator)
13 telephone, an executive-secretary system
14 dial; *also:* push-button keyboard
15 call buttons
16 receiver (telephone receiver)
17 dictating machine
18 position indicator
19 control buttons (operating keys)
20 cabinet
21 visitor's chair
22 safe
23 bolts
24 armour-plated (*Am.* armor-plated) lock area
25 confidential documents
26 patent
27 petty cash
28 picture
29 bar (drinks cabinet)
30 bar set
31-36 conference grouping
31 conference table
32 pocket-sized dictating machine, a micro-cassette recorder
33 ashtray
34 corner table
35 table lamp
36 two-seater sofa [part of the conference grouping]

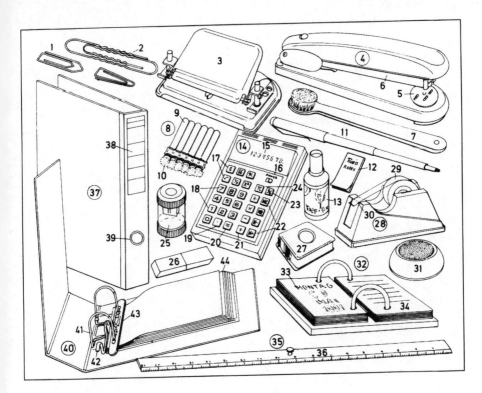

1-44 office equipment (office supplies, office materials)

1, 2 paper clips
3 punch
4 stapler (stapling machine)
5 anvil
6 spring-loaded magazine
7 type-cleaning brush
8 type cleaner (type-cleaning kit)
9 fluid container (fluid reservoir)
10 cleaning brush
11 felt tip pen
12 correcting paper [for typing errors]
13 correcting fluid [for typing errors]
14 electronic pocket calculator
15 eight-digit fluorescent display
16 on/off switch
17 function keys
18 number keys
19 decimal key
20 'equals' key
21 instruction keys (command keys)
22 memory keys
23 percent key (percentage key)
24 π-key (pi-key) for mensuration of circles
25 pencil sharpener
26 typewriter rubber
27 adhesive tape dispenser
28 adhesive tape holder (roller-type adhesive tape dispenser)
29 roll of adhesive tape
30 tear-off edge
31 moistener
32 desk diary
33 date sheet (calendar sheet)
34 memo sheet
35 ruler
36 centimetre and millimetre (*Am.* centimeter and millimeter) graduations
37 file (document file)
38 spine label (spine tag)
39 finger hole
40 arch board file
41 arch unit
42 release lever (locking lever, release/lock lever)
43 compressor
44 bank statement (statement of account)

1-48 open plan office
1 partition wall (partition screen)
2 filing drawer with suspension file system
3 suspension file
4 file tab
5 file (document file)
6 filing clerk
7 clerical assistant
8 note for the files
9 telephone
10 filing shelves
11 clerical assistant's desk
12 office cupboard
13 plant stand (planter)
14 indoor plants (houseplants)
15 programmer
16 data display terminal (visual display unit)
17 customer service representative
18 customer
19 computer-generated design
20 sound-absorbing partition
21 typist
22 typewriter
23 filing drawer
24 customer card index
25 office chair, a swivel chair
26 typing desk
27 card index box
28 multi-purpose shelving
29 proprietor
30 business letter
31 proprietor's secretary
32 shorthand pad (*Am.* steno pad)
33 audio typist
34 dictating machine
35 earphone
36 statistics chart
37 pedestal containing a cupboard or drawers
38 sliding-door cupboard
39 office furniture arranged in an angular configuration
40 wall-mounted shelf
41 letter tray

42 wall calendar
43 data centre (*Am.* center)
44 calling up information on the data
display terminal (visual display
unit)
45 waste paper basket
46 sales statistics
47 EDP print-out, a continuous fan-
fold sheet
48 connecting element

1 **electric typewriter,** a golf ball type-writer
2-6 keyboard
2 space bar
3 shift key
4 line space and carrier return key
5 shift lock
6 margin release key
7 tabulator key
8 tabulator clear key
9 on/off switch
10 striking force control (impression control)
11 ribbon selector
12 margin scale
13 left margin stop
14 right margin stop
15 golf ball (spherical typing element) bearing the types
16 ribbon cassette
17 paper bail with rollers
18 platen
19 typing opening (typing window)
20 paper release lever
21 carrier return lever
22 platen knob
23 line space adjuster
24 variable platen action lever
25 push-in platen variable
26 erasing table
27 transparent cover
28 exchange golf ball (exchange typing element)
29 type
30 golf ball cap (cap of typing element)
31 teeth
32 **photocopier** (copier, photocopying machine)
33 copyboard cover with single-copy (single-sheet) delivery tray
34 universal paper cassette
35 adjustable paper cassettes
36 front door
37 dual vertical transport unit
38 sorter
39 copy delivery bins
40-43 control panel displays and control keys
40 enlargement, reduction, and program selection keys
41 sort mode and two-sided copy keys
42 display with colour, exposure, format, and copy number selection keys
43 start key (copy start key)
44 **letter-folding machine**
45 paper feed
46 folding mechanism
47 receiving tray
48 **small offset press**
49 paper feed
50 lever for inking the plate cylinder
51, 52 inking unit (inker unit)
51 distributing roller (distributor)
52 ink roller (inking roller, fountain roller)
53 pressure adjustment
54 sheet delivery (receiving table)
55 printing speed adjustment
56 jogger for aligning the piles of sheets
57 pile of paper (pile of sheets)
58 folding machine
59 gathering machine (collating machine, assembling machine) for short runs
60 gathering station (collating station, assembling station)
61 adhesive binder (perfect binder) for hot adhesives
62 **magnetic tape dictating machine**
63 headphones (headset, earphones)
64 on/off switch
65 microphone cradle
66 foot control socket
67 telephone adapter socket
68 headphone socket (earphone socket, headset socket)
69 microphone socket
70 built-in loudspeaker
71 indicator lamp (indicator light)
72 cassette compartment
73 forward wind, rewind, and stop buttons
74 time scale with indexing marks
75 time scale stop

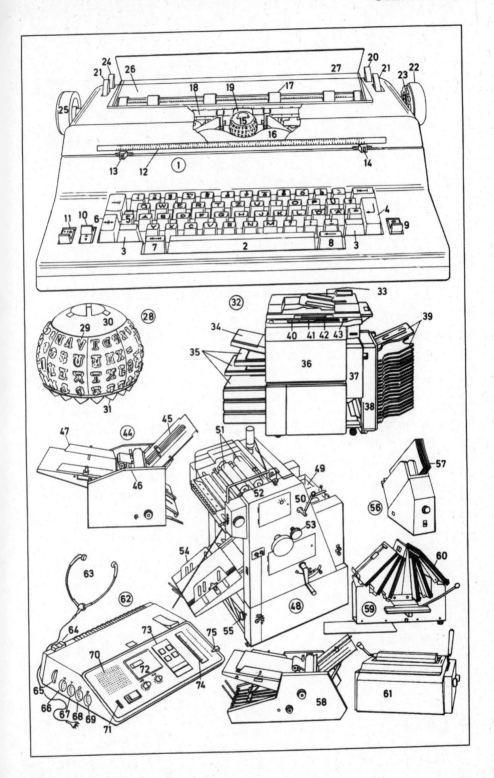

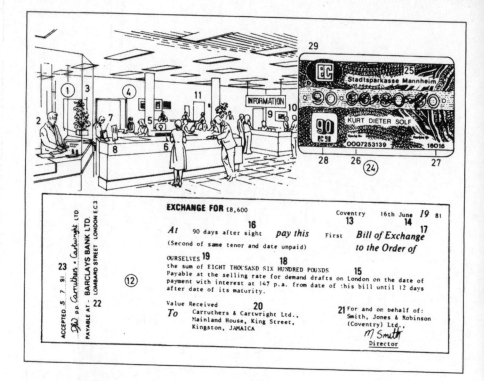

1-11 main hall
1 cashier's desk (cashier's counter)
2 teller (cashier)
3 bullet-proof glass
4 service counters (for service and advice on savings accounts, private and company accounts, personal loans)
5 bank clerk
6 customer
7 brochures
8 stock list (price list, list of quotations)
9 information counter
10 foreign exchange counter
11 entrance to strong room
12 **bill of exchange** (bill); *here:* a draft, an acceptance (bank acceptance)
13 place of issue
14 date of issue
15 place of payment
16 date of maturity (due date)
17 bill clause (draft clause)

18 value
19 payee (remittee)
20 drawee (payer)
21 drawer
22 domicilation (paying agent)
23 acceptance
24 Eurocheque card
25 issuing bank (drawee bank)
26 account number
27 card number
28 hologram, a white light hologram (rainbow hologram)
29 *(on the back:)* magnetic strip

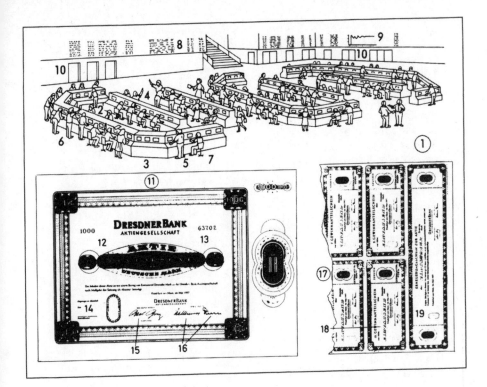

1-10 stock exchange

1 exchange hall (exchange floor)
2 market for securities
3 broker's post
4 sworn stockbroker (exchange broker, stockbroker, *Am.* specialist), an inside broker
5 kerbstone broker (kerbstoner, curbstone broker, curbstoner, outside broker), a commercial broker dealing in unlisted securities
6 member of the stock exchange (stockjobber, *Am.* floor trader, room trader)
7 stock exchange agent (boardman), a bank employee
8 quotation board
9 index curve
10 telephone box (telephone booth, telephone kiosk, call box)

11-19 securities; *kinds:* share (*Am.* stock), fixed-income security, annuity, bond, debenture bond, municipal bond (corporation stock), industrial bond, convertible bond

11 share certificate (*Am.* stock certificate); *here:* bearer share (share warrant)
12 par (par value, nominal par, face par) of the share
13 serial number
14 page number of entry in bank's share register (bank's stock ledger)
15 signature of the chairman of the board of governors
16 signature of the chairman of the board of directors
17 sheet of coupons (coupon sheet, dividend coupon sheet)
18 dividend warrant (dividend coupon)
19 talon

1-29 coins (coin, coinage, metal money, specie, *Am.* hard money); *kinds:* gold, silver, nickel, copper, or aluminium, *Am.* aluminum, coins

1 Athens: tetradrachm (tetradrachmon, tetradrachma)
2 the owl [emblem of the city of Athens]
3 aureus of Constantine the Great
4 bracteate of Emperor Frederick I Barbarossa
5 Louis XIV louis-d'or
6 Prussia: I reichstaler (speciestaler) of Frederick the Great
7 Federal Republic of Germany: 5 Deutschmarks (DM); 1 DM = 100 pfennigs
8 obverse
9 reverse (subordinate side)
10 mint mark (mintage, exergue)
11 legend (inscription on the edge of a coin)
12 device (type), a provincial coat of arms
13 Austria: 25 schillings; 1 sch = 100 groschen
14 provincial coats of arms
15 Switzerland: 5 francs; 1 franc = 100 centimes
16 France: 1 franc = 100 centimes
17 Belgium: 100 francs
18 Luxembourg (Luxemburg): 1 franc
19 Netherlands: 2 ½ guilders; 1 guilder (florin, gulden) = 100 cents
20 Italy: 200 lire (*sg.* lira)
21 Vatican City: 100 lire (*sg.* lira)
22 Spain: 1 peseta = 100 céntimos
23 Portugal: 1 escudo = 100 centavos
24 Denmark: 1 krone = 100 öre
25 Sweden: 1 krona = 100 öre
26 Norway: 1 krone = 100 öre
27 Czechoslovakia: 1 koruna = 100 heller

28 Yugoslavia: 1 dinar = 100 paras
29 United Kingdom of Great Britain and Northern Ireland: 1 pound sterling (£1) = 100 new pence (100 p) (*sg.* new penny, new p)
30-39 banknotes (*Am.* bills) (paper money, notes, treasury notes)
30 Federal Republic of Germany: 100 DM
31 bank of issue (bank of circulation)
32 watermark [a portrait]
33 denomination
34 USA: 1 dollar ($1) = 100 cents
35 facsimile signatures
36 impressed stamp
37 serial number
38 Greece: 1,000 drachmas (drachmae); 1 drachma = 100 lepta (*sg.* lepton)
39 portrait
40-44 striking of coins (coinage, mintage)
40, 41 coining dies (minting dies)
40 upper die
41 lower die
42 collar
43 coin disc (flan, planchet, blank)
44 coining press (minting press)

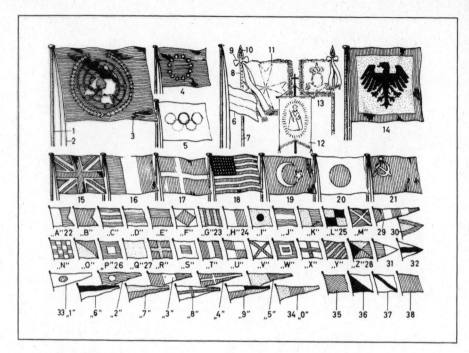

1-3 flag of the United Nations
1 flagpole (flagstaff) with truck
2 halyard (halliard, haulyard)
3 bunting
4 flag of the Council of Europe
5 Olympic flag
6 flag at half-mast (*Am.* at half-staff) [as a token of mourning]
7-11 flag
7 flagpole (flagstaff)
8 ornamental stud
9 streamer
10 pointed tip of the flagpole
11 bunting
12 banner (gonfalon)
13 cavalry standard (flag of the cavalry)
14 standard of the German Federal President [ensign of head of state]
15-21 national flags
15 the Union Jack (Great Britain)
16 the Tricolour (*Am.* Tricolor) (France)
17 the Danebrog (Dannebrog) (Denmark)
18 the Stars and Stripes (Star-Spangled Banner) (USA)
19 the Crescent (Turkey)
20 the Rising Sun (Japan)
21 the Hammer and Sickle (USSR)

22-34 signal flags, a hoist
22-28 letter flags
22 letter A, a burgee (swallow-tailed flag)
23 G, pilot flag
24 H ('pilot on board')
25 L ('you should stop, I have something important to communicate')
26 P, the Blue Peter ('about to set sail')
27 W ('I require medical assistance')
28 Z, an oblong pennant (oblong pendant)
29 code pennant (code pendant), used in the International Signals Code
30-32 substitute flags (repeaters), triangular flags (pennants, pendants)
33, 34 numeral pennants (numeral pendants)
33 number 1
34 number 0
35-38 customs flags
35 customs boat pennant (customs boat pendant)
36 'ship cleared through customs'
37 customs signal flag
38 powder flag ['inflammable (flammable) cargo']

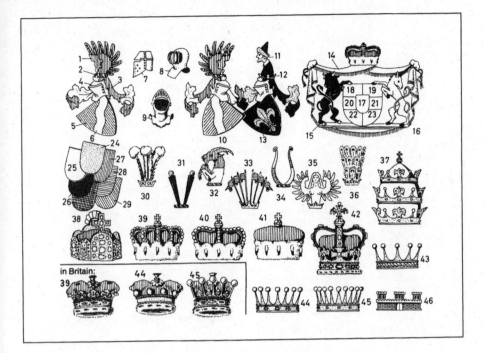

1-36 heraldry (blazonry)
1, 11, 30-36 crests
1-6 coat-of-arms (achievement of arms, hatchment, achievement)
1 crest
2 wreath of the colours (*Am.* colors)
3 mantle (mantling)
4, 7-9 helmets (helms)
4 tilting helmet (jousting helmet)
5 shield
6 bend sinister wavy
7 pot-helmet (pot-helm, heaume)
8 barred helmet (grilled helmet)
9 helmet affronty with visor open
10-13 marital achievement (marshalled, *Am.* marshaled, coat-of-arms)
10 arms of the baron (of the husband)
11-13 arms of the family of the femme (of the wife)
11 demi-man; *also:* demi-woman
12 crest coronet
13 fleur-de-lis
14 heraldic tent (mantling)
15, 16 supporters (heraldic beasts)
15 bull
16 unicorn
17-23 blazon
17 inescutcheon (heart-shield)
18-23 quarterings one to six
18, 20, 22 dexter (right)
18, 19 chief

19, 21, 23 sinister (left)
22, 23 base
24-29 tinctures
24, 25 metals
24 or (gold) [yellow]
25 argent (silver) [white]
26 sable
27 gules
28 azure
29 vert
30 ostrich feathers (treble plume)
31 truncheon
32 demi-goat
33 tournament pennons
34 buffalo horns
35 harpy
36 plume of peacock's feathers
37, 38, 42-46 crowns and coronets [continental type]
37 tiara (papal tiara)
38 Imperial Crown [German, until 1806]
39 ducal coronet (duke's coronet)
40 prince's coronet
41 elector's coronet
42 English Royal Crown
43-45 coronets of rank
43 baronet's coronet
44 baron's coronet (baronial coronet)
45 count's coronet
46 mauerkrone (mural crown) of a city crest

1-96 army **armament** (army weaponry)
1-28 **hand weapons**
1 P1 **pistol**
2 barrel
3 front sight (foresight)
4 hammer
5 trigger
6 pistol grip
7 magazine holder
8 MP2 **submachine gun**
9 shoulder rest (butt)
10 casing (mechanism casing)
11 barrel clamp (barrel-clamping nut)
12 cocking lever (cocking handle)
13 palm rest
14 safety catch
15 magazine
16 G3-A3 **self-loading rifle**
17 flash hider (flash eliminator)
18 trigger mechanism
19 notch (sighting notch, rear sight)
20 front sight block (foresight block) with front sight (foresight)
21 rifle butt (butt)
22 44 2A1 **light anti-tank rocket launcher**
23 rocket (projectile)
24 telescopic sight (telescope sight)
25 cheek rest
26 MG3 **machine gun** (Spandau)
27 recoil booster
28 belt-changing flap
29-61 **artillery weapons** mounted on self-propelled gun carriages
29 SFM 110 A2 **self-propelled howitzer**
30-32 gun carriage
30 drive wheel
31 track
32 road wheel
33 hull
34 spade
35 spade piston
36 hydraulic system
37 elevating piston
38 breech ring
39 barrel
40 muzzle
41 buffer (buffer recuperator)
42 M 109 A3 G **self-propelled howitzer**
43 armoured (*Am.* armored) turret
44 fighting compartment
45 barrel clamp
46 fume extractor
47 barrel recuperator
48 light anti-aircraft (AA) machine gun
49 SF Lance **missile launch system** (missile launcher)
50 skirt

51 tracked vehicle
52 missile (guided missile)
53 elevating gear
54 launching ramp
55 110 SF 2 **rocket launcher**
56 fire control system
57 launching tubes
58 tube bins
59 turntable
60 jack
61 driver's cab
62-87 **armoured** (*Am.* armored) **vehicles**
62 Leopard 2 **tank**
63 smooth-barrelled gun
64 driver's hatch
65 commander's periscope
66 smoke canister (smoke dispenser)
67 Luchs **armoured** (*Am.* armored) **reconnaissance vehicle,** an amphibious vehicle
68 cannon
69 hatch
70 antenna
71 propeller (for propulsion in water)
72 **Jagdpanzer** Jaguar 1 **ATGW vehicle** (HOT)
73 guidance system (upper part) with guidance unit
74 HOT guided-missile launcher
75 firing mechanism (upper part)
76 commander's cupola
77 Marder **armoured** (*Am.* armored) **personnel carrier**
78 searchlight
79 MILAN anti-tank guided-missile system
80 Fuchs **armoured** (*Am.* armored) **personnel and load carrier,** an amphibious vehicle
81 rear door
82 Gepard **anti-aircraft tank**
83 surveillance radar
84 tracking radar for fire control
85 twin 35 mm cannon
86 M113 A1 G **armoured** (*Am.* armored) **personnel carrier**
87 machine gun on a traversing mount
88-96 **helicopters**
88 CH-53 G **transport helicopter**
89 single rotor
90 turbine
91 stabilizing tail rotor
92 fuselage
93 cockpit
94 BO-105P **anti-tank helicopter**
95 skid
96 HOT anti-tank guided-missile launcher

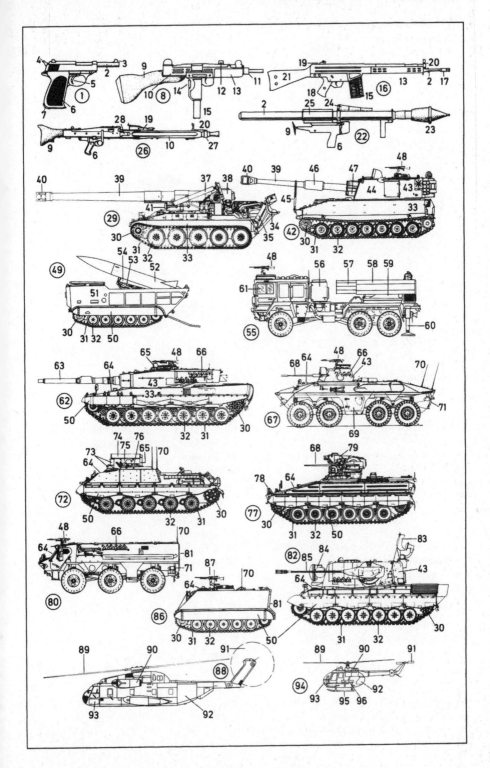

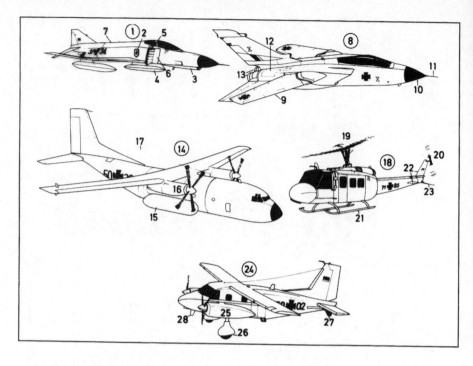

1 *McDonnell-Douglas F-4F Phantom II* **interceptor and fighter-bomber**
2 squadron marking
3 aircraft cannon
4 wing tank (underwing tank)
5 air intake
6 boundary layer control flap
7 in-flight refuelling (*Am.* refueling) probe (flight refuelling probe, air refuelling probe)
8 *Panavia 2000 Tornado* **multirole combat aircraft** (MRCA)
9 swing wing
10 radar nose (radome, radar dome)
11 pitot-static tube (pitot tube)
12 brake flap (air brake)
13 afterburner exhaust nozzles of the engines
14 *C160 Transall* **medium-range transport aircraft**
15 undercarriage housing (landing gear housing)

16 propeller-turbine engine (turbo-prop engine)
17 antenna
18 *Bell UH-ID Iroquois* **light transport and rescue helicopter**
19 main rotor
20 tail rotor
21 landing skids
22 stabilizing fins (stabilizing surfaces, stabilizers)
23 tail skid
24 *Dornier DO 28 D-2 Skyservant* **transport and communications aircraft**
25 engine pod
26 main undercarriage unit (main landing gear unit)
27 tail wheel
28 sword antenna

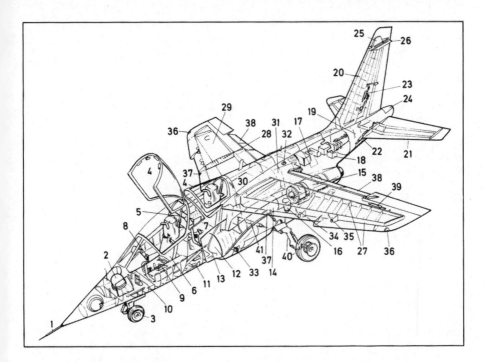

1-41 *Dornier-Dassault-Breguet Alpha Jet* Franco-German jet trainer
1 pitot-static tube (pitot tube)
2 oxygen tank
3 forward-retracting nose wheel
4 cockpit canopy (cockpit hood)
5 canopy jack
6 pilot's seat (student pilot's seat), an ejector seat (ejection seat)
7 observer's seat (instructor's seat), an ejector seat (ejection seat)
8 control column (control stick)
9 thrust lever
10 rudder pedals with brakes
11 front avionics bay
12 air intake to the engine
13 boundary layer control flap
14 air intake duct
15 turbine engine
16 reservoir for the hydraulic system
17 battery housing
18 rear avionics bay
19 baggage compartment
20 triple-spar tail construction
21 horizontal tail
22 servo-actuating mechanism for the elevator
23 servo-actuating mechanism for the rudder
24 brake chute housing (drag chute housing)
25 VHF (very high frequency) antenna (UHF antenna)
26 VOR (very high frequency omnidirectional range) antenna
27 twin-spar wing construction
28 former with integral spars
29 integral wing tanks
30 centre-section (*Am.* center-section) fuel tank
31 fuselage tanks
32 gravity fuelling (*Am.* fueling) point
33 pressure fuelling (*Am.* fueling) point
34 inner wing suspension
35 outer wing suspension
36 navigation lights (position lights)
37 landing lights
38 landing flap
39 aileron actuator
40 forward-retracting main undercarriage unit (main landing gear unit)
41 undercarriage hydraulic cylinder (landing gear hydraulic cylinder)

1 Hamburg class **guided-missile destroyer**
2 hull of flush-deck vessel
3 bow (stem)
4 flagstaff (jackstaff)
5 anchor, a stockless anchor (patent anchor)
6 anchor capstan (windlass)
7 breakwater (*Am.* manger board)
8 chine strake
9 main deck
10-28 superstructures
10 superstructure deck
11 life rafts
12 cutter (ship's boat)
13 davit (boat-launching crane)
14 bridge (bridge superstructure)
15 side navigation light (side running light)
16 antenna
17 radio direction finder (RDF) frame
18 lattice mast
19 forward funnel
20 aft funnel
21 cowl
22 aft superstructure (poop)
23 capstan
24 companion ladder (companionway, companion hatch)
25 ensign staff
26 stern, a transom stern
27 waterline
28 searchlight
29-37 armament
29 100 mm gun turret
30 four-barrel anti-submarine rocket launcher (missile launcher)
31 40 mm twin anti-aircraft (AA) gun
32 MM 38 anti-aircraft (AA) rocket launcher (missile launcher) in launching container
33 anti-submarine torpedo tube
34 depth-charge thrower
35 weapon system radar
36 radar antenna (radar scanner)
37 optical rangefinder
38 Lütjens class **guided-missile destroyer**
39 bower anchor
40 propeller guard
41 tripod lattice mast
42 pole mast
43 ventilator openings (ventilator grill)
44 exhaust pipe
45 ship's boat
46 antenna

47 radar-controlled 127 mm all-purpose gun in turret
48 127 mm all-purpose gun
49 launcher for Tartar missiles
50 anti-submarine rocket (ASROC) launcher (missile launcher)
51 fire control radar antennas
52 radome (radar dome)
53 Bremen class **frigate**
54 radar-controlled 76 mm rapid-fire gun
55 Sea Sparrow surface-to-air missiles
56 radar and fire control system
57 Harpoon surface-to-surface missiles
58 funnel
59 cowl
60 air/surface search radar
61 cutter
62 close-range surface-to-air missiles
63 helicopter deck
64 type 206 **submarine**
65 flooded foredeck
66 pressure hull
67 turret
68 retractable instruments
69 type 148 **missile-firing fast attack craft**
70 76 mm all-purpose gun with turret
71 missile-launching housing
72 deckhouse
73 40 mm anti-aircraft (AA) gun
74 propeller guard moulding (*Am.* molding)
75 type 143 **missile-firing fast attack craft**
76 breakwater (*Am.* manger board)
77 radome (radar dome)
78 torpedo tube
79 exhaust escape flue
80 type 331 **mine hunter**
81 reinforced rubbing strake
82 inflatable boat (inflatable dinghy)
83 davit
84 type 341 **minesweeper**
85 cable winch
86 towing winch (towing machine, towing engine)
87 mine-sweeping gear (paravanes)
88 crane (davit)
89 Barbe class **landing craft**
90 bow ramp
91 stern ramp
92 Rhein class **tender**
93 Lüneburg class **support ship**
94 Sachsenwald class **mine transport**
95 Helgoland class **salvage tug**
96 **replenishment tanker** 'Eifel'

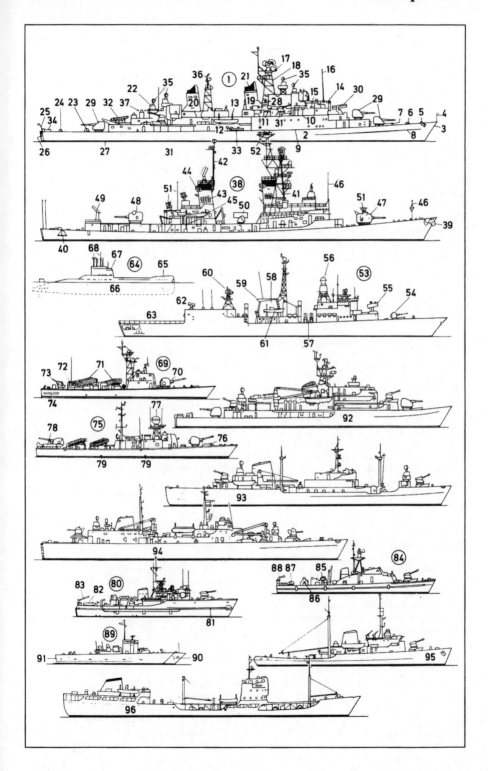

1 **nuclear-powered aircraft carrier** *Nimitz ICVN68* (USA)
2-11 body plan
2 flight deck
3 island (bridge)
4 aircraft lift (*Am.* aircraft elevator)
5 eight-barrel anti-aircraft (AA) rocket launcher (missile launcher)
6 pole mast (antenna mast)
7 antenna
8 radar antenna (radar scanner)
9 fully enclosed bow
10 deck crane
11 transom stern
12-20 deck plan
12 angle deck (flight deck)
13 aircraft lift (*Am.* aircraft elevator)
14 twin launching catapult
15 hinged (movable) baffle board
16 arrester wire
17 emergency crash barrier
18 safety net
19 caisson (cofferdam)
20 eight-barrel anti-aircraft (AA) rocket launcher (missile launcher)
21 *Kara class* **rocket cruiser** (missile cruiser) (USSR)
22 hull of flush-deck vessel
23 sheer
24 twelve-barrel underwater salvo rocket launcher (missile launcher)
25 twin anti-aircraft (AA) rocket launcher (missile launcher)
26 launching housing for 4 short-range rockets (missiles)
27 baffle board
28 bridge
29 radar antenna (radar scanner)
30 twin 76 mm anti-aircraft (AA) gun turret
31 turret
32 funnel
33 twin anti-aircraft (AA) rocket launcher (missile launcher)
34 automatic anti-aircraft (AA) gun
35 ship's boat
36 underwater 5-torpedo housing
37 underwater 6-salvo rocket launcher (missile launcher)
38 helicopter hangar
39 helicopter landing platform
40 variable depth sonar (VDS)
41 *California class* **rocket cruiser** (missile cruiser) (USA)
42 hull
43 forward turret
44 aft turret
45 forward superstructure
46 landing craft
47 antenna

48 radar antenna (radar scanner)
49 radome (radar dome)
50 surface-to-air rocket launcher (missile launcher)
51 underwater rocket launcher (missile launcher)
52 127 mm gun with turret
53 helicopter landing platform
54 **nuclear-powered fleet submarine**
55-74 middle section [diagram]
55 pressure hull
56 auxiliary engine room
57 rotary turbine pump
58 steam turbine generator
59 propeller shaft
60 thrust block
61 reduction gear
62 high and low pressure turbine
63 high-pressure steam pipe for the secondary water circuit (auxiliary water circuit)
64 condenser
65 primary water circuit
66 heat exchanger
67 nuclear reactor casing (atomic pile casing)
68 reactor core
69 control rods
70 lead screen
71 turret
72 snorkel (schnorkel)
73 air inlet
74 retractable instruments
75 **patrol submarine** with conventional (diesel-electric) drive
76 pressure hull
77 flooded foredeck
78 outer flap (outer doors) [for torpedoes]
79 torpedo tube
80 bow bilge
81 anchor
82 anchor winch
83 battery
84 living quarters with folding bunks
85 commanding officer's cabin
86 main hatchway
87 flagstaff
88-91 retractable instruments
88 attack periscope
89 antenna
90 snorkel (schnorkel)
91 radar antenna (radar scanner)
92 exhaust outlet
93 heat space (hot-pipe space)
94 diesel generators
95 aft diving plane and vertical rudder
96 forward vertical rudder

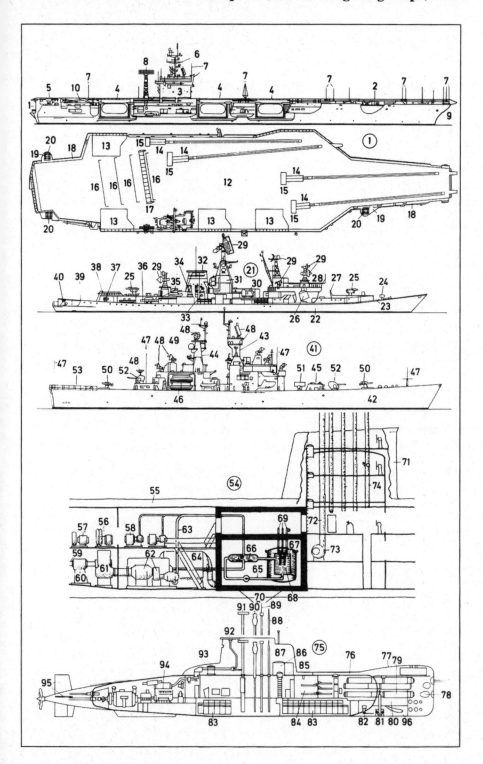

1-85 primary school
1-45 classroom
1 arrangement of desks in a horse-shoe
2 double desk
3 pupils (children) in a group (sitting in a group)
4 exercise book
5 pencil
6 wax crayon
7 school bag
8 handle
9 school satchel (satchel)
10 front pocket
11 strap (shoulder strap)
12 pen and pencil case
13 zip (*Am.* zipper)
14 fountain pen (pen)
15 loose-leaf file (ring file)
16 reader
17 spelling book
18 exercise book (notebook)
19 felt tip pen
20 pupil raising her hand
21 teacher
22 teacher's desk
23 register
24 pen and pencil tray
25 desk mat (blotter)
26 window painting with finger paints (finger painting)
27 pupils' (children's) paintings (watercolours, *Am.* watercolors)
28 cross
29 three-part blackboard
30 bracket for holding charts
31 chalk ledge
32 chalk
33 blackboard drawing
34 diagram
35 reversible side blackboard
36 projection screen
37 triangle
38 protractor
39 divisions
40 blackboard compass
41 sponge tray
42 blackboard sponge (sponge)
43 classroom cupboard
44 map (wall map)
45 brick wall
46-85 craft room
46 workbench
47 vice (*Am.* vise)
48 vice (*Am.* vise) bar
49 scissors
50-52 working with glue (sticking paper, cardboard, etc.)
50 surface to be glued
51 tube of glue
52 tube cap
53 fretsaw
54 fretsaw blade (saw blade)
55 wood rasp (rasp)
56 piece of wood held in the vice (*Am.* vise)
57 glue pot
58 stool
59 brush
60 pan (dustpan)
61 broken china
62 enamelling (*Am.* enameling)
63 electric enamelling (*Am.* enameling) stove
64 unworked copper
65 enamel powder
66 hair sieve
67-80 pupils' (children's) work
67 clay models (models)
68 window decoration of coloured (*Am.* colored) glass
69 glass mosaic picture (glass mosaic)
70 mobile
71 paper kite (kite)
72 wooden construction
73 polyhedron
74 hand puppets
75 clay masks
76 cast candles (wax candles)
77 wood carving
78 clay jug
79 geometrical shapes made of clay
80 wooden toys
81 materials
82 stock of wood
83 inks for wood cuts
84 paintbrushes
85 bag of plaster of Paris

1-45 grammar school; *also:* upper band of a comprehensive school (*Am.* alternative school)

1-13 chemistry

1 chemistry lab (chemistry laboratory) with tiered rows of seats
2 chemistry teacher
3 demonstration bench (teacher's bench)
4 water pipe
5 tiled working surface
6 sink
7 television monitor, a screen for educational programmes (*Am.* programs)
8 overhead projector
9 projector top for skins
10 projection lens with right-angle mirror
11 pupils' (*Am.* students') bench with experimental apparatus
12 electrical point (socket)
13 projection table

14-34 biology preparation room (biology prep room)

14 skeleton
15 casts of skulls
16 calvarium of Pithecanthropus erectus
17 skull of Steinheim man
18 calvarium of Peking man (of Sinanthropus)
19 skull of Neanderthal man, a skull of primitive man
20 Australopithecine skull (skull of Australopithecus)
21 skull of present-day man
22 dissecting bench
23 chemical bottles
24 gas tap
25 petri dish
26 measuring cylinder
27 work folder containing teaching material
28 textbook
29 bacteriological cultures
30 incubator

31 test tube rack
32 washing bottle
33 water tank
34 sink

35 language laboratory

36 blackboard
37 console
38 headphones (headset)
39 microphone
40 earcup
41 padded headband (padded headpiece)
42 programme (*Am.* program) recorder, a cassette recorder
43 pupil's (*Am.* student's) volume control
44 master volume control
45 control buttons (operating keys)

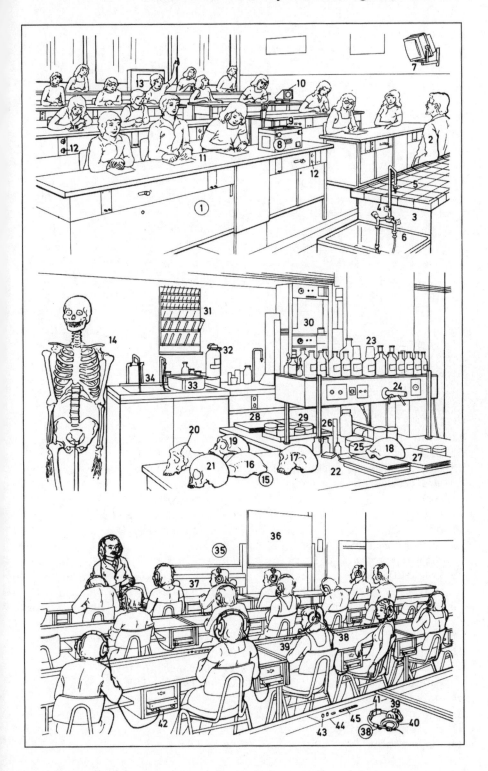

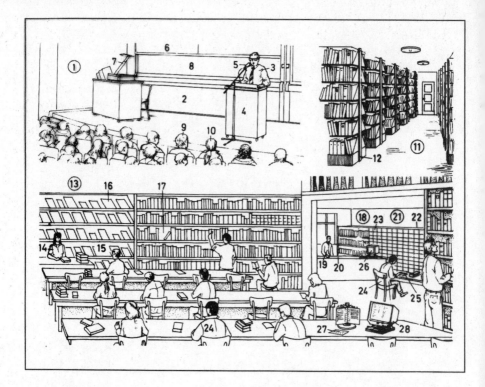

1-28 university (college)
1 lecture
2 lecture room (lecture theatre, *Am.* theater)
3 university lecturer (lecturer, college lecturer, *Am.* assistant professor)
4 lectern
5 microphone
6 remote-controlled blackboard
7 overhead projector
8 projection screen for projecting pictures by means of a film projector, slide projector, or an epidiascope
9, 10 students
11-28 university library; *sim.:* national library, regional or municipal scientific library
11 stack (book stack) with the stock of books
12 bookshelf, a steel shelf
13 reading room

14 member of the reading room staff, a librarian
15 periodicals rack with periodicals
16 newspaper shelf
17 reference library with reference books (handbooks, encyclopedias, dictionaries)
18 lending library and catalogue (*Am.* catalog) room
19 librarian
20 issue desk
21 main catalogue (*Am.* catalog)
22 card catalogue (*Am.* catalog)
23 card catalogue (*Am.* catalog) drawer
24 library user
25 borrower's ticket (library ticket)
26 issue terminal
27 microfiche (fiche)
28 microfiche reader

1-15 election meeting, a public meeting	**19** polling card with registration number (polling number)
1, 2 committee	
1 chairman	**20** ballot paper with the names of the parties and candidates
2 committee member	
3 committee table	**21** ballot envelope
4 pamphlet	**22** voter
5 election speaker (speaker)	**23** polling booth
6 rostrum	**24** elector (qualified voter)
7 microphone	**25** election regulations
8 meeting (audience)	**26** electoral register
9 man distributing leaflets	**27** election supervisor
10 stewards	**28** ballot box
11 armband (armlet)	**29** slot
12 banner	
13 placard	
14 proclamation	
15 heckler	
16-29 election	
16 polling station (polling place)	
17 polling officers	
18 electoral list	

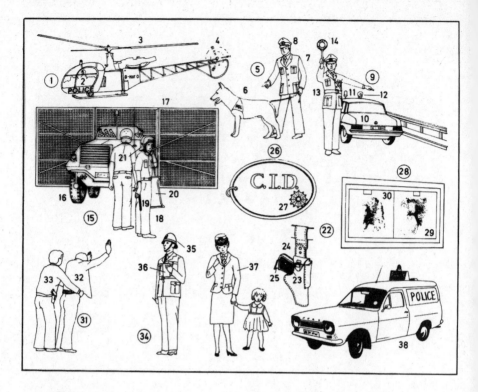

1-33 police duties
1 **police helicopter** (traffic helicopter) for controlling traffic from the air
2 cockpit
3 rotor (main rotor)
4 tail rotor
5 **use of police dogs**
6 police dog
7 uniform
8 uniform cap, a peaked cap with cockade
9 **traffic control** by a mobile traffic patrol
10 patrol car
11 blue light
12 loud hailer (loudspeaker)
13 patrolman (police patrolman)
14 police signalling (*Am.* signaling) disc (disk)
15 **riot duty**
16 special armoured (*Am.* armored) car
17 barricade
18 policeman (police officer) in riot gear
19 truncheon (baton)
20 riot shield
21 protective helmet (helmet)
22 **service pistol**
23 pistol grip
24 quick-draw holster
25 magazine
26 **police identification disc (disk)**
27 police badge
28 **fingerprint identification** (dactyloscopy)
29 fingerprint
30 illuminated screen
31 **search**
32 suspect
33 detective (plainclothes policeman)
34 English policeman
35 helmet
36 pocket book
37 policewoman
38 police van

1-31 **café;** *sim.:* espresso bar, tea room, ice-cream parlour (*Am.* parlor)
1 counter (cake counter)
2 coffee urn
3 tray for the money
4 gateau
5 meringue with whipped cream
6 trainee pastry cook
7 counter assistant
8 newspaper shelves (newspaper rack)
9 wall lamp
10 corner seat, an upholstered seat
11 café table
12 marble top
13 waitress
14 tray
15 bottle of lemonade
16 lemonade glass
17 chess players playing a game of chess
18 coffee set
19 cup of coffee
20 small sugar bowl
21 cream jug (*Am.* creamer)
22-24 café customers
22 gentleman
23 lady
24 man reading a newspaper
25 newspaper
26 newspaper holder
27 espresso
28 ice cream in assorted flavours (*Am.* flavors)
29 ice-cream dish (sundae dish)
30 iced coffee
31 (drinking) straw

1-27 restaurant
1-11 bar (counter)
1 beer pump (beerpull)
2 drip tray
3 beer glass
4 froth (head)
5 spherical ashtray for cigarette and cigar ash
6 beer glass (beer mug)
7 beer warmer
8 bartender (barman, *Am.* barkeeper, barkeep)
9 shelf for glasses
10 shelf for bottles
11 stack of plates
12 coat stand
13 hat peg
14 coat hook
15 wall ventilator
16 bottle
17 complete meal
18 waitress
19 tray

20 dessert, a slice of cake
21 menu (menu card)
22 cruet stand
23 toothpick holder
24 matchbox holder
25 customer
26 beer mat
27 meal of the day
28-44 wine restaurant (wine bar)
28 tablecloth
29 glass of water
30 wine waiter, a head waiter
31 wine list
32 wine carafe
33 wineglass
34 tiled stove
35 stove tile
36 stove bench
37 wooden panelling (*Am.* paneling)
38 corner seat
39 table reserved for regular customers
40 regular customer

41 cutlery chest	63 tray
42 wine cooler	64 tray counter
43 bottle of wine	65 food price list
44 ice cubes (ice, lumps of ice)	66 serving hatch
45-78 self-service restaurant	67 hot meal
45 stack of trays	68 beer pump (beerpull)
46 drinking straws (straws)	69 cash desk
47 serviettes (napkins)	70 cashier
48 cutlery holders	71 proprietor
49 cool shelf	72 rail
50 slice of honeydew melon	73 dining area
51 plate of salad	74 table
52 plate of cheeses	75 open sandwich
53 fish dish	76 ice-cream sundae
54 filled roll	77 salt cellar and pepper pot
55 meat dish with trimmings	78 table decoration (flower arrange-
56 half chicken	ment)
57 basket of fruit	
58 fruit juice	
59 drinks shelf	
60 bottle of milk	
61 bottle of mineral water	
62 vegetarian meal (diet meal)	

1-26 vestibule (foyer, reception hall)
1 doorman (commissionaire)
2 letter rack with pigeon holes
3 key rack
4 globe lamp, a frosted glass globe
5 indicator board
6 indicator light
7 chief receptionist
8 register (hotel register)
9 room key
10 number tag (number tab) showing room number
11 hotel bill
12 block of registration forms
13 passport
14 hotel guest
15 lightweight suitcase [for air travel]
16 wall desk
17 porter (*Am.* baggage man)
18-26 lobby (hotel lobby)
18 page (pageboy, *Am.* bell boy)
19 hotel manager
20 dining room (hotel restaurant)
21 chandelier
22 fireside
23 fireplace
24 mantelpiece (mantelshelf)
25 fire
26 armchair
27-38 hotel room, a double room with bath
27 double door
28 service bell panel
29 wardrobe (*Am.* clothes closet)
30 clothes compartment
31 linen compartment
32 double washbasin
33 room waiter
34 room telephone
35 velour (velours) carpet
36 flower stand
37 flower arrangement
38 double bed
39 function room (banqueting hall)
40-43 private party

40 speaker proposing a toast
41 42's neighbour (*Am.* neighbor)
42 43's partner
43 42's partner
44 bar trio
45 violinist
46 couple dancing (dancing couple)
47 waiter
48 napkin
49 cigarette
50 ashtray
51 **hotel bar**
52 foot rail
53 bar stool
54 bar
55 bar customer
56 cocktail glass (*Am.* highball glass)
57 whisky (whiskey) glass
58 champagne cork
59 champagne bucket (champagne cooler)
60 measuring beaker (measure)
61 cocktail shaker

62 bartender (barman, *Am.* barkeeper, barkeep)
63 barmaid
64 shelf for bottles
65 shelf for glasses
66 mirrored panel
67 ice bucket
68 hotel foyer

1 parking meter	21 broom
2 map of the town (street map)	22 rubbish (litter)
3 illuminated board	23 tramlines (*Am.* streetcar tracks)
4 key	24 pedestrian crossing (zebra crossing, *Am.* crosswalk)
5 litter bin (*Am.* trash bin)	25 tram stop (*Am.* streetcar stop, trolley stop)
6 street lamp (street light)	
7 street sign showing the name of the street	26 tram stop sign (*Am.* streetcar stop sign, trolley stop sign)
8 drain	27 tram timetable (*Am.* streetcar schedule, trolley schedule)
9 clothes shop (fashion house)	
10 shop window	28 ticket machine
11 window display (shop window display)	29 'pedestrian crossing' sign
	30 traffic policeman on traffic duty (point duty)
12 window decoration (shop window decoration)	31 traffic control cuff
13 entrance	32 white cap
14 window	33 hand signal
15 window box	34 motorcyclist
16 neon sign	35 motorcycle
17 tailor's workroom	36 pillion passenger (pillion rider)
18 pedestrian	37 bookshop
19 shopping bag	
20 road sweeper (*Am.* street sweeper)	

38 hat shop (hatter's shop); *for ladies' hats:* milliner's shop
39 shop sign
40 insurance company office
41 department store
42 shop front
43 advertisement
44 flags
45 illuminated letters
46 tram (*Am.* streetcar, trolley)
47 furniture lorry (*Am.* furniture truck)
48 flyover
49 suspended street lamp
50 stop line
51 pedestrian crossing (*Am.* crosswalk)
52 traffic lights
53 traffic light post
54 set of lights
55 pedestrian lights
56 telephone box (telephone booth, telephone kiosk, call box)
57 cinema (*Am.* movie) advertisement (film poster, *Am.* movie poster)
58 pedestrian precinct (paved zone)
59 street café
60 group seated (sitting) at a table
61 sunshade
62 steps to the public lavatories (public conveniences)
63 taxi rank (taxi stand)
64 taxi (taxicab, cab)
65 taxi sign
66 'taxi rank' ('taxi stand') sign
67 taxi telephone
68 post office
69 cigarette machine
70 advertising pillar
71 poster (advertisement)
72 white line
73 lane arrow for turning left
74 lane arrow for going straight ahead
75 news vendor (*Am.* news dealer)

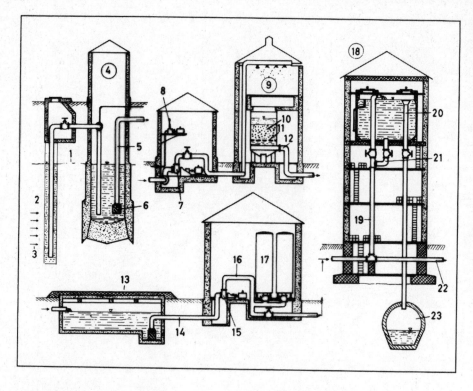

1-66 drinking water supply
1 water table (groundwater level)
2 water-bearing stratum (aquifer, aquafer)
3 groundwater stream (underground stream)
4 collector well for raw water
5 suction pipe
6 pump strainer with foot valve
7 bucket pump with motor
8 vacuum pump with motor
9 rapid-filter plant
10 filter gravel (filter bed)
11 filter bottom, a grid
12 filtered water outlet
13 purified water tank
14 suction pipe with pump strainer and foot valve
15 main pump with motor
16 delivery pipe
17 compressed-air vessel (air vessel, air receiver)
18 water tower
19 riser pipe (riser)
20 overflow pipe
21 outlet
22 distribution main
23 excess water conduit

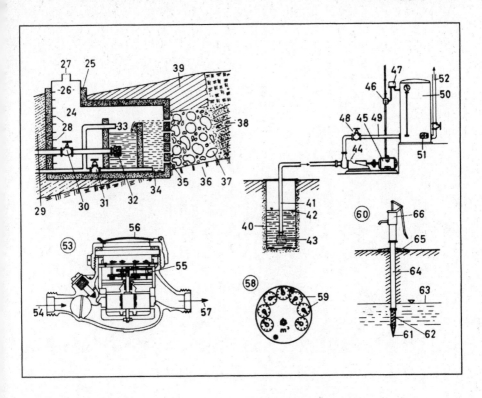

24-39 tapping a spring
24 chamber
25 chamber wall
26 manhole
27 ventilator
28 step irons
29 filling (backing)
30 outlet control valve
31 outlet valve
32 strainer
33 overflow pipe (overflow)
34 bottom outlet
35 earthenware pipes
36 impervious stratum (impermeable
    stratum)
37 rough rubble
38 water-bearing stratum (aquifer,
    aquafer)
39 loam seal (clay seal)
40-52 individual water supply
40 well
41 suction pipe
42 water table (groundwater level)
43 pump strainer with foot valve

44 centrifugal pump
45 motor
46 motor safety switch
47 manostat, a switching device
48 stop valve
49 delivery pipe
50 compressed-air vessel (air vessel,
    air receiver)
51 manhole
52 delivery pipe
53 water meter, a rotary meter
54 water inlet
55 counter gear assembly
56 cover with glass lid
57 water outlet
58 water-meter dial
59 counters
60 driven well (tube well, drive well)
61 pile shoe
62 filter
63 water table (groundwater level)
64 well casing
65 well head
66 hand pump

1-46 fire service drill (extinguishing, climbing, ladder, and rescue work)
1-3 fire station
1 engine and appliance room
2 firemen's (*Am*. firefighters') quarters
3 drill tower
4 fire alarm (fire alarm siren, fire siren)
5 fire engine
6 blue light (warning light), a flashing light (*Am*. flashlight)
7 horn (hooter)
8 motor pump, a centrifugal pump
9 motor turntable ladder (*Am*. aerial ladder)
10 ladder, a steel ladder (automatic extending ladder)
11 ladder mechanism
12 jack
13 ladder operator
14 extension ladder
15 ceiling hook (*Am*. preventer)
16 hook ladder (*Am*. pompier ladder)
17 holding squad
18 jumping sheet (sheet)
19 ambulance car (ambulance)
20 resuscitator (resuscitation equipment), oxygen apparatus
21 ambulance attendant (ambulance man)
22 armband (armlet, brassard)
23 stretcher
24 unconscious man
25 pit hydrant
26 standpipe (riser, vertical pipe)
27 hydrant key
28 hose reel (*Am*. hose cart, hose wagon, hose truck, hose carriage)
29 hose coupling
30 soft suction hose
31 delivery hose
32 dividing breeching
33 branch
34 branchmen
35 surface hydrant (fire plug)

36 officer in charge
37 fireman (*Am.* firefighter)
38 helmet (fireman's helmet, *Am.* fire hat) with neck guard (neck flap)
39 breathing apparatus
40 face mask
41 walkie-talkie set
42 hand lamp
43 small axe (*Am.* ax, pompier hatchet)
44 hoot belt
45 beltline
46 protective clothing of asbestos (asbestos suit) or of metallic fabric
47 breakdown lorry (*Am.* crane truck, wrecking crane)
48 lifting crane
49 load hook (draw hook, *Am.* drag hook)
50 support roll
51 water tender
52 portable pump
53 hose layer
54 flaked lengths of hose
55 cable drum
56 winch
57 face mask filter
58 active carbon (activated carbon, activated charcoal)
59 dust filter
60 air inlet
61 portable fire extinguisher
62 operating valve
63 hose with spray nozzle
64 foam-making branch (*Am.* foam gun)
65 fireboat
66 monitor (water cannon)
67 suction hose

1 cashier
2 electronic cash register (till) (scanner till)
3 number keys
4 scanner (light pen)
5 cash drawer (till)
6 compartments (money compartments) for coins and notes (*Am.* bills)
7 receipt (sales check)
8 amount [to be paid]
9 function keys
10 goods
11 glass-roofed well
12 men's wear department
13 showcase (display case, indoor display window)
14 wrapping counter
15 tray for purchases
16 customer
17 hosiery department
18 shop assistant (*Am.* salesgirl, saleslady)

19 price card
20 glove stand
21 duffle coat, a three-quarter length coat
22 escalator
23 fluorescent light (fluorescent lamp)
24 office (*e.g.* customer accounts office, travel agency, manager's office)
25 poster (advertisement)
26 theatre (*Am.* theater) and concert booking office (advance booking office)
27 shelves
28 ladies' wear department
29 ready-made dress (ready-to-wear dress, *coll.* off-the-peg dress)
30 dust cover
31 clothes rack
32 changing booth (fitting booth)
33 mirror
34 dummy
35 seat (chair)

36 fashion journal (fashion magazine)
37 tailor marking a hemline
38 measuring tape (tape measure)
39 tailor's chalk (French chalk)
40 hemline marker
41 loose-fitting coat
42 sales counter
43 warm-air curtain
44 stairs
45 lift (*Am.* elevator)
46 lift cage (lift car, *Am.* elevator car)
47 direction indicators
48 controls (lift controls, *Am.* elevator controls)
49 floor indicator
50 sliding door
51 lift shaft (*Am.* elevator shaft)
52 bearer cable
53 control cable
54 guide rail
55 customer
56 hosiery

57 linen goods (table linen and bed linen)
58 fabric department
59 roll of fabric (roll of material, roll of cloth)
60 head of department (department manager)
61 sales counter
62 jewellery (*Am.* jewelry) department
63 customer assistant
64 special counter (extra counter)
65 placard advertising special offers
66 curtain department
67 display on top of the shelves

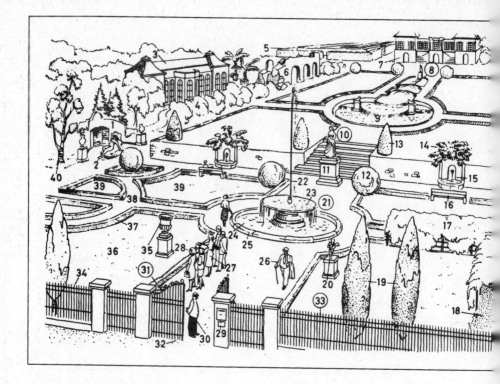

1-40 formal garden (French Baroque garden), palace gardens
1 grotto (cavern)
2 stone statue, a river nymph
3 orangery (orangerie)
4 boscage (boskage)
5 maze (labyrinth of paths and hedges)
6 open-air theatre (*Am.* theater)
7 Baroque palace
8 fountains
9 cascade (broken artificial waterfall, artificial falls)
10 statue, a monument
11 pedestal
12 globe-shaped tree
13 conical tree
14 ornamental shrub
15 wall fountain
16 park bench
17 pergola (bower, arbour, *Am.* arbor)
18 gravel path (gravel walk)
19 pyramid tree (pyramidal tree)
20 cupid (cherub, amoretto, amorino)
21 fountain
22 fountain
23 overflow basin
24 basin
25 kerb (curb)
26 man out for a walk
27 tourist guide
28 group of tourists
29 park by-laws (bye-laws)
30 park keeper
31 garden gates made of wrought iron
32 park entrance
33 park railings
34 railing (bar)
35 stone vase
36 lawn
37 border, a trimmed (clipped) hedge
38 park path
39 parterre
40 birch (birch tree)

41-72 landscaped park (jardin anglais)
41 flower bed
42 park bench (garden seat)
43 litter bin (*Am.* trash bin)
44 play area
45 stream
46 jetty
47 bridge
48 park chair
49 animal enclosure
50 pond
51-54 waterfowl
51 wild duck with young
52 goose
53 flamingo
54 swan
55 island
56 water lily
57 open-air café
58 sunshade
59 park tree (tree)
60 treetop (crown)
61 group of trees

62 fountain
63 weeping willow
64 modern sculpture
65 hothouse
66 park gardener
67 broom
68 minigolf course
69 minigolf player
70 minigolf hole
71 mother with pram (baby carriage)
72 courting couple (young couple)

1 table tennis	21 adventure playground
2 table	22 log ladder
3 table tennis net	23 lookout platform
4 table tennis racket (raquet) (table tennis bat)	24 slide
5 table tennis ball	25 litter bin (*Am.* trash bin)
6 badminton game (shuttlecock game)	26 teddy bear
7 shuttlecock	27 wooden train set
8 maypole swing	28 paddling pool
9 child's bicycle	29 sailing boat (yacht, *Am.* sailboat)
10 football (soccer)	30 toy duck
11 goal (goalposts)	31 pram (baby carriage)
12 football	32 high bar (bar)
13 goal scorer	33 go-cart (soap box)
14 goalkeeper	34 starter's flag
15 skipping (*Am.* jumping rope)	35 seesaw
16 skipping rope (*Am.* skip rope, jump rope, jumping rope)	36 robot
17 climbing tower	
18 rubber tyre (*Am.* tire) swing	
19 lorry tyre (*Am.* truck tire)	
20 bouncing ball	

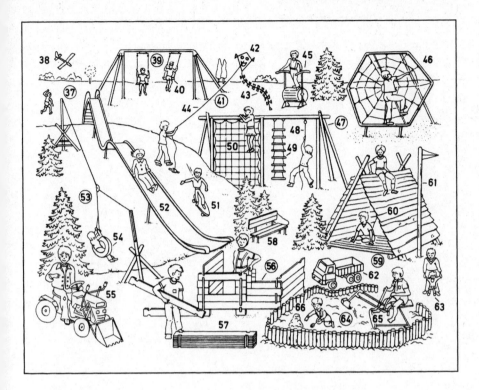

37 flying model aeroplanes (*Am.* airplanes)
38 model aeroplane (*Am.* airplane)
39 double swing
40 swing seat
41 flying kites
42 kite
43 tail of the kite
44 kite string
45 revolving drum
46 spider's web
47 climbing frame
48 climbing rope
49 rope ladder
50 climbing net
51 skateboard
52 up-and-down slide
53 rubber tyre (*Am.* tire) cable car
54 rubber tyre (*Am.* tire)
55 tractor, a pedal car
56 den
57 presawn boards
58 seat (bench)
59 Indian hut

60 climbing roof
61 flagpole (flagstaff)
62 toy lorry (*Am.* toy truck)
63 walking doll
64 sandpit (*Am.* sandbox)
65 toy excavator (toy digger)
66 sandhill

1-21 spa gardens
1-7 salina (salt works)
1 thorn house (graduation house)
2 thorns (brushwood)
3 brine channels
4 brine pipe from the pumping station
5 salt works attendant
6, 7 inhalational therapy
6 open-air inhalatorium (outdoor inhalatorium)
7 patient inhaling (taking an inhalation)
8 hydropathic (pump room) with kursaal (casino)
9 colonnade
10 spa promenade
11 avenue leading to the mineral spring
12-14 rest cure
12 sunbathing area (lawn)
13 deck-chair
14 sun canopy
15 pump room
16 rack for glasses
17 tap
18 patient taking the waters
19 bandstand
20 spa orchestra giving a concert
21 conductor

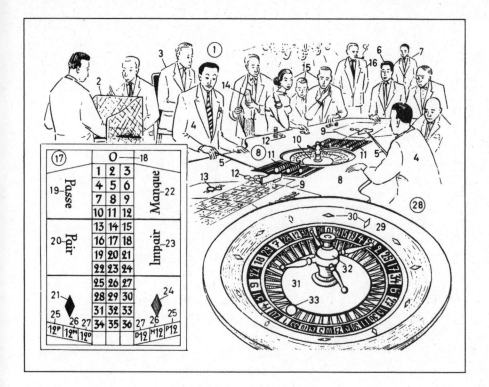

1-33 roulette, a game of chance (gambling game)
1 gaming room in the casino (in the gambling casino)
2 cash desk
3 tourneur (dealer)
4 croupier
5 rake
6 head croupier
7 hall manager
8 roulette table (gaming table, gambling table)
9 roulette layout
10 roulette wheel
11 bank
12 chip (check, plaque)
13 stake
14 membership card
15 roulette player
16 private detective (house detective)
17 roulette layout
18 zero (nought, 0)
19 passe (high) [numbers 19 to 36]
20 pair (even numbers)
21 noir (black)
22 manque (low) [numbers 1 to 18]
23 impair [odd numbers]
24 rouge (red)
25 douze premier (first dozen) [numbers 1 to 12]
26 douze milieu (second dozen) [numbers 13 to 24]
27 douze dernier (third dozen) [numbers 25 to 36]
28 roulette wheel (roulette)
29 roulette bowl
30 fret (separator)
31 revolving disc (disk) showing numbers 0 to 36
32 spin
33 roulette ball

1-16 chess, a game involving combinations of moves, a positional game
1 chessboard (board) with the men (chessmen) in position
2 white square (chessboard square)
3 black square
4 white chessmen (white pieces) [white = W]
5 black chessmen (black pieces) [black = B]
6 letters and numbers for designating chess squares in the notation of chess moves and chess problems
7 individual chessmen (individual pieces)
8 king
9 queen
10 bishop
11 knight
12 rook (castle)
13 pawn
14 moves of the individual pieces
15 mate (checkmate), a mate by knight
16 chess clock, a double clock for chess matches (chess championships)
17-19 draughts (*Am.* checkers)
17 draughtboard (*Am.* checkerboard)
18 white draughtsman (*Am.* checker, checkerman); *also:* piece for backgammon and nine men's morris
19 black draughtsman (*Am.* checker, checkerman)
20 salta
21 salta piece
22 backgammon board
23-25 nine men's morris
23 nine men's morris board
24 mill
25 double mill
26-28 halma
26 halma board
27 yard (camp, corner)
28 halma pieces (halma men) of vari-

ous colours (*Am.* colors)
29 dice (dicing)
30 dice cup
31 dice
32 spots (pips)
33 dominoes
34 domino (tile)
35 double
36 playing cards
37 playing card (card)
38-45 suits
38 clubs
39 spades
40 hearts
41 diamonds
42-45 German suits
42 acorns
43 leaves
44 hearts
45 bells (hawkbells)

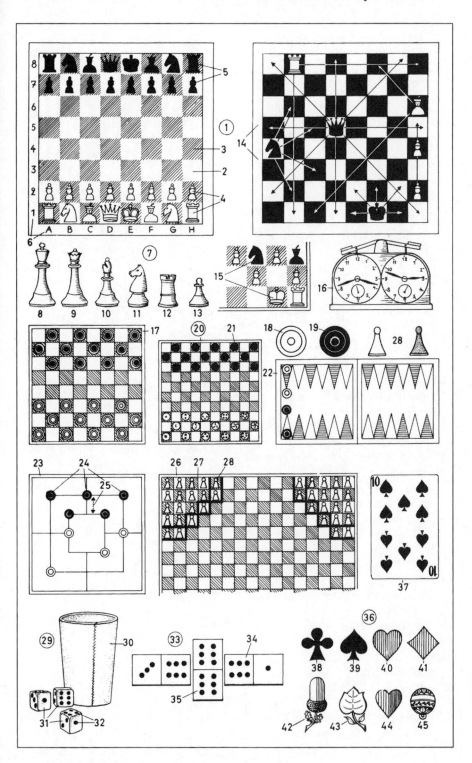

1-19 billiards
1 billiard ball, an ivory or plastic ball
2-6 billiard strokes
2 plain stroke (hitting the cue ball dead centre, *Am.* center)
3 top stroke [promotes extra forward rotation]
4 screw-back [imparts a direct recoil or backward motion]
5 side (running side, *Am.* English)
6 check side
7-19 billiard room (*Am.* billiard parlor, billiard saloon, poolroom)
7 billiards (English billiards); *sim.:* pool, carrom (carrom billiards)
8 billiard player
9 cue (billiard cue)
10 leather cue tip
11 white cue ball
12 red object ball
13 white spot ball (white dot ball)
14 billiard table
15 table bed with green cloth (billiard cloth, green baize covering)
16 cushions (rubber cushions, cushioned ledge)
17 billiard clock, a timer
18 billiard marker
19 cue rack

1-59 camp site (camping site, *Am.* campground)
1 reception (office)
2 site warden
3 folding trailer (collapsible caravan, collapsible trailer)
4 hammock
5, 6 washing and toilet facilities
5 toilets and washrooms (*Am.* lavatories)
6 washbasins and sinks
7 bungalow (chalet)
8-11 scout camp
8 bell tent
9 pennon
10 camp fire
11 boy scout (scout)
12 sailing boat (yacht, *Am.* sailboat)
13 landing stage (jetty)
14 inflatable boat (inflatable dinghy)
15 outboard motor (outboard)
16 trimaran

17 thwart (oarsman's bench)
18 rowlock (oarlock)
19 oar
20 boat trailer (boat carriage)
21 ridge tent
22 flysheet
23 guy line (guy)
24 tent peg (peg)
25 mallet
26 groundsheet ring
27 bell end
28 erected awning
29 storm lantern, a paraffin lamp
30 sleeping bag
31 air mattress (inflatable air-bed)
32 water carrier (drinking water carrier)
33 double-burner gas cooker for propane gas or butane gas
34 propane or butane gas bottle
35 pressure cooker

36 frame tent
37 awning
38 tent pole
39 wheelarch doorway
40 mesh ventilator
41 transparent window
42 pitch number
43 folding camp chair
44 folding camp table
45 camping eating utensils
46 camper
47 charcoal grill (barbecue)
48 charcoal
49 bellows
50 roof rack
51 roof lashing
52 caravan (*Am.* trailer)
53 box for gas bottle
54 jockey wheel
55 drawbar coupling
56 roof ventilator
57 caravan awning
58 inflatable igloo tent
59 camp bed (*Am.* camp cot)

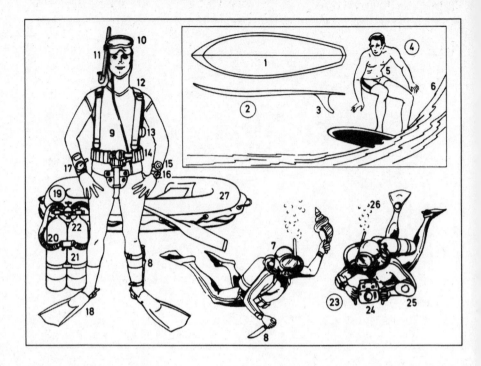

1-6 surf riding (surfing)
1 plan view of surfboard
2 section of surfboard
3 skeg (stabilizing fin)
4 big wave riding
5 surfboarder (surfer)
6 breaker
7-27 skin diving (underwater swimming)
7 skin diver (underwater swimmer)
8-22 underwater swimming set
8 knife
9 neoprene wetsuit
10 diving mask (face mask, mask), a pressure-equalizing mask
11 snorkel (schnorkel)
12 harness of diving apparatus
13 compressed-air pressure gauge (*Am.* gage)
14 weight belt
15 depth gauge (*Am.* gage)
16 waterproof watch for checking duration of dive
17 decometer for measuring stages of ascent
18 fin (flipper)
19 diving apparatus (aqualung, scuba) with two cylinders (bottles)
20 two-tube demand regulator
21 compressed-air cylinder (compressed-air bottle)
22 on/off valve
23 underwater photography
24 underwater camera
25 underwater flashlight
26 exhaust bubbles
27 inflatable boat (inflatable dinghy)

1 lifesaver (lifeguard)	24 beach bag
2 lifeline	25 bathing gown (bathing wrap)
3 lifebelt (lifebuoy)	26 bikini (ladies' two-piece bathing
4 storm signal	suit)
5 time ball	27 bikini bottom
6 warning sign	28 bikini top
7 tide table, a notice board showing	29 bathing cap (swimming cap)
times of low tide and high tide	30 bather
8 board showing water and air tem-	31 deck tennis (quoits)
perature	32 rubber ring (quoit)
9 bathing platform	33 inflatable rubber animal
10 pennon staff	34 beach attendant
11 pennon	35 sandcastle
12 paddle boat (pedal boat)	36 roofed wicker beach chair
13 surf riding (surfing) behind motor-	37 underwater swimmer
boat	38 diving goggles
14 surfboarder (surfer)	39 snorkel (schnorkel)
15 surfboard	40 hand harpoon (fish spear, fish
16 water ski	lance)
17 inflatable beach mattress	41 fin (flipper) for diving (for under-
18 beach ball	water swimming)
19-23 beachwear	42 bathing suit (swimsuit)
19 beach suit	43 bathing trunks (swimming trunks)
20 beach hat	44 bathing cap (swimming cap)
21 beach jacket	45 beach tent, a ridge tent
22 beach trousers	46 lifeguard station
23 beach shoe (bathing shoe)	

1-9 wave pool, an indoor pool
1 artificial waves
2 beach area
3 edge of the pool
4 swimming pool attendant (pool attendant, swimming bath attendant)
5 sun bed
6 lifebelt
7 water wings
8 bathing cap
9 channel to outdoor mineral bath
10 solarium
11 sunbathing area
12 sunbather
13 sun ray lamp
14 bathing towel
15 nudist sunbathing area
16 nudist (naturist)
17 screen (fence)
18 mixed sauna
19 wood panelling (*Am.* paneling)
20 tiered benches
21 sauna stove
22 stones
23 hygrometer
24 thermometer
25 towel
26 water tub for moistening the stones in the stove
27 birch rods (birches) for beating the skin
28 cooling room for cooling off (cooling down) after the sauna
29 lukewarm shower
30 cold bath
31 hot whirlpool (underwater massage bath)
32 step into the bath
33 massage bath
34 jet blower
35 hot whirlpool [diagram]
36 section of the bath
37 step
38 circular seat
39 water extractor
40 water jet pipe
41 air jet pipe

1-32 swimming pool, an open-air swimming pool
1 changing cubicle
2 shower (shower bath)
3 changing room
4 sunbathing area
5-10 diving boards (diving apparatus)
5 diver (highboard diver)
6 diving platform
7 ten-metre (*Am.* ten-meter) platform
8 five-metre (*Am.* five-meter) platform
9 three-metre (*Am.* three-meter) springboard (diving board)
10 one-metre (*Am.* one-meter) springboard
11 diving pool
12 straight header
13 feet-first jump
14 tuck jump (haunch jump)
15 swimming pool attendant (pool attendant, swimming bath attendant)
16-20 swimming instruction
16 swimming instructor (swimming teacher)
17 learner-swimmer
18 float; *sim.:* water wings
19 swimming belt (cork jacket)
20 land drill
21 non-swimmers' pool
22 footbath
23 swimmers' pool
24-32 freestyle relay race
24 timekeeper (lane timekeeper)
25 placing judge
26 turning judge
27 starting block (starting place)
28 competitor touching the finishing line
29 starting dive (racing dive)
30 starter
31 swimming lane
32 rope with cork floats
33-39 swimming strokes
33 breaststroke

34 butterfly stroke
35 dolphin butterfly stroke
36 side stroke
37 crawl stroke (crawl); *sim.:* trudgen stroke (trudgen, double overarm stroke)
38 diving (underwater swimming)
39 treading water
40-45 diving (acrobatic diving, fancy diving, competitive diving, highboard diving)
40 standing take-off pike dive
41 one-half twist isander (reverse dive)
42 backward somersault (double backward somersault)
43 running take-off twist dive
44 screw dive
45 armstand dive (handstand dive)
46-50 water polo
46 goal
47 goalkeeper
48 water polo ball
49 back
50 forward

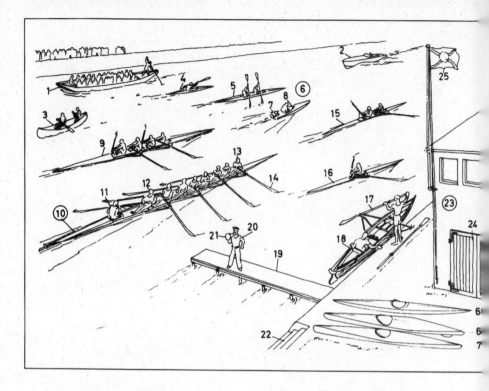

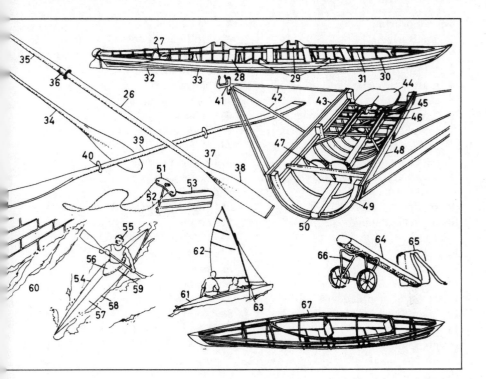

35	grip	**54**	one-man kayak
36	leather sheath	**55**	canoeist
37	shaft (neck)	**56**	spraydeck
38	blade	**57**	deck
39	double-bladed paddle (double-ended paddle)	**58**	rubber-covered canvas hull
		59	cockpit coaming (coaming)
40	drip ring	**60**	channel for rafts alongside weir
41-50	sliding seat	**61**	two-seater folding kayak, a touring kayak
41	rowlock (oarlock)		
42	outrigger	**62**	sail of folding kayak
43	saxboard	**63**	leeboard
44	sliding seat	**64**	bag for the rods
45	runner	**65**	rucksack
46	strut	**66**	boat trailer (boat carriage)
47	stretcher	**67**	frame of folding kayak
48	skin (shell, outer skin)	**68-70**	kayaks
49	frame (rib)	**68**	Eskimo kayak
50	kelson (keelson)	**69**	wild-water racing kayak
51-53	rudder (steering rudder)	**70**	touring kayak
51	yoke		
52	lines (steering lines)		
53	blade (rudder blade, rudder)		
54-66	folding boats (foldboats, canoes)		

1-9 windsurfing
1 windsurfer
2 sail
3 transparent window (window)
4 mast
5 surfboard
6 universal joint (movable bearing) for adjusting the angle of the mast and for steering
7 wishbone
8 retractable centreboard (*Am.* centerboard)
9 rudder
10-48 yacht (sailing boat, *Am.* sailboat)
10 foredeck
11 mast
12 trapeze
13 crosstrees (spreader)
14 hound
15 forestay
16 jib (Genoa jib)
17 jib downhaul
18 side stay (shroud)
19 lanyard (*also:* turnbuckle)
20 foot of the mast
21 kicking strap (vang)
22 jam cleat
23 foresheet (jib sheet)
24 centreboard (*Am.* centerboard) case
25 bitt
26 centreboard (*Am.* centerboard)
27 traveller (*Am.* traveler)
28 mainsheet
29 foresheet fairlead (jib fairlead)
30 toestraps (hiking straps)
31 tiller extension (hiking stick)
32 tiller
33 rudderhead (rudder stock)
34 rudder blade (rudder)
35 transom
36 drain plug
37 gooseneck
38 window
39 boom
40 foot

41 clew
42 luff (leading edge)
43 leech pocket (batten cleat, batten pocket)
44 batten
45 leech (trailing edge)
46 mainsail
47 headboard
48 racing flag (burgee)
49-65 yacht classes
49 Flying Dutchman
50 O-Joller
51 Finn dinghy (Finn)
52 pirate
53 12.00 m^2 sharpie
54 tempest
55 star
56 soling
57 dragon
58 5.5-metre (*Am.* 5.5-meter) class
59 6-metre (*Am.* 6-meter) R-class
60 30.00 m^2 cruising yacht (coastal cruiser)
61 30.00 m^2 dinghy cruiser
62 25.00 m^2 one-design keelboat
63 KR-class
64 catamaran
65 twin hull

1-13 points of sailing and wind directions
1 sailing downwind (running)
2 mainsail
3 jib
4 sails set goose-winged
5 centre (*Am.* center) line
6 wind direction
7 yacht stopped head to wind
8 sail, shivering
9 luffing
10 sailing close-hauled
11 sailing with wind abeam
12 sailing with free wind
13 quartering wind (quarter wind)

14-24 regatta course
14 starting and finishing buoy
15 committee boat
16 triangular course (regatta course)
17 buoy (mark) to be rounded
18 buoy to be passed
19 first leg
20 second leg
21 third leg
22 windward leg
23 downwind leg
24 reaching leg

25-28 tacking
25 tack
26 gybing (jibing)
27 going about
28 loss of distance during the gybe (jibe)

29-41 types of yacht hull
29-34 cruiser keelboat
29 stern
30 spoon bow
31 waterline
32 keel (ballast keel)
33 ballast
34 rudder
35 racing keelboat
36 lead keel
37-41 keel-centreboard (*Am.* centerboard) yawl
37 retractable rudder
38 cockpit

39 cabin superstructure (cabin)
40 straight stem
41 retractable centreboard (*Am.* centerboard)

42-49 types of yacht stern
42 yacht stern
43 square stern
44 canoe stern
45 cruiser stern
46 name plate
47 deadwood
48 transom stern
49 transom

50-57 timber planking
50-52 clinker planking (clench planking)
50 outside strake
51 frame (rib)
52 clenched nail (riveted nail)
53 carvel planking
54 ribband-carvel construction
55 ribband, a stringer
56 diagonal carvel planking
57 inner planking

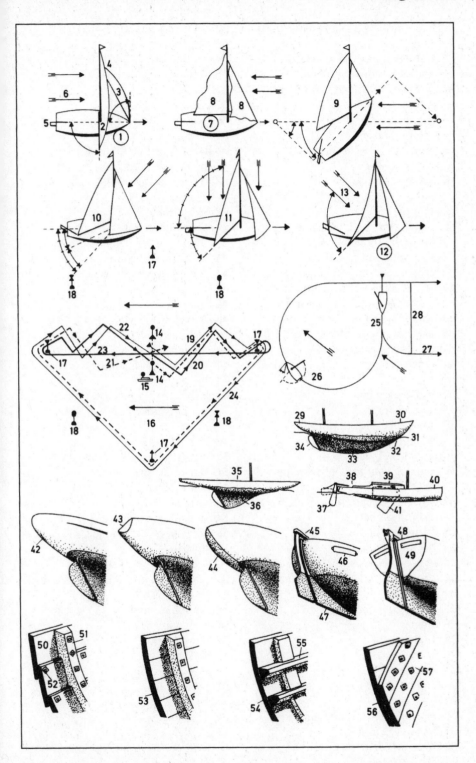

1-5 motorboats (powerboats, sportsboats)

1 inflatable sportsboat with outboard
motor (outboard inflatable)

2 Z-drive motorboat (outdrive
motorboat)

3 cabin cruiser

4 motor cruiser

5 30-metre (*Am.* 30-meter) ocean-
going cruiser

6 association flag

7 name of craft (*or:* registration
number)

8 club membership and port of reg-
istry (*Am.* home port)

9 association flag on the starboard
crosstrees

10-14 navigation lights of sportsboats
in coastal and inshore waters

10 white top light

11 green starboard sidelight

12 red port sidelight

13 green and red bow light (combined
lantern)

14 white stern light

15-18 anchors

15 stocked anchor (Admiralty
anchor), a bower anchor

16-18 lightweight anchor

16 CQR anchor (plough, *Am.* plow,
anchor)

17 stockless anchor (patent anchor)

18 Danforth anchor

19 life raft

20 life jacket

21-44 powerboat racing

21 catamaran with outboard motor

22 hydroplane

23 racing outboard motor

24 tiller

25 fuel pipe

26 transom

27 buoyancy tube

28 start and finish

29 start

30 starting and finishing line

31 buoy to be rounded

32-37 displacement boats

32-34 round-bilge boat

32 view of hull bottom

33 section of fore ship

34 section of aft ship

35-37 V-bottom boat (vee-bottom
boat)

35 view of hull bottom

36 section of fore ship

37 section of aft ship

38-44 planing boats (surface skimmers, skimmers)

38-41 stepped hydroplane (stepped
skimmer)

38 side view

39 view of hull bottom

40 section of fore ship

41 section of aft ship

42 three-point hydroplane

43 fin

44 float

45-62 water skiing

45 water skier

46 deep-water start

47 tow line (towing line)

48 handle

49-55 water-ski signalling (code of
hand signals from skier to boat
driver)

49 signal for 'faster'

50 signal for 'slower' ('slow down')

51 signal for 'speed OK'

52 signal for 'turn'

53 signal for 'stop'

54 signal for 'cut motor'

55 signal for 'return to jetty' ('back to
dock')

56-62 types of water ski

56 trick ski (figure ski), a monoski

57, 58 rubber binding

57 front foot binding

58 heel flap

59 strap support for second foot

60 slalom ski

61 skeg (fixed fin, fin)

62 jump ski

63 hovercraft (air-cushion vehicle)

64 propeller

65 rudder

66 skirt enclosing air cushion

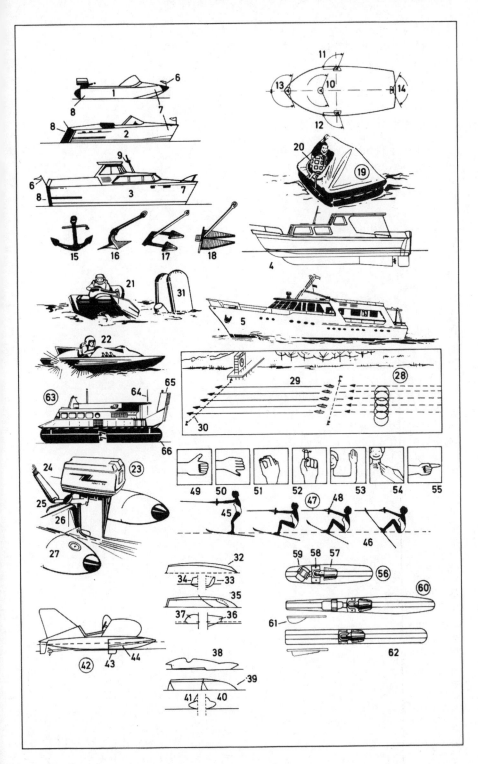

1 aeroplane (*Am.* airplane) tow
  launch (aerotowing)
2 tug (towing plane)
3 towed glider (towed sailplane)
4 tow rope
5 winched launch
6 motor winch
7 cable parachute
8 motorized glider (powered glider)
9 high-performance glider (high-performance sailplane)
10 T-tail (T-tail unit)
11 wind sock (wind cone)
12 control tower (tower)
13 glider field
14 hangar
15 runway for aeroplanes (*Am.* airplanes)
16 wave soaring
17 lee waves (waves, wave system)
18 rotor
19 lenticular clouds (lenticulars)
20 thermal soaring
21 thermal
22 cumulus cloud (heap cloud, cumulus, woolpack cloud)
23 storm-front soaring
24 storm front
25 frontal upcurrent
26 cumulonimbus cloud (cumulonimbus)
27 slope soaring
28 hill upcurrent (orographic lift)
29 multispar wing
30 main spar, a box spar
31 connector fitting
32 anchor rib
33 diagonal spar
34 leading edge
35 main rib
36 nose rib (false rib)
37 trailing edge
38 brake flap (spoiler)
39 torsional clamp
40 covering (skin)

41 aileron
42 wing tip
43 hang gliding
44 hang glider
45 hang glider pilot
46 control frame

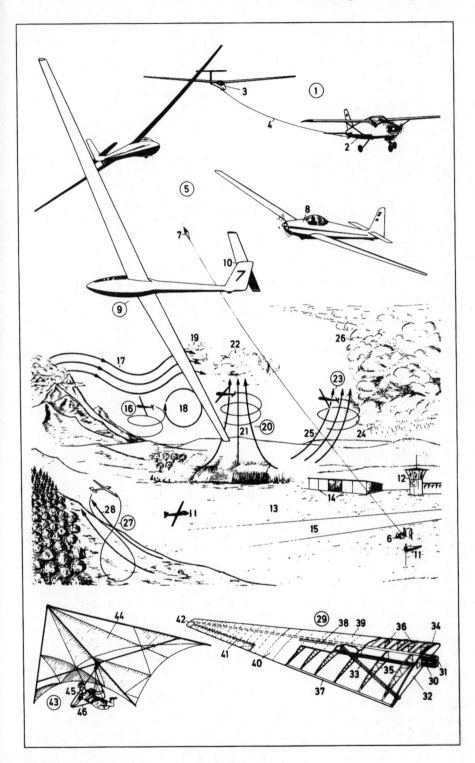

1-9 aerobatics (aerobatic manoeuvres, *Am.* maneuvers)
1 loop
2 horizontal eight
3 rolling circle
4 stall turn (hammer head)
5 tail slide (whip stall)
6 vertical flick spin
7 spin
8 horizontal slow roll
9 inverted flight (negative flight)
10 **cockpit**
11 instrument panel
12 compass
13 radio and navigation equipment
14 control column (control stick)
15 throttle lever (throttle control)
16 mixture control
17 radio equipment
18 **two-seater plane for racing and aerobatics**
19 cabin
20 antenna
21 vertical stabilizer (vertical fin, tail fin)
22 rudder
23 tailplane (horizontal stabilizer)
24 elevator
25 trim tab (trimming tab)
26 fuselage (body)
27 wing
28 aileron
29 landing flap
30 trim tab (trimming tab)
31 navigation light (position light) [red]
32 landing light
33 main undercarriage unit (main landing gear unit)
34 nose wheel
35 engine
36 propeller (airscrew)
37-62 parachuting (sport parachuting)
37 parachute
38 canopy
39 pilot chute
40 suspension lines
41 steering line
42 riser
43 harness
44 pack
45 system of slots of the sports parachute
46 turn slots
47 apex
48 skirt
49 stabilizing panel
50, 51 style jump

50 back loop
51 spiral
52-54 ground signals
52 signal for 'permission to jump' ('conditions are safe') (target cross)
53 signal for 'parachuting suspended–repeat flight'
54 signal for 'parachuting suspended–aircraft must land'
55 accuracy jump
56 target cross
57 inner circle [radius 25 m]
58 middle circle [radius 50 m]
59 outer circle [radius 100 m]
60-62 free-fall positions
60 full spread position
61 frog position
62 T position
63-84 ballooning
63 gas balloon
64 gondola (balloon basket)
65 ballast (sandbags)
66 mooring line
67 hoop
68 flight instruments (instruments)
69 trail rope
70 mouth (neck)
71 neck line
72 emergency rip panel
73 emergency ripping line
74 network (net)
75 rip panel
76 ripping line
77 valve
78 valve line
79 hot-air balloon
80 burner platform
81 mouth
82 vent
83 rip panel
84 balloon take-off
85-91 flying model aeroplanes (*Am.* airplanes)
85 radio-controlled model flight
86 remote-controlled free flight model
87 remote control radio
88 antenna (transmitting antenna)
89 control line model
90 mono-line control system
91 flying kennel, a K9-class model

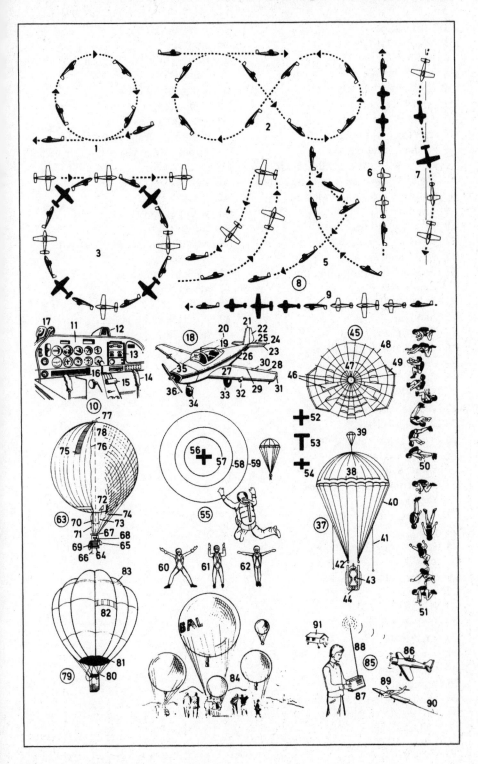

1-7 dressage
1 arena (dressage arena)
2 rail
3 school horse
4 dark coat (black coat)
5 white breeches
6 top hat
7 gait (*also:* school figure)
8-14 show jumping
8 obstacle (fence), an almost-fixed obstacle; *sim.:* gate, gate and rails, palisade, oxer, mound, wall
9 jumper
10 jumping saddle
11 girth
12 snaffle
13 red coat (hunting pink, pink; *also:* dark coat)
14 hunting cap (riding cap)
15 bandage
16-19 three-day event
16 endurance competition
17 cross-country
18 helmet (*also:* hard hat, hard hunting cap)
19 course markings
20-22 steeplechase
20 water jump, a fixed obstacle
21 jump
22 riding switch
23-40 harness racing (harness horse racing)
23 harness racing track (track)
24 sulky
25 spoke wheel (spoked wheel) with plastic wheel disc (disk)
26 driver in trotting silks
27 rein
28 trotter
29 piebald horse
30 shadow roll
31 elbow boot
32 rubber boot
33 number
34 glass-covered grandstand with totalizator windows (tote windows) inside

35 totalizator (tote)
36 number
37 odds (price, starting price, price offered)
38 winners' table
39 winner's price
40 time indicator
41-49 hunt, a drag hunt; *sim.:* fox hunt, paper chase (paper hunt, hare-and-hounds)
41 field
42 hunting pink
43 whipper-in (whip)
44 hunting horn
45 Master (Master of foxhounds, MFH)
46 pack of hounds (pack)
47 staghound
48 drag
49 scented trail (artificial scent)
50 horse racing (racing)
51 field (racehorses)
52 favourite (*Am.* favorite)
53 outsider

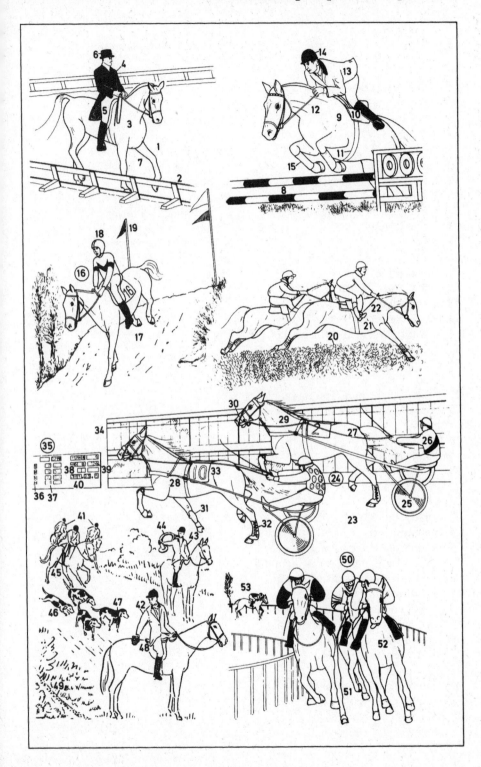

1-23 cycle racing
1 cycling track (cycle track); *here:* indoor track
2-7 six-day race
2 six-day racer, a track racer (track rider) on the track
3 crash hat
4 stewards
5 judge
6 lap scorer
7 rider's box (racer's box)
8-10 road race
8 road racer, a racing cyclist
9 racing jersey
10 water bottle
11-15 motor-paced racing (long-distance racing)
11 pacer, a motorcyclist
12 pacer's motorcycle
13 roller, a safety device
14 stayer (motor-paced track rider)
15 motor-paced cycle, a racing cycle
16 racing cycle (racing bicycle) for road racing (road race bicycle)
17 racing saddle, an unsprung saddle
18 racing handlebars (racing handlebar)
19 tubular tyre (*Am.* tire) (racing tyre)
20 chain
21 toe clip (racing toe clip)
22 strap
23 spare tubular tyre (*Am.* tire)
24-38 motorsports
24-28 motorcycle racing; *disciplines:* grasstrack racing, road racing, sand track racing, cement track racing, speedway [on ash or shale tracks], mountain racing, ice racing (ice speedway), scramble racing, trial, moto cross
24 sand track
25 racing motorcyclist (rider)
26 leather overalls (leathers)
27 racing motorcycle, a solo machine
28 number (number plate)
29 sidecar combination on the bend

30 sidecar
31 streamlined racing motorcycle [500 cc.]
32 gymkhana, a competition of skill; *here:* motorcyclist performing a jump
33 cross-country race, a test in performance
34-38 racing cars
34 Formula One racing car (a mono posto)
35 rear spoiler (aerofoil, *Am.* airfoil)
36 Formula Two racing car
37 Super-Vee racing car
38 prototype, a racing car

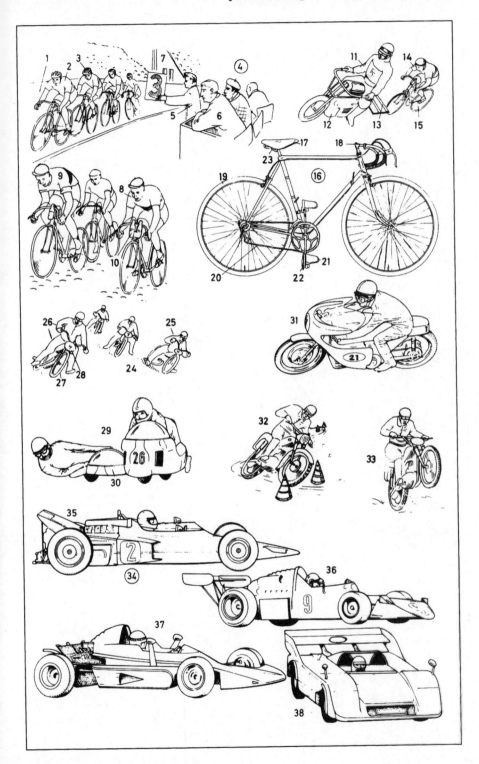

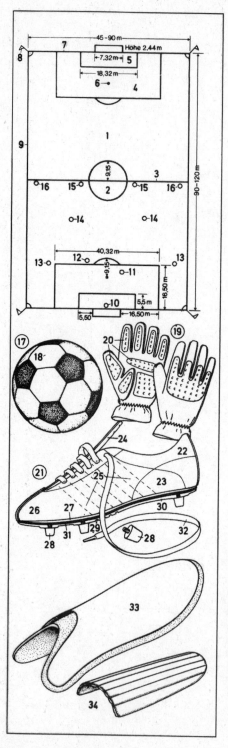

1-16 football pitch
1 field (park)
2 centre (*Am.* center) circle
3 half-way line
4 penalty area
5 goal area
6 penalty spot
7 goal line (by-line)
8 corner flag
9 touch line
10 goalkeeper
11 sweeper (libero)
12 inside defender
13 outside defender
14 midfield players
15 inside forward (striker)
16 outside forward (winger)
17 football
18 valve
19 goalkeeper's gloves
20 foam rubber padding
21 football boot
22 leather lining
23 counter
24 foam rubber tongue
25 bands
26 shaft
27 insole
28 screw-in stud
29 groove
30 nylon sole
31 inner sole
32 lace (bootlace)
33 football pad with ankle guard
34 shin guard
35 goal
36 crossbar
37 post (goalpost)
38 goal kick
39 save with the fists
40 penalty (penalty kick)
41 corner (corner kick)
42 offside
43 free kick
44 wall
45 bicycle kick (overhead bicycle kick)

46 header
47 pass (passing the ball)
48 receiving the ball (taking a pass)
49 short pass (one-two)
50 foul (infringement)
51 obstruction
52 dribble
53 throw-in
54 substitute
55 coach
56 shirt (jersey)
57 shorts
58 sock (football sock)
59 linesman
60 linesman's flag
61 sending-off
62 referee
63 red card; *also:* yellow card
64 centre (*Am.* center) flag

1 **handball** (indoor handball)
2 handball player, a field player
3 attacker, making a jump throw
4 defender
5 penalty line
6 **hockey**
7 goal
8 goalkeeper
9 pad (shin pad, knee pad)
10 kicker
11 face guard
12 glove
13 hockey stick
14 hockey ball
15 hockey player
16 striking circle
17 sideline
18 corner
19 **rugby** (rugby football)
20 scrum (scrummage)
21 rugby ball
22 **American football** (*Am.* football)
23 player (football player) carrying the ball
24 helmet
25 face guard
26 padded jersey
27 ball (pigskin)
28 **basketball**
29 basketball
30 backboard
31 backboard support
32 basket
33 basket ring
34 target rectangle
35 basketball player shooting
36 end line
37 restricted area
38 free-throw line
39 substitute
40-69 **baseball**
40-58 field (park)
40 spectator barrier
41 outfielder
42 short stop
43 second base
44 baseman

45 runner
46 first base
47 third base
48 foul line (base line)
49 pitcher's mound
50 pitcher
51 batter's position
52 batter
53 home base (home plate)
54 catcher
55 umpire
56 coach's box
57 coach
58 batting order
59, 60 baseball gloves (baseball mitts)
59 fielder's glove (fielder's mitt)
60 catcher's glove (catcher's mitt)
61 baseball
62 bat
63 batter at bat
64 catcher
65 umpire
66 runner
67 base plate
68 pitcher
69 pitcher's mound
70-76 **cricket**
70 wicket with bails
71 bowling crease
72 popping crease
73 wicket keeper of the fielding side
74 batsman
75 bat (cricket bat)
76 fielder (bowler)
77-82 **croquet**
77 winning peg
78 hoop
79 corner peg
80 croquet player
81 croquet mallet
82 croquet ball

1-42 tennis
1 tennis court
2-3 doubles sideline (sideline for doubles matches); *kinds of doubles:* men's doubles, women's doubles, mixed doubles
3-10 base line
4-5 singles sideline (sideline for singles matches); *kinds of singles:* men's singles, women's singles
6-7 service line
8-9 centre (*Am.* center) line
11 centre (*Am.* center) mark
12 service court
13 net (tennis net)
14 net strap
15 net post
16 tennis player
17 smash
18 opponent
19 umpire
20 umpire's chair
21 umpire's microphone
22 ball boy
23 net-cord judge
24 foot-fault judge
25 centre (*Am.* center) line judge
26 base line judge
27 service line judge
28 tennis ball
29 tennis racket (tennis racquet, racket, racquet)
30 racket handle (racquet handle)
31 strings (striking surface)
32 press (racket press, racquet press)
33 tightening screw
34 scoreboard
35 results of sets
36 player's name
37 number of sets
38 state of play
39 backhand stroke
40 forehand stroke
41 volley (forehand volley at normal height)
42 service
43, 44 badminton
43 badminton racket (badminton racquet)
44 shuttle (shuttlecock)
45-55 table tennis
45 table tennis racket (racquet) (table tennis bat)
46 racket (racquet) handle (bat handle)
47 blade covering
48 table tennis ball

49 table tennis players; *here:* mixed doubles
50 receiver
51 server
52 table tennis table
53 table tennis net
54 centre (*Am.* center) line
55 sideline
56-71 volleyball
56, 57 correct placing of the hands
58 volleyball
59 serving the volleyball
60 blocker
61 service area
62 server
63 front-line player
64 attack area
65 attack line
66 defence (*Am.* defense) area
67 referee
68 umpire
69 linesman
70 scoreboard
71 scorer
72-78 faustball
72 base line
73 tape
74 faustball
75 forward
76 centre (*Am.* center)
77 back
78 hammer blow
79-93 golf
79-82 course (holes)
79 teeing ground
80 rough
81 bunker (*Am.* sand trap)
82 green (putting green)
83 golfer, driving
84 follow-through
85 golf trolley
86 putting (holing out)
87 hole
88 pin (flagstick)
89 golf ball
90 tee
91 wood, a driver; *sim.:* brassie (brassy, brassey)
92 iron
93 putter

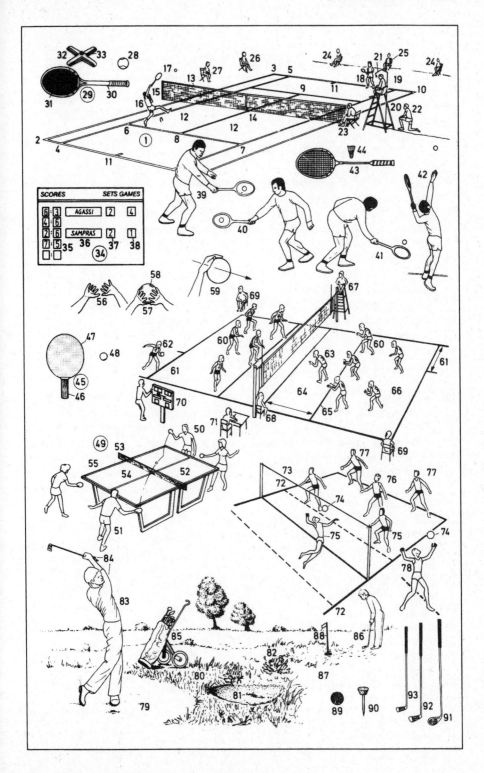

SCORES		SETS	GAMES
6:3	AGASSI	2	4
4:6			
2:6	SAMPRAS	2	1
7:5			

1-33 **fencing** (modern fencing)
1-18 foil
1 fencing master (fencing instructor)
2 piste
3 on guard line
4 centre (*Am.* center) line
5, 6 fencers (foil fencers, foilsmen, foilists) in a bout
5 attacker (attacking fencer) in lunging position (lunging)
6 defender (defending fencer), parrying
7 straight thrust, a fencing movement
8 parry of the tierce
9 line of fencing
10 the three fencing measures (short, medium, and long measure)
11 foil, a thrust weapon
12 fencing glove
13 fencing mask (foil mask)
14 neck flap (neck guard) on the fencing mask
15 metallic jacket
16 fencing jacket
17 heelless fencing shoes
18 first position for fencer's salute (initial position, on guard position)
19-24 sabre (*Am.* saber) fencing
19 sabreurs (sabre fencers, *Am.* saber fencers)
20 (light) sabre (*Am.* saber)
21 sabre (*Am.* saber) glove (sabre gauntlet)
22 sabre (*Am.* saber) mask
23 cut at head
24 parry of the fifth (quinte)
25-33 épée, with electrical scoring equipment
25 épéeist
26 electric épée; *also:* electric foil
27 épée point
28 scoring lights
29 spring-loaded wire spool
30 indicator light
31 wire

32 electronic scoring equipment
33 on guard position
34-45 **fencing weapons**
34 light sabre (*Am.* saber), a cut and thrust weapon
35 guard
36 épée, a thrust weapon
37 French foil, a thrust weapon
38 guard (coquille)
39 Italian foil
40 foil pommel
41 handle
42 cross piece (quillons)
43 guard (coquille)
44 blade
45 button
46 engagements
47 quarte (carte) engagement
48 tierce engagement (*also:* sixte engagement)
49 circling engagement
50 seconde engagement (*also:* octave engagement)
51-53 target areas
51 the whole body in épée fencing (men)
52 head and upper body down to the groin in sabre (*Am.* saber) fencing (men)
53 trunk from the neck to the groin in foil fencing (ladies and men)

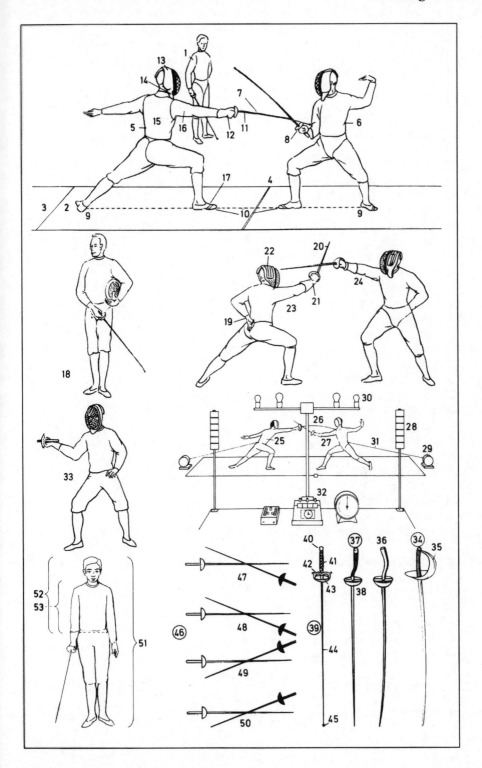

295 Free Exercise

1 basic position (starting position)
2 running posture
3 side straddle
4 straddle (forward straddle)
5 toe stand
6 crouch
7 upright kneeling position
8 kneeling position, seat on heels
9 squat
10 L seat (long sitting)
11 tailor seat (sitting tailor-style)
12 hurdle (hurdle position)
13 V-seat
14 side split
15 forward split
16 L-support
17 V-support
18 straddle seat
19 bridge
20 kneeling front support
21 front support
22 back support
23 crouch with front support
24 arched front support
25 side support
26 forearm stand (forearm balance)
27 handstand
28 headstand
29 shoulder stand (shoulder balance)
30 forward horizontal stand
   (arabesque)
31 rearward horizontal stand
32 trunk-bending sideways
33 trunk-bending forwards
34 arch
35 astride jump (butterfly)
36 tuck jump
37 astride jump
38 pike
39 scissor jump
40 stag jump (stag leap)
41 running step
42 lunge
43 forward pace
44 lying on back
45 prone position

46 lying on side
47 holding arms downwards
48 holding (extending) arms sideways
49 holding arms raised upward
50 holding (extending) arms forward
51 arms held (extended) backward
52 hands clasped behind the head

1-11 **gymnastics apparatus** in men's Olympic gymnastics
1 long horse (horse, vaulting horse)
2 parallel bars
3 bar
4 rings (stationary rings)
5 pommel horse (side horse)
6 pommel
7 horizontal bar (high bar)
8 bar
9 upright
10 stay wires
11 floor (12 m × 12 m floor area)
12-21 **auxiliary apparatus and apparatus for school and club gymnastics**
12 springboard (Reuther board)
13 landing mat
14 bench
15 box
16 small box
17 buck
18 mattress
19 climbing rope (rope)
20 wall bars
21 window ladder
22-39 **positions in relation to the apparatus**
22 side, facing
23 side, facing away
24 end, facing
25 end, facing away
26 outside, facing
27 inside, facing
28 front support
29 back support
30 straddle position
31 seated position outside
32 riding seat outside
33 hang
34 reverse hang
35 hang with elbows bent
36 piked reverse hang
37 straight inverted hang
38 straight hang
39 bent hang
40-46 **grasps** (kinds of grasp)
40 overgrasp on the horizontal bar

41 undergrasp on the horizontal bar
42 combined grasp on the horizontal bar
43 cross grasp on the horizontal bar
44 rotated grasp on the horizontal bar
45 outside grip on the parallel bars
46 rotated grasp on the parallel bars
47 leather handstrap
48-60 **apparatus exercises**
48 long-fly on the horse
49 rise to straddle on the parallel bars
50 crucifix on the rings
51 scissors (scissors movement) on the pommel horse
52 legs raising into a handstand on the floor
53 squat vault on the horse
54 double leg circle on the pommel horse
55 hip circle backwards on the rings
56 lever hang on the rings
57 rearward swing on the parallel bars
58 forward kip into upper arm hang on the parallel bars
59 backward underswing on the horizontal bar
60 backward grand circle on the horizontal bar
61-63 **gymnastics kit**
61 singlet (vest, *Am.* undershirt)
62 gym trousers
63 gym shoes
64 wristband

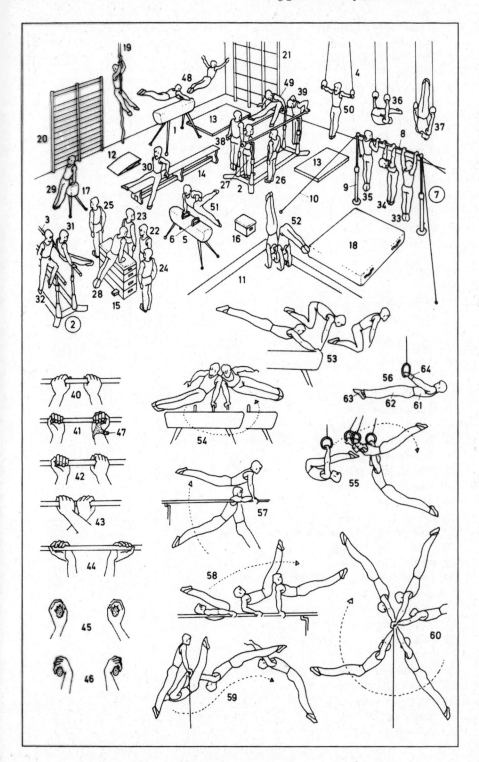

1-6 gymnastics apparatus in women's Olympic gymnastics
1 horse (vaulting horse)
2 beam
3 asymmetric bars (uneven bars)
4 bar
5 stay wires
6 floor (12 m × 12 m floor area)
7-14 auxiliary apparatus and apparatus for school and club gymnastics
7 landing mat
8 springboard (Reuther board)
9 small box
10 trampoline
11 sheet (web)
12 frame
13 rubber springs
14 springboard trampoline
15-32 apparatus exercises
15 backward somersault
16 spotting position (standing-in position)
17 vertical backward somersault on the trampoline
18 forward somersault on the springboard trampoline
19 forward roll on the floor
20 long-fly to forward roll on the floor
21 cartwheel on the beam
22 handspring on the horse
23 backward walkover
24 back flip (flik-flak) on the floor
25 free walkover forward on the floor
26 forward walkover on the floor
27 headspring on the floor
28 upstart on the asymmetric bars
29 free backward circle on the asymmetric bars
30 face vault over the horse
31 flank vault over the horse
32 back vault (rear vault) over the horse
33-50 gymnastics with hand apparatus
33 hand-to-hand throw
34 gymnastic ball
35 high toss
36 bounce
37 hand circling with two clubs
38 gymnastic club
39 swing
40 tuck jump
41 bar
42 skip
43 rope (skipping rope)
44 criss-cross skip
45 skip through the hoop
46 gymnastic hoop
47 hand circle
48 serpent
49 gymnastic ribbon
50 spiral
51, 52 gymnastics kit
51 leotard
52 gym shoes

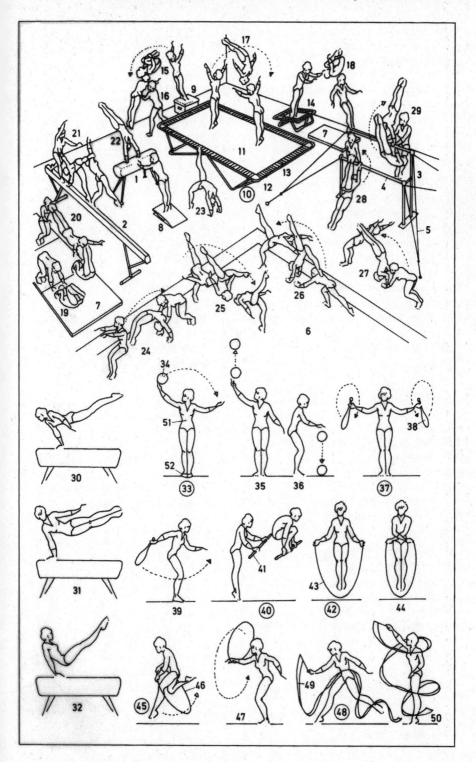

1-8 running
1-6 start
1 starting block
2 adjustable block (pedal)
3 start
4 crouch start
5 runner, a sprinter; *also:* middle-distance runner, long-distance runner
6 running track (track), a cinder track or synthetic track
7, 8 hurdles (hurdle racing); *sim.:* steeplechase
7 clearing the hurdle
8 hurdle
9-41 jumping and vaulting
9-27 high jump
9 Fosbury flop (Fosbury, flop)
10 high jumper
11 body rotation (rotation on the body's longitudinal and latitudinal axes)
12 shoulder landing
13 upright
14 bar (crossbar)
15 Eastern roll
16 Western roll
17 roll
18 rotation
19 landing
20 height scale
21 Eastern cut-off
22 scissors (scissor jump)
23 straddle (straddle jump)
24 turn
25 vertical free leg
26 take-off
27 free leg
28-36 pole vault
28 pole (vaulting pole)
29 pole vaulter (vaulter) in the pull-up phase
30 swing
31 crossing the bar
32 high jump apparatus (high jump equipment)
33 upright
34 bar (crossbar)

35 box
36 landing area (landing pad)
37-41 long jump
37 take-off
38 take-off board
39 landing area
40 hitch-kick
41 hang
42-47 hammer throw
42 hammer
43 hammer head
44 handle
45 grip
46 holding the grip
47 glove
48 shot put
49 shot (weight)
50 O'Brien technique
51-53 javelin throw
51 grip with thumb and index finger
52 grip with thumb and middle finger
53 horseshoe grip
54 binding

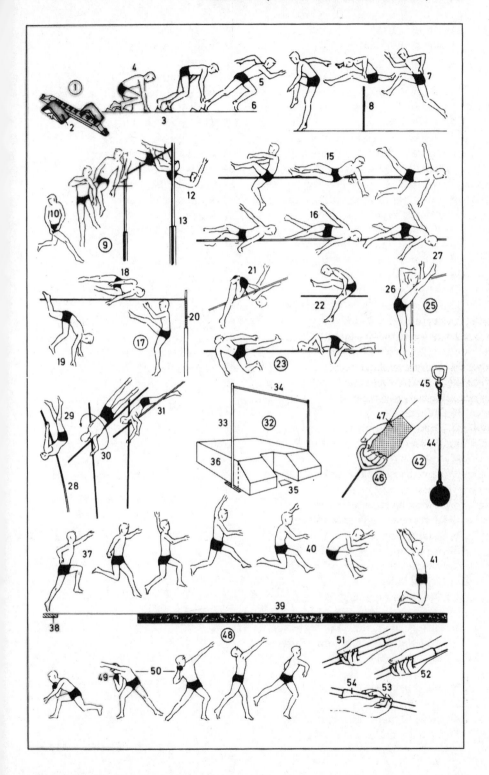

1-5 weightlifting
1 squat-style snatch
2 weightlifter
3 disc (disk) barbell
4 jerk with split
5 maintained lift
6-12 wrestling
6-9 Greco-Roman wrestling
6 standing wrestling (wrestling in standing position)
7 wrestler
8 on-the-ground wrestling (*here:* the referee's position)
9 bridge
10-12 freestyle wrestling
10 bar arm (arm bar) with grapevine
11 double leg lock
12 wrestling mat (mat)
13-17 judo (*sim.:* ju-jitsu, jiu-jitsu, ju-jutsu)
13 drawing the opponent off balance to the right and forward
14 judoka (judoist)
15 coloured (*Am.* colored) belt, as a symbol of Dan grade
16 referee
17 judo throw
18, 19 karate
18 karateka
19 side thrust kick, a kicking technique
20-50 boxing (boxing match)
20-24 training apparatus (training equipment)
20 spring-supported punch ball
21 punch bag (*Am.* punching bag)
22 speed ball
23 suspended punch ball
24 punch ball
25 boxer, an amateur boxer (boxes in a singlet, vest, *Am.* undershirt) or a professional boxer (boxes without singlet)
26 boxing glove
27 sparring partner
28 straight punch (straight blow)
29 ducking and sidestepping
30 headguard
31 infighting; *here:* clinch
32 uppercut
33 hook to the head; *here:* right hook
34 punch below the belt, a foul punch (illegal punch, foul)
35-50 boxing match (boxing contest), a title fight (title bout)
35 boxing ring (ring)
36 ropes
37 stay wire (stay rope)
38 neutral corner
39 winner
40 loser by a knockout
41 referee
42 counting out
43 judge
44 second
45 manager
46 gong
47 timekeeper
48 record keeper
49 press photographer
50 sports reporter (reporter)

1-57 mountaineering (mountain climbing, Alpinism)
1 hut (Alpine Club hut, mountain hut, base)
2-13 climbing (rock climbing) [rock climbing technique]
2 rock face (rock wall)
3 fissure (vertical, horizontal, or diagonal fissure)
4 ledge (rock ledge, grass ledge, scree ledge, snow ledge, ice ledge)
5 mountaineer (climber, mountain climber, Alpinist)
6 anorak (high-altitude anorak, snowshirt, padded jacket)
7 breeches (climbing breeches)
8 chimney
9 belay (spike, rock spike)
10 belay
11 rope sling (sling)
12 rope
13 spur
14-21 snow and ice climbing [snow and ice climbing technique]
14 ice slope (firn slope)
15 snow and ice climber
16 ice axe (*Am.* ax)
17 step (ice step)
18 snow goggles
19 hood (anorak hood)
20 cornice (snow cornice)
21 ridge (ice ridge)
22-27 rope (roped party)
22 glacier
23 crevasse
24 snow bridge
25 leader
26 second man (belayer)
27 third man (non-belayer)
28-30 roping down (abseiling, rapelling)
28 abseil sling
29 sling seat
30 Dülfer seat

31-57 mountaineering equipment (climbing equipment, snow and ice climbing equipment)
31 ice axe (*Am.* ax)
32 wrist sling
33 pick
34 adze (*Am.* adz)
35 karabiner hole
36 short-shafted ice axe (*Am.* ax)
37 hammer axe (*Am.* ax)
38 general-purpose piton
39 abseil piton (ringed piton)
40 ice piton (semi-tubular screw ice piton, corkscrew piton)
41 drive-in ice piton
42 mountaineering boot
43 corrugated sole
44 climbing boot
45 roughened stiff rubber upper
46 karabiner
47 screwgate
48 crampons (lightweight crampons, twelve-point crampons, ten-point crampons)
49 front points
50 point guards
51 crampon strap
52 crampon cable fastener
53 safety helmet (protective helmet)
54 helmet lamp
55 snow gaiters
56 climbing harness
57 sit harness

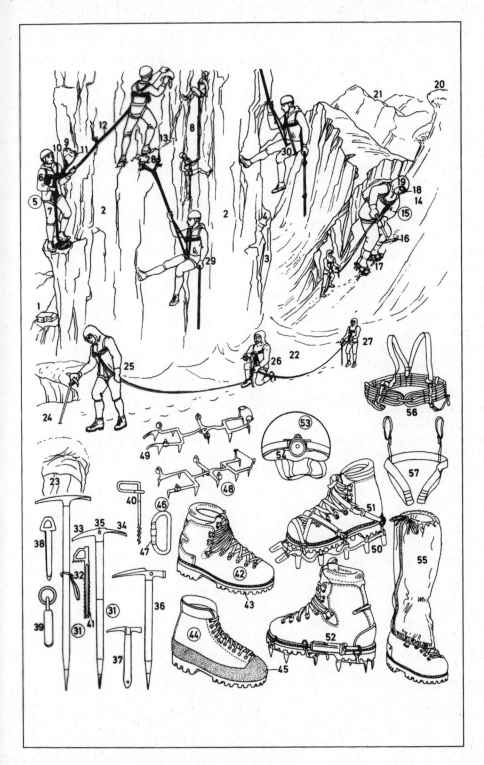

1-72 skiing
1 compact ski
2 safety binding (release binding)
3 strap
4 steel edge
5 ski stick (ski pole)
6 grip
7 loop
8 basket
9 ladies' one-piece ski suit
10 skiing cap (ski cap)
11 skiing goggles
12 cemented sole skiing boot
13 crash helmet
14-20 cross-country equipment
14 cross-country ski
15 cross-country rat trap binding
16 cross-country boot
17 cross-country gear
18 peaked cap
19 sunglasses
20 cross-country poles made of bamboo
21-24 ski-waxing equipment
21 ski wax
22 waxing iron (blowlamp, blowtorch)
23 waxing cork
24 wax scraper
25 downhill racing pole
26 herringbone, for climbing a slope
27 sidestep, for climbing a slope
28 ski bag
29 slalom
30 gate pole
31 racing suit
32 downhill racing
33 'egg' position, the ideal downhill racing position
34 downhill ski
35 ski jumping
36 lean forward
37 number
38 ski jumping ski
39 grooves (3 to 5 grooves)
40 cable binding
41 ski jumping boots
42 cross-country
43 cross-country stretch-suit

44 course
45 course-marking flag
46 layers of a modern ski
47 special core
48 laminates
49 stabilizing layer (stabilizer)
50 steel edge
51 aluminium (*Am.* aluminum) upper edge
52 synthetic bottom (artificial bottom)
53 safety jet
54-56 parts of the binding
54 automatic heel unit
55 toe unit
56 ski stop
57-63 ski lift
57 double chair lift
58 safety bar with footrest
59 ski lift
60 track
61 hook
62 automatic cable pulley
63 haulage cable
64 slalom
65 open gate
66 closed vertical gate
67 open vertical gate
68 transversal chicane
69 hairpin
70 elbow
71 corridor
72 Allais chicane

1-26 ice skating
1 ice skater, a solo skater
2 tracing leg
3 free leg
4 pair skaters
5 death spiral
6 pivot
7 stag jump (stag leap)
8 jump-sit-spin
9 upright spin
10 holding the foot
11-19 compulsory figures
11 curve eight
12 change
13 three
14 double-three
15 loop
16 change loop
17 bracket
18 counter
19 rocker
20-25 ice skates
20 speed skating set (speed skate)
21 edge
22 hollow grinding (hollow ridge, concave ridge)
23 ice hockey set (ice hockey skate)
24 ice skating boot
25 skate guard
26 speed skater
27, 28 skate sailing
27 skate sailor
28 hand sail
29-37 ice hockey
29 ice hockey player
30 ice hockey stick
31 stick handle
32 stick blade
33 shin pad
34 headgear (protective helmet)
35 puck, a vulcanized rubber disc (disk)
36 goalkeeper
37 goal
38-40 ice-stick shooting (Bavarian curling)

38 ice-stick shooter (Bavarian curler)
39 ice stick
40 block
41-43 curling
41 curler
42 curling stone (granite)
43 curling brush (curling broom, besom)
44-46 ice yachting (iceboating, ice sailing)
44 ice yacht (iceboat)
45 steering runner
46 outrigged runner

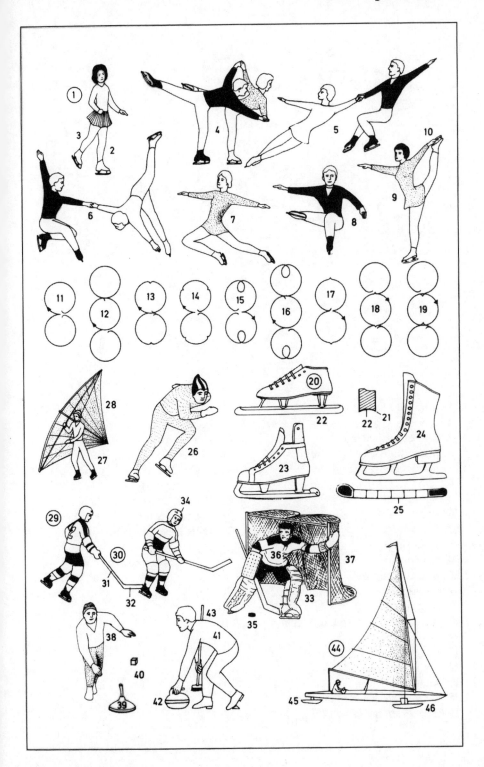

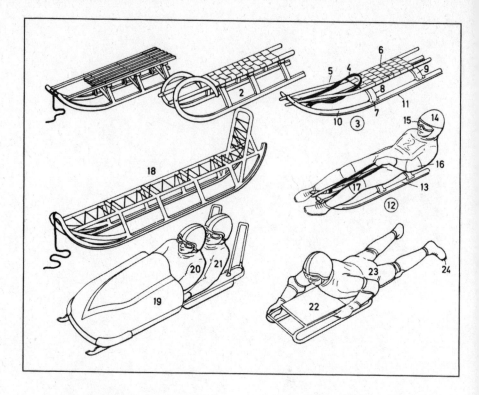

1 toboggan (sledge, *Am.* sled)
2 toboggan (sledge, *Am.* sled) with seat of plaid straps
3 junior luge toboggan (junior luge, junior toboggan)
4 rein
5 bar (strut)
6 seat
7 bracket
8 front prop
9 rear prop
10 movable runner
11 metal face
12 luge tobogganer
13 luge toboggan (luge, toboggan)
14 crash helmet
15 goggles
16 elbow pad
17 knee pad
18 Nansen sledge, a polar sledge
19-21 bobsleigh (bobsledding)

19 bobsleigh (bobsled), a two-man bobsleigh (a boblet)
20 steersman
21 brakeman
22-24 skeleton tobogganing (Cresta tobogganing)
22 skeleton (skeleton toboggan)
23 skeleton rider
24 rake, for braking and steering

1 avalanche (snow avalanche, *Am.* snowslide); *kinds:* wind avalanche, ground avalanche
2 avalanche wall, a deflecting wall (diverting wall); *sim.:* avalanche wedge
3 avalanche gallery
4 snowfall
5 snowdrift
6 snow fence
7 avalanche forest [planted as protection against avalanches]
8 street-cleaning lorry (street cleaner)
9 snow plough (*Am.* snowplow) attachment
10 snow chain (skid chain, tyre chain, *Am.* tire chain)
11 radiator bonnet (*Am.* radiator hood)
12 radiator shutter and shutter opening (louvre shutter)
13 snowman
14 snowball fight

15 snowball
16 ski bob
17 slide
18 boy, sliding
19 icy surface (icy ground)
20 covering of snow (on the roof)
21 icicle
22 man clearing snow
23 snow push (snow shovel)
24 heap of snow
25 horse-drawn sleigh (horse sleigh)
26 sleigh bells (bells, set of bells)
27 foot muff (*Am.* foot bag)
28 earmuff
29 handsledge (tread sledge); *sim.:* push sledge
30 slush

1-13 skittles
1-11 skittle frame
1 front pin (front)
2 left front second pin (left front second)
3 running three [left]
4 right front second pin (right front second)
5 running three [right]
6 left corner pin (left corner), a corner (copper)
7 landlord
8 right corner pin (right corner), a corner (copper)
9 back left second pin (back left second)
10 back right second pin (back right second)
11 back pin (back)
12 pin
13 landlord
14-20 tenpin bowling
14 frame
15 bowling ball (ball with finger holes)
16 finger hole
17-20 deliveries
17 straight ball
18 hook ball (hook)
19 curve
20 back-up ball (back-up)
21 **boules;** *sim.:* Italian game of boccie, green bowls (bowls)
22 boules player
23 jack (target jack)
24 grooved boule
25 group of players
26 **rifle shooting**
27-29 shooting positions
27 standing position
28 kneeling position
29 prone position
30-33 targets
30 target for 50 m events (50 m target)
31 circle
32 target for 100 m events (100 m target)
33 bobbing target (turning target, running-boar target)
34-39 ammunition
34 air rifle cartridge
35 rimfire cartridge for zimmerstutzen (indoor target rifle), a smallbore German single-shot rifle
36 case head
37 caseless round
38 .22 long rifle cartridge
39 .222 Remington cartridge
40-49 sporting rifles
40 air rifle
41 optical sight

42 front sight (foresight)
43 smallbore standard rifle
44 international smallbore free rifle
45 palm rest for standing position
46 butt plate with hook
47 butt with thumb hole
48 smallbore rifle for bobbing target (turning target)
49 telescopic sight (riflescope, telescope sight)
50 optical ring sight
51 optical ring and bead sight
52-66 archery (target archery)
52 shot
53 archer
54 competition bow
55 riser
56 point-of-aim mark
57 grip (handle)
58 stabilizer
59 bow string (string)
60 arrow
61 pile (point) of the arrow
62 fletching
63 nock
64 shaft
65 cresting
66 target
67 Basque game of **pelota** *(jai alai)*
68 pelota player
69 wicker basket (cesta)
70-78 skeet (skeet shooting), a kind of clay pigeon shooting
70 skeet over-and-under shotgun
71 muzzle with skeet choke
72 ready position on call
73 firing position
74 shooting range
75 high house
76 low house
77 target's path
78 shooting station (shooting box)
79 **aero wheel**
80 handle
81 footrest
82 **go-karting** (karting)
83 go-kart (kart)
84 number plate (number)
85 pedals
86 pneumatic tyre (*Am.* tire)
87 petrol tank (*Am.* gasoline tank)
88 frame
89 steering wheel
90 bucket seat
91 protective bulkhead
92 two-stroke engine
93 silencer (*Am.* muffler)

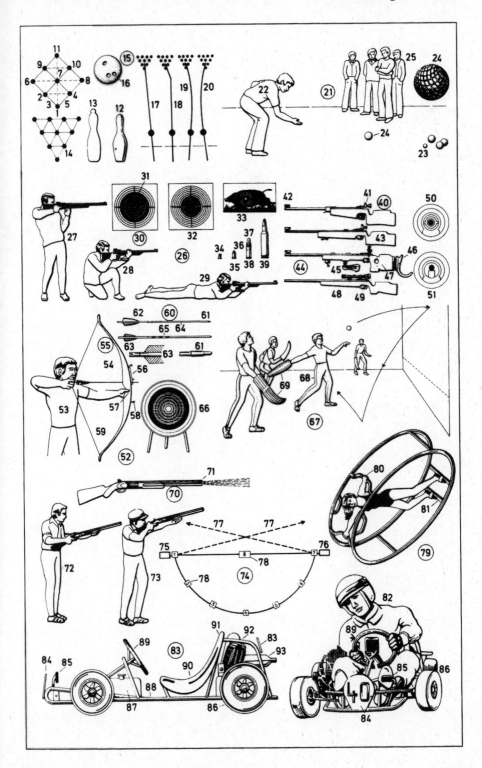

1-48 masked ball (masquerade, fancy-dress ball)
1 ballroom
2 dance band
3 pop musician
4 paper lantern
5 festoon (string of decorations)
6-48 disguise (fancy dress) at the masquerade
6 witch
7 mask
8 fur trapper (trapper)
9 Apache girl
10 net stocking
11 first prize in the tombola (raffle), a hamper
12 pierette
13 half mask (domino)
14 devil
15 domino
16 hula-hula girl (Hawaii girl)
17 garland
18 grass skirt (hula skirt)
19 pierrot
20 ruff
21 midinette
22 Biedermeier dress
23 poke bonnet
24 décolletage with beauty spot
25 bayadère (Hindu dancing girl)
26 grandee
27 Columbine
28 maharaja (maharajah)
29 mandarin, a Chinese dignitary
30 exotic girl (exotic)
31 cowboy; *sim.:* gaucho (vaquero)
32 vamp, in fancy dress
33 dandy (fop, beau)
34 rosette
35 harlequin
36 gipsy (gypsy) girl
37 cocotte (demi-monde, demi-mondaine, demi-rep)
38 owl-glass, a fool (jester, buffoon)
39 foolscap (jester's cap and bells)
40 rattle

41 odalisque, Eastern female slave in Sultan's seraglio
42 chalwar (pantaloons)
43 pirate (buccaneer)
44 tattoo
45 paper hat
46 false nose
47 clapper (rattle)
48 slapstick
49-54 fireworks
49 percussion cap
50 cracker
51 banger
52 jumping jack
53 cannon cracker (maroon, maroon)
54 rocket
55 paper ball
56 jack-in-the-box
57-70 carnival procession
57 carnival float (carnival truck)
58 King Carnival

59 bauble (fool's sceptre, *Am.* scepter)
60 fool's badge
61 Queen Carnival
62 confetti
63 giant
64 beauty queen
65 fairy-tale figure
66 paper streamer
67 majorette
68 king's guard
69 buffoon, a clown
70 lansquenet's drum

1-63 travelling (*Am.* traveling) circus
1 circus tent (big top), a four-pole tent
2 tent pole
3 spotlight
4 lighting technician
5 trapeze platform
6 trapeze
7 trapeze artist
8 rope ladder
9 bandstand
10 circus band
11 ring entrance (arena entrance)
12 wings
13 tent prop (prop)
14 safety net
15 seats for the spectators
16 circus box
17 circus manager
18 agent
19 entrance and exit
20 steps
21 ring (arena)
22 ring fence
23 musical clown (clown)
24 clown
25 comic turn (clown act), a circus act
26 circus riders (bareback riders)
27 ring attendant, a circus attendant
28 pyramid
29 support
30, 31 performance by liberty horses
30 circus horse, performing the levade (pesade)
31 ringmaster
32 vaulter

33 emergency exit
34 caravan (circus caravan, *Am.* trailer)
35 springboard acrobat (springboard artist)
36 springboard
37 knife thrower
38 circus marksman
39 assistant
40 tightrope dancer
41 tightrope
42 balancing pole
43 throwing act
44 balancing act
45 support
46 pole (bamboo pole)
47 acrobat
48 equilibrist (balancer)
49 wild animal cage, a round cage
50 bars of the cage
51 passage (barred passage, passage for the wild animals)
52 tamer (wild animal tamer)
53 whip
54 fork
55 pedestal
56 wild animal (tiger, lion)
57 stand
58 hoop (jumping hoop)
59 seesaw
60 ball
61 camp
62 cage caravan
63 menagerie

1-69 fair (annual fair)
1 fairground
2 children's merry-go-round (whirligig), a roundabout (*Am.* carousel)
3 refreshment stall (drinks stall)
4 chairoplane
5 up-and-down roundabout
6 show booth (booth)
7 box (box office)
8 barker
9 medium
10 showman
11 try-your-strength machine
12 hawker
13 balloon
14 paper serpent
15 windmill
16 pickpocket (thief)
17 vendor
18 nougat
19 ghost train
20 monster

21 dragon
22 monster
23 beer marquee
24 sideshow
25-28 travelling (*Am.* traveling) artistes (travelling show people)
25 fire eater
26 sword swallower
27 strong man
28 escapologist
29 spectators
30 ice-cream vendor (ice-cream man)
31 ice-cream cornet, with ice cream
32 sausage stand
33 grill (*Am.* broiler)
34 bratwurst (grilled sausage, *Am.* broiled sausage)
35 sausage tongs
36 fortune teller
37 big wheel (Ferris wheel)
38 orchestrion (automatic organ), an automatic musical instrument
39 scenic railway (switchback)

40 toboggan slide (chute)	**62** dodgems (bumper cars)
41 swing boats	**63** dodgem (bumper car)
42 swing boat, turning full circle	**64-66** pottery stand
43 full circle	**64** barker
44 lottery booth (tombola booth)	**65** market woman
45 wheel of fortune	**66** pottery
46 devil's wheel (typhoon wheel)	**67** visitors to the fair
47 throwing ring (quoit)	**68** waxworks
48 prizes	**69** wax figure
49 sandwich man on stilts	
50 sandwich board (placard)	
51 cigarette seller, an itinerant trader (a hawker)	
52 tray	
53 fruit stall	
54 wall-of-death rider	
55 hall of mirrors	
56 concave mirror	
57 convex mirror	
58 shooting gallery	
59 giant swing boat	
60 junk stalls (second-hand stalls)	
61 first aid tent (first aid post)	

1 treadle sewing machine
2 flower vase
3 wall mirror
4 cylindrical stove
5 stovepipe
6 stovepipe elbow
7 stove door
8 stove screen
9 coal scuttle
10 firewood basket
11 doll
12 teddy bear
13 barrel organ
14 orchestrion
15 metal disc (disk)
16 radio (radio set, *joc.:* 'steam radio'),
   a superheterodyne (superhet)
17 baffle board
18 'magic eye', a tuning indicator valve
19 loudspeaker aperture
20 station selector buttons (station
   preset buttons)
21 tuning knob
22 frequency bands

23 crystal detector (crystal set)
24 headphones (headset)
25 folding camera
26 bellows
27 hinged cover
28 spring extension
29 salesman
30 box camera
31 gramophone
32 record (gramophone record)
33 needle head with gramophone needle
34 horn
35 gramophone box
36 record rack
37 portable tape recorder
38 flashgun
39 flash bulb
40, 41 electronic flash (electronic flashgun)
40 flash head
41 accumulator
42 slide projector
43 slide holder
44 lamphouse

45 candlestick
46 scallop shell
47 cutlery
48 souvenir plate
49 drying rack for photographic plates
50 photographic plate
51 delayed-action release
52 tin soldiers (*sim.:* lead soldiers)
53 beer mug (stein)
54 bugle
55 second-hand books
56 grandfather clock
57 clock case
58 pendulum
59 time weight
60 striking weight
61 rocking chair
62 sailor suit
63 sailor's hat
64 washing set
65 washing basin
66 water jug
67 washstand
68 dolly
69 washtub

70 washboard
71 humming top
72 slate
73 pencil box
74 adding machine
75 paper roll
76 number keys
77 abacus
78 inkwell, with lid
79 typewriter
80 [hand-operated] calculating machine (calculator)
81 operating handle
82 result register (product register)
83 rotary counting mechanism (rotary counter)
84 kitchen scales
85 waist slip (underskirt)
86 wooden handcart
87 wall clock
88 bed warmer
89 milk churn

1-13 film studios (studio complex, *Am.* movie studios)
1 lot (studio lot)
2 processing laboratories (film laboratories, motion picture laboratories)
3 cutting rooms
4 administration building (office building, offices)
5 film (motion picture) storage vault (film library, motion picture library)
6 workshop
7 film set (*Am.* movie set)
8 power house
9 technical and research laboratories
10 groups of stages
11 concrete tank for marine sequences
12 cyclorama
13 hill
14-60 shooting (filming)
14 music recording studio (music recording theatre, *Am.* theater)
15 'acoustic' wall lining

16 screen (projection screen)
17 film orchestra
18 exterior shooting (outdoor shooting, exterior filming, outdoor filming)
19 camera with crystal-controlled drive
20 cameraman
21 assistant director
22 boom operator (boom swinger)
23 recording engineer (sound recordist)
24 portable sound recorder with crystal-controlled drive
25 microphone boom
26-60 shooting (filming) in the studio (on the sound stage, on the stage, in the filming hall)
26 production manager
27 leading lady (film actress, film star, star)
28 leading man (film actor, film star, star)
29 film extra (extra)
30 arrangement of microphones for stereo and sound effects

31 studio microphone	**48** soundproof housing (soundproof cover, blimp)
32 microphone cable	
33 side flats and background	**49** camera crane (dolly)
34 clapper boy	**50** hydraulic stand
35 clapper board (clapper) with slates (boards) for the film title, shot number (scene number), and take number	**51** mask (screen) for protection from spill light (gobo)
	52 tripod spotlight (fill-in light, filler light, fill light, filler)
36 make-up artist (hairstylist)	**53** spotlight catwalk
37 lighting electrician (studio electrician, lighting man, *Am.* gaffer)	**54** recording room
	55 recording engineer (sound recordist)
38 diffusing screen	
39 continuity girl (script girl)	**56** mixing console (mixing desk)
40 film director (director)	**57** sound assistant (assistant sound engineer)
41 cameraman (first cameraman)	
42 camera operator, an assistant cameraman (camera assistant)	**58** magnetic sound recording equipment (magnetic sound recorder)
43 set designer (art director)	**59** amplifier and special effects equipment, e.g. for echo and sound effects
44 director of photography	
45 filmscript (script, shooting script, *Am.* movie script)	**60** sound recording camera (optical sound recorder)
46 assistant director	
47 soundproof film camera (soundproof motion picture camera), a wide screen camera (cinemascope camera)	

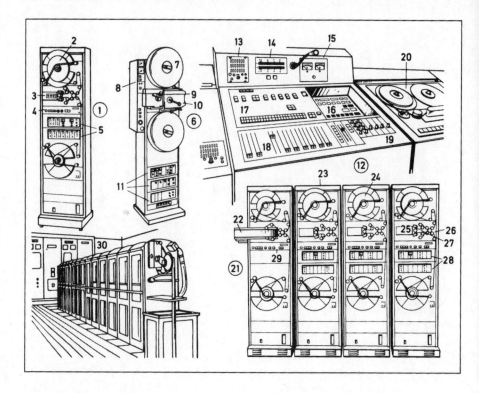

31 echo chamber
32 echo chamber loudspeaker
33 echo chamber microphone
34-36 sound mixing (sound dubbing, mixing of several sound tracks)
34 mixing room (dubbing room)
35 mixing console (mixing desk) for mono or stereo sound
36 dubbing mixers (recording engineers, sound recordists) dubbing (mixing)
37-41 synchronization (syncing, dubbing, post-synchronization, post-syncing)
37 dubbing studio (dubbing theatre, *Am.* theater)
38 dubbing director
39 dubbing speaker (dubbing actress)
40 boom microphone
41 microphone cable
42-46 cutting (editing)

42 cutting table (editing table, cutting bench)
43 film editor (cutter)
44 film turntables for picture and sound tracks
45 projection of the picture
46 loudspeaker

1-23 **film projection** (motion picture projection)
1 cinema (picture house, *Am.* movie theater, movie house)
2 cinema box office (*Am.* movie theater box office)
3 cinema ticket (*Am.* movie theater ticket)
4 usherette
5 cinemagoers (filmgoers, cinema audience, *Am.* moviegoers, movie audience)
6 safety lighting (emergency lighting)
7 emergency exit
8 stage
9 rows of seats (rows)
10 stage curtain (screen curtain)
11 screen (projection screen)
12 projection room (projection booth)
13 lefthand projector
14 righthand projector
15 projection room window with projection window and observation port

16 reel drum (spool box)
17 house light dimmers (auditorium lighting control)
18 rectifier, a selenium or mercury vapour rectifier for the projection lamps
19 amplifier
20 projectionist
21 rewind bench for rewinding the film
22 film cement (splicing cement)
23 slide projector for advertisements
24-52 **film projectors**
24 sound projector (film projector, cinema projector, theatre projector, *Am.* movie projector)
25-38 projector mechanism
25 fireproof reel drums (spool boxes) with circulating oil cooling system
26 feed sprocket (supply sprocket)
27 take-up sprocket
28 magnetic head cluster
29 guide roller (guiding roller) with framing control

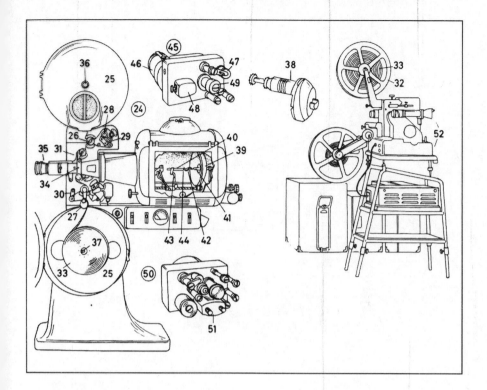

30 loop former for smoothing out the intermittent movement; *also:* film break detector
31 film path
32 film reel (film spool)
33 reel of film
34 film gate (picture gate, projector gate) with cooling fan
35 projection lens (projector lens)
36 feed spindle
37 take-up spindle with friction drive
38 maltese cross mechanism (maltese cross movement, Geneva movement)
39-44 lamphouse
39 mirror arc lamp, with aspherical (non-spherical) concave mirror and blowout magnet for stabilizing the arc (*also:* high-pressure xenon arc lamp)
40 positive carbon (positive carbon rod)

41 negative carbon (negative carbon rod)
42 arc
43 carbon rod holder
44 crater (carbon crater)
45 optical sound unit [also designed for multi-channel optical stereophonic sound and for push-pull sound tracks]
46 sound optics
47 sound head
48 exciter lamp in housing
49 photocell in hollow drum
50 attachable four-track magnetic sound unit (penthouse head, magnetic sound head)
51 four-track magnetic head
52 narrow-gauge (*Am.* narrow-gage) cinema projector for mobile cinema

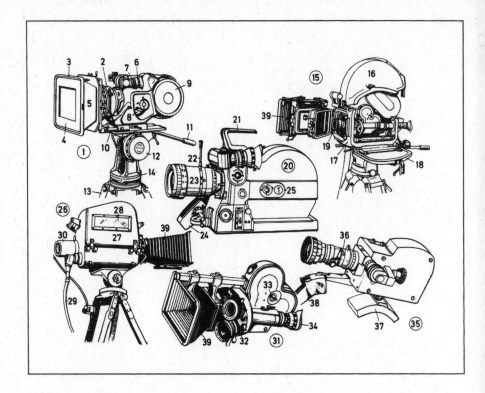

1-39 motion picture cameras (film cameras)
1 standard-gauge (*Am.* standard-gage) motion picture camera (standard-gauge, *Am.* standard-gage, 35 mm camera)
2 lens (object lens, taking lens)
3 lens hood (sunshade) with matte box
4 matte (mask)
5 lens hood barrel
6 viewfinder eyepiece
7 eyepiece control ring
8 opening control for the segment disc (disk) shutter
9 magazine housing
10 slide bar for the lens hood
11 control arm (control lever)
12 pan and tilt head
13 wooden tripod
14 degree scale
15 soundproof (blimped) motion picture camera (film camera)
16-18 soundproof housing (blimp)
16 upper section of the soundproof housing
17 lower section of the soundproof housing
18 open sidewall of the soundproof housing
19 camera lens
20 lightweight professional motion picture camera

21 grip (handgrip)
22 zooming lever
23 zoom lens (variable focus lens, varifocal lens) with infinitely variable focus
24 handgrip with shutter release
25 camera door
26 sound camera (newsreel camera) for recording sound and picture
27 soundproof housing (blimp)
28 window for the frame counters and indicator scales
29 pilot tone cable (sync pulse cable)
30 pilot tone generator (signal generator, pulse generator)
31 professional narrow-gauge (*Am.* narrow-gage) motion picture camera, a 16 mm camera
32 lens turret (turret head)
33 housing lock
34 eyecup
35 high-speed camera, a special narrow-gauge (*Am.* narrow-gage) camera
36 zooming lever
37 rifle grip
38 handgrip with shutter release
39 lens hood bellows

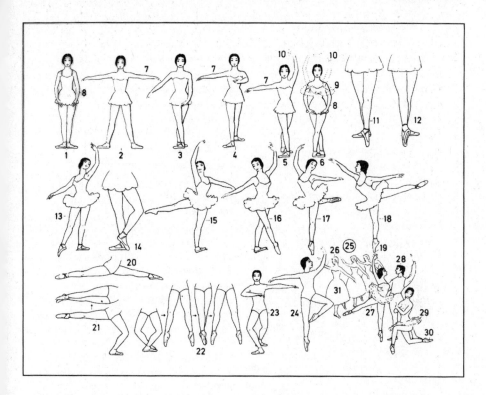

1-6 the five positions (ballet positions)
1 first position
2 second position
3 third position
4 fourth position [open]
5 fourth position [crossed; extended
fifth position]
6 fifth position
7-10 ports de bras (arm positions)
7 port de bras à coté
8 port de bras en bas
9 port de bras en avant
10 port de bras en haut
11 dégagé à la quatrième devant
12 dégagé à la quatrième derrière
13 effacé
14 sur le cou-de-pied
15 écarté
16 croisé
17 attitude
18 arabesque
19 à pointe (on full point)

20 splits
21 cabriole (capriole)
22 entrechat (entrechat quatre)
23 préparation [e.g. for a pirouette]
24 pirouette
25 corps de ballet
26 ballet dancer (ballerina)
27, 28 pas de trois
27 prima ballerina
28 principal male dancer (leading
soloist)
29 tutu
30 point shoe, a ballet shoe (ballet
slipper)
31 ballet skirt

315 Theatre (*Am.* Theater) I

1-4 types of curtain operation
1 draw curtain (side parting)
2 tableau curtain (bunching up side-ways)
3 fly curtain (vertical ascent)
4 combined fly and draw curtain
5-11 cloakroom hall (*Am.* checkroom hall)
5 cloakroom (*Am.* checkroom)
6 cloakroom attendant (*Am.* checkroom attendant)
7 cloakroom ticket (*Am.* check)
8 playgoer (theatregoer, *Am.* theatergoer)
9 opera glass (opera glasses)
10 commissionaire
11 theatre (*Am.* theater) ticket, an admission ticket
12, 13 foyer (lobby, crush room)
12 usher; *form.:* box attendant
13 programme (*Am.* program)
14-27 auditorium and stage
14 stage
15 proscenium
16-20 auditorium
16 gallery (balcony)
17 upper circle
18 dress circle (*Am.* balcony, mezzanine)
19 front stalls
20 seat (theatre seat, *Am.* theater seat)
21-27 rehearsal (stage rehearsal)
21 chorus
22, 23 singer
24 orchestra pit
25 orchestra
26 conductor
27 baton (conductor's baton)
28-42 paint room, a workshop
28 stagehand (scene shifter)
29 catwalk (bridge)
30 set piece
31 reinforcing struts
32 built piece (built unit)
33 backcloth (backdrop)
34 portable box for paint containers

35 scene painter
36 paint trolley
37 stage designer (set designer)
38 costume designer
39 design for a costume
40 sketch for a costume
41 model stage
42 model of the set
43-52 dressing room
43 dressing room mirror
44 make-up gown
45 make-up table
46 greasepaint stick
47 chief make-up artist (chief make-up man)
48 make-up artist (hairstylist)
49 wig
50 props (properties)
51 theatrical costume
52 call light

1-60 stagehouse with machinery
(machinery in the flies and below
stage)
1 control room
2 control console (lighting console,
lighting control console) with preset control for presetting lighting
effects
3 lighting plot (light plot)
4 grid (gridiron)
5 fly floor (fly gallery)
6 sprinkler system for fire preven-
tion (for fire protection)
7 fly man
8 fly lines (lines)
9 cyclorama
10 backcloth (backdrop, background)
11 arch, a drop cloth
12 border
13 compartment (compartment-type,
compartmentalized) batten (*Am.*
border light)
14 stage lighting units (stage lights)
15 horizon lights (backdrop lights)
16 adjustable acting area lights (acting
area spotlights)
17 scenery projectors (projectors)
18 monitor (water cannon) (piece of
safety equipment)
19 travelling (*Am.* traveling) lighting
bridge (travelling lighting gallery)
20 lighting operator (lighting man)
21 portal spotlight (tower spotlight)
22 adjustable proscenium
23 curtain (theatrical curtain)
24 iron curtain (safety curtain, fire
curtain)
25 forestage (apron)
26 footlight (footlights, floats)
27 prompt box
28 prompter
29 stage manager's desk
30 stage director (stage manager)
31 revolving stage
32 trap opening
33 lift (*Am.* elevator)
34 bridge (*Am.* elevator), a rostrum

35 pieces of scenery
36 scene
37 actor
38 actress
39 extras (supers, supernumeraries)
40 director (producer)
41 prompt book (prompt script)
42 director's table (producer's table)
43 assistant director (assistant producer)
44 director's script (producer's script)
45 stage carpenter
46 stagehand (scene shifter)
47 set piece
48 mirror spot (mirror spotlight)
49 automatic filter change (with
colour filters, colour mediums,
gelatines)
50 hydraulic plant room
51 water tank
52 suction pipe
53 hydraulic pump
54 pressure pipe
55 pressure tank (accumulator)
56 pressure gauge (*Am.* gage)
57 level indicator (liquid level indicator)
58 control lever
59 operator
60 rams

1	bar	**22**	tuner
2	barmaid	**23**	amplifier
3	bar stool	**24**	records (discs)
4	shelf for bottles	**25**	disc jockey
5	shelf for glasses	**26**	mixing console (mixing desk,
6	beer glass		mixer)
7	wine and liqueur glasses	**27**	tambourine
8	beer tap (tap)	**28**	mirrored wall
9	bar	**29**	ceiling tiles
10	refrigerator (fridge, *Am.* icebox)	**30**	ventilators
11	bar lamps	**31**	toilets (lavatories, WC)
12	indirect lighting	**32**	long drink
13	colour (*Am.* color) organ (clavilux)	**33**	cocktail (*Am.* highball)
14	dance floor lighting		
15	speaker (loudspeaker)		
16	dance floor		
17, 18	dancing couple (dancers)		
19	record player		
20	microphone		
21	tape recorder		
22, 23	stereo system (stereo equipment)		

1-33 nightclub (night spot)
1 cloakroom (*Am.* checkroom)
2 cloakroom attendant (*Am.* checkroom attendant)
3 band
4 clarinet
5 clarinettist (*Am.* clarinetist)
6 trumpet
7 trumpeter
8 guitar
9 guitarist (guitar player)
10 drums
11 drummer
12 speaker (loudspeaker)
13 bar
14 barmaid
15 bar
16 bar stool
17 tape recorder
18 receiver
19 spirits
20 cine projector for porno films (sex
films, blue movies)

21 box containing screen
22 stage
23 stage lighting
24 spotlight
25 festoon lighting
26 festoon lamp (lamp, light bulb)
27-32 striptease act (striptease number)
27 striptease artist (stripper)
28 suspender (*Am.* garter)
29 brassiere (bra)
30 fur stole
31 gloves
32 stocking
33 hostess

1-33 bullfight (corrida, corrida de toros)
1 mock bullfight
2 novice (aspirant matador, novillero)
3 mock bull (dummy bull)
4 novice banderillero (apprentice banderillero)
5 bullring (plaza de toros) [diagram]
6 main entrance
7 boxes
8 stands
9 arena (ring)
10 bullfighters' entrance
11 torril door
12 exit gate for killed bulls
13 slaughterhouse
14 bull pens (corrals)
15 paddock
16 lancer on horseback (picador)
17 lance (pike pole, javelin)
18 armoured (*Am.* armored) horse
19 leg armour (*Am.* armor)
20 picador's round hat
21 banderillero, a torero
22 banderillas (barbed darts)
23 shirtwaist
24 bullfight
25 matador (swordsman), a torero
26 queue, a distinguishing mark of the matador
27 red cloak (capa)
28 fighting bull
29 montera [hat made of tiny black silk chenille balls]
30 killing the bull (kill, estocada)
31 matador in charity performances [without professional uniform]
32 estoque (sword)
33 muleta
34 rodeo
35 young bull
36 cowboy
37 stetson (stetson hat)
38 scarf (necktie)
39 rodeo rider
40 lasso

1, 2 medieval (mediaeval) notes
1 plainsong notation (neumes, neums, pneumes, square notation)
2 mensural notation
3-7 musical note (note)
3 note head
4 note stem (note tail)
5 hook
6 stroke
7 dot indicating augmentation of note's value
8-11 clefs
8 treble clef (G-clef, violin clef)
9 bass clef (F-clef)
10 alto clef (C-clef)
11 tenor clef
12-19 note values
12 breve (brevis, *Am.* double-whole note)
13 semibreve (*Am.* whole note)
14 minim (*Am.* half note)
15 crotchet (*Am.* quarter note)
16 quaver (*Am.* eighth note)
17 semiquaver (*Am.* sixteenth note)
18 demisemiquaver (*Am.* thirty-second note)
19 hemidemisemiquaver (*Am.* sixty-fourth note)
20-27 rests
20 breve rest
21 semibreve rest (*Am.* whole rest)
22 minim rest (*Am.* half rest)
23 crotchet rest (*Am.* quarter rest)
24 quaver rest (*Am.* eighth rest)
25 semiquaver rest (*Am.* sixteenth rest)
26 demisemiquaver rest (*Am.* thirty-second rest)
27 hemidemisemiquaver rest (*Am.* sixty-fourth rest)
28-42 time (time signatures, measure, *Am.* meter)
28 two-eight time
29 two-four time
30 two-two time
31 four-eight time
32 four-four time (common time)
33 four-two time
34 six-eight time
35 six-four time
36 three-eight time
37 three-four time
38 three-two time
39 nine-eight time
40 nine-four time
41 five-four time
42 bar (bar line, measure line)
43, 44 staff (stave)
43 line of the staff
44 space
45-49 scales
45 C major scale naturals: c, d, e, f, g, a, b, c
46 A minor scale [natural] naturals: a, b, c, d, e, f, g, a
47 A minor scale [harmonic]
48 A minor scale [melodic]
49 chromatic scale
50-54 accidentals (inflections, key signatures)
50, 51 signs indicating the raising of a note
50 sharp (raising the note a semitone or half-step)
51 double sharp (raising the note a tone or full-step)
52, 53 signs indicating the lowering of a note
52 flat (lowering the note a semitone or half-step)
53 double flat (lowering the note a tone or full-step)
54 natural
55-68 keys (major keys and the related minor keys having the same signature)
55 C major (A minor)
56 G major (E minor)
57 D major (B minor)
58 A major (F sharp minor)
59 E major (C sharp minor)
60 B major (G sharp minor)
61 F sharp major (D sharp minor)
62 C major (A minor)
63 F major (D minor)
64 B flat major (G minor)
65 E flat major (C minor)
66 A flat major (F minor)
67 D flat major (B flat minor)
68 G flat major (E flat minor)

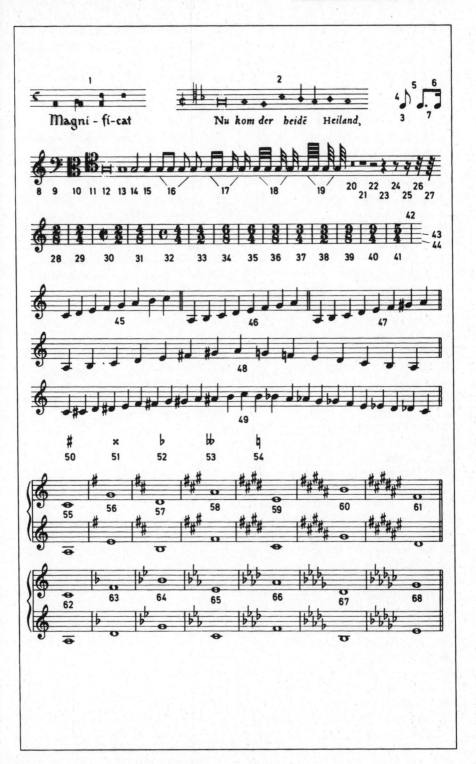

321 Musical Notation II

1-5 **chord**
1-4 triad
1 major triad
2 minor triad
3 diminished triad
4 augmented triad
5 chord of four notes, a chord of the seventh (seventh chord, dominant seventh chord)

6-13 **intervals**
6 unison (unison interval)
7 major second
8 major third
9 perfect fourth
10 perfect fifth
11 major sixth
12 major seventh
13 perfect octave

14-22 **ornaments** (graces, grace notes)
14 long appoggiatura
15 acciaccatura (short appoggiatura)
16 slide
17 trill (shake) without turn
18 trill (shake) with turn
19 upper mordent (inverted mordent, pralltriller)
20 lower mordent (mordent)
21 turn
22 arpeggio

23-26 other signs in musical notation
23 triplet; *corresponding groupings:* duplet (couplet), quadruplet, quintuplet, sextolet (sextuplet), septolet (septuplet, septimole)
24 tie (bind)
25 pause (pause sign)
26 repeat mark

27-41 **expression marks** (signs of relative intensity)
27 marcato (marcando, markiert, attack, strong accent)
28 presto (quick, fast)
29 portato (lourer, mezzo staccato, carried)
30 tenuto (held)
31 crescendo (increasing gradually in power)

32 decrescendo (diminuendo, decreasing or diminishing gradually in power)
33 legato (bound)
34 staccato (detached)
35 piano (soft)
36 pianissimo (very soft)
37 pianissimo piano (as soft as possible)
38 forte (loud)
39 fortissimo (very loud)
40 forte fortissimo (double fortissimo, as loud as possible)
41 forte piano (loud and immediately soft again)

42-50 **divisions of the compass**
42 subcontra octave (double contra octave)
43 contra octave
44 great octave
45 small octave
46 one-line octave
47 two-line octave
48 three-line octave
49 four-line octave
50 five-line octave

1 lur, a bronze trumpet
2 panpipes (Pandean pipes, syrinx)
3 aulos, a double shawm
4 aulos pipe
5 phorbeia (peristomion, capistrum, mouth band)
6 crumhorn (crummhorn, cromorne, krumbhorn, krummhorn)
7 recorder (fipple flute)
8 bagpipe; *sim.:* musette
9 bag
10 chanter (melody pipe)
11 drone (drone pipe)
12 curved cornett (zink)
13 serpent
14 shawm (schalmeyes); *larger:* bombard (bombarde, pommer)
15 cythara (cithara); *sim. and smaller:* lyre
16 arm
17 bridge
18 sound box (resonating chamber, resonator)
19 plectrum, a plucking device
20 kit (pochette), a miniature violin
21 cittern (cithern, cither, cister, citole), a plucked instrument; *sim.:* pandora (bandora, bandore)
22 sound hole
23 viol (descant viol, treble viol, a viola da gamba); *larger:* tenor viol, bass viol (viola da gamba, gamba), violone (double bass viol)
24 viol bow
25 hurdy-gurdy (vielle à roue, symphonia, armonie, organistrum)
26 friction wheel
27 wheel cover (wheel guard)
28 keyboard (keys)
29 resonating body (resonator, sound box)
30 melody strings
31 drone strings (drones, bourdons)
32 dulcimer
33 rib (resonator wall)
34 beater for the Valasian dulcimer
35 hammer (stick) for the Appenzell dulcimer
36 clavichord; *kinds:* fretted or unfretted clavichord
37 clavichord mechanism
38 key (key lever)
39 balance rail
40 guiding blade
41 guiding slot
42 resting rail
43 tangent
44 string
45 harpsichord (clavicembalo, cembalo), a wing-shaped stringed keyboard instrument; *sim.:* spinet (virginal)
46 upper keyboard (upper manual)
47 lower keyboard (lower manual)
48 harpsichord mechanism
49 key (key lever)
50 jack
51 slide (register)
52 tongue
53 quill plectrum
54 damper
55 string
56 portative organ, a portable organ; *larger:* positive organ (positive)
57 pipe (flue pipe)
58 bellows

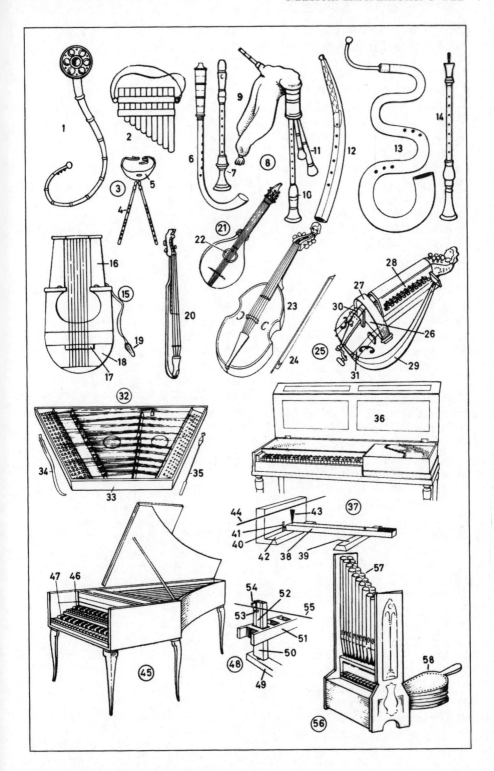

323 Musical Instruments II

1-62 **orchestral instruments**
1-27 **stringed instruments,** bowed
instruments
1 violin
2 neck of the violin
3 resonating body (violin body,
sound box of the violin)
4 rib (side wall)
5 violin bridge
6 F-hole, a sound hole
7 tailpiece
8 chin rest
9 strings (violin strings, fiddle
strings): G-string, D-string, A-
string, E-string
10 mute (sordino)
11 resin (rosin, colophony)
12 violin bow (bow)
13 nut (frog)
14 stick (bow stick)
15 hair of the violin bow (horsehair)
16 violoncello (cello), a member of
the da gamba violin family
17 scroll
18 tuning peg (peg)
19 pegbox
20 nut
21 fingerboard
22 spike (tailpin)
23 double bass (contrabass, violone,
double bass viol, *Am.* bass)
24 belly (top, soundboard)
25 rib (side wall)
26 purfling (inlay)
27 viola
28-38 **woodwind instruments** (wood-
winds)
28 bassoon; *larger:* double bassoon
(contrabassoon)
29 tube with double reed
30 piccolo (small flute, piccolo flute,
flauto piccolo)
31 flute (German flute), a cross flute
(transverse flute, side-blown flute)
32 key
33 fingerhole
34 clarinet; *larger:* bass clarinet

35 key (brille)
36 mouthpiece
37 bell
38 oboe (hautboy); *kinds:* oboe
d'amore; tenor oboes: oboe da cac-
cia, cor anglais; heckelphone (bari-
tone oboe)
39-48 **brass instruments** (brass)
39 tenor horn
40 valve
41 French horn (horn, waldhorn), a
valve horn
42 bell
43 trumpet; *larger:* Bb cornet; *smaller:*
cornet
44 bass tuba (tuba, bombardon); *sim.:*
helicon (pellitone), contrabass
tuba
45 thumb hold
46 trombone; *kinds:* alto trombone,
tenor trombone, bass trombone
47 trombone slide (slide)
48 bell
49-59 **percussion instruments**
49 triangle
50 cymbals
51-59 membranophones
51 side drum (snare drum)
52 drum head (head, upper head, batter
head, vellum)
53 tensioning screw
54 drumstick
55 bass drum (Turkish drum)
56 stick (padded stick)
57 kettledrum (timpano), a screw-ten-
sioned drum; *sim.:* machine drum
(mechanically tuned drum)
58 kettledrum skin (kettledrum vellum)
59 tuning screw
60 harp, a pedal harp
61 strings
62 pedal

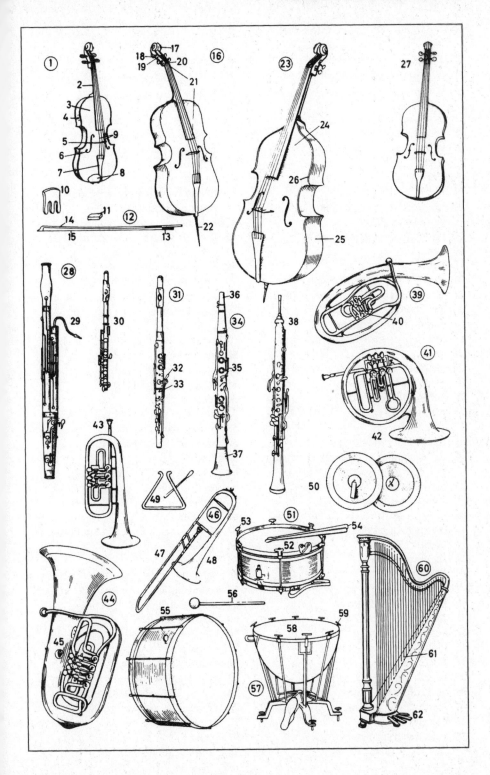

1-46 popular musical instruments (folk instruments)

1-31 stringed instruments

1 lute; *larger:* theorbo, chitarrone

2 resonating body (resonator)

3 soundboard (belly, table)

4 string fastener (string holder)

5 sound hole (rose)

6 string, a gut (catgut) string

7 neck

8 fingerboard

9 fret

10 head (bent-back pegbox, swan-head pegbox, pegbox)

11 tuning peg (peg, lute pin)

12 guitar

13 string holder

14 string, a gut (catgut) or nylon string

15 resonating body (resonating chamber, resonator, sound box)

16 mandolin (mandoline)

17 sleeve protector (cuff protector)

18 neck

19 pegdisc

20 plectrum

21 zither (plucked zither)

22 pin block (wrest pin block, wrest plank)

23 tuning pin (wrest pin)

24 accompaniment strings (bass strings, unfretted strings, open strings)

25 melody strings (fretted strings, stopped strings)

26 semicircular projection of the resonating sound box (resonating body)

27 ring plectrum

28 balalaika

29 banjo

30 tambourine-like body

31 parchment membrane

32 ocarina, a globular flute

33 mouthpiece

34 fingerhole

35 mouth organ (harmonica)

36 accordion; *sim.:* piano accordion, concertina, bandoneon

37 bellows

38 bellows strap

39 melody side (keyboard side, melody keys)

40 keyboard (keys)

41 treble stop (treble coupler, treble register)

42 stop lever

43 bass side (accompaniment side, bass studs, bass press-studs, bass buttons)

44 bass stop (bass coupler, bass register)

45 tambourine

46 castanets

47-78 jazz band instruments (dance band instruments)

47-58 percussion instruments

47-54 drum kit (drum set, drums)

47 bass drum

48 small tom-tom

49 large tom-tom

50 high-hat cymbals (choke cymbals, Charleston cymbals, cup cymbals)

51 cymbal

52 cymbal stand (cymbal holder)

53 wire brush

54 pedal mechanism

55 conga drum (conga)

56 tension hoop

57 timbales

58 bongo drums (bongos)

59 maracas; *sim.:* shakers

60 guiro

61 xylophone; *form.:* straw fiddle; *sim.:* marimbaphone (steel marimba), tubaphone

62 wooden slab

63 resonating chamber (sound box)

64 beater

65 jazz trumpet

66 valve

67 finger hook

68 mute (sordino)

69 saxophone

70 bell

71 crook

72 mouthpiece

73 struck guitar (jazz guitar)

74 hollow to facilitate fingering

75 vibraphone (*Am.* vibraharp)

76 metal frame

77 metal bar

78 tubular metal resonator

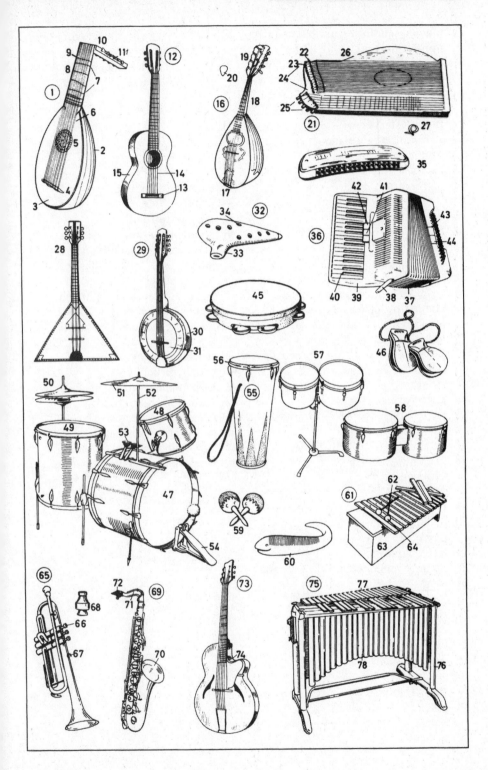

1 **piano** (pianoforte, upright piano, upright, vertical piano, spinet piano, console piano), a keyboard instrument (keyed instrument); *smaller form:* cottage piano (pianino); *earlier forms:* pantaleon; celesta, with steel bars instead of strings

2-18 piano action (piano mechanism)

2 iron frame

3 hammer; *collectively:* striking mechanism

4, 5 keyboard (piano keys)

4 white key (ivory key)

5 black key (ebony key)

6 piano case

7 strings (piano strings)

8, 9 piano pedals

8 right pedal (sustaining pedal, damper pedal; *loosely:* forte pedal, loud pedal) for raising the dampers

9 left pedal (soft pedal; *loosely:* piano pedal) for reducing the striking distance of the hammers on the strings

10 treble strings

11 treble bridge (treble belly bridge)

12 bass strings

13 bass bridge (bass belly bridge)

14 hitch pin

15 hammer rail

16 brace

17 tuning pin (wrest pin, tuning peg)

18 pin block (wrest pin block, wrest plank)

19 metronome

20 tuning hammer (tuning key, wrest)

21 tuning wedge

22-39 key action (key mechanism)

22 beam

23 damper-lifting lever

24 felt-covered hammer head

25 hammer shank

26 hammer rail

27 check (back check)

28 check felt (back check felt)

29 wire stem of the check (wire stem of the back check)

30 sticker (hopper, hammer jack, hammer lever)

31 button

32 action lever

33 pilot

34 pilot wire

35 tape wire

36 tape

37 damper (damper block)

38 damper lifter

39 damper rest rail

40 **grand piano** (horizontal piano, grand, concert grand; *smaller:* baby grand piano, boudoir piano; *sim.:* square piano, table piano)

41 grand piano pedals; right pedal for raising the dampers; left pedal for softening the tone (shifting the keyboard so that only one string is struck 'una corda')

42 pedal bracket

43 **harmonium** (reed organ, melodium)

44 draw stop (stop, stop knob)

45 knee lever (knee swell, swell)

46 pedal (bellows pedal)

47 harmonium case

48 harmonium keyboard (manual)

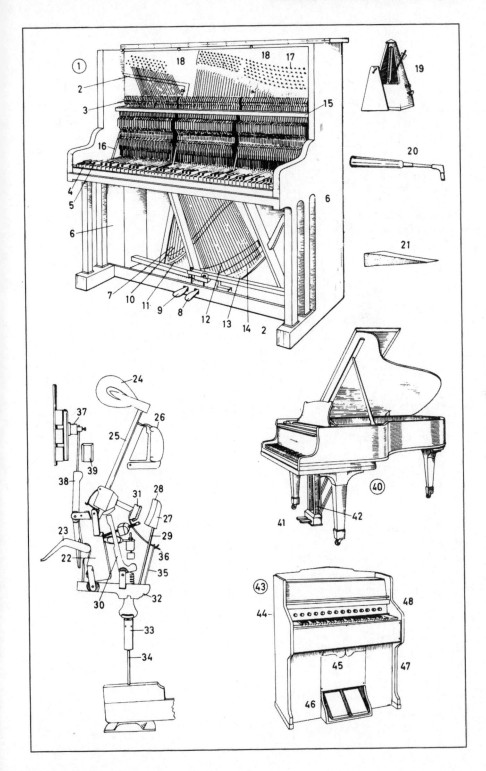

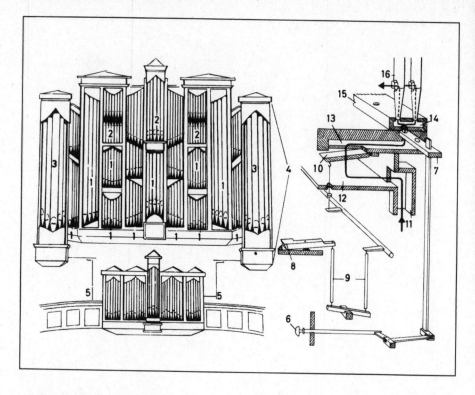

1-52 **organ** (church organ)
1-5 front view of organ (organ case)
  [built according to classical princi-
  ples]
1-3 display pipes (face pipes)
1 Hauptwerk
2 Oberwerk
3 pedal pipes
4 pedal tower
5 Rückpositiv
6-16 tracker action (mechanical
  action); *other systems:* pneumatic
  action, electric action
6 draw stop (stop, stop knob)
7 slider (slide)
8 key (key lever)
9 sticker
10 pallet
11 wind trunk
12-14 wind chest, a slider wind chest;
  other types: sliderless wind chest
  (unit wind chest), spring chest,
  kegellade chest (cone chest),
  diaphragm chest

12 wind chest (wind chest box)
13 groove
14 upper board groove
15 upper board
16 pipe of a particular stop
17-35 organ pipes (pipes)
17-22 metal reed pipe (*set of pipes:*
  reed stop), a posaune stop
17 boot
18 shallot
19 tongue
20 block
21 tuning wire (tuning crook)
22 tube
23-30 open metal flue pipe, a salicional
23 foot

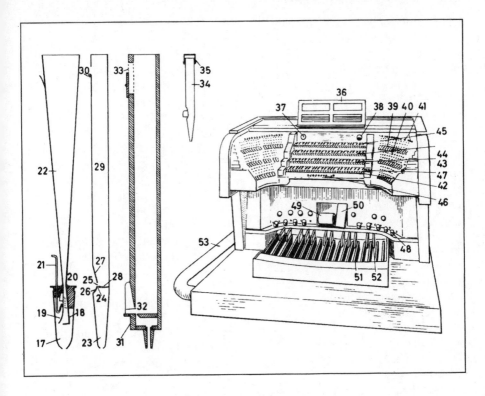

24 flue pipe windway (flue pipe duct)
25 mouth (cutup)
26 lower lip
27 upper lip
28 languid
29 body of the pipe (pipe)
30 tuning flap (tuning tongue), a tuning device
31-33 open wooden flue pipe (open wood), principal (diapason)
31 cap
32 ear
33 tuning hole (tuning slot), with slide
34 stopped flue pipe
35 stopper
36-52 organ console (console) of an electric action organ
36 music rest (music stand)
37 crescendo roller indicator
38 voltmeter
39 stop tab (rocker)
40 free combination stud (free combination knob)

41 cancel buttons for reeds, couplers etc.
42 manual I, for the Rückpositiv
43 manual II, for the Hauptwerk
44 manual III, for the Oberwerk
45 manual IV, for the Schwellwerk
46 thumb pistons controlling the manual stops (free or fixed combinations) and buttons for setting the combinations
47 switches for current to blower and action
48 toe piston, for the coupler
49 crescendo roller (general crescendo roller)
50 balanced swell pedal
51 pedal key [natural]
52 pedal key [sharp or flat]
53 cable (transmission cable)

327 Fabulous Creatures (Fabled Beings)

1-61 fabulous creatures (fabulous animals), mythical creatures
1 dragon
2 serpent's body
3 claws (claw)
4 bat's wing
5 fork-tongued mouth
6 forked tongue
7 unicorn [symbol of virginity]
8 spirally twisted horn
9 Phoenix
10 flames or ashes of resurrection
11 griffin (griffon, gryphon)
12 eagle's head
13 griffin's claws
14 lion's body
15 wing
16 chimera (chimaera), a monster
17 lion's head
18 goat's head
19 dragon's body
20 sphinx, a symbolic figure
21 human head
22 lion's body
23 mermaid (nix, nixie, water nixie, sea maid, sea maiden, naiad, water nymph, water elf, ocean nymph, sea nymph, river nymph); *sim.:* Nereids, Oceanids (sea divinities, sea deities, sea goddesses); *male:* nix (merman, seaman)
24 woman's trunk
25 fish's tail (dolphin's tail)
26 Pegasus (favourite, *Am.* favorite, steed of the Muses, winged horse); *sim.:* hippogryph
27 horse's body
28 wings
29 Cerberus (hellhound)
30 three-headed dog's body
31 serpent's tail
32 Lernaean (Lernean) Hydra
33 nine-headed serpent's body
34 basilisk (cockatrice)
35 cock's head
36 dragon's body
37 giant (titan)
38 rock
39 serpent's foot
40 triton, a merman (demigod of the sea)
41 conch shell trumpet
42 horse's hoof
43 fish's tail
44 hippocampus
45 horse's trunk
46 fish's tail
47 sea ox, a sea monster
48 monster's body
49 fish's tail
50 seven-headed dragon of St. John's Revelation (Revelations, Apocalypse)
51 wing
52 centaur (hippocentaur), half man and half beast
53 man's body with bow and arrow
54 horse's body
55 harpy, a winged monster
56 woman's head
57 bird's body
58 siren, a daemon
59 woman's body
60 wing
61 bird's claw

328 Prehistory

1-40 prehistoric finds
1-9 Old Stone Age (Palaeolithic, Paleolithic, period) and **Mesolithic period**
1 hand axe (*Am.* ax) (fist hatchet), a stone tool
2 head of throwing spear, made of bone
3 bone harpoon
4 head
5 harpoon thrower, made of reindeer antler
6 painted pebble
7 head of a wild horse, a carving
8 Stone Age idol, an ivory statuette
9 bison, a cave painting (rock painting) [cave art, cave painting]
10-20 New Stone Age (Neolithic period)
10 amphora [corded ware]
11 bowl [menhir group]
12 collared flask [Funnel-Beaker culture]
13 vessel with spiral pattern [spiral design pottery]
14 bell beaker [bell beaker culture]
15 pile dwelling (lake dwelling, lacustrine dwelling)
16 dolmen (cromlech), a megalithic tomb (*coll.:* giant's tomb); *other kinds:* passage grave, gallery grave (long cist); *when covered with earth:* tumulus (barrow, mound)
17 stone cist, a contracted burial
18 menhir (standing stone), a monolith
19 boat axe (*Am.* ax), a stone battle axe
20 clay figurine, an idol
21-40 Bronze Age and **Iron Age;**
epochs: Hallstatt period, La Tène period
21 bronze spear head
22 hafted bronze dagger
23 socketed axe (*Am.* ax), a bronze axe with haft fastened to rings
24 girdle clasp
25 necklace (lunula)
26 gold neck ring
27 violin-bow fibula (safety pin)
28 serpentine fibula; *other kinds:* boat fibula, arc fibula
29 bulb-head pin, a bronze pin
30 two-piece spiral fibula; *sim.:* disc (disk) fibula
31 hafted bronze knife
32 iron key
33 ploughshare (*Am.* plowshare)
34 sheet-bronze situla, a funerary vessel
35 pitcher [chip-carved pottery]
36 miniature ritual cart (miniature ritual chariot)
37 Celtic silver coin
38 face urn, a cinerary urn; *other kinds:* domestic urn, embossed urn
39 urn grave in stone chamber
40 urn with cylindrical neck

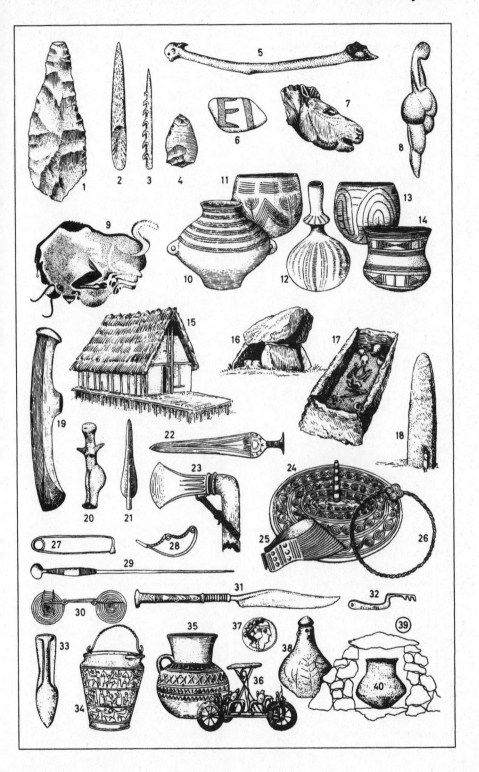

1 **knight's castle** (castle)
2 inner ward (inner bailey)
3 draw well
4 keep (donjon)
5 dungeon
6 battlements (crenellation)
7 merlon
8 tower platform
9 watchman
10 ladies' apartments (bowers)
11 dormer window (dormer)
12 balcony
13 storehouse (magazine)
14 angle tower
15 curtain wall (curtains, enclosure wall)
16 bastion
17 angle tower
18 crenel (embrasure)
19 inner wall
20 battlemented parapet
21 parapet (breastwork)
22 gatehouse
23 machicolation (machicoulis)
24 portcullis
25 drawbridge
26 buttress
27 offices and service rooms
28 turret
29 chapel
30 great hall
31 outer ward (outer bailey)
32 castle gate
33 moat (ditch)
34 approach
35 watchtower (turret)
36 palisade (pallisade, palisading)
37 moat (ditch, fosse)
38-65 **knight's armour** (*Am.* armor)
38 suit of armour (*Am.* armor)
39-42 helmet
39 skull
40 visor (vizor)
41 beaver
42 throat piece
43 gorget
44 épaulière
45 pallette (pauldron, besageur)
46 breastplate (cuirass)

47 brassard (rear brace and vambrace)
48 cubitiere (coudiere, couter)
49 tasse (tasset)
50 gauntlet
51 habergeon (haubergeon)
52 cuisse (cuish, cuissard, cuissart)
53 knee cap (knee piece, genouillère, poleyn)
54 jambeau (greave)
55 solleret (sabaton, sabbaton)
56 pavis (pavise, pavais)
57 buckler (round shield)
58 boss (umbo)
59 iron hat
60 morion
61 light casque
62 types of mail and armour (*Am.* armor)
63 mail (chain mail, chain armour, *Am.* armor)
64 scale armour (*Am.* armor)
65 plate armour (*Am.* armor)
66 **accolade** (dubbing, knighting)
67 liege lord, a knight
68 esquire
69 cup bearer
70 minstrel (minnesinger, troubadour)
71 **tournament** (tourney, joust, just, tilt)
72 crusader
73 Knight Templar
74 caparison (trappings)
75 herald (marshal at tournament)
76 tilting armour (*Am.* armor)
77 tilting helmet (jousting helmet)
78 panache (plume of feathers)
79 tilting target (tilting shield)
80 lance rest
81 tilting lance (lance)
82 vamplate
83-88 horse armour (*Am.* armor)
83 neck guard (neck piece)
84 chamfron (chaffron, chafron, chamfrain, chanfron)
85 poitrel
86 flanchard (flancard)
87 tournament saddle
88 rump piece (quarter piece)

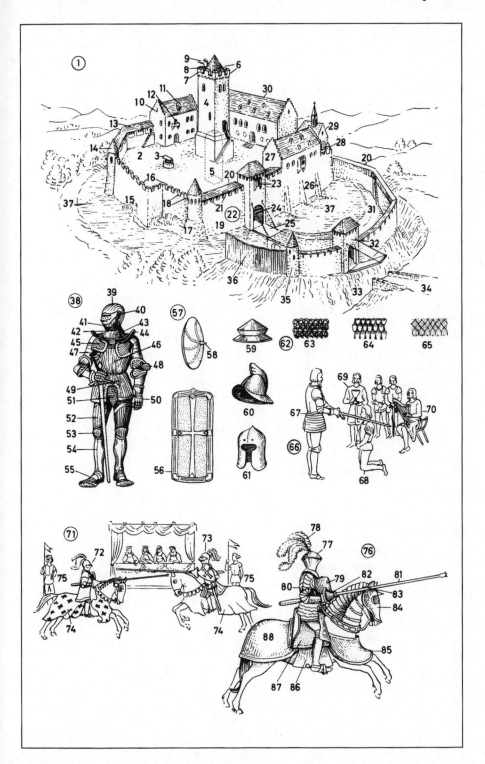

330 Church I

1-30 Protestant church
1 chancel
2 lectern
3 altar carpet
4 altar (communion table, Lord's table, holy table)
5 altar steps
6 altar cloth
7 altar candle
8 pyx (pix)
9 paten (patin, patine)
10 chalice (communion cup)
11 Bible (Holy Bible, Scriptures, Holy Scripture)
12 altar crucifix
13 altarpiece
14 church window
15 stained glass
16 wall candelabrum
17 vestry door (sacristy door)
18 pulpit steps
19 pulpit
20 antependium
21 canopy (soundboard, sounding board)
22 preacher (pastor, vicar, clergyman, rector) in his robes (vestments, canonicals)
23 pulpit balustrade
24 hymn board showing hymn numbers
25 gallery
26 verger (sexton, sacristan)
27 aisle
28 pew; *collectively:* pews (seating)
29 churchgoer (worshipper); *collectively:* congregation
30 hymn book
31-62 Roman Catholic church
31 altar steps
32 presbytery (choir, chancel, sacrarium, sanctuary)
33 altar
34 altar candles
35 altar cross
36 altar cloth
37 lectern

38 missal (mass book)
39 priest
40 server
41 sedilia
42 tabernacle
43 stele (stela)
44 paschal candle (Easter candle)
45 paschal candlestick (Easter candlestick)
46 sanctus bell
47 processional cross
48 altar decoration (foliage, flower arrangement)
49 sanctuary lamp
50 altarpiece, a picture of Christ
51 Madonna (statue of the Virgin Mary)
52 pricket
53 votive candles
54 station of the Cross
55 offertory box
56 literature stand
57 literature (pamphlets, tracts)
58 verger (sexton, sacristan)
59 offertory bag
60 offering
61 man praying
62 prayer book

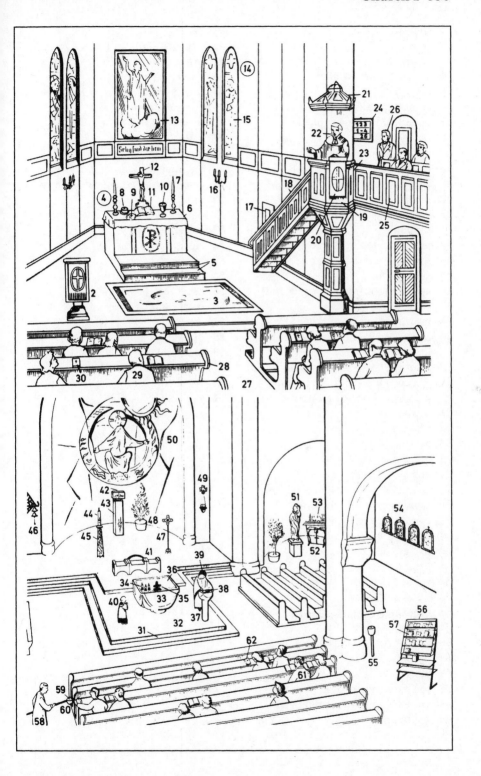

1 **church**
2 steeple
3 weathercock
4 weather vane (wind vane)
5 spire ball
6 church spire (spire)
7 church clock (tower clock)
8 belfry window
9 electrically operated bell
10 ridge cross
11 church roof
12 memorial chapel
13 vestry (sacristy), an annexe (annex)
14 memorial tablet (memorial plate, wall memorial, wall stone)
15 side entrance
16 church door (main door, portal)
17 churchgoer
18 graveyard wall (churchyard wall)
19 graveyard gate (churchyard gate, lichgate, lychgate)
20 vicarage (parsonage, rectory)
21-41 **graveyard** (churchyard, God's acre, *Am.* burying ground)
21 mortuary
22 grave digger
23 grave (tomb)
24 grave mound
25 cross
26 gravestone (headstone, tombstone)
27 family grave (family tomb)
28 graveyard chapel
29 child's grave
30 urn grave
31 urn
32 soldier's grave
33-41 funeral (burial)
33 mourners
34 grave
35 coffin (*Am.* casket)
36 spade
37 clergyman
38 the bereaved
39 widow's veil, a mourning veil
40 pallbearers

41 bier
42-50 **procession** (religious procession)
42 processional crucifix
43 cross bearer (crucifer)
44 processional banner, a church banner
45 acolyte
46 canopy bearer
47 priest
48 monstrance with the Blessed Sacrament (consecrated Host)
49 canopy (baldachin, baldaquin)
50 nuns
51 participants in the procession
52-58 **monastery**
52 cloister
53 monastery garden
54 monk, a Benedictine monk
55 habit (monk's habit)
56 cowl (hood)
57 tonsure
58 breviary
59 **catacomb,** an early Christian underground burial place
60 niche (tomb recess, arcosolium)
61 stone slab

1 Christian baptism (christening)
2 baptistery (baptistry)
3 Protestant clergyman
4 robes (vestments, canonicals)
5 bands
6 collar
7 child to be baptized (christened)
8 christening robe (christening dress)
9 christening shawl
10 font
11 font basin
12 baptismal water
13 godparents
14 church wedding (wedding ceremony, marriage ceremony)
15, 16 bridal couple
15 bride
16 bridegroom (groom)
17 ring (wedding ring)
18 bride's bouquet (bridal bouquet)
19 bridal wreath
20 veil (bridal veil)
21 [myrtle] buttonhole
22 clergyman
23 witnesses [to the marriage]
24 bridesmaid
25 kneeler
26 Holy Communion
27 communicants
28 Host (wafer)
29 communion cup
30 rosary
31 paternoster
32 Ave Maria; *set of 10:* decade
33 crucifix
34-54 liturgical vessels (ecclesiastical vessels)
34 monstrance
35 Host (consecrated Host, Blessed Sacrament)
36 lunula (lunule)
37 rays
38 censer (thurible), for offering incense (for incensing)
39 thurible chain
40 thurible cover

41 thurible bowl
42 incense boat
43 incense spoon
44 cruet set
45 water cruet
46 wine cruet
47 holy water basin
48 ciborium containing the sacred wafers
49 chalice
50 dish for communion wafers
51 paten (patin, patine)
52 altar bells
53 pyx (pix)
54 aspergillum
55-72 forms of Christian crosses
55 Latin cross (cross of the Passion)
56 Greek cross
57 Russian cross
58 St. Peter's cross
59 St. Anthony's cross (tau cross)
60 St. Andrew's cross (saltire cross)
61 Y-cross
62 cross of Lorraine
63 ansate cross
64 patriarchal cross
65 cardinal's cross
66 papal cross
67 Constantinian cross, a monogram of Christ (CHR)
68 crosslet
69 cross moline
70 cross of Jerusalem
71 cross botonnée (cross treflée)
72 fivefold cross (quintuple cross)
73 Celtic cross

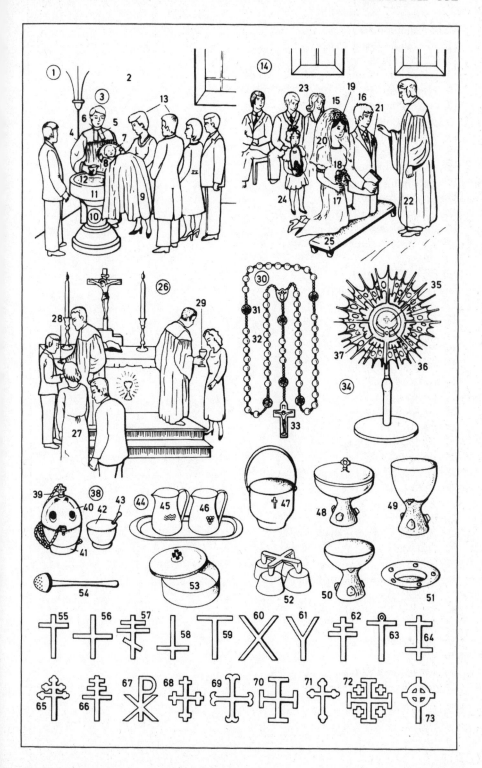

1-18 Egyptian art
1 pyramid, a royal tomb
2 king's chamber
3 queen's chamber
4 air passage
5 coffin chamber
6 pyramid site
7 funerary temple
8 valley temple
9 pylon, a monumental gateway
10 obelisks
11 Egyptian sphinx
12 winged sun disc (sun disk)
13 lotus column
14 knob-leaf capital (bud-shaped capital)
15 papyrus column
16 bell-shaped capital
17 palm column
18 ornamented column
19, 20 Babylonian art
19 Babylonian frieze
20 glazed relief tile
21-28 art of the Persians
21 tower tomb
22 stepped pyramid
23 double bull column
24 projecting leaves
25 palm capital
26 volute (scroll)
27 shaft
28 double bull capital
29-36 art of the Assyrians
29 Sargon's Palace, palace buildings
30 city wall
31 castle wall
32 temple tower (ziggurat), a stepped (terraced) tower
33 outside staircase
34 main portal
35 portal relief
36 portal figure
37 art of Asia Minor
38 rock tomb

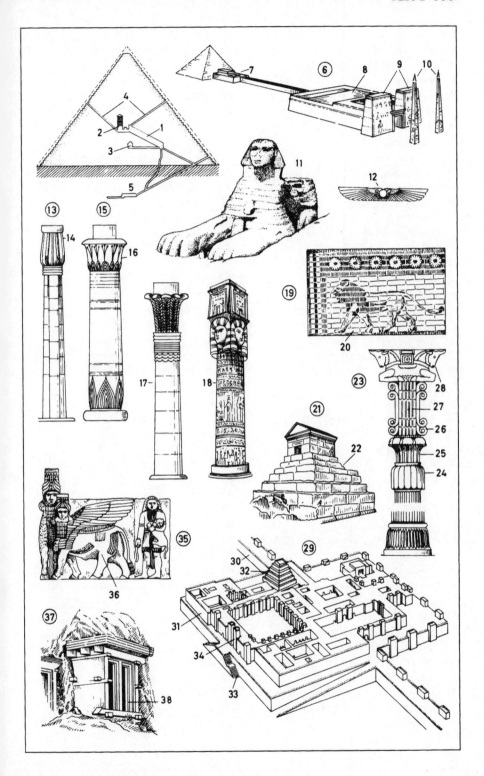

1-48 Greek art
1-7 the Acropolis
1 the Parthenon, a Doric temple
2 peristyle
3 pediment
4 crepidoma (stereobate)
5 statue
6 temple wall
7 propylaea
8 Doric column
9 Ionic column
10 Corinthian column
11-14 cornice
11 cyma
12 corona
13 mutule
14 dentils
15 triglyph
16 metope, a frieze decoration
17 regula
18 epistyle (architrave)
19 cyma (cymatium, kymation)
20-25 capital
20 abacus
21 echinus
22 hypotrachelium (gorgerin)
23 volute (scroll)
24 volute cushion
25 acanthus
26 column shaft
27 flutes (grooves, channels)
28-31 base
28 [upper] torus
29 trochilus (concave moulding, *Am.* molding)
30 [lower] torus
31 plinth
32 stylobate
33 stele (stela)
34 acroterion (acroterium, acroter)
35 herm (herma, hermes)
36 caryatid; *male:* Atlas
37 Greek vase
38-43 Greek ornamentation (Greek decoration, Greek decorative designs)

38 bead-and-dart moulding (*Am.* molding), an ornamental band
39 running dog (Vitruvian scroll)
40 leaf ornament
41 palmette
42 egg and dart (egg and tongue, egg and anchor) cyma
43 meander
44 Greek theatre (*Am.* theater)
45 scene
46 proscenium
47 orchestra
48 thymele (altar)
49-52 Etruscan art
49 Etruscan temple
50 portico
51 cella
52 entablature
53-60 Roman art
53 aqueduct
54 conduit (water channel)
55 centrally-planned building (centralized building)
56 portico
57 reglet
58 cupola
59 triumphal arch
60 attic
61-71 Early Christian art
61 basilica
62 nave
63 aisle
64 apse
65 campanile
66 atrium
67 colonnade
68 fountain
69 altar
70 clerestory (clearstory)
71 triumphal arch
72-75 Byzantine art
72, 73 dome system
72 main dome
73 semidome
74 pendentive
75 eye, a lighting aperture

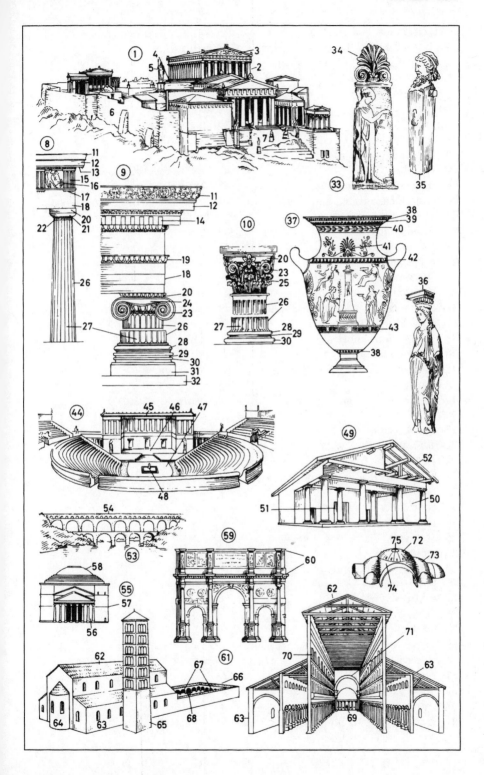

1-21 Romanesque art
1-13 Romanesque church, a cathedral
1 nave
2 aisle
3 transept
4 choir (chancel)
5 apse
6 central tower (*Am.* center tower)
7 pyramidal tower roof
8 arcading
9 frieze of round arcading
10 blind arcade (blind arcading)
11 lesene, a pilaster strip
12 circular window
13 side entrance
14-16 Romanesque ornamentation
   (Romanesque decoration,
   Romanesque decorative designs)
14 chequered (*Am.* checkered) pattern (chequered design)
15 imbrication (imbricated design)
16 chevron design
17 Romanesque system of vaulting
18 transverse arch
19 barrel vault (tunnel vault)
20 pillar
21 cushion capital
22-41 Gothic art
22 Gothic church [westwork, west
   end, west façade], a cathedral
23 rose window
24 church door (main door, portal), a
   recessed portal
25 archivolt
26 tympanum
27-35 Gothic structural system
27, 28 buttresses
27 buttress
28 flying buttress
29 pinnacle
30 gargoyle
31, 32 cross vault (groin vault)
31 ribs (cross ribs)
32 boss (pendant)
33 triforium
34 clustered pier (compound pier)

35 respond (engaged pillar)
36 pediment
37 finial
38 crocket
39-41 tracery window, a lancet window
39, 40 tracery
39 quatrefoil
40 cinquefoil
41 mullions
42-54 Renaissance art
42 Renaissance church
43 projection, a projecting part of the
   building
44 drum
45 lantern
46 pilaster (engaged pillar)
47 Renaissance palace
48 cornice
49 pedimental window
50 pedimental window with round
   gable
51 rustication (rustic work)
52 string course
53 sarcophagus
54 festoon (garland)

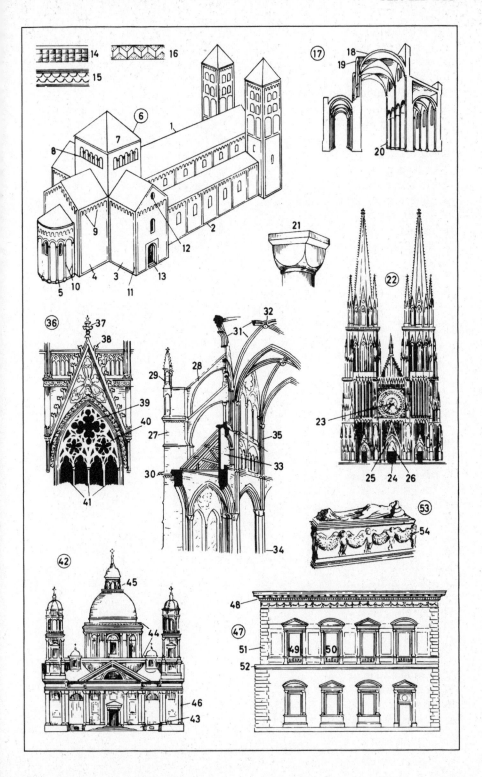

1-8 Baroque art
1 Baroque church
2 bull's eye
3 bulbous cupola
4 dormer window (dormer)
5 curved gable
6 twin columns
7 cartouche
8 scrollwork

9-13 Rococo art
9 Rococo wall
10 coving, a hollow moulding (*Am.* molding)
11 framing
12 ornamental moulding (*Am.* molding)
13 rocaille, a Rococo ornament
14 table in Louis Seize style (Louis Seize table)
15 neoclassical building (building in neoclassical style), a gateway
16 Empire table (table in the Empire style)
17 Biedermeier sofa (sofa in the Biedermeier style)
18 Art Nouveau easy chair (easy chair in the Art Nouveau style)

19-37 types of arch
19 arch
20 abutment
21 impost
22 springer, a voussoir (wedge stone)
23 keystone
24 face
25 intrados
26 extrados
27 round arch
28 segmental arch (basket handle)
29 parabolic arch
30 horseshoe arch
31 lancet arch
32 trefoil arch
33 shouldered arch
34 convex arch
35 tented arch
36 ogee arch (keel arch)
37 Tudor arch

38-50 types of vault
38 barrel vault (tunnel vault)
39 crown
40 side
41 cloister vault (cloistered vault)
42 groin vault (groined vault)
43 rib vault (ribbed vault)
44 stellar vault
45 net vault
46 fan vault
47 trough vault
48 trough
49 cavetto vault
50 cavetto

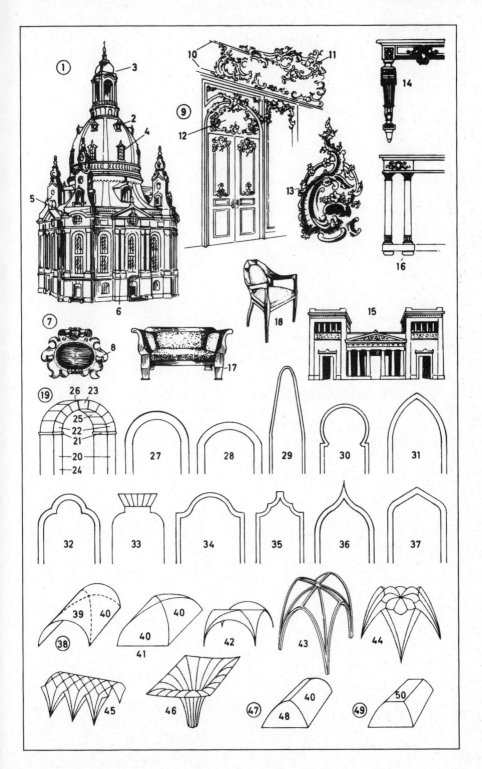

1-6 Chinese art

1 pagoda (multi-storey, multistory, pagoda), a temple tower
2 storey (story) roof (roof of storey)
3 pailou (pailoo), a memorial archway
4 archway
5 porcelain vase
6 incised lacquered work

7-11 Japanese art

7 temple
8 bell tower
9 supporting structure
10 bodhisattva (boddhisattva), a Buddhist saint
11 torii, a gateway

12-18 Islamic art

12 mosque
13 minaret, a prayer tower
14 mihrab
15 minbar (mimbar, pulpit)
16 mausoleum, a tomb
17 stalactite vault (stalactitic vault)
18 Arabian capital

19-28 Indian art

19 dancing Siva (Shiva), an Indian god
20 statue of Buddha
21 stupa (Indian pagoda), a mound (dome), a Buddhist shrine
22 umbrella
23 stone wall (*Am.* stone fence)
24 gate
25 temple buildings
26 shikara (sikar, sikhara, temple tower)
27 chaitya hall
28 chaitya, a small stupa

1-43 studio
1 studio skylight
2 painter, an artist
3 studio easel
4 chalk sketch, a rough draft
5 crayon (piece of chalk)
6-19 painting materials
6 flat brush
7 camel hair brush
8 round brush
9 priming brush
10 box of paints (paintbox)
11 tube of oil paint
12 varnish
13 thinner
14 palette knife
15 spatula
16 charcoal pencil (charcoal, piece of charcoal)
17 tempera (gouache)
18 watercolour (*Am.* watercolor)
19 pastel crayon
20 wedged stretcher (canvas stretcher)
21 canvas

22 piece of hardboard, with painting surface
23 wooden board
24 fibreboard (*Am.* fiberboard)
25 painting table
26 folding easel
27 still life group, a motif
28 palette
29 palette dipper
30 platform
31 lay figure (mannequin, manikin)
32 nude model (model, nude)
33 drapery
34 drawing easel
35 sketch pad
36 study in oils
37 mosaic (tessellation)
38 mosaic figure
39 tesserae
40 fresco (mural)
41 sgraffito
42 plaster
43 cartoon

1 sculptor
2 proportional dividers
3 calliper (caliper)
4 plaster model, a plaster cast
5 block of stone (stone block)
6 modeller (*Am.* modeler)
7 clay figure, a torso
8 roll of clay, a modelling (*Am.* modeling) substance
9 modelling (*Am.* modeling) stand
10 wooden modelling (*Am.* modeling) tool
11 wire modelling (*Am.* modeling) tool
12 beating wood
13 claw chisel (toothed chisel, tooth chisel)
14 flat chisel
15 point (punch)
16 iron-headed hammer
17 gouge (hollow chisel)
18 spoon chisel
19 wood chisel, a bevelled-edge chisel

20 V-shaped gouge
21 mallet
22 framework
23 baseboard
24 armature support (metal rod)
25 armature
26 wax model
27 block of wood
28 wood carver (wood sculptor)
29 sack of gypsum powder (gypsum)
30 clay box
31 modelling (*Am.* modeling) clay
32 statue, a sculpture
33 low relief (bas-relief)
34 modelling (*Am.* modeling) board
35 wire frame, wire netting
36 circular medallion (tondo)
37 mask
38 plaque

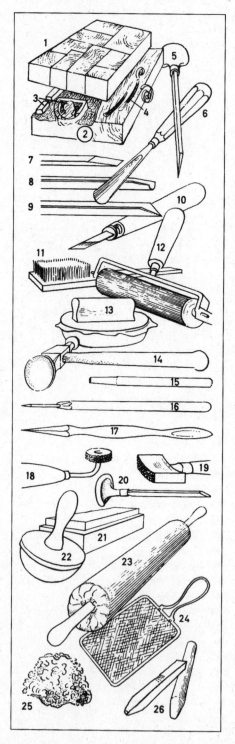

1-13 wood engraving (xylography), a relief printing method (a letterpress printing method)

1 end-grain block for wood engravings, a wooden block
2 wooden plank for woodcutting, a relief image carrier
3 positive cut
4 plank cut
5 burin (graver)
6 U-shaped gouge
7 scorper (scauper, scalper)
8 scoop
9 V-shaped gouge
10 contour knife
11 brush
12 roller (brayer)
13 pad (wiper)

14-24 copperplate engraving (chalcography), an intaglio process; *kinds:* etching, mezzotint, aquatint, crayon engraving

14 hammer
15 burin
16 etching needle (engraver)
17 scraper and burnisher
18 roulette
19 rocking tool (rocker)
20 round-headed graver, a graver (burin)
21 oilstone
22 dabber (inking ball, ink ball)
23 leather roller
24 sieve

25, 26 lithography (stone lithography), a planographic printing method

25 sponge for moistening the lithographic stone
26 lithographic crayons (greasy chalk)

27-64 graphic art studio, a printing office (*Am.* printery)
27 broadside (broadsheet, single sheet)
28 full-colour (*Am.* full-color) print (colour print, chromolithograph)
29 platen press, a hand press
30 toggle
31 platen
32 type forme (*Am.* form)
33 feed mechanism
34 bar (devil's tail)
35 pressman
36 copperplate press
37 tympan
38 pressure regulator
39 star wheel
40 cylinder
41 bed
42 felt cloth
43 proof (pull)
44 copperplate engraver

45 lithographer (litho artist), grinding the stone
46 grinding disc (disk)
47 grain (granular texture)
48 pulverized glass
49 rubber solution
50 tongs
51 etching bath for etching
52 zinc plate
53 polished copperplate
54 cross hatch
55 etching ground
56 non-printing area
57 lithographic stone
58 register marks
59 printing surface (printing image carrier)
60 lithographic press
61 lever
62 scraper adjustment
63 scraper
64 bed

341 Script I

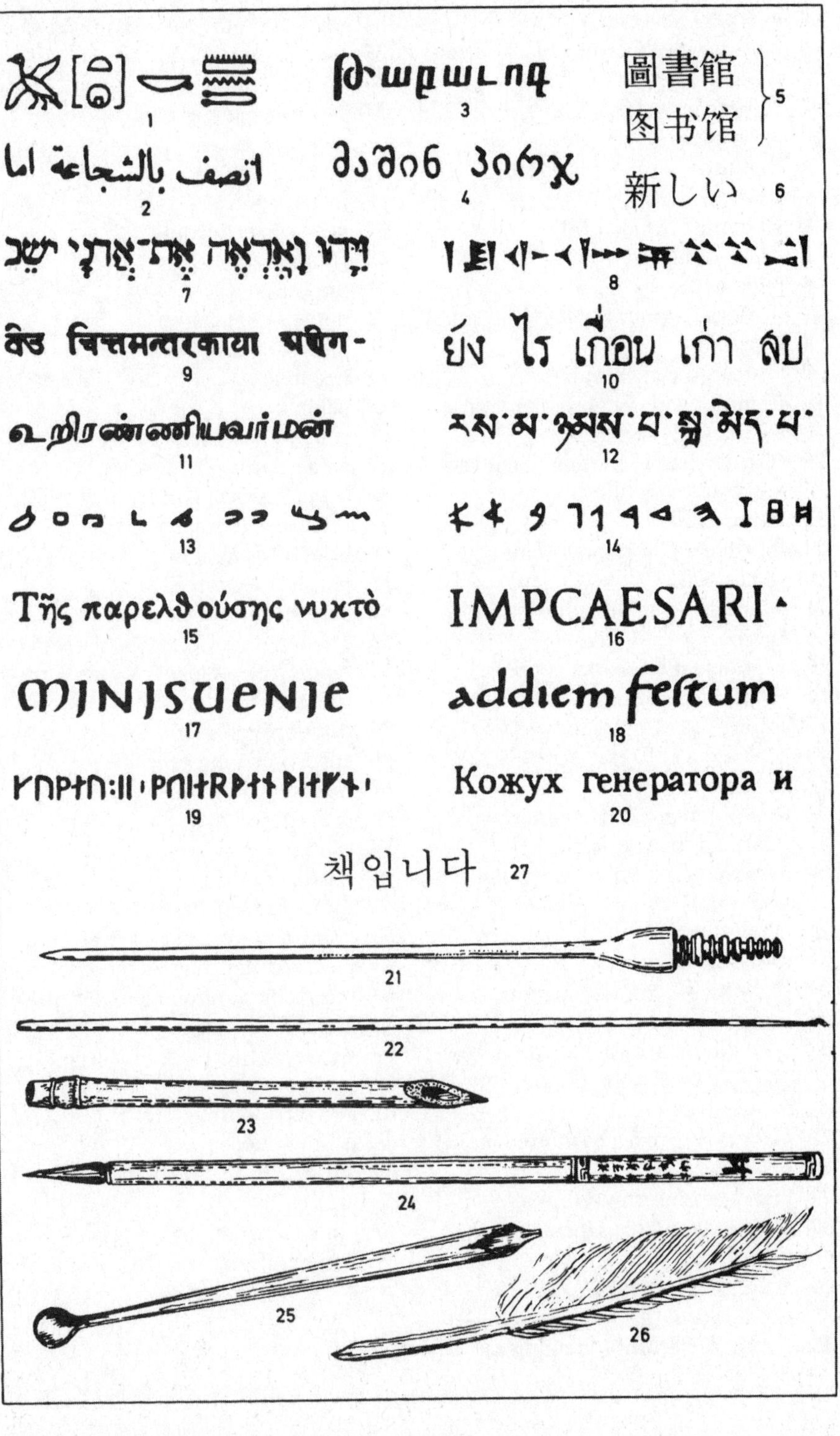

1

انصف بالشجاعة ا

2

3

4

圖書館
图书馆

5

新しい

6

7

8

9

10

11

12

13

14

Τῆς παρελθούσης νυκτὸ

15

IMPCAESARI·

16

ⱮINJSUENJE

17

addiem feſtum

18

19

Кожух генератора и

20

책입니다

27

21

22

23

24

25

26

1-15 types (type faces)
1 Gothic type (German black-letter type)
2 Schwabacher type (German black-letter type)
3 Fraktur (German black-letter type)
4 Humanist (Mediaeval)
5 Transitional
6 Didone
7 Sanserif (Sanserif type, Grotesque)
8 Egyptian
9 typescript (typewriting)
10 English hand (English handwriting, English writing)
11 German hand (German handwriting, German writing)
12 Latin script
13 shorthand (shorthand writing, stenography)
14 phonetics (phonetic transcription)
15 Braille
16-29 punctuation marks (stops)
16 full stop (period, full point)
17 colon
18 comma
19 semicolon
20 question mark (interrogation point, interrogation mark)
21 exclamation mark (*Am.* exclamation point)
22 apostrophe
23 dash (em rule)
24 parentheses (round brackets)
25 square brackets
26 quotation mark (double quotation marks, paired quotation marks, inverted commas)
27 guillemet (French quotation mark)
28 hyphen
29 marks of omission (ellipsis)
30-35 accents and diacritical marks (diacritics)
30 acute accent (acute)
31 grave accent (grave)
32 circumflex accent (circumflex)
33 cedilla [under c]

34 diaeresis (*Am.* dieresis) [over e]
35 tilde [over n]
36 section mark
37-70 newspaper, a national daily newspaper
37 newspaper page
38 front page
39 newspaper heading
40 contents
41 price
42 date of publication
43 place of publication
44 headline
45 column
46 column heading
47 column rule
48 leading article (leader, editorial)
49 reference to related article
50 brief news item
51 political section
52 page heading
53 cartoon
54 report by newspaper's own correspondent
55 news agency's sign
56 advertisement (*coll.* ad)
57 sports section
58 press photo
59 caption
60 sports report
61 sports news item
62 home and overseas news section
63 news in brief (miscellaneous news)
64 television programmes (*Am.* programs)
65 weather report
66 weather chart (weather map)
67 arts section (feuilleton)
68 death notice
69 advertisements (classified advertising)
70 job advertisement, a vacancy (a situation offered)

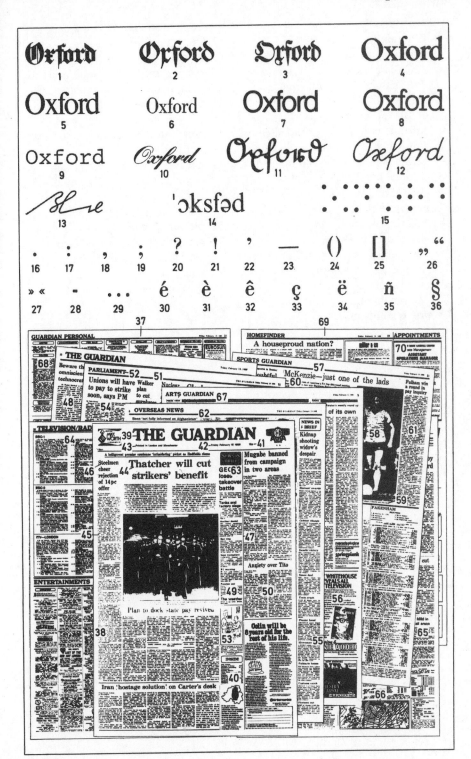

𝕺𝖝𝖋𝖔𝖗𝖉
1

𝕺𝖝𝖋𝖔𝖗𝖉
2

𝕺𝖝𝖋𝖔𝖗𝖉
3

Oxford
4

Oxford
5

Oxford
6

Oxford
7

Oxford
8

Oxford
9

Oxford
10

Oxford
11

Oxford
12

13

ˈɒksfəd
14

15

.
16

:
17

,
18

;
19

?
20

!
21

'
22

—
23

()
24

[]
25

„ "
26

» «
27

-
28

...
29

é
30

è
31

ê
32

ç
33

ë
34

ñ
35

§
36

Script II (samples of newspaper text — The Guardian)

1-26 arithmetic
1-22 numbers
1 Roman numerals
2 Arabic numerals
3 abstract number, a four-figure
  number [8: units; 5: tens; 6: hun-
  dreds; 9: thousands]
4 concrete number (physical quantity
  consisting of the numerical value
  and the unit or unit symbol)
5 cardinal number (cardinal)
6 ordinal number (ordinal)
7 positive number [with plus sign]
8 negative number [with minus sign]
9 algebraic symbols
10 mixed number [3: whole number
  (integer); $^{1}/_{3}$: fraction]
11 even numbers
12 odd numbers
13 prime numbers

14 complex number [3: real part; $2\sqrt{-1}$
  imaginary part]
15, 16 vulgar fractions
15 proper fraction [2: numerator, hor
  izontal line; 3: denominator]
16 improper fraction, also the reciproca
  of item 15
17 compound fraction (complex fraction)
18 improper fraction [when cancelled
  down produces a whole number]
19 fractions of different denomina-
  tions [35: common denominator]
20 proper decimal fraction with decimal point and decimal places [3:
  tenths; 5: hundredths; 7: thou-
  sandths]
21, 22 recurring decimal

①	I	II	III	IV	V	VI	VII	VIII	IX	X
②	1	2	3	4	5	6	7	8	9	10

①	XX	XXX	XL	XLIX	IL	L	LX	LXX	LXXX	XC
②	20	30	40	49		50	60	70	80	90

①	XCIX	IC	C	CC	CCC	CD	D	DC	DCC	DCCC
②	99		100	200	300	400	500	600	700	800

①	CM	CMXC	M
②	900	990	1000

③ 9658   ④ 5 kg.   ⑤ 2   ⑥ 2nd   ⑦ +5   ⑧ -5

23-26 fundamental arithmetical operations

23 addition (adding) [3 and 2: the terms of the sum; + : plus sign; = : equals sign; 5: the sum]

24 subtraction (subtracting); [3: the minuend; – : minus sign; 2: the subtrahend; 1: the remainder (difference)]

25 multiplication (multiplying); [3: the multiplicand; ×: multiplication sign; 2: the multiplier; 2 and 3: factors; 6: the product]

26 division (dividing); [6: the dividend; ÷: division sign; 2: the divisor; 3: the quotient]

⑨ a,b,c...   ⑩ $3\frac{1}{3}$ ⑪ 2,4,6,8   ⑫ 1,3,5,7

⑬ 3,5,7,11   ⑭ $3+2\sqrt{-1}$ ⑮ $\frac{2}{3}$ ⑯ $\frac{3}{2}$

⑰ $\dfrac{\frac{5}{6}}{\frac{3}{4}}$ ⑱ $\frac{12}{4}$ ⑲ $\frac{4}{5}+\frac{2}{7}=\frac{38}{35}$ ⑳ 0·357

㉑ $0\cdot6666....=0\cdot\overline{6}$ ㉒   ㉓ 3+2=5

㉔ 3−2=1   ㉕ 3 · 2 = 6   ㉖ 6÷2=3
               3 × 2 = 6

① $3^2 = 9$ ② $\sqrt[3]{8} = 2$ ③ $\sqrt{4} = 2$

④ $3x + 2 = 12$

⑥

⑤ $4a + 6ab - 2ac = 2a(2 + 3b - c)$ $\log_{10} 3 = 0.4771$

⑦ $\dfrac{P[£1000] \times R[5\%] \times T[2\,\text{years}]}{100} = I[£100]$

1-24 arithmetic
1-10 advanced arithmetical operations
1 raising to a power [three squared (3^2): the power; 3: the base; 2: the exponent (index); 9: value of the power]
2 evolution (extracting a root); [cube root of 8: cube root; 8: the radical; 3: the index (degree) of the root; √: radical sign; 2: value of the root]
3 square root
4, 5 algebra
4 simple equation [3, 2: the coefficients; ×: the unknown quantity]
5 identical equation; [a, b, c: algebraic symbols]
6 logarithmic calculation (taking the logarithm, log); [log: logarithm sign; 3: number whose logarithm is required; 10: the base; 0: the characteristic; 4771: the mantissa; 0.4771: the logarithm]

7 simple interest formula [P: the principal; R: rate of interest; T: time; I: interest (profit); %: percentage sign]
8-10 rule of three (rule-of-three sum, simple proportion)
8 statement with the unknown quantity ×
9 equation (conditional equation)
10 solution
11-14 higher mathematics
11 arithmetical series with the elements 2, 4, 6, 8
12 geometrical series
13, 14 infinitesimal calculus
13 derivative [dx, dy: the differentials; d: differential sign]
14 integral (integration) [x: the variable; C: constant of integration; ∫: the integral sign; dx: the differential]

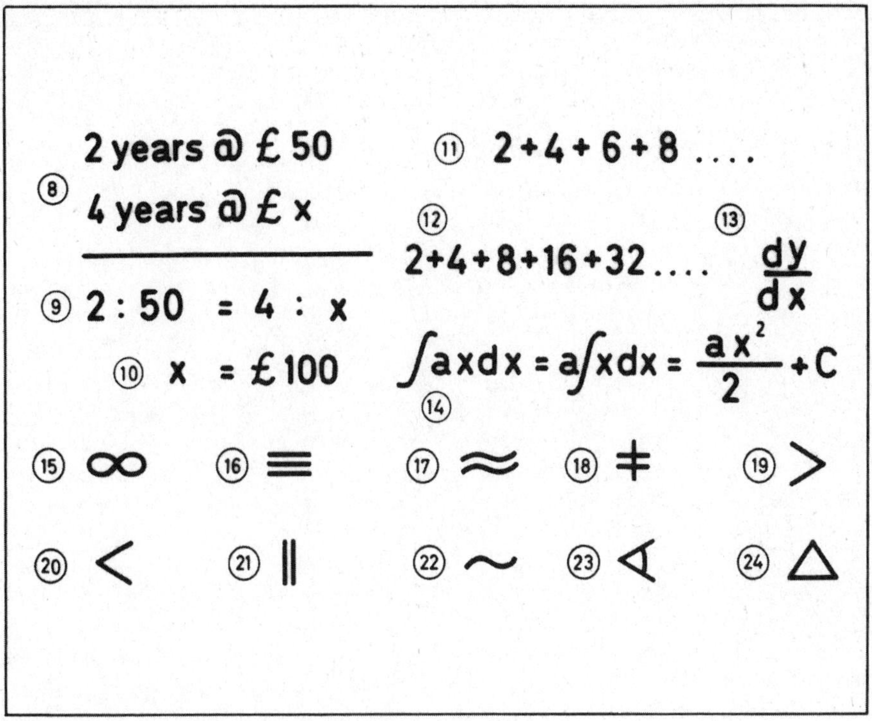

⑧ $\dfrac{\begin{array}{l}\text{2 years @ £ 50}\\[4pt]\text{4 years @ £ x}\end{array}}{}$

⑪ $2+4+6+8\ldots.$

⑫ $2+4+8+16+32\ldots.$

⑬ $\dfrac{dy}{dx}$

⑨ $2:50\ =4:x$

⑩ $x\ =£100$

⑭ $\displaystyle\int a x\,dx = a\!\int x\,dx = \dfrac{a x^{2}}{2}+C$

⑮ ∞ ⑯ $\equiv$ ⑰ $\approx$ ⑱ $\neq$ ⑲ $>$

⑳ $<$ ㉑ $\parallel$ ㉒ $\sim$ ㉓ $\sphericalangle$ ㉔ $\triangle$

15-24 mathematical symbols
15 infinity
16 identically equal to (the sign of identity)
17 approximately equal to
18 unequal to
19 greater than
20 less than
21-24 geometrical symbols
21 parallel (sign of parallelism)
22 similar to (sign of similarity)
23 angle symbol
24 triangle symbol

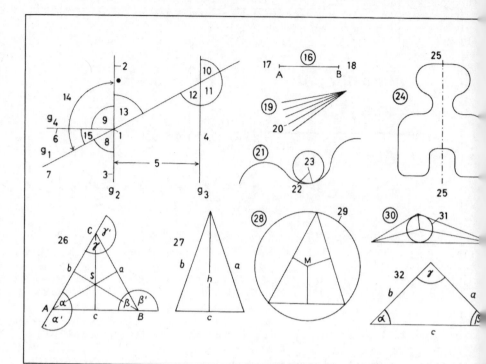

1-58 plane geometry (elementary geometry, Euclidian geometry)

1-23 point, line, angle

1 point [point of intersection of g_1 and g_2], the angular point of **8**

2, 3 straight line g_2

4 the parallel to g_2

5 distance between the straight lines g_2 and g_3

6 perpendicular (g_4) on g_2

7, 3 the arms of **8**

8, 13 vertically opposite angles

8 angle

9 right angle [90°]

10, 11, 12 reflex angle

10 acute angle, also the alternate angle to **8**

11 obtuse angle

12 corresponding angle to **10**

13, 9, 15 straight angle [180°]

14 adjacent angle; *here:* supplementary angle to 13

15 complementary angle to **8**

16 straight line AB

17 end A

18 end B

19 pencil of rays

20 ray

21 curved line

22 radius of curvature

23 centre (*Am.* center) of curvature

24-58 plane surfaces

24 symmetrical figure

25 axis of symmetry

26-32 plane triangles

26 equilateral triangle [A, B, C: the vertices; a, b, c: the sides; α (alpha), β (beta), γ (gamma): the interior angles; α', β', γ': the exterior angles; S: the centre (*Am.* center)]

27 isosceles triangle [a, b: the sides (legs); c: the base; h: the perpendicular, an altitude]

28 acute-angled triangle with perpendicular bisectors of the sides

29 circumcircle (circumscribed circle)

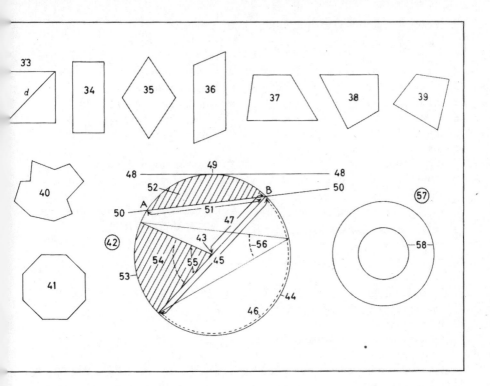

30 obtuse-angled triangle with bisectors of the angles
31 inscribed circle
32 right-angled triangle and the trigonometrical functions of angles [a, b: the catheti; c: the hypotenuse; γ: the right angle; $a/c = \sin \alpha$ (sine); $b/c = \cos \alpha$ (cosine); $a/b = \tan \alpha$ (tangent); $b/a = \cot \alpha$ (cotangent)]
33-39 quadrilaterals
33-36 parallelograms
33 square [d: a diagonal]
34 rectangle
35 rhombus (rhomb, lozenge)
36 rhomboid
37 trapezium
38 deltoid (kite)
39 irregular quadrilateral
40 polygon
41 regular polygon
42 **circle**
43 centre (*Am.* center)

44 circumference (periphery)
45 diameter
46 semicircle
47 radius (r)
48 tangent
49 point of contact (P)
50 secant
51 the chord AB
52 segment
53 arc
54 sector
55 angle subtended by the arc at the centre (*Am.* center) (centre, *Am.* center, angle)
56 circumferential angle
57 ring (annulus)
58 concentric circles

347 Mathematics IV (Geometry II)

1 **system of right-angled coordinates**
2, 3 axes of coordinates (coordinate axes)
2 axis of abscissae (x-axis)
3 axis of ordinates (y-axis)
4 origin of ordinates
5 quadrant [I-IV: 1st to 4th quadrant]
6 positive direction
7 negative direction
8 points [P_1 and P_2] in the system of coordinates; x_1 and y_1 [and x_2 and y_2 respectively] their coordinates
9 values of the abscissae [x_1 and x_2] (the abscissae)
10 values of the ordinates [y_1 and y_2] (the ordinates)
11-29 conic sections
11 **curves** in the system of coordinates
12 plane curves [a: the gradient (slope) of the curve; b: the ordinates' intersection of the curve; c: the root of the curve]
13 inflected curves
14 **parabola,** a curve of the second degree
15 branches of the parabola
16 vertex of the parabola
17 axis of the parabola
18 **a curve of the third degree**
19 maximum of the curve
20 minimum of the curve
21 point of inflexion (of inflection)
22 **ellipse**
23 transverse axis (major axis)
24 conjugate axis (minor axis)
25 foci of the ellipse [F_1 and F_2]
26 **hyperbola**
27 foci [F_1 and F_2]
28 vertices [S_1 and S_2]
29 asymptotes [a and b]
30-46 solids
30 cube
31 square, a plane (plane surface)
32 edge

33 corner
34 quadratic prism
35 base
36 parallelepiped
37 triangular prism
38 cylinder, a right cylinder
39 base, a circular plane
40 curved surface
41 sphere
42 ellipsoid of revolution
43 cone
44 height of the cone (cone height)
45 truncated cone (frustum of a cone)
46 quadrilateral pyramid

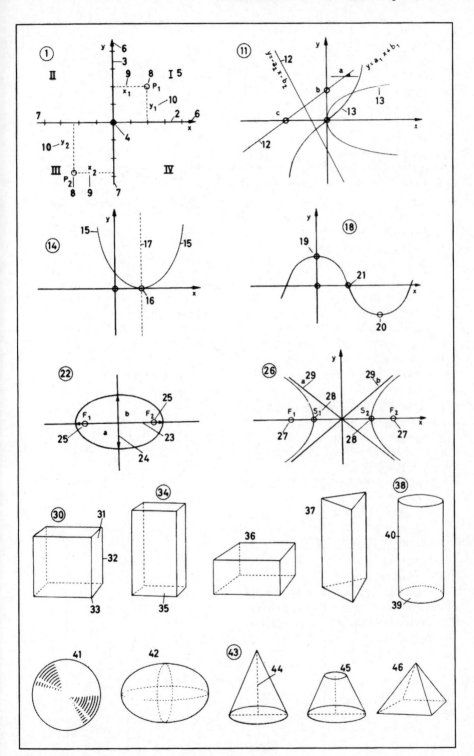

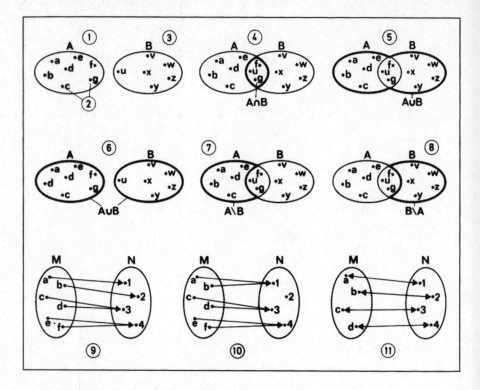

1 the set A, the set {a, b, c, d, e, f, g}
2 elements (members) of the set A
3 the set B, the set {u, v, w, x, y, z}
4 intersection of the sets A and B,
   $A \cap B = \{f, g, u\}$
5, 6 union of the sets A and B, $A \cup B$
   = {a, b, c, d, e, f, g, u, v, w, x, y, z}
7 complement of the set B, B' = {a,
   b, c, d, e}
8 complement of the set A, A' = {v,
   w, x, y, z}
9-11 mappings
9 mapping of the set M *onto* the set N
10 mapping of the set M *into* the set N
11 one-to-one mapping of the set M
   on to the set N

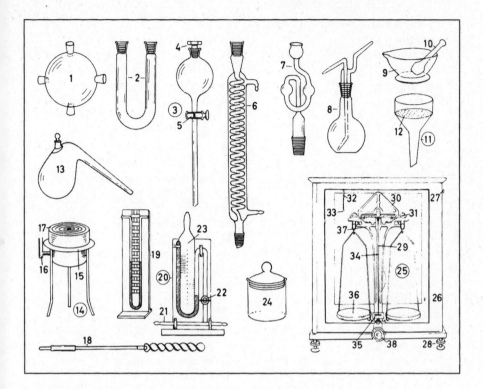

1-38 laboratory apparatus (laboratory equipment)
1 Scheidt globe
2 U-tube
3 separating funnel
4 octagonal ground-glass stopper
5 tap (*Am.* faucet)
6 coiled condenser
7 air lock
8 wash-bottle
9 mortar
10 pestle
11 filter funnel (Büchner funnel)
12 filter (filter plate)
13 retort
14 water bath
15 tripod
16 water gauge (*Am.* gage)
17 insertion rings
18 stirrer
19 manometer for measuring positive and negative pressures

20 mirror manometer for measuring small pressures
21 inlet
22 tap (*Am.* faucet)
23 sliding scale
24 weighing bottle
25 analytical balance
26 case
27 sliding front panel
28 three-point support
29 column (balance column)
30 balance beam (beam)
31 rider bar
32 rider holder
33 rider
34 pointer
35 scale
36 scale pan
37 stop
38 stop knob

1-63 laboratory apparatus (laboratory equipment)
1 Bunsen burner
2 gas inlet (gas inlet pipe)
3 air regulator
4 Teclu burner
5 pipe union
6 gas regulator
7 stem
8 air regulator
9 bench torch
10 casing
11 oxygen inlet
12 hydrogen inlet
13 oxygen jet
14 tripod
15 ring (retort ring)
16 funnel
17 pipe clay triangle
18 wire gauze
19 wire gauze with asbestos centre (*Am.* center)
20 beaker
21 burette (for measuring the volume of liquids)
22 burette stand
23 burette clamp
24 graduated pipette
25 pipette
26 measuring cylinder (measuring glass)
27 measuring flask
28 volumetric flask
29 evaporating dish (evaporating basin), made of porcelain
30 tube clamp (tube clip, pinchcock)
31 clay crucible with lid
32 crucible tongs
33 clamp
34 test tube
35 test tube rack
36 flat-bottomed flask
37 ground glass neck
38 long-necked round-bottomed flask
39 Erlenmeyer flask (conical flask)
40 filter flask

41 fluted filter
42 one-way tap
43 calcium chloride tube
44 stopper with tap
45 cylinder
46 distillation apparatus (distilling apparatus)
47 distillation flask (distilling flask)
48 condenser
49 return tap, a two-way tap
50 distillation flask (distilling flask, Claisen flask)
51 desiccator
52 lid with fitted tube
53 tap
54 desiccator insert made of porcelain
55 three-necked flask
56 connecting piece (Y-tube)
57 three-necked bottle
58 gas-washing bottle
59 gas generator (Kipp's apparatus, *Am.* Kipp generator)
60 overflow container
61 container for the solid
62 acid container
63 gas outlet

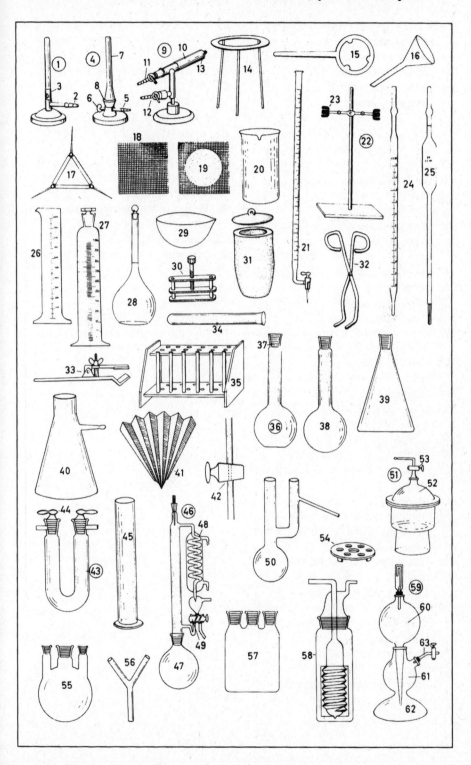

1-26 basic crystal forms and crystal combinations [structure of crystals]
1-17 regular (cubic, tesseral, isometric) **crystal system**
1 tetrahedron (four-faced polyhedron) [tetrahedrite, fahlerz, fahl ore]
2 hexahedron (cube, six-faced polyhedron), a holohedron [rock salt]
3 centre (*Am.* center) of symmetry (crystal centre)
4 axis of symmetry (rotation axis)
5 plane of symmetry
6 octahedron (eight-faced polyhedron) [gold]
7 rhombic dodecahedron [garnet]
8 pentagonal dodecahedron [pyrite, iron pyrites]
9 pentagon (five-sided polygon)
10 triakis-octahedron [diamond]
11 icosahedron (twenty-faced polyhedron), a regular polyhedron
12 icositetrahedron (twenty-four-faced polyhedron) [leucite]
13 hexakis-octahedron (hexoctahedron, forty-eight-faced polyhedron) [diamond]
14 octahedron with cube [galena]
15 hexagon (six-sided polygon)
16 cube with octahedron [fluorite, fluorspar]
17 octagon (eight-sided polygon)
18, 19 tetragonal crystal system
18 tetragonal dipyramid (tetragonal bipyramid)
19 protoprism with protopyramid [zircon]
20-22 hexagonal crystal system
20 protoprism with protopyramid, deutero-pyramid and basal pinacoid [apatite]
21 hexagonal prism
22 hexagonal (ditrigonal) biprism with rhombohedron [calcite]

23 orthorhombic pyramid (rhombic crystal system) [sulphur, *Am.* sulfur]
24, 25 monoclinic crystal system
24 monoclinic prism with clinoprinacoid and hemipyramid (hemihedron) [gypsum]
25 orthopinacoid (swallowtail twin crystal) [gypsum]
26 triclinic pinacoids (triclinic crystal system) [copper sulphate, *Am.* copper sulfate]
27-33 apparatus for measuring crystals (for crystallometry)
27 contact goniometer
28 reflecting goniometer
29 crystal
30 collimator
31 observation telescope
32 divided circle (graduated circle)
33 lens for reading the angle of rotation

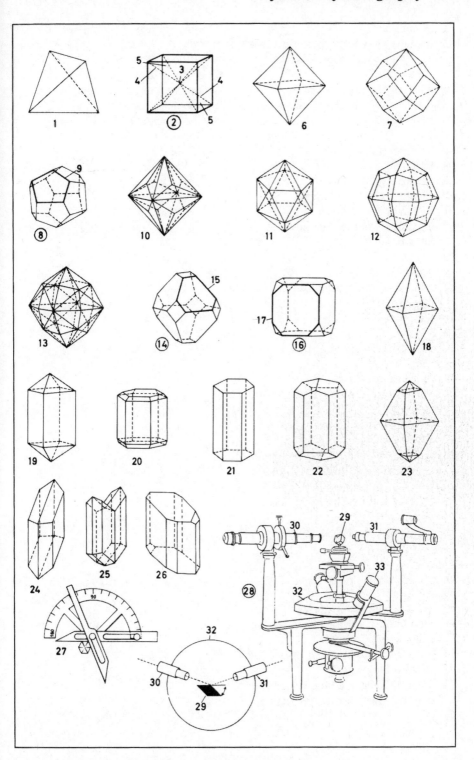

1 totem pole
2 totem, a carved and painted pictorial or symbolic representation
3 plains Indian
4 mustang, a prairie horse
5 lasso, a long throwing-rope with running noose
6 pipe of peace
7 wigwam (tepee, teepee)
8 tent pole
9 smoke flap
10 squaw, an Indian woman
11 Indian chief
12 headdress, an ornamental feather headdress
13 war paint
14 necklace of bear claws
15 scalp (cut from enemy's head), a trophy
16 tomahawk, a battle axe (*Am.* ax)
17 leggings
18 moccasin, a shoe of leather and bast
19 canoe of the forest Indians
20 Maya temple, a stepped pyramid
21 mummy
22 quipa (knotted threads, knotted code of the Incas)
23 Indio (Indian of Central and South America); *here:* highland Indian
24 poncho, a blanket with a head opening used as an armless cloak-like wrap
25 Indian of the tropical forest
26 blowpipe
27 quiver
28 dart
29 dart point
30 shrunken head, a trophy
31 bola (bolas), a throwing and entangling device
32 leather-covered stone or metal ball
33 pile dwelling
34 duk-duk dancer, a member of a duk-duk (men's secret society)
35 outrigger canoe (canoe with outrigger)
36 outrigger
37 Australian aborigine
38 loincloth of human hair
39 boomerang, a wooden missile
40 throwing stick (spear thrower) with spears

1 Eskimo
2 sledge dog (sled dog), a husky
3 dog sledge (dog sled)
4 igloo, a dome-shaped snow hut
5 block of snow
6 entrance tunnel
7 blubber-oil lamp
8 wooden missile
9 lance
10 harpoon
11 skin float
12 kayak, a light one-man canoe
13 skin-covered wooden or bone frame
14 paddle
15 reindeer harness
16 reindeer
17 Ostyak (Ostiak)
18 passenger sledge
19 yurt (yurta), a dwelling tent of the
   western and central Asiatic nomads
20 felt covering
21 smoke outlet
22 Kirghiz
23 sheepskin cap
24 shaman
25 decorative fringe
26 frame drum
27 Tibetan
28 flintlock with bayonets
29 prayer wheel
30 felt boot
31 houseboat (sampan)
32 junk
33 mat sail
34 rickshaw (ricksha)
35 rickshaw coolie (cooly)
36 Chinese lantern
37 samurai
38 padded armour (*Am.* armor)
39 geisha
40 kimono
41 obi
42 fan
43 coolie (cooly)
44 kris (creese, crease), a Malayan dagger
45 snake charmer
46 turban
47 flute
48 dancing snake

1 camel caravan
2 riding animal
3 pack animal
4 oasis
5 grove of palm trees
6 bedouin (beduin)
7 burnous
8 Masai warrior
9 headdress (hairdress)
10 shield
11 painted ox hide
12 long-bladed spear
13 negro
14 dance drum
15 throwing knife
16 wooden mask
17 figure of an ancestor
18 slit gong
19 drumstick
20 dugout, a boat hollowed out of a
    tree trunk
21 negro hut
22 negress
23 lip plug (labret)
24 grinding stone
25 Herero woman
26 leather cap
27 calabash (gourd)
28 beehive-shaped hut
29 bushman
30 earplug
31 loincloth
32 bow
33 knobkerry (knobkerrie), a club
    with round, knobbed end
34 bushman woman making a fire by
    twirling a stick
35 windbreak
36 Zulu in dance costume
37 dancing stick
38 bangle
39 ivory war horn
40 string of amulets and bones
41 pigmy
42 magic pipe for exorcising evil spirits
43 fetish

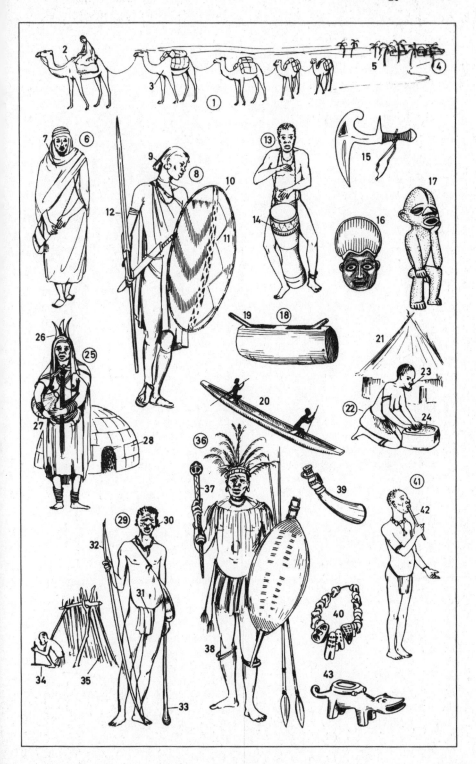

1 Greek woman
2 peplos
3 Greek
4 petasus (Thessalonian hat)
5 chiton, a linen gown worn as a basic garment
6 himation, woollen (*Am.* woolen) cloak
7 Roman woman
8 toupee wig (partial wig)
9 stola
10 palla, a coloured (*Am.* colored) wrap
11 Roman
12 tunica (tunic)
13 toga
14 purple border (purple band)
15 Byzantine empress
16 pearl diadem
17 jewels
18 purple cloak
19 long tunic
20 German princess [13th cent.]
21 crown (diadem)
22 chinband
23 tassel

24 cloak cord
25 girt-up gown (girt-up surcoat, girt-up tunic)
26 cloak
27 German dressed in the Spanish style [ca. 1575]
28 wide-brimmed cap
29 short cloak (Spanish cloak, short cape)
30 padded doublet (stuffed doublet, peasecod)
31 stuffed trunk-hose
32 lansquenet (German mercenary soldier) [ca. 1530]
33 slashed doublet (paned doublet)
34 Pluderhose (loose breeches, paned trunk-hose, slops)
35 woman of Basle [ca. 1525]
36 overgown (gown)
37 undergown (petticoat)
38 woman of Nuremberg [ca. 1500]
39 shoulder cape
40 Burgundian [15th cent.]
41 short doublet

42	piked shoes (peaked shoes, copped shoes, crackowes, poulaines)
43	pattens (clogs)
44	young nobleman [ca. 1400]
45	short, padded doublet (short, quilted doublet, jerkin)
46	dagged sleeves (petal-scalloped sleeves)
47	hose
48	Augsburg patrician lady [ca. 1575]
49	puffed sleeve
50	overgown (gown, open gown, sleeve-less gown)
51	French lady [ca. 1600]
52	millstone ruff (cartwheel ruff, ruff)
53	corseted waist (wasp waist)
54	gentleman [ca. 1650]
55	wide-brimmed felt hat (cavalier hat)
56	falling collar (wide-falling collar) of linen
57	white lining
58	jack boots (bucket-top boots)
59	lady [ca. 1650]
60	full puffed sleeves (puffed sleeves)
61	gentleman [ca. 1700]
62	three-cornered hat
63	dress sword
64	lady [ca. 1700]
65	lace fontange (high headdress of lace)
66	lace-trimmed loose-hanging gown (loose-fitting housecoat, robe de chambre, negligée, contouche)
67	band of embroidery
68	lady [ca. 1880]
69	bustle
70	lady [ca. 1858]
71	poke bonnet
72	crinoline
73	gentleman of the Biedermeier period
74	high collar (choker collar)
75	embroidered waistcoat (vest)
76	frock coat
77	pigtail wig
78	ribbon (bow)
79	ladies in court dress [ca. 1780]
80	train
81	upswept Rococo coiffure
82	hair decoration
83	panniered overskirt

1 outdoor enclosure
2 rocks
3 moat
4 enclosing wall
5 animals on show; *here:* a pride of
   lions
6 visitor to the zoo
7 notice
8 aviary
9 elephant enclosure
10 animal house (*e.g.* carnivore house,
   giraffe house, elephant house,
   monkey house)
11 outside cage (summer quarters)
12 reptile enclosure
13 Nile crocodile
14 terrarium and aquarium
15 glass case
16 fresh-air inlet
17 ventilator
18 underfloor heating
19 aquarium
20 information plate
21 flora in artificially maintained climate

1-12 **unicellular** (one-celled, single-celled) **animals** (protozoans)
1 amoeba, a rhizopod
2 cell nucleus
3 protoplasm
4 pseudopod
5 excretory vacuole (contractile vacuole, an organelle)
6 food vacuole
7 Actinophrys, a heliozoan
8 radiolarian; *here:* siliceous skeleton
9 slipper animalcule, a Paramecium (ciliate infusorian)
10 cilium
11 macronucleus (meganucleus)
12 micronucleus
13-39 **multicellular animals** (metazoans)
13 bath sponge, a porifer (sponge)
14 medusa, a discomedusa, a coelenterate
15 umbrella
16 tentacle
17 red coral (precious coral), a coral animal (anthozoan, reef-building animal)

18 coral colony
19 coral polyp
20-26 worms (Vermes)
20 leech, an annelid
21 sucker
22 Spirographis, a bristle worm
23 tube
24 earthworm
25 segment
26 clitellum [accessory reproductive organ]
27-36 molluscs (*Am.* mollusks)
27 edible snail, a snail
28 creeping foot
29 shell (snail shell)
30 stalked eye
31 tentacles (feelers)
32 oyster
33 freshwater pearl mussel
34 mother-of-pearl (nacre)
35 pearl
36 mussel shell
37 cuttlefish, a cephalopod
38, 39 echinoderms
38 starfish (sea star)
39 sea urchin (sea hedgehog)

1, 2 crustaceans
1 mitten crab, a crab
2 water slater
3-39, 48-56 insects
3 water nymph (dragonfly), a homopteran (homopterous insect)
4 water scorpion (water bug), a rhynchophore
5 raptorial leg
6 mayfly (dayfly, ephemerid)
7 compound eye
8 green grasshopper (green locust, meadow grasshopper), an orthopteron (orthopterous insect)
9 larva (grub)
10 adult insect, an imago
11 leaping hind leg
12 caddis fly (spring fly, water moth), a neuropteran
13 aphid (greenfly), a plant louse
14 wingless aphid
15 winged aphid
16-20 dipterous insects (dipterans)
16 gnat (mosquito, midge), a culicid
17 proboscis (sucking organ)
18 bluebottle (blowfly), a fly
19 maggot (larva)
20 chrysalis (pupa)
21-23 Hymenoptera
21, 22 ant
21 winged female
22 worker
23 bumblebee (humblebee)
24-39 beetles (Coleoptera)
24 stag beetle, a lamellicorn beetle
25 mandibles
26 trophi
27 antenna (feeler)
28 head
29, 30 thorax
29 thoracic shield (prothorax)
30 scutellum
31 tergites
32 stigma
33 wing (hind wing)
34 nervure
35 point at which the wing folds

36 elytron (forewing)
37 ladybird (*Am.* ladybug), a coccinellid
38 Ergates faber, a longicorn beetle (longicorn)
39 dung beetle, a lamellicorn beetle
40-47 arachnids
40 Euscorpius flavicandus, a scorpion
41 cheliped with chelicer
42 maxillary antenna (maxillary feeler)
43 tail sting
44-46 spiders
44 wood tick (dog tick)
45 cross spider (garden spider), an orb spinner
46 spinneret
47 spider's web (web)
48-56 Lepidoptera (butterflies and moths)
48 mulberry-feeding moth (silk moth), a bombycid moth
49 eggs
50 silkworm
51 cocoon
52 swallowtail, a butterfly
53 antenna (feeler)
54 eyespot
55 privet hawkmoth, a hawkmoth (sphinx)
56 proboscis

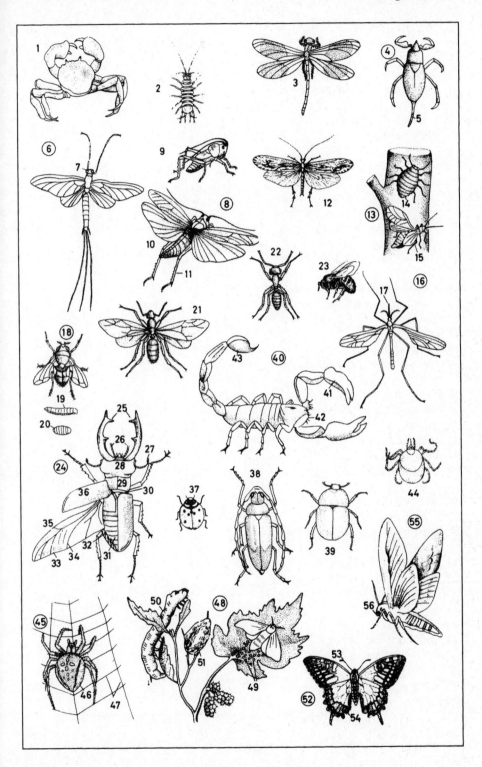

1-3 flightless birds
1 cassowary; *sim.:* emu
2 ostrich
3 clutch of ostrich eggs [12 - 14 eggs]
4 king penguin, a penguin, a flightless bird
5-10 web-footed birds
5 white pelican
6 webfoot (webbed foot)
7 web (palmations) of webbed foot
  (palmate foot)
8 lower mandible with gular pouch
9 northern gannet (gannet, solan
  goose), a gannet
10 green cormorant (shag), a cormorant displaying with spread
  wings
11-14 long-winged birds (seabirds)
11 common sea swallow, a sea swallow (tern), diving for food
12 fulmar
13 guillemot, an auk
14 black-headed gull (mire crow), a
  gull
15-17 Anseres
15 goosander (common merganser), a
  sawbill
16 mute swan, a swan
17 knob on the bill
18 common heron, a heron
19-21 plovers
19 stilt (stilt bird, stilt plover)
20 coot, a rail
21 lapwing (green plover, peewit,
  pewit)
22 quail, a gallinaceous bird
23 turtle dove, a pigeon
24 swift
25 hoopoe, a roller
26 erectile crest
27 spotted woodpecker, a woodpecker; *related:* wryneck
28 entrance to the nest
29 nesting cavity
30 cuckoo

360 Birds II (European Birds)

1, 3, 4, 5, 7, 9, 10 songbirds
1 goldfinch, a finch
2 bee eater
3 redstart (star finch), a thrush
4 bluetit, a tit (titmouse), a resident
   bird (non-migratory bird)
5 bullfinch
6 common roller (roller)
7 golden oriole, a migratory bird
8 kingfisher
9 white wagtail, a wagtail
10 chaffinch

1-20 songbirds
1-3 Corvidae (corvine birds, crows)
1 jay (nutcracker)
2 rook, a crow
3 magpie
4 starling (pastor, shepherd bird)
5 house sparrow
6-8 finches
6, 7 buntings
6 yellowhammer (yellow bunting)
7 ortolan (ortolan bunting)
8 siskin (aberdevine)
9 great titmouse (great tit, ox eye), a
 titmouse (tit)
10 golden-crested wren (goldcrest);
 sim.: firecrest, one of the
 Regulidae
11 nuthatch
12 wren
13-17 thrushes
13 blackbird
14 nightingale (*poet.:* philomel,
 philomela)

15 robin (redbreast, robin redbreast)
16 song thrush (throstle, mavis)
17 thrush nightingale
18, 19 larks
18 woodlark
19 crested lark (tufted lark)
20 common swallow (barn swallow,
 chimney swallow), a swallow

1-13 **diurnal birds of prey**
1-4 falcons
1 merlin
2 peregrine falcon
3 leg feathers
4 tarsus
5-9 eagles
5 white-tailed sea eagle (white-tailed eagle, grey sea eagle, erne)
6 hooked beak
7 claw (talon)
8 tail
9 common buzzard
10-13 accipiters
10 goshawk
11 common European kite (glede, kite)
12 sparrow hawk (spar-hawk)
13 marsh harrier (moor buzzard, moor harrier, moor hawk)
14-19 **owls**
14 long-eared owl (horned owl)
15 eagle-owl (great horned owl)
16 plumicorn (feathered ear, ear tuft, ear, horn)
17 barn owl (white owl, silver owl, yellow owl, church owl, screech owl)
18 facial disc (disk)
19 little owl (sparrow owl)

363 Birds V (Exotic Birds)

1 sulphur-crested cockatoo, a parrot
2 blue-and-yellow macaw
3 blue bird of paradise
4 sappho
5 cardinal (cardinal bird)
6 toucan (red-billed toucan), one of
   the Piciformes

1-18 fishes

1 man-eater (blue shark, requin), a shark
2 nose (snout)
3 gill slit (gill cleft)
4 mirror carp
5 gill cover (operculum)
6 dorsal fin
7 pectoral fin
8 pelvic fin (abdominal fin, ventral fin)
9 anal fin
10 caudal fin (tail fin)
11 scale
12 catfish (sheatfish, sheathfish, wels)
13 barbel
14 herring
15 brown trout
16 pike (northern pike)
17 freshwater eel (eel)
18 sea horse (Hippocampus, horse-fish)
19 tufted gills

20-26 Amphibia (amphibians)

20-22 salamanders

20 greater water newt (crested newt), a water newt
21 dorsal crest
22 fire salamander, a salamander

23-26 salientians (anurans, batrachians)

23 European toad, a toad
24 tree frog (tree toad)
25 vocal sac (vocal pouch, croaking sac)
26 adhesive disc (disk)

27-41 reptiles

27, 30-37 lizards

27 sand lizard
28 hawksbill turtle (hawksbill)
29 carapace (shell)
30 basilisk
31 desert monitor, a monitor lizard (monitor)
32 common iguana, an iguana
33 chameleon, one of the Chamaeleontidae (Rhiptoglossa)
34 prehensile foot
35 prehensile tail
36 wall gecko, a gecko
37 slowworm (blindworm), one of the Anguidae

38-41 snakes

38 ringed snake (ring snake, water snake, grass snake), a colubrid
39 collar
40, 41 vipers (adders)
40 common viper, a poisonous (venomous) snake
41 asp (asp viper)

365 Lepidoptera (Butterflies and Moths)

1-6 butterflies
1 red admiral
2 peacock butterfly
3 orange tip (orange tip butterfly)
4 brimstone (brimstone butterfly)
5 Camberwell beauty (mourning
   cloak, mourning cloak butterfly)
6 blue (lycaenid butterfly, lycaenid)
7-11 moths (Heterocera)
7 garden tiger
8 red underwing
9 death's-head moth (death's-head
   hawkmoth), a hawkmoth (sphinx)
10 caterpillar
11 chrysalis (pupa)

1 platypus (duck-bill, duck-mole), a monotreme (oviparous mammal)

2, 3 marsupial mammals (marsupials)

2 New World opossum, a didelphid

3 red kangaroo (red flyer), a kangaroo

4-7 insectivores (insect-eating mammals)

4 mole

5 hedgehog

6 spine

7 shrew (shrew mouse), one of the Soricidae

8 nine-banded armadillo (peba)

9 long-eared bat (flitter-mouse), a flying mammal (chiropter, chiropteran)

10 pangolin (scaly ant-eater), a scaly mammal

11 two-toed sloth (unau)

12-19 rodents

12 guinea pig (cavy)

13 porcupine

14 beaver

15 jerboa

16 hamster

17 water vole

18 marmot

19 squirrel

20 African elephant, a proboscidean (proboscidian)

21 trunk (proboscis)

22 tusk

23 manatee (manati, lamantin), a sirenian

24 South African dassie (das, coney, hyrax), a procaviid

25-31 ungulates

25-27 odd-toed ungulates

25 African black rhino, a rhinoceros (nasicorn)

26 Brazilian tapir, a tapir

27 zebra

28-31 even-toed ungulates

28-30 ruminants

28 llama

29 Bactrian camel (two-humped camel)

30 guanaco

31 hippopotamus

1-10 ungulates, ruminants
1 elk (moose)
2 wapiti (*Am.* elk)
3 chamois
4 giraffe
5 black buck, an antelope
6 mouflon (moufflon)
7 ibex (rock goat, bouquetin, stein-bock)
8 water buffalo (Indian buffalo, water ox)
9 bison
10 musk ox
11-22 carnivores (beasts of prey)
11-13 Canidae
11 black-backed jackal (jackal)
12 red fox
13 wolf
14-17 martens
14 stone marten (beach marten)
15 sable
16 weasel
17 sea otter, an otter
18-22 seals (pinnipeds)
18 fur seal (sea bear, ursine seal)
19 common seal (sea calf, sea dog)
20 walrus (morse)
21 whiskers
22 tusk
23-29 whales
23 bottle-nosed dolphin (bottle-nose dolphin)
24 common dolphin
25 sperm whale (cachalot)
26 blowhole (spout hole)
27 dorsal fin
28 flipper
29 tail flukes (tail)

1-11 carnivores (beasts of prey)
1 striped hyena, a hyena
2-8 felines (cats)
2 lion
3 mane (lion's mane)
4 paw
5 tiger
6 leopard
7 cheetah (hunting leopard)
8 lynx
9-11 bears
9 raccoon (racoon, *Am.* coon)
10 brown bear
11 polar bear (white bear)
12-16 primates
12, 13 monkeys
12 rhesus monkey (rhesus, rhesus macaque)
13 baboon
14-16 anthropoids (anthropoid apes, great apes)
14 chimpanzee
15 orang-utan (orang-outan)
16 gorilla

1 Gigantocypris agassizi
2 Eupharynx pelecanoides (pelican
   eel, pelican fish)
3 Metacrinus (feather star), a sea
   lily, an echinoderm
4 Lycoteuthis diadema (jewelled
   squid), a cuttlefish [luminescent]
5 Atolla, a deep-sea medusa, a coelenterate
6 Melanocetes, a pediculate [lumi-
   nescent]
7 Lophocalyx philippensis, a glass
   sponge
8 Mopsea, a sea fan [colony]
9 Hydrallmania, a hydroid polyp, a
   coelenterate [colony]
10 Malacosteus indicus, a stomiatid
   [luminescent]
11 Brisinga endecacnemos, a sand star
   (brittle star), an echinoderm [lumi-
   nescent only when stimulated]
12 Pasiphaea, a shrimp, a crustacean
13 Echiostoma, a stomiatid, a fish
   [luminescent]
14 Umbellula encrinus, a sea pen (sea
   feather), a coelenterate [colony,
   luminescent]
15 Polycheles, a crustacean
16 Lithodes, a crustacean, a crab
17 Archaster, a starfish (sea star), an
   echinoderm
18 Oneirophanta, a sea cucumber, an
   echinoderm
19 Palaeopneustes niasicus, a sea
   urchin (sea hedgehog), an echinoderm
20 Chitonactis, a sea anemone
   (actinia), a coelenterate

1 tree
2 bole (tree trunk, trunk, stem)
3 crown of tree (crown)
4 top of tree (treetop)
5 bough (limb, branch)
6 twig (branch)
7 bole (tree trunk) [cross section]
8 bark (rind)
9 phloem (bast sieve tissue, inner fibrous bark)
10 cambium (cambium ring)
11 medullary rays (vascular rays, pith rays)
12 sapwood (sap, alburnum)
13 heartwood (duramen)
14 pith
15 **plant**
16-18 root
16 primary root
17 secondary root
18 root hair
19-25 shoot (sprout)
19 leaf
20 stalk
21 side shoot (offshoot)
22 terminal bud
23 flower
24 flower bud
25 leaf axil with axillary bud
26 **leaf**
27 leaf stalk (petiole)
28 leaf blade (blade, lamina)
29 venation (veins, nervures, ribs)
30 midrib (nerve)
31-38 leaf shapes
31 linear
32 lanceolate
33 orbicular (orbiculate)
34 acerose (acerous, acerate, acicular, needle-shaped)
35 cordate
36 ovate
37 sagittate
38 reniform
39-42 compound leaves
39 digitate (digitated, palmate, quinquefoliolate)
40 pinnatifid
41 abruptly pinnate
42 odd-pinnate
43-50 leaf margin shapes
43 entire
44 serrate (serrulate, saw-toothed)
45 doubly toothed
46 crenate
47 dentate
48 sinuate
49 ciliate (ciliated)
50 cilium
51 **flower**

52 flower stalk (flower stem, scape)
53 receptacle (floral axis, thalamus, torus)
54 ovary
55 style
56 stigma
57 stamen
58 sepal
59 petal
60 ovary and stamen [section]
61 ovary wall
62 ovary cavity
63 ovule
64 embryo sac
65 pollen
66 pollen tube
67-77 inflorescences
67 spike (racemose spike)
68 raceme (simple raceme)
69 panicle
70 cyme
71 spadix (fleshy spike)
72 umbel (simple umbel)
73 capitulum
74 composite head (discoid flower head)
75 hollow flower head
76 bostryx (helicoid cyme)
77 cincinnus (scorpioid cyme, curled cyme)
78-82 roots
78 adventitious roots
79 tuber (tuberous root, swollen taproot)
80 adventitious roots (aerial roots)
81 root thorns
82 pneumatophores
83-85 blade of grass
83 leaf sheath
84 ligule (ligula)
85 leaf blade (lamina)
86 embryo (seed, germ)
87 cotyledon (seed leaf, seed lobe)
88 radicle
89 hypocotyl
90 plumule (leaf bud)
91-102 fruits
91-96 dehiscent fruits
91 follicle
92 legume (pod)
93 siliqua (pod)
94 schizocarp
95 pyxidium (circumscissile seed vessel)
96 poricidal capsule (porose capsule)
97-102 indehiscent fruits
97 berry
98 nut
99 drupe (stone fruit) (cherry)
100 aggregate fruit (compound fruit) (rose hip)
101 aggregate fruit (compound fruit) (raspberry)
102 pome (apple)

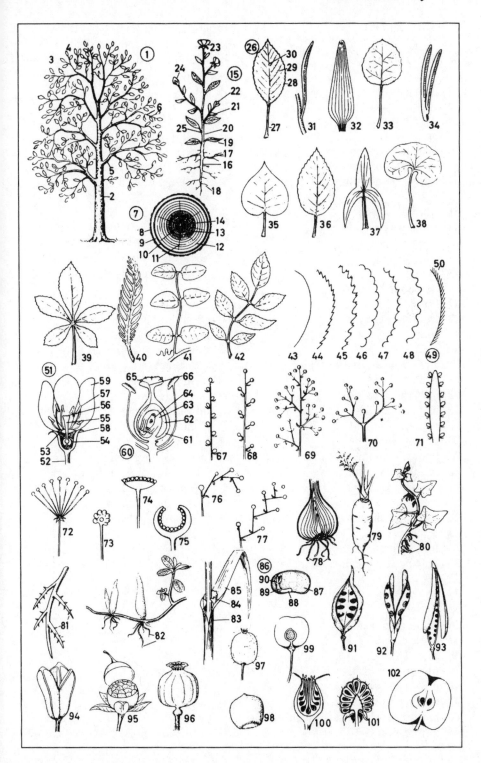

1-73 deciduous trees
1 oak (oak tree)
2 flowering branch
3 fruiting branch
4 fruit (acorn)
5 cupule (cup)
6 female flower
7 bract
8 male inflorescence
9 birch (birch tree)
10 branch with catkins, a flowering branch
11 fruiting branch
12 scale (catkin scale)
13 female flower
14 male flower
15 poplar
16 flowering branch
17 flower
18 fruiting branch
19 fruit
20 seed
21 leaf of the aspen (trembling poplar)
22 infructescence
23 leaf of the white poplar (silver poplar, silverleaf)
24 sallow (goat willow)
25 branch with flower buds
26 catkin with single flower
27 branch with leaves
28 fruit
29 osier branch with leaves
30 alder
31 fruiting branch
32 branch with previous year's cone
33 beech (beech tree)
34 flowering branch
35 flower
36 fruiting branch
37 beech nut
38 ash (ash tree)
39 flowering branch
40 flower
41 fruiting branch
42 mountain ash (rowan, quickbeam)
43 inflorescence
44 infructescence
45 fruit [longitudinal section]
46 lime (lime tree, linden, linden tree)
47 fruiting branch
48 inflorescence
49 elm (elm tree)
50 fruiting branch
51 flowering branch
52 flower
53 maple (maple tree)
54 flowering branch
55 flower
56 fruiting branch
57 maple seed with wings (winged maple seed)
58 horse chestnut (horse chestnut tree, chestnut, chestnut tree, buckeye)
59 branch with young fruits
60 chestnut (horse chestnut)
61 mature (ripe) fruit
62 flower [longitudinal section]
63 hornbeam (yoke elm)
64 fruiting branch
65 seed
66 flowering branch
67 plane (plane tree)
68 leaf
69 infructescence and fruit
70 false acacia (locust tree)
71 flowering branch
72 part of the infructescence
73 base of the leaf stalk with stipules

1-71 coniferous trees (conifers)
1 silver fir (European silver fir, common silver fir)
2 fir cone, a fruit cone
3 cone axis
4 female flower cone
5 bract scale (bract)
6 male flower shoot
7 stamen
8 cone scale
9 seed with wing (winged seed)
10 seed [longitudinal section]
11 fir needle (needle)
12 spruce (spruce fir)
13 spruce cone
14 cone scale
15 seed
16 female flower cone
17 male inflorescence
18 stamen
19 spruce needle
20 pine (Scots pine)
21 dwarf pine
22 female flower cone
23 short shoot with bundle of two leaves
24 male inflorescences
25 annual growth
26 pine cone
27 cone scale
28 seed
29 fruit cone of the arolla pine (Swiss stone pine)
30 fruit cone of the Weymouth pine (white pine)
31 short shoot [cross section]
32 larch
33 flowering branch
34 scale of the female flower cone
35 anther
36 branch with larch cones (fruit cones)
37 seed
38 cone scale
39 arbor vitae (tree of life, thuja)
40 fruiting branch
41 fruit cone

42 scale
43 branch with male and female flowers
44 male shoot
45 scale with pollen sacs
46 female shoot
47 juniper (juniper tree)
48 female shoot [longitudinal section]
49 male shoot
50 scale with pollen sacs
51 fruiting branch
52 juniper berry
53 fruit [cross section]
54 seed
55 stone pine
56 male shoot
57 fruit cone with seeds [longitudinal section]
58 cypress
59 fruiting branch
60 seed
61 yew (yew tree)
62 male flower shoot and female flower cone
63 fruiting branch
64 fruit
65 cedar (cedar tree)
66 fruiting branch
67 fruit scale
68 male flower shoot and female flower cone
69 mammoth tree (Wellingtonia, sequoia)
70 fruiting branch
71 seed

373 Ornamental Shrubs and Trees I

1 forsythia
2 ovary and stamen
3 leaf
4 yellow-flowered jasmine (jasmin, jessamine)
5 flower [longitudinal section] with styles, ovaries, and stamens
6 privet (common privet)
7 flower
8 infructescence
9 mock orange (sweet syringa)
10 snowball (snowball bush, guelder rose)
11 flower
12 fruits
13 oleander (rosebay, rose laurel)
14 flower [longitudinal section]
15 red magnolia
16 leaf
17 japonica (japanese quince)
18 fruit
19 common box (box, box tree)
20 female flower
21 male flower
22 fruit [longitudinal section]
23 weigela (weigelia)
24 yucca [part of the inflorescence]
25 leaf
26 dog rose (briar rose, wild briar)
27 fruit
28 kerria
29 fruit
30 cornelian cherry
31 flower
32 fruit (cornelian cherry)
33 sweet gale (gale)

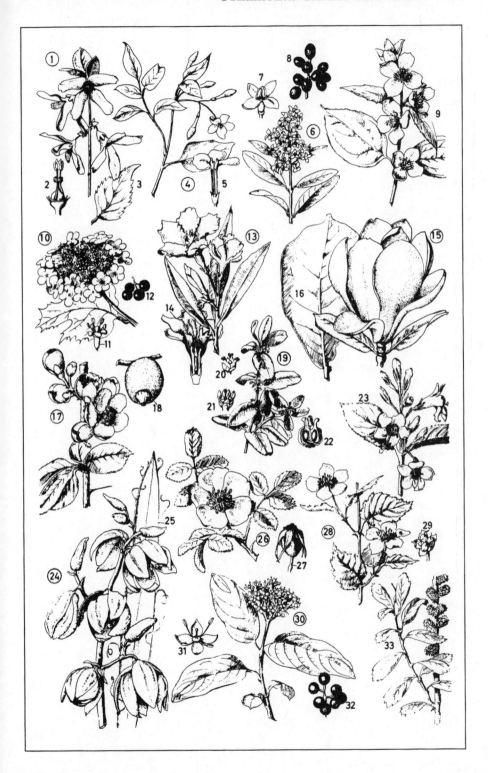

1 tulip tree (tulip poplar, saddle tree, whitewood)
2 carpels
3 stamen
4 fruit
5 hyssop
6 flower [front view]
7 flower
8 calyx with fruit
9 holly
10 androgynous (hermaphroditic, hermaphrodite) flower
11 male flower
12 fruit with stones exposed
13 honeysuckle (woodbine, woodbind)
14 flower buds
15 flower [cut open]
16 Virginia creeper (American ivy, woodbine)
17 open flower
18 infructescence
19 fruit [longitudinal section]
20 broom
21 flower with the petals removed
22 immature (unripe) legume (pod)
23 spiraea
24 flower [longitudinal section]
25 fruit
26 carpel
27 blackthorn (sloe)
28 leaves
29 fruits
30 single-pistilled hawthorn (thorn, may)
31 fruit
32 laburnum (golden chain, golden rain)
33 raceme
34 fruits
35 black elder (elder)
36 elder flowers
37 elderberries

1 rotundifoliate (rotundifolious) saxifrage (rotundifoliate breakstone)
2 leaf
3 flower
4 fruit
5 anemone (windflower)
6 flower [longitudinal section]
7 fruit
8 buttercup (meadow buttercup, but-
terflower, goldcup, king cup, crow-
foot)
9 basal leaf
10 fruit
11 lady's smock (ladysmock, cuckoo
flower)
12 basal leaf
13 fruit
14 harebell (hairbell, bluebell)
15 basal leaf
16 flower [longitudinal section]
17 fruit
18 ground ivy (ale hoof)
19 flower [longitudinal section]
20 flower [front view]
21 stonecrop
22 speedwell
23 flower
24 fruit
25 seed
26 moneywort
27 dehisced fruit
28 seed
29 small scabious
30 basal leaf
31 ray floret (flower of outer series)
32 disc (disk) floret (flower of inner
series)
33 involucral calyx with pappus bristles
34 ovary with pappus
35 fruit
36 lesser celandine
37 fruit
38 leaf axil with bulbil
39 annual meadow grass
40 flower
41 spikelet [side view]

42 spikelet [front view]
43 caryopsis, an indehiscent fruit
44 tuft of grass (clump of grass)
45 comfrey
46 flower [longitudinal section]
47 fruit

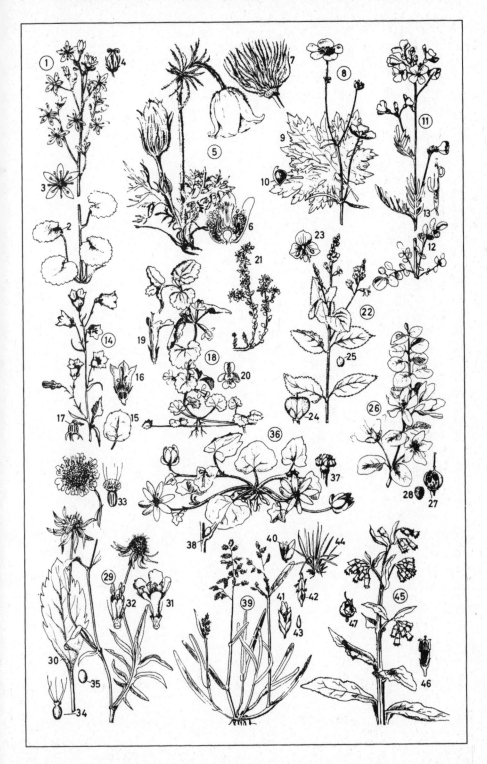

1 daisy (*Am.* English daisy)
2 flower
3 fruit
4 oxeye daisy (white oxeye daisy, marguerite)
5 flower
6 fruit
7 masterwort
8 cowslip
9 great mullein (Aaron's rod, shepherd's club)
10 bistort (snakeweed)
11 flower
12 knapweed
13 common mallow
14 fruit
15 yarrow
16 self-heal
17 bird's foot trefoil (bird's foot clover)
18 horsetail (equisetum) [a shoot]
19 flower (strobile)
20 campion (catchfly)
21 ragged robin (cuckoo flower)
22 birthwort
23 flower
24 crane's bill
25 wild chicory (witloof, succory, wild endive)
26 common toadflax (butter-and-eggs)
27 lady's slipper (Venus's slipper, *Am.* moccasin flower)
28 orchis (wild orchid), an orchid

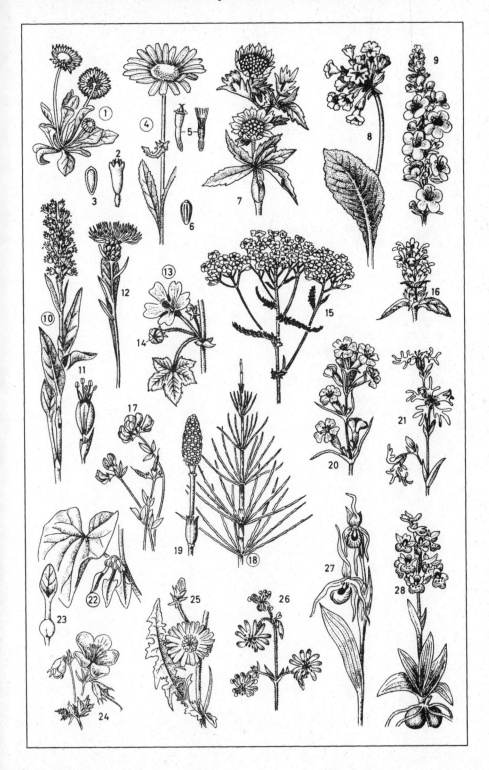

1 wood anemone (anemone, windflower)
2 lily of the valley
3 cat's foot (milkwort); *sim.*: sand-
   flower (everlasting)
4 turk's cap (turk's cap lily)
5 goatsbeard (goat's beard)
6 ramson
7 lungwort
8 corydalis
9 orpine (livelong)
10 daphne
11 touch-me-not
12 staghorn (stag horn moss, stag's
   horn, stag's horn moss, coral ever-
   green)
13 butterwort, an insectivorous plant
14 sundew; *sim.*: Venus's flytrap
15 bearberry
16 polypody (polypod), a fern; *sim.*:
   male fern, brake (bracken, eagle
   fern), royal fern (royal osmund,
   king's fern, ditch fern)
17 haircap moss (hair moss, golden
   maidenhair), a moss
18 cotton grass (cotton rush)
19 heather (heath, ling); *sim.*: bell
   heather (cross-leaved heather)
20 rock rose (sun rose)
21 marsh tea
22 sweet flag (sweet calamus, sweet
   sedge)
23 bilberry (whortleberry, huckleber-
   ry, blueberry); *sim.*: cowberry (red
   whortleberry), bog bilberry (bog
   whortleberry), crowberry (crake-
   berry)

1-13 alpine plants
1 alpine rose (alpine rhododendron)
2 flowering shoot
3 alpine soldanella (soldanella)
4 corolla opened out
5 seed vessel with the style
6 alpine wormwood
7 inflorescence
8 auricula
9 edelweiss
10 flower shapes
11 fruit with pappus tuft
12 part of flower head (of capitulum)
13 stemless alpine gentian
14-57 aquatic plants (water plants) **and marsh plants**
14 white water lily
15 leaf
16 flower
17 Queen Victoria water lily (Victoria regia water lily, royal water lily, Amazon water lily)
18 leaf
19 underside of the leaf
20 flower
21 reed mace bulrush (cattail, cat's tail, cattail flag, club rush)
22 male part of the spadix
23 male flower
24 female part
25 female flower
26 forget-me-not
27 flowering shoot
28 flower [section]
29 frog's bit
30 watercress
31 stalk with flowers and immature (unripe) fruits
32 flower
33 siliqua (pod) with seeds
34 two seeds
35 duckweed (duck's meat)
36 plant in flower
37 flower
38 fruit
39 flowering rush
40 flower umbel

41 leaves
42 fruit
43 green alga
44 water plantain
45 leaf
46 panicle
47 flower
48 honey wrack, a brown alga
49 thallus (plant body, frond)
50 holdfast
51 arrow head
52 leaf shapes
53 inflorescence with male flowers [above] and female flowers [below]
54 sea grass
55 inflorescence
56 Canadian waterweed (Canadian pondweed)
57 flower

1 aconite (monkshood, wolfsbane,
   helmet flower)
2 foxglove (Digitalis)
3 meadow saffron (naked lady,
   naked boys)
4 hemlock (Conium)
5 black nightshade (common nightshade, petty morel)
6 henbane
7 deadly nightshade (belladonna,
   banewort, dwale), a solanaceous
   herb
8 thorn apple (stramonium, stramo-
   ny, *Am.* jimson weed, jimpson
   weed, Jamestown weed,
   stinkweed)
9 cuckoo pint (lords-and-ladies, wild
   arum, wake-robin)
10-13 poisonous fungi (poisonous
   mushrooms, toadstools)
10 fly agaric (fly amanita, fly fungus),
   an agaric
11 amanita
12 Satan's mushroom
13 woolly milk cap

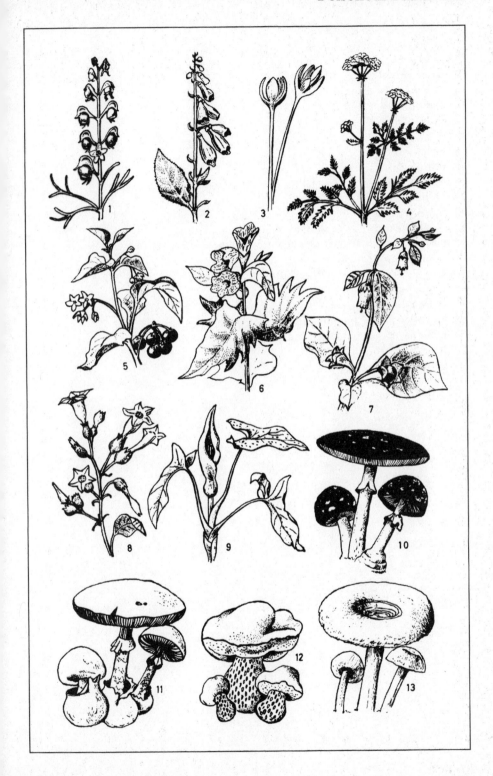

1 camomile (chamomile, wild camomile)
2 arnica
3 peppermint
4 wormwood (absinth)
5 valerian (allheal)
6 fennel
7 lavender
8 coltsfoot
9 tansy
10 centaury
11 ribwort (ribwort plantain, ribgrass)
12 marshmallow
13 alder buckthorn (alder dogwood)
14 castor-oil plant (Palma Christi)
15 opium poppy
16 senna (cassia); *the dried leaflets:* senna leaves
17 cinchona (chinchona)
18 camphor tree (camphor laurel)
19 betel palm (areca, areca palm)
20 betel nut (areca nut)

381 Edible Fungi (Esculent Fungi)

1 meadow mushroom (field mushroom)
2 mycelial threads (hyphae, myceli-
  um) with fruiting bodies
3 mushroom [longitudinal section]
4 cap (pileus) with gills
5 veil (velum)
6 gill [section]
7 basidia [on the gill with
  basidiospores]
8 germinating basidiospores (spores)
9 truffle
10 truffle [external view]
11 truffle [section]
12 interior showing asci [section]
13 two asci with the ascospores
   (spores)
14 chanterelle (chantarelle)
15 Chestnut Boletus
16 cep (cepe, squirrel's bread, Boletus
   edulis)
17 layer of tubes (hymenium)
18 stem (stipe)
19 puffball (Bovista nigrescens)
20 devil's tobacco pouch (common
   puffball)
21 Brown Ring Boletus (Boletus
   luteus)
22 Birch Boletus (Boletus scaber)
23 Russula vesca
24 scaled prickle fungus
25 slender funnel fungus
26 morel (Morchella esculenta)
27 morel (Morchella conica)
28 honey fungus
29 saffron milk cap
30 parasol mushroom
31 hedgehog fungus (yellow prickle
   fungus)
32 yellow coral fungus (goatsbeard,
   goat's beard, coral Clavaria)
33 little cluster fungus

382 Tropical Plants used as Stimulants, Spices, and Flavourings (*Am.* Flavorings)

1 coffee tree (coffee plant)
2 fruiting branch
3 flowering branch
4 flower
5 fruit with two beans [longitudinal section]
6 coffee bean; *when processed:* coffee
7 tea plant (tea tree)
8 flowering branch
9 tea leaf; *when processed:* tea
10 fruit
11 maté shrub (maté, yerba maté, Paraguay tea)
12 flowering branch with androgynous (hermaphroditic, hermaphrodite) flowers
13 male flower
14 androgynous (hermaphroditic, hermaphrodite) flower
15 fruit
16 cacao tree (cacao)
17 branch with flowers and fruits
18 flower [longitudinal section]
19 cacao beans (cocoa beans); *when processed:* cocoa, cocoa powder
20 seed [longitudinal section]
21 embryo
22 cinnamon tree (cinnamon)
23 flowering branch
24 fruit
25 cinnamon bark; *when crushed:* cinnamon
26 clove tree
27 flowering branch
28 flower bud; *when dried:* clove
29 flower
30 nutmeg tree
31 flowering branch
32 female flower [longitudinal section]
33 mature (ripe) fruit
34 nutmeg with mace, a seed with laciniate aril
35 seed [cross section]; *when dried:* nutmeg
36 pepper plant
37 fruiting branch

38 inflorescence
39 fruit [longitudinal section] with seed (peppercorn); *when ground:* pepper
40 Virginia tobacco plant
41 flowering shoot
42 flower
43 tobacco leaf; *when cured:* tobacco
44 mature (ripe) fruit capsule
45 seed
46 vanilla plant
47 flowering shoot
48 vanilla pod; *when cured:* stick of vanilla
49 pistachio tree
50 flowering branch with female flowers
51 drupe (pistachio, pistachio nut)
52 sugar cane
53 plant in bloom
54 panicle
55 flower

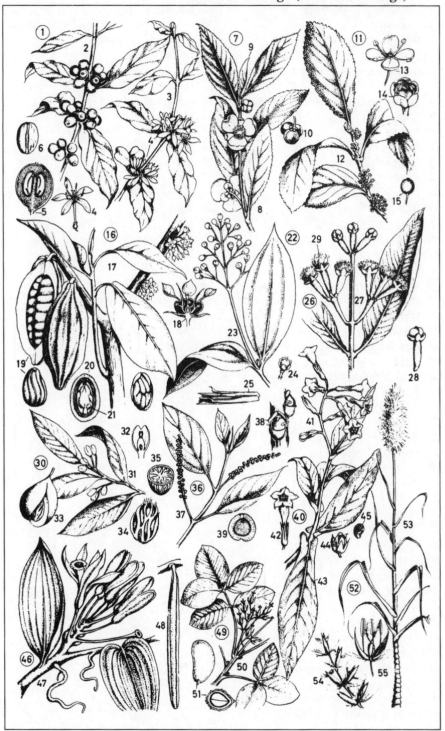

383 Plants used in Industry

1 rape (cole, coleseed)
2 basal leaf
3 flower [longitudinal section]
4 mature (ripe) siliqua (pod)
5 oleiferous seed
6 flax
7 peduncle (pedicel, flower stalk)
8 seed vessel (boll)
9 hemp
10 fruiting female (pistillate) plant
11 female inflorescence
12 flower
13 male inflorescence
14 fruit
15 seed
16 cotton
17 flower
18 fruit
19 lint [cotton wool]
20 silk-cotton tree (kapok tree, capoc tree, ceiba tree)
21 fruit
22 flowering branch
23 seed
24 seed [longitudinal section]
25 jute
26 flowering branch
27 flower
28 fruit
29 olive tree (olive)
30 flowering branch
31 flower
32 fruit
33 rubber tree (rubber plant)
34 fruiting branch
35 fig
36 flower
37 gutta-percha tree
38 flowering branch
39 flower
40 fruit
41 peanut (ground nut, monkey nut)
42 flowering shoot
43 root with fruits
44 nut (kernel) [longitudinal section]
45 sesame plant (simsim, benniseed)
46 flowers and fruiting branch
47 flower [longitudinal section]
48 coconut palm (coconut tree, coco palm, cocoa palm)
49 inflorescence
50 female flower
51 male flower [longitudinal section]
52 fruit [longitudinal section]
53 coconut (cokernut)
54 oil palm
55 male spadix
56 infructescence with fruit
57 seed with micropyles (foramina) (foraminate seed)
58 sago palm
59 fruit
60 bamboo stem (bamboo culm)
61 branch with leaves
62 spike
63 part of bamboo stem with joints
64 papyrus plant (paper reed, paper rush)
65 umbel
66 spike

384 Southern Fruits (Tropical, Subtropical, and Mediterranean Fruits)

1 date palm (date)
2 fruiting palm
3 palm frond
4 male spadix
5 male flower
6 female spadix
7 female flower
8 stand of fruit
9 date
10 date kernel
11 fig
12 branch with pseudocarps
13 fig with flowers [longitudinal section]
14 female flower
15 male flower
16 pomegranate
17 flowering branch
18 flower [longitudinal section, corolla removed]
19 fruit
20 seed [longitudinal section]
21 seed [cross section]
22 embryo
23 lemon; *sim.:* tangerine (mandarin), orange, grapefruit
24 flowering branch
25 orange flower [longitudinal section]
26 fruit
27 orange [cross section]
28 banana plant (banana tree)
29 crown
30 herbaceous stalk with overlapping leaf sheaths
31 inflorescence with young fruits
32 infructescence (bunch of fruit)
33 banana
34 banana flower
35 banana leaf [diagram]
36 almond
37 flowering branch
38 fruiting branch
39 fruit
40 drupe containing seed [almond]
41 carob
42 branch with female flowers

43 female flower
44 male flower
45 fruit
46 siliqua (pod) [cross section]
47 seed
48 sweet chestnut (Spanish chestnut)
49 flowering branch
50 female inflorescence
51 male flower
52 cupule containing seeds
53 Brazil nut
54 flowering branch
55 leaf
56 flower [from above]
57 flower [longitudinal section]
58 opened capsule containing seeds
59 Brazil nut [cross section]
60 nut [longitudinal section]
61 pineapple plant (pineapple)
62 pseudocarp with crown of leaves
63 syncarp
64 pineapple flower
65 flower [longitudinal section]

Ordering

In this index the entries are ordered as follows:
1. Entries consisting of single words, e.g.: 'hair'.
2. Entries consisting of noun + adjective. Within this category the adjectives are entered alphabetically, e.g. 'hair, bobbed' is followed by 'hair, closely-cropped'. Where adjective and noun are regarded as elements of a single lexical item, they are not inverted, e.g.: 'blue spruce', not 'spruce, blue'.
3. Entries consisting of other phrases, e.g. 'hair curler', 'ham on the bone', are alphabetized as headwords.

Where a whole phrase makes the meaning or use of a headword highly specific, the whole phrase is entered alphabetically. For example 'ham on the bone' follows 'hammock'.

Index

References

The numbers in bold type refer to the sections in which the word may be found, and those in normal type refer to the items named in the pictures. Homonyms, and in some cases uses of the same word in different fields, are distinguished by section headings (in italics), some of which are abbreviated, to help to identify at a glance the field required. In most cases the full form referred to by the abbreviations will be obvious. Those which are not explained are shown in the following list:

Agr.	Agriculture/Agricultural	*Hydr. Eng.*	Hydraulic Engineering
Alp. Plants	Alpine Plants	*Impl.*	Implements
Art. Studio	Artist's Studio	*Inf. Tech.*	Information Technology
Bldg.	Building	*Intern. Combust. Eng.*	Internal Combustion Engine
Carp.	Carpenter	*Moon L.*	Moon Landing
Cement Wks.	Cement Works	*Music Not.*	Musical Notation
Cost.	Costumes	*Overh. Irrign.*	Overhead Irrigation
Cyc.	Cycle	*Platem.*	Platemaking
Decid.	Deciduous	*Plant. Propagn.*	Propagation of Plants
D.I.Y.	Do-it-yourself	*Rm.*	Room
Dom. Anim.	Domestic Animals	*Serv. Stat.*	Service Station
Equest.	Equestrian Sport	*Sp.*	Sports
Fabul. Creat.	Fabulous Creatures	*Text.*	Textile[s]
Gdn.	Garden	*Veg.*	Vegetable[s]

A

Aaron's rod **376** 9
abacus **309** 77
abacus *Art* **334** 20
abattoir **94**
abbreviated dialling key **237** 13
abdomen *Man* **16** 35–37, 36
abdomen *Bees* **77** 10–19
abdomen *Forest Pests* **82** 9
abdomen, lower ~ **16** 37
abdomen, upper ~ **16** 35
abductor hallucis **18** 49
abductor of the hallux **18** 49
aberdevine **361** 8
aborigine, Australian ~ **352** 37
abrasion platform **13** 31
abrasive wheel combination **111** 28, 35
abscissa **347** 9
abseiling **300** 28–30
abseil piton **300** 39
abseil sling **300** 28
absinth **380** 4
absorber attachment **27** 44
absorption dynamometer **143** 97–107
absorption muffler **190** 16
absorption silencer **190** 16
abutment *Bridges* **215** 27, 29, 45
abutment *Art* **336** 20
abutment pier **215** 29
acanthus **334** 25
acceleration lane **15** 16
acceleration rocket **234** 22, 4
accelerator **191** 46
accelerator lock **85** 17
accelerator pedal **191** 46, 94
accelerometer **230** 10
accent, acute ~ **342** 30
accent, circumflex ~ **342** 32
accent, grave ~ **342** 31
accent, strong ~ **321** 27
accents **342** 30–35
acceptance **250** 12, 23

access arm **244** 47
access balcony **37** 72–76
access flap **62** 1, 25
accessories **115** 54–74
accessory shoe **114** 4; **115** 4
accessory shop **196** 24
access ramp **199** 15
access slot **244** 42
acciaccatura **321** 15
accipiters **362** 10–13
accolade **329** 66
accommodation **146** 33
accommodation bureau **204** 28
accommodation ladder **221** 98
accommodation module **146** 33
accompaniment side **324** 43
accompaniment string **324** 24
accordion **324** 36
account, private ~ **250** 4
accounting machine **236** 26
account number **250** 26
accumulator **309** 41
accumulator *Theatre* **316** 55
accumulator railcar **211** 55
accuracy jump **288** 55
acerate **370** 34
acerose **370** 34
acerous **370** 34
acetylene connection **141** 31
acetylene control **141** 32
acetylene cylinder **141** 2, 22
achene **58** 23
achievement **254** 1–6
achievement, marital ~ **254** 10–13
achievement of arms **254** 1–6
Achilles' tendon **18** 48
acicular **370** 34
acid container **350** 62
Ackermann steering system **85** 31, 37
acolyte **331** 45
aconite **379** 1
acorn **371** 4
acorns **276** 42
acoustic coupler **237** 48; **244** 66

acrobat **307** 47
Acropolis **334** 1–7
acroter **334** 34
acroterion **334** 34
acroterium **334** 34
acting area light **316** 16
acting area spotlight **316** 16
actinia **369** 20
Actinophrys **357** 7
action **326** 6–16
action lever **325** 32
activated blade attachment **84** 33
actor **316** 37
actress **316** 38
actuating transistor **195** 19
actuator **244** 47
acuity projector **111** 47
acute **342** 30
ad **342** 56
Adam's apple **19** 13
adapter **112** 55
adapter, four-socket ~ **127** 8
adapter, four-way ~ **127** 8
adapter ring **115** 55
added-feature telephone **237** 9, 19, 22
adders **364** 40 *u.* 41
adding **344** 23
adding machine **309** 74
addition **344** 23
address **236** 42
address bus **244** 52
address display **236** 41
addressing machine, transfer-type ~ **245** 7
address label **236** 4
address system, ship's ~ **224** 30
A-deck **223** 28–30
adhesion railcar **214** 1
adhesive, hot ~ **249** 61
adhesive binder *Bookbind.* **184** 1
adhesive binder *Office* **249** 61
adhesive tape dispenser **247** 27
adhesive tape dispenser, roller-type ~ **247** 28

bag *Doc.* **22** 33
bag *Hunt* **86** 38
bag *Music. Instr.* **322** 9
bag, girl's ~ **29** 56
bag, heat-sealed ~ **76** 29
bag, paper ~ **98** 48
bag, postman's ~ **236** 54
bag filter **83** 54
bag-full indicator **50** 61, 73
baggage compartment **257** 15
baggage loader **233** 22
baggage man **267** 17
'baggage reclaim' **233** 38
baggage terminal **233** 5, 16
bagging nozzle **83** 55
bag net **77** 54
bagpipe **322** 8
bagsealer **40** 47
baguette **97** 12
bag wig **34** 4
bail **292** 70
bailey, inner ~ **329** 2
bailey, outer ~ **329** 31
bait **86** 21
bait, poisoned ~ **83** 31
bait, weighted ~ **89** 36
bait needle **89** 41
baits **89** 65–76
bait tin **89** 24
bakehouse **97** 55–74
baker's shop **97** 1–54
bakery **97; 97** 55–74
baking ingredient **99** 62
baking ingredients **98** 8–11
balalaika **324** 28
Balance *Astron.* **3** 19; **4** 59
balance *Paperm.* **173** 9
balance beam **349** 30
balance cable **214** 46
balance cable sleeve **214** 74
balance column **349** 29
balance control **241** 54
balancer **307** 48
balance rail **322** 39
balance wheel **110** 31
balancing act **307** 44
balancing knob **116** 39
balancing pole **307** 42
balcony *Dwellings* **37** 18, 69, 73
balcony *Theatre* **315** 16; **315** 18
balcony *Chivalry* **329** 12
balcony, projecting ~ **218** 57
baldachin **331** 49
baldaquin **331** 49
bald patch **34** 21
bale **55** 31; **63** 34; **75** 7; **83** 13; **169** 34; **170** 62; **206** 10, 11, 23
bale arm **89** 62
bale breaker **163** 7
bale loader, hydraulic ~ **63** 37
bale opener **163** 7
baler, high-pressure ~ **63** 35
baling press **169** 33
balk **63** 3
ball *Infant Care etc.* **28** 16
ball *Bicycle* **187** 31
ball *Aircraft* **230** 12
ball *Ball Games* **292** 27
ball *Circus* **307** 60
ball, ivory ~ **277** 1
ball, metal ~ **352** 32

ball, paper ~ **306** 55
ball, plastic ~ **277** 1
ball, steel ~ **143** 70
ball, stone ~ **352** 32
ball and socket head **114** 47
ballast *Station* **205** 61
ballast *Railw.* **212** 66
ballast *Sailing* **285** 33
ballast *Airsports* **288** 65
ballast keel **285** 32
ballast tank **223** 78
ball bearing **143** 69; **187** 56, 68
ball boy **293** 22
ballerina **314** 26
ballet **314**
ballet dancer **314** 26
ballet positions **314** 1–6
ballet shoe **314** 30
ballet skirt **314** 31
ballet slipper **314** 30
ball games **291; 292; 293**
ballistics **87** 73
ball mill **161** 1
ball of clay **161** 9
ball of the foot **19** 58
ball of the thumb **19** 75
balloon **308** 13
balloon, gas ~ **288** 63
balloon, hot-air ~ **288** 79
balloon, manned ~ **7** 16
balloon basket **288** 64
ballooning **288** 63–84
ballot box **263** 28
ballot envelope **263** 21
ballot paper **263** 20
ball race **187** 68
ballroom **306** 1
Balmer series **1** 21
baluster **38** 29; **123** 51
balustrade **38** 25; **123** 22, 50
bamboo cane **136** 31
bamboo culm **383** 60
bamboo stem **383** 60, 63
banana **99** 90; **384** 33
banana flower **384** 34
banana-handling terminal **226** 22
banana leaf **384** 35
banana plant **384** 28
banana saddle **188** 59
banana tree **384** 28
band *Ball Games* **291** 25
band *Nightclub* **318** 3
band *Church* **332** 5
band, fluorescent ~ **199** 8
band, iron ~ **130** 16
band, ornamental ~ **334** 38
band, steel ~ **163** 5
bandage *First Aid* **21** 9
bandage *Equest.* **289** 15
bandages, emergency ~ **21** 1–13
band brake **143** 104
banderilla **319** 22
banderillero **319** 4, 21
band of barrel **130** 8
bandoneon **324** 36
bandora **322** 21
bandsaw **134** 50; **157** 48
bandsaw, horizontal ~ **157** 48
bandsaw blade **157** 53
band selection button **241** 45
bandstand **274** 19; **307** 9

band wheel **104** 15
band wheel cover **133** 32
banewort **37** 97
banger **306** 51
bangle *Jewell.* **36** 17
bangle *Ethnol.* **354** 38
bangle, asymmetrical ~ **36** 26
bangs **34** 36
banjo **324** 29
bank *Phys. Geog.* **13** 4
bank *Bank* **250**
bank *Roulette* **275** 11
bank acceptance **250** 12
bank branch **204** 31
bank clerk **250** 5
bank employee **251** 7
banknotes **252** 30–39
bank of circulation **252** 31
bank of issue **252** 31
bank of oars **218** 12
bank protection **216** 51–55
bank slope **217** 28
bank stabilization **216** 51–55
bank statement **247** 44
banner *Flags* **253** 12
banner *Election* **263** 12
banner, processional ~ **331** 44
banqueting hall **267** 39
bantam **74** 56
baptism, Christian ~ **332** 1
baptistery **332** 2
bar *Horse* **71** 41
bar *Office* **246** 29
bar *Restaurant* **266** 1–11
bar *Hotel* **267** 54
bar *Park* **272** 34
bar *Playground* **273** 32
bar *Gymn.* **296** 3, 8; **297** 4, 41
bar *Athletics* **298** 14, 34
bar *Winter Sp.* **303** 5
bar *Circus* **307** 50
bar *Disco* **317** 1, 9
bar *Nightclub* **318** 13, 15
bar *Music. Not.* **320** 42
bar *Graphic Art* **340** 34
bar, flat ~ **143** 10
bar, metal ~ **324** 77
bar, round ~ **143** 8
bar, sliding ~ **75** 21
bar arm **299** 10
barb *Bees* **77** 10
barb *Fish Farm.* **89** 80
barb *Mach. Parts etc.* **143** 44
Barbe class landing craft **258** 89
barbecue **278** 47
barbel **364** 13
bar bender **119** 21
barber **106** 1
barber's shop **106** 1–42
barchan **13** 40
barchane **13** 40
bar customer **267** 55
bareback rider **307** 26
barge **216** 22, 25; **225** 8
barge and push tug assembly **221** 92
bargeboard **37** 8
bargee **216** 26
bargeman **216** 26
barge sucker **216** 59
bark *Carp.* **120** 86

bow wave **223** 81
box *Livestock* **75** 2
box *Carriages* **186** 8
box *Gymn.* **296** 15
box *Athletics* **298** 35
box *Fair* **30** 87
box *Bullfight etc.* **319** 7
box, centrifugal ~ **169** 17
box, coach's ~ **292** 56
box, crossing keeper's ~ **202** 43
box, gateman's ~ **202** 43
box, racer's ~ **290** 7
box, rider's ~ **290** 7
box, small ~ **296** 16; **297** 9
box attendant **315** 12
box camera **309** 30
boxcar **213** 14, 22
boxer *Dog* **70** 10
boxer *Sports* **299** 25
box feeder **159** 7
box gutter **122** 83
boxing **299** 20–50
boxing contest **299** 35–50
boxing glove **299** 26
boxing match **299** 20–50, 35
boxing ring **299** 35
box office **308** 7
box pile **217** 6
boxroom door **38** 20
box spar **287** 30
box spur **71** 50
box trap **86** 20
box tree **373** 19
boy scout **278** 11
bra **32** 1; **318** 29
bra, longline ~ **32** 4
brace *Bldg. Site* **119** 63
brace *Carp.* **120** 27, 54
brace *Roof* **121** 41, 58, 69, 82
brace *Ship* **219** 67
brace *Music. Instr.* **325** 16
brace, diagonal ~ *Bldg. Site* **118** 88; **119** 51
brace, diagonal ~ *Bridges* **215** 4
bracelet **36** 3
bracelet, cultured pearl ~ **36** 9
bracelet, gemstone ~ **36** 25
bracelet watch **36** 33
braces **29** 26, 34; **32** 30
braces, adjustable ~ **33** 45
braces clip **32** 31
brachioradialis **18** 39
bracing **215** 3
bracing, diagonal ~ **119** 14
bracken **15** 5; **377** 16
bracket *Doc.* **23** 10
bracket *Plumb. etc* **12** 66
bracket *Bicycle* **187** 77
bracket *School* **260** 30
bracket *Winter Sp.* **302** 17; **303** 7
bracket, chrome ~ **188** 60
bracket, round ~ **342** 24
bracket, square ~ **342** 25
Brackett series **1** 23
bract **371** 7; **372** 5
bracteate **252** 4
bract scale **372** 5
braid, floral ~ **30** 28
braid embroidery **102** 31
braid work **102** 31
Braille **342** 15

brain stem **17** 47; **18** 24
brake *Mills* **91** 8
brake *Carriages* **186** 2, 16
brake *Car* **191** 45
brake *Air Force* **257** 10
brake *Forest Plants etc.* **377** 16
brake, automatic ~ **181** 47
brake, auxiliary ~ **212** 10
brake, covered ~ **186** 33
brake, front ~ **187** 5
brake, hydraulic ~ **212** 44
brake arm **187** 66
brake arm cone **187** 67
brake axle **143** 99
brake band **143** 105
brake block *Mach. Parts etc.* **143** 100
brake block *Carriages* **186** 16
brake cable **188** 37; **189** 12
brake casing **187** 70
brake chute housing **257** 24
brake cone **187** 71
brake cylinder pressure gauge **212** 7
brake disc **191** 17; **192** 48
brake drum **138** 11, 20
brake flap *Aircraft* **229** 44
brake flap *Air Force* **256** 12
brake flap *Gliding* **287** 38
brake fluid reservoir **191** 49
brake line *Motorcycle* **189** 12
brake line *Car* **192** 53
brake lining *Blacksm.* **138** 13
brake lining *Mach. Parts etc.* **143** 106
brake lining *Car* **192** 52
brake lock **56** 38
brake magnet **143** 102
brakeman **303** 21
brake pedal *Gdn. Tools* **56** 40
brake pedal *Offset Platem.* **179** 12, 30
brake pedal *Car* **191** 45, 95
brake pressure gauge **210** 50
brake pulley **143** 98
brake shaft **143** 99
brake shoe *Blacksm.* **138** 12
brake shoe *Mach. Parts etc.* **143** 100
brake shoe *Car* **192** 51
brake system, dual-circuit ~ **191** 72
brake-testing equipment **138** 16
brake weight **143** 103
brake wheel **91** 7
braking disc **191** 17; **192** 48
braking distance **203** 29
braking roller **138** 18
branch *Railw.* **203** 48
branch *Fire Brig.* **270** 33
branch *Maths.* **347** 15
branch *Bot.* **370** 5, 6
branch *Decid. Trees* **371** 10, 25, 27, 32, 59
branch *Conifers* **372** 36, 43
branch *Trop. Plants* **382** 17
branch *Industr. Plants* **383** 61
branch *South. Fruits* **384** 12, 42
branch, flowering ~ **58** 32, 52; **59** 1, 26, 37
branch, fruit-bearing ~ **59** 19, 48

branch, fruiting ~ **59** 30
branch, left ~ **203** 47
branch, right ~ **203** 46
branch line **15** 23
branchman **270** 34
brandy **98** 59
brandy glass **45** 88
brashing **84** 12
brass **323** 39–48
brassard *Fire Brig.* **270** 22
brassard *Chivalry* **329** 47
brassica **57** 32
brassicas **57** 28–34
brassie **293** 91
brassière **32** 1; **318** 29
brassière, longline ~ **324**
brass instruments **323** 39–48
brayer **340** 12
Brazil Current **14** 35
Brazil nut **384** 53, 59
breach **13** 34
bread **45** 22; **97** 2
bread, kinds of ~ **97** 6–12; **99** 11
bread, wrapped ~ **97** 48–50
bread and cheese **266** 75
bread basket **45** 20
bread counter **99** 9
bread crust **97** 4
breadth scale **157** 58
bread unit **97** 56–57
break *Brew.* **93** 2
break *Typesett. Rm.* **175** 15
break *Carriages* **186** 2
break, covered ~ **186** 33
break-bulk cargo, unitized ~ **226** 11
break-bulk cargo elevator, floating ~ **226** 31
break-bulk cargo transit shed **225** 9
break-bulk carrier **225** 14; **226** 13
breakdown lorry **270** 47
breaker *Overh. Irrign.* **67** 34
breaker *Swim.* **279** 6
breaker spring **67** 35
break removal **93** 1–5
breakstone, rotundifoliate ~ **375** 1
breakwater *Hydr. Eng* **217** 16
breakwater *Docks* **225** 65
breakwater *Warships* **258** 7, 76
breast *Man* **16** 28–29
breast *Horse* **72** 19
breast beam **166** 46
breast beam board **166** 16
breastbone *Man* **17** 8
breastbone *Meat* **95** 27
breastbox **173** 11
breast collar **71** 28
breast collar ring **71** 27
breast drill **140** 58
breast harness **71** 26–36
breast of veal **95** 4
breastplate **329** 46
breast pocket **33** 9
breasts **16** 28–29
breaststroke **282** 33
breast work **329** 21
breather **153** 10
breathing apparatus **26** 1; **270** 39
breathing tube **27** 37
breccia **11** 27

breeches **300** 7
breeches, loose ~ **355** 34
breeches, white ~ **289** 5
breeches buoy **228** 13
breech ring **255** 38
breeding comb **77** 46
breeds of dog **70**
breeze **120** 44; **156** 14
Bremen class frigate **258** 53
breve **320** 12
breve rest **320** 20
breviary **331** 58
brevier **175** 25
brevis **320** 12
brewer **92** 49
brewery **93** 1–31
brewhouse **93** 1–31
brewing **92**; **93**
briar grain **107** 41
briar rose **373** 26
brick **118** 40
brick, green ~ **159** 16
brick, perforated ~ **159** 21 u. 22, 21
brick, radial ~ **159** 25
brick, radiating ~ **159** 25
brick, solid ~ **159** 20
brick, standard ~ **118** 58
brick, unfired ~ **159** 16
brick cutter **159** 15
brickfield **159**
brick hammer **118** 53
brick kiln **159** 19
bricklayer **118** 18
bricklayer's tools **118** 50–57
brickmason **118** 18
brickmason's tools **118** 50–57
brick-pressing machine **159** 11
brickwork, frost-resistant ~ **122** 39
brickwork, base **123** 15
brickworks *Map* **15** 89
brickworks **159**
brickyard **159**
bride **332** 15
bridegroom **332** 16
bridesmaid **332** 24
bridge *Map* **15** 44
bridge *Opticn.* **111** 11
bridge *Station* **205** 3
bridge *Ship* **221** 6, 12; **223** 12–18
bridge *Shipbuild.* **222** 26
bridge *Warships* **258** 14; **259** 3, 28
bridge *Park* **272** 47
bridge *Free Exerc.* **295** 19
bridge *Sports* **299** 9
bridge *Theatre* **315** 29; **316** 34
bridge *Music. Instr.* **322** 17
bridge, cable-stayed ~ **215** 46
bridge, covered ~ **215** 32
bridge, cross-section of ~ **215** 1
bridge, dental ~ **24** 26
bridge, flat ~ **215** 52
bridge, iron ~ **15** 56
bridge, reinforced concrete ~ **215** 49
bridge, rope ~ **215** 15
bridge, solid ~ **215** 19
bridge, stone ~ **15** 50
bridge bearing **215** 55
bridge deck **223** 12–18

bridge over railway **15** 40
bridge ring **89** 58
bridges **215**
bridge strut **215** 30
bridge superstructure **258** 14
bridge support **222** 12
bridge under railway **15** 42
bridle **71** 7–13
bridle path **12** 46
briefcase **41** 17
briefs **32** 26
brig **220** 17
brigantine **220** 14
brightness control **240** 33
brille **323** 35
brilliant **175** 21
brilliant cut **36** 44
brimstone butterfly **365** 4
brine channel **274** 3
brine pipe **274** 4
briolette, faceted ~ **36** 86
Brisinga endecacnemos **369** 11
brisket, hind ~ **95** 25
brisket, middle ~ **95** 26
brisket of beef **95** 23
bristle **88** 52
bristles *Hairst. etc.* **34** 23
bristles *Household* **50** 47
bristletail **81** 14
bristle worm **357** 22
broach **109** 8
broaching tap **93** 14
broach roof **121** 22
broach roof, conical ~ **121** 24
B road **15** 36
broad axe **120** 70
broad bean *Veg.* **57** 8
broad bean *Fodder Plants* **69** 15
broadcasting **238**; **239**; **240**
broadcasting centre **238** 16–26
broadcasting satellite **237** 70, 80
broadcasting station **15** 33
broadsheet **340** 27
broadside **340** 27
broadside fire **218** 59
broadtail *Ladies' Wear* **30** 60
broadtail *Furrier* **131** 21
brochure **250** 7
broderie anglaise **102** 11
broiler **98** 6; **308** 33
broiler chicken **74** 12
broiler rearing **74** 11–17
broken thread detector roller **16** 44
broken thread stop motion **165** 19
broker, commercial ~ **251** 5
broker, inside ~ **251** 4
broker, outside ~ **251** 5
bronchus **20** 5
Bronze Age **328** 21–40
brooch, ivory ~ **36** 30
brooch, modern-style ~ **36** 19
brooch, pearl ~ **36** 7
brood bud bulblet **54** 27, 29
brood cell **77** 31
brood chamber **77** 46
brooder **74** 3
brook **13** 8; **15** 80
broom **38** 36; **50** 46; **62** 5; **199** 6; **268** 21; **272** 67
broom *Shrubs etc.* **374** 20

broom, circular ~ **199** 40
broom, cylinder ~ **199** 42
broom, inverted ~ **224** 99
broom, upward-pointing ~ **224** 100
broom handle **38** 37; **50** 49
broom head **50** 48
broomstick **38** 37; **50** 49
brougham **186** 3
brow antler **88** 6
browband **71** 9
brown **343** 5
brown ale **93** 26
brown bear **368** 10
brown leaf-eating weevil **80** 49
Brown Ring Boletus **381** 21
brown-tail moth **80** 28
brown trout **364** 15
brow point **88** 6
brow snag **88** 6
brow tine **88** 6
brush *Roof & Boilerr.* **38** 32
brush *Household* **50** 42, 53
brush *Bees* **77** 7
brush *Forestry* **84** 5
brush *Game* **88** 47
brush *School* **260** 59
brush *Graphic Art* **340** 11
brush *Script* **341** 24
brush, camel hair ~ **338** 7
brush, dry ~ **128** 49
brush, flat ~ *Painter* **129** 17
brush, flat ~ *Art. Studio* **338** 6
brush, rotating ~ **168** 46
brush, round ~ **33** 88
brush, stiff-bristle ~ **105** 16
brush, wire ~ *Gas Weld.* **141** 26
brush, wire ~ *Arc Weld.* **142** 18
brush, wire ~ *Music. Instr.* **324** 53
brush head **50** 79
brush head, detachable ~ **49** 30
brushwood *Map* **15** 15
brushwood *Forestry* **84** 5
brushwood *Spa* **274** 2
Brussels lace **102** 18
Brussels sprout **57** 30
bubble bath **49** 3
bubble chamber **1** 58
bubble float, oval ~ **89** 47
buccaneer **306** 43
Büchner funnel **349** 11
buck *Dom. Anim.* **73** 18
buck *Game* **88** 28, 40, 59
buck *Gymn.* **296** 17
buck, young ~ **88** 39
bucket *Household* **50** 54
bucket *Mills* **91** 36
bucket *Bldg. Site* **118** 82
bucket *Road Constr.* **200** 5
bucket chain **226** 42
bucket dredger **226** 41
bucket elevator **200** 49; **201** 2
bucket elevator chain **216** 57
bucket ladder **226** 43
bucket pump **269** 7
bucket seat **305** 90
bucket teeth **200** 6
bucket-top boot **355** 58
buckeye **371** 58
buckle **101** 52
buckle and knife folder **185** 8

buzzer, electric ~ **127** 15
buzz saw **119** 19; **125** 24; **134** 50
buzz saw blade **132** 59
by-line **291** 7
bypass air flow **232** 50
bypass duct **232** 41, 44
bypass engine **232** 46
bypass switch **211** 25

C

cab *Carriages* **186** 26, 28
cab *Lorries etc.* **194** 2
cab *Railw.* **209** 4
cab *Town* **268** 64
cab, driver's ~ **64** 36; **194** 2, 15; **200** 11; **208** 14; **209** 4; **210** 39–63, 49; **211** 19, 57; **212** 5; **213** 2; **255** 61
cab, engineer's ~ **208** 14; **209** 4; **210** 39–63, 49; **211** 19, 57; **212** 5; **213** 2
cabbage, green ~ **57** 32
cabbage, red ~ **57** 32
cabbage, round ~ **57** 32
cabbage lettuce ~ **57** 36
cabbage white butterfly ~ **80** 47, 48
cab frame **65** 21
cab heating switch **211** 39
cab horse **186** 28
cabin *Railw.* **214** 20, 25, 28
cabin *Ship* **218** 45
cabin *Sailing* **285** 39
cabin *Airsports* **288** 19
cabin, admiral's ~ **218** 27
cabin, captain's ~ **223** 13
cabin, commanding officer's ~ **259** 85
cabin, coxswain's ~ **228** 31
cabin, crane driver's ~ **119** 35; **222** 16; **226** 52
cabin, de luxe ~ **223** 30
cabin, double-berth ~ **223** 29
cabin, large-capacity ~ **214** 52
cabin, officer's ~ **223** 21
cabin, single-berth ~ **223** 46; **228** 32
cabin cruiser **286** 3
cabinet **22** 40; **246** 20
cabinet maker **132** 38
cabin pulley cradle **214** 66
cabin superstructure **285** 39
cable *Sea Fish* **90** 26
cable *Power Plant* **153** 41
cable *Music. Instr.* **326** 53
cable, auxiliary ~ **214** 47
cable, electric ~ **56** 32
cable, endless ~ **214** 21
cable, high-voltage ~ **153** 42
cable, lower ~ **214** 46
cable, moisture-proof ~ **127** 42
cable, thermoplastic ~ **127** 42
cable, three-core ~ **127** 44
cable binding **301** 40
cable boom **195** 15
cable box **153** 33
cable clip **127** 40
cable connection *Moon L.* **6** 26
cable connection *Post* **237** 88
cable connection panel **239** 3
cable crane berth **222** 11–18

cable drum **85** 39; **270** 55
cable duct **234** 29, 47; **235** 61
cable ferry **216** 1
cable guide **201** 7
cable guide rail **214** 33
cablehead station **237** 83
cable manhole **198** 17
cable network **237** 87
cable parachute **287** 7
cable pattern **30** 39
cable pulley, automatic ~ **301** 62
cable railway **214** 12
cable release **23** 9; **114** 38; **115** 62
cable release socket **117** 6
cable support **214** 76
cable suspension lines **214** 15–38
cable television **237** 79
cable tunnel **152** 20
cable vault **152** 21
cableway **214** 30
cableway, endless ~ **214** 16–24, 19
cableway gondola **214** 52
cableways **214** 15–38
cable winch **85** 38, 46; **258** 85
cabochon, high ~ **36** 79
cabochon, octagonal ~ **36** 81
cabochon, oval ~ **36** 80
cabochon, round ~ **36** 78
cabochon, simple ~ **36** 78
cabochons **36** 78–81
caboose **223** 42
cabriole **314** 21
cabriolet **186** 29
cabriolet sports car **193** 14
cabriolet sports coupé **193** 14
cacao bean **382** 19
cacao tree **382** 16
cachalot **367** 25
cache controller **244** 9
cache memory **244** 9
caddis fly **358** 12
caecum **20** 17
café **265** 1–31
café, open-air ~ **272** 57
café customers **265** 22–24
café table **265** 11
cage *Fish Farm.* **89** 1
cage *Coal* **144** 23
cage *Circus* **307** 50
cage , crane driver's ~ **119** 35; **222** 16; **226** 52
cage, outside ~ **356** 11
cage, rotating ~ **168** 17
cage, round ~ **307** 49
cage, stepped ~ **74** 20
cage, tiered ~ **74** 20
cage caravan **307** 62
cage system **74** 18
cage-winding system **144** 23
caisson **217** 33; **222** 32; **259** 19
cake **169** 19–27, 22
cake, slice of ~ **266** 20
cake counter **99** 9; **265** 1
cake plate **97** 25
cakes **97** 17–47
cake tin **40** 28, 29
calabash **354** 27
calcaneum **17** 27
calcite **351** 22
calcium chloride tube **350** 43
calculating machine **309** 80

calculation, logarithmic ~ **345** 6
calculator **309** 80
calculator, electronic ~ **246** 12
calculator dial *Photog.* **114** 57
calculator dial *Photograv.* **182** 19
calculus, infinitesimal ~ **345** 13–14
calendar **22** 10
calendar clock **110** 11
calendar sheet **247** 33
calender **173** 36
calendering machine **168** 38
calender roll **173** 26, 38
calender roller **163** 20, 37, 59
calf *Man* **16** 53
calf *Farm Bldgs.* **62** 33
calf *Dom. Anim.* **73** 1
calf *Game* **88** 1
calf *Meat* **95** 1–13
caliber **87** 40
calibre **87** 40
California Current **14** 39
caliper *see* calliper
call box **236** 8; **251** 10; **268** 56
call button **25** 6; **127** 3; **246** 1
call button, follow-on ~ **237** 34
call indicator **237** 18
calliper *Car* **191** 18
calliper *Sculpt. Studio* **339** 3
calliper, fixed ~ **192** 49
calliper, inside ~ **135** 23
calliper, outside ~ **135** 18
calliper gauge **149** 59
calliper square **85** 10
call light **315** 52
callosity **72** 27
calls for luring game **87** 43–47
calm **91** 1
calm belts **9** 46–47
calms, equatorial ~ **9** 46
calvarium **261** 16, 18
calyx **58** 8; **374** 8
calyx, involucral ~ **375** 33
calyx, renal ~ **20** 30
cam **190** 60
Camberwell beauty **365** 5
cambium ring **370** 10
camcorder **243** 1–4
camcorder, video-8 ~ **243** 2
came **124** 13
camel **366** 29
camel caravan **354** 1
camera *Atom* **1** 60
camera *Optic. Instr.* **112** 14, 20
camera *Cine Film* **117** 28
camera *Video* **243** 1
camera *Films* **310** 19
camera, cartridge-loading ~ **114** 11
camera, compact ~ *Cine Film* **117** 51
camera, compact ~ *Photo-mech. Reprod.* **177** 32
camera, folding ~ **114** 49; **309** 25
camera, high-speed ~ **313** 35
camera, large-format ~ *Optic. Instr.* **112** 25, 36
camera, large-format ~ *Photog.* **114** 49, 61
camera, miniature ~ *Doc.* **23** 7
camera, miniature ~ *Optic. Instr.* **112** 26

cleaning tank **178** 1
cleaning tow **87** 63
cleanout door **38** 39
cleansing pond **8** 96
clear-felling system **84** 4–14
clearing *Map* **15** 2
clearing *Forestry* **84** 13
clearstory **334** 70
cleat *Carp.* **120** 45
cleat *Floor etc. Constr.* **123** 67
cleaver, butcher's ~ **94** 18
cleaving hammer **85** 5
clefs **320** 8–11
cleft, anal ~ **16** 41
clench planking **258** 50–52
clerestory **334** 70
clergyman **330** 22; **331** 37; **332** 22
clergyman, Protestant ~ **332** 3
clerical assistant **24** 87
clew **284** 41
click **110** 26
click beetle **80** 37, 38
click wheel **110** 27
cliff **13** 28
cliff face **13** 28
cliffline **13** 25–31
cliffs **13** 25–31
climate, artificially maintained ~ **356** 21
climate, boreal ~ **9** 56
climate, equatorial ~ **9** 53
climates **9** 53–58
climates, polar ~ **9** 57–58
climatic map **9** 40–58
climatology **9**
climber *Flower Gdn.* **51** 5
climber *Fruit & Veg. Gdn.* **52** 5
climber *Indoor Plants* **53** 2
climber *Veg.* **57** 8
climber *Mountain* **300** 5
climbing **300** 2–13
climbing boot **300** 44
climbing breeches **300** 7
climbing equipment **300** 31–57
climbing frame **273** 47
climbing harness **300** 56
climbing net **273** 50
climbing plant **53** 2
climbing roof **273** 60
climbing rope **273** 48; **296** 19
climbing tower **273** 17
clinch **299** 31
clinker cooler **160** 9
clinker pit **152** 8
clinker planking **285** 50–52
clinker store **160** 10
clinoprinacoid **351** 24
clip *Atom* **218**
clip *Bicycle* **187** 62
clip *Railw.* **202** 9
clipper display **238** 44
clippers, electric ~ **105** 21; **106** 32
clipper ship, English ~ **220** 36
clitellum **357** 26
clitoris **20** 88
Clivia minata **53** 8
cloak **355** 18, 26
cloak, red ~ **319** 27
cloak, short ~ **355** 29
cloak, Spanish ~ **355** 29
cloak, woollen ~ **355** 6

cloak cord **355** 24
cloakroom **48** 34; **207** 70; **315** 5; **318** 1
cloakroom attendant **315** 6; **318** 2
cloakroom hall **315** 5–11
cloakroom ticket **315** 7
cloche **35** 12
clock **191** 38; **211** 37; **212** 16
clock, double ~ **276** 16
clock, electric ~ **191** 79
clock, main ~ **245** 18
clock case **110** 18; **309** 57
clockmaker **109** 1
clocks **110**
clockwork **110** 28
clockwork drive **10** 14
clockwork mechanism **110** 28
clod **63** 7
clog **101** 44; **355** 43
cloister **331** 52
cloister vault **336** 41
closed vertical gate **301** 66
close-range surface-to-air missile **258** 62
close-up bellows attachment **115** 58
close-up lens **117** 55
closing gear **90** 27
closing head **143** 59
closure rail **202** 26
cloth **166** 12; **271** 59
cloth, damask ~ **45** 2
cloth, felt ~ **340** 42
cloth, flannel ~ **128** 48
cloth, linen ~ **206** 11
cloth, sterile ~ **26** 38
cloth, unraised ~ **168** 33
clothes, children's ~ **29**
clothes, teenager's ~ **29** 48–68
clothes brush **50** 44; **104** 31
clothes closet **43** 1
clothes closet door **46** 2
clothes compartment **212** 63; **267** 30
clothes line **38** 23; **50** 33
clothes louse **81** 41
clothes moth **81** 13
clothes rack **271** 31
clothes rack, movable ~ **103** 7
clothes shop **268** 9
clothing, protective ~ **84** 26; **270** 46
cloth roller **166** 20
cloth-shearing machine, rotary ~ **168** 42
cloth take-up motion **166** 19
cloth take-up roller **166** 47
cloth temple **166** 13
cloud, lenticular ~ **287** 19
cloud chamber photograph **2** 26
cloud chamber track **2** 27
cloud cover **9** 20–24
clouds **8** 1–19, 1–4, 5–12, 13–17
clouds, luminous ~ **7** 22
clouds, noctilucent ~ **7** 22
clout **121** 94
clout nail **121** 94; **122** 96
clove **382** 28
clove carnation **60** 7
clove pink **60** 7
clover, four-leaf ~ **6** 95

clover broadcaster **66** 26
clove tree **382** 26
clown **306** 69; **307** 24
clown, musical ~ **307** 23
clown act **307** 25
club **283** 23
club hammer **126** 77
clubhouse **283** 23
club membership **286** 8
club rush **378** 21
clubs **276** 38
clump of grass **375** 44
cluster of eggs **80** 2, 30
cluster of grapes **78** 5
cluster of stars **3** 26
clutch **191** 44
clutch, dry ~ **190** 78
clutch, fluid ~ **65** 37
clutch, main ~ **65** 39
clutch, multi-plate ~ **190** 78
clutch, single-plate ~ **190** 71
clutch coupling **227** 23
clutch flange **177** 55
clutch lever **188** 32
clutch pedal **191** 44, 96; **192** 28
C major **320** 55, 62
C major scale **320** 45
C minor **320** 65
coach *Lorries etc.* **194** 17
coach *Ball Games* **291** 55; **292** 57
coach, four-axled ~ **208** 3
coach body **186** 5; **207** 2; **208** 6
coach bolt **202** 7
coach box **186** 8
coach door **186** 11
coaches **186** 1–3, 26–39, 45, 51–54
coach horse **186** 28
coachman **186** 32
coach screw **202** 7
coach step **186** 13
coach wagons **186** 1–3, 26–39, 45, 51–54
coagulating bath **169** 15
coal **170** 1
coal bunker **152** 2; **225** 19
coal conveyor **152** 1
coal distillation, dry ~ **170** 2
coal feed conveyor **199** 37
coal mill **152** 4
coal mine **144** 1–51
coal scuttle **309** 9
coal seam **144** 50
coal shovel **38** 43
coal tar **170** 3
coal tar extraction **156** 18
coal wharf **225** 18
coaming **283** 59
coarse dirt hose **50** 84
coarse fishing **89** 20–31
coastal cruiser **284** 60
coastal lake **13** 44
coaster **221** 99
coaster brake **187** 63
coasting vessel **221** 99
coat **29** 54; **30** 60; **33** 2
coat, black ~ **289** 4
coat, braided ~ **186** 23
coat, cloth ~ **30** 61; **33** 66
coat, dark ~ **289** 4, 13
coat, fur ~ **30** 60
coat, gallooned ~ **186** 23

collimator **111** 46; **351** 30
colon **342** 17
colon, ascending ~ **20** 19
colon, descending ~ **20** 21
colon, transverse ~ **20** 20
colonnade **274** 9; **334** 67
colophony **323** 11
color *see* colour
Colorado beetle **80** 52
colour **343**
colour analyser **116** 36
colour analyser lamp **116** 37
colour chemicals **116** 52
colour computer **177** 51
colour conversion filter step **117** 38
colour correction, selective ~ **177** 51
colour correction unit **177** 39
colour decoder module **240** 5
colour developer **116** 10
colour enlarger **116** 40
colour filter **316** 49
colour indicator **127** 37
colour light distant signal **203** 9, 14
colour light signal **203** 3
colour medium **316** 49
colour-mixing knob **116** 43–45
colour organ **317** 13
colour output stage module **240** 13
colour pickup tube **240** 36
colour picture tube **240** 15
colour print **340** 28
colour printing paper **116** 51
colour processing chemicals **116** 52
colour selection key **249** 42
colours of the rainbow **343** 14
colour television receiver **240** 1
colour television set **240** 1
colposcope **23** 5
coltsfoot **380** 8
colubrid **364** 38
Columbian **175** 30
columbine *Gdn. Flowers* **60** 10
Columbine *Carnival* **306** 27
column *Photog.* **116** 42
column *Forging* **139** 10
column *Mach. Tools* **150** 10
column *Bookbind.* **185** 65
column *Script* **342** 45
column *Chem.* **349** 29
column, angled ~ **116** 28
column, bent ~ **113** 21
column, central ~ **114** 46
column, Corinthian ~ **334** 10
column, Doric ~ **334** 8
column, Ionic ~ **334** 9
column, ornamented ~ **333** 18
column, rotating ~ **150** 37
column, spinal ~ **17** 2–5
column, vertebral ~ **17** 2–5
column box **119** 11, 73
column heading **342** 46
column rule **342** 47
column shaft **334** 26
coma position **21** 24
comb *Infant Care etc.* **28** 8
comb *Dom. Anim.* **73** 22
comb *Hairdresser* **105** 6

comb, adjustable ~ **165** 26
comb, top ~ **163** 67
combat sports **299**
comber **163** 56, 63
comber draw box **163** 60
comb foundation **77** 43
combination, two-piece ~ **30** 45
combination cutting pliers **126** 60; **127** 53
combination lever **210** 30
combination rib weave **171** 25
combination toolholder **149** 41
combine **64** 1–33
combined grasp **296** 42
combine harvester **63** 31; **64** 1–33
combing cylinder **163** 68
combing machine **163** 56
comb setting **165** 36
combustion chamber **232** 37
combustion chamber, external ~ **147** 16
comfrey **375** 45
comic turn **307** 25
comma **342** 18
command key **247** 21
command module **6** 9
command section **234** 65
command window **176** 33
command window, typographic ~ **176** 33
commencement of speed restriction **203** 39, 42
commissionaire **267** 1; **315** 10
commissure, labial ~ **16** 14; **19** 19
committee **263** 1–2
committee boat **285** 15
committee member **263** 2
committee table **263** 3
common box **373** 19
common buzzard **362** 9
common comfrey **69** 13
common denominator **344** 19
common dolphin **367** 24
common European kite **362** 11
common flea **81** 42
common groundsel **61** 12
common heron **359** 18
common housefly **81** 2
common iguana **364** 32
common mallow **376** 13
common merganser **359** 15
common myrtle **53** 11
common nightshade **379** 5
common orache **61** 24
common pheasant **88** 77
common privet **373** 6
common puffball **381** 20
common roller **360** 6
common salt **170** 13
common seal **367** 19
common sea-swallow **359** 11
common silver fir **372** 1
common swallow **361** 20
common time **320** 32
common toadflax **376** 26
common vetch **69** 18
common viper **364** 40
communicant **332** 27
communication line **127** 23
communications module **237** 68
communications satellite **237** 63

communion cup **330** 10; **332** 29
communion table **330** 4
communion wafer **332** 50
commutator cover **211** 18
compact disc **242** 61
compact disc player **241** 8; **242** 28
compact disc rack **241** 10
compact hi-fi system **242** 64
compact stereo system **242** 64
compact telephone **237** 9
companion hatch **258** 24
companion ladder **221** 123; **223** 24; **258** 24
companionway **221** 123; **222** 23; **223** 24; **258** 24
company account **250** 4
company messenger **236** 17
compartment *Forestry* **84** 2
compartment *Railw.* **207** 13; **208** 24
compartment *Store* **271** 6
compartment, secretarial ~ **205** 37
compartment, special ~ **205** 26
compartment, twin-berth ~ **207** 38
compartment, two-berth ~ **207** 38
compartment, two-seat ~ **207** 38
compartment batten **316** 13
compartment door **207** 14
compartment window **207** 52; **208** 8
compass *Drawing Off.* **151** 52
compass *Airsports* **288** 12
compass, divisions of ~ **321** 42–50
compass, fluid ~ **224** 46
compass, gyroscopic ~ **224** 31, 51–53
compass, liquid ~ **224** 46
compass, magnetic ~ **223** 6; **224** 46; **230** 6
compass, mariner's ~ **223** 6
compass, ratchet-type ~ **151** 64
compass, spirit ~ **224** 46
compass, wet ~ **224** 46
compass bowl **224** 49
compass brick **159** 25
compass bridge **223** 4–11; **227** 24
compass card **224** 47
compasses **224** 46–53
compass flat **223** 4–11; **227** 24
compass head **151** 53
compass plane **132** 28
compass platform **223** 4–11; **227** 24
compass repeater **224** 31, 52, 53
compass saw **120** 63; **126** 70; **132** 3
compendium of games **47** 18
compensating airstream **192** 4
compensating roller **181** 45
compensation pendulum **109** 33
compensator **181** 45
compensator level **112** 69
competition bow **305** 54
competitor **282** 28
complementary angle **346** 15
complement of set **348** 7, 8
composing frame **174** 2
composing room **174; 175**
composing rule **174** 14
composing stick **174** 13
composition *Typesett. Rm.* **175** 1–17

frame, aluminium ~ **50** 19
frame, annular ~ **235** 47
frame, bone ~ **353** 13
frame, C-shaped ~ **26** 19; **27** 17
frame, ferroconcrete ~ **119** 2
frame, heated ~ **55** 16
frame, iron ~ **325** 2
frame, lower ~ **148** 20
frame, metal ~ *Opticn.* **111** 7
frame, metal ~ *Music. Instr.* **324** 76
frame, plate glass ~ **179** 15
frame, reinforced concrete ~ **119** 2
frame, sectional ~ **65** 56
frame, shell ~ **111** 8
frame, tortoiseshell ~ **111** 8
frame, tubular ~ **188** 9, 49
frame, upper ~ **148** 19
frame, wire ~ **339** 35
frame, wooden ~ **353** 13
frame bar **64** 51
frame-clamping machine **133** 42
frame counter **115** 37; **313** 28
frame-cramping machine **133** 42
frame drum **353** 26
frame end plate **164** 26
frame hive **77** 45–50
frame-mounting device **133** 48
frame number **187** 51
frame sample **124** 2
frame-sanding pad **133** 34
frame saw, vertical ~ **157** 2
frame section, aft ~ **234** 49
frame section, forward ~ **234** 45
frame slipway **222** 19–21
frame stand **133** 43
frame tent **278** 36
frame timber **119** 64
frame timber, bolted ~ **119** 74
frame vent **55** 17
frame wood **124** 3
frame wood sample **124** 2
framework **339** 22
framework support **214** 77
framing **336** 11
framing chisel **132** 11
framing control **312** 29
framing table **132** 62
franc **252** 15, 16, 17, 18
Frankfurter **96** 8
Frankfurter garland cake **97** 42
Frankfurter sausage **96** 8
franking machine **22** 24; **236** 7, 27, 47
free backward circle **297** 29
free combination knob **326** 40
free combination stud **326** 40
free exercise **295**
free-fall positions **288** 60–62
free flight model, remote controlled ~ **288** 86
free kick **291** 43
free leg *Athletics* **298** 27
free leg *Winter Sp.* **302** 3
free leg, vertical ~ **298** 25
free port **225** 2
freestyle relay race **282** 24–32
freestyle wrestling **299** 10–12
free-throw line **292** 38
free walkover forward **297** 25

freeway *Map* **15** 16
freeway *Docks* **225** 54
free-wheel hub **187** 63
freezer **22** 63; **96** 21; **97** 65; **98** 74; **99** 57
freezer, upright ~ **39** 7
freezing compartment **39** 5
free zone enclosure **225** 3
free zone frontier **225** 3
freight agent **206** 28
freight barge **216** 25
freight car **206** 6
freight car, flat ~ **206** 21
freight car, open ~ **213** 8, 33
freight car, special ~ **213** 33
freight depot *Map* **15** 91
freight depot *Station* **206**
freighter **221** 57
freight house **206** 7, 26–39
freight house door **206** 37
freight office **206** 26
freight truck **206** 15
French chalk **271** 39
French horn **323** 41
French lady **355** 51
French toast **97** 54
French window **37** 21
frequency **241** 47; **242** 55
frequency band **309** 22
frequency divider **110** 43
frequency selection button **241** 45
fresco **338** 40
fresh-air inlet **356** 16
fresh-air inlet and control **191** 85
fresh-air regulator **191** 86
fresh meat counter **99** 51
fresh milk filling and packing plant **76** 20
fresh milk tank **76** 15
fresh oil tank **65** 46
freshwater eel **364** 17
freshwater pearl mussel **357** 33
fresh water tank **221** 70; **223** 79
fret *Roulette* **275** 30
fret *Music. Instr.* **324** 9
fretsaw **135** 12; **260** 53
fretsaw blade **135** 13; **260** 54
friction drive **116** 33; **312** 37
friction pad **192** 49
friction tape **127** 34
friction wheel **322** 26
fridge *Kitch.* **39** 2
fridge *Flat* **46** 33
fridge *Disco* **317** 10
frieze **335** 9
frieze, Babylonian ~ **333** 19
frieze decoration **334** 16
frill **31** 34; **32** 44
frill collar **31** 46
frill front **32** 44
fringe **34** 36
fringe, decorative ~ **353** 25
fringe region **7** 34
frit **162** 2
frit feeder **162** 13
frit funnel **162** 13
frock coat **355** 76
frog *Agr. Mach.* **65** 8
frog *Road Constr.* **200** 26
frog *Railw.* **202** 24
frog *Music. Instr.* **323** 13

frog position **288** 61
frog's bit **378** 29
frond **378** 49
front **305** 1
front, cold ~ **8** 13; **9** 27
front, extended ~ **200** 10
front, hinged ~ **213** 10
front, occluded ~ **9** 25
front, warm ~ **8** 5; **9** 26
frontalis **19** 4
front axle pivot pin **65** 48
front axle suspension **65** 49
front band **71** 9
front door **249** 36
front fan-jet **232** 33
front-line player **293** 63
front panel, sliding ~ **349** 27
front roller underclearer **164** 44
fronts **9** 25–29
fronts, cold ~ **8** 13–17
fronts, warm ~ **8** 5–12
front sight block **255** 20
front support *Free Exerc.* **295** 21, 23
front support *Gymn.* **296** 28
front wheel drive **191** 52
front wheel drum brake **188** 36
froth **266** 4
fruit *Weeds* **61** 11, 20, 23
fruit *Restaurant* **266** 57
fruit *Decid. Trees* **371** 4, 19, 28, 45, 69
fruit *Conifers* **372** 53, 64
fruit *Shrubs etc.* **373** 12, 18, 22, 27, 29, 32; **374** 4, 8, 12, 19, 25, 29, 31, 34
fruit *Flowers etc.* **375** 4, 7, 10, 13, 17, 24, 35, 37, 47; **376** 3, 6, 14
fruit *Alp. Plants etc.* **378** 11, 38, 42
fruit *Trop. Plants* **382** 3, 5, 10, 15, 17, 24, 39
fruit *Industr. Plants* **383** 14, 18, 21, 28, 32, 40, 43, 52, 56, 59
fruit *South. Fruits* **384** 19, 26, 39, 45
fruit, aggregate ~ *Soft Fruit* **58** 28
fruit, aggregate ~ *Bot.* **370** 100, 101
fruit, canned ~ **98** 16
fruit, compound ~ *Soft Fruit* **58** 28
fruit, compound ~ *Bot.* **370** 100, 101
fruit, dehisced ~ **375** 27
fruit, immature ~ **378** 31
fruit, indehiscent ~ **375** 43
fruit, mature ~ *Decid. Trees* **371** 61
fruit, mature ~ *Trop. Plants* **382** 33
fruit, ripe ~ *Decid. Trees* **371** 61
fruit, ripe ~ *Trop. Plants* **382** 33
fruit, soft ~ **58** 1–30
fruit, stewed ~ **45** 30
fruit, unripe ~ **378** 31
fruit, young ~ *Decid. Trees* **371** 59
fruit, young ~ *South. Fruits* **384** 31
fruit and vegetable counter **99** 80
fruit and vegetable garden **52** 1–32
fruit bowl **45** 29, 40
fruit capsule, mature ~ **382** 44
fruit capsule, ripe ~ **382** 44

high house **305** 75
high jump **298** 9–27
high jump apparatus **298** 32
high jump equipment **298** 32
high jumper **298** 10
highland Indian **352** 23
high-moor bog **13** 19
high-mountain region **12** 39–47
high performance sailplane **287** 9
high-pile lining **101** 3
high-pressure area **9** 6
high-pressure belt **9** 47
high-pressure manometer **141** 4
high-pressure xenon arc lamp **312** 39
high-resolution colour monitor **244** 60
high-resolution graphics screen **176** 30
high-rise handlebar **188** 57
high-riser **188** 56
high school **261**
high school riding **71** 1–6
high seat **86** 14
high-speed plate, automatic ~ **39** 15
high-tension voltage indicator **211** 29
high tide **280** 7
high toss **297** 35
high-water line **13** 35
high-water mark **13** 35
hiking boot **101** 18
hiking stick **284** 31
hiking strap **284** 30
hill *Phys. Geog.* **13** 66
hill *Films* **310** 13
hillside spring **12** 38
hill upcurrent **287** 28
himation **355** 6
hind **86** 13
hind, young ~ **88** 1
hinge **188** 2
hip *Man* **16** 33
hip *Horse* **72** 32
hip *Roof* **121** 12
hip bone **17** 18
hip circle backwards **296** 55
hip dormer window **121** 13
hip end **121** 11
hip grip **21** 38
hipped-gable roof **121** 16
hippocampus *Fabul. Creat.* **327** 44
Hippocampus *Fish etc.* **364** 18
hippocentaur **327** 52
hippogryph **327** 26
hippopotamus **366** 31
hip rafter **121** 62
hip roof **37** 64; **121** 10, 60
hip tile **122** 9
historical ship, types of ~ **218**
hitch **65** 61
hitch, adjustable ~ **64** 60
hitch, front ~ **65** 50
hitch-kick **298** 40
hitch pin **325** 14
hive **77** 45–50, 52
hive-bee **77** 1–25
hock **72** 37
hockey **292** 6
hockey ball **292** 14

hockey player **292** 15
hockey stick **292** 13
hod **122** 22
hod hook **122** 23
hoe **66** 24
hoe and fork, combined ~ **56** 7
hoe handle **66** 2
hog **94** 11
hogpen **62** 8; **75** 35
hoist *Oil, Petr.* **145** 11
hoist *Flags* **253** 22–34
hoist, builder's ~ **118** 31
hoist, inclined ~ **158** 16; **159** 5
hoisting gear **206** 56; **217** 74
hoisting gear bridge **217** 73
hoisting gear cabin **217** 71
hoisting rope **120** 37
hold **223** 55, 75
hold, insulated ~ **223** 56
hold, underfloor ~ **231** 21
hold-down, automatic ~ **157** 65
holdfast *Carp.* **120** 66
holdfast *Alp. Plants etc.* **378** 50
holding device **157** 47
holding forceps **23** 12
holding press **183** 4
holding squad **270** 17
hold pillar **222** 61
hole *Phys. Geog.* **13** 34
hole *PC* **244** 39
hole *Ball Games* **293** 79–82, 87
hole, elongated ~ **240** 17
hole, square ~ **140** 43
holing out **293** 86
hollowing tool **135** 17
hollow of the throat **16** 20
hollow-shaft boring bit **133** 7
holly **374** 9
hologram **250** 28
hologram, rainbow ~ **250** 28
hologram, white light ~ **250** 28
holohedron **351** 2
holster **264** 24
Holy Bible **330** 11
Holy Communion **332** 26
Holy Scripture **330** 11
holy table **330** 4
holy water basin **332** 47
home and overseas news section **342** 62
home base **292** 53
homeplate **292** 53
home port **286** 8
homogenizer **76** 12
homopteran **358** 3
honey **77** 33, 62 *u.* 63
honey, strained ~ **77** 62 *u.* 63
honey bag **77** 18
honey-bee **77** 1–25
honey cell **77** 33
honeycomb **77** 31–43, 45
honeycomb, artificial ~ **77** 42
honeycomb, natural ~ **77** 60
honeycomb weave **171** 29
honeydew melon **266** 50
honey extractor **77** 61
honey fungus **381** 28
honey gland **59** 18
honey in the comb **77** 64
honey jar **77** 63
honey pail **77** 62

honey sac **77** 18
honey separator **77** 61
honeysuckle **374** 13
honey super **77** 45
honey wrack **378** 48
hood *Infant Care etc.* **28** 26
hood *Child. Clothes* **29** 2
hood *Ladies' Wear* **30** 69
hood *Headgear* **35** 2
hood *Blacksm.* **137** 7
hood *Carriages* **186** 42
hood *Car* **191** 8
hood *Garage* **195** 36
hood *Aircraft* **230** 39
hood *Mountain.* **300** 19
hood *Church* **331** 56
hood, automatic ~ **193** 16
hood, collapsible ~ **186** 52
hood, detachable ~ **31** 21
hood, falcon's ~ **86** 44
hood, folding ~ **28** 35
hood, power-operated ~ **193** 16
hood, protective ~ **157** 65
hood drawstring **29** 64
hood support **195** 37
hoof *Home* **72** 26
hoof *Game* **88** 24
hoof, horse's ~ **327** 42
hoof prints **86** 8
hook *Roof & Boilerr.* **38** 22
hook *Horse* **71** 14
hook *Shoem.* **100** 62
hook *Oil, Petr.* **145** 9
hook *Sports* **299** 33
hook *Winter Sp.* **301** 61
hook *Sports* **305** 18, 46
hook *Music. Not.* **320** 5
hook, blunt ~ **26** 50
hook, butcher's ~ **96** 55
hook, closed ~ **89** 85
hook, concealed ~ **89** 75
hook, double ~ **89** 83
hook, open ~ **89** 83
hook, treble ~ **89** 85
hookah **107** 42
hook-and-ride band **140** 50
hook ball **305** 18
hook belt **270** 44
hook disgorger **89** 40
hook ladder **270** 16
hooks **89** 79–87
hoop *Airsports* **288** 67
hoop *Ball Games* **292** 78
hoop *Circus* **307** 58
hoopoe **359** 25
hoop of barrell **130** 8
hooter *Motorcycles etc.* **188** 53
hooter *Fire Brig.* **270** 7
hop boiler **92** 52
hop garden **15** 114
hop growing **83** 27
hopper *Agr. Mach.* **64** 59
hopper *Wine Grow.* **78** 18
hopper *Mills* **91** 13
hopper *Cotton Spin.* **163** 31
hopper *Music. Instr.* **325** 30
hopper, endless-floor ~ **64** 84
hopper barge **226** 46
hopper delivery roller, wooden ~ **163** 32
hopper feeder **163** 33

lady's smock **375** 11
lager **93** 26
lager cellar **93** 12
lagging **38** 72
lagoon **13** 33
lake **13** 3
lake, coastal ~ **13** 44
lake, ox-bow ~ **15** 75
lake dwelling **328** 15
lamantin **366** 23
lamb **73** 13; **75** 11
lamb's lettuce **57** 38
lamellicorn **82** 1
lamellicorn beetle **358** 24, 39
lamina **68** 20; **370** 28, 85
laminate **301** 48
lamp *Dent.* **24** 19
lamp *Dining Rm.* **44** 12
lamp *Watchm.* **109** 12
lamp *Carriages* **186** 9
lamp *Street Sect.* **198** 18
lamp *Nightclub* **318** 26
lamp, directional ~ **22** 44
lamp, fluorescent ~ **49** 32; **271** 23
lamp, front ~ **188** 29
lamp, individual ~ **26** 11
lamp, pendant ~ **44** 12
lamp, rear ~ **187** 46
lamp, side ~ **191** 20
lamp bracket *Photomech. Reprod.* **177** 16
lamp bracket *Bicycle* **187** 6
lamp compartment **177** 41
lampholder **127** 60
lamphouse **112** 28, 59; **116** 29; **309** 44; **312** 39–44
lamphouse connector **112** 60
lamp housing **116** 29
lamp post **198** 18
lam rod **166** 54
lance *Gdn. Tools* **56** 25
lance *Bullfight. etc.* **319** 17
lance *Chivalry* **329** 81
lance *Ethnol.* **353** 9
lanceolate **370** 32
lancer **319** 16
lance rest **329** 80
lancet arch **336** 31
lancet window **335** 39–41
land **87** 39
landau **186** 36
landaulette **186** 36
land drill **282** 20
landfill, sanitary ~ **199** 10
landing *Floor etc. Constr.* **123** 34–41
landing *Athletics* **298** 19
landing, intermediate ~ **123** 52–62
landing area **298** 36, 39
landing beam **123** 34, 55
landing beam, main ~ **123** 66
landing craft **259** 46
landing flap **229** 42; **230** 53; **257** 38; **288** 29
landing gear, hydraulically operated ~ **235** 31
landing gear, main ~ **235** 31
landing gear, retractable ~ **232** 10
landing gear housing **256** 15
landing gear hydraulic cylinder **257** 41

landing gear unit, forward retracting ~ **257** 40
landing gear unit, main ~ **230** 41; **231** 28; **257** 40; **288** 33
landing gear unit, retractable ~ **231** 28
landing light **230** 49; **257** 37; **288** 32
landing mat **296** 13; **297** 7
landing net **89** 2
landing pad *Moon L.* **6** 33
landing pad *Athletics* **298** 36
landing pontoon **225** 63
landing skid **232** 15; **256** 21
landing stage **225** 63; **278** 13; **283** 19
landing unit, main ~ **256** 26
landlord **305** 7, 13
landside **65** 5, 67
landslide **11** 46
landslip **11** 46
land surveying **14** 46–62
land wheel **65** 15
lane *Map* **15** 112
lane *Forestry* **84** 1
lane arrow **268** 73, 74
lane timekeeper **282** 24
language laboratory **261** 35
language select button **237** 33
languid **326** 28
lansquenet **355** 32
lantern *Carriages* **186** 9
lantern *Ship* **218** 44; **221** 48
lantern *Navig.* **224** 105
lantern *Art* **335** 45
lantern, Chinese ~ **353** 36
lantern, combined ~ **286** 13
lantern, paper ~ **52** 15; **306** 4
lantern mast **224** 82
lantern tower **224** 82
lanyard **284** 19
lap *Dom. Anim.* **73** 23
lap *Roof* **122** 100
lap *Cotton Spin.* **163** 58, 64
lap, carded ~ **163** 47
lapboard **136** 7
lap cradle **163** 15
lapel **31** 23; **33** 5
lapel, silk ~ **33** 8
lapping plate **125** 4
lap riveting **143** 56
lap scorer **290** 6
laptop **244** 1
lap-turner, movable ~ **163** 19
lapwing **359** 21
larch **372** 32
larch cone **372** 36
lard **96** 5
large cabbage white butterfly **80** 47
larks **361** 18–19
larkspur **60** 13
larmier **88** 14
larry **144** 8; **156** 6
larry car **144** 8; **156** 6
larva **58** 64; **77** 29; **80** 6, 19, 36, 38, 41, 46; **81** 20; **82** 12, 25, 36; **358** 9, 19
larva, first-generation ~ **80** 23
larva, mature ~ **80** 53
larva, second-generation ~ **80** 24

larva, young ~ **77** 28; **80** 54
larynx **20** 2–3
laser disc, large ~ **243** 41
laser disc, small ~ **243** 40
laser head **243** 45
laser head tracing spindle **243** 44
laser printer **176** 12; **244** 61
laser scanning system **243** 42
laser unit **243** 45
lashing *Bldg. Site* **118** 30
lashing *Ship* **218** 32; **221** 119
lasso **319** 40; **352** 5
last **100** 34
last, iron ~ **100** 54
last, wooden ~ **100** 32
latch **244** 34
latch bolt **140** 37
latch needle **167** 12, 56, 61
lateen sail **218** 29; **220** 3
lateen spanker **218** 29
lateen yard **218** 30
La Tène period **328** 21–40
lateral **144** 30
lath **123** 70
lath, double ~ **122** 43
lath, tilting ~ **122** 43
lath, toothed ~ **122** 26
lath axe **122** 21
lathe **135** 1
lathe, watchmaker's ~ **109** 20
lathe bed **135** 2; **149** 31
lathe carrier **149** 54
lathe foot **149** 12
lathe spindle **149** 20
lathe tool **149** 48, 52
lathe tools **149** 45–53
lathing **123** 71
latissimus dorsi **18** 59
latitude **14** 6
latrine **118** 49
lattice casing **221** 84
lattice girder **235** 12
lattice mast **258** 18
lattice swing bridge **215** 63
launch **225** 25
launcher **258** 49
launching container **258** 32
launching housing **259** 26
launching ramp **255** 54
launching tube **255** 57
launch phase escape tower **234** 66
lauter battery **92** 51
lauter tun **92** 50
lava plateau **11** 14
lava stream **11** 18
lavatories **317** 31
lavatory **49** 12; **146** 29; **207** 16, 42, 72; **211** 59; **231** 31; **278** 5
lavatory, public ~ **268** 62
lavender **380** 7
lawn **37** 46; **51** 33; **272** 36; **274** 12
lawn aerator **56** 15
lawn mower, electric ~ **56** 31
lawn mower, motor ~ **56** 28
lawn rake **51** 3; **56** 3
lawn sprinkler **37** 43; **56** 43
lay-by **217** 27
layer **54** 11, 12
layer, bituminous ~ **200** 58
layer, bust ~ **54** 35
layer, level ~ **123** 39

Z

zap flap **229** 50
Z-drive motorboat **286** 2
zebra **366** 27
zebra crossing **198** 11; **268** 24
Zechstein, leached ~ **154** 62
Zechstein, lixiviated ~ **154** 62
Zechstein shale **154** 68
zenith *Astron.* **4** 11
zenith *Hunt.* **87** 77
zero **275** 18
zero adjustment **2** 7
zero isotherm **9** 41

zero level **7** 6, 20
ziggurat **333** 32
zimmerstutzen **305** 35
zinc plate **179** 9; **180** 53; **340** 52
zinc plate, etched ~ **178** 40
zinc plate, photoprinted ~ **178** 32
zink **322** 12
zinnia **60** 22
zip **31** 55; **33** 28; **260** 13
zip, front ~ **29** 18
zip, inside ~ **101** 6
zip code **236** 43
zipper *see* zip

zircon **351** 19
zither **324** 21
zone, arid ~ **9** 54
zone, paved ~ **268** 58
zone, tropical ~ **9** 53
zoo **356**
zoological gardens **356**
zooming lever **117** 54; **313** 22, 36
zoom lens **112** 41; **115** 23, 48; **240** 34; **243** 3; **313** 23
zoom lens, interchangeable ~ **117** 2
zoom stereomicroscope **112** 40
Zulu **354** 36